PICTORIAL PRICE GUIDE
TO AMERICAN ANTIQUES

FOURTH EDITION

PICTORIAL PRICE GUIDE TO AMERICAN ANTIQUES

and Objects Made for the American Market

OVER 5000 OBJECTS IN 300 CATEGORIES ILLUSTRATED AND PRICED

BY

Dorothy Hammond

A Dutton **dep** Paperback

E. P. DUTTON / NEW YORK

For information contact: Elsevier-Dutton Publishing Co., Inc.,
2 Park Avenue, New York, N.Y. 10016
Library of Congress Catalog Card Number: 80-65353

ISBN: 0-525-47660-1

Published simultaneously in Canada by Clarke, Irwin & Company
Limited, Toronto and Vancouver

10 9 8 7 6 5 4 3 2 1

CONTENTS

INTRODUCTION

The fourth edition of PICTORIAL PRICE GUIDE TO AMERICAN ANTIQUES includes approximately 6,000 illustrated items sold at auction galleries in the United States between January 1, 1980 and April 1, 1981. The majority of the items included here date from the nineteenth or early twentieth century, with information necessary to make accurate identification.

Each entry is keyed to the auction house where the item was actually sold. A state abbreviation has been included for the readers' convenience, since prices vary in different locations across the country. Additionally, the year and the month the item was sold has been indicated. This unique method of pricing objects sets this price guide apart from all others on the market. Moreover, when the book becomes dated, it will serve as a reference guide for future generations.

In spite of a 10 percent buyers' premium added by many leading auction galleries and the shaky world economy, records continued to be set throughout 1980. It was the quality objects that fetched the hefty figures. Though grand sums paid oftentimes indicated a rising market in some fields, they as easily may signal one man's passion.

American furniture from all periods is still at the top of the market in popularity. Contrarily, massive European imports went down in price while prices for Victorian, Centennial, and custom-made furniture from the nineteenth century and well into the present century, continued to gain strength in the market — now that earlier period furniture is priced beyond the average buyer's means. Furniture that Gustav Stickley promoted in his Craftsman Magazine from 1901 to 1916, has brought staggering prices during the past year. And some of the better known furniture manufacturers, such as Kittinger, have seen early pieces of their fine furniture literally soar in price in recent months . . . which indicates that functional pieces are very popular collectibles these days.

Hand crafted textiles are still very much in demand and prices continue to soar, especially for choice quilts and coverlets. Voluminous scholarly attention given the Shakers attests to a steadily growing interest in their textiles.

Prices of lamps broke records at many leading auction galleries, and the most dramatic news was in the field of ceramics, when a Rookwood vase by Matt Daly, picturing a Sioux warrior sold for $32,000. Quality art glass, paperweights, and rare bottles sold very well, and there was a brisk market for dolls and toys. Overall, almost nothing in the antiques market showed a downward trend, which proves that the values of antiques rose faster than inflation during 1980.

Dorothy Hammond

ACKNOWLEDGEMENTS

I wish to express my sincere gratitude to the many auction galleries that have so generously provided pictorial material for this volume. Thanks are especially due to: Richard A. Bourne, Co., Hyannis Port, MA; Paul W. Calkins Auction Gallery, Peru, NY; Clements, Forney, TX; Paul Dias, Inc.; Early Auction Company, Milford, OH; Robert C. Eldred Co. Inc., East Dennis, MA; Garth Auctions, Inc., Delaware, OH; Laws Auction & Antiques, Manassas, VA; Morton's Auction Exchange, New Orleans, LA; Lloyd W. Ralston; Robert W. Skinner, Inc., Bolton, MA; Stratford Auction Center, Delaware, OH; and Adam A. Weschler & Son, Washington, D.C.

To Modena Spurlock, secretary, and Gail Hendry, project coordinator, go my deepest thanks for their countless hours of patient typing, proofreading, and organizing the many entries. Because the photographs contribute so much that is essential to this book, I am very grateful to Charles Thompson for his excellent work, and a special thank you to John Huey for cover photography.

ABBREVIATIONS USED WITHIN THIS BOOK AND THEIR MEANING

A . . . . Auction	Irid. . . . . Iridescent	Sgn. . . . . Signed
A.B.C. . . . . Acid Cut Back	Litho. . . . . Lithograph	W/ . . . . With
Am. . . . . American	Lrg. . . . . Large	Wh. . . . . White
Amt. . . . . Amount	Lt. . . . . Light	Wrt. . . . . Wrought
Attrib. . . . . Attributed	Mfg. . . . . Manufactured	
Blk. . . . . Black	M.O.P. . . . . Mother of Pearl	State Abbreviations used within this volume are:
Br. . . . . Brown	Mkd. . . . . Marked	CT . . . . Connecticut
Comb. . . . . Combination	M.W. . . . . Mt. Washington	DE . . . . Delaware
Cond. . . . . Condition	N. Eng. . . . . New England	LA . . . . Louisiana
Const. . . . . Construction	N.E.G.W. . . . . New England Glass Works	ME . . . . Maine
Decor. . . . . Decorated	Orig. . . . . Original	MD . . . . Maryland
Drk. . . . . Dark	Patt. . . . . Pattern	MA . . . . Massachusetts
D.Q.M.O.P. . . . . . Diamond Quilted Mother of Pearl	Pcs. . . . . Pieces	NH . . . . New Hampshire
Eng. . . . . English	Pr. . . . . Pair	NJ . . . . New Jersey
Escut. . . . . Escutcheon	Q.A. . . . . Queen Anne	NY . . . . New York
Ext. . . . . Exterior	Ref. . . . . Refinished	OH . . . . Ohio
Fr. . . . . French	Remov. . . . . Removable	PA . . . . Pennsylvania
Gr. . . . . Green	Repl. . . . . Replaced	TX . . . . Texas
Ht. . . . . Height	Repr. . . . . Repair	VA . . . . Virginia
Inc. . . . . Incomplete	Repro. . . . . Reproduction	WV . . . . West Virginia
Int. . . . . Interior	Sq. . . . . Square	WA D.C. . . . . Washington D.C.

A-MA May 1980   *Paul J. Dias, Inc.*
ROW I, L To R
INDIAN PORTRAITS, In Colors, Perry
Picture Co., 5¢ Each, Ca. 1898, F. A. Rine-
hart, Framed, 10" x 12" $90.00
STORE CARD, Fleischmann's Yeast,
Upper Left Corner Missing, Holes In Cor-
ners, Framed, 9½" x 11½" $17.50
ROW II, L To R
PHOTO, Ward's Cakes Bakery Truck,
Blk. & Wh., Framed, 6½" x 9¼" . . . $20.00
SIGN ON BOARD, Blk. & Wh. Whiskey,
4 Dogs Smoking Pipes & Drinking Whiskey,
Framed, 9" x 13½" $55.00

A-MA May 1980   *Paul J. Dias, Inc.*
L To R
REGULATOR CLOCK, Sauer's Flavor-
ing Extracts, Walnut Case, In Working
Cond., Orig. Gold Lettering, 39½" x 14½"
. . . . $725.00
TIN LITHO. CABINET, Dr. A. C. Daniels
Dog & Cat Remedies, Complete W/Mar-
quee: "Keep The Pets Well" By Chase
Emerson, Lift Up Doors In Back, 13" x 20" x
5" $1100.00

A-MA May 1980   *Paul J. Dias, Inc.*
L To R
TIN VACUUM, National Vacuum Cleaner,
Gr. W/Eagle Decal, Ca. 1911, 51" H. . . . $50.00
FOLK FIGURE, Wooden Uncle Sam, Paint-
ed, Double-Sided, Gr. Jacket, Red, Wh.
Striped Pants & Hat, Hands-Feet Missing, 5'
H. $75.00
SIGN ON CARDBOARD, Blue Label
Ketchup, Orig. Frame, Curtice Bros., Ro-
chester, NY, Sl. Water Staining Around
Edges, 18½" x 30" $50.00

A-MA May 1980   *Paul J. Dias, Inc.*
PORCELAIN SIGN, Hood Tires, Red,
Wh. & Blue, Few Lrg. Chips, 5' x 18"
. . . . $137.50
WOODEN SIGN, Blk. & Wh., Frank
Rand, Horse & Carriage Shoer & Black-
smith, Horse Shoe In The Middle, 7' x 19"
. . . . $187.50

A-MA Feb 1980   *Robert W. Skinner Inc.*
DESCRIPTIVE BROADSIDE, Ensigns &
Thayer, NY, 29" x 21¼" $150.00*

A-MA April 1980   *Richard A. Bourne Co., Inc.*
CURRIER & IVES TRADE CARDS
ROW I, L To R
AMATEUR MUSCLE IN THE SHELL
. . . . $20.00
CAUGHT ON THE FLY $25.00
ROW II, L To R
CAUGHT NAPPING $25.00
CROWING MATCH $25.00
ROW III, L To R
GETTING A HOIST $25.00
HORSE SHED STAKES $25.00
ROW IV, L To R
**NO MA'AM, I DIDN'T COME TO
SHOOT BIRDS** $25.00
YOUNG CADETS $25.00

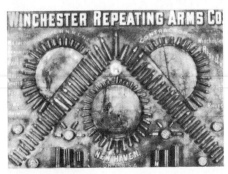

A-MA Feb 1980   *Robert W. Skinner, Inc.*
CARTRIDGE DISPLAY BOARD, Winchester Repeating Arms Co., Some Sam-
ples Repl. & Others Missing, Board
Stained & Discolored, N. Eng., Ca. 1880,
38" x 27" $450.00*

A-MA Mar 1980   *Richard A. Bourne Co., Inc.*
**COLLECTION OF ADVERTISING
CARDS,** Framed, 9 Cards $60.00

*Price does not include 10% buyer fee.

A-MA May 1980   *Paul J. Dias, Inc.*
L To R
LITHO. ON PAPER HANGING SIGN,
Allen & Ginter, "State Flags", Lrg. U.S.
Shield W/Eagle & Cards Of All The States,
Metal Ends For Hanging, Sm. Tear, 15″ x
21½″ $55.00
CARDBOARD FIGURAL STAND UP,
Moxie, Bend At Bottle Neck, 21″ H. . . . $30.00

A-MA May 1980   *Paul J. Dias, Inc.*
LITHO. ON CARDBOARD SIGN, La-
Preferencia Cigar, "30 Minutes In Havana",
Orig. Frame, Upper Left Corner Missing,
Edge Tears, 29½″ x 19½″ $100.00
LITHO. ON CARDBOARD SIGN, Hon-
est Scrap Tobacco, Orig. Frame, Sm. Nail
Holes On Margins, Sl. Wear, 18½″ x 26″
.... $262.50
STAND UP STORE DISPLAY, Now's
The Time For Jello, Cardboard Cut-Out,
23″ W., 56″ H. $112.50

A-MA May 1980   *Paul J. Dias, Inc.* ►
POLITICAL HANDKERCHIEF, Our
Choice, Harrison & Morton, Protection &
Prosperity, No Competition W/Half Paid
Labor, Framed, Red W/Wh. Stars . . $95.00
LITHO. ON PAPER POSTER, Uncle
Tom's Cabin, "Topsy's Recreation", Re-
paired Tear, Framed, 19″ x 27″ . . . $137.50

A-MA May 1980   *Paul J. Dias, Inc.*
STONEWARE DISPENSER, Dr. Swetts
Orig. Root Beer, Boston, MA, Tan W/Blk.
Lettering, Orig. Spigot, Wooden Lid Not
Orig., 7″ D., 12″ H. $150.00
**PORCELAIN SODA FOUNTAIN DIS-
PENSER,** Schuster's Root Beer 5¢, Br. &
Wh. W/Gold Lettering, 6¾″ D., 16″ H.
.... $100.00
PORCELAIN DISPENSER, Hires Root
Beer, Hour Glass Shaped, Orig. Pump,
Chip On Base, 7½″ D., 15″ H. . . . $175.00
**PORCELAIN SODA FOUNTAIN DIS-
PENSER,** Jersey Creme, The Perfect Drink,
Embossed Wh. W/Gr., Red & Gold, Orig.
Pump Top W/Crack On 1 Side, 7″ D., 16″ H.
.... $150.00
CABINET, Diamond Dye, The Washer-
woman, Oak Case W/Embossed Tin Front,
29½″ x 21½″ x 9½″ $400.00
CABINET, DeLaval Cream Separator, Oak
Case W/Embossed Tin Front, Int. W/Draw-
ers, 26″ x 17½″ x 10½ $325.00

A-MA May 1980   *Paul J. Dias, Inc.*
ADVERTISING BROADSIDE, Gr. Moun-
tain Balm Of Gilead & Cedar Plaster, Blk. &
Tan, Ca. 1868, Framed, 15½″ x 19½″
.... $70.00
LITHO ON PAPER SIGN, Arm & Ham-
mer Soda, Comic Man W/Lrg. Head & Blue
Coast W/Soda Buttons Holding Baby, 14″ x
20″ $150.00
TROLLEY CARD, Savon Cadum, The
Great Fr. Complexion Soap, Gray Ground,
Stained Across Top, Framed, 10½″ x 20½″
.... $25.00
PRINT, Winchester Repeating Arms. Co.,
By W. Leigh, Some Creasing, 1 Hole In Left
Side, Framed, 15″ x 19″ $40.00

A-MA May 1980   *Paul J. Dias, Inc.*
ROW I, L To R
LITHO. ON PAPER, U.S. Ammunition,
U.S. Cartridge Co., "The Blk. Shells", Re-
paired, Framed, 21″ x 45½″ $225.00
REVERSE PAINTING ON GLASS SIGN,
Estey Pianos, NY, Blk. W/Gold Lettering,
Trade Mrk. In Center, Framed, 20″ x 29½″
.... $145.00
ROW II, L To R
LITHO. ON PAPER SIGN, Red Indian
Cut Plug Tobacco, 5¢, Must Have It, Yellow
Ground, Framed, 22″ x 28″ $150.00
LITHO. ON PAPER, International Stock
Food, 3 Feeds For 1 Cent, Sow and Suckling
Piglets, Framed, 20″ x 28″ $150.00

A-MA May 1980   *Paul J. Dias, Inc.*
L To R

TIN SIGN, You Can Rely On Lewando's, Fancy Dyes, Fr. Cleaners, Boston, MA, Embossed, 19½″ x 13½″ $300.00

TIN SIGN, Delaval Separator Co., Self-Framed, Advertising On Edge Painted Over, Rusted Overall, 26″ D. $150.00

TIN SIGN, John P. Squire & Co., Boston, Self-Framed, Blue Ground, "I Make Squires Pure Food Products, Lt. Rust, 14½″ x 18½″ $500.00

TIN SIGN, C.P.F. Meerschaum & Briar Pipes, Self-Framed, Some Rust & Wear To Frame, 19″ x 16¼″ $112.50

A-MA May 1980   *Paul J. Dias, Inc.*
TIN APOTHECARY TRADE SIGN, Beaker Going Into Jar W/Scales, 30″ x 26″ $125.00
WOODEN BROADAXE, Advertising A.O.E. Of A. Foresters, Symbols On 1 Side, Plain On Other, 32″ L. $75.00

A-MA May 1980   *Paul J. Dias, Inc.*
L To R
TIN SIGN, C.D. Kenny Coffee, Self-Framed, 2 Girls Having Outdoor Tea, 8½″ x 12″ $100.00
TIN LITHO. PLATE, Peter Rabbit, Blue, 8″ D. $45.00

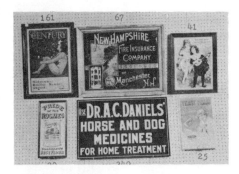

A-MA May 1980   *Paul J. Dias, Inc.*
ROW I, L To R
CENTURY POSTER By Maxfield Parrish, Ca. 1894, 2nd Prize In Centry Magazine Poster Contest, Midsummer Holiday Number, August, Framed, 19½″ x 13½″ $800.00

TIN SIGN, NH Fire Insurance Co. Of Manchester, Silver & Gold On Blk. Ground, Sl. Rusting On Bottom Of Sign, Framed, 18″ x 24″ $150.00

LITHO. ON PAPER, West Street Grocery, Quality Meats, Fruits & Vegetables, Girl & Boy Playing Mandolin, 10½″ x 14½″ $30.00

ROW II, L To R
PAPER ADVERTISEMENT, Pride Of The Rockies Flour, Colorado's Best Flour, Bag Of Flour W/Factory Inside, Framed, 7½″ x 15¼″ $65.00

TIN SIGN, Dr. A.C. Daniels Horse & Dog Medicines For Home Treatment, Embossed W/Blk. & Wh. Lettering, 18″ x 28″ .. $40.00

LITHO. STORE HANGING AD, Yeast Foam Makes Delicious Buckwheat Cakes $52.50

A-MA May 1980   *Paul J. Dias, Inc.*
ROW I, L To R
TIN STAND-UP SIGN, Munsingwear, Perfect Fitting Union Suits, Sign Faded, Scratches & Rust Spots, 19″ x 20″ .. $155.00
LITHO. ON PAPER, Palmer & Goodrich Tires, "Gwendolen", Advertising In Upper Left Corner, Tears Repaired, Ca. 1904, Framed, 21″ x 26½″ $90.00
ROW II, L To R
PAPER ADVERTISING, Egyptian Deities, The Utmost In Cigarettes, Framed, 15″ x 19″ $125.00
LITHO. ON PAPER, Worcester Salt, "The Best For Table, Kitchen & Dairy", Mounted On Linen, Tears Repaired, Water Stains, Framed, 14″ x 23½″ $50.00

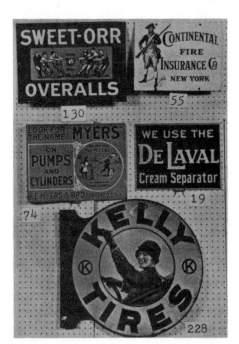

A-MA May 1980   *Paul J. Dias, Inc.*
ROW I, L To R
PORCELAIN SIGN, Sweet-Orr Overalls, Blue, Yellow & Wh., Men Playing Tug Of War W/Trousers, 14″ x 20″ $212.50
PORCELAIN SIGN, Continental Fire Insurance Co., NY, Blue Lettering On Wh., Revolutionary Soldier Holding Musket, 12″ x 16″ $87.50
ROW II, L To R
DOUBLE-SIDED TIN SIGN, Look For The Name "Myers" On Pumps & Cylinders, F.E. Myers & Bro., Ashland, OH, Yellow W/Blue & Red, 14″ x 18″ $95.00
PORCELAIN SIGN, We Use The DeLaval Cream Separator, Blue W/Yellow Letters, 12″ x 16″ $35.00
ROW III
DOUBLE-SIDED TIN HANGING SIGN, Kelly Tires, Woman In Red Driving Car, 1 Side Rusty, 24″ D. $150.00

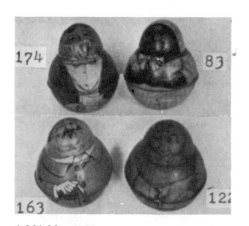

A-MA May 1980   Paul J. Dias, Inc.
ROW I, L To R
TIN ROLY POLY, Mayo's Cut Plug, The
Singing Waiter $250.00
ROLY POLYS, Lot Of 2, (1 Illus.), Mayo's
Cut Plug & Red Indian Cut Plug .. $325.00
ROW II, L To R
TIN ROLY POLY, Mayo's Cut Plug, The
Inspector From Scotland Yard.... $450.00
TIN ROLY POLY, Mayo's Cut Plug, The
Dutchman, Tin Darkened........ $275.00

A-MA May 1980   Paul J. Dias, Inc.
L To R
LITHO. ON PAPER, Ayer's Sarsaparilla,
Purifies The Blood, Makes The Weak Strong,
Ca. 1889, Mounted On Linen, Edge Tears
Repaired, Framed, 14" x 28" $375.00
LITHO. ON PAPER, Ayer's Cherry Pec-
toral,, Lowell, MA, Cures Coughs, Colds,
Throat & Lung Disorders, Mounted On
Linen, Tears Repaired, Ca. 1889, Framed,
14" x 28" $350.00

A-MA May 1980   Paul J. Dias, Inc.
FACTORY LITHO. ON PAPER, C. L.
Centlivre Brewing Co., Fort Wayne, IN,
Framed, 24½" x 38" $250.00

Left
A-MA May 1980   Paul J. Dias, Inc.
LITHO. ON PAPER, Seal Of NC Smoking
Tobacco, "Look Out Dar, I Is Comin' ",
Matted & Framed, 10½" x 13½" .. $200.00

Right
A-MA Feb 1980   Robert W. Skinner Inc.
POLITICAL POSTER, Currier & Ives,
NY, Minor Foxing & Tape Marks, Am.
.... $110.00*

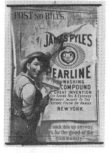 

A-MA May 1980   Paul J. Dias, Inc.
L To R
PAPER LITHO. ON CANVAS, James
Pyle's Pearline Washing Compound, Work-
man W/Paint Brush Putting Poster On
Fence, Minor Edge Tears, Framed, 28" x 42"
.... $612.50
LITHO. ON CANVAS SIGN, Houk Wire
Wheels, By G. L. Simmons, "Quick Change",
Framed, 21½" x 31½" $225.00

A-MA May 1980   Paul J. Dias, Inc.
L To R
CABINET, Diamond Dye, The Governess,
Cherry Case W/Embossed Tin Front, Case
Ref., 30½" x 23" x 10" $550.00
CABINET, Diamond Dye, The Maypole,
Cherry Case W/Embossed Tin Front, Reds
Faded To Pink, 30" x 22" x 10" ... $325.00

A-MA May 1980   Paul J. Dias, Inc.
L To R
GLOBE, Chrysler Sales Service, Milk Glass
Frame, Red, Yellow & Blk. W/Emblem In
Center $100.00
COUNTRY STORE FIGURE, Dutch Boy
Paint, Papier Mache, 31" H. $137.50
GLOBE, Fleet-Wing, Milk Glass Frame,
Red & Wh. W/Flying Bird $50.00

A-MA May 1980   Paul J. Dias, Inc.
L To R
WOODEN BARBER POLE, Painted Red,
Wh. & Blue, 42" H. $100.00
ADVERTISING CHAIR, Piedmont, Blue
& Wh. Porcelain Back, Double Sided
.... $50.00

A-MA May 1980   Paul J. Dias, Inc.
L To R
COFFEE TIN, Campbell Brand, 4-Lb.,
Red & Yellow W/Arabs & Camels .. $50.00
BOX, E. R. Durkee & Co. Spices, Paper
Label On Front & Inside Lid, 16" x 7¼" x 4"
.... $50.00
COUNTER TIN, Old Eng. Curve Cut Pipe
Tobacco, Slant Front, Red & Gray W/Gen-
tleman In Red Coat, 13" x 8½" x 10½"
.... $80.00

*Price does not include 10% buyer fee.

A-CT Oct 1980   Lloyd W. Ralston
L To R
GLOBE SAFE, Electroplated Steel & Iron,
5½" H. $80.00
CAPTAIN KIDD, Cast Iron, Repaint, 5¾" H.
. . . . $160.00

A-CT Oct 1980   Lloyd W. Ralston
L To R
BARREL W/ARMS, Cast Iron, 3¾" H.
. . . . $450.00
BARREL W/ARMS, Brass, 3½" H. . . . $80.00

A-CT Oct 1980   Lloyd W. Ralston
L To R
PIG, "I Made Chicago Famous", Cast Iron,
2¼" H. $100.00
PIG, "I Made Chicago Famous", Cast Iron,
No Paint, 2¾" H. 150.00

A-CT Oct 1980   Lloyd W. Ralston
L To R
CAT, Cast Iron, 4½" H. $260.00
CAT, Cast Iron, Gilded, 2¾" H. . . $160.00

A-CT Oct 1980   Lloyd W. Ralston
CAMEL, Cast Iron, 7¼" H. $285.00

A-CT Oct 1980   Lloyd W. Ralston
L To R
WATER WHEELS, Nickeled Cast Iron &
Pressed Steel, 4¼" H. $2100.00
RABBIT, Cast Iron, 5" H. $90.00

A-CT Oct 1980   Lloyd W. Ralston
L To R
RABBIT, Cast Iron, 4¾" H. $160.00
RABBIT, Cast Iron, No Paint, 6½" H.
. . . . $100.00

A-CT Oct 1980   Lloyd W. Ralston
L To R
SEATED MONKEY, Pottery, 6" H.
. . . . $20.00
MODERN OWL, Cast Iron, 4" H. . . $30.00

A-CT Oct 1980   Lloyd W. Ralston
L To R
THRIFTY PIG, Cast Iron, 6¾" H. . . $75.00
MONEY BAG, Cast Iron, 3½" H. . . . $775.00
SEATED PIG, Nickeled Cast Iron, 2¾" H.
. . . . $65.00

A-CT Oct 1980   Lloyd W. Ralston
L To R
OWL, Cast Iron, 4¼" H. $100.00
OWL ON STUMP, Cast Iron, 5" H.
. . . . $115.00

A-CT Oct 1980   Lloyd W. Ralston
L To R
TURKEY, Cast Iron, 4¾" H. $500.00
TURKEY, Cast Iron, 3¾" H. $110.00

A-CT Oct 1980   Lloyd W. Ralston
CAMEL W/Pack, Cast Iron, Repaired, Poor
Paint, 2¾" H. $420.00

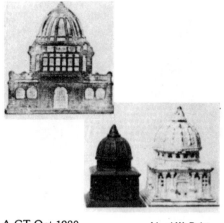

A-CT Oct 1980   Lloyd W. Ralston
L To R
COLUMBIA BANK, Electroplated Cast
Iron, 6″ x 4½″ $170.00
COLUMBIA BANK, Cast Iron, Overpaint,
5″ x 5¼″ $175.00
COLUMBIAN EXPO, Cast Iron, 5″ x 5¼″
. . . . $90.00

A-CT Oct 1980   Lloyd W. Ralston
L To R
BANK BUILDING, Cast Iron, Repaired,
3¾″ x 1¾″ $15.00
BANK BUILDING, Cast Iron, 5½″ x 2½″
. . . . $80.00

A-CT Oct 1980   Lloyd W. Ralston
L To R
HARPER THRONE 1953, Electroplated
Cast Iron, 8¼″ H. $55.00
THRONE, Eng., Aluminum, 3½″ H.
. . . . $65.00

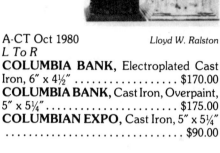

A-CT Oct 1980   Lloyd W. Ralston
L To R
BANK BUILDING, Cast Iron, 4½″ x 4¼″
. . . . $25.00
BANK BUILDING, Cast Iron, 6½″ x 4¼″
. . . . $80.00

A-CT Oct 1980   Lloyd W. Ralston
L To R
I LOVE A COPPER, Eng., Jappaned, Cast
Iron, 6″ H. $975.00
EVERY COPPER HELPS, Eng., Cast
Iron, 4¾″ H. $925.00
EVERY COPPER HELPS, Eng., Alumi-
num, 5¾″ H. $115.00

A-CT Oct 1980   Lloyd W. Ralston
L To R
WESTMINSTER ABBEY, Eng., Cast Iron,
6¼″ x 3¼″ $75.00
WESTMINSTER ABBEY, Eng., Raised
Letters, Cast Iron, Flush Front, 6⅜″ H.
. . . . $85.00

A-CT Oct 1980   Lloyd W. Ralston
BEAR STEALING PIG, Overpaint, Cast
Iron, 5½″ x 2¼″ $950.00

A-CT Oct 1980   Lloyd W. Ralston
STORK W/BABIES, Hanging, Eng., Cast
Iron, 8¾″ H. $425.00

A-CT Oct 1980   Lloyd W. Ralston
L To R
3-TOWERS BANK, Eng., Cast Iron, 7¼″
H. $450.00
CASTLE, Cast Iron, Repair, 3¾″ H.
. . . . $265.00

A-CT Oct 1980   Lloyd W. Ralston
PIG, Cast Iron, No Paint, 4″ W. $45.00

A-CT Oct 1980   *Lloyd W. Ralston*
L To R
EDISON RADIO, Pot Metal, 4″ H.
.... $60.00
PHONOGRAPH, Save For Your Bruns-
wick, Pot Metal, 5″ H. $60.00

A-CT Oct 1980   *Lloyd W. Ralston*
BERT WHITING BANK, Ca. 1969, Orig.,
5½″ x 6″ $90.00

A-CT Oct 1980   *Lloyd W. Ralston*
L To R
BUNKER HILL MONUMENT, Cast Iron,
7″ x 3¾″ $1100.00
BUNKER HILL MONUMENT, "Centen-
nial", Painted Tin, 6½″ H. $450.00

A-CT Oct 1980   *Lloyd W. Ralston*
L To R
EUREKA #410 GAS STOVE, Eng., Tin,
5¼″ x 3″ $35.00
REVO STOVE, Tin, Eng., 5½″ x 3½″
.... $45.00
RADIATION STOVE, Eng., Tin, 8½″ H.
.... $90.00

A-CT Oct 1980   *Lloyd W. Ralston*
PLASTIC BANKS, Lot Of 3, Emerson
Radio, Hopalong Cassidy & Serval Refrig-
erator $10.00

A-CT Oct 1980   *Lloyd W. Ralston*
INDEPENDENCE HALL, Cast Iron, 10″
x 9¼″ $500.00

A-CT Oct 1980   *Lloyd W. Ralston*
AIRPLANES, Lot Of 2, 1 Nickel Plated
Steel, Other Die Cast $220.00

A-CT Oct 1980   *Lloyd W. Ralston*
L To R
STATUE OF LIBERTY, Cast Iron, 9½″ H.
.... $475.00
STATUE OF LIBERTY, Cast Iron, 6½″ H.
.... $35.00
STATUE OF LIBERTY, Cast Iron, 6¼″ H.
.... $40.00

A-CT Oct 1980   *Lloyd W. Ralston*
INDEPENDENCE HALL, Cast Iron, 9″ x
6¾″ $625.00

A-CT Oct 1980 *Lloyd W. Ralston*
L To R
STATE, Key Lock Door, Cast Iron, 6¾ x 5½″
.... $50.00
BANK BUILDING, Cast Iron, 5¾″ x 4¼″
.... $50.00

A-CT Oct 1980 *Lloyd W. Ralston*
L To R
BUILDING, Cast Iron, 5″ x 3″ ... $425.00
BUILDING, Cast Iron, 4″ x 2″ ... $390.00

A-CT Oct 1980 *Lloyd W. Ralston*
L To R
BANK, Cast Iron, Stenciling, 5½″ x 4¼″
.... $200.00
BANK, Cast Iron, 4¼″ x 3¼″ $35.00

A-CT Oct 1980 *Lloyd W. Ralston*
L To R
HOUSE W/PORCH, Cast Iron, 3″ H.
.... $30.00
2-STORY HOUSE, Cast Iron, 4″ x 3¾″
.... $55.00

A-CT Oct 1980 *Lloyd W. Ralston*
L To R
BARREL, Brass, 3″ H. $10.00
TANKARD, Covered, Brass, 3¾″ H. ..$20.00

A-CT Oct 1980 *Lloyd W. Ralston*
HOUSE W/PORCH, Cast Iron, Blue Roof,
Poor Cond., 3″ x 2½″ $30.00

A-CT Oct 1980 *Lloyd W. Ralston*
FORTUNE SHIP, Cast Iron, 4″ x 5½″
.... $1300.00

A-CT Oct 1980 *Lloyd W. Ralston*
PHONOGRAPH, Save For Your Sunny
Suds, Advertising, Pot Metal, 4¾″ H.
.... $75.00

A-CT Oct 1980 *Lloyd W. Ralston*
MERMAID, Cast Iron, 4½″ x 4″ .. $900.00

A-CT Oct 1980 *Lloyd W. Ralston*
L To R
BLACK BUST, Aluminum, 5″ H. ...$180.00
PICCANINNY, Cast Iron, 5¼″ x 4½″
.... $150.00

A-CT Oct 1980 *Lloyd W. Ralston*
BATTLESHIP MAINE, Cast Iron, 4½″ x
4½″ $250.00

A-CT Oct 1980 *Lloyd W. Ralston*
DOLPHIN, Cast Iron, 4½″ x 4″ .. $450.00

A-CT Oct 1980 *Lloyd W. Ralston*
CAMPBELL KIDS, Cast Iron, 3¼″ x 4¼″
.... $165.00

A-CT Oct 1980   *Lloyd W. Ralston*
L To R
JUG, Cast Iron, 4″ H. $150.00
MAJESTIC REFRIGERATOR, Cast Iron
& Tin, 4½″ H. $170.00

A-CT Oct 1980   *Lloyd W. Ralston*
BANK BUILDING, Cast Iron, 5½″ x 4¼″
. . . . $60.00

A-CT Oct 1980   *Lloyd W. Ralston*
SMILING PIG, Variation, Cast Iron, Overpaint, 2¾″ x 5¼″ $55.00

A-CT Oct 1980   *Lloyd W. Ralston*
SEATED PIG, Cast Iron, 3″ H. . . . $15.00

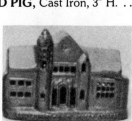

A-CT Oct 1980   *Lloyd W. Ralston*
REID LIBRARY, Cast Iron, 3½″ H. . . $175.00

A-CT Oct 1980   *Lloyd W. Ralston*
L To R
STATE BANK, For Our New Church,
Cast Iron, 4″ x 3″ $90.00
STATE BANK, Cast Iron, 5½″ x 4″ . . $50.00

A-CT Oct 1980   *Lloyd W. Ralston*
BOSTON STATE HOUSE, Cast Iron,
5¼″ H. $700.00

A-CT Oct 1980   *Lloyd W. Ralston*
L To R
STOVE, Norman, Nickel Plated Cast Iron,
2″ x 3″ $200.00
TIGER, Porcelain Over Iron, 4″ x 3¾″
. . . . $75.00

A-CT Oct 1980   *Lloyd W. Ralston*
L To R
STATE BANK, Key Lock Opening Door,
Cast Iron, 8½″ H. $220.00
STATE BANK, Key Lock Door, Cast Iron,
5¾″ H. $60.00
STATE BANK, Cast Iron, 3″ x 2¼″ . . $135.00

A-CT Oct 1980   *Lloyd W. Ralston*
L To R
STATE, Cast Iron, 8″ x 7″ $200.00
STATE, Cast Iron, 5½″ x 4¼″ $45.00
STATE, Cast Iron, 6¾″ x 5½″ $80.00

A-CT Oct 1980   *Lloyd W. Ralston*
L To R
BANK BUILDING, Cast Iron, 5½″ x 4¼″
. . . . $55.00
BANK BUILDING, Cast Iron, 5¼″ x 3¾″
. . . . $60.00

A-CT Oct 1980   *Lloyd W. Ralston*
L To R
HOME SAVINGS BANK, Cast Iron, 5¾″ H.
. . . . $70.00
BANK BUILDING, Cast Iron, 3″ x 2¾″
. . . . $35.00

BANKS **17**

A-CT Oct 1980 *Lloyd W. Ralston*
SCOTTIE DOG, Cast Iron, 3¼" H. . . . $80.00

A-CT Oct 1980 *Lloyd W. Ralston*
L To R
GEM FURNACE, Cast Iron, No Paint, 4½"
H. $70.00
**SAVE YOUR MONEY & BUY A GAS
STOVE,** Tin & Cast Iron, 5½" x 4" . . $80.00

A-CT Oct 1980 *Lloyd W. Ralston*
L To R
SOLDIER-MINUTE MAN, Cast Iron, 6" H.
. . . . $425.00
WWI SOLDIER, Cast Iron, 7" H. . . $500.00

A-CT Oct 1980 *Lloyd W. Ralston*
L To R
MARSHALL FURNACE, Cast Iron, 3¾" H.
. . . . $85.00
GILSON MAGIC FURNACE, Cast Iron,
5" H. $110.00

A-CT Oct 1980 *Lloyd W. Ralston*
KELVINATOR REFRIGERATOR, Orig.
Arcade Label, Cast Iron & Tin, 4" H.
. . . . $115.00

A-CT Oct 1980 *Lloyd W. Ralston*
L To R
WWI TANK, Brass, 2¼" x 5" $290.00
GENERAL PERSHING, Electroplated
Cast Iron, 7¾" H. $70.00

 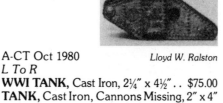

A-CT Oct 1980 *Lloyd W. Ralston*
L To R
WWI TANK, Cast Iron, 2¼" x 4½" . . $75.00
TANK, Cast Iron, Cannons Missing, 2" x 4"
. . . . $60.00

A-CT Oct 1980 *Lloyd W. Ralston*
DONKEY, Cast Iron, Poor Cond., 6¾" H.
. . . . $70.00

A-CT Oct 1980 *Lloyd W. Ralston*
L To R
SHELL, Nickel Plated Cast Iron, 7¾" H.
. . . . $25.00
SHELL, Electroplated Cast Iron, 7¾" H.
. . . . $25.00

 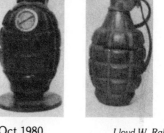

A-CT Oct 1980 *Lloyd W. Ralston*
L To R
HAND GRENADE ON PEDESTAL, Cast
Iron, 4" H. $85.00
WWI HAT, Tin, 2" x 3¾" $45.00
HAND GRENADE, Tin & Iron, 4½" H.
. . . . $50.00

A-CT Oct 1980 *Lloyd W. Ralston*
PIG, Cast Iron, 2¼" x 3¾" $500.00

A-CT Oct 1980 *Lloyd W. Ralston*
TINY PIG, Cast Iron, 1¾" x 3" . . $2600.00

A-CT Nov 1980 *Lloyd W. Ralston*
L To R
ARTILLERY BANK, Mechanical, Shepard, Nickel Plated & Brass Plated Cast Iron $375.00
TRICK PONY BANK, Mechanical, Shepard, Painted Cast Iron, Repl. Trap .. $335.00

A-CT Nov 1980 *Lloyd W. Ralston*
DEER BANKS, Lot Of 2, Still, Painted Cast Iron, 9½″ H. $120.00

A-CT Nov 1980 *Lloyd W. Ralston*
L To R
FERRIS WHEEL BANK, Mechanical, Hubley/Bauer, Painted Cast Iron & Pressed Tin, Clockwork Working, Restorations, 17″ W., 22″ H. $1800.00
BREMER STADTMUSIKANTEN BANK, Still, Pot Metal, Nursery Rhyme Bank, 5½″ H. $700.00
CAMEL BANK, Still, Painted Cast Iron, 7¼″ H. $150.00

A-CT Nov 1980 *Lloyd W. Ralston*
MAIN STREET TROLLEY BANK, Still, Cast Iron, 6¾″ L. $350.00

A-MA Dec 1980 *Robert W. Skinner Inc.*
CAST IRON MECHANICAL BANKS
L To R
DRK. TOWN BATTERY, Orig. Paint, Coin Release Door Missing, J. & E. Stevens Co., CT, Late 19th C., 10″ L. $875.00*
PUNCH & JUDY BANK, Orig. Cond., Pat. July, 1884, Shepard Hdw. Co., NY, 7½″ H. $825.00*
INDIAN MAIDEN, Am., Late 19th C. $750.00*

A-CT Nov 1980 *Lloyd W. Ralston*
L To R
BOY ROBBING NEST BANK, Mechanical, Stevens, Painted Cast Iron, Some Restoration $900.00
CAT & MOUSE BANK, Mechanical, Stevens, Painted Cast Iron $1400.00

A-CT Nov 1980 *Lloyd W. Ralston*
L To R
BABY DUCK BANKS, Lot Of 2, Still, Painted Cast Iron, 5″ H. $150.00
STILL BANKS, Lot Of 2, Fido & Mosque, Painted Cast Iron, 5″ H. $60.00
FROWNING MAN BANK, Still, Hanging Wall Plaque, Old Iron, No Paint, 5¾″ H. $550.00

A-MA Dec 1980 *Robert W. Skinner Inc.*
BANKS
L To R
MECHANICAL, Cast Iron Novelty Bank, J. & E. Stevens Co., CT, 4½″ Sq., 6⅞″ H. $290.00*
CAST IRON STILL, State Bank, Orig. Finish, Am., Late 19th C., 8½″ H. $110.00*
PAINTED TIN HOUSE, Vic.-Style, Sl. Alligatoring On Roof, Am., Late 19th C., 7½″ H. $130.00*
CAST IRON HIP ROOF, Am., Late 19th C., 5⅜″ H. $30.00*

A-CT Nov 1980 *Lloyd W. Ralston*
L To R
VICTORIA CANDY VENDING BANK, Mechanical, Stollwerck, Tin & Glass, 10¾″ H. $500.00
SIGNAL CABIN BANK, Mechanical, German Tin, 4″ L., 6″ H. $360.00

A-MA Dec 1980 *Robert W. Skinner, Inc.*
CAST IRON MECHANICAL BANKS
L To R
FROG ON DRUM, Patd., Aug. 29, 1872, Am. $200.00*
2 FROGS, Glass Eyes, Lrg. Frog Damaged, J. & E. Stevens Co., CT, Ca. 1882, 4048¾″ L. $210.00*
FROG ON STUMP, Am., Late 19th C., 3⅛″ H. $150.00*

A-CT Oct 1980 *Lloyd W. Ralston*
STILL BANKS
L To R
CAT ON TUB, Cast Iron, 4″ H. .. $120.00
DOG ON TUB, Cast Iron, 4″ H. .. $100.00

*Price does not include 10% buyer fee.

A-CT Oct 1980   *Lloyd W. Ralston*
L To R
HUMPTY DUMPTY, Litho. Tin, 5¼" H.
.... $50.00
MICKEY MOUSE POST OFFICE, Litho.
Tin, 6" H. $45.00
MICKEY MOUSE POST OFFICE, Litho.
Tin, 4½" H. $25.00

A-CT Oct 1980   *Lloyd W. Ralston*
L To R
NATIONAL CANNERS ASSOCIATION,
Advertising, Litho. Tin, 4" H. $20.00
LI'L ABNER, Advertising, Litho. Tin, 4¼" H.
.... $40.00

A-CT Oct 1980   *Lloyd W. Ralston*
L To R
**COIN REGISTERING CALENDAR
BANK,** Advertising, Litho. Tin, 7¾" H.
.... $35.00
BUILDING W/POST BOX, Litho. Tin, 7"
H. $160.00

A-CT Oct 1980   *Lloyd W. Ralston*
L To R
TELEPHONE BOOTH, Litho. Tin, 5¾" H.
.... $20.00
TELEPHONE BOOTH, Litho. Tin, 5¾" H.
.... $30.00

A-CT Oct 1980   *Lloyd W. Ralston*
HOUSE BANKS, Lot Of 3, 1 Litho. Tin, 1
Painted Tin $85.00

A-CT Oct 1980   *Lloyd W. Ralston*
L To R
STOP & GO TRAFFIC LIGHT, Twist
Action, Litho. & Painted Tin, 4½" H.
.... $40.00
POST OFFICE SAVINGS BANK, Cleared
At Christmas, Paper Label, Painted Tin,
Eng., 7½" H. $70.00
POST OFFICE, Painted Tin, Paper Label,
Eng., 4" H. $10.00

◄ A-CT Oct 1980   *Lloyd W. Ralston*
L To R
CAMERA, Litho. Tin, 2¾" x 3" .. $220.00
SAILOR BOY AT SHORE, Photo In Paint-
ed Tin Box, 3½" x 2¼" $125.00

A-CT Oct 1980   *Lloyd W. Ralston*
L To R
HANSEL & GRETEL, Litho. Tin, 2¼" H.
.... $95.00
RUSTIC COTTAGE, Litho. Tin, 2¼" H.
.... $35.00

A-CT Oct 1980   *Lloyd W. Ralston*
COTTAGE, Geo. Brown, Painted & Stenciled Tin, 6" H. $450.00

A-CT Oct 1980   *Lloyd W. Ralston*
L To R
MASTER SIMPSON BOOK, Litho. Tin,
7" x 5" $90.00
STANDING BEAR, Cast Iron, 7" H.
.... $400.00

A-CT Oct 1980   *Lloyd W. Ralston*
L To R
SEATED BRONZE MONKEY, Cast Iron,
Separate Hat, 4" H. $375.00
HOMEY BEAR, Cast Iron, 2½" H. .. $700.00
BEAR STANDING, Cast Iron, 5¼" H.
.... $50.00

A-CT Oct 1980   *Lloyd W. Ralston*
ARMY-NAVY BANK, Nickel Plated Cast
Iron, 6″ H. $275.00

A-CT Oct 1980   *Lloyd W. Ralston*
L To R
TIME SAFE, Nickel Plated Cast Iron, 7¼″ H.
. . . . $300.00

BANK OF INDUSTRY, Nickel Plated
Cast Iron, 5½″ H. $70.00

A-CT Oct 1980   *Lloyd W. Ralston*
L To R
O EYE C, Paper Litho. On Wood, 6½″ x 5¼″
. . . . $90.00

TIME LOCK SAFE, Paper Label, Embossed, Litho. Tin, 5½″ H. $70.00

◄ A-CT Oct 1980   *Lloyd W. Ralston*
L To R
MASCOT SAFE ON WHEELS, Litho.
Tin, 4″ x 3″ $70.00
MASCOT SAFE ON WHEELS, Litho.
Tin, 5¼″ x 3¾″ $70.00

A-CT Oct 1980   *Lloyd W. Ralston*
GEM SAFE, Painted Wood, 9″ x 7¼″
. . . . $100.00

A-CT Oct 1980   *Lloyd W. Ralston*
L To R
KEYLESS SAVINGS BANK, Advertis-
ing, Painted & Stenciled Tin, 5¼″ H.
. . . . $75.00
NATIONAL SAFE DEPOSIT, Cast Iron
& Steel, 6″ H. $110.00

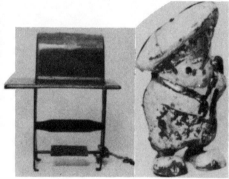

A-CT Oct 1980   *Lloyd W. Ralston*
L To R
SINGER SEWING MACHINE, Litho. &
Painted Tin, Orig. Key, 5½″ H. . . $1000.00

SAILOR BOY W/TELESCOPE, German,
Painted Tin, 5¾″ H. $105.00

A-CT Oct 1980   *Lloyd W. Ralston*
L To R
WATCH ME GROW, Man W/Straw Hat,
Litho. Tin, 5½″ H. $35.00
JOCKEY HEAD, German, Litho. Tin, 2¼″ H.
. . . . $150.00
KANTER'S BABY BELL TELEPHONE,
Painted Tin, 10″ H. $110.00

A-CT Oct 1980   *Lloyd W. Ralston*
L To R
COLLEGE HAT, Litho. Tin, Advertising,
4″ H. $135.00
SAVINGS BANK, Painted & Stenciled
Tin, 4¼″ H. $35.00

A-CT Oct 1980   *Lloyd W. Ralston*
L To R
BOOT, Do It For The Kids W/Shoes, Tin,
3″ H. $150.00
MILITARY HAT, Painted Tin, 3½″ H.
. . . . $85.00
GOTHIC, Painted & Stenciled Tin, 4¼″ H.
. . . . $135.00

A-CT Oct 1980   *Lloyd W. Ralston*
L To R
PUNCH & JUDY PUPPET SHOW, Litho.
Tin, 3″ H. $225.00
BRICK HOUSE, Litho. & Painted Tin, 3¼″
H. $35.00
JOHN BULL'S MONEY BOX BARREL,
Litho. Tin, 2½″ x 3″ $55.00

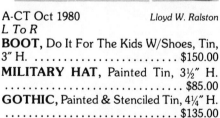

A-CT Oct 1980   *Lloyd W. Ralston*
L To R
POST OFFICE GR VI, Litho. & Painted Tin, Eng., 5¼″ H. $15.00
FAMILY JOURNAL MONEY BOX, Litho. Tin, Eng., 4½″ H. $10.00

A-CT Oct 1980   *Lloyd W. Ralston*
L To R
HORSE, Beauty, Cast Iron, 4″ H. .. $30.00
POST OFFICE, Litho. Tin, Canada, 4½″ H. $30.00

A-CT Oct 1980   *Lloyd W. Ralston*
L To R
LION, Cast Iron, 2½″ H. $135.00
3 MONKEYS, Cast Iron, 3¼″ H. .. $165.00

A-CT Oct 1980   *Lloyd W. Ralston*
L To R
SEATED RABBIT, Cast Iron, 3½″ H. $70.00
RABBIT LAYING DOWN, Cast Iron, 2¼″ H. $475.00

A-CT Oct 1980   *Lloyd W. Ralston*
L To R
BEAR, Cast Iron, No Paint, 2½″ H. .. $85.00
SAVINGS BANK, Tammany Tiger, Cast Iron, No Paint, 4″ H. $3200.00

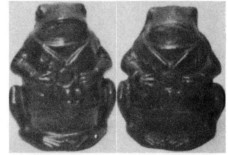

A-CT Oct 1980   *Lloyd W. Ralston*
L To R
PROF. PUG FROG, Cast Iron, 3¼″ H. $210.00
PROF. PUG FROG, Lead, 3¼″ H. ..$50.00

A-CT Oct 1980   *Lloyd W. Ralston*
L To R
SEATED ELEPHANT, Cast Iron, 4½″ H. $450.00
ELEPHANT, Cast Iron, 2¾″ H. .. $35.00

A-CT Oct 1980   *Lloyd W. Ralston*
Top To Bottom
COW, Cast Iron, 3½″ H. $90.00
BULL, Cast Iron, Overpaint, 3½″ H. $105.00

◄ A-CT Oct 1980   *Lloyd W. Ralston*
L To R
SADDLE HORSE, Confederate, Cast Iron, 4½″ H. $325.00
HORSE, Cast Iron, 2¾″ H. $325.00

A-CT Oct 1980   *Lloyd W. Ralston*
Top To Bottom
LION, Cast Iron, 5¼″ H. $55.00
LION, Cast Iron, 3″ H. $25.00

A-CT Oct 1980   *Lloyd W. Ralston*
L To R
LION, Cast Iron, 4″ H. $10.00
BEAR, Cast Iron, No Paint, 2½″ H. .. $90.00

A-CT Oct 1980   *Lloyd W. Ralston*
L To R
DONKEY, Cast Iron, 6½″ H. ... $145.00
DONKEY, Cast Iron, 4¼″ H. ... $120.00

A-CT Oct 1980   *Lloyd W. Ralston*
L To R
LION, Cast Iron, 3¾″ H. $30.00
FROG ON LATTICE, Cast Iron, 4¾″ H. $300.00

A-CT Oct 1980   *Lloyd W. Ralston*
TABERNACLE SAVINGS BANK, Cast Iron, 2¼″ H. $925.00

A-CT Oct 1980   *Lloyd W. Ralston*
L To R
LINCOLN CABIN, Center Chimney Variation, Cast Iron, 2½″ x 3½″ $110.00
LINCOLN CABIN, Cast Iron, 2½″ x 3½″
.... $125.00

A-CT Oct 1980   *Lloyd W. Ralston*
L To R
BANK BUILDING, 6-Sided, Cast Iron, 2½″ x 2½″ $200.00
BUILDING, 6-Sided, Cast Iron, 3¼″ x 3¼″
.... $310.00
OVAL BANK, Cast Iron, 3″ x 3″ .. $280.00

A-CT Oct 1980   *Lloyd W. Ralston*
L To R
COUNTY BANK, Cast Iron, 4¼″ x 5¼″
.... $130.00
BANK BUILDING, Cast Iron, 2¾″ x 2¼″
.... $40.00

A-CT Oct 1980   *Lloyd W. Ralston*
L To R
CHURCH, Cast Iron, Eng., 3″ x 2¾″
.... $165.00
MOSQUE, Cast Iron, Regilded, 2¾″ x 2½″
.... $40.00

A-CT Oct 1980   *Lloyd W. Ralston*
L To R
DUTCH BOY, Cast Iron, 6¾″ H. . .$750.00
DUTCH GIRL, Cast Iron, 6½″ H. . .$575.00

A-CT Oct 1980   *Lloyd W. Ralston*
L To R
CLOWN, Cast Iron, 6¼″ H. $75.00
MASCOT-BOY, On Baseball, Cast Iron, 5¾″ H. $1800.00
FOOTBALL PLAYER, Cast Iron, 5¾″ H.
.... $275.00

A-CT Oct 1980   *Lloyd W. Ralston*
L To R
BOY W/FOOTBALL, Varnished Nickel, 5″ H. $2800.00
SAILOR, Cast Iron, 5¾″ H. $170.00

A-CT Oct 1980   *Lloyd W. Ralston*
CLOTHES BASKET, Tin, Repaired, 2½″ x 4″ $220.00

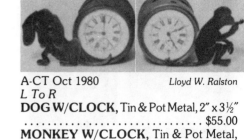

A-CT Oct 1980   *Lloyd W. Ralston*
L To R
DOG W/CLOCK, Tin & Pot Metal, 2″ x 3½″
.... $55.00
MONKEY W/CLOCK, Tin & Pot Metal, 2″ x 3¼″ $50.00

A-CT Oct 1980   *Lloyd W. Ralston*
L To R
CAT, MOUSE & CRACKER BARREL, Pot Metal & Tin, Eng., 2½″ x 3″ .. $360.00
DOG & DRUM, Tin & Pot Metal, 2″ x 2¾″
.... $50.00

A-CT Oct 1980   *Lloyd W. Ralston*
L To R
ELEPHANT W/BARREL, Pot Metal, 4½″ H. $110.00
LINDBERG BUST, Aluminum, 6¼″ H.
.... $70.00

A-CT Oct 1980   *Lloyd W. Ralston*
L To R
CHIMNEY SWEEP, Pot Metal, 4¼″ x 3″
.... $575.00
MAN IN BARREL, Composition, 4¼″ H.
.... $120.00

A-CT Oct 1980   *Lloyd W. Ralston*
AUTO, Plated Pot Metal, 2¼″ x 5″ .. $55.00

A-CT Oct 1980   *Lloyd W. Ralston*
L To R
RADIO, Cast Iron, 4″ H. $75.00
RADIO, Cast Iron, 2¾″ H. $110.00

A-CT Oct 1980   *Lloyd W. Ralston*
L To R
RADIO, Cast Iron, 3¼″ H. $55.00
RADIO, Cast Iron, 3¾″ H. $95.00

A-CT Oct 1980   *Lloyd W. Ralston*
L To R
MAJESTIC RADIO, Electroplated Cast
Iron, 4½″ H. $60.00
TEMPLETONE RADIO BANK, Tin &
Cast Iron, 4¼″ H. $110.00

A-CT Oct 1980   *Lloyd W. Ralston*
WHITE CITY PUZZLE BANK, Paper
Label, Electroplated, Cast Iron, 4½″ H.
.... $400.00

A-CT Oct 1980   *Lloyd W. Ralston*
TOY RADIO BANK, Nickel Plated Cast
Iron & Tin, Repro. Trap, Repaint Over
Nickel, 2¾″ H. $155.00

A-CT Oct 1980   *Lloyd W. Ralston*
L To R
WHITE CITY PUZZLE BARREL, Nickel
Plated Cast Iron, 3½″ H. $95.00
WHITE CITY PUZZLE SAFE, Paper
Label, Electroplated, Cast Iron, 2¾″ H.
.... $140.00

A-CT Oct 1980   *Lloyd W. Ralston*
L To R
WHITE CITY PUZZLE SAFE, Electro-
plated Cast Iron, 5″ H. $110.00
WHITE CITY PUZZLE SAFE, Nickel
Plated Cast Iron, 4¼″ H. $65.00

A-CT Oct 1980   *Lloyd W. Ralston*
L To R
BANK OF COMMERCE, Electroplated
Cast Iron, 6¾″ H. $180.00
WHITE CITY PUZZLE BANK, Orig.
Handle, Nickel Plated Cast Iron, 3¼″ H.
.... $50.00

A-CT Oct 1980   *Lloyd W. Ralston*
L To R
TOWER BANK, Cast Iron, No Paint, 4¼″ H.
.... $190.00
BUILDING, Cast Iron, 4¾″ x 2½″ .. $70.00
SAVE & SMILE, Hanging, Eng., Cast Iron,
Old Repaint, 7¼″ x 2″ $385.00

A-CT Oct 1980   *Lloyd W. Ralston*
L To R
EIFFEL TOWER, Variation, Cast Iron,
10½″ H. $625.00
EIFFEL TOWER, Cast Iron, 9″ H. .. $625.00

A-CT Oct 1980   *Lloyd W. Ralston*
L To R
HUMPTY DUMPTY, Cast Iron, Eng., Ear
Screws, 6″ H. $650.00
JARMULOWSKY BUILDING, Cast Iron,
Damaged Base Plate, 7¾″ x 5″ ... $250.00

A-CT Oct 1980   *Lloyd W. Ralston*
BATTLESHIP MAINE, Cast Iron, Jappaned, 4¾″ x 4½″ $210.00

A-CT Oct 1980   *Lloyd W. Ralston*
OREGON, Cast Iron, Recast Twist Pin, 5″
x 6¼″ $240.00

A-CT Oct 1980   *Lloyd W. Ralston*
L To R
CHURCH W/CLOCK STEEPLE, Painted
& Stenciled Tin, 12½" H. $1800.00
CHURCH W/LRG. BELL, Painted & Sten-
ciled Tin, 5" H. $55.00
SAVINGS BANK, Painted & Stenciled Tin,
4½" H. $45.00

A-CT Oct 1980   *Lloyd W. Ralston*
L To R
ADA COTTAGE, Converted Toy, Painted
Tin, 8" H. $170.00
EAGLE, Cast Iron, Old Repaint, 4" H.
.... $470.00

A-CT Oct 1980   *Lloyd W. Ralston*
L To R
LIBERTY BELL, 1876, Cast Iron, Wood Base,
Paper Label, 4¾" H. $55.00
LIBERTY BELL, G. Washington, Cast
Iron, 2¾" H. $190.00
SAVINGS BANK, Painted & Stenciled
Tin, 3" H. $30.00

A-CT Oct 1980   *Lloyd W. Ralston*
L To R
LIBERTY BELL, Electroplated Cast Iron,
3½" H. $25.00
LIBERTY BELL, Electroplated Cast Iron, 4" H.
.... $290.00

A-CT Oct 1980   *Lloyd W. Ralston*
L To R
LIBERTY BELL, Sesqui 1926 Centennial,
Cast Iron, 4" H. $30.00
LIBERTY BELL, Modern 1976, Cast Iron,
4¼" H. $25.00

A-CT Oct 1980   *Lloyd W. Ralston*
LIBERTY BELLS, Set of 3, 1776, 1 Milk
Glass, 2 Patt. Glass, Tin Closures .. $150.00

A-CT Oct 1980   *Lloyd W. Ralston*
ORIENTAL GIRL W/Mandolin, Cast Iron,
7" H. $245.00

A-CT Oct 1980   *Lloyd W. Ralston*
L To R
RETRIEVER, Cast Iron, Old Repaint, 4½" H.
.... $150.00
BOSTON BULL DOG, Cast Iron, 4½" H.
.... $75.00

A-CT Oct 1980   *Lloyd W. Ralston*
L To R
ELEPHANT W/Howdah, Cast Iron, 3¾" H.
.... $65.00
ELEPHANT, Cast Iron, 3½" H. .. $110.00

A-CT Oct 1980   *Lloyd W. Ralston*
ELEPHANT, Cast Iron, Bolted, 5" H.
.... $185.00

A-CT Oct 1980   *Lloyd W. Ralston*
DOG, On Cushion, Cast Iron, 6" H. .. $100.00

A-CT Oct 1980   *Lloyd W. Ralston*
L To R
GLOBE SAVINGS, Cast Iron, Complete
& Working, 7″ H. $900.00
WOOLWORTH BUILDING, On Platform,
Cast Iron, 8¼″ H. $220.00

A-CT Oct 1980   *Lloyd W. Ralston*
L To R
CORONATION BANK, Cast Iron, Eng.,
7″ H. $400.00
CORONATION, Cast Iron, Eng., 6½″ H.
.... $90.00

A-CT Oct 1980   *Lloyd W. Ralston*
L To R
SAVE MONEY W/MO-HE-CO, Cast Iron,
4¼″ H. $200.00
PARLOR STOVE, Cast Iron, 7″ H.
.... $175.00
MELLOW FURNACE, Cast Iron, 3½″ H.
.... $60.00

A-CT Oct 1980   *Lloyd W. Ralston*
L To R
IRONMASTER'S HOUSE, Cast Iron, MA,
4¼″ H. $350.00
WOOLWORTH BUILDING, Cast Iron,
Partial Overpaint, 5¾″ H. $30.00

A-CT Oct 1980   *Lloyd W. Ralston*
L To R
ROYAL BANK, Cast Iron, Eng., Poor
Paint, 5½″ H. $105.00
CROWN, Cast Iron W/Bronze Crown, Eng.,
3¾″ H. $65.00

A-CT Oct 1980   *Lloyd W. Ralston*
L To R
PARLOR STOVE-YORK, Electroplated
Cast Iron, 4″ H. $200.00
STOVE, Cast Iron, 4½″ H. $60.00

A-CT Oct 1980   *Lloyd W. Ralston*
L To R
BUILDING, 6-Sided W/Cupid, Cast Iron,
7″ H. $190.00
BUILDING, 6-Sided W/Bird Of Paradise,
Cast Iron, Eng., 6½″ H. $75.00
BEEHIVE, Cast Iron, Overpaint, Eng., 6¼″
H. $150.00

A-CT Oct 1980   *Lloyd W. Ralston*
L To R
GOLLYWOG, Cast Iron, 6¼″ H. . .$290.00
GOLLYWOG, Aluminum, Googly Eyes,
6¼″ H. $90.00

A-CT Oct 1980   *Lloyd W. Ralston*
L To R
BEEHIVE SPARBANK, Brass, 3½″ H.
.... $160.00
TROLLEY CAR, Cast Iron, Repl. Wheels,
Poor Cond., 4½″ H. $80.00

◄ A-CT Oct 1980   *Lloyd W. Ralston*
L To R
GLOBE, Embossed Base, Cast Iron, 4¼″ H.
.... $105.00
GLOBE, On Arc, Cast Iron, 5¼″ H. . .$90.00

A-CT Oct 1980   *Lloyd W. Ralston*
FIREPLACE & TALL CHEST, Litho.
Tin, 4½″ H. $100.00

A-OH May 1980   *Garth's Auctions, Inc.*
ROW I, L To R
CAST BRONZE BANK, Bear Clutching
Pig, 5⅜″ H. $30.00
CAST IRON BANK, Globe W/Eagle Finial,
Mkd. "Engerprise Mfg. Co., Philadelphia",
Rusted & Worn Paint, 5½″ H. $110.00
TIN BANK, "Sweet Thrift Bank", 6″ H.
. . . . $197.50
CAST IRON BANK, Rooster W/Old Gold
& Red Paint, 4¾″ H. $90.00
CAST IRON BANK, Bear, Old Gold Paint,
5⅜″ H. $60.00
ROW II, L To R
CAST WHITE METAL BANK, Bull Dog
W/Pipe & Sm. Brass Padlock, Old Paint, 3″
H. $325.00
CAST IRON BANK, Domed Building W/
Old Bronze & Gold Paint, 3¼″ H. . . $40.00
CAST IRON BANK, Mechanical, "Hall's
Liliput Bank", Old Paint Has Wear, 4¼″ H.
. . . . $200.00
TIN BANK, Red W/Blk. Transfer Of Eagle,
2⅞″ H. $20.00
CAST IRON BANK, "Billiken", Worn Gold
Paint, 4¼″ H. $30.00
ROW III, L To R
CAST WHITE METAL BANK, "Hi-Did-
dle-Diddle", Bronzed, 5⅜″ H. $20.00
CAST IRON BANK, Mechanical, Building
W/Pop Out Coin Slot, "Presto", Worn Gold
& Red Paint, 4½″ H. $95.00
CAST IRON TOY, Touring Car, Worn
Gr. Paint, 5¾″ L. $650.00
ROW IV
CAST IRON TOY, Train W/Engine &
Coal Car & 3 Open Cars, Worn Red & Blk.
Paint, 22″ L. $80.00

 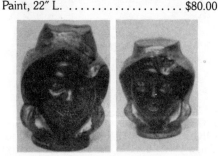

A-CT Oct 1980   *Lloyd W. Ralston*
L To R
BUFFALO, Cast Iron, 3″ H. $120.00
GOOSE, Cast Iron, 5″ H. $95.00

A-CT Oct 1980   *Lloyd W. Ralston*
L To R
BIRD ON STUMP, Cast Iron, 5″ H.
. . . . $210.00
DUCK, Cast Iron, 4″ H. $245.00

A-CT Oct 1980   *Lloyd W. Ralston*
L To R
STANDING CAT, Cast Iron, Bronze Fin-
ish, 6¾″ H. $1200.00
ZENITH RADIO, Die Cast, 3½″ H. . .$80.00

A-CT Oct 1980   *Lloyd W. Ralston*
L To R
PUMP, Brass, 4¼″ H. $95.00
CAMEL, Cast Iron, 4¾″ H. $100.00

―――――――――――――――――――

◄ A-CT Oct 1980   *Lloyd W. Ralston*
L To R
2-FACED WOMAN, Cast Iron, 4″ H.
. . . . $170.00
2-FACED WOMAN, Cast Iron, 3¼″ H.
. . . . $70.00

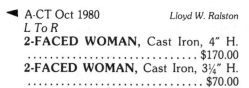

A-CT Oct 1980   *Lloyd W. Ralston*
2 KIDS, Cast Iron, 4½″ H. $1050.00

A-CT Oct 1980   *Lloyd W. Ralston*
ALPHABET, Cast Iron, 3¼″ H. . . $2400.00

A-CT Oct 1980   *Lloyd W. Ralston*
L To R
CUBE, 12-Sided, Brass, 3″ H. $15.00
DOC JAK, Cast Iron, 4¾″ H. . . . $450.00

A-CT Oct 1980   *Lloyd W. Ralston*
L To R
EVERY COPPER HELPS, Eng., Cast
Iron, 6″ H. $415.00
CHRISTIAN POLICE HAT, Eng., Tin,
4½″ H. $275.00

A-CT Oct 1980   *Lloyd W. Ralston*
LITHOGRAPHED TIN BOOK BANKS
L To R
MY OWN BOOK, 5¾" H. $45.00
BABES IN THE WOOD $15.00
ENDEAVOUR $25.00
ALLADIN $20.00
JACK & THE BEANSTALK $30.00
WESTWARD HO $20.00
HAPPY DAYS $25.00
DICK WHITTINGTON $40.00
TREASURE ISLAND $30.00

A-CT Oct 1980   *Lloyd W. Ralston*
3 LITTLE PIGS, CHURCH, NEW DEAL,
Chein, Litho. Tin $80.00

A-CT Oct 1980   *Lloyd W. Ralston*
L To R
ROUND WIRE BANK, Cast Iron, Wire
Mesh, Hairline Crack, 4" H. $25.00
CASH REGISTER, Cast Iron, Wire Mesh,
3¾" H. $80.00

A-OH May 1980   *Garth's Auctions, Inc.*
BANKS
ROW I, L To R
CAST IRON, Lighthouse, Old Red & Gold
Paint, 10¼" H. $560.00
CAST IRON, Mechanical, "Hall's Excel-
sior Bank", Wooden Cashier, Old Paint W/
Minor Wear, 5⅛" H. $130.00
CAST IRON, Mechanical, "Monkey
Bank", Old Paint W/Minor Wear, 7⅝" H.
. . . . $135.00
CAST IRON, Mechanical, "Uncle Sam",
Old Paint Faded & Shows Wear, Door Miss-
ing, 11¼" H. $175.00
ROW II, L To R
CAST IRON, Mechanical, "Novelty Bank",
Old Paint Darkened Some & Shows Wear,
6½" H. $215.00
CAST IRON, Aunt Jemima, Old Drk.
Paint, 6" H. $60.00
CAST IRON, Mechanical, "Jonah & The
Whale", 10¼" L. $750.00
CAST IRON, Boy Scout, Old Worn Gold
Paint, 6" H. $70.00
CAST IRON, Mechanical, "Punch & Judy
Bank", Old Paint W/Some Wear, Old Screws
Soldered In Place On Back, 7⅜" H. . . . $325.00
ROW III, L To R
CAST IRON, Mechanical, Lion & Monkeys,
Complete, Old Paint Shows Wear, 8½" H.
. . . . $375.00
NICKEL PLATED, Mechanical, Pig Baby
In High Chair, 6" H. $395.00
CAST IRON, Frog Body W/Human Head,
Inscription On Arms, Old Worn Paint, 6½" H.
. . . . $2050.00
CAST IRON, Mechanical, Leprechaun &
Pig, Old Yellowed Paint Shows Wear, 3" H.
. . . . $625.00

A-CT Oct 1980   *Lloyd W. Ralston*
L To R
RHINO, Cast Iron, 2¾" H. $225.00
BEAR W/TOP HAT, Pot Metal, 5½" H.
. . . . $90.00

A-CT Oct 1980   *Lloyd W. Ralston*
L To R
CRYSTAL BANK, Cast Iron & Glass, 3¾"
H. $35.00
HORSE SHOE WIRE BANK, Cast Iron,
Wire Mesh, 3½" H. $45.00

A-CT Oct 1980   *Lloyd W. Ralston*
L To R
UPRIGHT CONSOLE, Comb. Lock,
Nickeled Cast Iron, Tin, 4½" H. . . . $55.00
RADIO, Nickeled Cast Iron, 3¼" H. . . $100.00

A-CT Oct 1980   *Lloyd W. Ralston*
CROSLEY RADIO #70, Variation, Tin &
Cast Iron, 5" H. $150.00

A-CT Oct 1980   *Lloyd W. Ralston*
L To R
GOOSE, Cast Iron, 4" H. $550.00
RED GOOSE SCHOOL SHOES, Cast
Iron, 3¾" H. $95.00

A-CT Oct 1980   *Lloyd W. Ralston*
L To R
PRESTO STILL, Cast Iron, Overpaint, 4" H.
.... $50.00
PRESTO STILL, Cast Iron, 3¼" H. . .$40.00

A-CT Oct 1980   *Lloyd W. Ralston*
BUSTER BROWN & TIGE CASHIER,
Cast Iron, Orig. Drawer, 6¾" H. . . $250.00

A-CT Oct 1980   *Lloyd W. Ralston*
L To R
FLAT IRON BUILDING ON PEDESTAL,
Cast Iron, 6" H. $40.00
FLAT IRON BUILDING, Cast Iron, 8½" H.
.... $280.00

A-CT Oct 1980   *Lloyd W. Ralston*
L To R
INDIAN CHIEF, Pot Metal, 3¼" H. . .$60.00
INDIAN MAIDEN, Pot Metal, 3½" H.
.... $75.00
INDIAN CHIEF, Pot Metal, 3½" H. . .$80.00

A-OH May 1980   *Garth's Auctions, Inc.*
CAST IRON BANKS
ROW I, L To R
DINAH, Mechanical, "Made In England",
Old Paint Has Some Wear, 6½" H. . .$235.00
BLACK MAMMY, Mechanical, Repaired,
Traces Of Old Paint, 7½" H. $345.00
UNCLE SAM, Mechanical, Paint Has Touch
Up & Wear, Has Door & Key, 11¼" H.
.... $375.00
STANDING RABBIT, Worn Gr. Repaint,
6¾" H. $85.00
JOLLY NIGGER, Broken & Glued, Old
Worn Paint, 7¼" H. $75.00
ROW II, L To R
INDEPENDENCE HALL TOWER, Bell
Rings, Old Paint W/Little Wear, 9½" H.
.... $265.00
DOG, Mechanical, Old Worn Gold Paint,
4¾" H. $155.00
TRICK DOG, Mechanical, Old Paint Has
Little Wear, 7¼" H. $500.00
HALL'S EXCELSIOR BANK, Mechani-
cal, Old Paint, Cashier Has Some Touch
Up, 5" H. $125.00
TOWER BANK, Traces Of Gold Paint &
No Bell, 9¼" H. $205.00
ROW III, L To R
DARK TOWN BATTERY, Old Paint W/
Good Color & Some Wear, 7" H. . . $650.00
HORSE RACE, Mechanical, Mkd. "Pat-
ented Aug. 15, 1871", Top Plate Cracked,
Old Paint W/Minor Wear, 6" D. . . $2100.00
MULE, Mechanical, "Always Did 'Spise A
Mule", Old Paint W/Minor Wear, 7¾" H.
.... $500.00

A-CT Oct 1980   *Lloyd W. Ralston*
L To R
WINDMILL W/DOG, Tin, Pot Metal, 4" H.
.... $110.00
AMISH BOY & PIG ON BALE OF HAY,
Pot Metal, 4¾" H. $90.00

A-CT Oct 1980   *Lloyd W. Ralston*
L To R
BEGGING DOG, Pot Metal, 4½" H.
.... $65.00
TREE TRUNK, Pot Metal, 2½" H. . .$180.00

A-CT Oct 1980   *Lloyd W. Ralston*
L To R
DOG & BALL, Pot Metal & Tin, 2¼" H.
.... $75.00
GIRL AT BARREL, Pot Metal, 2" H.
.... $210.00

A-CT Oct 1980   *Lloyd W. Ralston*
CHILD'S SAFES, 3, Litho, Tin, 4", 2¾",
5½" H. $130.00

A-CT Oct 1980   *Lloyd W. Ralston*
HANSEL & GRETEL, Litho, Tin, Advertising Inside, 7¼" H. $100.00

A-OH May 1980   *Garth's Auctions, Inc.*
ROW I, L To R
CAST IRON BANK, Globe W/Worn Red
Paint, 5½″ H. $105.00
CAST IRON BANK, Horse W/Old Blk.
Repaint, 4¼″ H. $20.00
CAST WH. METAL BANK, Scottie W/
Worn Blk. Paint, 5½″ H. $35.00
CAST IRON BANK, Good Luck Horse,
Old Worn Blk. Paint, 4¼″ H. $35.00
CAST IRON BANK, Begging Bear, Old
Worn Gold Paint, 5¾″ H. $45.00
ROW II, L To R
CAST IRON BANK, Doe, Worn Gold
Repaint, 4⅞″ H. $105.00
CAST IRON BANK, Stag, Repl. Screw &
Traces Of Paint, Rock Incomplete, 6″ H.
. . . . $50.00
CAST IRON BANK, Rearing Horse, Old
Gold Paint, 7″ H. $30.00
CAST IRON BANK, Good Luck Horse,
Old Blk. & Gold Paint, 4½″ H. . . . $135.00
CAST IRON BANK, Prancing Horse, Old
Red Paint, 4¼″ H. $45.00
ROW III, L To R
CAST IRON TOY, Fire Engine Pumper,
Old Wh., Red & Blk. Paint Shows Wear, No
Driver, 8¼″ L. $85.00
CAST IRON BANK, Horse W/"Beauty",
Worn Blk. Paint, 4⅛″ H. $45.00
CAST IRON BANK, Donkey, Traces Of
Gold Paint, 4¾″ H. $40.00
CAST IRON PULL TOY, Wild Mule
Jack, Heart Wheels & Old Worn Paint,
Wheels Repl., 8″ L. $175.00

A-CT Oct 1980   *Lloyd W. Ralston*
L To R
MOSQUE, Cast Iron, 3¼″ H. $55.00
MOSQUE, Cast Iron, 5″ H. $140.00

A-CT Oct 1980   *Lloyd W. Ralston*
L To R
MAIL BOX, Cast Iron, 4¾″ H. . . . $50.00
MAIL BOX, Cast Iron, 4″ H. $45.00

A-OH May 1980   *Garth's Auctions, Inc.*
CAST IRON BANKS
ROW I, L To R
BUILDING, Old Gray Paint, 4¾″ H.
. . . . $20.00
NATIONAL SAFE, Some Tin W/Old Gold
Repaint Over Red, 4¾″ H. $35.00
SKYSCRAPER, Old Silver & Gold Paint,
5½″ H. $32.50
RABBIT, Traces Of Old Gold Paint, 6½″ H.
. . . . $85.00
BUILDING W/DOME, Old Silver & Gold
Paint, 4¾″ H. $30.00
ROW II, L To R
LION, Worn Old Paint & Little Rust, 5″ H.
. . . . $40.00
CHIEF BIG MOON, Mechanical, Worn
Paint, 10″ L. $450.00
MAN W/RIFLE, Mechanical, Old Paint
Shows Wear, 6¾″ H. $225.00
ROW III, L To R
LION & MONKEY, Complete, Mechanical,
Old Paint Shows Wear, 8½″ H. . . $375.00
EAGLE & EAGLETS, Mechanical, Squeak-
er Works & Old Paint Shows Wear, 6″ H.
. . . . $355.00
WILLIAM TELL, Mechanical, Old Paint
Shows Wear & Sl. Faded, 6¾″ H. . . $325.00

A-CT Oct 1980   *Lloyd W. Ralston*
L To R
MAIL BOX, Cast Iron, 3½″ H. . . . $30.00
6 SIDED BUILDING, Cast Iron, 3½″ H.
. . . . $65.00

A-OH May 1980   *Garth's Auctions, Inc.*
CAST IRON BANKS
ROW I, L To R
CIRCUS LION, Old Worn Paint, 5½″ H.
. . . . $62.50
REVOLVING CARROUSEL, Worn Red,
Blk. & Gold Paint W/Some Rust, 4¾″ H.
. . . . $7.50
SHED, Mechanical, Broom Lever Repl.,
Old Paint Shows Wear, 3¾″ H. . . . $125.00
REVOLVING CARROUSEL, Old Poly-
chrome Paint Shows Wear, 4¾″ H. . $115.00
U.S. MAIL, Old Gr. Paint, 4¼″ H. . . $37.50
ROW II, L To R
LION, Traces Of Gold Paint, 3¾″ H.
. . . . $17.50
BUILDING W/DOME, Worn Silver Paint,
3¼″ H. $25.00
SKYSCRAPER, Worn Silver & Gold Paint,
3½″ H. $22.50
BUILDING W/DOME, Worn Silver &
Gold Paint, 3″ H. $22.50
LION, Traces Of Gold Paint, 3½″ H.
. . . . $22.50
ROW III, L To R
BILLIKEN, Traces Of Gold Paint, New
Screw, 4″ H. $32.50
TURKEY, Worn Gold Paint & Some Rust,
3½″ H. $35.00
CAMEL, Old Repaint, 4¾″ H. $87.50
ELEPHANT, Worn Gold Paint, Base In-
scribed "Ivory Salt, Worcester Salt, Iodized
Salt", 4⅜″ H. $62.50
BILLIKEN, Worn Gold Paint, 4¼″ H.
. . . . $30.00

A-CT Oct 1980   *Lloyd W. Ralston*
L To R
8 SIDED BUILDING, Cast Iron, 4″ H.
. . . . $240.00
SM. HOUSE, Cast Iron, 3¼″ H. . . $85.00
BANK BUILDING, Cast Iron, 3½″ H.
. . . . $40.00

A-OH May 1980   *Garth's Auctions, Inc.*
BANKS
ROW I, L To R
CAST IRON HALL'S EXCELSIOR, Mechanical W/Wooden Cashier, Old Paint Has Minor Wear, 5⅛″ H. $65.00
CAST IRON PRESTO, Worn Red & Gold Paint, 4½″ H. $95.00
CAST WHITE FIGURES, Mutt & Jeff, Worn Paper Label On Back, Advertising Label On Base For Bank In Logan, OH, 5¾″ H. $535.00
POLISHED NICKEL STEEL SAFE, "Kenton Brand", Orig. Paper Label Combination, 5″ H. $30.00
CAST IRON HALL'S EXCELSIOR, Mechanical, 5⅛″ H. $65.00
ROW II, L To R
CAST IRON OWL, Mechanical, Old Paint Has Minor Wear, 7½″ H. $195.00
CAST IRON WILLIAM TELL, Mechanical, Old Paint Has Minor Wear, 6¾″ H. $315.00
CAST IRON CLOCK, Old Red & Gold Paint, 6″ H. $410.00
CAST IRON TAMMANY, Mechanical, Old Paint Has Some Wear, 5¾″ H. ...$150.00
ROW III, L To R
CAST IRON TRICK PONY, Mechanical, Old Paint Shows Minor Wear, 7¾″ H. $460.00
CAST IRON INDIAN, Mechanical, Old Paint Has Minor Touch-Up, 7½″ H. ...$195.00
CAST IRON SPEAKING DOG, Mechanical, Old Paint Shows Wear, Bottom Plate Repaired, 7″ H. $305.00

A-OH May 1980   *Garth's Auctions, Inc.*
CAST IRON BANKS
ROW I, L To R
BUILDING, Old Silver & Gold Paint, Some Wear & Little Rust, 6½″ H. $50.00
TAMMANY BANK, Mechanical, Crack In Back, Old Paint Shows Wear, 5¾″ H. $65.00
UNCLE SAM, Mechanical, Paint Shows Wear, Door Has Key, 11″ H. $500.00
BUILDING, Worn Old Silver & Gold Paint, 5½″ H. $30.00
CLOWN, Mechanical, Old Paint Worn, 8″ H. $225.00
ROW II, L To R
HALL'S EXCELSIOR BANK, Mechanical, Teller Has Some Repaint, Door Knob Repl. W/ Bead, 5¼″ H. $45.00
SHACK, Mechanical, Paint Shows Wear, 3¾″ H. $150.00
CREEDMORE BANK, Mechanical, Old Paint Shows Wear, 6¾″ H. $225.00
TAMMANY BANK, Mechanical, Old Paint Shows Little Wear, 5¾″ H. $85.00
ORGAN, Mechanical, Good Paint, 5¾″ H. $200.00
ROW III, L To R
EAGLE & EAGLETS, Mechanical, Old Paint W/Minor Wear, 6″ H. $245.00
LEAP-FROG, Mechanical, Old Paint Shows Some Wear, 4⅞″ H. $725.00
ARTILLERY BANK, Mechanical, Old Paint Shows Wear, 6″ H. $550.00

A-CT Oct 1980   *Lloyd W. Ralston*
L To R
HORSE ON TUB, No Saddle, Cast Iron 5¼″ H. $110.00
HORSE ON TUB, Cast Iron, 5¼″ H. $160.00

A-CT Oct 1980   *Lloyd W. Ralston*
DUTCH GIRL & BOY, Cast Iron, Repainted, 5¼″ H., 5¾″ H. $60.00

A-CT Oct 1980   *Lloyd W. Ralston*
L To R
ELEPHANT ON TUB, Cast Iron, 5¼″ H. $100.00
ELEPHANT ON TUB, Cast Iron, 5¼″ H. $85.00

A-CT Oct 1980   *Lloyd W. Ralston*
L To R
LION ON TUB, Cast Iron, Regilded, 4¼″ H. $50.00
ELEPHANT ON BENCH ON TUB, Cast Iron, Regilded, 4″ H. $75.00

A-CT Oct 1980   *Lloyd W. Ralston*
L To R
SOLDIER, Cast Iron, 5½″ H. ... $250.00
BILLY BOUNCE, Cast Iron, 4¾″ H. $425.00

A-CT Oct 1980   *Lloyd W. Ralston*
L To R
LION ON WHEELS, Cast Iron, Regilded, 5″ H. $120.00
LION ON WHEELS, Cast Iron, Poor Paint, 5″ H. $245.00

A-OH May 1980   *Garth's Auctions, Inc.*
STILL BANKS
ROW I, L To R
TIN, Clown, "J. Chein", 5" H. $35.00
CAST IRON, Building W/Dome, Old Silver & Gold Paint, 4¾" H. $35.00
TIN, Monkey, 5" H. $22.50
ROW II, L To R
CAST IRON, Building W/Tower, Some Rust, 3" H. $20.00
CAST IRON, Bank Building, 3⅜" H. . . $40.00
CAST IRON, "Home Safe", 3¼" H. ... $27.00
CAST IRON BANK, Tiny Safe "The Daisy", Has Key, Old Silver Paint, 2⅛" H. . . $40.00
TIN, Round W/Pierced Sides & Worn Red & Gr. Paint, 2¾" H. $15.00
ROW III, L To R
TIN, Globe, 4½" H. $5.00
CAST IRON, Baby In Cradle, Worn Paint & Some Rust, 4" L. $45.00
TIN, "Alarm Safety Deposit Vault", Clock Shaped, 3¾" H. $32.50

A-CT Oct 1980   *Lloyd W. Ralston*
L To R
BASEBALL PLAYER, Cast Iron, 5¾" H. $85.00
MUTT & JEFF, Cast Iron, 5¼" H. . . $125.00
FIREMAN, Cast Iron, 5½" H. ... $130.00

A-CT Oct 1980   *Lloyd W. Ralston*
COFFIN BANK, Nickeled Cast Iron, 4½" H.
.... $85.00

A-OH May 1980   *Garth's Auctions, Inc.*
ROW I, L To R
CAST IRON BANK, Mechanical, Trick Dog, Old Paint W/Minor Wear, 7½" H.
.... $205.00
CAST IRON BANK, "Wireless Bank" W/Tin & Wood, Electro Magnet Locking Device Powered By Battery, Last Patent Date Of 1918, Worn Transfer & Paint, 4¾" H.
.... $180.00
CAST IRON BANK, Building W/Cupola, Old Worn Paint, 5½" H. $75.00
CAST IRON TOY, Mechanical, "Always Did 'Spise A Mule", Wheels Missing, Paint Worn W/Old Touch Up, Hat Bill Repl., 9¾" L.
.... $65.00
ROW II, L To R
CAST IRON BANK, Mechanical, William Tell Shoots Apple Off Child's Head, Old Paint W/Some Wear, 6¾" H. $235.00
CAST IRON BANK, Mechanical, "Tammany Bank", Old Paint W/Wear, 5¾" H.
.... $115.00
NICKEL PLATED BANK, "Benton Brand", 4¼" H. $40.00
CAST IRON BANK, Mechanical, Speaking Dog, Old Paint W/Wear, 7" H. . $375.00
ROW III, L To R
CAST IRON BANK, Mechanical, "Dark Town Battery", Old Worn & Faded Paint, 9⅞" L. $475.00
CAST IRON BANK, Mechanical, Trick Dog, Old Paint W/Wear, 8¾" L. .. $205.00
CAST ALUMINUM BANK, Mechanical, Jolly Nigger, "Starkies Patent", Worn Old Paint, 6" H. $40.00
CAST IRON BANK, Bull Dog, Old Paint W/Wear, 7¾" H. $175.00

A-CT Oct 1980   *Lloyd W. Ralston*
L To R
MARY & LAMB, Cast Iron, 4½" H.
.... $525.00
BUSTER BROWN & TIGE, Cast Iron, 5" H. $55.00

A-CT Oct 1980   *Lloyd W. Ralston*
L To R
ELEPHANT ON WHEELS, Cast Iron, Regilded, 4" H. $85.00
HORSE ON WHEELS, Cast Iron, Poor Paint, 5" H. $250.00

A-MA Mar 1980   *Richard A. Bourne Co., Inc.*
ROW I
STILL BANKS, 4, 1st Dated Over Doorway "1878", Orig. Paint, 3" To 3½" H. . . $120.00
ROW II, L To R
STILL BANK, Minor Loss Of Paint, 5" H.
.... $70.00
STILL BANK, "1882" Over Doorway, Some Loss Of Paint, 5½" H. $90.00
MECHANICAL, Blk. Boy Standing In Doorway Of Shack, June 1885, Orig. Decor. W/Minimal Wear, Mechanism Working, 3¾" H. $200.00
ROW III, L To R
MECHANICAL, William Tell W/Crossbow, Pcs. Missing, Restorations Needed, 10½" L., 6½" H. $70.00
MECHANICAL, Creedmore, Orig. Decor. Worn & Rusted, Not Working But Restorable, 6½" H. $100.00

A-CT Oct 1980   *Lloyd W. Ralston*
L To R
FEED MY SHEEP, Pot Metal, 3" x 4"
.... $110.00
STATE BANK, Cast Iron, Poor Cond., 3¼" H. $45.00

A-CT Oct 1980   *Lloyd W. Ralston*
L To R
YOUNG AMERICA SAFE, Cast Iron,
4¼″ x 3″ $110.00
SPORT SAFE, Cast Iron, 3″ x 2¼″
.... $50.00

A-CT Oct 1980   *Lloyd W. Ralston*
L To R
FURNACE, Wood, Age Cracks, 4¾″ H.
.... $10.00
SCHOOL HOUSE SAVINGS BANK,
Paper Litho. On Wood, 4″ x 4″ $45.00

A-CT Oct 1980   *Lloyd W. Ralston*
L To R
FOOTED CHEST, Wood, 7″ x 5¼″ x 4¾″
.... $50.00
CANNISTER, "GMP Jan. 19, 1905", Wood,
4½″ H. $5.00

A-CT Oct 1980   *Lloyd W. Ralston*
L To R
ARABIAN SAFE, Cast Iron, No Paint, 4¾″
x 4″ $40.00
FRUIT BASKET, Nickel Plated Cast Iron,
3″ x 3¾″ $310.00

A-CT Oct 1980   *Lloyd W. Ralston*
L To R
FEZ, Steel, 3¼″ x 3¾″ $75.00
FEZ, Pot Metal, 5½″ x 5¼″ $145.00

A-CT Oct 1980   *Lloyd W. Ralston*
CHURCH PASTORAL AID BANK, Paper
Litho. On Wood, 4″ x 4¾″ $15.00

A-CT Oct 1980   *Lloyd W. Ralston*
L To R
BEES & FARM BOY, Brass, 4″ x 4½″
.... $180.00
TRUNK, Nickel Plated Cast Iron, 2¾″ x 3½″
.... $20.00

A-CT Oct 1980   *Lloyd W. Ralston*
L To R
LADIES SLIPPER, Plated Pot Metal, 3¼″ x
5½″ $135.00
LADIES SLIPPER, Plated Pot Metal, 2¾″ x
5¼″ $80.00

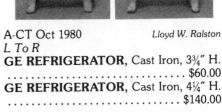

A-CT Oct 1980   *Lloyd W. Ralston*
L To R
GE REFRIGERATOR, Cast Iron, 3¾″ H.
.... $60.00
GE REFRIGERATOR, Cast Iron, 4¼″ H.
.... $140.00

A-CT Oct 1980   *Lloyd W. Ralston*
L To R
PASS AROUND THE HAT, Lincoln High
Hat, Cast Iron, 2½″ x 3″ $80.00
PASS AROUND THE HAT, Lincoln High
Hat, Nickel Plated Cast Iron, 2½″ x 3″
.... $70.00

A-CT Oct 1980   *Lloyd W. Ralston*
L To R
WINDMILL, Brass, Poor Cond., 3¾″ x 2¾″
.... $60.00
SCHOOL HOUSE CLOCK, Trick Open-
ing, Inlaid Wood, 9¾″ H. $75.00

A-CT Oct 1980   *Lloyd W. Ralston*
PIANO, Musical, Nickel Plated Cast Iron,
6½″ x 7″ $400.00

ABC PLATES - Alphabet plates were made especially for children as teaching aids. They date from the late 1700s, and were made of various material including porcelain, pottery, glass, pewter, tin and ironstone.

AMPHORA ART POTTERY was made at the Amphora Porcelain Works in the Teplitz-Turn area of Bohemia during the late 19th and early 20th centuries. Numerous potteries were located here.

BATTERSEA ENAMELS - The name "Battersea" is a general term for those metal objects decorated with enamels, such as pill, patch, and snuff boxes, door knobs, etc. The process of fusing enamel onto metal—usually copper—began about 1750 in the Battersea District of London. Today, the name has become a generic term for similar objects—mistakenly called "Battersea."

BELLEEK porcelain was first made at Fermanagh, Ireland in 1857. Today, this ware is still being made in buildings within walking distance of the original clay pits according to the skills and traditions of the original artisans. Irish Belleek is famous for its thinness and delicacy. Similar type wares were also produced in other European countries as well as the United States.

BENNINGTON POTTERY - The first pottery works in Bennington, Vermont was established by Captain John Norton in 1793; and, for 101 years, it was owned and operated by succeeding generations of Nortons. Today, the term "Bennington" is synonymous with the finest in American ceramics because the town was the home of several pottery operations during the last century—each producing under different labels. Today, items produced at Bennington are now conveniently, if inaccurately, dubbed "Bennington." One of the popular types of pottery produced here is known as "Rockingham." The term denotes the rich, solid brown glazed pottery from which many household items were made. The ware was first produced by the Marquis of Rockingham in Swinton, England—hence the name.

BISQUE - The term applies to pieces of porcelain or pottery which have been fired, but left in an unglazed state.

BLOOR DERBY - "Derby" porcelain dates from about 1755 when William Duesbury began the production of porcelain at Derby. In 1769, he purchased the famous Chelsea Works and operated both factories. During the Chelsea-Derby period, some of the finest examples of English porcelains were made. Because of their fine quality, in 1773 King George III gave Duesbury the patent to mark his porcelain wares "Crown Derby." Duesbury died in 1796. In 1810, the factory was purchased by Robert Bloor, a senior clerk. Bloor revived the Imari styles which had been so popular. After his death in 1845, former workmen continued to produce fine porcelains using the traditional Derby patterns. The firm was reorganized in 1876 and in 1878, a new factory was built. In 1890, Queen Victoria appointed the company "Manufacturers to Her Majesty," with the right to be known as Royal Crown Derby.

BUFFALO POTTERY -The Buffalo Pottery of Buffalo, New York, was organized in 1901. The firm was an adjunct of the Larkin Soap Company, which was established to produce china and pottery permiums for that company. Of the many different types produced, the Buffalo Pottery is most famous for their "Deldare" line which was developed in 1905.

CANARY LUSTRE earthenware dates to the early 1800s, and was produced by potters in the Staffordshire District of England. The body of this ware is a golden yellow and decorated with transfer printing, usually in black.

CANTON porcelain is a blue-and-white decorated ware produced near Canton, China, from the late 1700s through the last century. Its hand-decorated Chinese scenes have historical as well as mythological significance.

CAPO-di-MONTE, originally a soft paste porcelain, is Italian in origin. The first ware was made during the 1700s near Naples. Although numerous marks were used, the most familiar to us is the crown over the letter "N." Mythological subjects, executed in either high or low relief and tinted in bright colors on a light ground, were a favorite decoration. The earlier ware has a peculiar grayish color as compared to later examples which have a whiter body.

CARLSBAD porcelain was made by several factories in the area from the late 1800s and exported to the United States. When Carlsbad became a part of Czechoslovakia after World War I, wares were frequently marked "Karlsbad." Items marked "Victoria" were made for Lazarus & Rosenfeldt, Importers.

CASTLEFORD earthenware was produced in England from the late 1700s until around 1820. Its molded decoration is similar to Pratt Wares.

CHINESE EXPORT PORCELAIN was made in quantity in China during the 1700s and early 1800s. The term identifies a variety of porcelain wares made for export to Europe and the United States. Since many thought the product to be of joint Chinese and English manufacture, it has also been known as "Oriental or Chinese Lowestoft."

As much as this ware was made to order for the American and European market, it was frequently adorned with seals of states or the coats of arms of individuals, in addition to eagles, sailing scenes, flowers, religious and mythological scenes.

CLEWS POTTERY - see also, Historical Staffordshire - was made by George Clews & Co., of Brownhill Pottery, Tunstall, England from 1806-1861.

CLIFTON POTTERY was founded by William Long in Clifton, New Jersey, in 1905.

COALPORT porcelain has been made by the Coalport Porcelain Works in England since 1795. The ware is still being produced at Stroke-on-Trent.

COPELAND-SPODE - The firm was founded by Josiah Spode in 1770 in Staffordshire, England. From 1847 W.T. Copeland & Sons, Ltd., succeeded Spode, using the designation "Late Spode" to their wares. The firm is still in operation.

COPPER LUSTRE - See Lustre Wares

CROWN DUCAL - English porcelain made by the A.G. Richardson & Co., Ltd., since 1916.

CUP PLATES were used where cups were handleless and saucers were deep. During the early 1800s, it was very fashionable to drink from a saucer. Thus, a variety of fancy small plates were produced for the cup to rest in. The lacy Sandwich examples are very collectible.

DAVENPORT pottery and porcelain were made at the Davenport Factory in Longport, Staffordshire, England, by John Davenport—from 1793 until 1887 when the pottery closed. Most of the wares produced here—porcelains, creamwares, ironstone, earthenwares and other products—were marked.

DEDHAM - (Chelsea Art Works) - The firm was founded in 1872 at Chelsea, Massachusetts by James Robertson & Sons, and closed in 1889. In 1891, the pottery was reopened under the name of The Chelsea Pottey, U.S. The first and most popular blue underglaze decoration for the desirable "Cracqule Ware" was the rabbit motif—designed by Joseph L. Smith. In 1893, construction was started on the new pottery in Dedham, Massachusetts, and production began in 1895. The name of the pottery was then changed to "Dedham Pottery," to eliminate the confusion with the English Chelsea Ware. The famed crackleware finish became synonymous with the name. Because of its popularity, over fifty patterns of tableware were made.

DELFT - Holland is famous for its fine examples of tin-glazed pottery dating from the 16th century. Although blue and white is the most popular color, other colors were also made. The majority of the ware found today is from the late Victorian period and, when the name Holland appears with the Delft factory mark, this indicates that the item was made after 1891.

DORCHESTER POTTERY was established by George Henderson in Dorchester, a part of Boston, in 1895. Production included stonewares, industrial wares, and later some decorated tablewares. The pottery is still in production.

DOULTON - The Pottery was established in Lambeth in 1815 by John Doulton and John Watts. When Watts retired in 1845, the firm became known as Doulton & Company. In 1901, King Edward VII conferred a double honor on the company by presentation of the Royal Warrant, authorizing their chairman to use the word "Royal" in describing products.

A variety of wares has been made over the years for the American market. The firm is still in production.

DRESDEN. See Meissen

FLOWING BLUE ironstone is a highly glazed dinnerware made at Staffordshire by a variety of potters. It became popular about 1825. Items were printed with the patterns (oriental), and the color flowed from the design over the white body so that the finished product appeared smeared. Although purple and brown colors were also made, the deep cobalt blue shades were the most popular. Later wares were less blurred, having more white ground.

GAUDY DUTCH is the most spectacular of the Gaudy wares. It was made for the Pennsylvania Dutch market from about 1785 until the 1820s. This soft paste tableware is lightweight and frail in appearance. Its rich cobalt blue decoration was applied to the biscuit, glazed and fired—then other colors were applied over the first glaze—and the object was fired again. No lustre is included in its decoration.

GAUDY IRONSTONE was made in Staffordshire from the early 1850s until around 1865. This ware is heavier than Gaudy Welsh or Gaudy Dutch, as its texture is a mixture of pottery and porcelain clay.

GAUDY WELSH, produced in England from about 1830, resembles Gaudy Dutch in decorations, but the workmanship is not as fine and its texture is more comparable to that of spatterware. Lustre is usually included with the decoration.

HISTORICAL STAFFORDSHIRE - The term refers to a particular blue-on-white, transfer-printed earthenware produced in quantity during the early 1800s by many potters in the Staffordshire District. The central decoration was usually an American city scene or landscape, frequently showing some mode of transportation in the foreground. Other designs included portraits and patriotic emblems. Each potter had a characteristic border which is helpful to identify a particular ware, as many pieces are unmarked. Later transfer-printed wares were made in sepia, pink, green and black, but the early cobalt blue examples are the most desirable.

IRONSTONE is a heavy, durable, utilitarian ware made from the slag of iron furnaces, ground and mixed with clay. Charles Mason of Lane Delft, Staffordshire, patented the formula in 1813. Much of the early ware was decorated in imitation of Imari, in addition to transfer-printed blue ware, flowing blues and browns. During the mid-nineteenth century, the plain white enlivened only by embossed designs became fashionable. Literally hundreds of patterns were made for export.

JACKFIELD POTTERY is English in origin. It was first produced during the 17th century, however most items available today date from the last century. It is a red-bodied pottery, oftentimes decorated with scrolls and flowers in relief, then covered with a black glaze.

JUGTOWN POTTERY - This North Carolina pottery has been made since the 18th century. In 1915, Jacques Busbee organized what was to become the Jugtown Pottery in 1921. Production was discontinued in 1958.

KING'S ROSE is a decorated creamware produced in the Staffordshire district of England during the 1820-1840 period. The rose decorations are usually in red, green, yellow and pink. This ware is often referred to as "Queen's Rose."

LEEDS POTTERY was established by Charles Green in 1758 at Leed, Yorkshire, England. Early wares are unmarked. From 1775, the impressed mark, "Leeds Pottery" was used. After 1800, the name "Hartly, Green & Co." was added, and the impressed or incised letters "L P" were also used to identify the ware.

LIMOGES - The name identifies fine porcelain wares produced by many factories at Limoges, France, since the mid-1900s. A variety of different marks identify wares made here including Haviland china.

LIVERPOOL POTTERY - The term applies to wares produced by many potters located in Liverpool, England, from the early 1700s, for American trade. Their print-decorated pitchers—referred to as "jugs" in England—have been especially popular. These featured patriotic emblems, prominent men, ships, etc., and can be easily identified as nearly all are melon-shaped with a very pointed lip, strap handle and graceful curved body.

LUSTRE WARES - John Hancock of Hanley, England, invented this type of decoration on earthenwares during the early 1800s. The copper, bronze, ruby, gold, purple, yellow, pink and mottled pink lustre finishes were made from gold-painted on the glazed objects, then fired. The latter type is often referred to as "Sunderland Lustre." Its pinkish tones vary in color and pattern. The silver lustres were made from platinum.

McCOY POTTERY - The J.W. McCoy Pottery was established in 1899. Production of art pottery did not begin until after 1926, when the name was changed to Brush McCoy.

METTLACH, Germany, located in the Zoar Basin, was the location of the famous Villeroy & Boch factories from 1836 until 1921 when the factory was destroyed by fire. Steins (dating from about 1842) and other stonewares with bas relief decoration were their speciality.

MOCHA WARE - This banded creamware was first produced in England during the late 1700s. The early ware was lightweight and thin, having colorful bands of bright colors decorating its cream-colored to very light brown body. After 1840, the ware became heavier in body and the color was oftentimes quite light—almost white. Mocha Ware can easily be identified by its colorful banded decorations—on and between the bands, including feathery ferns, lacy trees, seaweeds, squiggly designs and lowly earthworms.

NILOAK POTTERY with its prominent swirled, marbleized designs, is a 20th century pottery first produced at Benton, Arkansas, in 1911 by the Niloak Pottery Company. Production ceased in 1946.

NIPPON porcelain has been produced in quantity for the American market since the late 19th century. After 1891, when it became obligatory to include the country of origin on all imports, the Japenese trademark "Nippon" was used. Numerous other marks appear on this ware identifying the manufacturer, artist or importer. The hand painted Nippon examples are extremely popular today and prices are on the rise.

OWENS POTTERY was made from 1891 to 1928 at Zanesville, Ohio. The first art pottery was produced after 1896. Their different lines included Utopian Ware, Navarre, Feroza, Cyrano and Henri Deux. Art pottery was discontinued about 1907.

PISGAH FOREST POTTERY - The pottery was founded near Mt. Pisgah in North Carolina in 1914 by Walter B. Stephen. the pottery remains in operation.

REDWARE is one of our most popular forms of country pottery. It has a soft, porous body and its color varies from reddish-brown tones to deep wine to light orange. It was produced in mostly utilitarian forms by potters in small factories or by potters working on their farms, to fill their everyday needs. Glazes were used to intensify the color. The most desirable examples are the slip-decorated pieces, or the rare and expensive "sgraffito" examples which have scratched or incised line decoration. This type of decoration was for ornamentation, since examples were rarely used for ordinary utilitarian purposes, but were given as gifts. Hence, these highly prized pieces rarely show wear, indicating that they were treasured as ornaments only. Slip decoration was made by tracing the design on the redware shape with a clay having a creamy consistency in contrasting colors. When dried, the design was slightly raised above the surface. Because these pieces were made for practical usage, the potter then pressed or beat the slip decoration into the surface of the object.

RED WING POTTERY of Red Wing, MN, was founded in 1878. The firm began producing art pottery during the 1920s. The pottery closed in 1967.

ROCKINGHAM, See Bennington Pottery.

ROOKWOOD POTTERY - The Rookwood Pottery began production at Cincinnati, Ohio, in 1880 under the direction of Maria Longworth Nichols Storer, and operated until 1960. The name was derived from the family estate, "Rookwood," because of the "rooks" or "crows" which inhabited the wooded areas. All pieces of this art pottery are marked, usually bearing the famous flame.

RORSTRAND FAIENCE - The firm was founded in 1726 near Stockholm, Sweden. Items dating from the early 1900s and having an "art nouveau" influence are very much in demand these days and expensive.

ROSE MEDALLION ware dates from the eighteenth century. It was decorated and exported from Canton, China, in quanitity. The name generally applied to those pieces having medallions with figures of people alternating with panels of flowers, birds and butterflies. When all the medallions were filled with flowers, the ware was differentiated as Rose Canton.

ROSEVILLE POTTERY - The Roseville Pottery was organized in 1890 in Roseville, Ohio. The firm produced utilitarian stoneware in the plant formerly owned by the Owens Pottery. In 1898, the firm acquired the Midland Pottery of Roseville, also producers of stoneware, and the Linden Avenue Plant at Zanesville, Ohio, originally built by the Clark Stoneware Company. In 1900, an art line of pottery was created to compete with Owens and Weller lines. The new ware was named "Rozane," and it was produced at the Zanesville location. Following its success, other prestige lines were created. The Azurine line was introduced about 1902.

ROYAL BAYREUTH manufactory began in Tettau in 1794 at the first porcelain factory in Bavaria. Wares made here were on the same par with Meissen. Fire destroyed the original factory during the 1800s. Much of the wares available today were made at the new factory which began production in 1897. These include Rose Tapestry, Sunbonnet Baby novelties and the Devil and Card items. The Royal Bayreuth blue mark has the 1794 founding date incorporated with the mark.

ROYAL BONN - The trade name identifies a variety of porcelain items made during the 19th century by the Bonn China Manufactory, established in 1755 by Clemers August. Most of the ware found today is from the Victorian period.

ROYAL DOULTON wares have been made from 1901, when King Edward VII conferred a double honor on the Doulton Pottery by the presentation of the Royal Warrant, authorizing their chairman to use the word "Royal" in describing products. A variety of wares have been produced for the American market. The firm is still in production.

ROYAL DUX was produced in Bohemia during the late 1800s. Large quantitites of this decorative porcelain ware were exported to the United States. Royal Dux figurines are especially popular.

ROYAL WORCESTER - The Worcester factory was established in 1751 in England. This is a tastefully decorated porcelain noted for its creamy white lustreless surface. Serious collectors prefer items from the Dr. Wall (the activator of the concern) period of production which extended from the time the factory was established to 1785.

ROYCROFT POTTERY was made by the Roycrofter community of East Aurora, NY, during the late 19th and early 20th centuries. The firm was founded by Elbert Hubbard. Products produced here included pottery, furniture, metalware, jewelry and leatherwork.

R.S. PRUSSIA porcelain was produced during the mid-1800s by Erdman Schlegelmilch in Suhl. His brother Reinhold founded a factory in 1869 in Tillowitz in lower Silesia. Both made fine quality porcelain, using both satin and high gloss finishes with comparable decoration. Addtionally, both brothers used the same R.S. mark in the same colors, the initials being in memory of their father, Rudolph Schlegelmilch. It has not been determined when production at the two factories ceased.

SAMPSON WARE dates from the early 19th century. The firm was founded in Paris, and reproduced a variety of collectibles wares including Chelsea, Meissen and Oriental Lowestoft, with marks which distinguish their wares as reproductions. The firm is still in production.

SATSUMA is a Japanese pottery having a distinctive creamy crackled glaze decorated with bright enamels and oftentimes Japanese faces. The majority of the ware available today includes the mass produced wares dating from the 1850s. Their quality does not compare to the fine early examples.

SPATTERWARE is a soft paste tableware, laboriously decorated with hand-drawn flowers, birds, buildings, trees, etc., with "spatter" decoration chiefly as a background. It was produced in considerable quantity from the early 1800s to around 1850.

To achieve this type decoration, small bits of sponge was cut into different shapes— leaves, hearts, rosettes, vines, geometrical patterns, etc.—and mounted on the end of a short stick for convenience in dipping into the pigment.

SPONGEWARE, as it is known, is a decoreated white earthenware. Color—usually blue, blue/green, brown/tan/blue, or blue/brown—was applied to the white clay base. Because the color was often applied with a color-soaked sponge, the term "spongeware" became common for this ware. A vareity of utilitarian items were produced—pitchers, cookie jars, bean pots, water coolers, etc. Marked examples are rare.

STAFFORDSHIRE is a district in England where a variety of pottery and porcelain wares have been produced by many factories in the area.

STICKSPATTER - The term identifies a type of decoration that combines hand painting and transfer-painted decoration. "Spattering" was done with either a sponge or a brush containing a moderate supply of pigment. Stick-spatter was developed from the traditional Staffordshire spatterware, as the earlier ware was time-consuming and expensive to produce. Although the majority of this ware was made in England from the 1850s to the late 1800s, it was also produced in Holland, France and elsewhere.

TEA LEAF is a lightweight stone china decorated with copper or gold "tea leaf" sprigs. It was first made by Anthony Shaw of Longport, England, during the 1850s. By the late 1800s, other potters in Staffordshire were producing the popular ware for export to the United States. As the result, there is a noticeable version in decoration.

TECO POTTERY, an art pottery line made by the Terra Cotta Tile Works of Terra Cotta, IL. The firm was organized in 1881 by William D. Gates. The Teco line was first made in 1902 and was discontinued during the 1920s.

VAN BRIGGLE POTTERY was established at Colorado Springs, Colorado, in 1900 by Artus Van Briggle and his wife Anna. Most of the ware was marked. The first mark included two joined "A's," representing their first two initials. The firm is still in operation.

VILLEROY & BOCH - See Mettlock

WEDGWOOD POTTERY was established by Josiah Wedgwood in 1759 in England. A tremendous variety of fine wares have been produced through the years including basalt, lustre wares, creamware, jasperware, bisque, agate, Queens's Ware and others. The system of marks used by the firm clearly indicates when each piece was made.

Since 1940, the new Wedgwood factory has been located at Barleston.

WELLER POTTERY - Samuel A. Weller established the Weller Pottery in 1872 in Fultonham, Ohio. In 1888, the pottery was moved to Piece Street in Putnam, Ohio—now a part of Zanesville, Ohio. The producaton of art pottery began in 1893 and, by late 1897, several prestige lines were being produced including Samantha, Touranda and Dickens' Ware. Other later types included Weller's Louwelsa, Eosian, Aurora, Turada and the rare Sicardo which is the most sought after and most expensive today. The firm closed in 1948.

A-OH April 1980   *Garth's Auctions, Inc.*
HISTORICAL BLUE STAFFORDSHIRE
ROW I, L To R
PLATE, Med. Drk. Blue "Southampton, Hampshire", Impressed "E. Wood & Sons", 7½" D. $135.00
PLATE, Drk. Blue, "Falls Of Mont Morenci", Impressed "E. Wood & Sons", 9⅜" D. $150.00
PLATE, Med. Blue, "View Of Trenton Falls", Impressed "Wood", Minor Surface Pitting, 7⅝" D. $95.00
ROW II, L To R
PLATE, Drk. Blue, "Chief Justice Marshall, Troy", Impressed "E. Wood & Sons", Rim Flake, 8½" D. $185.00
TEA POT, Drk. Blue, Sm Flakes On Spout, Lid Chipped, Unmarked, 7½" H. .. $155.00
PLATE, Med. Blue, "The Landing Of The Fathers At Plymouth", Impressed "Enoch Wood & Sons", Minor Surface Wear, 8⅝" D. $115.00
ROW III, L To R
PLATE, Med. Drk. Blue, "Peace & Plenty", Impressed "Clews", Rim Flakes, 10⅛" D. $255.00
PLATE, Med. Drk. Blue, "America & Independence", 10½"D. $205.00
PLATE, Drk. Blue, "Pine Orchard House Catskill Mountains", Impressed "E. Wood & Sons", 10⅛" D. $200.00

A-OH April 1980   *Garth's Auctions, Inc.*
HISTORICAL BLUE STAFFORDSHIRE
ROW I, L To R
CUP & SAUCER, Drk. Blue, "Christmas Eve", Impressed "Clews" $135.00
PLATTER, Drk. Blue, Doctor Syntax "The Advertisement For A Wife", Impressed "Clews", 15⅜" L. $420.00
CUP & SAUCER, Drk. Blue, "Wadsworth Tower", Impressed "E. Wood & Sons" $195.00
ROW II, L To R
PLATE, Drk. Blue, "Doctor Syntax Painting A Portrait", Impressed "Clews", Sm. Rim Repair, 10" D. $25.00
TUREEN & TRAY, Drk. Blue Doctor Syntax Scenes, Edge Wear & Sm. Chips, Impressed "Clews", 9¾" L. $625.00
LADLE, Med. Blue, Minor Edge Wear On Bowl, 6½" L. $105.00
SOUP PLATE, Drk. Blue, "Doctor Syntax Mistakes A Gentleman's House For A Inn", Impressed "Clews", 9⅞" D. $150.00
ROW III, L To R
PLATE, Drk. Blue, "Doctor Syntax & The Bees", Impressed "Clews", 10" D. .. $155.00
PLATE, Med. Drk. Blue, "Doctor Syntax Star Gazing", Impressed "Clews", Rim Hairline & Sm. Flake, 8⅛" D. $15.00
SOUP PLATE, Drk. Blue, "Sancho Panza At The Boar Hunt", Sm. Hairline, 9⅝" D. $145.00

A-OH April 1980   *Garth's Auctions, Inc.*
HISTORICAL BLUE STAFFORDSHIRE
ROW I, L To R
PLATE, Med. Drk. Blue, "Nahant Hotel Near Boston", 9" D. $175.00
SOUP PLATE, Med. Drk. Blue, "The Beach At Brighton", Impressed "Wood", 10⅛" D. $180.00
PLATE, Drk. Blue, "Christmas Eve", From Wilkie's Designs", Impressed "Clews Warranted Staffordshire", 8⅞" D. $95.00
ROW II, L To R
PLATE, Drk. Blue, "Doctor Syntax", Impressed "Clews Warranted Staffordshire", Minor Hairlines, 10⅛" D. $115.00
PLATE, Med. Blue, "Doctor Syntax Star Gazing", Impressed "Clews Warranted Staffordshire", 8⅞" D. $95.00
SOUP PLATE, Med. Drk. Blue, "Doctor Syntax Mistakes A Gentlemans House For An Inn", Impressed "Clews Warranted Staffordshire", 9⅞" D. $185.00
ROW III, L To R
PLATE, Med. Drk. Blue, "Doctor Syntax Returned From His Tour", Impressed "Clews Warranted Staffordshire", 8⅞" D. .. $105.00
PLATE, Med. Blue, "Doctor Syntax & The Bees", Impressed "Clews Warranted Staffordshire", 10⅛" D. $125.00
PLATE, Med. Drk. Blue, "Doctor Syntax Reading His Tour", Impressed "Clews Warranted Staffordshire", 8⅞" D. .. $115.00

A-MA April 1980   *Richard A. Bourne Co., Inc.*
L To R
DELFT PLAQUE, Sgn., 19th C., 15½" L. $225.00
SHELF CLOCK W/Delft Case, 19th C., Works Not Guaranteed, Age Cracks, 15½" H. $450.00
DELFT BOWL, 18th C., Floral Spray On Int., Glaze Roughage On Rim, Retouching Of Decor., 10¾" D. $350.00

*Price does not include 10% buyer fee.

A-WA D.C. May 1980 *Adam A. Weschler & Son* ▶
EDWARD MARSHALL BOEHM BIRDS
ROW I, L To R
FLEDGLIN KINGFISHER, Printed Marks, Patt. Number, Ca. 1960, 3¾" L., 6" H. $100.00*
BABY EASTERN BLUEBIRD, Printed Marks, Patt. Number, Ca. 1958, 3½" L., 4½" H. $75.00*
BABY ROBIN, Printed Marks, Patt. Number, Ca. 1957, 3¾" H. $80.00*
ROW II
CANADA GEESE, Pr., Printed Marks, Patt. Number, Ca. 1953, 5½" H., 7½" H. $400.00*

A-OH Aug 1980   *Garth's Auctions, Inc.*
HISTORICAL BLUE STAFFORDSHIRE
ROW I, L To R
CUP & SAUCER, Drk. Blue, Country Scene W/Shell Border, Flake On Table Ring
.... $90.00
CUP & SAUCER, Drk. Blue W/Vase Of Flowers, Impressed "Adams", Flake On Saucer Table Ring $50.00
CUP & SAUCER, Med. Blue, Flowers, Hairline In Cup & Flake On Saucer Table Ring $12.50
CUP & SAUCER, Drk. Blue, "Landing Of Gen. LaFayette" On Saucer, Edge Wear & Flakes On Base Of Cup & Saucer Rim
.... $195.00
ROW II, L To R
PLATE, Drk. Blue, Men Pulling Boat Ashore W/Early Steamboat, 8″ D. $130.00
PLATE, Lt. Blue, 2 Men Fishing, Rim Hairline & Edge Flake, 8″ D. $10.00
PLATE, Med. Blue, Fruit, 7½″ D. .. $70.00
ROW III, L To R
PLATE, Med. Drk. Blue, "Pains Hill, Surrey", 10⅛″ D. $55.00
PLATES, 2, (1 Illus.), Drk. Blue, Cupid Behind Bars, Impressed "Wood", 1 W/Sm. Hairline, 9¼″ D. $80.00
PLATES, 3, (1 Illus.), Med. Blue, Fruit Center & Foliage Rim, 9¾″ D. $105.00

A-WA D.C. May 1980 *Adam A. Weschler & Son*
BOEHM KESTRELS, Pr., Printed Marks, Patt. Number, Ca. 1968, Limited Edition, 16½″ H., 14″ H. $1200.00*

*Price does not include 10% buyer fee.

A-OH June 1980   *Garth's Auctions, Inc.*
HISTORICAL BLUE STAFFORDSHIRE
ROW I, L To R
CUPS & SAUCERS, 2, (1 Illus.), Med. Drk. Blue W/Beehive & Churn, Minor Rim Flakes
.... $30.00
CUP & SAUCER, Med. Drk. Blue, Flower & Urn, Sm. Chips On Table Ring Of Saucer
.... $10.00
CUP & SAUCER, Med. Drk. Blue, Flower & Urn, Impressed "Clews", Pinpoint Flakes
.... $47.50
ROW II, L To R
PLATE, Med. Drk. Blue, Fruit Center, 8½″ D.
.... $15.00
TEAPOT, Med. Drk. Blue, Girl At Well, Cracked In Several Places & Lid Chips, 7¾″ H. $55.00
PLATE, Drk. Blue, "Castles" By "R. Stevenson", Flake On Back Of Rim, 8″ D.
.... $47.50
ROW III, L To R
PLATE, Med. Drk. Blue, Cows, Impressed "Adams", Wear & Sm. Flakes, 10⅜″ D.
.... $25.00
CREAMER, Med. Drk. Blue, Flowers, Edge Chips, 4⅝″ D. $42.50
PLATE, Med. Drk. Blue, "Ponte Rotto", Minor Rim Flakes $15.00

A-MA Aug 1980   *Robert C. Eldred Co., Inc.*
BLUE STAFFORDSHIRE
ROW I, L To R
PLATE, "Athenaeum, Boston", Beauties Of America Series By J. & W. Ridgway, 1814/1830, 6¼″ D. $190.00
PLATE, "The Landing Of The Fathers", By Enoch Wood & Sons, 10″ D. $130.00
ROW II, L To R
PLATE, "Marine Hospital, Louisville, KY", By Enoch Wood & Sons, 9½″ D. .. $250.00
PLATE, "New York From Brooklyn Heights", By A. Stevenson, 1816/1830, 2 Rim Repairs, 10¼″ D. $250.00
ROW III, L To R
SOUP PLATE, "Table Rock, Niagara", By Enoch Wood & Sons, 10″ D. $320.00
PLATE, "City Of Albany, State Of NY", By Enoch Wood, Worn & Reverse Side Stained, 10″ D. $180.00
ROW IV, L To R
PLATE, "Building, Sheep On Lawn", From America & Independence Series By Clews, 8¾″ D. $110.00
PLATE, "Landing of LaFayette", By Clews, 9″ D. $210.00

◄ A-OH April 1980   *Garth's Auctions, Inc.*
HISTORICAL BLUE STAFFORDSHIRE
TOP
PLATTER, Med. Drk. Blue, "Landing Of Gen. LaFayette", 18½″ L. $1100.00
BOTTOM
PLATTER, Drk. Blue, "Castle Garden Battery NY", Impressed "E. Wood & Sons", Knife Scratches & Sm. Surface Chips, 18½″ L.
.... $1250.00

A-OH April 1980   *Garth's Auctions, Inc.*

HISTORICAL BLUE STAFFORDSHIRE
ROW I, L To R
SUGAR BOWL, Med. Blue, Impressed "Adams", Chipped, 5½" H. $75.00
PLATE, Drk. Blue, "The Valentine From Wilkie's Designs", Sm. Flakes, Impressed "Clews", 9" D. $135.00
PLATE, Med. Drk. Blue, "Highlands At West Point, Hudson River", Impressed "E. Wood & Sons", Sm. Flake, 6½" D. $240.00
ROW II, L To R
SUGAR BOWL, Med. Drk. Blue, "Landing Of Gen. LaFayette", Minor Rim Wear & Chips, Lid Rep., 6⅛" H. $180.00
PLATE, Med. Drk. Blue, "Landing Of Gen. LaFayette", Impressed "Clews", 10¼" H. $255.00
CUP & SAUCER, Med. Drk. Blue, "Landing Of Gen. LaFayette", Impressed "Clews", Pinpoint Flakes $275.00
ROW III, L To R
PLATE, Drk. Blue, "Landing Of Gen. La-Fayette", Impressed "Clews", 8⅞" D. $200.00
PLATE, Med. Drk. Blue, "The Baltimore & Ohio Railroad", Impressed "E. Wood & Son", 9" D. $525.00
PLATE, Med. Blue, "Landing Of Gen. La-Fayette", Impressed "Clews", Sm. Flake, 8⅞" D. $155.00

A-OH April 1980   *Garth's Auctions, Inc.*

HISTORICAL BLUE STAFFORDSHIRE
ROW I, L To R
SUGAR BOWL, Drk. Blue, Washington At Tomb By Wood, Minor Hairlines & Chips, Int. Lid Flanges W/Old Rep., 6¾" H. $275.00
PLATE, Drk. Blue, "Union Line", Impressed "Wood", Minor Surface Wear & Knife Scratches, 10¼" D. $305.00
CREAMER, Drk. Blue, Wadsworth Tower, Minor Edge Wear, 4⅜" H. $235.00
ROW II, L To R
PLATE, Drk. Blue, "The Baltimore & Ohio Railroad", Impressed "E: Baltimore & Sons, Burslem", 10⅛" D. $560.00
TEAPOT, Drk. Blue, Wadsworth Tower, Minor Flake, 7½" H. $310.00
PLATE, Drk. Blue, "Marine Hospital, Louisville, KY", Impressed "E. Wood & Sons, Burslem", 9¼" D. $335.00
ROW III, L To R
SOUP PLATE, Drk. Blue, Cadmus, "E. Wood & Sons, Burslem", Minor Surface Wear & Scratches, Sm. Rim Flake, 10⅛" D. $195.00
PITCHER, Med. Blue, "Mt. Vernon", Minor Wear & Glaze Flakes, Rim & Spout Have Rep., 8¼" H. $350.00
PLATE, Drk. Blue, "Commodore MacDonnoughs Victory", 10¼" D. $360.00

A-OH April 1980   *Garth's Auctions, Inc.*

HISTORICAL BLUE STAFFORDSHIRE
ROW I, L To R
PLATE, Drk. Blue, "La Grange, Residence Of The Marquis De LaFayette", Rim Flake, 10¼" D. $140.00
DOME TOP COFFEE POT, Med. Blue, "Franklin" Tomb By Wood, Minor Wear & Rep., 10½" H. $1425.00
PLATE, Drk. Blue, "Landing Of Gen. La-Fayette", Impressed "Clews", Tiny Flake, 10⅛" D. $175.00
ROW II, L To R
CREAMER, Drk. Blue, "Franklin" Tomb, Impressed "Wood", Minor Glaze Wear, 5¾" H. $225.00
TEA POT, Drk. Blue, "Franklin" Tomb, Impressed "Wood", Flakes & Minor Glaze Wear, 7½" H. $410.00
CUP & SAUCER, Drk. Blue, "Franklin" Tomb, Saucer Impressed "E. Wood & Sons, Burslem", Color Varies Slightly ... $185.00
SUGAR BOWL, Drk. Blue, "Franklin" Tomb, Chips & Rep., 6¾" H. $100.00
ROW III, L To R
PLATE, Drk. Blue, "City Of Albany", Impressed "E. Wood & Sons, Burslem", 10¼" D. $510.00
PLATE, Med. Drk. Blue, "Bank Of The United States, Philadelphia", 10⅛" D. $230.00
PLATE, Drk. Blue, "City Of Albany", Impressed "E. Wood & Sons", 10¼" D. $350.00

A-WA D.C. May 1980 *Adam A. Weschler & Son*
DOUGHTY BALTIMORE ORIOLES, Pr., Tulip Trees, Ca. 1938, Limited Edition, 9½" H. $3500.00*

A-WA D.C. May 1980 *Adam A. Weschler & Son*
DOUGHTY LADYBIRDS, Pr., Ca. 1950, Limited Edition, 10¾" H. $1200.00*

A-WA D.C. May 1980 *Adam A. Weschler & Son*
BOEHM EASTERN BLUEBIRDS, Pr., Maker's Marks, Patt. Number, Ca. 1959, Limited Edition, 12" H., 14" H. ... $3900.00*

*Price does not include 10% buyer fee.

A-WA D.C. May 1980 *Adam A. Weschler & Son*
L To R
BOEHM ROSE, Queen's Masterpiece, Printed Marks, Eng., Ca. 1971, 7″ L. $100.00*
BOEHM IRIS, Printed Marks, Eng., Ca. 1972, 12″ L. $250.00*

A-OH July 1980 *Stratford Auction Center*
L To R
WELLER JARDINEER, 2-Part, Both W/ Impressed Weller Sgn., 11½″ D., 39″ H. $650.00
WELLER JARDINEER & STAND, Br. Shiny Glaze W/Yellow Daffodils, Unsigned, 12″ D., 31″ H. $360.00

A-OH July 1980 *Stratford Auction Center* ▶
L To R
WELLER UMBRELLA STAND, Scalloped Mouth, Br. Shiny Glaze, W/Bl.-Yellow Berries, Artist Sgn. "A. Haubrick", 21″ H. $425.00
WELLER UMBRELLA STAND, 3 Footed, Br. Shiny Glaze, Yellow Daffodils, Chips On Foot, Hairline At Rim, Unsigned, 21¾″ H. $95.00

Left
A-OH July 1980 *Stratford Auction Center*
WELLER VASE, Blueware, Classical Musicians, Imp. Sgn., 16½″ H. $300.00
Right
A-WA D.C. May 1980 *Adam A. Weschler & Son*
BOEHM MOURNING DOVES, Printed Marks, Patt. Number, Ca. 1958, Limited Edition, 10″ L., 14″ H. $650.00*

A-OH July 1980 *Stratford Auction Center*
WELLER WALL POCKET, Wh. Daisies On Burnt Orange-Cream Speckled Ground, Unsigned, Short Hairline, 10¾″ L. .. $35.00
WELLER BOWL W/Flower Frog, Coppertone, Stamped Ink Sgn., 11¼″ H. $65.00
WELLER WALL POCKET, Woodcraft Owl, Some Flakes, Unsigned, 11″ L. $65.00
WELLER WALL POCKET, 4 Fingered, Sydonia Patt., Blue-Gr., Incised "Weller Pottery", 10″ L. $10.00
WELLER FROG DISH, Coppertone, Stamped Ink Sgn., 6¼″ L. $50.00
WELLER WALL POCKET, Blue Ware, Classical Lady, Imp. Sgn., 10½″ L. .. $45.00

A-OH July 1980 *Stratford Auction Center*
ROW I, L To R
WELLER VASE. Dickensware, Matt Finish, Incised Portrait W/Artist Sgn. By G. Mull, 9½″ H. $650.00
ROOKWOOD VASE, Shiny Br. Glaze W/Cream Flowers, Artist Sgn. By Maryann Mitchell, Imp. Rookwood Mrk. 1901, 8¼″ H. $350.00
WELLER VASE, Forest Design, Stamped Ink Sgn., 8¼″ H. $65.00
WELLER HANDLED VASE, Shiny Br. Glaze W/Blk. Eyed Susan, Imp. Floretta Sgn., 5″ H. $50.00
WELLER VASE, Baldwin Patt., Unsigned, 9½″ H. $50.00
ROW II L To R
WELLER VASE, Shiny Br. Glaze W/Wh.- Bittersweet Flower, Imp. Weller Sgn., Artist Sgn. By Cora Davis, Glazing Imperfect On 1 Side, 7¼″ H. $50.00
ROZANE VASE, Shiny Br. Glaze, 2 Handles, Lily, Chip On 1 Foot & 1 On Rim, Imp. Sgn., 4¼″ H. $25.00
WELLER VASE, Dickensware, Matt Finished Vase, Chip At Rim, Impressed Sgn., 7½″ H. $75.00
WELLER VASE, Louwelsea, Shiny Br. Glaze W/Clover, Imp. Sgn., 5½″ H. .. $75.00
WELLER VASE, Louwelsa, Shiny Br. Glaze W/Wh. Roses, Imp. Sgn., Glaze Wear On Body, 7¼″ H. $45.00
ROW III, L To R
WELLER VASE, Gr. Leaves In Relief, Imp. Sgn., 6¼″ H. $35.00
WELLER VASE, Shiny Br. Glaze W/ Molded Designs, Imp. Floretta Sgn., 3 Minute Flakes At Rim, 8″ H. $50.00
MOSAIC BEAR, Imp. "Mosaic Tile Co." Sgn., 9½″ L., 6″ H. $70.00
WELLER VASE, Louwelsa, Shiny Br. Glaze W/Orange-Yellow Flower, Imp. Sgn., 7″ H. $90.00
WELLER CROCUS POT, Greora Patt., 5″ H. $30.00

A-OH Jan 1980 *Garth's Auctions, Inc.*
ROW I, L To R
KITCHEN SPATTER CREAMER, Yellow Ware W/Blue & Br. Sponging, Minor Glaze Grazing, 3" H. $80.00
KITCHEN SPATTER PIG BANK, Yellow Ware W/Blue & Br. Sponging, Flakes Around Coin Slot, 4" L. $105.00
KITCHEN SPATTER MINI. JUG, Blue & Wh., 3¼" H. $92.50
STONEWARE HOUSE BANK, Chips At Coin Slot & Chimney Broken, OH, 3¼" H.
.... $180.00
ROW II, L To R
TIN QUEEN BEE CARRIER, Swivel Cover On Lid, Honeycomb Inside, 3" D. . . $85.00
KITCHEN SPATTER CAT HEAD BANK, Wh. Clay W/Tan & Blk. Sponging & Amber Glaze, Minor Flake On Base, 4" H. . .$275.00
CHRISTMAS TREE LIGHT, Deep Red, Thousand Eye Patt., 3⅝" H. $35.00
ROW III, L To R
KITCHEN SPATTER PIG BANK, Running Blue & Amber Sponging, 6" L. . .$100.00
KITCHEN SPATTER BOWL, Blue & Wh., 4⅝" D. $90.00
KITCHEN SPATTER PIG BANK, Blue & Br. Sponging, Old Chips Around Coin Slot, 5¾" L. $195.00

A-OH Sept 1980 *Garth's Auctions, Inc.*
ROW I, L To R
GAUDY STICK SPATTER CUPS & SAUCERS, 6 Sets, (1 Illus.), Red, Mkd. "Auld Heather Wear, Scotland", 1 Cup W/ Hairline $78.00
GAUDY STICK SPATTER PLATES, Set Of 6, (1 Illus.), Matches Above, 1 W/Glued Rim Break...................... $66.00
GAUDY STICK SPATTER OVAL PLATTER, Matches Above, 10¾" L. $47.50
GAUDY STICK SPATTER SAUCERS, Set Of 6, (1 Illus.), Matches Above, 5½" D.
.... $90.00
ROW II, L To R
GAUDY IRONSTONE PLATE, Red & Gr. Floral Enamel Is Worn, 9½" D. . . $35.00
GAUDY IRONSTONE CREAMER, Urn Of Flowers, 5¾" H. $85.00
GAUDY SUGAR BOWL, Matches Above, 6¾" H. $105.00
GAUDY IRONSTONE PLATE, Floral Design, Enamel Shows Wear, 8¾" D.
.... $45.00
ROW III, L To R
GAUDY STICK SPATTER BOWLS, 2, Mkd. "Belgium", 11" D. $20.00
STICK SPATTER PLATES, Set Of 6, (1 Illus.), Matches Items In 1st Row, 1 W/Hairline, 9" D. $78.00

A-OH April 1980 *Garth's Auctions, Inc.*
ROW I, L To R
MINI. SPATTERWARE CUP & SAUCER, Red & Blue, Sm. Flake $125.00
RAINBOW SPATTERWARE, Blk. & Purple, 5" L. $85.00
MINI. SPATTERWARE CUP & SAUCER, Blue W/Design In Green & Blk., Sm. Flake & Rim Roughage $210.00
ROW II, L To R
SEWING KIT, Turned Wooden Keg Shaped Container, Decor. Iron Hinge & Latch, Int. Lined W/Purple Velvet 3¼" H. $35.00
PORCELAIN DISHES, 2, (1 Illus.), Leaf Shaped W/Embossed Veins On Back, Blue & Wh., Rim Chips, 3⅞" L. & 4½" L. ...$25.00
STIRRUP CUP, Wh. Porcelain, 4½" L.
.... $90.00
DRINKING VESSEL, Persian Silver Footed W/Engravings, Sl. Battered, 2¾" H. . . $28.00
FAIRYLAND LUSTRE FOOTED SAUCE, Gilt Decor. On Sides, Int. Butterfly, Mkd. "Wedgwood England", 3" H. . . .$390.00
ROW III, L To R
SPATTERWARE CUP PLATE, Gr. W/Peafowl In Blue, Red, Ochre & Blk, 3⅞" D.
.... $330.00
SPATTERWARE MINI. CUP & SAUCER, Gr. W/Peafowl In Blue, Red, Ochre & Blk.
.... $150.00
HISTORICAL BLUE STAFFORDSHIRE TODDY, Drk. Blue, "Landing Of Gen. LaFayette", Impressed "Clews Warranted Staffordshire", Minor Glaze Wear, 4⅜" D.
.... $330.00

Left
A-MA April 1980 *Richard A. Bourne Co., Inc.*
WELLER POTTERY VASE, Floral Decor., Incised Sgn. "Aurelian/Weller", 11¼" H.
.... $250.00

Right
A-OH July 1980 *Stratford Auction Center*
WELLER VASE, Sicard, Ribbed Body, Stamped Sgn. 14¾" H. $370.00

A-MA Sept 1980 *Richard A. Bourne Co., Inc.*
L To R
FLINT ENAMEL COVERED COFFEE URN, Plate 109, Bennington Pottery & Porcelain By Barret, Chip Under Rim Back Side, 20½" H. $2100.00
FLINT ENAMEL COFFEE POT, Imp. "U" In Bottom, Plate 136, Above Book, 13¼" H. $1300.00

A-MA Sept 1980 *Richard A. Bourne Co., Inc.*
L To R
FLINT ENAMEL LIDDED SUGAR BOWL W/Faint "1849" Mark (See Barret, Plate 126), Age Crack In Side, 2 Chips In Foot Ring, 8½" H. $500.00
ROCKINGHAM GLAZE ALTERNATE RIB TOBACCO JAR W/"1849" Mark (See Barret, Plates 129 & 130), Chip In Edge Of Cover, 7" H. $375.00

A-OH July 1980   *Stratford Auction Center*
ROW I, L To R
VASE, Shiny Br. Glaze, Cream-Orange Flowers, Peters & Reed, Unsigned, 10½" H. $70.00
WELLER VASE, Louwelsea, Shiny Br. Glaze W/3 Pansies, 2 Flakes On Rim, 5½" H. $25.00
WELLER VASE, Hudson, Blue & Gr. Ground W/Raised Blue-Yellow-Pink-Wh. Flowers, Incised & Ink Sgn., 7" H. .. $125.00
ROOKWOOD VASE, Shiny Br. Glaze W/Wh. Violets, Artist Sgn., 4 Feet 1 W/Chip, 5" x 5½" $55.00
WELLER VASE, Dickensware, Shiny Br. Glaze W/Blueberries & Leaves, Impressed Block Letters Sgn., 10½" H. $125.00
ROW II, L To R
WELLER VASE, Hudson Timberlake, Iris, Impressed & Stamped Ink Sgn., 8½" H. $205.00
WELLER CANDLESTICK, Warwick, Stamped Ink Sgn., 7¼" H. $20.00
WELLER CLOCK, Louwelsea, Shiny Br. Glaze W/Leaves, Stamped Sgn. .. $450.00
WELLER VASE, LaSa, Chip At Rim, Unsigned, 6¼" H. $22.50
WELLER VASE, Hudson, Artist Sgn. Leffler, Berries & Leaves, 7" H. $195.00
ROW III, L To R
WELLER CANDLESTICKS, Pr. Pink Flower On Cream Ground, Gilded Trim, Gr. Candle Sockets, 1 Stick W/2 Flakes At Rim, 9¼" H. $110.00
WELLER VASE, Sicard, Unsigned, 7½" H. $65.00
WELLER VASE, Shiny Br. Glaze W/Gr.-Br.-Cream Leaves, Unsigned, Sm. Wear On 1 Side, 5½" H. $45.00
WELLER VASE, LaSa, Mountains & Trees, Unsigned, 6½" H. $125.00

A-OH July 1980   *Stratford Auction Center*
ROW I L To R
WELLER VASE, Sicard, Sgn. In Script On Decor., 8½" H. $160.00
WELLER VASE, Etna, Shaded Gray-Blue Ground W/ Pink Berries, Unsigned, 6½" H. $50.00
WELLER VASE, LaSa, Palm Trees & Clouds, Unsigned, 7¼" H. $50.00
POTTERY VASE, 2 Handled, Shiny Br. Glaze W/Orange & Yellow Flowers, Unsigned, Imp. 31 On Bottom, 11" H. $70.00
POTTERY VASE, Gourd Shaped, Shiny Br. Glaze W/2 Pansies, 8" H. $55.00
WELLER VASE, Rows Of Splotching Decor., Incised Script Sgn., 7¾" H. $160.00
ROW II, L To R
MCCOY POTTERY BOWL, 4 Footed, Shiny Br. Glaze W/Yellow-Russet Tulips, Imp. Block Sgn., "Loy-Nel-Art", 4¼" x 4¼" $55.00
WELLER VASE, LaSa, Palm Trees, Mountains & Clouds, Unsigned, 5¼" H. $110.00
WELLER VASE, Sicard, Shiny Red Metalic, Imp. Weller Sgn., 5¾" H. $150.00
POTTERY VASE, Shiny Br. Glaze W/Yellow Flower, Unsigned, 4½" H. $27.50
CAMBRIDGE POTTERY VASE, Yellow-Gr. Berries, Imp. Mark, 5½" H. $160.00
ROW III, L To R
LONHUDA VASE, 3 Footed, Shiny Br. Glaze W/Wh.-Yellow Flower, Incised Sgn., 1 Foot W/Several Flakes, 6½" H. $65.00
ROZANE VASE, 2 Handled, Shiny Br. Glaze, Repaired Chips & Crack On Ruffled Edge, Cartouche On Bottom Damaged, 9½" H. $375.00
WELLER VASE, Woodcraft, Embossed Leaves, Imp. Sgn., 7½" L., 5½" H. .. $95.00

◄ A-MA Sept 1980   *Richard A. Bourne Co., Inc.*
BLUE JASPERWARE TILE, Sgn. Turner, Raised Figures, Natural Separations In Raised Wh. Molding, 5½" x 8" $175.00

A-OH July 1980   *Stratford Auction Center*
ROW I, L To R
WELLER LAMP BASE, Roma, Polychrome Flowers, Unsigned, 9½" H. $17.50
ROSEVILLE VASE, 2 Handled, Wh. Roses, 4½" x 4½" $20.00
HULL PLANTER, Swan, 10¾" x 8½" $15.00
WELLER VASE, Hudson, Shaded Pink & Wh. Flowers On Shaded Blue-Gr. Ground, 4½" x 4½" $120.00
WELLER VASE, Roma, Yellow-Pink Berries On Wh. Ground, Unsigned, 8¼" H. $15.00
ROW II, L To R
ROSEVILLE VASE, 2 Spouted, 9" H. $7.50
WELLER PLANTER, Duck, Gr.-Cream, 5" L. $40.00
WELLER VASE, Hudson, Dogwood On Rose To Blue-Gr. Ground, Artist Sgn. "Hattie Mitchell", 7¼" H. $225.00
WELLER PLANTER, Swan, Wh. Ground W/Yellow-Gr. Leaves, Yellow Beak, 4½" L. $35.00
WELLER FLOWER FROG, Muskota, Lady W/Swan, 8" x 8" $110.00
ROW III, L To R
ROSEVILLE VASE, 2 Handled, Wh. Rose, Minute Flakes On Rim. 6¼" H. $12.50
ROSEVILLE BOWL, 3 Footed, Shiny Glaze, Artist Sgn. "C. Neff", 4" x 4" $70.00
WELLER PLANTER, Muskota, Swan, 5" x 9½" $90.00
WELLER VASE, Hudson, Artist Sgn. 5¾" H. $65.00
WELLER VASE, 3 Footed, Flower W/Butterfly On Shaded Gr. Ground, Gloria Patt., 5¼" x 5" $17.50

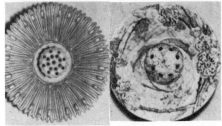

A-OH July 1980   *Stratford Auction Center*
L To R
WELLER BOWL W/Flower Frog, Ardsley, Stamped Ink Sgn., 17" D. $100.00
WELLER BOWL, Silvertone W/Matching Frog, Stamped Ink Sgn., 12" D. ... $35.00

A-OH July 1980   *Stratford Auction Center*
ROW I, L To R
WELLER VASE, Eocean, Blue Ground W/Flowers, 5½" H. $60.00
CREAMWARE VASE, Footed, 2 Handled, Reserves Of Classical Ladies, Leads, Pierced Rim, Imp. Weller Sgn., Flake On 1 Foot, 4¾" x 2¼" $7.50
WELLER VASE, 2 Handled, Eocean, Gray Ground, Violet Pansy, Faint Imp. Sgn., 5" H. $80.00
WELLER VASE, Eocean, Shaded Blue Ground W/Pink-Cream Flower, 5½ H. $60.00
ROW II, L To R
BURNTWOOD MUG, Unsigned Weller, 4¾" H. $30.00
WELLER CARD HOLDER, Etna, Gray-Gr. Ground, 3½" x 4½" $250.00
BURNTWOOD MUG, Unsigned Weller, 4½" H. $32.50
ROW III, L To R
WELLER COMIC DOG, Muskota, Incised Sgn. 4" H. $225.00
ROSEVILLE FLOWER FROG, 2 Handled, Gr. W/ Pink Tulip, Raised Sgn., 4½" H. $17.50
MEDALLION OF LINCOLN, Wh. On Blue, Mosaic Tile Co., Sgn. On Back, 3" H. $10.00

A-OH July 1980   *Stratford Auction Center*
ROW I, L To R
TANKARD PITCHER, Redware, Matt Glaze, Embossed Grapes, Incised Sgn. "Ferrell", Chip At Mouth & Some Flakes, 12" H. $5.00
WELLER TALL CANDLESTICK, Louwelsa, Br. Shiny Glaze, Red-Yellow Clover, 1 Chip On Lip, Artist Impressed Sgn., 10¾" H. $17.50
EWER, Br. Shiny Glaze, Yellow Pansies, Repaired Chip On Rim, Unsigned, 10½" H. $70.00
ROSEVILLE VASE, Mostique, Unsigned, 10" H. $27.50
ROW II, L To R
WELLER VASE, Louwelsa, Br. Shiny Glaze W/Some Wear, Burnt Orange Flowers, Imp. Sgn., 9¾" H. $40.00
WELLER PLANTER, Forest, Unsigned, 17¾" x 7½" $210.00
WELLER VASE, Louwelsa, Br. Shiny Glaze, Bachelor Buttons In Yellow-Orange-Wh. & Gr. Leaves, Imp. Sgn., 8½" H. $50.00
ROW III, L To R
WELLER CLOCK, Louwelsa, 3 Feet, Handle, Br. Shiny Glaze, Imp. Sgn., 7½" H. $300.00
WELLER VASE, Golden Glow, 2 Handles Going Into Molded Leaves, Script Incised Sgn., 4½" D., 7" H. $45.00
WELLER VASE, 3 Sections In Top, Blue Ground, Red Roses, Imp. Sgn., 6" H. $12.50
ROOKWOOD VASE, Br. Shiny Glaze, Berries & Flowers, "1897", Artist Sgn. Charles Schmidt, 6½" H. $575.00

A-OH July 1980   *Stratford Auction Center*
ROW I, L To R
WELLER VASE, Louwelsea, Shiny Br. Glaze W/Berries, Imp., Sgn., 13½" H. $150.00
WELLER EWER, Louwelsea, Dainty Flowers Imp. Sgn., 6¼" H. $50.00
WELLER VASE, Shiny Br. Glaze W/Pansies, 3 Sm. Flakes On Rim, Unsigned, 12" H. $40.00
HULL POTTERY SWAN PLANTER, Imp. Sgn., 8" L. $5.00
WELLER VASE, Shiny Br. Glaze W/Roses, Imp. "Weller", 11¼" $150.00
ROW II, L To R
WELLER MUG, Eocean, Blueberries, Imp. Sgn., 5½" H. $140.00
WELLER LUSTRE VASE, Unsigned, 8¼" H. $25.00
WELLER VASE, Hudson, Pink-Wh. Flowers, Imp. Sgn., 10½" H. $125.00
WELLER VASE, Lamar Patt., Paper Sgn. "Weller Ware", 8" H. $185.00
ROSEVILLE VASE, 2 Handled, Magnolia, Raised Sgn., 6¼" H. $17.50
ROW III, L To R
WELLER JARDINEER, Shiny Br. Glaze, Orange-Yellow Pansies, Artist Sgn. M.C., 6½" x 8" $60.00
WELLER JARDINEER, Shiny Br. Glaze, Yellow Daffodils, Unsigned, 9" x 10" $60.00
WELLER JARDINEER, Shiny Br. Glaze, Swirl Molded Body, Flakes On Rim, 8" x 7¼" $25.00

Left
A-OH July 1980   *Stratford Auction Center*
WELLER CLAYWOOD JARDINEER, Satyrs In Vinyard, Imp. Sgn., 13" D. $350.00

Right
A-MA July 1980   *Robert W. Skinner, Inc.*
DOULTON IMPASTO VASE, Gold Enameled Rolled Rim, Sgn. "J. Kelsall", Eng., 19th C., 15½" H. $750.00*

*Price does not include 10% buyer fee.

A-OH July 1980   *Stratford Auction Center* ▶
L To R
ROSEVILLE VASE, 2 Handled, Wh. Roses On Pumpkin Ground, Raised Sgn., 18½" H. $50.00
WELLER VASE, LaSa, Trees, Mountains & Clouds, Unsigned, Minute Flake At Bottom, 14" H. $225.00

A-OH July 1980   *Stratford Auction Center*
L To R
WELLER UMBRELLA STAND, Art Nouveau Lady In Lavender, Golden Glaze Ground, Gr. Glazed Int., 27" H. . . $550.00
WELLER UMBRELLA STAND, Br. Shiny Glaze, Yellow Iris, Some Flaking Of Glaze Around Bottom, Unsigned, 21" H $105.00

A-OH April 1980   *Garth's Auctions, Inc.*
ROW I, L To R
ROCKINGHAM SUGAR BOWL, Rebecca At The Well, 6¼" H. $70.00
ROCKINGHAM SOAP DISH, 5" D., 2½" H. $45.00
ROCKINGHAM BOWL, 5⅜" D. .. $27.50
ROCKINGHAM COW CREAMER, Chip In Lid, 5⅜" H. $185.00
ROW II, L To R
ROCKINGHAM PLATES, Pr., Embossed Border, Sm. Flake, 9" Sq. $210.00
ROCKINGHAM LOVING CUP, Int. Frog, Embossed Scene, Tiny Glaze Flakes & 1 Int. Flake, 6½" H. $165.00
ROW III, L To R
BENNINGTON FLINT ENAMEL CANDLESTICKS, 2, Sm. Flakes, 8¼" H. $770.00
ROCKINGHAM MUG, 3" H. ... $60.00
ROCKINGHAM BOWL, Out Of Round, 10¼" D. $50.00
ROCKINGHAM MUG, 3" H. ... $70.00

*Price does not include 10% buyer fee.

A-OH April 1980   *Garth's Auctions, Inc.*
SPATTERWARE
ROW I, L To R
CUP & SAUCER, Red W/Blue Shield Design, Impressed "Stone China" .. $475.00
CUP & SAUCER, Purple W/Buildings & Trees, Flake $175.00
SUGAR BOWL, Blue W/Tree Design, 2 Rim Hairlines, 4¾" H. $210.00
CUP & SAUCER, Purple W/Adam's Rose Design $135.00
CUP & SAUCER, Brown W/Fort Patt., Sm. Chip $225.00
ROW II, L To R
PLATE, Yellow W/Red & Gr. Tulip Design, Faded Slightly, 8½" D. $375.00
SUGAR BOWL, Red & Purple Rainbow, Rim Flakes & Hairlines, 4½" H. .. $150.00
CUP & SAUCER, Red & Yellow Rainbow, Thistle Is Red & Gr. $350.00
PLATE, Gr. W/Trees & Castles, 8⅜" D. $290.00
ROW III, L To R
PLATE, Red W/Schoolhouse Design In Red, Gr. & Blk., 10¼" D. $1200.00
CUP & SAUCER, Purple W/Thistle In Red & Gr. $225.00
CUP & SAUCER, Red W/Trees & Castles $175.00
PLATE, Blue W/Schoolhouse Design In Red, Gr., & Blk., 10¼" D. $1050.00

Left
A-MA Mar 1980   *Robert W. Skinner, Inc.*
ROOKWOOD COVERED JAR, Gold Incised Bands, Base W/Incised Trademark & "A.R.V", OH, Ca. 1888, 7" H. .. $1700.00*

Right
A-MA Sept 1980   *Richard A. Bourne Co., Inc.*
CHALK WARE FIGURE, Reclining Stag, Horns Chipped, 15½" L., 15" H. .. $100.00

A-MA July 1980   *Robert W. Skinner Inc.* ►
ROSEVILLE ROZANE VASE, Sgn. "E.B.", OH, Late 19th Or Early 20th C., 8¼" H. $725.00*

A-OH Jan 1980   *Garth's Auctions, Inc.*
ROW I, L To R
SPATTERWARE SAUCER, Blue, Red & Green Rose Center, Tiny Rim Flake ...$95.00
STAFFORDSHIRE PLATE, Blue, Eagle & Shield Transfer, Edge Wear & Sm. Flakes $25.00
SPATTERWARE SAUCER, Blue & Green W/Red & Green Rose Center $40.00
ROW II, L To R
SPATTERWARE HANDLELESS CUP, Red W/Peafowl In Blue, Green, & Red, Int. Blister $45.00
RAINBOW SPATTERWARE PLATTER, Red & Blue, Edge Flake, 13½" L. $475.00
SPATTERWARE HANDLELESS CUP, Blue W/Peafowl In Red, Green & Ochre $65.00
ROW III, L To R
SPATTERWARE PLATE, Blue, Peafowl In Red, Green & Blue, Old Crack, Impressed "Adams", 8¾" D. $85.00
SPATTERWARE SOUP PLATE, Blue, Peafowl In Blue, Green & Red, Sm. Rim Hairline & Rim Wear, 10" D. $165.00
SPATTERWARE PLATE, Red, Peafowl In Blue, Green & Red, Impressed "Adams", 9½" D. $195.00

A-WA D.C. Oct 1980   *Adam A. Weschler & Son*
L To R
FAIENCE TANKARD, German, Pewter Mounded, Armorial Crest, 15¼″ H.
.... $500.00*
METTLACH TANKARD, Pewter Mounted, 2 Vikings Drinking From Horns, 15¾″ H.
.... $425.00*
METTLACH TANKARD, Pewter Mounted, Blue & Wh. Salt Glaze W/Frolicking Figures, 14½″ H. $400.00*
METTLACH TANKARD, Pewter Mounted, Armorial Crest, 14½″ H. $225.00*
METTLACH TANKARD, Pewter Mounted, Floral Decor., 13½″ H. $300.00*
METTLACH STEIN, 1-Litre, Pewter Mounted, Muchen Standing Beside Keg, 10″ H. $675.00*
METTLACH TANKARD, Blue & Wh. Salt Glaze, 5 Singing Men, Removable Domed Top, 11½″ H. $275.00*

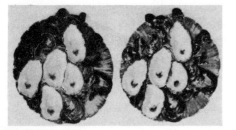

A-MA Aug 1980   *Robert C. Eldred Co., Inc.*
LIMOGES OYSTER PLATES, Set Of 5, (2 Illus.), Blue Ground, Mkd. W/Am. Eagle, 8½″ D. $900.00

A-WA D.C. Dec 1980   *Adam A. Weschler & Son*
LIMOGES PARTIAL DINNER SERVICE, Haviland & Co., Wh. Ground W/ Floral Bouquet & Gild Border, 113 Pcs.
.... $775.00*

A-WA D.C. Oct 1980   *Adam A. Weschler & Son*
BAVARIAN DINNER SERVICE, Maria Patt. By Rosenthal, 101 Pcs. $950.00*

Price does not include 10% buyer fee.

A-MA April 1980   *Richard A. Bourne Co., Inc.*
COPPER LUSTRE
ROW I, L To R
JUG, Yellow & Pink Swag Band, Spout Repaired, Decor. Worn, 6″ H. $60.00
JUG, Yellow Bank W/Raised Polychromed Flower Decor., Mask Spout, Sl. Flaking Of Decor., 6″ H. $175.00
JUG, Canary Band, Transfer Scenes Of Mother & Child At Play, 5¾″ H. .. $150.00
ROW II, L To R
JUG, Double Gr. Band W/Pink Decor., Sl. Nicks, 6½″ H. $50.00
LRG. JUG, Raised Classical Scenes, Wh. Glazed Area Toned To Br. Shade, 7″ H.
.... $125.00

A-WA D.C. Oct 1980   *Adam A. Weschler & Son*
ROW I, L To R
ROOKWOOD VASE, Aqua Glaze, Dated 1925, Underglaze Scroll Decor., 6″ H.
.... $70.00*
ROOKWOOD VASE, Chartreuse Glaze, Decor. By A.M. Bookprinter, Dated 1886, 8″ H. $120.00*
FULPER VASE, 7-Sided, Gr.-Br. Irid. Glaze, Early 20th C., 8½″ H. $45.00*
VAN BRIGGLE VASE, Persian Rose Glaze, Indian Mask On Shoulder, Mid-20th C., 11½″ H. $175.00*
REDWARE BULB BOWL, Turquoise Glaze, 20th C., 10″ D. $35.00*
ROW II, L To R
ROOKWOOD TOBACCO HUMIDOR, Blue Glaze, Dated 1929, 5½″ H. .. $150.00*
BATCHELDER BOWL, Lavender Glaze, Flared Rim, 20th C., Lt. Blue Int., 7″ D.
.... $60.00*
ROOKWOOD INK STAND, Lavender Splash Glaze, Dated 1924, Orig. Ink Pot, 3¾″ H. $125.00*
ROOKWOOD FLORIFORM VASE, Celadon Glaze, Dated 1949, Underglaze Water Lily & Pad Decor., 6¼″ H. $100.00*

A-WA D.C. Oct 1980   *Adam A. Weschler & Son*
ROW I, L To R
ROOKWOOD LONG NECK VASE, Canary Crackleware Glaze, Dated 1917, 8¾″ H. $45.00*
ROOKWOOD VASE, Blue Glaze, Dated 1923, Art Deco Form, 5¾″ H. $40.00*
ROOKWOOD VASE, Canary Yellow Glaze, Dated 1910, Art Deco Stylized Underglaze Decor., 9½″ H. $100.00*
ROW II, L To R
ROYCROFT VASE, Blue Speckled, Mei P'ing Form, 7″ H. $45.00*
ROOKWOOD BULB BOWL, Aqua Glaze, Dated 1921, Underglaze Lobed Base, 3¼″ H.
.... $50.00*
ROOKWOOD ROSE JAR, Turquoise Glaze, Dated 1927, Inner Cover, Removable Pierced Lid, 4½″ H. $100.00*
ROOKWOOD FLORIFORM VASE, Splash Blue Glaze, Dated 1931, 5¼″ H.
.... $60.00*
ROOKWOOD VASE, Blue Flower Glaze, Decor. By Louise Abel, Dated 1926, Int. Painted W/Blue Flowers, 6½″ D., 5½″ H.
.... $85.00*

A-WA D.C. Oct 1980   *Adam A. Weschler & Son*
ROW I, L To R
POTTERY VASE, Lavender Flambe Glaze, Am. Art Grecian-Form, Attrib. To Fulper, 20th C., 8″ H. $35.00*
ROOKWOOD VASE, Decor. By C.S. Todd, Ca. 1892, Irises On Gold-To-Carmel-To-Gr. Ground, 5″ H. $275.00*
ROYCROFT VASE, Celadon, Crackleware Glaze, 20th C., 9¾″ H. $80.00*
ROW II, L To R
LITTLEFIELD FOOTED JAR, Blue Speckled Glaze, Pear-Form, 20th C., Removable Wood Top, 4½″ H. $40.00*
VAN BRIGGLE EWER, Carmel Glaze, Mid-20th C., 5″ H. $40.00*
COWAN VASE, Silver Irid. Glaze, Early 20th C., 10¾″ H. $60.00*
COWAN CANDLESTICKS, Pr., Orange Irid. Glaze, Early 20th C., 7″ H. $35.00*

A-WA D.C. Oct 1980 *Adam A. Weschler & Son*
LIMOGES DINNER SERVICE, C. Ahrenfeldt, Retailed By Wright, Tyndale & Van Roden, Phil., Early 20th C., 151 Pcs. $850.00*

A-MA July 1980 *Robert W. Skinner Inc.*
COPPER LUSTRE PITCHERS, Set Of 3, Eng., Early 19th C., 5¼", 6½", 7" H. $175.00*

A-MA April 1980 *Richard A. Bourne Co., Inc.*
ROW I, L To R
ROYAL COPENHAGEN CABINET VASE, Decor. Of Fishing Boat, 3-Rivers Mark, 3⅞" H. $25.00
ROYAL COPENHAGEN VASE, Decor. Of Plant, 3-Rivers Mark, 5" H. $30.00
BING & GRONDAHL VASE, Decor. Of Blue Crocus, 5⅜" H. $25.00
ROYAL COPENHAGEN FIGURINE, Boy Whittling, 3-Rivers Mark, 7½" H. $160.00
ROYAL COPENHAGEN VASE, Decor. Of Wh. Morning Glory, 3-Rivers Mark, 6½" H. $35.00
ROW II, L To R
ROYAL COPENHAGEN DISHES, Pr., Shell Formed, Raised Figures Of Crab & Lobster, 3-Rivers Mark, 6½" D. . . . $50.00
BING & GRONDAHL VASE, Lrg. Gourd-Form, Decor. W/Wh. Flowers, 10" H. $50.00

*Price does not include 10% buyer fee.

A-OH July 1980 *Garth's Auctions, Inc.*
ROW I, L To R
COPPER LUSTRE CREAMER, Gr. Band W/Applied Polychrome Decor, Hairlines, 5¾" H. $20.00
COPPER LUSTRE CREAMER, Orange Band W/Applied Polychrome Decor., Flakes on Spout, 4¾" H. $30.00
SALT GLAZE CREAMER, Br. W/Applied Decor., Vintage Rim, Glaze Imperfection, 4⅝" H. $135.00
COPPER LUSTRE CREAMER, Blue Band W/Raised Polychrome Decor., Flakes, 4⅜" H. $30.00
COPPER LUSTRE CREAMER, Blue Band W/Raised Polychrome Decor., 3⅜" H. $30.00
ROW II, L To R
MOCHA PITCHER, Drk. Br. Seaweed Decor. On Tan Ground, Crowsfoot In Bottom 7" H. $375.00
COPPER LUSTRE PITCHER, Rust Band W/3 Oval Reserves, Minor Wear & Crack, 6⅜" H. $175.00
MOCHA PITCHER, Gr. Embossed Band, Br. Stripes, Drk. Br. Seaweed On Tan, Sm. Flakes On Rim & Foot, 5¼" H. . . . $310.00
STAFFORDSHIRE PITCHER, Blk. Transfer, Rim Flake, 5" H. $95.00
ROW III, L To R
SUNDERLAND LUSTRE PITCHER, Blk. Transfer, Polychrome Enameling, 8⅜" H. $300.00
STAFFORDSHIRE COW CREAMER, Wh. Clay W/Br. Running Glaze, Lid W/Fly, Sm. Flakes, Tips of Horns Broken, 6⅛" H. $175.00
CANARY LUSTRE COFFEEPOT, Gaudy Floral Decor, Flake On Rim, Edge of Lid & Top Of Handle, 9½" H. $575.00

A-WA D.C. Dec 1980 *Adam A. Weschler & Son* ►
TOP
CROWN DERBY EWER, Retailed By Tiffany & Co., Early 20th C., 8½" H. $175.00*
BOTTOM
ROYAL WORCESTER PITCHERS, 2, Ewer-Form & Keg-Form, Early 20th C., 6½" H., 8" H. $275.00*

A-OH Mar 1980 *Garth's Auctions, Inc.*
ROW I, L To R
ENGLISH IRONSTONE PLATES, 3 (1 Illus.), Drk. Red Transfer W/Red, Blk. & Gold Enameling, Impressed "Ashworth Real Ironstone China", 7¼" D. $18.00
ENGLISH IRONSTONE PLATTER, Matches 1st Item, 15¼" L. $75.00
ENGLISH IRONSTONE PLATES, 5 (1 Illus.), Matches 1st Item, 10¼" D. . . $125.00
ROW II, L To R
ENGLISH PORECLAIN CUP & SAUCER, Blue Oriental Transfer W/Red & Gr. Enameling $27.50
ENGLISH IMARI MUG, Dragon Handle W/Br. Transfer & Gr., Red, Purple, & Yellow Enamaling & Underglaze Blue, Mkd. "Mason's", Handle Rep., 4½" H. . . $65.00
PLATE, Similar To Previous Item, "Mason's", 7½" D. $25.00
GAUDY WELSH CUP & SAUCER, Tulip Design $30.00
ROW III, L To R
IRONSTONE PLATE, Br. Transfer, Mkd. "Pratt 123 Fenton", 7⅜" D. $30.00
ENGLISH IMARI PLATE, 10¼" D. $45.00
STAFFORDSHIRE MUG, Br. Transfer, Hairline At Base Of Handle, 4" H. . . $35.00

A-OH Jan 1980   *Garth's Auctions, Inc.*
ROW I, L To R
LEEDS SAUCER. 3 Color Floral Decor., Sm. Rim Flake, 4" D. $65.00
LEEDS PLATE, Blue Feather Edge W/Floral Swags In 4 Colors $155.00
MINI. GAUDY WELSH MUG, 1¾" H. $55.00
MINI. LEEDS SAUCER, Blue Border W/Swags & Floral Center In 4 Colors, 3¾" D. $55.00
ROW II, L To R
MINI LEEDS COVERED POT, Floral Decor. In 3 Colors, Hairline & Sm. Chip In Rim, 2¾" D., 2" H. $40.00
STAFFORDSHIRE CAT, Yellow & Blk. Sponging, Chips & Glued Rep., 4¼" H. $40.00
MINI. LEEDS PLATTER, Floral Decor. In 3 Colors, 4¾" L. $255.00
STAFFORDSHIRE SEATED DOG, Blk. & Amber On Wh., Chip On Base, 3½" H. $25.00
MINI. GAUDY LEEDS CREAMER, Floral Decor. In 3 Colors, Hairline & Rim Flake, 2½" H. $85.00
ROW III, L To R
MINI. GAUDY LEEDS HANDLELESS CUPS & SAUCERS, Set Of 4, 1 Saucer W/Glaze Flakes & Slightly Faded, 2 Cups W/Rim Chips & Hairlines & 1 W/Minor Flake On Table Ring $80.00

A-MA April 1980   *Richard A. Bourne Co., Inc.*
ROYAL COPENHAGEN
ROW I, L To R
CHRISTMAS PLATE, 1945, Peaceful Motif, Sl. Bruise, 7¼" D. $110.00
CHRISTMAS PLATE, 1949, Church Of Our Lady, 7¼" D. $65.00
CHRISTMAS PLATE, 1951, Christmas Angel, 7¼" D. $140.00
ROW II, L To R
CHRISTMAS PLATE, 1954, Amalienborg Palace, 7⅛" D. $50.00
CHRISTMAS PLATE, 1955, Fano Girl, 7⅛" D. $90.00
CHRISTMAS PLATE, 1959, Christmas Night, 7¼" D. $70.00

*Price does not include 10% buyer fee.

A-MA Mar 1980   *Richard A. Bourne Co., Inc.*
ROW I, L To R
TOLE MOLASSES SYRUP JUG, Blk. W/Stenciled Decor., Wear To Paint, 4¼"H. $80.00
CHINA SYRUP JUG, Flowing Blue W/Pewter Top, Sl. Wear, 4¼" H. ... $90.00
STONEWARE SYRUP JUG, Cobalt Blue, Raised Decor., Pewter Top, Age Crack In Rim, 6⅝" O.H. $30.00
ROW II, L To R
ETUSCAN MAJOLICA SYRUP PITCHER, Sgn. "Sunflower", Patt., Pewter Top, Top Bent & Discolored, 8" O.H. $60.00
SYRUP JUG, Mottled Blue, Br. & Wh., "Morley & Co", Age Crack & Pewter Top Bent, 8¼" H. $60.00
MAJOLICA PITCHER, Pewter Lid, Raised Decor., 8½" H. $100.00
ROW III, L To R
STAFFORDSHIRE PITCHER, Hinged Pewter Lid, Overall Transfer Design, Age Crack & Sm. Glaze Chip Reglued, 8½" H. $70.00
STONE CHINA SYRUP JUG, Flowing Blue, Hinged Pewter Lid, Gold Decor., 10¾" O.H. $130.00
MAJOLICA FISH SYRUP JUG, Hinged Pewter Top, Slightly Discolored, 11" H. $100.00

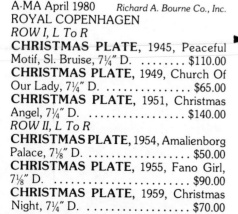

A-OH July 1980   *Stratford Auction Center*
POTTERY
ROW I, L To R
EWER, Shiny Br. Glaze, Autumn Leaves, Imp. Sgn. "Owens Utopian", Flake On Rim, 6" H. $35.00
ROSEVILLE VASE, Shaded Gr. W/Leaf, Silhouette Patt., Raised Sgn., 5¼" H. ...$10.00
WELLER MUG, Shiny Br. Glaze W/Cherries, Unsigned, 4½" H. $80.00
ROW II, L To R
ROOKWOOD CREAMER & SUGAR, Shiny Br. Glaze W/Yellow Blossoms, Imp. Mrk. For 1893, Artist Sgn. Sadie Markland, Sugar Not Illus., 3" x 4" $360.00
OWENS BOWL, Cyrano, Drk. Br. Ground W/Raised Orange Flowers & Cream Beading, 2½" x 4½" $105.00
ROSEVILLE VASE, 2 Handled, Bushberry, Raised Roseville Sgn., 3½" x 3½" $5.00
ROW III, L To R
WELLER MUG, Orange Tulips In Relief, Sgn. Block Letter Imp. "Art Nouveau Mat" In Circle, 5" H. $270.00
OWENS MUG, Shiny Br. Glaze W/Berries In Blk.-Orange, Imp. Sgn., Artist Sgn. T.S. In Glaze, 4½" H. $95.00
MUG, Shiny Br. Glaze, Orange Flower, Unsigned, 4½" H. $60.00
MUG, Shiny Br. Glaze, Bittersweet Rose, Unsigned, 5" H. $65.00

Left
A-MA July 1980   *Robert W. Skinner, Inc.*
PRATTWARE PITCHER, Polychrome Relief Decor., Handle Damaged & Rep., Eng., Early 19th C., 7¾" H. $210.00*

Right
A-MA Sept 1980   *Robert W. Skinner Inc.*
PRATTWARE TEA CADDY, Cover Missing, Eng., Early 19th C. $250.00*

A-MA Sept 1980   *Richard A. Bourne Co., Inc.*
ROW I, L To R
SPATTERWARE, 3 Pcs., Creamer, Covered Sugar & Child's Covered Sugar, 2 Pcs. W/Cracks $65.00
NEWHALL CREAMER, Eng., Decor. W/ Oriental Figures, 4½" H. $40.00
STAFFORDSHIRE CREAMER, 19th C., Raised Flowers On Grayish-Br. Glaze, 4½" H.
.... $35.00

ROW II, L To R
LIVERPOOL TEAPOT, Transfers Of Verse In Blk. On Both Sides, Cracked, Finial Repaired, Sm. Chips $55.00
NEWHALL CHINA, 4 Pcs., (2 Illus.), Discoloration & Wear, Age Cracks ... $85.00

ROW III, L To R
WHIELDON PLATE, Embossed Rim, Sm. Rim Chip, 9½" D. $220.00
LIVERPOOL JUG, Polychrome Transfers, Age Cracks, 8¼" H. $200.00
WHIELDON PLATTERS, Br., Gr. & Blue On Cream, Pr. (1 Illus.), 1 Chipped & Cracked $425.00

A-MA Aug 1980   *Robert C. Eldred Co., Inc.*
L To R
ROYAL WORCHESTER IVORYWARE EWERS, Pr., (1 Illus.), Gilt Floral Decor., Openwork Handles, Relief Decor. Around Neck, Ca. 1889, 19½" H. $250.00
ROYAL WORCHESTER VASES, Pr., (1 Illus.), Japanese Decor., Gold Flecked Red Lacquer Ground, Bronze Glazed Base, 8½" H. $550.00
ROYAL WORCHESTER PORCELAIN VASE, Dolphin Handles, Raised Gilt Highlighting, Clear Yellow Ground, Ca. 1884, 10¾" H. $300.00
ROYAL CROWN DERBY PORCELAIN VASE, Raised Gilt Flowers & Jeweling, Pierced Cover & Knop, Ca. 1880 .... $450.00

A-OH April 1980   *Garth's Auctions, Inc.*
ROW I, L To R
SOFT PASTE CUP & SAUCER, Br. Classical Scene W/Polychrome Transfer, Sm. Flakes $65.00
LEEDS PLATE, Gaudy 5 Color Decor., 5⅜" D. $125.00
LEEDS PLATE, Octagonal W/Green Feather Edge, Sm. Flakes, 6¼" D. ...$240.00
CREAMWARE CUP & SAUCER, Polychrome Decor., Cup W/Minor Rim Flakes $55.00

ROW II, L To R
LEEDS PLATE, 5 Color House Design, 8⅛" D. $360.00
LEEDS PLATE, Scalloped Blue Feather Edge, 8¼" D. $460.00
LEEDS PLATE, 4 Color House Design, Sm. Rim Damage, 8⅛" D. $200.00

ROW III, L To R
LEEDS PLATES, Pr., Pheasant Center & 5 Colors, Minor Rim Flakes, 10" D. .. $600.00
MOCHA TUMBLER, Footed, Blue & Cream Band W/Drk. Br. Stripes, 4" H.
.... $42.50
MINI. LEEDS CUP & SAUCER, Gaudy Blue & Ochre Design, Sm. Flake .. $70.00

A-MA April 1980   *Richard A. Bourne Co., Inc.*
OCCUPATIONAL SHAVING MUGS
ROW I, L To R
COBBLER'S By Limoges, Bearing Name "A.S. Bieler", Decor. W/Shoes & Boots, Sl. Wear To Decor. $130.00
RAILROAD BY Limoges, Bearing Name "Harry C. Stem", Decor. Worn... $170.00

ROW II, L To R
TRAINMAN'S, Bearing Name "Theodore Buck", Decor. Worn $160.00
TRAINMAN'S By Limoges, Bearing Name "Harry C. Stem" $170.00

A-OH July 1980   *Stratford Auction Center*
ROW I, L To R
WELLER VASE, Hudson, Purple & Wh. Crabapple W/Blk. Stems, Chip On Lip, Impressed Sgn., 13" H. $65.00
POTTERY VASE, Shiny Br. Glaze, Ear Of Corn, "Olympia" Impressed, Chip On Rim Of Foot, 11¼" H. $50.00
WELLER VASE, Chengtu, Chinese Orange-Red, Unsigned, 13¾" H. $60.00
WELLER VASE, Louwelsea, Yellow, Burnt Orange & Gr., Impressed Sgn., 11¼" H.
.... $95.00
ROSEVILLE WOODLAND VASE, Matt Ground W/Yellow, Burnt Orange & Gr., 2 Flakes On Bottom, Unsigned, 10¾" H.
.... $260.00

ROW II, L To R
WELLER VASE, Marbelized Design, Unsigned, 7" H. $15.00
ROZANE VASE, Shiny Br. Glaze W/Yellow & Gr. Molded Swirl, Cartouche Sgn. "Rozane Ware Royal", 6¾" H. $85.00
POTTERY VASE, 4 Footed, Shiny Br. Glaze W/Bittersweet & Gr., Impressed Sgn. Unreadable, 5¼" H. $85.00
ROZANE VASE, Shiny Br. Glaze, Clover Flower, Round Cartouche Sgn. "Rozane Ware", 7¼" H. $135.00
WELLER VASE, "Eocean" Sgn. In Script, Gray Shaded To Gr., Bubbles In Glaze, 7" H.
.... $65.00

ROW III, L To R
POTTERY VASE, Shiny Br. Glaze W/ Yellow & Orange Daffodil, Factory Drilled For Lamp Base, Impressed "O.S.", 8½" H.
.... $35.00
TRIANGULAR VASES, Pr., 3 Footed, "Weller" Tutone, Pink-Gr. W/Raised Flowers, Stamped Ink Sgn., 4¾" H. $35.00
WELLER FROG FIGURE, Coppertone, Stamped Ink Sgn., Hairline In Base, 6" H.
.... $105.00
POTTERY VASE, Shiny Br. Glaze, Yellow-Bittersweet Tulip, Impressed "O.S.", Factory Drilled For Lamp Base, 8¼" H. .. $55.00

A-OH Oct 1980   *Garth's Auctions, Inc.*
ROW I, L To R
STONEWARE STEIN, Embossed Blue &
Gray, "O.5L", Int. Frog, 5½" H. . . . $15.00
POTTERY STEIN, Pewter Lid, Gr. &
Blk., "Zumwohl", 4⅝" H. $30.00
STEIN, Frog Form W/Pewter Fittings, Gr.,
Red & Blk. On Wh., 7¾" H. $55.00
PORCELAIN STEIN, Pewter Lid, Poly-
chrome Farewell Scene, Lithophane Bot-
tom, Sgn. "Jagergrub", 8⅝" H. . . . $115.00
STONEWARE STEIN, Embossed Blue &
Gray, Pewter Lid W/Polychrome Porcelain
Insert, 5¾" H. $25.00
ROW II, L To R
METTLACH STEIN, Polychrome Scene,
Sgn. "Heinr Schlitt", Impressed Castle Mrk.,
9¼" H. $375.00
STONEWARE BOTTLE, Embossed Blue
& Gray, Impressed "D.W. Kitchens Whis-
kies & Wines, Mineola, TX", 9¼" H. . . .$35.00
POTTERY STEIN, Pewter Lid, Embossed
W/Blue, Gr., Blk. & Tan, Mkd. "R.H. Ger-
many", 9¼" H. $45.00

A-WA D.C. Oct 1980   *Adam A. Weschler & Son*
L To R
METTLACH STEIN, ½-Litre, Pewter
Mounted, Art Deco Gr. Hops, Early 20th
C., 7" H. $225.00*
METTLACH STEIN, ½-Litre, Pewter
Mounted, 3 Panels Depicting Hunting
Scenes, Early 20th C., 6¾" H. $250.00*
METTLACH STEIN, ½-Litre, Pewter
Mounted, Man Smoking, Early 20th C., 6¾"
H. $200.00*
METTLACH STEIN, ½-Litre, Pewter
Mounted, Elves Smoking Pipe, Early 20th
C., 9½" H. $200.00*
METTLACH STEIN, ½-Litre, Pewter
Mounted, Tavern Scene, Early 20th C., 9¼"
H. $325.00*
METTLACH STEIN, 1-Litre, Pewter
Mounted, Housetops, Early 20th C., 7¼" H.
. . . . $400.00*
METTLACH STEIN, 1-Litre, Pewter
Mounted, Man In Armour, Hinged Lid
W/Figural Thumbpiece W/Cone Roof Top,
Mid-20th C., 11" H. $700.00*

*Price does not include 10% buyer fee.

A-MA Aug 1980   *Robert C. Eldred Co., Inc.*
L To R
PORCELAIN STEIN, German, Pewter
Lid, Late 19th C., 11" H. $260.00
PORCELAIN STEIN, German, Form Of
Head Of Prussian Officer, 19th C., 7½" H.
. . . . $170.00
METTLACH ½ LITRE STEIN, Man Sera-
nading Lady, Inlaid Top, 9" H. . . . $475.00
PORCELAIN STEIN, German, Regimental
Crest, 10" H. $70.00

A-MA Sept 1980   *Richard A. Bourne Co., Inc.*
SHAVING MUGS
ROW I, L To R
TRAINMAN'S MUG, "Albert G. Bogert"
By C.F. Haviland-Limoges, Gold Decor.
Worn $150.00
BARTENDER'S MUG, "Joe Schweitzer"
. . . . $175.00
CABINET MAKER'S MUG, "Chas.
Oppel", Sl. Wear To Gold $175.00
LIGHTHOUSE KEEPER'S MUG, "Joseph
Roitmuer", Name Worn $275.00
ROW II, L To R
PATRIOTIC MUG, "Herman Abramowitz"
. . . . $30.00
COBBLER'S MUG, "A. Mule", Handle
Missing, Age Cracks, Gold Worn . . . $80.00
JEWELER'S MUG, "C.W. Ross", Decor.
Worn $100.00
BLK. & GOLD MUG, "J.F. Gilman"
. . . . $20.00

A-MA Sept 1980   *Richard A. Bourne Co., Inc.*
SHAVING MUGS
ROW I, L To R
TRAINMAN'S MUG, "C.H. Jacobus",
Gold Lettering Shows Some Wear . . $160.00
TROLLEYMAN'S MUG By Limoges, No
Name Of Owner, Chip On Foot Ring
. . . . $100.00
TUGBOAT MAN'S MUG, "Harold Meyer"
. . . . $400.00
MAILMAN'S MUG, "John Cole", Sl. Wear
To Gold Decor. $275.00
ROW II, L To R
UNDERTAKER'S MUG, Modern Copy
. . . . $80.00
**FRUIT & VEGETABLE PEDDLER'S
MUG,** "John Hagenburgh", Made In Ger-
many, Sl. Wear To Gold Decor. . . $175.00
GROCER'S MUG, "F.B. Smith & Son", By
Limoges, Age Crack, Gold Worn . . $175.00
PHOTOGRAPHER'S MUG, "C.M. Willis"
. . . . $275.00
ROW III, L To R
BRICKLAYER'S MUG, "Frank Gionia/
1911", Made In Germany, Age Cracks,
Gold Shows Wear $140.00
TELEGRAPHER'S MUG, Name Unread-
able, Chip In Rim $170.00
MECHANIC'S MUG, Name Unreadable,
Gold Decor. Worn $75.00
BUTCHER'S MUG, "Henry Herzel"
. . . . $160.00

A-MA July 1980   *Robert W. Skinner Inc.*
L To R
PORCELAIN PLATE, Hand Painted,
Gold Embossed Decor., Sgn. "Kaufman",
Blue Beehive Mark In Center, Austria, Late
19th C., 9" D. $375.00*
PORCELAIN PLATE, Hand Painted,
Gold Embossed Decor., Sgn. "Kaufman",
Blue Beehive Mark In Center, Austria, Late
19th C., 9" D. $375.00*

◄ A-MA Aug 1980   *Robert C. Eldred Co., Inc.*
L To R
PORCELAIN SERVING DISH, Pale Yellow
& Gilt Border, Floral Cartouches, Ormolu
Mounts, Sgn. Ruten, 17¼" L. $450.00
PORCELAIN EWER, Relief Figural
Decor. In Wh. On Gray-Gr. Ground, Gilt
Highlights, Some Chips, 18" H. . . $450.00

A-WA D.C. Feb 1980 *Adam A. Weschler & Son*
MANTEL URNS, Pr., Late 19th C., Paris, 16″ H. $1000.00*

A-MA Jan 1981   *Robert W. Skinner Inc.*
L To R
ROYAL WORCESTER COVERED JAR, Eng., Late 19th C., Oriental Decor. W/Gr. Trademark $1400.00*

ROYAL WORCESTER COVERED PIT-CHER, Eng., Polychrome Floral Motif On Cream Ground, Gold Highlights, Base Mkd. W/Gr. Trademark, Covered W/Purple Trade-mark, Ca. 1884, 10½″ H. $450.00*

A-MA Jan 1981   *Robert W. Skinner Inc.*
L To R
DEDHAM POTTERY VOLCANIC GLAZE VASE, MA, Thick Drizzled Glaze In Mottled Shades Of Gr. & Red, Base Incised, Hairline Crack, Ca. 1896, 9¼″ H. $850.00*
ROOKWOOD POTTERY VASE, OH, Drk. Blue Neck Shading To Pale Gr., Artist Sgn. "Sara Sax", Ca. 1907, 10½″ H. $2750.00*

A-WA D.C. Feb 1980 *Adam A. Weschler & Son*
PORCELAIN MANTEL VASES, Pr., French, Mid 19th C., 11″ H. $275.00*

A-MA Jan 1981   *Robert W. Skinner Inc.*
L To R
ROYAL WORCESTER COVERED URN, Eng., Pierced & Molded Arabesque Cover & Neck, Gold Highlighted Polychrome Decor., Base Mkd. W/Purple Trademark, Ca. 1889, 15½″ H. $850.00*

ROYAL WORCESTER COVERED URN, Eng., Late 19th C., Polychrome Floral Decor. Body W/Gold Highlights, 18½″ H. $1400.00*

ROYAL WORCESTER FRUIT BOWL, Eng., Pierced Loop Border, Ext. Molded Leaves, Int. Decor. W/Gold Highlighted Poly-chrome Floral Motif, Base Mkd. W/Purple Trademark, Ca. 1897, 9¼″ D. $550.00*

Left
A-MA Nov 1980   *Robert W. Skinner Inc.*
WEDGWOOD BLK. BASALT VASE, Eng., Late 19th C., Raised Polychrome Floral Motif, Lip Repaired, 6″ H. $110.00*
Right
A-OH Oct 1980   *Early Auction Co.*
WELLER DICKENSWARE VASE, Sgn. M. G. On Side, Repaired & Reglazed, 16″ H. $350.00*

A-MA Jan 1981   *Robert W. Skinner Inc.*
ALBERTINE COVERED JAR, MA, Beige & Gold Oak Leaf & Acorn Motif, Ca. 1885 .... $525.00*

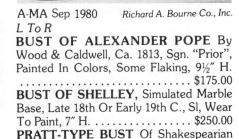

A-MA Sep 1980   *Richard A. Bourne Co., Inc.*
L To R
BUST OF ALEXANDER POPE By Wood & Caldwell, Ca. 1813, Sgn. "Prior", Painted In Colors, Some Flaking, 9½″ H. $175.00
BUST OF SHELLEY, Simulated Marble Base, Late 18th Or Early 19th C., Sl, Wear To Paint, 7″ H. $250.00
PRATT-TYPE BUST Of Shakespearian Actor, 18th C., 7⅛″ H. $350.00

A-MA Jan 1981   *Robert W. Skinner Inc.*
WEDGWOOD BLUE JASPERWARE, 3 Pcs., Eng., Late 19th & 20th C., Baluster Shaped Bud Vase, Cracker Jar W/Plated Silver Cover & Handle, Tankard Shaped Milk Pitcher..................... $200.00*

A-OH Oct 1980   *Early Auction Co.* ▶
L To R
WELLER LOUWELSA VASE, Sgn. "K" On Bottom, Yellow & Red Rose Decor., Roughness At Top, 11½″ H. $200.00*
WELLER LOUWELSA VASE, Full Sgn. On Side: Hester W. Pillsbury, Thistle Decor., Br. Glazed Style, Sl. Roughness On Lip, 17″ H. $325.00*

*Price does not include 10% buyer fee.

A-MA Sept 1980   *Richard A. Bourne Co., Inc.*
STAFFORDSHIRE FIGURES
ROW I, L To R
BENJAMIN FRANKLIN, Erroneously
Titled "The Old English Gentleman", 15½" H.
.... $700.00
BENJAMIN FRANKLIN, Erroneously
Titled "Gen. Washington", Sm. Chip &
Glaze Crazing, 15½" H. $500.00
MAN, Figure Holding Handkerchief & Eye-
glasses, 14¾" H. $150.00
ROW II, L To R
MOODY, Wears Blk. Coat, 17¼" H.
.... $200.00
PRINCE OF WALES, Full Uniform W/
Medals, Glaze Worn On Rt. Elbow, 17¾" H.
.... $200.00

A-MA Sept 1980   *Richard A. Bourne Co., Inc.*
STAFFORDSHIRE FIGURINES
ROW I, L To R
2 SHEEP, Late 18th C., Both W/Sm. Dam-
ages, Largest: 4" H. $70.00
MONKEY, 18th C., Wh. W/Br. Spots,
Chips & Age Cracks, 2¼" H. $150.00
SM. DOGS, Pr., Early 19th C., Wh. W/
Reddish-Br. Spots, Yellow Baskets W/Gr.
Contents, Both W/Surface Wear & Sl.
Damage, 3½" H. $150.00

A-MA April 1980   *Richard A. Bourne Co., Inc.*
Top
PORCELAIN WING VASES, Pr., Euro-
pean, 19th C., Sl. Wear To Gold Decor., 11"
H. $225.00
Bottom
PORCELAIN WING VASES, Pr., Euro-
pean, 19th C., 1 Vase Damaged, 15" H.
.... $175.00

A-MA Mar 1980   *Robert W. Skinner Inc.*
L To R
ROOKWOOD VELLUM VASE, Soft
Shades of Blue, Green, & Cream, Rook-
wood Trademark & Artists Initials, Ca.
1920, 7¾" H. $550.00*
PORCELAIN VASE, Raised Gold Center-
ing Hand Painted Medallion "Ruth", Sgn.
"Wagner", European, Late 19th C., 12" H.
.... $525.00*

► A-MA July 1980   *Robert W. Skinner, Inc.*
L To R
ROOKWOOD VASE, Incised Base, Sgn.
"AMB", OH, Ca. 1885, 9" D. $700.00*
**AUSTRIAN BEEHIVE PORCELAIN
DESSERT PLATES,** Set Of 11, 9 Are
Artist Sgn. "Neumann", 19th C., 7" D.
.... $425.00*

A-MA Sept 1980   *Richard A. Bourne Co., Inc.*
STAFFORDSHIRE FIGURES
ROW I, L To R
ROWLAND HILL & HOPE, Minor Dam-
ages, 6¾" H. $125.00
GIRL ON PONY, Rt. Hand Broken Off,
6¼" H. $40.00
LADY IN BED, 4¾" H. $200.00
3 MEN, 5¼" H. $50.00
ROW II, L To R
KATE NICKLEBY, Sgn. "Published June
15 1830/By Ridgway & Robey/Hanley/Staf-
fordshire Potteries", 8" H. $350.00
WOMAN, CHILD & DOLPHIN, Repaired
Poorly, 8½" H. $25.00
GIN & WATER, Hat W/Sm. Chip, 8½" H.
.... $50.00
WOMAN, 2 Chips In Base, 8" H. .. $30.00
ROW III, L To R
MERCURY, 10" H. $300.00
NELSON, Drk. Coat Holding Spyglass,
End Of Spyglass Broken Off, 9½" H.
.... $190.00
MOURNING WOMEN, Pr., Both Dam-
aged, 9¼" H. $120.00

A-MA Aug 1980   *Robert C. Eldred Co., Inc.*
MEISSEN PORCELAIN TEA SET, Salmon & Gilt Decor. On Wh. Ground, Ca. 1900
.... $500.00

A-OH July 1980 *Stratford Auction Center*
POTTERY
ROW I, L To R
WALL POCKETS, Pr., Roma, Cream Ground W/Pink Roses, Imp. Weller, 7¼" H. $20.00
WALL POCKET, Wood Rose, Imp. Weller, 7" H. $15.00
WELLER WALL POCKET, Glendale, Yellow Bird W/Nest, Stamped Ink Sgn., 7¼" H. $45.00
POTTERY WALL POCKET, Marbelized Shades Of Rose, Gr., Gold, Unsigned, 8¼" H. $30.00
ROW II, L To R
POTTERY WALL POCKET, Deco. Designs Shaded Gr.-Yellow, Unsigned, 11¼" H. $30.00
WELLER OVAL BOWL W/Pierced Handles, Warwick Patt., Stamped Ink Sgn., 13½" L. $35.00
WELLER WALL POCKET, Woodcraft, Imp. Sgn., 9½" H. $60.00
ROW III, L To R
WELLER CANDLESTICKS, Pr., Warwick Patt., Stamped Ink Sgn., 5¼" D. ... $20.00
GR. POTTERY ASHTRAY, Unsigned, 8½" L. $15.00

A-WA D.C. May 1980 *Adam A. Weschler & Son*
ROYAL DOULTON FIGURINES
L To R
EASTER DAY, Ca. 1945 .... $175.00 *
THE GOSSIPS .... $150.00 *
DAFFY DOWN DILLY, Ca. 1935 . $125.00 *
THE BRIDE, Ca. 1955 .... $100.00 *
SWEET & TWENTY .... $150.00 *
THE LEISURE HOUR, Ca. 1949 ...$200.00 *

A-MA Aug 1980 *Robert C. Eldred Co., Inc.* ►
BRONZE & PORCELAIN CANDELABRA, Pr., French, Celeste Blue W/Floral & Musical Motif, 1 W/Plaque Mkd. Legendre, Ca.1809, 9" H. $200.00
SEVRES PORCELAIN CONFITURIER, 2 Feathered Blue & Floral Decor. Cups On Lozenge Shaped Tray, All W/Ormolu Mounts, Ca. 1777, 9¾" L. $550.00

*Price does not include 10% buyer fee.

A-MA Sept 1980 *Richard A. Bourne Co., Inc.*
STAFFORDSHIRE FIGURINES
ROW I, L To R
TOBY-STYLE PITCHER, Depicting Major Rodney, Early 19th C., Sm. Rim Chip, Age Cracks, 7" H. $150.00
TOBY TOBACCO JAR, Early 19th C., Restorations & Age Crack, 6" H. .. $60.00
ST. GEORGE SLAYING DRAGON, Late 18th Or Early 19th C., Lance Not Orig., Reglued Chip, Age Crack, 11¼" H. ... $650.00
ROW II, L To R
RALPH WOOD-TYPE LRG. TOBY, Ca. 1765, Age Cracks, Worn Glaze, Pipe Missing, 11¼" H. $375.00
BEGGING SPANIEL PITCHER, Reddish-Br. On Wh., 19th C., Reglued Chip, 10½" H. $70.00
BEGGING SPANIEL PITCHER, Blk. On Wh., Eng., 19th C., 10½" H. $125.00

A-MA Sept 1980 *Richard A. Bourne Co., Inc.*
STAFFORDSHIRE FIGURINES
L To R
RALPH WOOD BUST, "The Revd./John Wesley MA/Aged 88", Late 18th C., Restorations, Blk. Paint Flaking, 11" H. $400.00
BUST OF WILLIAM SHAKESPEARE, All Wh., 19th C., Minor Damages, 10½" H. $100.00

A-MA Aug 1980 *Robert C. Eldred Co., Inc.*
RUSSIAN ENAMEL & SILVER
ROW I, L To R
DOMED BOX, Pierced Apron & Gallery, 18th C., 5" H. $475.00
TEA GLASS HOLDER, Wh. Flowers On Deep Gr. Ground, Made By Berlin Firm, Touched 84 & St. George, 4" H. .. $275.00
CUP & SAUCER, Sky Blue Flowers On Deep Red Ground W/Blue Border, Mkd. Vasilii Agafanov, 84 & St. George, Saucer, 5⅛" D. $450.00
ROW II
DEMI TASSE SET, 3-Pcs., Sawtooth Patt. In Blue & Wh. W/Touches Of Yellow, Cyrillic Mrks., Star & 916 .... $525.00
ROW III, L To R
CHALICE, Blue & Gr. Floral Scrolling W/Red & Turquoise Border, 3½" D., 3¼" H. $450.00
EASTER EGG, Diamond & Circular Motifs Between Blue Beaded Borders, No Marks, 2⅝" L $1600.00
LOBED BEAKER, Touched 84, Kokoshnik, & Cyrillic Sgn., 4¼" D., 3¾" H. $1500.00

A-WA D.C. Oct 1980 *Adam A. Weschler & Son*
MEISSEN COVERED URNS, Pr., Cobalt & Gilt Ground Centering 2 Medallions, Each W/Underglaze Blue Crossed Swords & Impressed Numbers, Both Entitled, Late 19th C., 16½" H. $750.00*

A-OH April 1980   *Garth's Auctions, Inc.*

ROW I, L To R

ROCKINGHAM MUG, Sm. Glaze Flake, 3¼″ H. $57.50

REDWARE HANDLED BOWL, Greenish Amber Glaze, Incised "Made In Stahl's Pottery By Thomas Stahl, Feb. 22-1940", 4″ D. $40.00

ROCKINGHAM BOWL, 9¼″ H. . $50.00

ROCKINGHAM BOWL, Rim Chips, 5½″ D. $20.00

ROCKINGHAM BOWL, 3″ D. .. $75.00

ROW II, L To R

ROCKINGHAM PLATES, 4, (2 Illus.), Rayed W/Scalloped Rim, 8″ D. $210.00

REDWARE CUSTARD CUP, Int. Glaze, 2¾″ H. $30.00

REDWARE JAR, Greenish Amber Glaze, Incised Sgn. "Made By I.S. Stahl, Sept. 30/1942, Clear & Cool", 4¼″ H. ... $55.00

REDWARE CUSTARD CUP, Gr. Int. Glaze, Incised Sgn. "Made By I.S. Stahl, 10/19/42", 2⅞″ H. $40.00

ROW III, L To R

REDWARE SAUCE BOAT W/Cover, Greenish Amber Blaze W/Blue Stripe, Incised Sgn. "Made By I.S. Stahl, Feb. 12th, 1942, Cold & Wind, Buy Bonds & Keep Um Flying", 4¾″ H. $160.00

REDWARE PITCHER, Gr. Glaze, Incised Sgn. "Made By R.R. Stahl, Weather Clear & Cool, 10/19/48", Minor Edge Wear, 5¼″ H. $65.00

ROCKINGHAM DISH, Embossed Rim W/ Ribbed Corners, 8¾″ x 8¾″ $90.00

REDWARE CUP & SAUCER, Greenish Amber Glaze, Incised Sgn. "Made By I.S. Stahl, 7/26/1946", Cup Has Rim Damage $70.00

REDWARE CANDLESTICK W/Applied Handle, Brownish Amber Glaze, Sgn. "Made By I.S. Stahl, 7/16/1946, Clear & Warm", 5″ D. $80.00

A-WA D.C. Dec 1980   *Adam A. Weschler & Son*
BLUE & GRAY SALT GLAZED STONEWARE
L To R

CROCK, 3-Gal., Cartouche "3", 19th C., 10″ H. $70.00*

CROCK, 3-Gal., 19th C., 14″ H. . $175.00*

CROCK, Imp. Maker's Mark, Molded Rim, NJ, 4-Gal., 19th C., 11″ H. $60.00*

CROCK, Baluster-Form, 19th C., 12″ H. $150.00*

CROCK, 19th C., 11″ H. $80.00*

*Price does not include 10% buyer fee.

A-NY May 1980   *Calkins Auction Gallery*
STONEWARE
ROW I, L To R

CROCK, 2 GAL., Cobalt Blue Decor., By C. Hart, NY, Rim Chips, 9″ D. $80.00

CROCK, 2 GAL., Cobalt Blue Decor., By C. Hart, NY, Ca. 1850, 8½″ D., 13½″ H. $110.00

ROW II, L To R

CROCK, 2 GAL., Cobalt Blue Decor., By W. Hart, NY, 9″ D., 11½″ H. $100.00

CROCK, 4 GAL., Cobalt Blue Decor., By W. Roberts, NY, 11½″ D., 11½″ H. ... $140.00

CROCK, 2 GAL., Cobalt Blue Decor., 8½″ D., 11″ H. $120.00

A-MA Feb 1980   *Robert W. Skinner, Inc.*
L To R

INDIAN POTTERY JAR, Santa Domingo, Stylized Decor. On Cover & Top Half Of Jar W/Red Band Around Middle, Blk. On Cream, 12″ D., 13″ H. $800.00*

INDIAN POTTERY OLA, Acoma, Slip Decor., Blk., Red & Cream, 12″ D., 9″ H. $350.00*

___

A-WA D.C. Dec 1980   *Adam A. Weschler & Son*
BLUE & GRAY SALT GLAZED STONE-WARE
ROW I, L To R

BUTTER CHURN, Ca. 1848, 16½″ H. $225.00*

JUG, Medallion In Gr.-Brown, Teardrop Splashes, 19th C., 20″ H. $125.00*

ROW II, L To R

CROCK, Gray, 19th C., 15½″ H. ... $80.00*

CROCK, Br. Slipping To Gold, 19th C., 17″ H. $50.00*

JUG, Smith & Thompson, NJ, Blue & Gray W/Maker's Marks, 2-Gal., 19th C., 14″ H. $425.00*

A-WA D.C. Dec 1980   *Adam A. Weschler & Son*
GLAZED STONEWARE
L To R

JUG, Blue & Gray Salt, Maker's Mark, PA, 1½″ Gal., 19th C., 14″ H. $125.00*

MILK PITCHER, Blue & Gray Salt, Baluster-Form, 19th C., 10½″ H. $375.00*

JUG, Gr. Iron, Wire & Treen Bail Handle, Applied Finger Notch On Bottom, 1½ Gal., 10½″ H. $70.00*

JUG, Blue & Gray Salt, 19th C., 12″ H. $125.00*

JUG, Blue & Gray Salt, 19th C., 12″ H. $80.00*

A-WA D.C. Dec 1980   *Adam A. Weschler & Son*
SALT GLAZED STONEWARE
L To R

BUTTER CHURN CROCK, Blue & Gray, T. R. Reppert, PA, 19th C., 10″ H. .. $75.00*

CROCK, Blue & Gray, 1½ Gal., 19th C., 11″ H. $90.00*

CROCK, Blue & Gray, T. F. Connly Mfg., NJ, 19th C., 12″ H. $75.00*

CROCK, Blue & Br., 2-Gal., 19th C., 9½″ H. $75.00*

CROCK, Blue & Gray, 19th C., 11″ H. $75.00*

CROCK, Blue & Gray, 19th C., 8″ H. $75.00*

Left

A-MA June 1980   *Robert W. Skinner Inc.*
FED. BANJO TIMEPIECE, Mahogany, Brass Bezel, Painted Dial, 8-Day Weight Driven Move., Repl. Dial & Eglomise Tablets, N. Eng., Ca. 1820, 32″ O.H. $1000.00*

Right

A-MA July 1980   *Robert W. Skinner Inc.*
FED. BANJO TIMEPIECE, Brass Bezel, Painted Iron Dial, 8-Day Brass T Bridge Move., "S. Willard's Patent", Pierced Brass Sidearms, MA, Early 19th C., 32½″ H. $2500.00*

Left

A-MA April 1980   *Robert W. Skinner, Inc.*
BANJO WALL TIMEPIECE, Mahogany, No Maker's Name, Needs Restoration, Damage To Gesso Frame, Dial Replaced, Early 19th C., 10″ W., 33½″ H. .. $1050.00*

Right

A-MA July 1980   *Robert W. Skinner Inc.*
FED. BANJO WALL CLOCK, Mahogany, Case W/Wood Bezel, Pierced Brass Sidearms, Striking Rack & Snail Move., NH, Ca. 1820, 29½ H. $3000.00*

A-MA July 1980   *Robert W. Skinner, Inc.*
GARNITURE CLOCK SET, 3-Pcs., Enamel & Brass Spring-Driven Time & Strike Move., Branch Candelabras W/Conforming Design & Decor., Late 19th C., Clock: 19½″ H., Candelabra: 17″ H. $4000.00*

Left

A-WA D.C. May 1980 *Adam A. Weschler & Son*
FEDERAL TALL CASE CLOCK, Mahogany, Sgn. Aaron Willard, Jr., MA, Ca. 1810-1820, 97″ H. $4900.00*

Right

A-MA Aug 1980   *Robert W. Skinner Inc.*
FEDERAL TALL CASE CLOCK, Poplar, Paint & Gilt Dial, 30-Hr. Movement, Ref., N. Eng., Ca. 1790, 89″ H. .. $1000.00*

◄ A-WA D.C. May 1980 *Adam A. Weschler & Son*
L To R
LOUIS XV BRACKET CLOCK, Ormolu Mounted, Tortoise, Late 19th-Early 20th C., 28″ H. $675.00*

LOUIS XVI CARRIAGE CLOCK, Wh. Enamel W/Blk. Arabic Numeral Dial, Wh. Marble Housing, Ormolu Applied Scrolling, Ca. 1900 .... $600.00*

Left

A-WA D.C. May 1980 *Adam A. Weschler & Son*
LOUIS XV BRACKET CLOCK & STAND, Late 19th C., 15″ H. ... $425.00*

Right

A-WA D.C. Oct 1980   *Adam A. Weschler & Son*
MANTEL CLOCK, Champleve Blue Enamel & Crystal, French, Late 19th C., 11″ H. $600.00*

Left

A-MA July 1980   *Robert W. Skinner Inc.*
CALENDAR WALL CLOCK, Rosewood, Wooden Bezel Over Painted Tin Dial, 8-Day Move., Label: "L F & W Carter & B B Lewis", CT, Ca. 1862, 40″ H. ... $1100.00*

Right

A-MA July 1980   *Robert W. Skinner Inc.*
CUCKOO CLOCK, Blk. Forest Walnut Decor., Porcelain & Wood Dial, Pine Cone Weights, German, Ca. 1900, 25″ W., 46″ H. $875.00*

Left

A-MA Aug 1980   *Richard A. Bourne Co., Inc.*
WHALE'S TOOTH, Mounted As Watch Holder, Engraved Military Figures On Both Sides, Tiffany 8-Day Watch In Center, Blk. & Red Engraving, Walnut Base, Back Cover Missing, 8¼″ O.L., 6½″ O.H. $800.00

Right

A-MA Mar 1980   *Robert W. Skinner Inc.*
SETH THOMAS MANTEL CLOCK, Bronze W/8-Day Time & Strike Move., CT, Early 20th C. $250.00*

*Price does not include 10% buyer fee.

Left

A-MA July 1980   *Robert W. Skinner Inc.*
REGULATOR TIMEPIECE, Mahogany
Case W/Reverse Painted Tablet, Paper
Label: "E. Ingraham & Co", CT, Ca. 1865,
22″ H. $525.00*

Right

A-MA Oct 1980   *Robert W. Skinner, Inc.*
FEDERAL MANTEL CLOCK, Mahogany
Pillar & Scroll, Englomise Tablet, Painted
Wooden Dial, Wooden Movement, Attrib.
To Eli Terry, Minor Repair, CT, Ca. 1817-
1818, 16¼″ W., 4½″ D., 30½″ H. . . . $2750.00*

Left

A-VA April 1980   *Laws Auction & Antiques*
TALL CASE CLOCK, Am., Mahogany,
Face W/Orig. Hand Painted Decor., Brass
Works, Ca. 1790, 88″ H. $1600.00

Right

A-MA Mar 1980   *Richard A. Bourne Co., Inc.*
TALL CASE CLOCK, Am., Early 19th C.,
34 Hr. Wooden Works, Pine Case W/Grained
Finish, Orig. Painted Wooden Dial, Door
Glass Cracked, 90″ H. $950.00

Left

A-MA April 1980   *Robert W. Skinner, Inc.*
TALL CASE CLOCK, Pine, Painted, 30-
Hr. Movement, ME, Ca. 1820, 86″ H.
. . . . $1000.00*

Right

A-MA April 1980   *Robert W. Skinner, Inc.*
CHIPPENDALE TALL CASE CLOCK,
Mahogany Inlaid, Restored, MA, Ca.1770,
95″ O.H. $2000.00*

Left

A-NY May 1980   *Calkins Auction Gallery*
TALL CASE CLOCK, Wooden Works,
Early 19th C., Br. & Tan Graining, Com-
pletely Orig., Working Cond., Am., 7′ 2″ H.
. . . . $850.00

Right

A-WA D.C. May 1980   *Adam A. Weschler & Son*
TALL CASE CLOCK, Carved Wood,
19th C., Clock Dial Inscribed Newport, 86″
H. $450.00*

Left

A-VA April 1980   *Laws Auction & Antiques*
TALL CASE CLOCK, Scottish, Hand
Painted Dial Sgn. "Thomas Marriott Botley",
Brass 8-Day Works, Ca. 1830, 89″ H.
. . . . $1600.00

Right

A-WA D.C. May 1980   *Adam A. Weschler & Son*
TALL CASE CLOCK, New Eng., Cherry
& Tiger Maple, Ca. 1810, Tole & Blk. Arabic
Numeral Dial W/Floral Pediment, 96″ H.
. . . . $800.00

A-MA Mar 1980   *Robert W. Skinner Inc.*
VIC. MANTEL CLOCK, Mahogany Ve-
neered Case W/Wooden Bezel W/Blk. &
Gold Door Glass, 8-Day Move., Hadley
Brothers & Estell, IL, Ca. 1870, 20½″ H.
. . . . $575.00*

*Price does not include 10% buyer fee.

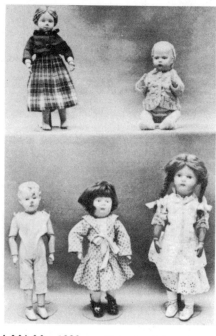

A-MA Mar 1980   *Richard A. Bourne Co., Inc.*
SCHOENHUT SPECIALTY FIGURES
ROW I, L To R
BISQUE-HEADED BAREBACK RIDER,
Orig. Costume, Tiny Firing Marks, 8¼″ H.
.... $260.00
WOODEN-HEAD HOBO, Orig. Clothing,
Sl. Paint Flecking On Face, 7½″ H. ...$100.00
WOODEN HEAD MAN, Redressed, Prob-
ably Repainted, 7¾″ H. $75.00
ROW II, L To R
COCO THE CLOWN, Orig. Costume,
Some Crazing To Paint In Facial Areas,
10¾″ H. $100.00
WOODEN HEAD CLOWN, Redressed,
Left Ear Missing, 7¾″ H. $60.00

A-MA Mar 1980   *Richard A. Bourne Co., Inc.*
SCHOENHUT DOLLS
ROW I, L To R
ALL WOOD GIRL, Incised "Schoenhut
Doll/Pat. Jan 17 11 USA/& Foreign Coun-
tries", Face Washed, Nose Rub, Some
Crazing, 14″ H. $625.00
ALL-WOOD GIRL, Sticker On Back
W/"C" In Circle & Paper Label, Repainted,
12″ H. $175.00
ROW II, L To R
ALL—WOOD BOY, Incisement Faint,
Paint Flecking On Face & Sl. Flaking On
Body, 14″ H. $360.00
WOOD-HEAD GIRL, C Sticker On Head
& Typical Sticker On Back, Chipped On
Left Cheek, 13½″ H. $200.00
WOOD-HEAD GIRL, Paper Sticker On
Back, Repainted, 16½″ H. $175.00

A-MA Mar 1980   *Richard A. Bourne Co., Inc.*
SCHOENHUT DOLLS
ROW I, L To R
ALL-WOOD GIRL, Incised "Schoenhut
Doll/Pat. Jan 17 11 USA/Foreign Countries",
Repainted, 14¾″ H. $425.00
ALL-WOOD GIRL, Incisement Same As
Preceding But Faint, Head Repainted, 14¾″
H. $300.00
ALL-WOOD BOY, Sticker On Back
"Schoenhut Doll/Pat. Jan. 17 1911/USA",
Crazing, Restoration To Forehead & Nose,
15″ H. $150.00
ROW II, L To R
MAN MANEKIN, All Wood, Paper Label
"Schoenhut Doll/Pat. Jan 17, 1911/USA",
Minor Paint Flecks, 19″ H. $1550.00
ALL-WOOD GIRL, Orig. Underwear,
Modern Dress, 15″ H. $325.00
ALL-WOOD GIRL, Paint Chip On Nose,
Flaking Line, Both Toes Chipped, 15″ H.
.... $200.00

Left
A-MA Dec 1980   *Robert W. Skinner Inc.*
CHARACTER BABY, All Bisque, Sta-
tionary Glass Eyes, Imp. "J.D.K. Made In
Germany", 1 Finger Missing, Late 19th C.,
12″ L. $425.00*

Right
A-MA Dec 1980   *Robert W. Skinner Inc.*
CHARACTER BABY, Bisque Head, Sleep-
ing Glass Eyes, Imp. "Made In Germany",
Jointed Comp. Body, Hands Damaged,
Late 19th C., 13″ H. $200.00*

*Price does not include 10% buyer fee.

A-MA Mar 1980   *Richard A. Bourne Co., Inc.*
L To R
PRE-GREINER, Orig. Clothes, Slight
Wear To Paint, Some Cracks, Arms Not Matched,
27″ H. $550.00
**PAPIER-MACHE SHOULDER-HEAD
LADY,** Face Washed & Worn, Crazing Lines,
Minor Damages, Leather Hands
Badly Worn, 27½″ H. $340.00
**SHOULDER-HEAD COMPOSITION
LADY,** Redressed, Tip Of Thumb Missing, Sl.
Paint Wear To Face, 29″ H. $300.00

A-MA Mar 1980   *Richard A. Bourne Co., Inc.*
L To R
BISQUE-HEADED BYE-LO BABY, Head
Incised "Cop'r. By/Grace S. Putnam/Made
In Germany", Body Mkd. "Bye-Lo Baby/Pat-
ent Applied For Grace Storey Putnam",
Cloth Body W/Celluloid Hands, Blue Sleep
Eyes, 11″ L. $250.00
BISQUE-HEADED BYE-LO BABY, Head
Mkd. "(C In Circle) 1923 By/Grace S. Putnam/
Made In Germany", No Marks On Body,
Comp. Wrist Hands, Br. Sleep Eyes, Paint
Flaking On Hands, 11″ H. $275.00

A-MA Mar 1980   *Richard A. Bourne Co., Inc.*
BISQUE–HEADED DOLLHOUSE DOLLS
ROW I, L To R
BEARDED GENTLEMAN, Redressed,
7¼″ H. $500.00
LADY W/Incised S & H Mark, Orig.
Clothing Melting, 6½″ H. $275.00
MAN, Orig. Suit, Left Foot Missing, 7″ H.
.... $400.00
LADY, Orig. Clothing, Toes Of Both Feet
Missing, 6″ H. $90.00
ROW II, L To R
GENTLEMAN, Orig. Suit & Top Hat,
Both Feet Missing, 7¼″ O.H. $160.00
LADY Orig. Dress, Left Leg & Right Foot
Missing, Fingers Chipped Off On Right
Hand, 6¾″ H. $100.00
LADY Orig. Dress Melting, Left Hand
Missing, 6¾″ H. $70.00
GENTLEMAN, Orig. Blk. Evening Suit &
Top Hat, 7½″ H. $250.00
ROW III, L To R
LADY, Orig. Clothing, Left Foot Missing,
6¼″ H. $100.00
LADY, Orig. Clothing, Body Soft At
Waistline, 6¼″ H. $70.00
Maid, Orig. Clothing, Slightly Faded, 6½″
H. $90.00
MILITARY GENTLEMAN, Orig. Cloth-
ing Including Sword, Body Reinforced,
Holes In Clothes, 7″ H. $270.00

A-MA Mar 1980   *Richard A. Bourne Co., Inc.*
BISQUE-HEADED DOLLHOUSE DOLLS
L To R
MAN, Orig. Clothing, 6½″ H. $100.00
MAN, Orig. Clothing, 6¼″ H. $100.00
MAN, Orig. Clothing, 6¼″ H. $80.00
MAN, Orig. Clothing, 6¼″ H. $80.00

*Price does not include 10% buyer fee.

A-MA Mar 1980   *Richard A. Bourne Co., Inc.*
ROW I, L To R
CHINA SHOULDER-HEAD DOLL, In-
cised On Back "Germany/189 (Bell Sym-
bol)", Wear To Glaze, 13¼″ H. $80.00
CHINA SHOULDER-HEAD DOLL,
Crack In Center Front Shoulder Plate, Min-
ute Wear To Hair & Boots, Chip On Left
Toe, 16″ H. $50.00
CHINA SHOULDER-HEAD DOLL, Orig.
Undergarments, Sl. Wear To Back Of Head,
Minor Chips On Both Hands, Dress Sl.
Motheaten, 14½″ H. $75.00
ROW II, L To R
CHINA SHOULDER-HEAD DOLL,
Shoulder Plate Restored, Glaze Worn On
Nose & Hair, Minute Firing Marks On
Cheek, Sl. Glaze Wear To Forehead, Dress
Melting, 17½″ H. $80.00
PARIAN SHOULDER-HEAD DOLL, Re-
paired Shoulder Plate, Sl. Roughage To
Ends Of Fingers, Minute Nick To Ear, 16″ H.
.... $180.00

A-MA Mar 1980   *Richard A. Bourne Co., Inc.*
L To R
PARIAN SHOULDER-HEAD DOLL,
Orig. Dress Melting, Orig. Undergarments,
Body Shows Wear & Discoloration, 16½″ H.
.... $275.00
BISQUE SHOULDER-HEAD DOLL,
Orig. Undergarments, Tips Of Fingers Slight-
ly Flaked, 13½″ H. $500.00
FRENCH FASHION DOLL, No Visible
Marks, Body Shows Crazing, 17″ H.
.... $1600.00

A-MA July 1980   *Robert W. Skinner Inc.*
STUFFED DOLLS, Painted Cloth Faced
& Cloth Bodies, Am., Ca. 1910 ... $175.00*

A-MA Mar 1980   *Robert A. Bourne Co., Inc.*
DOLLS
ROW I, L To R
ALL-BISQUE GIRL, Slight Chip At End
Of Feather, 4¾″ H. $50.00
ALL-BISQUE GIRL, Mkd. "Germany",
Roughage At Left Hip Joint, Some Firing
Marks On Face, 4¼″ H. $40.00
**MINI. BLK. CHINA FROZEN CHAR-
LOTTE,** Slight Paint Fleck On Elbow Of
Right Arm, 2½″ H. $80.00
ALL-BISQUE GIRL, Mkd. "2½/Ger-
many", 4¾″ H. $80.00
ROW II, L To R
ALL- BISQUE BOY, Tassel On Top Of
Hat Missing, Mold Mark On Left Arm, 6¾″ H.
.... $55.00
ALL-BISQUE GIRL, 7″ H. $60.00
ALL-BISQUE INDIAN, Sm. Lifting Of
Flocking, Rough Spot At End Of Feather,
Mold Imperfection On Forehead, 6¼″ H.
.... $80.00
ROW III, L To R
ALL-BISQUE GIRL, 5¼″ H. $80.00
ALL-BISQUE GIRL, No Visible Markings,
5¼″ H. $70.00
ALL-BISQUE GIRL, Mold Mark On But-
tocks, Flat Chip In Neck Area, Repaired
Brow & Eyes Reset, 5¾″ H. $80.00

A-WA D.C. Dec 1980 *Adam A. Weschler & Son*
WINDSOR ARROW-BACK CHAIRS,
Set Of 5, Painted, 1 Armchair (Not Illus.), 4
Side Chairs, Plank Seats, Simulated Bamboo Turned Legs, Ca. 1820 . . . . . . $600.00*

A-MA Jan 1981 *Robert W. Skinner Inc.*
SHAKER LADDER-BACK SIDE CHAIRS,
N. Eng., Mid 19th C., Maple & Ash, Some
Leg Restorations, 40½" H. $3000.00*

Left
A-MA Jan 1981 *Robert W. Skinner Inc.*
WINDSOR ARM CHAIR, N. Eng., Mid
18th C., Saddle Seat, Orig. Blk. Paint, 35¾"
H. $2700.00*

Right
A-MA Feb 1980 *Robert W. Skinner Inc.*
WM. & MARY CORNER CHAIR, 1 Spanish Foot, Rush Seat, 1 Stretcher Repl., N.
Eng., Ca. 1700-1730, 32" H. $700.00*

A-MA Feb 1980 *Robert W. Skinner Inc.*
WRITING ARM WINDSOR CHAIR W/
Drawer, Am., Late 18th C., 29" H.
. . . . $1800.00*

A-MA Sept 1980 *Richard A. Bourne Co., Inc.*
L To R
WINDSOR SIDE CHAIR, Am., Early 19th
C., Bamboo Turnings, Old Natural Finish
. . . . $200.00
CAPTAIN'S CHAIR, Am., Early 19th C.,
Eagle Decor. On Orig. Gr. Paint, Converted
To Commode Chair, Dry Rot Rt. Arm
. . . . $100.00
WRITING ARM CAPTAIN'S CHAIR,
Am., 19th C., Old Worn Natural Finish
. . . . $350.00

Left
A-VA Jan 1980 *Laws Auction & Antiques*
LADDER-BACK ARM CHAIR, Orig. Half
Ball Turned Feet, Bulbous Double Stretcher,
Later Simulated Rush Seat, Partial Old Finish, PA, Ca. 1740 . . . . $1400.00
Right
A-MA Feb 1980 *Robert W. Skinner Inc.*
WINDSOR ARMCHAIR, Am., Ca. 1770,
39" H. $950.00*

Left
A-WA D.C. Dec 1980 *Adam A. Weschler & Son*
WINDSOR BOW-BACK ARMCHAIR,
N. Eng., 7-Spindle, Shaped Saddle Seat,
Painted Drk. Gr., Ca. 1780 . . . . . . $1100.00*
Right
A-MA Oct 1980 *Robert W. Skinner Inc.*
WINDSOR BOW-BACK ARMCHAIR, 7
Spindles, Blk. Paint, N. Eng., Late 18th C.,
37¾" H. $950.00*

Left
A-MA April 1980 *Robert W. Skinner Inc.*
WINDSOR ARM CHAIR, Maple, Pine &
Ash, Break In Bow, Loser ½ Of Knuckle Arm
Missing, N. Eng. Mid 18th C., 36½"
O.H. $1300.00*

Right
A-MA Feb 1980 *Robert W. Skinner Inc.*
FAN BACK WINDSOR SIDE CHAIR,
Am., Mid 18th C., 36" H. $600.00*

A-MA Sept 1980 *Richard A. Bourne Co., Inc.*
L To R
WINDSOR ARMCHAIR, Am., Early 19th
C., Bamboo Turnings, Old Worn Blk. Paint
W/Traces Of Orig. Cream $150.00
WINDSOR COMB-BACK ROCKER,
Am., Early 19th C., Bamboo Turnings, Old
Natural Finish $400.00
WINDSOR ARMCHAIR, Am., Early 19th
C., Bamboo Style, Seat Patched, Once
Used As Commode Chair, Old Finish Worn
. . . . $120.00

A-MA Aug 1980 *Robert W. Skinner, Inc.*
FAN-BACK WINDSOR SIDE CHAIRS,
Set Of Three, 7 Spindle W/Bobbin Turned
Stretchers, Ring & Reel Turned Legs, Am.,
Mid 18th C., 36" H. $1500.00*

*Price does not include 10% buyer fee.

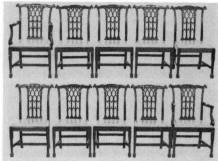

A-MA Mar 1980   *Robert W. Skinner Inc.*
CHIPPENDALE DINING CHAIRS, Set of 10, Mahogany, Am., 20th C., 39″ H.
.... $2000.00*

A-MA Mar 1980   *Richard A. Bourne Co., Inc.*
L To R
LADDER-BACK SIDE CHAIR, Am., Ca. 1837, Blk.-Painted W/Gold Highlights, New Seat $175.00
Q.A. SIDE CHAIR, Fruitwood, Am., 18th C., New Seat, Ref. $250.00
BANISTER-BACK SIDE CHAIR, N. Eng. 18th C., Fruitwood & Other Woods, New Seat, Ref. $350.00

A-MA Feb 1980   *Robert W. Skinner Inc.*
WM. & MARY BANISTER BACK SIDE CHAIRS, Pr., Blk. & Gold Paint, 1 Rear Leg Pierced, 19th C., Am., Ca. 1700-1730, 40″ H.
.... $600.00*

A-MA Feb 1980   *Robert W. Skinner Inc.*
Q. A. SIDE CHAIRS, Pr., Rush Seat, Orig. Blk. Paint, N. Eng., Ca. 1730-1760, 41″ H.
.... $900.00*

A-NY May 1980   *Calkins Auction Gallery*
L To R
FAN-BACK WINDSOR, 18th C., N. Eng., Old Red & Blk. Graining Over Red Paint, 35″ O.H. $360.00
BOW-BACK WINDSOR SIDE CHAIR, 18th C., N. Eng. Br. Varnish Finish, Repaired Seat, 35½″ O.H. $260.00
FAN-BACK WINDSOR SIDE CHAIR, Early 19th C., Traces Of Old Red Paint, 36″ O.H. $200.00

A-MA July 1980   *Robert W. Skinner Inc.*
Q. A. DINING CHAIRS, Set Of 10, Mahogany, Hand Made By The Nathan Margolis Shop, Hartford, CT, 20th C., 43″ H.
.... $1900.00*

A-MA Mar 1980   *Robert W. Skinner, Inc.*
MINI. MORRIS CHAIR, Mahogany, Tufted Cushions, Fitted W/Game Box, Am., Early 20th C., 9″ W., 9½″ D., 12″ H.
.... $425.00*

A-WA D.C. Oct 1980   *Adam A. Weschler & Son*
Q.A. CHAIRS, Set Of 6, Walnut, PA, Ca. 1740-60, Upholstered Slip Seats, Thumb-molded Edge Seats $12000.00*

A-WA D.C. Dec 1980   *Adam A. Weschler & Son*
NEW ENGLAND YOUTH FURNITURE
L To R
LADDER-BACK ARM ROCKER, Cherry, Rush Seat, 19th C. $175.00*
LADDER-BACK SIDE CHAIR, Cherry, Rush Seat, 19th C. $100.00*
LADDER-BACK ARM CHAIR, Cherry & Hickory, Rush Seat, 19th C. $225.00*
LADDER-BACK ARM CHAIR, Maple & Hickory, Rush Seat, 19th C. $100.00*

*Price does not include 10% buyer fee.

A-MA April 1980 *Robert W. Skinner, Inc.*
WINDSOR SIDE CHAIRS, Set Of 4, Mustard Yellow, Crest Rails Decor., Seats Sponge Grained, N.E., 19th C., 35″ H.
.... $3300.00*

Left
A-WA D.C. Oct 1980 *Adam A. Weschler & Son*
BOSTON ROCKER, Ca. 1820 . . . $225.00*

Right
A-WA D.C. Dec 1980 *Adam A. Weschler & Son*
BOSTON ROCKER, Painted & Turned, 7-Spindle, Plank Seat, Rouge & Drk. Br., Ca. 1800 .... $275.00*

Left
A-MA July 1980 *Robert W. Skinner Inc.*
VIC. ARMCHAIR, Laminated & Carved Rosewood, Mid 19th C., Am., 42½″ H.
.... $2100.00*

Right
A-WA D.C. May 1980 *Adam A. Weschler & Son*
VIC. OPEN ARMCHAIR, Carved Walnut, Ca. 1865-70, Upholstered In Floral & Vine Cut Velvet W/Tufted Back . . . $275.00*

_____

A-MA July 1980 *Robert W. Skinner Inc.*
VIC. PARLOR SET, Incised Walnut & Burl Veneer, Sofa, 2 Gentleman's Chairs, 3 Lady's Chairs, Am., Ca. 1870, Sofa: 74″ L.
.... $850.00*

A-MA June 1980 *Robert W. Skinner, Inc.*
VIC. PARLOR SET, Rosewood, Setee, Armchair & 4 Side Chairs, Am., Late 19th C., Settee: 80″ W. $4000.00*

A-MA July 1980 *Robert W. Skinner Inc.*
L To R
VIC. GENTLEMAN'S CHAIR, Carved Walnut, Am., Late 19th C., 44″ H. . . . $425.00*
VIC. GENTLEMAN'S CHAIR, Carved Walnut, Am., Late 19th C., 45″ H. . . . $425.00*

A-MA Feb 1980 *Robert W. Skinner Inc.*
VIC. LADY'S & GENTLEMAN'S CHAIRS, Am., Walnut, Ca. 1865, 36½″ H., 39½″ H. $450.00*

A-WA D.C. May 1980 *Adam A. Weschler & Son*
CHARLES II ARMCHAIRS, Set Of 6, (2 Illus.), Carved Oak & Cane, Mid 19th C.
.... $1200.00

A-MA July 1980 *Robert W. Skinner Inc.*
L To R
WICKER PLATFORM ROCKER, Wicker Cover For Feet Missing, Am., Late 19th C., 46″ H. $175.00*
WICKER ARMCHAIR, Fan Back, Minor Breaks, Am., Ca. 1900, 48″ H. . . . $175.00*

A-WA D.C. May 1980 *Adam A. Weschler & Son*
LOUIS XV PARLOR SUITE, 3-Pc., Fruitwood, Floral Needle & Petitpoint Upholstery
.... $875.00*

A-MA Mar 1980 *Richard A. Bourne Co., Inc.*
COBBLER'S BENCH, 1 Drawer & Leather Seat, Restored & Ref., 47″ L.
.... $250.00

A-MA Feb 1980   *Robert W. Skinner Inc.*
Q. A. TALL CHEST, Maple, Bun Feet, Retains Most Orig. Finish, Some Drawer Edges Broken, N. Eng., Ca. 1730, 37″ W., 17″ D., 47″ H. $2250.00*

A-MA Feb 1980   *Robert W. Skinner Inc.*
CHIPPENDALE TALL CHEST, Maple, Orig. Red Finish, Repl. Brasses, New Eng., Ca. 1760-1785, 36″ W., 18″ D., 46″ H. $3500.00*

A-VA April 1980   *Laws Auction & Antiques*
CHIPPENDALE CHEST, Walnut, PA, Thumbnail Molding, Brass Bail Plates, Orig. Ogee Molded Feet, Ca. 1775-80, 39½″ W., 22″ D., 36½″ H. $1900.00

A-MA Aug 1980   *Robert W. Skinner Inc.*
CHIPPENDALE CHEST, Maple Base To Chest On Chest, Applied Molded Edge, Pad Feet, Attrib. To Dunlap School, NH, Cherry Top Added, Drawer Lip Repl., Mid 18th C., 38½″ W., 17½″ D., 36″ H. $1500.00*

A-MA Feb 1980   *Robert W. Skinner Inc.*
FEDERAL CHEST OF DRAWERS, Grain Painted, Orig. Brasses, Am., Ca. 1795, 41″ W., 18½″ D., 36½″ H. $2300.00*

◄ A-MA Oct 1980   *Robert W. Skinner Inc.*
CHIPPENDALE TALL CHEST OF DRAWERS, Maple, Cornice Molding, Lipped Drawers, N. Eng., Mid 18th C., 37½″ W., 18¼″ D., 49½″ H. $1850.00*

A-WA D.C. Oct 1980   *Adam A. Weschler & Son*
CHIPPENDALE BLOCK-FRONT CHEST OF DRAWERS, Mahogany, MA, Ca. 1770, 36″ W., 23″ D., 34″ H. $14500.00*

A-VA Jan 1980   *Laws Auction & Antiques*
CHIPPENDALE CHEST OF DRAWERS, Bow Front, Cherry & Tiger Maple, Brass Bail Pulls, Ca. 1780 .... $1800.00

A-MA Mar 1980   *Richard A. Bourne Co., Inc.*
EMPIRE CHEST OF DRAWERS, Mahogany, Minor Repairs Necessary To Veneer, 43¼″ L. $400.00

*Price does not include 10% buyer fee.

A-NY May 1980   *Calkins Auction Gallery*
HEPPLEWHITE CHEST OF DRAWERS,
Cherry, N. Eng., Early 19th C., Dovetailed
Drawers, Orig. Finish, Brasses Repl., 37½"
W., 18" D., 38" H. $750.00

A-OH Jan 1980   *Garth's Auctions, Inc.*
HEPPLEWHITE CHEST OF DRAWERS,
N. E., Bass Wood W/Br. Over Natural
Wood Gr., Dovetailed Drawers, Orig. Oval
Brasses Except Top Drawer W/Old Replace-
ments, 40" W., 21" D., 37½" H. . . . $7500.00

A-MA Mar 1980   *Richard A. Bourne Co., Inc.*
SHERATON CHEST OF DRAWERS,
Mahogany, Swell-Front, Am., Early 19th C.,
Rep. To Veneer, 40½" W. $1450.00

*Price does not include 10% buyer fee.

A-VA April 1980   *Laws Auction & Antiques*
FEDERAL DRESSING BUREAU, Veneered Slip Mirror Frame, Satinwood Faced
Drawers, Cross Banded Veneer & Cockbeaded Moldings, 42" W., 21" D., 6' H.
. . . . $600.00

A-MA Oct 1980   *Robert W. Skinner Inc.*
CHEST OF DRAWERS, Pine, Applied
Molding, Polychromed Decor., CT., Ca.
1710, 42" W., 19½" D., 41" H. $23000.00*

◀ A-NY May 1980   *Calkins Auction Gallery*
FOOT STOOL, Carved & Painted, Blk.
Over Red, 18th C., 1 Spoke Missing, 17" L.,
8" W., 8" H. $85.00

A-MA Jan 1981   *Robert W. Skinner Inc.*
PEWTER DRESSER, Am., 18th C., Pine,
Old Red Color, Repairs, 81" W., 17" D., 86"
H. $4500.00*

A-NY May 1980   *Calkins Auction Gallery*
WARDROBE, Am., Carved & Painted,
Early 19th C., Orig. Red Paint, 39½" W., 16"
D., 75" H. $625.00

A-VA April 1980   *Laws Auction & Antiques*
WM. & MARY HIGHBOY, Am., Mahogany, Banded Inlay, Cotter Pin Teardrop Pulls, Cockbeaded Edging, Ca. 1730-40, 40½" W., 20" D., 68" H. $1425.00

A-VA April 1980   *Laws Auction & Antiques*
Q.A. HIGHBOY, Am., Curly Maple, Thumbnail Molding, Orig. Batwing Brasses, Ca. 1730-50, 38" W., 21" D., 66" H. . . . $2900.00

A-MA Aug 1980   *Robert C. Eldred Co., Inc.*
TALL CHEST, Am., Maple W/Pine Sides, Some Curl To Drawer Fronts, Repl. Brasses, Molded Top, Restorations Needed, 40½" W., 21" D., 60" H. $2500.00

A-MA Aug 1980   *Robert C. Eldred Co., Inc.*
HIGHBOY, Cherry, CT, Molded Cornice, Repl. Brasses, Minor Damage To Some Drawer Corners, 40" W., 78½" H. . .$8000.00

*Price does not include 10% buyer fee.

A-OH May 1980   *Garth's Auctions, Inc.*
CHIPPENDALE CHEST ON CHEST, Cherry & Maple, Dovetailed Cockbeaded Drawers, Top 2 Drawers Have Orig. Brass Bails, Rest Of Hdw. Repl., Ref., 19¾" x 39½", 73¼" H. $4800.00

A-MA July 1980   *Robert W. Skinner Inc.*
CHIPPENDALE CHEST ON CHEST, Maple, NH, Late 18th C., 38" W., 18½" D., 77" H. $10500.00*

A-MA Feb 1980   Robert W. Skinner Inc.
Q.A. HIGHBOY, Maple, MA, Ca. 1730-1760
38½″ W., 18½″ D., 71″ H. $1200.00*

A-MA Feb 1980   Robert W. Skinner Inc.
CHIPPENDALE HIGHBOY, Maple, Restorations, N. Eng., Ca. 1770, 39″ W., 20½″ D., 75″ H. $2300.00*

A-VA April 1980   Laws Auction & Antiques
CHIPPENDALE CHEST-ON-CHEST, Walnut Chester Co., PA, Thumbnail Molding, Post & Bail Hdw., Ca. 1760, Repl. Finials, 41″ W., 32″ D., 86″ H. $2400.00

A-MA Mar 1980   Robert W. Skinner Inc.
CHIPPENDALE HIGHBOY, Mahogany, Am., 20th C., 40″ W., 22″ D., 85″ H.
.... $2100.00*

A-MA Mar 1980   Richard A. Bourne Co., Inc.
Q. A. HIGHBOY, Curly Maple, Am., 18th C., Marriage Pc., Ref. & Restored, Replaced Hdw., 36¼″ W., 19½″ D., 68¼″ O.H.
.... $2100.00

A-VA Jan 1980   Laws Auction & Antiques
Q.A. HIGHBOY, Maple, New Eng., Orig. Cabriole Legs, Padded Dutch Feet, Cast Brass Willow Hdw. Later Repl., Ca. 1730-1760, 37½″ W., 20½″ D., 6'2″ H. .. $3000.00

*Price does not include 10% buyer fee.

A-NY May 1980   *Calkins Auction Gallery*
SHAKER DESK, Pine, 19th C., Slanted Lift Top Writing Surface W/Well Below, 31½″ L., 19″ D., 32½″ H. $235.00

A-MA Jan 1981   *Robert W. Skinner Inc.*
CUSTOM MADE WM. & MARY HIGH-BOY, Am., 20th C., Walnut & Burl Veneer Inlaid, 39¾″ W., 20½″ D., 62½″ H. ...$800.00*

A-MA Jan 1981   *Robert W. Skinner Inc.*
CUSTOM Q.A. HIGHBOY, Am., 20th C., 31½″ W., 19″ D., 74½″ H. $1400.00*

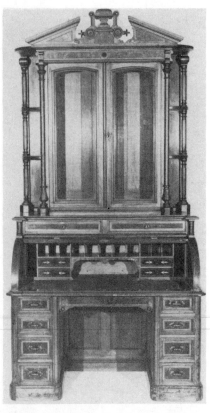

A-MA Jan 1981   *Robert W. Skinner Inc.*
RENAISSANCE REVIVAL ROLL TOP SECRETARY, PA, Walnut & Burl Veneer, Int. Drawers Are Cherry, Other Secondary Wood Is Wh. Wood, Ca. 1865, 53″ W., 28½″ D., 111″ H. $3000.00*

A-MA Jan 1981   *Robert W. Skinner Inc.*
CUSTOM CHIPPENDALE CHEST ON CHEST, Am., Late 19th C., Mahogany & Mahogany Veneer Block Front, 40″ W., 19½″ D., 92″ O.H. $3100.00*

A-MA Jan 1981   *Robert W. Skinner Inc.*
CUSTOM CHIPPENDALE MAHOGANY & MAHOGANY VENEER CHEST ON CHEST, Am., Late 19th C., 89½″ H., 39″ W., 21″ D. $1400.00*

*Price does not include 10% buyer fee.

A-MA June 1980   *Robert W. Skinner, Inc.*
CHIPPENDALE SLANT TOP DESK,
Curly Maple, By Ralph Wakefield, ME, Ca.
1960, 45″ W., 21″ D., 46½″ H. . . . $4000.00*

A-MA Feb 1980   *Robert W. Skinner Inc.*
CHIPPENDALE SLANT TOP DESK,
Maple, Stepped Int. W/Pinwheel & Fan
Carved Drawers, Am., Ca. 1755-1785, 40″
W., 19½″ D., 43″ H. $5000.00*

A-NY May 1980   *Calkins Auction Gallery*
HEPPLEWHITE SECRETARY, 2-Part,
Cherry, Ca. 1780-1800, Orig. Varnish Fin-
ish, N. Eng., Brasses Repl., 36″ W., 5′ 8″ H.
. . . . $1350.00

A-WA D.C. May 1980 *Adam A. Weschler & Son*
CHIPPENDALE FALL-FRONT DESK,
Maple, 20th C., Thumbmolded Edge Lid,
37″ W., 19″ D., 41″ H. $700.00*

A-MA Mar 1980   *Richard A. Bourne Co., Inc.*
HEPPLEWHITE SLANT-LID DESK,
Cherry, Am., Ca. 1800, Bird's-eye Maple
Int., Ref., Minor Loss Of Veneer On Base,
Orig. Hdw., Minor Split On Front Edge,
43⅞″ L. $1700.00

A-WA D.C. Oct 1980 *Adam A. Weschler & Son*
**CHIPPENDALE BLOCK-FRONT
DESK,** Mahogany, MA, Thumbmolded
Slanting Writing Lid, Orig. Brasses, Val-
anced Secret Drawer, Ca. 1770, 39″ W., 22″
D., 43″ H. $21000.00*

A-TX June 1980   *Clements Auctions*
DESK, Walnut, Am., Made By Wooten
Desk Co., Ca. 1860 . . . . $8400.00

A-MA July 1980   *Robert W. Skinner Inc.*
**CHIPPENDALE BONNET TOP SECRE-
TARY,** Cherry, CT, Ca, 1755, 40″ W., 20½″
D., 88½″ H. $9000.00*

*Price does not include 10% buyer fee.

A-VA April 1980 *Laws Auction & Antiques*
HEPPLEWHITE SECRETARY DESK,
Mahogany, 2-Part, Glazed Diamond Paneled
Doors, Brass Steeple Finials $850.00

A-MA July 1980 *Robert W. Skinner Inc.*
FED. SECRETARY, Mahogany, Am., Ca.
1900, 42″ W., 19½″ D., 88″ H. $950.00*

A-VA April 1980 *Laws Auction & Antiques*
FEDERAL SECRETARY DESK, Carved
& Inlaid Fan, Molded Cornice, Oval Plate &
Bail Pulls, 41″ W., 20½″ D., 92″ H. ... $1900.00

A-MA Aug 1980 *Robert C. Eldred Co., Inc.*
Q.A. HIGHBOY, Bonnet Top, Maple, Parts
Orig., Reworked In 1920, 40″ W., 20½″ D.,
84″ H. $5750.00

A-MA Aug 1980 *Robert W. Skinner Inc.*
FEDERAL SECRETARY/BOOKCASE,
Mahogany, 2 Glazed Doors, Cornice Re-
stored, New Eng., Ca. 1800, 39½″ W., 18¾″
D., 78″ H. $2800.00*

A-MA Aug 1980 *Robert W. Skinner Inc.*
CHIPPENDALE SECREATARY, Maple,
Repl. Brasses, Glass Panels Possible Repl.,
New Eng., Ca. 1770, 40″ W., 19¼″ D., 85½″
H. $5750.00*

*Price does not include 10% buyer fee.

A-WA D.C. May 1980 *Adam A. Weschler & Son*
JAMES I COURT CUPBOARD, Carved
Oak, Ca. 1623, 60" W., 21" D., 74" H.
.... $700.00*

A-MA Aug 1980 *Robert W. Skinner Inc.*
CHIPPENDALE CORNER CUPBOARD,
Walnut, Double Glass Doors W/Shaped
Shelved Int., PA, Mid 18th C., 56" W., 105" H.
.... $900.00*

A-VA Jan 1980 *Laws Auction & Antiques*
CHIPPENDALE CORNER CUPBOARD,
Pine, Dentil Molding, 2 Doors W/8 Glazed
Panels & 2 Lower Cabinet Doors W/Molded
3 Panel Bodies, Am., Ca. 1780, 90" H.
.... $1450.00

A-VA Jan 1980 *Laws Auction & Antiques*
PIE SAFE, Cherry W/Pierced Tin Sides &
Doors $675.00

A-WA D.C. May 1980 *Adam A. Weschler & Son*
CORNER CUPBOARD, Am., Cherry,
Ca. 1920, 2 Parts, 39" W., 24" D., 89" H.
.... $1500.00*

A-OH July 1980 *Garth's Auctions, Inc.*
CORNER CUPBOARD, 2-Pc., Poplar
W/Orig. Red Paint, Cockbeaded Drawers &
Doors, Sm. Section Of Molding Missing, 51"
W., 92" H. $4500.00

A-MA Aug 1980 *Robert C. Eldred Co., Inc.*
LIFT-TOP CHEST, PA, Pine W/Paneled
Front, Orig. Painted Decor., Mkd. "BPI",
Ca. 1760, 44" L., 25" H. $1100.00

*Price does not include 10% buyer fee.

A-OH Mar 1980   *Garth's Auctions, Inc.*
CORNER CUPBOARD, 2-Pc., Poplar, Orig. Worn Red Paint & Cast Iron Thumb Latches W/Porcelain Knobs, 45" W., 82" H. $775.00
CARVED WOODEN DECOY, Mallard Drake, Wm. E. Pratt Mfg. Co., Joliet, IL, Ca. 1920-1935, Glass Eyes & Worn Orig. Paint, 17½" L. $45.00

A-MA Mar 1980   *Richard A. Bourne Co., Inc.*
CORNER CABINET, Pine, Am., Late 18th Or Early 19th C., Ref. & Traces Of Old Blue Paint Beneath, Restored, 50" W., 22" D., 73½" H. $700.00

A-MA Aug 1980   *Robert W. Skinner Inc.*
CUPBOARD, Pine, Double Glazed Panel Doors, Shelved Int., Old Yellow Mustard Paint, Am., Ca. 1800, 46" W., 18" D., 78" H. $1400.00*

A-MA Mar 1980   *Richard A. Bourne Co., Inc.*
CORNER CABINET, Pine, Am., 18th C., 2-Pc. Const., Facings Ref., Needs Restorations, 47" W., 19" D., 87½" O.H. .. $900.00

A-MA July 1980   *Robert W. Skinner Inc.*
CHIPPENDALE CORNER CUPBOARD, Pine, Am., 18th C., 48" W., 92" H. $3000.00*

A-NY May 1980   *Calkins Auction Gallery*
STEP BACK CUPBOARD, 18th Or Early 19th C., Dovetailed Drawers, Wrought Nails, Orig. Red Paint, 56" W., 7' 6" H. $950.00

A-VA Jan 1980   *Laws Auction & Antiques*
CHIPPENDALE BLANKET CHEST, Orig. Blue Paint W/Hinged Top, Dovetailed Case, 3 Drawers, Ca. 1760-70 .... $850.00

*Price does not include 10% buyer fee.

A-MA July 1980   *Robert W. Skinner Inc.*
LOUIS XVI DISPLAY CABINET,
Mahogany W/Brass Gallery, Am., Ca. 1900
. . . . $800.00*

A-MA Jan 1981   *Robert W. Skinner Inc.*
WALL CABINET, Late 18th C., Maple,
Dovetailed Const., Br. Stained Finish, 49½″
H. $2100.00*

A-VA Jan 1980   *Laws Auction & Antiques*
CORNER CUPBOARD, Cherry, 18th C.
. . . . $2400.00

A-MA Aug 1980   *Richard A. Bourne Co., Inc.*
VIC. DESK, Walnut, Am., Ca. 1860-1870,
Orig. Cond., 50½″ L., 25″ D., 48¾″ H.
. . . . $675.00

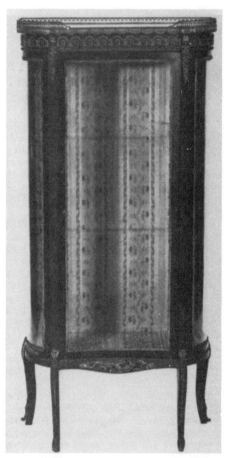

A-MA Mar 1980   *Robert W. Skinner Inc.*
FRENCH-STYLE CURIO CABINET, Ma-
hogany, Red Marble Top W/Brass Gallery
Decor. W/Embossed Motif, Int. Lined W/
Floral Fabric, Am., Late 19th C., 26″ W.,
12½″ D., 55″ H. $850.00*

A-MA Jan 1981   *Robert W. Skinner Inc.*
CUPBOARD, Pine, N. Eng., Late 18th C.,
Repl. "H" Hinges, Old Red Paint, 32½″ W.,
18″ D., 79″ H. $1300.00*

◄ A-MA Jan 1981   *Robert W. Skinner Inc.*
SIDE CHAIRS, Set Of 4, Mid 18th C.,
Maple & Ash, Rush Seats, Traces Of Old
Red Paint, 43″ H. $550.00*

*Price does not include 10% buyer fee.

A-OH Mar 1980   *Garth's Auctions, Inc.*
ROPE BED, Birch, Old Worn Finish, Splits
In Headboard, Side Rails Replaced, 1 Finial
Split, 53" x 82", 60" H. $260.00

A-OH Jan 1980   *Garth's Auctions, Inc.*
TALL POST CANOPY BED, Single Size,
Birch, Pine Head Board W/Orig. Rails &
Canopy Frame, Ref., Posts: 59" H., Bed: 36"
x 77" $1500.00

A-VA April 1980   *Laws Auction & Antiques*
4-POSTER ROPE BED, Walnut, Converted To Take Standard Mattress, Ca. 1850,
91" H. $450.00

A-MA Jan 1981   *Robert W. Skinner Inc.*
BEDROOM SET, Am., Late 19th C., Bam-
boo Turned Maple & Maple Veneer, Includes
Bed, Night Table, 2 Side Chairs, Lock End
Tall Chest Of Drawers W/Mirror, Dressing
Table W/Mirror & Chest Of Drawers W/3
Drawer Facade & Mirror, Some Damages
.... $5000.00*

A-VA April 1980   *Laws Auction & Antiques*
SHERATON CRADLE ON FRAME, San-
to Domingo Mahogany, Ca. 1790-1800
.... $1500.00

A-NY May 1980   *Calkins Auction Gallery*
STEP BACK CUPBOARD, Pine, NY,
19th C., Old Worn Gray Paint, 52" W., 7' H.
.... $400.00

A-MA Jan 1981   *Robert W. Skinner Inc.*
VIC. CRADLE ON STAND, Am., 19th C.,
Walnut W/Monogrammed Hanger, Some
Damage, 36" H. $200.00*

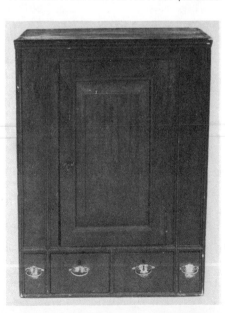

◄ A-MA Aug 1980   *Robert W. Skinner Inc.*
Q. A. RUM CUPBOARD, Pine, Orig.
Engraved Brasses, Old Br. Paint, Ca. 1740, 2
Int. Shelves, 23½" W., 11¾" D., 31¾" H.
.... $3900.00*

*Price does not include 10% buyer fee.

A-MA Mar 1980   *Richard A. Bourne Co., Inc.*
DOME-TOP CHEST, Orig. Wallpaper Covering, Replaced Hinges, Slight Age Crack & Some Loss Of Paper, 30¼" L.
. . . . $400.00

A-NY May 1980   *Calkins Auction Gallery*
DOME TOP CHEST, Early 19th C., Painted Red W/Blk. Decor., 41½" L., 21" D., 19½" H.
. . . . $250.00

A-MA June 1980   *Robert W. Skinner Inc.*
BLANKET BOX ON FRAME, Camphor Wood, Dovetail Const., China, 19th C., 34" W., 17" D., 31" H. $525.00*

A-NY May 1980   *Calkins Auction Gallery*
BLANKET CHEST, Pine, N. Eng., Early 19th C., Dovetailed, Orig. Red Stain, 33" L., 14" D., 17" H. $150.00

*Price does not include 10% buyer fee.

A-MA Aug 1980   *Richard A. Bourne Co., Inc.*
Top To Bottom
SEA CHEST, Dovetailed Pine, Inset Engraved Whalebone Escut., Orig. Beckets, Lock Missing, 35½" L. $500.00
SEA CHEST, Dovetailed Pine, Side Handles W/Repl. Ropes, Orig. Grained Finish, 38" L. $100.00
SEA CHEST, Dovetailed Pine, Orig. Handles W/Beckets, Ref., Restorations, 41" L.
. . . . $200.00

A-WA D.C. Oct 1980 *Adam A. Weschler & Son*
L To R
CHIPPENDALE MIRROR, Mahogany, RI, Pierced Arch Pediment W/Applied Concave Shell, Glass W/Gilt Lip, Ca. 1760-80, 27½" x 13" $700.00*
CHIPPENDALE MIRROR, Mahogany, PA, Parcel Gilt Constitution Mirror, Ca. 1780-90, 48" x 24" $1800.00*

A-MA Aug 1980   *Robert C. Eldred Co., Inc.*
FEDERAL DRESSER MIRROR, Am., Mahogany W/Ormolu Rosettes & Pulls, Ca. 1800, 21" W., 25" H. $310.00*

A-WA D.C. May 1980 *Adam A. Weschler & Son*
CELLARETTE ON STAND, Am., Satinwood Inlaid Walnut, Ca. 1780, 26" W., 16" D., 28" H. $2900.00*

A-MA Aug 1980   *Robert C. Eldred Co., Inc.*
FAN-BACK WINDSOR SIDE CHAIRS, Pr., 7-Spindle, Blk. Paint, Ca. 1770 . . $800.00
TAVERN TABLE, Breadboard Top, Peg Const., Single Drawer Old But Not Orig., Old Red Paint, Am., 31" W., 55" L., 28" H.
. . . . $325.00

◄ *Left*
A-VA April 1980   *Laws Auction & Antiques*
CHIPPENDALE MIRROR, Am. Gilt Carved Inner Border, Gilt Pierced Carved Phoenix Bird, Orig. Mirror Glass & Backboard, Ca. 1780, 19" W., 37" L. . . $500.00
Right
A-WA D.C. Dec 1980 *Adam A. Weschler & Son*
FEDERAL CONVEX MIRROR, Gilt, Ca. 1800, 42" W., 56" H. $800.00*

A-MA Mar 1980   Robert W. Skinner Inc.
VIC. PRINCESS BUREAU, Walnut & Burl Veneer, Br. Marble Top On Base W/1 Carved & Paneled Drawer, Am., Ca. 1870, 47" W., 20" D., 96" H. $800.00*

A-MA Aug 1980   Robert W. Skinner Inc.
SEWING CABINET, Pine, Pull-Out Work Surface, Dovetailed Bracket Base, Repl. Wooden Knobs & Facing To 1 Drawer Repaired, Ca. 1830, 23" W., 21" D., 36½" H. $1900.00*

*Price does not include 10% buyer fee.

A-MA July 1980   Robert W. Skinner Inc.
EMPIRE CARD TABLE, Mahogany, Am., Mid 19th C., 32" H. , 30" W. $300.00*

A-WA D.C. Oct 1980   Adam A. Weschler & Son
VIC. POLE SCREEN, 67" H. . . . $300.00*

A-OH May 1980   Garth's Auctions, Inc.
Q.A. CHEST ON FRAME, Curly Maple, Dovetailed, Restorations Including Repl. Brasses, 37¾" W., 17¾" D., 58" H. $2800.00
FIRE SIDE SHELF, Brass, English, 10" x 14", 11" H. $275.00

A-MA Mar 1980   Richard A. Bourne Co., Inc.
L To R
QUEEN ANNE TAVERN TABLE, Am., 18th C., Maple Top W/Turned Maple Legs, Restored & Ref., 30" L., 23½" W., 26" H. $1500.00
BANISTER-BACK ARM CHAIR, Am., Early 18th C., Ref., Reseated, Restored $425.00

A-WA D.C. Oct 1980   Adam A. Weschler & Son
L To R
Q.A. TEA TABLE, Mahogany, Kittinger, Williamsburg Repro., 29" L., 18" W., 26" H. $675.00*
Q.A. TRIFID WASH STAND, Mahogany, Kittinger, Williamsburg Repro., 33" H. $250.00*

A-MA Feb 1980   Robert W. Skinner, Inc.
CHIPPENDALE CANDLESTAND W/Cherry Tray Top, Am., Ca. 1755-1785, 15" x 14½" $900.00*

A-MA Mar 1980   *Richard A. Bourne Co., Inc.*
PEDESTAL-BASE END TABLES, Mahogany, Pr., Embossed Leather Tops, Single Drawers $200.00
Q. A. WING CHAIR, Williamsburg, Branded "Kittinger", W/Mahogany Frame, Damask Upholstery $925.00

A-VA Jan 1980   *Laws Auction & Antiques*
L To R
SHERATON STAND, Sgn. Wallace Nutting, 1-Drawer, Boxwood & Ebony Inlay, Top: 14¼" x 14¼", 27½" H. $475.00
ARM CHAIR, Sgn. Wallace Nutting, 15-Spindle Back $400.00
OVAL TIP-TOP TABLE, Maple, Sgn. Wallace Nutting, 35" x 25", 28" H. $500.00

A-WA D.C. Oct 1980   *Adam A. Weschler & Son*
VIC. SIDE CABINET, Burl Walnut, Ebonized, Ca. 1870, 49" W., 19" D., 46" H.
.... $600.00*

◄ A-NY May 1980   *Calkins Auction Gallery*
CRADLE, 18th C., Pine & Maple In Orig. Red Paint, 3 Wooden Knobs On Each Side, 37" L., 23½" H. $195.00

*Price does not include 10% buyer fee.

A-VA April 1980   *Laws Auction & Antiques*
L To R
SHERATON WASHSTAND, Am., Dovetailed & Scrolled Gallery Back, Storage Shelf W/Drawer Beneath, Ca. 1810 ..$250.00
Q. A. DUMBWAITER, Mahogany, Ca. 1750-70, 24" D., 46" H. $800.00

A-MA July 1980   *Robert W. Skinner Inc.*
CYLINDER MUSIC BOX ON STAND, Marquietry Inlaid, Switzerland, Late 19th C., 21½" W., 39" L., 40" H. $4700.00*

Left
A-VA April 1980   *Laws Auction & Antiques*
CHIPPENDALE CELLARET, Am. Mahogany, Orig. Feet & Brass Fittings, Beaded Edges, Molded Base, Orig. Brass Castors, Ca. 1770-80, 15" W., 15" D., 16" H. ...$800.00
Right
A-MA July 1980   *Robert W. Skinner Inc.*
VIC. CANTERBURY, Carved Rosewood, Brass Castors & Caps, Am., Ca. 1860, 23½" W., 14¼" D., 22" H. $325.00*

A-WA D.C. Oct 1980   *Adam A. Weschler & Son*
STEINWAY BABY GRAND PIANO, Mahogany, Bench Included, Ca. 1949 . . $5200.00*

A-MA July 1980   *Robert W. Skinner, Inc.*
OAK PIANO, Bronze Candle Brackets, Mfg. By Vose & Sons, MA, Ca. 1910, 60½" W., 26½" D., 53" H. $3400.00*

A-WA D.C. May 1980   *Adam A. Weschler & Son*
EMPIRE MELODEON, Rosewood, George A. Prince & Co., NY, Ca. 1840, Electrified, 44½" W., 23" D., 32" H. $400.00*

A-MA Feb 1980 *Robert W. Skinner Inc.*
VIC. CANTERBURY, Walnut & Burl, Eng.,
Ca. 1840, 24" W., 15" D., 20" H. ... $450.00*

A-NY May 1980 *Calkins Auction Gallery*
FLAX WHEEL, Am., Late 18th Or Early
19th C., Complete & In Working Cond.,
Ref., 36" L., 38" H. $225.00

A-MA April 1980 *Robert W. Skinner, Inc.*
CHIPPENDALE WALL BOX, Walnut,
Sliding Front Door, Sm. Break To Backboard
Mid 18th C., 20" H. $525.00*

*Price does not include 10% buyer fee.

Left
A-MA Feb 1980 *Robert W. Skinner, Inc.*
PIPE BOX W/Drawer, Mahogany, Chips
To Rt. Side, Am., 18th C., 16½" H. .. $1400.00*
Right
A-MA July 1980 *Robert W. Skinner Inc.*
LIGHTING DEVICE STAND, Orig. Red
Paint, Double Candle Sockets, Am., Early
18th C., 44" H. $550.00*

A-MA Feb 1980 *Robert W. Skinner Inc.*
REGENCY CANTERBURY, Rosewood,
Eng., Ca. 1800, 19" W., 15" D., 22" H.
.... $250.00*

A-VA Jan 1980 *Laws Auction & Antiques*
L To R
BANISTER BACK SIDE CHAIR, Woven
Seat, Orig. Blk. Paint, 18th C. $250.00
OVAL TOP TAVERN TABLE, Cleated
Top, Ca. 1770, Top: 27" x 41", 29" H.
.... $625.00

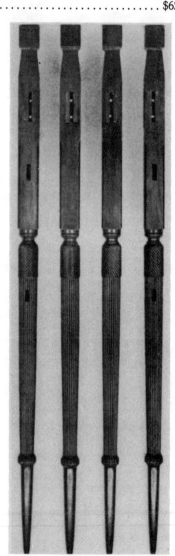

A-WA D.C. May 1980 *Adam A. Weschler & Son*
FEDERAL TESTER BED, Mahogany, Mid-
19th C., W/Canopy, 59" W., 96" H. .. $1300.00*

◄ A-MA May 1980 *Paul J. Dias, Inc.*
SPOOL CABINET, J & P Coats, 6-Draw-
ers, Ref. Cherry Cabinet W/Embossed
Drawers, Brass Pulls, Advertising Panel On
Back $487.50

A-MA July 1980   *Robert W. Skinner Inc.*
Q.A. SOFA, Mahogany, Needlepoint Upholstery, Am., Ca. 1900 .... $700.00*

A-OH May 1980   *Garth's Auctions, Inc.*
SHERATON SOFA, Mahogany, Upholstered In Ecru, Burgandy & Blue Striped Satin, Some Wear, 72¼" L. $1000.00

A-VA Jan 1980   *Laws Auction & Antiques*
LOUIS XVI SALON SUITE, Canape, 4 Arm Chairs & 2 Side Chairs (3 Illus.), All Upholstered In Figural & Floral Tapestry, Carved Gilt Framing, Ca. 1850 .. $5500.00

A-MA Feb 1980   *Robert W. Skinner Inc.*
GRECO ROMAN REVIVAL SOFA, Mahogany, Carved Decor., Am., Ca. 1820, 88" L.
.... $350.00*

A-MA July 1980   *Robert W. Skinner Inc.*
ROCOCO SOFA, Carved & Laminated Rosewood, Restorations To Carvings, 1 Leg Repaired, Ca. 1860, NY, 75½" L., 47" H.
.... $1400.00*

A-MA July 1980   *Robert W. Skinner Inc.*
VIC. PARLOR SET, Walnut & Burly Veneer, Sofa, 4 Side Chairs, Lady's & Gentleman's Chairs, Side Chairs Braced, Am., Mid 19th C.
.... $1150.00*

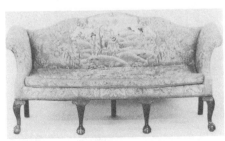

A-WA D.C. Oct 1980 *Adam A. Weschler & Son*
GEORGE III SOFAS, Pr., (1 Illus.), Camel Back, Needle & Petitpoint Upholstery, Ca. 1790-1810, 75" L., 36" H. $3800.00*

◄ A-MA July 1980   *Robert W. Skinner Inc.*
CHIPPENDALE SETTEE, Mahogany, Am., Ca. 1900, 55"W., 36½" H. .. $1100.00*

A-MA Jan 1981   *Robert W. Skinner Inc.*
VIC. RENAISSANCE REVIVAL PARLOR SET, Am., Rosewood, Set Includes Pr. Of Sofas, 2 Armchairs & 2 Side Chairs, Rose & Vine Carved Crests, Upholstered Oval Medallion Backs, Some Damage, Ca. 1860
.... $2300.00*

A-MA Jan 1981   *Robert W. Skinner Inc.*
RENAISSANCE REVIVAL PARLOR SET, Am., Setee, Lady's Chair & Gentleman's Chair $800.00*

A-NY May 1980   *Calkins Auction Gallery*
DECORATED WINDSOR SETTEE, PA, Ca. 1830, Orig. Paint, 6' L., 21" D., 36" O.H. $725.00

A-MA June 1980   *Robert W. Skinner Inc.*
Q.A. SLANT TOP DESK, Maple, Restorations, N. Eng., Ca. 1760, 38½" W., 20" D., 43" H. $2200.00*

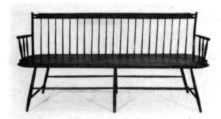

A-MA Aug 1980   *Robert W. Skinner Inc.*
WINDSOR SETTEE, Bamboo Turned Legs
& Stretchers, Am., Ca. 1800, 69½" L.
.... $1500.00*

A-WA D.C. Dec 1980 *Adam A. Weschler & Son*
HITCHCOCK ROCKING SETTEE,
Painted & Stenciled, N. Eng., 19 Turned
Spindles, Plank Seat, Blue & Gold Decor.
On Simulated Rosewood Ground, 69" L.,
30" H. $350.00*

A-WA D.C. Dec 1980 *Adam A. Weschler & Son*
HITCHCOCK DEACON'S BENCH,
Painted & Stenciled, Plank Seat, Ca. 1830-
40, 71" L., 35" H. $650.00*

A-VA April 1980   *Laws Auction & Antiques*
WINDSOR SETTEE, Bamboo Turned
Banisters, Single Board Seat, Ca. 1760-70,
90" L. $340.00

A-VA Jan 1980   *Laws Auction & Antiques*
FEDERAL LOVESEAT, Mahogany, Up-
holstered In Floral Tapestry, Winged Paw
Feet, 64" L. $500.00

A-VA April 1980   *Laws Auction & Antiques*
CANED SETTEE, Ornately Carved, Ca.
1800 .... $250.00

A-VA April 1980   *Laws Auction & Antiques*
HEPPLEWHITE SOFA, Floral Rose Damask, Brass Cups & Castors, 82" L. .. $1000.00

A-VA April 1980   *Laws Auction & Antiques*
CHIPPENDALE SETTEE, Chinese, Santo
Domingo Mahogany, Upholstered In Gr.
Embossed Damask, Ca. 1790, 72" L., 22" D.,
40" H. $2100.00

◀ A-MA July 1980   *Robert W. Skinner Inc.*
WICKER SETTEE, Painted Wh., Am.,
Ca. 1900, 24"W., 46" L., 32½" H. .. $500.00*

A-MA July 1980   *Robert W. Skinner Inc.*
SETTEE, Mahogany, Am., Ca. 1830, 66"
L. $675.00*

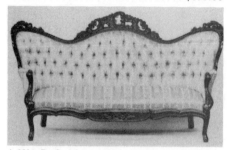

A-WA D.C. May 1980 *Adam A. Weschler & Son*
VIC. SETTEE, Carved Walnut, Ca. 1865-
70, Floral Brocade Pink Striped Upholstery
W/Tufted Back, 68" L., 38" H. ... $400.00*

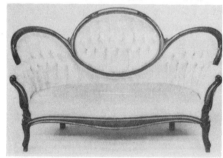

A-WA D.C. May 1980 *Adam A. Weschler & Son*
VIC. SETTEE, Carved Walnut, Ca. 1865-
70, Gold Velvet Upholstery, 65" L., 38" H.
.... $475.00*

A-WA D.C. May 1980 *Adam A. Weschler & Son*
DUNCAN PHYFE SOFA, Carved Ma-
hogany, Brass Paw Caster Feet, Gr. Damask
Upholstery, 88" L., 33" H. $650.00*

A-WA D.C. May 1980 *Adam A. Weschler & Son*
L To R
VIC. OPEN ARMCHAIRS, Pr., Walnut,
Upholstered In Floral Brocaded Silk .. $250.00*
VIC. SETTEES, Pr., Ca. 1865, Walnut,
Blue Floral Damask Upholstery, 70" L., 42" H.
.... $500.00*

*Price does not include 10% buyer fee.

A-MA Jan 1981   *Robert W. Skinner Inc.*
CHIPPENDALE GAME TABLE, Boston, Mahogany, Orig. Brass Pull, Maple & Wh. Pine Secondary Wood, Minor Restoration, Ca. 1760, 33½″ W., 31¼″ D., 28″ H. $21000.00*

A-MA Jan 1981   *Robert W. Skinner Inc.*
WM. & MARY TAVERN TABLE, N. Eng., Early 18th C., Maple & Pine, Color On Base Not Orig., 40″ W., 27⅛″ D., 26¾″ H. $1800.00*

A-MA Jan 1981   *Robert W. Skinner Inc.*
FEDERAL TILT TOP CANDLESTAND, Am., Mahogany, Carved String Decor., Ca. 1800, 22″ x 14″ $650.00*

Left
A-MA July 1980   *Robert W. Skinner Inc.*
WM. & MARY TAVERN TABLE, Pine & Maple, N. Eng., Ca. 1700, Top: 25″ x 19″, 24″ H. $1100.00*
Right
A-WA D.C. May 1980 *Adam A. Weschler & Son*
Q.A. TEA TABLE, Walnut & Maple, N. Eng., Ca. 1740, 30″ W., 21″ D., 26″ H. $4800.00*

A-MA Jan 1981   *Robert W. Skinner Inc.*
Q. A. BUTTERFLY TABLE, N. Eng., Mid 18th C., Cherry & Hickory, 40″ x 34″ $1200.00*

A-MA Jan 1981   *Robert W. Skinner Inc.*
Q. A. TEA TABLE, N. Eng., Walnut, Porriger Top, Ca. 1730, 22½″ x 33½″ . . . $4000.00*

A-WA D.C. Oct 1980 *Adam A. Weschler & Son*
L To R
Q.A. TEA TABLE, Walnut, PA, Dish-Top, Bird-Cage, Ca. 1760, 34″ D., 29″ H. . . $2500.00*
CHIPPENDALE TEA TABLE, Mahogany, PA, Dish-Top, Bird-Cage, Ca. 1780, 24″ D., 29″ H. $900.00*

A-MA Feb 1980   *Robert W. Skinner Inc.*
CHIPPENDALE TILT TOP CANDLE STAND, Maple & Tiger Maple, Restored, N. Eng., Ca. 1810, 28½″ H. $250.00

A-MA Mar 1980   *Robert W. Skinner, Inc.*
VIC. TIP TABLE, Inlaid Mother-Of-Pearl Border Of Grapes & Leaves Centering A Basket Of Flowers W/Painted Highlights, Base Restored, Eng., Mid 19th C., 27″ W., 22″ D., 29″ H. $275.00*

*Price does not include 10% buyer fee.

A-MA Feb 1980   *Robert W. Skinner Inc.*
CHIPPENDALE DROP LEAF TABLE, Mahogany, Repaired Knothole, Minor Scoring On Top, PA, Ca. 1755-1785, Top: 48" x 60" $3000.00*

A-WA D.C. Oct 1980   *Adam A. Weschler & Son*
Q. A. DROP-LEAF TABLE, Cherry, Ca. 1750-70, 35" D., 27" H. $3100.00*

A-MA April 1980   *Robert W. Skinner Inc.*
Q.A. TEA TABLE, Maple, N. Eng., Ca. 1750, 21¾" D., 31" W., 25" H. ... $2000.00*

A-MA Feb 1980   *Robert W. Skinner Inc.*
Q. A. DROP LEAF DINING TABLE, Maple, Circular Top, Cabriole Legs W/Pad Feet, Orig. Blk. Paint, MA, Ca. 1730-1760, Top: 36" D. $5700.00*

A-VA April 1980   *Laws Auction & Antiques*
PEMBROKE TABLE, Am., Mahogany, 1-Drawer W/Orig. Brass Hdw., Double Drop Leaves W/Triple Banded Line Inlay, Ca. 1780-90, 21½" W., 33" L., 28½" H. ..$1950.00

A-MA Jan 1981   *Robert W. Skinner Inc.*
GRECO-ROMAN REVIVAL TABLE, Am., 19th C., Walnut W/Wh. Marble Top, Part Of Apron Missing, Legs Repaired, 33" W., 41" L., 28½" H. $350.00*

◄ A-MA Aug 1980   *Robert W. Skinner Inc.*
FEDERAL SIDEBOARD, Mahogany Inlaid, Cockbeaded Drawers, N. Eng., Ca. 1790, 65" W., 24½" D., 40" H. .. $3500.00*

A-MA Mar 1980   *Richard A. Bourne Co., Inc.*
HEPPLEWHITE 3-PART BANQUET TABLE, Am., Late 18th C., Drop-Leaf Center, Base Const. Of Chestnut W/Brass Casters, Top Pcs. Of Pine, Ref., 8' 6¾" L., 3' 11" W., 29" H. $2600.00

A-NY May 1980   *Calkins Auction Gallery*
HEPPLEWHITE PEMBROKE TABLE, Mahogany, Ca. 1790, Dovetailed Drawer W/ Bail Brass, 31½" L., 21½" W., 28½" H. $350.00

A-NY May 1980   *The Auction Gallery*
TEN-SIDED TABLE, Grain Painted, NY, 19th C., 40" D., 28½" H. $175.00

A-MA Mar 1980   *Robert W. Skinner Inc.*
VIC. TABLE, Walnut W/Marble Top, Am., 19th C., 38" L., 29" D., 28" H. $650.00*

*Price does not include 10% buyer fee.

A-MA Mar 1980   *Richard A. Bourne Co., Inc.*
HUTCH TABLE, Pine, Am., 18th C.,
Restored & Ref., Pegs Missing, 6' L., 37½"
W., 29" H. $600.00

A-MA Feb 1980   *Robert W. Skinner Inc.*
CHAIR TABLE, Pine, Shoe Feet, Am., 18th
C., Top: 46" D. $1400.00*

A-MA Feb 1980   *Robert W. Skinner Inc.*
CHAIR TABLE, Pine & Maple, Am., 18th
C., Top: 47" D., 26" H. $1150.00*

A-MA Feb 1980   *Robert W. Skinner Inc.*
WM. & MARY TAVERN TABLE, Pine
Breadboard Top, Old Tan Paint To Base, 1
End To Top Missing, Am., Ca. 1700-1730,
Top: 24" x 37" $2000.00*

A-WA D.C. Dec 1980   *Adam A. Weschler & Son*
HUTCH TABLE, N. Eng., Cherry, Thumb-
molded Drawers, Breadboard End Hinged
Top, 19th C., 60" W., 31" D., 28½" H.
.... $600.00*

A-WA D.C. Dec 1980   *Adam A. Weschler & Son*
BUTTERFLY TABLE, Pine, N. Eng., Ca.
1680-1710, 38" L., 26" H. $400.00*

A-VA April 1980   *Laws Auction & Antiques*
Q. A. DROP LEAF TABLE, Walnut, MA,
2 Legs Swing To Support Leaves, Ca. 1730-
50, Restorations, 50" W., 18" L. (Closed),
58" L. (Open) 28" H. $1500.00

A-WA D.C. Oct 1980   *Adam A. Weschler & Son*
DROP-LEAF TABLE, Pine, Ca. 1820, 36"
W., 29" H. $275.00*

A-MA Oct 1980   *Robert W. Skinner Inc.*
WM. & MARY GATELEG TABLE, N.
Eng., Ca. 1730, 45" D., 42¼" L., 26½" H.
.... $2400.00*

A-WA D.C. Oct 1980   *Adam A. Weschler & Son*
GATE-LEG TABLE, Maple, N. Eng., Ca.
1720-30, 42" W., 28" H. $4200.00*

*Price does not include 10% buyer fee.

AGATA GLASS was patented by Joseph Locke of the New England Glass Company of Cambridge, Massachusetts, in 1877. The application of a metallic stain left a mottled design characteristic of agata, hence the name.

AMBER GLASS is the name of any glassware having a yellowish-brown color. It became popular during the last quarter of the nineteenth century.

AMBERINA GLASS was patented by The New England Glass Company in 1883. It is generally recognized as a clear yellow glass shading to a deep red or fuschia at the top. When the colors are opposite, it is known as reversed amberina. It was machine-pressed into molds, free blown, cut and pattern molded. Almost every glass factory here and in Europe produced this ware, however, few pieces were ever marked.

AMETHYST GLASS - The term identifies any glassware made in the proper dark purple shade. It became popular after the Civil War.

ART GLASS is a general term given to various types of ornamental glass made to be decorative rather than functional. It dates primarily from the late Victorian period to the present day and, during the span of time glassmakers have achieved fantastic effects of shape, color, pattern, texture and decoration.

AVENTURINE GLASS - The Venetians are credited with the discovery of Aventurine during the 1860s. It was produced by various mixes of copper in yellow glass. When the finished pieces were broken, ground or crushed, they were used as a decorative material by glassblowers. Therefore, a piece of Aventurine glass consists of many tiny glittering particles on the body of the object, suggestive of sprinkled gold crumbs or dust. Other colors in Aventurine are known to exist.

BACCARAT GLASS was first made in France in 1765 by La Compagnie des Cristalleries de Baccarat—until the firm went bankrupt. Production began for the second time during the 1820s and the firm is still in operation, producing fine glassware and paperweights. Baccarat is famous for its earlier paperweights made during the last half of the 19th century.

BOHEMIAN GLASS is named for its country of origin. It is an ornate, overlay, or flashed glassware, popular during the Victorian era.

BRISTOL GLASS is a lightweight opaque glass, oftentimes having a light bluish tint, and decorated with enamels. The ware is a product of Briston, England—a glass center since the 1700s.

BURMESE - Frederick Shirley developed this shaded art glass at the now famous old Mt. Washington Glass Company in New Bedford, Massachusetts, and patented his discovery under the name of "Burmese" on December 15, 1885. The ware was also made in England by Thomas Webb & Sons.

Burmese is a hand-blown glass with the exception of a few pieces that were pattern molded. The latter are either ribbed, hobnail or diamond quilted in design. This ware is found in two textures or finishes: the original glazed or shiny finish, and the dull, velvety, satin finish. It is a homogeneous glass (single-layered) that was never lined, cased or plated. Although its color varies slightly, it always shades from a delicate yellow at the base to a lovely salmon-pink at the top. The blending of colors is so gradual that it is difficult to determine where one color ends and the other begins.

CAMBRIDGE glasswares were produced by the Cambridge Glass Company in Ohio from 1901 until the firm closed in 1954.

CAMEO GLASS can be defined as any glass in which the surface has been cut away to leave a design in relief. Cutting is accomplished by the use of hand cutting tools, wheel cutting and hydrofluoric acid. This ware can be clear or colored glass of a single layer, or glass with multiple layers of clear or colored glass.

Although Cameo glass has been produced for centuries, the majority available today dates from the late 1800s. It has been produced in England, France and other parts of Europe, as well as the United States. The most famous of the French masters of Cameo wares was Emile Galle'.

CANDY CONTAINERS were used for holding tiny candy pellets. These were produced in a variety of shapes—locomotives, cars, boats, guns, etc. for children.

CARNIVAL GLASS was an inexpensive, pressed, iridescent glassware made from about 1900 through the 1920s. It was made in quantities by Northwood Glass Company; Fenton Art Glass Company and others, to compete with the expensive art glass of the period. Originally called "Taffeta" glass, the ware became known as "Carnival" glass during the 1920s when carnivals gave examples as premiums or prizes.

CORALENE - The term Coralene denotes a type of decoration rather than a kind of glass—consisting of many tiny beads, either of colored or transparent glass—decorating the surface. The most popular design used resembled coral or seaweed—hence the name.

CRACKLE GLASS - This type of art glass was an invention of the Venetians that spread rapidly to other countries. It is made by plunging red-hot glass into cold water, then reheating and reblowing it, thus producing an unusual outer surface which appears to be covered with a multitude of tiny fractures, but is perfectly smooth to the touch.

CRANBERRY GLASS - The term "Cranberry Glass" refers to color only, not to a particular type of glass. It is undoubtedly the most familiar colored glass known to collectors. This ware was blown or molded, and oftentimes decorated with enamels.

CROWN MILANO glass was made by Frederick Shirley at the Mt. Washington Glass Company, New Bedford, MA, from 1886-1888. It is ivory in color with satin finish, and was embellished with floral sprays, scrolls and gold enamel.

CROWN TUSCAN glass has a pink-opaque body. It was originally produced in 1936 by A.J. Bennett, President of the Cambridge Glass Company of Cambridge, Ohio. The line was discontinued in 1954. Occasionally referred to as Royal Crown Tuscan, this ware was named for a scenic area in Italy, and it has been said that its color was taken from the flesh-colored sky at sunrise. When trans-illuminated, examples do have all of the blaze of a sunrise—a characteristic that is even applied to new examples of the ware reproduced by Mrs. Elizabeth Degenhart of Crystal Art Glass, and Harold D. Bennett, Guernsey Glass Company of Cambridge, Ohio.

CUSTARD GLASS was manufactured in the United States for a period of about thirty years (1885-1915). Although Harry Northwood was the first and largest manufacturer of custard glass, it was also produced by the Heisey Glass Company, Diamond Glass Company, Fenton Art Glass Company and a number of others.

The name Custard Glass is derived from its "custard yellow" color which may shade light yellow to ivory to light green glass that is opaque to opalescent. Most pieces have fiery opalescence when held to light. Both the color and glow of this ware comes from the use of uranium salts in the glass. It is generally a heavy type pressed glass made in a variety of different patterns.

CUT OVERLAY - The term identifies pieces of glassware usually having a milk-white exterior that has been cased with cranberry, blue or amber glass. Other type examples are deep blue, amber or cranberry on crystal glass, and the majority of pieces have been decorated with dainty flowers. Although Bohemian glass manufacturers produced some very choice pieces during the nineteenth century, fine examples were also made in America, as well as in France and England.

DAUM NANCY is the mark found on pieces of French cameo glass made by August and Antonin Daum, after 1875.

DURAND ART GLASS was made by Victor Durand from 1879 to 1935 at the Durand Art Glass Works in Vineland, New Jersey. The glass resembles Tiffany in quality. Drawn white feather designs and thinly drawn glass threading (quite brittle) applied around the main body of the ware, are striking examples of Durand creations on an iridescent surface.

FLASHED WARES were popular during the late 19th century. They were made by partially coating the inner surface of an object with a thin plating of glass or another, more dominant color — usually red. These pieces can readily be identified by holding the object to the light and examining the rim, as it will show more than one layer of glass. Many pieces of "Rubina Crystal" (cranberry to clear), "Blue Amberina" (blue to amber), and "Rubina Verde" (cranberry to green), were manufactured in this way.

FINDLAY or ONYX art glass was manufactured about 1890 for only a short time by the Dalzell Gilmore Leighton Company of Findlay, Ohio.

FRANCISWARE is a hobnail glassware with frosted or clear glass hobs and stained amber rims and tops. It was produced during the late 1880s by Hobbs, Brockunier & Company.

FRY GLASS was made by the H. C. Fry Company, Rochester, PA from 1901, when the firm was organized, until 1934 when operations ceased. The firm specialized in the manufacture of cut glassware. The production of their famous "Foval" glass did not begin until the 1920s. The firm also produced a variety of glass specialties, oven wares and etched glass.

GALLE' glass was made in Nancy, France by Emile Galle' at the Galle Factory founded in 1874. The firm produced both enameled and cameo glass, pottery, furniture and other Art Nouveau items. After Galle's death in 1904, the factory continued operating until 1935.

GREENTOWN glass was made in Greentown, IN by the Indiana Tumbler & Goblet Company from 1894 until 1903. The firm produced a variety of pressed glass wares in addition to milk and chocolate glass.

GUNDERSON peachblow is a more recent type art glass produced in 1952 by the Gunderson-Pairpoint Glass Works of New Bedford, MA, successors to the Mt. Washington Glass Co. Gunderson pieces have a soft satin finish shading from white at the base to a deep rose at the top.

HOBNAIL – The term hobnail identifies any glassware having "bumps" — flattened, rounded or pointed — over the outer surface of the glass. A variety of patterns exists. Many of the fine early examples were produced by Hobbs, Brockunier & Co., Wheeling, W. Va., and The New England Glass Company.

HOLLY AMBER, originally known as "Golden Agate," is a pressed glass pattern which features holly berries and leaves over its glossy surface. Its color shades from golden

brown tones to opalescent streaks. This ware was produced by the Indiana Tumbler and Goblet Company for only six months, from January 1, to June 13, 1903. Examples are rare and expensive.

IMPERIAL GLASS – The Imperial Glass Company of Bellaire, Ohio, was organized in 1901 by a group of prominent citizens of Wheeling, West Virginia. A variety of fine art glass, in addition to Carnival glass, was produced by the firm. The two trademarks which identified the ware were issued in June, 1914. One consisted of the firm's name, "Imperial," and the other included a cross formed by double-pointed arrows. The latter trademark was changed in September of the same year from the arrow cross to what was known as a "German" cross. The overlapping "IG" cipher was adopted by Imperial in 1949, and appears on practically all of their present production —including reproduced Carnival glass.

LATTICINO is the name given to articles of glass in which a network of tiny milk-white lines appear, crisscrossing between two walls of glass. It is a type of Filigree glassware developed during the 16th century by the Venetians.

LEGRAS GLASS – cameo, acid cut and enameled glass wares — were made by August J. F. Legras at Saint-Denis, France from 1864-1914.

LOETZ GLASS was made in Austria just before the turn of the century. As Loetz worked in the Tiffany factory before returning to Austria, much of his glass is similar in appearance to Tiffany wares. Loetz glass is oftentimes marked "Loetz" or "Loetz-Austria."

LUTZ GLASS was made by Nicholas Lutz, a Frenchman, who worked at the Boston and Sandwich Glass Company from 1870 to 1888 when it closed. He also produced fine glass at the Mt. Washington Glass Company and later at the Union Glass Company. Lutz is noted for two different types of glass — striped and threaded wares. Other glass houses also produced similar glass and these wares were known as Lutz-type.

MARY GREGORY was an artist for the Boston & Sandwich Glass Company during the last quarter of the 19th century. She decorated glass ware with white enamel figures of young children engaged in playing, collecting butterflies, etc. in white on transparent glass, both clear and colored. Today, the term "Mary Gregory" glass applies to any glassware that remotely resembles her work.

MERCURY GLASS is a double-walled glass that dates from the 1850s to about 1910. It was made in England as well as the United States during this period. Its interior, usually in the form of vases, is lined with flashing mercury, giving the items an allover

silvery appearance. The entrance hole in the base of each piece was sealed over. Many pieces were decorated.

MILK GLASS is an opaque pressed glassware, usually of milk-white color, although green, amethyst, black, and shades of blue were made. Milk glass was produced in quantity in the United States during the 1880s, in a variety of patterns.

MILLEFIORI – This decorative glassware is considered to be a specialty of the Venetians. It is sometimes called "glass of a thousand flowers," and has been made for centuries. Very thin colored glass rods are arranged in bundles, then fused together with heat. When the piece of glass is sliced across, it has a design like that of many small flowers. These tiny wafer thin slices are then embedded in larger masses of glass, enlarged and shaped.

MOSER GLASS was made by Kolomon Moser at Carlsbad. The ware is considered to be another type of Art Nouveau glass as it was produced during its heyday — during the early 1900s. Principal colors included amethyst, cranberry, green and blue, with fancy enameled decoration.

MOTHER-OF-PEARL, is often abbreviated in descriptions as M.O.P., is glass composed of two or more layers, with a pattern showing through to the outer surface. The pattern, caused by internal air traps, is created by expanding the inside layer of molten glass into molds with varying designs. And when another layer of glass is applied, this brings out the design. Then the final layer of glass is then acid dipped, and the result is Mother of Pearl Satin Ware. Patterns are numerous. The most frequently found are the Diamond Quilted, Raindrop and Herringbone. This ware can be one solid color, a single color shading light to dark, two colors blended or a variety of colors which includes the rainbow effect. In addition, many pieces are decorated with colorful enamels, coralene beading, and other applied glass decorations.

NAILSEA glass was first produced in England from 1788 to 1873. The characteristics that identify this ware are the "pulled" loopings and swirls of colored glass over the body of the object.

NEW ENGLAND PEACHBLOW was patented in 1886 by the New England Glass Company. It is a single-layered glass shading from opaque white at the base to deep rose-red or from opaque white at the base to deep rose-red or raspberry at the top. Some pieces have a glossy surface, but most were given to acid bath to produce a soft, matte finish.

NEW MARTINSVILLE PEACHBLOW GLASS was produced from 1901-1907 at New Martinsville, PA.

OPALESCENT GLASS – The term refers to glasswares which have a milky white effect in the glass, usually on a colored ground. There are three basic types of this ware. Presently, the most popular includes pressed glass patterns found in table settings. Here, the opalescence appears at the top rim, the base, or a combination of both. On blown or mold-blown glass, the pattern itself consists of this milky effect — such as Spanish Lace. Another example is the opalescent points on some pieces of hobnail glass. These wares are lighter weight. And the third group includes opalescent novelties, primarily of the pressed variety.

PAMONA glass was invented in 1884 by Joseph Locke at the New England Glass Company.

PEKING GLASS is a type of Chinese cameo glass produced from the 1700s, well into the nineteenth century.

PHOENIX GLASS – The firm was established in Beaver County, Pennsylvania during the late 1800s, and produced a variety of commercial glasswares. During the 1930s the factory made a desirable sculptured gift-type glassware which has become very collectible in recent years. Vases, lamps, bowls, ginger jars, candlesticks, etc. were made until the 1950s in various colors with a satin finish.

PIGEON BLOOD is a bright reddish-orange glass ware dating from the early 1900s.

PRESSED GLASS was the inexpensive glassware produced in quantity to fill the increasing demand for tablewares when Americans moved away from the simple table utensils of pioneer times. During the 1820s, ingenious Yankees invented and perfected machinery for successfully pressing glass. And about 1865, manufacturers began to color their products. Literally hundreds of different patterns were produced.

ROSALINE GLASS is a product of the Steuben Glass Works of Corning, NY. The firm was founded by Frederick Carter & T. C. Hawkes, Sr. Rosaline is a rose-colored jade glass or colored alabaster. The firm is now owned by the Corning Glass Company, which is presently producing fine glass of exceptional quality.

ROYAL FLEMISH ART GLASS was made by the Mt. Washington Glass Works during the 1880s. It has an acid finish which may consist of one or more colors, decorated with raised gold enameled lines separating into sections. Fanciful painted enamel designs also decorate this ware. Royal Flemish glass is marked "RF," with the letter "R" reversed and backed to the letter "F", within a four-sided orange-red diamond mark.

SANDWICH GLASS – One of the most interesting and enduring pages from America's past is Sandwich Glass produced by the famous Boston and Sandwich Glass Company at Sandwich, Massachusetts. The firm began operations in 1825, and the glass

flourished until 1888 when the factory closed. Despite the popularity of Sandwich Glass, little is known about its founder, Deming Jarvis.

The Sandwich Glass house turned out hundreds of designs in both plain and figured patterns, in colors and crystal, so that no one type could be considered entirely typical — but the best known is the "lacy" glass produced here. The variety and multitude of designs and patterns produced by the company over the years is a tribute to its greatness.

SILVER DEPOSIT GLASS was made during the late 19th and early 20th centuries. Silver was deposited on the glass surface by a chemical process so that a pattern appeared against a clear or colored ground. This ware is sometimes referred to as "silver overlay."

SLAG GLASS was originally known as "Mosaic" and "Marble Glass" because of its streaked appearance. Production in the United States began about 1880. The largest producer of this ware was Challinor, Taylor & Company. The various slag mixtures are: purple, butterscotch, blue, orange, green and chocolate. A small quantity of Pink Slag was also produced in the Inverted Fan & Feather pattern. Examples are rare and expensive.

SPANISH LACE is a Victorian glass pattern that is easily identified by its distinct opalescent flower and leaf pattern. It belongs to the shaded opalescent glass family.

STEUBEN – The Steuben Glass Works was founded in 1904 by Frederick Carter, an Englishman, and T. G. Hawkes, Sr., at Corning, new York. In 1918, the firm was purchased by the Corning Glass Company. However, Steuben remained with the firm, designing a bounty of fine art glass of exceptional quality.

STIEGEL-TYPE GLASS – Henry William Stiegel founded America's first flint glass factory during the 1760s at Manheim, PA. Stiegel glass is flint or crystal glass, it is thin and clear, and has a bell-like ring when tapped. The ware is quite brittle and fragile. Designs were painted free-hand on the glass — birds, animals and architectural motifs, surrounded by leaves and flowers. The engraved glass resulted from craftsmen etching the glass surface with a copper wheel, then cutting the desired patterns.

It is extremely difficult to identify with certainty, a piece of original Stiegel glass. Part of the problem resulted from the lack of an identifying mark on the products. Additionally, many of the craftsmen moved to other areas after the Stiegel plant closed — producing a similar glass product. Therefore, when one is uncertain about the origin of this type ware, it is referred to as "Stiegel-type" glass.

TIFFANY GLASS was made by Louis Comfort Tiffany, one of America's outstanding glass designers of the Art Nouveau

period, from about 1870 to the 1930s. Tiffany's designs included a variety of lamps, bronze work, silver, pottery and stained glass windows. Practically all items made were marked "L. C. Tiffany" or "L.C.T." in addition to the word "Favrille" — the French word for color.

TORTOISE SHELL GLASS – As the name indicates, this type glassware resembles the color of tortoise shell and has deep rich brown tones combined with amber and cream-colored shades. Tortoise Shell Glass was originally produced in 1880 by Francis Pohl, a German chemist. It was also made in the United States by the Sandwich Glass Works and other glass houses during the late 1800s.

VAL ST. LAMBERT Cristalleries, located in Belgium, was founded in 1825 and the firm is still in operation.

VASA MURRHINA glassware was produced in quantity at the Vasa Murrhina Art Glass Company of Sandwich, MA during the late 1900s. John C. DeVoy, Assignor to the firm, registered a patent on July 1, 1884, for the process of decorating glassware with particles of mica flakes (coated with copper, gold, nickel or silver) sandwiched between an inner layer of glass which is opaque, and an outer layer of clear or transparent colored glass. The ware was also produced by other American glass firms and in England.

VASELINE GLASS – The term "Vaseline" refers to color only, as it resembles the greenish-yellow color typical of the oily petroleum jelly known as Vaseline. This ware has been produced in a variety of patterns both here and in Europe — from the late 1800s. It has been made in both clear and opaque yellow, Vaseline combined with clear glass, and occasionally the two colors are combined in one piece.

WAVECREST GLASS is an opaque white glassware made from the late 1890s by French factories and the Pairpoint Manufacturing Company at New Bedford, Mass. Items were decorated by the C. F. Monroe Company of Meriden, Ct., with painted pastel enamels. The name Wavecrest was used after 1898 with the initials of the Company "C.F.M. Co." Operations ceased during World War II.

WEBB GLASS was made by Thomas Webb & Sons of Stourbridge, England during the late Victorian period. The firm produced a variety of different types of art and cameo glass.

WHEELING PEACHBLOW – With its simple lines and delicate shadings, Wheeling Peachblow was produced soon after 1883 by J. H. Hobbs, Brockunier & Company at Wheeling, West Virginia. It is a two-layered glass lined or cased inside with an opaque, milk-white type of plated glassware. The outer layer shades from a bright yellow at the base to a mahogany red at the top. The majority of pieces produced are in the glossy finish.

Left

A-MA Nov 1980   *Robert W. Skinner Inc.*
WHEELING PEACHBLOW VASE, Shiny Finish, Appl. Amber Foot, Ca. 1890, 8¾" H.
. . . . $275.00*

Right

A-MA Jan 1981   *Robert W. Skinner Inc.*
MT. WASHINGTON PEACHBLOW VASE, N. Eng., Ca. 1890, 4¼" H.
. . . . $2500.00*

A-OH Oct 1980   *Early Auction Co.*
L To R
RAINBOW PELOTON VASE, Swirled Frosted Rigaree Decor., 13¼" H. . . $175.00*
EPERGNE, Crainberry W/Pull-Up Technique, Base Mkd. N. E. Glass Co., 13½" H.
. . . . $250.00*
WHEELING PEACHBLOW MILK PITCHER, Shiny W/Amber Handle, Sm. Line In Inner Lining, 5" H. $325.00*

A-OH Oct 1980   *Early Auction Co.*
L To R
D.Q.M.O.P. FAIRY LAMP & HOLDER, Blue Satin Glass $150.00*
CANDLE LAMPS, Pr., Gr. Satin W/Frosted Petal Bases, 9¼" H. $350.00*
FAIRY LAMP, Satin Glass W/Lemon Shade $150.00*
FAIRY LAMP, Satin Glass W/Ribbed Pink Shade, Clear Glass Holder Mkd. Cricklite Clarkes $120.00*

A-OH Oct 1980   *Early Auction Co.*
L To R
MT. WASHINGTON BURMESE LILY VASE, Acid Finish, 12½" H. $185.00*
PEACHBLOW LILY VASE, Shiny, N. Eng., 17½" H. $425.00*
AMBERINA LILY VASE, N. Eng., Ribbed, 15¾" H. $265.00*

A-OH Oct 1980   *Early Auction Co.*
L To R
AMBERINA BASKET, Swirled W/Gold Floral Decor., Appl. Amber Feet, 15½" H.
. . . . $300.00*
AMBERINA BOWL, Swirled W/Gilt Metal Base, 13¼" H. $350.00*

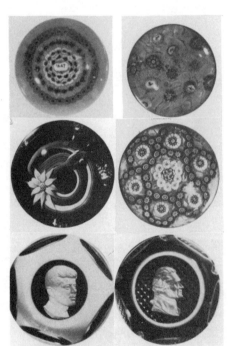

A-MA Aug 1980   *Robert C. Eldred Co., Inc.*
BACCARAT PAPERWEIGHTS
ROW I, L To R
BACCARAT PAPERWEIGHT, Dated Cane In Center "1847", 2⅜" D. . . $650.00
BACCARAT PAPERWEIGHT, Blue Spiraling, Gauze Cable Canes, Sgn. & Dated "B 1848", 2⅜" D. $850.00

ROW II, L To R
BACCARAT PAPERWEIGHT, Gr. & Yellow Snake, Etched On Base "1970" & Baccarat Mark, 3¼" D. $400.00
BACCARAT PAPERWEIGHT, Stylized Flowers On Wh. Muslin Ground, Unsigned, 3" D. $2200.00

ROW III, L To R
JOHN F. KENNEDY, Opaque Wh. Overlay, Sulphide Portrait, Cobalt Cushion, Etched Mark On Base, 3⅛" D. . . . $225.00
THOMAS JEFFERSON, Red & Wh. Double Overlay, Sulphide Portrait, Clear Cushion, "G.P. 1953" On Cameo, 3⅛" D.
. . . . $200.00

A-OH Oct 1980   *Early Auction Co.*
L To R
M.O.P. PICKLE CASTER, Apricot Satin Herringbone, Silver Plated Frame W/Tongs
. . . . $300.00*
AMBERINA PICKLE CASTER, N. Eng., Thumbprint Patt., Enamel Floral & Fruit Decor., Silver Plated Holder, Mkd. Rogers Bros. $375.00*
PEACHBLOW PICKLE CASTER, Swirled, In Homan Silver Plated Frame W/Tongs $200.00*

A-OH Oct 1980   *Early Auction Co.*
L To R
AMBERINA CRUET, Plated . . . $2000.00*
AMBERINA CRUET & SALT & PEPPER, Mt. Washington, Pairpoint Silver Plated Holder $385.00*
AMBERINA JUG, Swirled W/Stopper, 8" H. $300.00*

*Price does not include 10% buyer fee.

◄ A-OH Oct 1980 *Early Auction Co.*

ROW I, L To R

CAMEO VASE, Fr., Decor. W/Thistle & Multicolored Leaves & Pods On Lt. Tan Ground, 14¼" H. $625.00*

D.Q.M.O.P. MINI. LAMP, Rainbow W/ Frosted Petal Base & Appl. Frosted Rigaree Around Top Of Base, Orig. Ruffled-Top Shade $1900.00*

GALLE CAMEO VASE, Sgn., Decor. In Red Foliage Over Frosted Gray Ground, 8" H. $900.00*

D.Q.M.O.P. EPERGNE, Glossy Pink W/ Center Stem & 3 Arms, Mirrored Plateau $550.00*

CAMEO VASE, Fr., Decor. W/Flowers & Leaves In Gr. & Red On Pink Ground, Sgn. G. Raspiller, 10" H. $550.00*

QUEZAL STICK VASE, Sgn., Irid. Blues, Gr. & Purple W/Silver Overlay, Mkd., 9¾" H. $1050.00*

CAMEO A.C.B. VASE, Fuchsia On Purple-To-Cream Ground, Sgn. Daum Nancy, 13¾" H. $600.00*

ROW II, L To R

AGATA CRUET $1100.00*

ROOKWOOD LOVING CUP, 3-Handled, Portrait Of Am. Indian On Standard Glaze, Artist: Lenore Asbury, Ca. 1897, 7½" H. $6000.00*

AMBERINA PITCHER, Plated, 7" H. $1700.00*

ROOKWOOD WHISKEY JUG, Corn Decor. On Standard Glaze, Comp. W/ Stopper, Artist: Lenore Asbury, 7½" H. $1000.00*

PELOTON CRUET, Clear Appl. Handle & Faceted Stopper................ $375.00*

CAMEO VASE, Eng., Deep Blue, Cut W/Wh. Floral Decor., Imperfection At Base, 5½" H. $500.00*

WEBB CAMEO VASE, Blue, Cut W/Butterfly & Wh. Flowers On Pink Ground, Chip At Base, 4⅞" H. $900.00*

ROW III, L To R

CAMEO VASE, Fr., Sgn. Le Verre Francais, Decor. In Burnt Orange & Yellow, 18" H. $800.00*

DECOR. VASE, Garnet Red, Mkd. L.C. Tiffany-Favrille, 3½" H. $2300.00*

ROOKWOOD TANKARD PITCHER, Standard Glaze, Artist: Harriet E. Wilcox, Chip On Spout, Age Crack, Ca. 1891, 9½" H. $1000.00*

*Price does not include 10% buyer fee.

ROYAL FLEMISH EWER, Cooling Check At Handle, 12" H. $500.00*

ROOKWOOD VASE, Scenic Vellum, Artist: E. T. Hurley, No Crazing, Ca. 1931, 13½" H. $1000.00*

PEACHBLOW VASE, Appl. Glass Plums, Leaves & Vines On Amber Appl. Feet, 14¼" H. $550.00*

VASE, Peacock Blue, Sgn. L. C. Tiffany, Inc.-Favrille, 9¾" H. $525.00*

ROW IV, L To R

LILY VASE, Irid. Gold, Sgn. Aurene, 8" H. $425.00*

WHEELING PEACHBLOW STICK VASE, Acid Finish, 8¼" H. $375.00*

WHEELING PEACHBLOW STICK VASE, Shiny Finish, 8¼" H. $400.00*

ROOKWOOD VASE, Gr. Scenic Vellum, Artist: Ed Diers, Ca. 1931, 9½" H. $1000.00*

ROOKWOOD TANKARD, Pine Cone Spray On Standard Glaze, Artist: O. G. Reed, Ca. 1893, 9½" H. $600.00*

WHEELING PEACHBLOW SALT & PEPPER, Shiny Finish, 1 W/Nick $175.00*

ROOKWOOD VASE, Blue Scenic Vellum, Artist: Ed Diers, Ca. 1931, 9½" H. $1050.00*

PEACHBLOW LILY VASE, N. Eng., Acid Finish, Orig. Label: "Wild Rose, N.E.G.W., Pat. March 2, 1886," 8" H. $575.00*

PEACHBLOW LILY VASE, N. Eng., Shiny Finish, 8" H. $375.00*

TIFFANY OVERLAY VASE, Br. Cut To Wh., Wafer Pontil, Sgn. L. C. Tiffany-Favrille, 8" H. $2100.00*

ROW V, L To R

WHEELING PEACHBLOW GOURD VASE, Shiny Finish, 7" H. $800.00*

GALLE CAMEO VASE, Sgn., Decor. W/ Blue Flower, Br. & Gr. Leaves On Tan Ground, 5½" H. $600.00*

CREAMER & SUGAR, N. Eng. Peachblow Ribbed Satin Finish, Decor. W/"World's Fair, 1893" In Gold $400.00*

AGATA VASE, Acid Finish W/Tri-Con Folded Top, 5" H. $950.00*

GALLE CAMEO VASE, Sgn., Lavender Flowers On Gold Ground, 5" H. .. $400.00*

WHEELING PEACHBLOW MILK PITCHER, Shiny Finish W/Amber Handle, Sm. Line In Inner Lining, 5" H. $325.00*

A-OH Oct 1980 *Early Auction Co.*
L To R
D.Q.M.O.P. WATER PITCHER, Pink Satin W/Coralene & Enamel Decor, Camphor Handle........................ $500.00*
RUBINA VERDE WATER PITCHER, Hobnail Patt., Matching Tumbler $165.00*

A-OH Oct 1980 *Early Auction Co.*
L To R
M.O.P. EWER, Glossy Herringbone W/ Clear Thorn Handle, 14" H. $160.00*
D.Q.M.O.P. EWER, Pink On Pedestal Base, Frosted Thorn Handle, Sm. Blister, 14" H. $90.00*

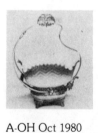

A-OH Oct 1980 *Early Auction Co.*
L To R
M.O.P. BRIDE'S BOWL, Red-To-Pink Herringbone, Satin In Silver Plated Holder, 10" H. $350.00*

ART GLASS VASE, Decor. W/Appl. Glass Flowers & Amber Leaves Which Form Handles, 1 Leaf Missing On Back, 10½" H. $850.00*

A-MA Nov 1980 *Robert W. Skinner Inc.*
L To R
CUT GLASS BOWL, Cut From Blue To Amber To Clear In Vintage Patt., Am., 19th C., 5" D., 2½" H. $525.00*

A-MA Jan 1981 *Robert W. Skinner Inc.*
TUTHILL GLASS TRAY, Sgn., NY, 20th C., Sl. Chips, 13½" L. $525.00*

A-OH Oct 1980   *Early Auction Co.*

ROW I, L To R

CAMEO VASE, Eng., Wh. Floral & Leaf Cutting On Red Ground, Sgn. R. G. Rowley No. 8, 12″ H. $2250.00*

CITRON CAMEO VASE, Eng., Sgn. Thomas Webb & Sons, Floral & Butterfly Decor., 7⅞″ H. $1350.00*

TABLE LAMP, Mkd. Duffner & Kimberly, Bronze Egyptian Base, Shade W/Egyptian Figure In Each Leaded Panel $5500.00*

CAMEO FINGER BOWL & UNDER- PLATE, Eng., 3-Color, Decor. W/Flowers & Butterfly, Sgn. Thomas Webb & Sons $3250.00*

GOLD VASE, Wh. Paperweight Flowers & intaglio Foliage, Wafer Pontil, Sgn. Louis C. Tiffany Furnaces, inc., L.C.T.-Favrile, 15½″ H. $2250.00*

ROW II, L To R

ROCKWOOD CHOCOLATE POT, Decor. W/Clover Blossoms & Bees, Artist: Carl Schmidt, Ca. 1900, 8½″ H. $1150.00*

WOODALL CAMEO VASE, 2 Handles & Pedestal Base, Overall Carving, Sgn. Thomas Webb & Sons, Gem Cameo, 16″ H. $52500.00*

WOODALL CAMEO VASE, Bottom Mkd. Loves Areo & Tiffany & Co.-Paris Exposition 1880 & Thomas Webb & Sons, S1. Nick, 7½″ H. $6500.00*

CAMEO VASE, Eng., Blue Floral Decor. W/2 Handles, Sgn. G. Woodall On Side, Bottom Sgn. Thomas Webb & Sons-Gem Cameo, Stamped Theodore B. Starr, NY, 11″ H. $11500.00*

CAMEO VASE, Eng. Raisin Colored W/2 Handles, Sgn. G. Woodall, Sgn. On Bottom Thomas Webb & Sons-Gem Cameo, 9″ H. $10500.00*

WHEELING PEACHBLOW WATER PIT- CHER, Acid Finish W/Sq. Top & Frosted Amber Handle, 8″ H. $1400.00*

ROW III, L To R

ROCKWOOD VASE, Scenic Vellum, Artist: E. T. Hurley, No Crazing, Ca. 1940, 8″ H. $2000.00*

ROCKWOOD BISQUE VASE, Ginger Clay, Fired Overglaze Gold, Artist: Albert R. Valentien, Ca. 1883, 9¼″ H. $1000.00*

FLOWER FORM VASE, Wh. Opalescent Ribbed Base W/Leaves Terminating At Wh. Top, Gold Liner, 14″ H. $1850.00*

ROOKWOOD VASE, Decor. W/Pr. Of Blue Jays On Crystalline Glaze, Artist: Ora King, Ca. 1949, 11½″ H. $1025.00*

ROOKWOOD VASE, Scenic Vellum, Artist: E. T. Hurley, No Crazing, Ca. 1931, 13½″ H. $1000.00*

ROOKWOOD VASE, Venetian Canal Scene On Iris Glaze, Artist: Carl Schmidt, Ca. 1923, 7¼″ H. $4000.00*

ROOKWOOD JUG, Standard Glaze W/ Wheat Decor., Artist: O. Geneva Reed, Ca. 1893, 6½″ H. $475.00*

PLAQUE, William E. Gladstone By George Wodall, Sgn. Thomas Webb & Sons-Gem Cameo, 2½″ H. $2500.00*

AMBERINA CREAM PITCHER, Plated, 4⅝″ W., 2⅝″ H. $2800.00*

AMBERINA SUGAR BOWL, Plated, 4″ W., 2″ H. $2750.00*

*Price does not include 10% buyer fee.

Left

A-WA D.C. Feb 1980   *Adam A. Weschler & Son*

TIFFANY FAVRILLE PAPERWEIGHT VASE, Glass, Daffodil, Sgn. L.C. Tiffany/ Favrille, 15″ H. $2100.00*

Right

A-MA Aug 1980   *Robert C. Eldred Co., Inc.*

TIFFANY FAVRILLE TRUMPET VASE, Mkd., 10″ H. $1300.00

Left

A-MA Jan 1981   *Robert W. Skinner Inc.*

CUT GLASS VASE, Am., Late 19th C., Hobstar, Cane & Crosshatch Cutting, 10″ H. $350.00*

STERLING OVERLAY VASE, Loetz- Type, Blue Irid. Glass W/Floral & Scroll Motif, Ca. 1900, 7″ H. $650.00*

Right

A-MA Nov 1980   *Robert W. Skinner Inc.*

TIFFANY PEPPER SHAKER, Early 20th C., NY, Gold Irid. W/Silver Top, Base Sgn. "L.C.T.-Favrille, 2¾″ H. $175.00*

A-MA Nov 1980   *Robert W. Skinner Inc.*

L To R

CUT GLASS CORDIAL BOTTLE, Pale Cranberry Cut To Clear, Europe, 20th C., Sterling Silver Collar, Neck Chipped, 10½″ H. $300.00*

CUT GLASS WATER PITCHER, Late 19th C., Am., Russian Patt., 6½″ H. $700.00*

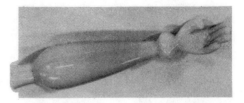

A-MA Mar 1980   *Robert W. Skinner Inc.*

BURMESE PERFUME BOTTLE, Rim Chip, N. Eng., Late 19th C., 6¾″ L. $450.00*

Left

A-MA Nov 1980   *Robert W. Skinner Inc.*

CUT GLASS COMPOTE, Opaque Wh. Cut To Emerald Gr., Polychrome Floral Decor., Europe, Late 19th C., 9¾″ D., 8″ H. $300.00*

Right

A-MA Jan 1981   *Robert W. Skinner Inc.*

CUT GLASS PUNCH BOWL, Am., Late 19th C., 2-Part W/Scalloped Sawtooth Rim Tulip Shaped Bowl On Knopped Standard, 14″ D., 14½″ H. $1000.00*

A-MA Nov 1980   *Robert W. Skinner Inc.*

Top To Bottom

HAWKES CUT GLASS FRUIT BOWL, Hobstar & Crosshatch Cutting, Corning, NY, Ca. 1900, 12″ D., 3¾″ H. $450.00*

CUT GLASS BOWLS, 2, Late 19th C. $375.00*

A-MA April l980   *Robert W. Skinner Inc.*

HISTORICAL FLASK, Eagle-Cornucopia, ½″ Pt., Pale Amethyst, Kensington Glass Works, PA, Ca. 1820-1840 ...... $3400.00*

301

B-63

B-63

408

B-62

B-62

350

200

234

480

401

272

272

282

421

B-61

B-61

B-60

B-60

388

440

199

323

398

497

399

◄ A-OH Oct 1980   *Early Auction Co.*
ROW I, L To R

MINI. LAMP, Rainbow Swirl Patt. W/Clear Appl. Leaf Feet $975.00*

MOCKINGBIRDS W/BINDWEED, Pr., By Edward Marshall Boehm W/Boehm Hallmark $2000.00*

SCARLET TANAGERS & WHITE OAK, Pr., By Dorothy Doughty $2000.00*

DAUM NANCY CAMEO NIGHT LIGHT, Sgn., Dome Shade Decor. W/Red Rose, Vines & Leaves, Matching Base W/3 Frosted Feet $1000.00*

AMBERINA PITCHER, Plated, 7″ H. $3500.00*

ROW II, L To R

SLAG COVERED BUTTER DISH, Pink W/Inverted Fan Patt. $600.00*

CROWN MILANO SWEET MEAT JAR, Sgn., Burmese W/Dainty Flowers, Silver Plated Lid Mkd. MW $700.00*

FINDLAY SPOONER, Red W/Wh. Flowers $450.00*

MT. WASHINGTON BURMESE CRUET, Ribbed Acid Finish..............$700.00*

AMBERINA WATER PITCHER & PUNCH CUPS, N. Eng., Inverted Thumbprint Patt. W/Etched Fern Decor.............$375.00*

MT. WASHINGTON PEACHBLOW FINGER BOWL, Acid Finish.........$900.00*

CORALENE VASE, Pink Satin W/Gold Washed Pedestal $500.00*

MT. WASHINGTON PEACHBLOW PITCHER, Acid Finish, 6″ H. $1900.00*

ROW III, L To R

YELLOW-HEADED BLACKBIRDS & SPIDERWORT, Pr., By Dorothy Doughty $2000.00*

CACTUS WRENS & PRICKLY PEAR, Pr., By Dorothy Doughty............$2500.00*

ROW IV, L To R

MILLEFIORI PLAQUE, Attrib. To Frederick Carder, 10¼″ H. $1100.00*

CROWN MILANO BRIDE'S BOWL, Mkd., Decor. In Gold Floral On Peach Ground, Silver Plated Holder, 13″ H. $1300.00*

SLAG WATER PITCHER, Pink W/Inverted Fan Patt. $1200.00*

CROWN MILANO VASE, Sgn. ..$900.00*

ROW V, L To R

CAMEO PLAQUE, Fr., Sgn. Jacques Gruber, 19¾″ x 5¼″ H. $700.00*

RAINBOW VASE, Sgn. Tartan, 6″ H. $375.00*

PASTEL TAZZA, Pink W/Decor. Bowl & Stretch Border, Sgn. L.C.T.-Favrile, 6¾″ H. $375.00*

PASTEL TAZZA, Gr. W/Leaf-Decor. Bowl & Stretch Border, Sgn. L.C.T.-Favrile, 6¼″ H. $325.00*

*Price does not include 10% buyer fee.

Left

A-MA Jan 1981   *Robert W. Skinner Inc.*
GOLD AURENE ATOMIZER, Corning, NY, Unsigned, Cabochon Amber Glass Finial, Ca. 1910, 9½″ H. $200.00*

Right

A-MA Nov 1980   *Robert W. Skinner Inc.*
CORALENE & RUBINA GLASS VASE, Am., Late 19th C., 7¾″ H. $200.00*

A-WA D.C. May 1980 *Adam A. Weschler & Son*
STEUBEN AURENE
ROW I
SHERBERTS, 3 Unsigned Steuben Aurene & Calcite, 3¾″ H. $150.00*
ROW II, L To R
FAN-SHAPED VASES, Pr., Inscribed, Early 20th C., 8¾″ H. $600.00*
VASE, Early 20th C., 8¼″ H. $400.00*

A-MA July 1980   *Robert W. Skinner, Inc.*
STEUBEN VASE, Floral Decor., Burst Bubble, NY, Ca. 1900, 7½″ H. ... $650.00*

A-OH Oct 1980   *Early Auction Co.*
STEUBEN A.C.B. VASE, Sgn., Ivory W/ Gazelles...................... $600.00*

Left

A-MA Mar 1980   *Robert W. Skinner Inc.*
DURAND GLASS VASE, Sapphire Blue, Irid. Feather Design, Unsigned, Am., Early 20th C., 12½″ H. $600.00*

Right

A-OH Oct 1980   *Early Auction Co.*
DECOR. VASE, Br., Sgn. L. C. Tiffany-Favrile, 19″ H. $3250.00*

A-OH Oct 1980   *Early Auction Co.*
L To R

PITCHER, Gr. Opaque Glass, Decor. W/ Indian Chief & Mallard Ducks, 7″ H. $625.00*

CASTER SET, Gr. Opaque, Silver Plated Holder, Mkd. Barbour Bros. Silver Co. $425.00*

A-MA Nov 1980   *Robert W. Skinner Inc.*
L To R

CASTOR SET, Am., Late 19th C., Papier Mache & Mother Of Pearl, Ormolu Handle W/Cut Glass Bottles, Missing Mustard Top $150.00*

NORTHWOOD CARNIVAL GLASS, Punch Bowl & 11 Cups, Purple Grape & Cable Patt., All Sgn., Ca. 1910, 10″ O.H. $400.00*

◄ A-OH Oct 1980   *Early Auction Co.*

ROW I, L To R
CORALENE VASE, Pink Satin W/Gold Washed Pedestal $500.00*
QUEZAL FOOTED VASE, Sgn., Burnt Orange Body W/Irid. Gold Feet, 10" H.
. . . . $675.00*
GALLE CAMEO VASE, Sgn., 4-Color, 11" H. $2100.00*
TIFFANY LILY TABLE LAMP, Gold Shades, Bronze Base Sgn. Tiffany Studios NY . . . . Passed
CAMEO VASE, Fr., 3-Color Acid Cut, Sgn. On Bottom Cristallene de Quinim, 14" H.
. . . . $800.00*
WEBB BURMESE EPERGNE, Acid Finish, Stem W/Swirled Ribbing, 9¼" H.
. . . . $350.00*
DURAND CAMEO VASE, Sgn. & Numbered, Cut W/Wh. Decor. Over Coral Ground, 10" H. $2000.00*

ROW II, L To R
D.Q.M.O.P. PITCHER, Rainbow W/Frosted Handle, 4¼" H. $400.00*
NORTHWOOD VASE, Mkd. Patent, 6" H.
. . . . $450.00*
MT. WASHINGTON BURMESE LILY VASE, 7" H. $225.00*
M.O.P. BASKET, Herringbone Rainbow Satin, Twisted Camphor Thorn Handle
. . . . $850.00*
ALEXANDRITE SHERBET & UNDERPLATE, 3" H. $575.00*
D.Q.M.O.P. VASE, Shiny Rainbow, 8" H.
. . . . $350.00*
ALEXANDRITE BUD VASE, 6" H.
. . . . $475.00*
BISCUIT JAR, Mkd. Smith Bros., Satin Melon Decor. W/Gold Flowers . . . $500.00*
D.Q.M.O.P. TUMBLER, Rainbow . . . .
. . . . $275.00*

ROW III, L To R
CAMEO VASE, Sgn. Thomas Webb & Sons, Blue, Eng., 9" H. $2700.00*
D.Q.M.O.P. VASE, Pink, Appl. Camphor Decor., 9¾" H. $350.00*
VASE, Sgn. Steuben Aurene, Gr. Decor., 9¾" H. $1050.00*
FLOWER FORM VASE, Sgn. Tiffany, Gr. Leaves On Wh. Opalescent Ground, 11½" H.
. . . . $1000.00*
D.Q.M.O.P. WATER PITCHER, Satin W/ Enamel Floral Decor., Reeded Camphor Handle, 9" H. $425.00*
D.Q.M.O.P. VASE, Silver Overlay, Blue Ground, Mkd. Sterling, 8¼" H. . . . $300.00*

ROW IV, L To R
M.O.P. PITCHER, Blue & Gold Decor. Herringbone Ribbed Satin, Lavender Liner, Frosted Handle, Mkd. In Red On Bottom
. . . . $750.00*
ROSE BOWL, Shiny Peachblow-Colored, Appl. Decor., Handles & Amber Feet
. . . . $350.00*
VASE, Gr. & Gold Lily Pad Decor., Gold Liner, Mkd. Kew Blas, 4½" H. $575.00*
STEUBEN CALCITE BASKET, Blue, 15" H. $1900.00*
ROSALINE COVERED JAR, Alabaster Base & Finial, 9½" H. $145.00*
D.Q.M.O.P. WEBB VASE, Satin W/2 Frosted Handles $400.00*
D.Q.M.O.P. CRUET, Blue W/Camphor Handle & Thorn Stopper $400.00*

ROW V, L To R
HOLLY AMBER PARFAIT $400.00*
HOLLY AMBER ROUND TRAY, 9¼" D.
. . . . $450.00*
HOLLY AMBER COVERED BUTTER DISH. $850.00*
SQ. HOLLY AMBER PLATE, 7½" D.
. . . . $400.00*
HOLLY AMBER CREAMER, 4½" H.
. . . . $250.00*

Left
A-OH Oct 1980   *Early Auction Co.*
L To R
IMPERIAL VASE, Orange Background Decor. W/Lily Pads, Orig. Label, 6½" H.
. . . . $200.00*

DURAND FOOTED VASE, Butterscotch Ground W/Gr. Lily Pad Decor., Sgn., 12" H.
. . . . $525.00*

Right
A-MA Nov 1980   *Robert W. Skinner Inc.*
FINDLAY ONYX COVERED SUGAR BOWL, Opalescent In Floral Patt., Minor Chips, Ca. 1890, 5¾" H. $175.00*

A-MA Nov 1980   *Robert W. Skinner Inc.*
AGATA WATER PITCHER & TUMBLERS, N. Eng., Appl. Handle, Ca. 1890
. . . . $700.00*

A-OH Oct 1980   *Early Auction Co.*
L To R
CAMEO VASE, Fr., Red Poppy & Blk. Leaf Decor. On Lt. Ground, Sgn. Muller, Luneville, 5⅞" H. $900.00*
DAUM NANCY COVERED BOX, Sgn., Pink Roses & Gr. Leaves On Lt. Ground, 5" L., 2½" H. $575.00*
CAMEO VASE, Fr., Decor. W/Burgundy Trumpet Flowers & Vines, Sgn. D'Argental W/Cross Of Lorraine, 14" H. $650.00*
CAMEO VASE, Fr., Decor. W/Trees In Shades Of Br. & Gr. On Lt. Pink Ground, Sgn. Galle' W/Star, 9¾" H. $800.00*

A-MA April 1980   *Richard A. Bourne Co., Inc.*
L To R
LOETZ-TYPE ART GLASS VASE, Austrian, Irid. Gold & Gr. Lily Pads W/Sterling Silver Overlay, 5½" H. $500.00
CAMEO GLASS VASE By Legras, Mulberry-Colored Prunus Blossoms On Shaded & Frosted Ground, 8" H. $350.00

Left
A-MA Nov 1980   *Robert W. Skinner Inc.*
CAMEO GLASS VASE, Europe, 20th C., Purple Cut To Amber W/Irid. Textured Ground, Highlighted In Gold, Illegibly Sgn., 6" H. $80.00*

Right
A-MA Jan 1981   *Robert W. Skinner Inc.*
EPERGNE, Am., Late 19th C., 3-Branch W/Cranberry To Clear Glass, 20½" H.
. . . . $175.00*

*Price does not include 10% buyer fee.

A-MA April 1980   *Richard A. Bourne Co., Inc.*
ROW I, L To R
ART NOUVEAU VASE, Austrian, Irid. Blue W/Silver Overlay, Sgn. In Pontil "Mercur/721/A", 7¼" H. $500.00
CUT GLASS MAYONNAISE DISH, Swag & Draper Style Cutting, Rim Roughage & Sm. Chips, 6¼" D. ... $30.00
ROW II, L To R
CUT GLASS QT. DECANTER W/Stopper, Sm. Flakes & Chips, W/ Chemical Deposits $225.00
CUT GLASS DECANTER, Lrg. Hobstar Cutting, W/Chemical Deposit, 10" O.H. $130.00

A-MA Aug 1980   *Robert C. Eldred Co., Inc.*
CUT GLASS PUNCH BOWL, Sunburst Design, 13½" D. $525.00

A-MA April 1980   *Richard A. Bourne Co., Inc.*
CUT GLASS
ROW I, L To R
SM. BOWL, Rim Chips, Lt. Roughage, 7" D. $40.00
LRG. BOWL, Deeply Cut, Minimal Rim Roughage, 8" D. $70.00
ROW II, L To R
TAZZA, Floral Cutting W/ Pressed Leaves, 6⅛" D., 5¼" H. $45.00
SHALLOW BOWL, Minimal Rim Roughage, 8¾" D. $80.00

A-MA April 1980   *Richard A. Bourne Co., Inc.*
HEAVY CUT GLASS
ROW I
TUMBLERS, Lot Of 6, Set Of 5 By J. Hoare & Co., Sgn., 2 W/Rim Chips, Non-Matching Tumbler W/Chips $90.00
ROW II, L To R
TEAPOT, Sinclair, Corning, NY, Sgn. Under Base Of Handle, Cover Missing, Spout Has Chips, 5¾" D. $210.00
PUNCH BOWL, Separate Base, Sm. Chips, Roughages, 10" D., 9¾" H. .. $325.00
DECANTER W/Stopper, Sl. Film Of Chemical Deposits On Inside, 15" O.H. $425.00

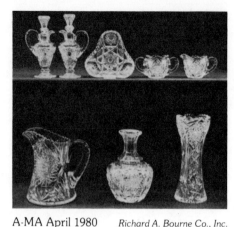

A-MA April 1980   *Richard A. Bourne Co., Inc.*
CUT GLASS
ROW I, L To R
CRUETS, Pr., Orig, Matching Stoppers, Sl. Roughage On Lip Of 1 ...... $400.00
TRIANGULAR DISH, Sl, Rim Nicks & Roughage, 6½" W., 6½" L......... $30.00
SUGAR & CREAMER, Sl. Roughage On Both $45.00
ROW II, L To R
WATER PITCHER, Hobstar Cutting, 8½" H $150.00
CARAFE, Hobstar & Other Cutting, 8¼" H $125.00
VASE Chips & Sl. Roughage, 10" H. $40.00

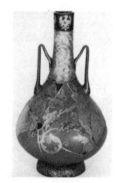

Left
A-WA D.C. Feb 1980   *Adam A. Weschler & Son*
CUT GLASS DECANTER, Ruby To Clear, Silver Mounted, Am., 20th C., 11" H. $2700.00*

Right
A-MA Mar 1980   *Robert W. Skinner Inc.*
ROYAL FLEMISH VASE, Body Decor. In Stained Glass Effect & Highlighted W/Gold Enamel, N. Eng., Late 19th C., 13½" H. $2550.00*

◄ A-WA D.C. May 1980 *Adam A. Weschler & Son*
TIFFANY FAVRILE GLASS COMPOTE, Inscribed L.C.T. Favrile Gr. Bowl W/Opaque Glass Stem, 5½" D., 4¾" H. $425.00*

CUT GLASS TALL VASE, Amethyst To Clear Cut, Carlsbad, 20th C., Lobed Int., 13½" H. $75.00*

STEUBEN FOOTED BOWL, Calcite Glass, Lacy Rim, Early 20th C., 14" L., 6½" H. $200.00*

A-MA July 1980   *Robert W. Skinner Inc.*
SUGAR & CREAMER, Foot Cut Glass W/Hobstar & Cornucopia Cutting, Am., Late 19th C., 3½" H. $300.00*

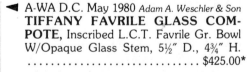

A-WA D.C. Dec 1980 *Adam A. Weschler & Son*
EUROPEAN CUT GLASS
ROW I, L To R
FOOTED COMPOTE, Early 20th C., Irish, Diamond & Pineapple Plume Patt. . . . $120.00*
CANDLESTICKS, Pr., Diamond Patt., Irish, 20th C., 14" H. $450.00*
COVERED JARS, Pr., Early 20th C., Irish, 11½" H. $225.00*
ROW II, L To R
DECANTERS, Pr., Pineapple Plume W/ Arched Diamond Panels, Early 20th C., Irish, 10½" H. $200.00*
BOWL, Pineapple Plume Rim Above Diamond Body, Early 20th C., Irish, 13" D. $125.00*
VASES, Set Of 3, (1 Illus.), Early 20th C., Irish $75.00*

A-MA July 1980 *Robert W. Skinner Inc.*
GLASS COLOGNE BOTTLES, Ruby W/Overall Gilt Decor. & Applied Medallion, Europe, Late 19th C., 11½" H. $525.00*

A-MA Aug 1980 *Robert C. Eldred Co., Inc.*
ST. LOUIS CUT GLASS SEALS, 2, 4⅛" H. $275.00
ST. LOUIS CUT GLASS PENHOLDER, Paperweight Base, 5⅛" H. $275.00

*Price does not include 10% buyer fee.

Left
A-MA April 1980 *Richard A. Bourne Co., Inc.*
CAMEO GLASS STICK VASE, Attrib. To Webb, Raspberry-Red Frosted Ground, 9¼" H. $2000.00
Right
A-MA Aug 1980 *Robert C. Eldred Co., Inc.*
GALLE CAMEO GLASS VASE, Yellowish Br. & Clambroth W/Pine Cone Decor., Sgn., 13" H. $625.00

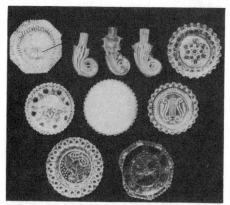

A-OH July 1980 *Garth's Auctions, Inc.*
ROW I, L To R
CLEAR LACY CUP PLATE, Edge Chips, 3½" D. $30.00
CLEAR BLOWN SCENT W/Wh. Loops & Applied Rigaree, 2⅞" L. . . $65.00
CLEAR BLOWN SCENT W/Swirled Ribs & Applied Regaree, Rim Flake, 3" L. $75.00
CLEAR BLOWN SCENT W/Wh. Loops & Applied Rigaree, 3" L. $95.00
CLEAR LACY CUP PLATE, 3 7/16" D. $35.00
ROW II, L To R
CLEAR LACY CUP PLATES, Set of 3 . . . . $115.00
OPALESCENT LACY CUP PLATE, 3½" D. $65.00
CLEAR LACY CUP PLATES, Set of 3, Rim Chips $55.00
ROW III, L To R
CLEAR LACY CUP PLATE, Eagle & "Fort Patt.", Rim Uneven, 3 11/16" D. $45.00
CLEAR LACY CUP PLATE, Side Wheeler & "Union Glass Works, Pittsburgh 1831", Lrg. Pc. Broken From Rim, 3½" D. $100.00

A-WA D.C. May 1980 *Adam A. Weschler & Son*
L To R
GALLE CAMEO GLASS VASE, Sgn., Early 20th C., Rose-Gr. Ground Cut W/Rose-Amber Flowers, 6¼" H. . . $450.00
CAMEO GLASS VASE, Sgn., Early 20th C., Pink Ground W/Floral & Leaf In Purple-Amethyst, 8" H. $475.00
GALLE CAMEO GLASS VASE, Sgn., Purple Cut To Frosted, Berry & Leaf Decor., 3½"H. $200.00
DE VEZ CAMEO GLASS LAMP BASE, Sgn., Early 20th C., Yellow-Orange Ground W/Forest Scene, Raised On Footed Bronze Base, 11" O.H. $650.00
GALLE CAMEO GLASS VASE, Sgn., Early 20th C., Pink Ground W/Berry, Leaf & Vine Decor., 13" H. $850.00
GALLE CAMEO GLASS BUD VASE, Sgn., Early 20th C., Opaque & Amethyst Ground Cut To Floral & Vine In Purple, 3½" H. $225.00
CAMEO GLASS SCENT BOTTLE, Early 20th C., Cranberry Ground W/Wh. Latticework Overlaid In Opaque Wh., Repl. Faceted Stopper, 7¼" O.H. $400.00

Left
A-WA D.C. May 1980 *Adam A. Weschler & Son*
GALLE CAMEO GLASS VASE, Sgn., Ca. 1900, 18¼" H. $1050.00*

Right
A-MA July 1980 *Robert W. Skinner Inc.*
DAUM NANCY VASE, Mottled Glass, Inscribed, Fr., Early 20th C., 31" H. $400.00*

A-MA April 1980   *Richard A. Bourne Co., Inc.*
L To R
CAMEO GLASS LAMP GLOBE, Scene Of Deer In Forest, Ruby On Frosted Wh., Sm. Chip, 9½" D., 10" H. $250.00
CAMEO GLASS LAMP, Sgn. By Emile Galle, Gr. Leaves On Amber & Frosted Ground, 29" O.H. $500.00
LIBBY CUT GLASS VASE, Sgn. In Pontil, Panels Of Tulips, 13¾" H. $100.00

A-MA April 1980   *Richard A. Bourne Co., Inc.*
SYRUP JUGS
ROW I, L To R
MILK GLASS, Raised Floral Patt. .. $70.00
MILK GLASS, Waffle-Like Swirls & Raised Flowers.................. $110.00
MILK GLASS, Melon-Ribbed W/Floral Decor., Spring-Hinged Brass Lid... $50.00
MILK GLASS, Net-Like Panels W/Raised Oak Leaves $40.00
ROW II, L To R
MILK GLASS, Decor. W/Violets .. $75.00
MILK GLASS, Decor. W/Fruit, Pewter Handle & Spring-Hinged Top $85.00
HEAVY MILK GLASS, Attrib. To Boston & Sandwich Glass Co., Decor. Of Heron Midst Cat-O-Nine-Tails $130.00
MILK GLASS, Pear-Shaped, Decor. W/Flowers, Pewter Handle & Spring Hinged Top..................... $50.00
ROW III, L To R
MILK GLASS, Acorn Shaped, Decor. W/Flowers $45.00
FLUTED MILK GLASS, Floral Decor., Handle Check $45.00
MILK GLASS. Raised Coral-Like Design, Decor, W/Flowers, Molded-In Handle $65.00
GLOBULAR MILK GLASS, Decor. W/Blue Cornflowers, Finish Worn Off Top $35.00

A-OH June 1980   *Garth's Auctions, Inc.*
ROW I, L To R
CLEAR FLINT DECANTER W/Diamond Point Stopper, Horn Of Plenty Patt., Base Of Stopper Chipped, 8¾" O.H. ... $70.00
CLEAR LACY BOWL, Feather Patt. W/ Quatrefoil Center, Rim Flake, 9½" D. $45.00
CLEAR FLINT LAMP, Star & Punty Patt., Hexagonal Base, Brass Collar, Minor Flake On Foot, 11¼" H. $115.00
ROW II, L To R
CLEAR LACY BOWL, Peacock Eye Patt., Rim Flake, 7½" H. $30.00
CLEAR LACY OBLONG BOWL, Minor Flakes, 10½" L. $85.00
CLEAR LACY BOWL, Peacock Eye Patt. W/Rayed Center, Minor Flakes, 7½" D. $65.00

A-WA D.C. Feb 1980   *Adam A. Weschler & Son*
AMERICAN CUT GLASS
CANDELABRA, Pr., 2-Light, T.G. Hawkes & Co., NY, Early 20th C., 10" H. .. $270.00*
PUNCH BOWL ON STAND, Early 20th C., Wheat & Chrysanthemum Patt., 12" D., 11½" H. $425.00*
FOOTED CREAMER & SUGAR, Early 20th C., Roosevelt Patt. $125.00*
TUMBLERS, Set Of 8, (2 Illus.), T.B. Clark & Co., PA, 20th C., Roosevelt Patt., 3¾" H. $325.00*
ICE TUB, Sterling Mounted, Wilcox, Alhambra Patt., 6" D., 5¼" H. $120.00*
CREAMER & SUGAR, Early 20th C., Chrysanthemum & Diamond Patt., 4½" H. $150.00*
CREAMER & SUGAR, Early 20th C., Comb. Patt., 3½" H. $100.00*

A-MA April l980   *Richard A. Bourne Co., Inc.*
SYRUP JUGS
ROW I, L To R
MILK GLASS, Ribbed W/Raised Panels Of Beehive & Tropical Landscape, Pewter Top $110.00
MILK GLASS, "Peace & Plenty" Patt., Pewter Top $130.00
OPALESCENT, Attrib. To Boston & Sandwich Glass Co., Panel Decor., Tin Top $160.00
FLUTED MILK GLASS, ... $40.00
ROW II, L To R
MILK GLASS, Thistle Patt., Pewter Top, Thumb-Tab Broken Off Top $90.00
MILK GLASS, Rosette In Bottom, Pewter Top $45.00
MILK GLASS, Acorn & Bluebell Patt., Tin Top, Damaged $20.00
MILK GLASS, 2-Panel Raised Decor., Pewter Top.................... $160.00
ROW III, L To R
MILK GLASS, Palmette Patt., Pewter Top $90.00
MILK GLASS, Cable Patt., ... $50.00
MILK GLASS, Acanthus-Like Patt., Pewter Top......................... $130.00
MILK GLASS, Strawberry Patt., In Deep Relief $100.00

Left

A-MA Mar 1980   *Robert W. Skinner Inc.*
QUEZAL ROSE BOWL, Gold Irid. Rim & Pull Up Decor. Over Gr. Feather Motif On Alabaster Glass, Int. Gold Irid., Base Engraved NY, Late 19th C., 3¾" H. $1200.00*

Right

A-MA Aug 1980   *Robert C. Eldred Co., Inc.*
ART GLASS BOWL, Decorative Metal Stand, 19th C., 10" W., 16" L., 10" H. $475.00

A-MA July 1980   *Robert W. Skinner Inc.*
CAMEO GLASS PERFUME, 2-Color, Gilt Metal Covered Rim. Eng., Early 20th C., 5¼" H $1450.00*

A-OH July 1980   *Garth's Auctions, Inc.*
ROW I, L To R
CLEAR BLOWN CANDLESTICKS, Pr., Applied Domed Foot, Applied Socket, 12½" H. $950.00
CLEAR BLOWN VASES, Pr., Opalescent Loops & Matching Witch Balls, Pittsburgh, Shallow Broken Blister, 7¾" H. . . $750.00
CLEAR FLINT COMPOTE, Diamond Block & Thumbprint, Minor Roughness, 8¼" D., 6½" H. $65.00
ROW II, L To R
CLEAR BLOWN COMPOTE, Pittsburgh, 8½" D., 9¼" H. $300.00
CLEAR GLASS COVERED COMPOTE, Westword-Ho Patt., Sm. Bruise On Edge, 11¾" H. $205.00

A-OH Mar 1980   *Garth's Auctions, Inc.*
BOTTLES & PLATES
ROW I, L To R
SCENT, Cobalt Blue W/Swirled Ribs, 3⅛" L. $60.00
SCENT, Cobalt Blue W/Verticle Ribs, 2¾" L. $45.00
SCENT, Drk. Amethyst W/Thread Brass Cap, 2½" L. $40.00
SCENT, Amethyst W/Threaded Pewter Cap, 2½" L. $50.00
SCENT, Cobalt Blue W/Threaded Pewter Cap, 2¾" L. $45.00
SCENT, Sapphire Blue W/Swirled Ribs, 2¾" L. $60.00
SCENT, Cobalt Blue W/Swirled Ribs & Wide Mouth, 3" L. $45.00
ROW II, L To R
CUP PLATE, Opalescent W/Star Flower Border, Minor Rim Roughness, 3" D. $47.50
BLOWN BULLSEYE, Amber W/Folded Rim, 4" D. $30.00
CUP PLATE, Sapphire Blue W/Star Center, Minor Rim Flakes, 3" D. $90.00
ROW III, L To R
SCENT, Cobalt Blue W/Swirled Ribs, 2⅞" L. $80.00
SCENT, Violet Cobalt Blue W/Verticle Ribs, Minor Rim Flakes, 3" L. $25.00
SCENT, Amethyst W/Threaded Pewter Cap, 2½" L. $40.00
SCENT, Cobalt Blue W/Threaded Pewter Cap, 3¼" L. $20.00
SCENT, Cobalt Blue W/Threaded Lip, Cap Missing, 2½" L. $9.00
SCENT, Violet Blue W/Verticle Ribs, 2⅞" L. $65.00
SCENT, Amethyst W/Threaded Lip, Cap Missing, 2 1/3" L. $5.00

A-OH May 1980   *Garth's Auctions, Inc.*
ROW I, L To R
ENAMELED GLASS VASES, Pr., Silver Plated Bases, Rim Chip & Hairline, 7⅛" H. $90.00
FOOTED TUMBLERS, Set Of 9, (1 Illus.), Blown Gr. W/Polychrome Enameled Decor., 4½" H. $54.00
FOOTED TUMBLERS, Set Of 12, (1 Illus.), Matches Above, 1 W/Rim Flake, 7" H. $72.00
TUMBLERS, Set Of 7, (1 Illus.), Matches Above, 3¾" H. $50.00
ROW II, L To R
D.Q.M.O.P. TUMBLER, Shades From Blue To White, 3⅞" H. $30.00
DRESDEN BASKETS, 4, (1 Illus.), Porcelain W/Applied Flowers, Minor Chips & Repaired Arms, 3½" H. $64.00
SILVER JIGGERS, Pr., Glued Steel Inlay, Persian, 2¼" H. $30.00
CARVED JADE MEDALLION, Wooden Frame, 4" H. $80.00
BOHEMIAN VASE, Ruby Flashed W/Wh. & Gilt Enameling, German, 4½" H. . . $20.00
ROW III, L To R
TUMBLER, Pale Blue W/Gold Enameling, 3⅞" H. $20.00
TUMBLER, Clear W/Gold Enameled Spirals, 4" H. $15.00
TUMBLER, Cranberry W/Gold, Silver, Blue & Wh. Enameling, 4" H. $62.50
TUMBLER, Cranberry W/Gold, Pink & Blue Enameling, 4⅛" H. $90.00
TUMBLER, Clear W/Gold & Silver Enameling, 4¼" H. $25.00

Left
A-WA D.C. Feb 1980 *Adam A. Weschler & Son*
GALLE CAMEO GLASS LANDSCAPE VASE, Sgn., Ca. 1900, 10" H. . . $1000.00*

Right
A-MA July 1980   *Robert W. Skinner Inc.*
BLUE AURENE DECORATED VASE, Sgn., Steuben Glass Works, NY, Ca. 1905 . . . . $1700.00*

A-MA July 1980   *Robert W. Skinner Inc.*
OVERLAY GLASS, Red & Wh., Pr. Of Lustres, 3 Vases, All W/Gilt Decor., Some Chips Late 19th C., Approx. 11" H. . . $700.00*

*Price does not include 10% buyer fee.

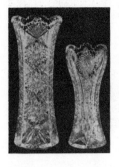

A-MA Aug 1980   *Robert C. Eldred Co., Inc.*
ROW I, L To R
SANDWICH PAPERWEIGHT, Blue Poinsettia W/Purple Stripes On Petals, Red & Wh. Floret At Center, 3″ D. $450.00
NEW ENG. PAPERWEIGHT, Pear, Shading From Yellow To Deep Pink, Clear Cushion, 2⅝″ D. $800.00
ROW II, L To R
ST. LOUIS PAPERWEIGHT, Sulphide Portrait Of Q. Elizabeth II, Turquoise Cushion, Etched On Base "Couronement 2-6-53, St. Louis, Fr.", 2⅞″ D. $80.00
ST. LOUIS PAPERWEIGHT, Mabrie Swirl In Blue-Wh.-Gr., "SL 1971", 3¼″ D. ..$160.00

A-OH July 1980   *Garth's Auctions, Inc.*
ROW I, L To R
WHEELING VASES, Pr., Wh. Cased W/Shaded Peachblow Int., Amber Applied Rim, Hairline Check On Side, 11½″ H. .. $170.00
OPALESCENT BLOWN VASES, Pr., Opaque Wh. Witch Balls, Pittsburgh, 7¼″ & 7½″ H. $400.00
OVERLAY LAMP, Blk. Pressed Base & Opaque Wh. Cut To Clear & Frosted Font, Stem & Collar Are Brass W/Worn Gilding, Sev. Flat Ground Spots On Base, 8¾″ H.
.... $125.00
ROW II, L To R
PITTSBURGH COMPOTE, Bowl & Lid Are Opalescent, Applied Baluster Stem & Foot Are Opaque Wh., Minor Rim Flakes, 8½″ H. $350.00
CLEAR COLOGNE, Swirled W/Mary Gregory Wh. Enameling, Stopper Missing, 4¾″ H. $95.00
WHEELING VASE, Wh. Cased W/Shaded Peachblow Int., Applied Amber Rim, Minor Chips, 9⅞″ H. $85.00
ROSE BOWLS, Pr., Cased Satin Peachblow, 1 Illus., 5⅜″ H. $55.00
ROW III, L To R
HAND LAMP, Opaque Wh., Brass Collar, 3¾″ H. $145.00
COMPOTE, Opaque Wh., 3¼″ D., 8″ H.
.... $35.00
HOBNAIL BOWL, Opalescent, 5″ D.
.... $35.00

Left
A-WA D.C. Oct 1980   *Adam A. Weschler & Son*
L To R
CUT GLASS TALL VASE, Am., Stenciled Libbey, Hobstar, Diamond, Pineapple Leaf Patt., Early 20th C., 15¾″ H.
.... $225.00*
CUT GLASS VASE, Am., Hobstar Patt., Early 20th C., 12″ H. $150.00*

Right
A-MA Mar 1980   *Robert W. Skinner Inc.*
RED LALIQUE VASE, Brambles Patt., Sgn. In Block Letters On Base & Script On Side, Drilled For Lamp, France, 20th C., 9½″ H. $375.00

A-MA April 1980   *Robert W. Skinner Inc.*
FLATTENED POISON FLASK, ½ Pt., Cobalt Bl., 19th C. $220.00*

Left
A-WA D.C. May 1980 *Adam A. Weschler & Son*
STEUBEN BOWL ON STAND, Clear Cut Glass, Early 20th C., Incised Sidney Waugh, Separate Base, 6½″ D., 7″ H.
.... $1500.00*
Right
A-WA D.C. Oct 1980 *Adam A. Weschler & Son*
STEUBEN FOOTED VASE, Calcite & Blue Irid., Orig. Paper Label, 10″ D., 7½″ H.
.... $400.00*

A-MA April 1980   *Robert W. Skinner, Inc.*
L To R
CONCENTRIC RING FLASK, Pt., Lt. Yellow Gr., New Eng. Glass Co., MA, Ca. 1815-1825 .... $4800.00*
SWIRLED GLOBULAR BOTTLE, Qt., Citron, Body Bubble Burst, Midwestern, Ca. 1815-1830 .... $425.00*

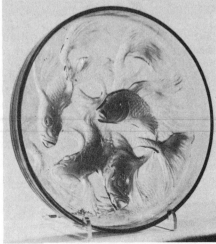

A-MA April 1980   *Richard A. Bourne Co., Inc.*
LALIQUE CANDY BOX, Sgn., Fabric-Covered Pasteboard Bottom W/Opalescent-Amber Cover, 10⅛″ D. $1700.00

Left
A-MA Aug 1980   *Robert C. Eldred Co., Inc.*
DAUM NANCY CAMEO GLASS VASE, Frost Lavender & Gr. W/ Blk.-Gray Trees, 4¾″ H. $800.00

Right
A-MA Mar 1980   *Robert W. Skinner Inc.*
WEBB LAMP BASE, Cameo Cut, Brass Collar Stamped "Messenger's Patent", Base Etched W/Webb Circular Trademark, England, Late 19th C., 7¼″ D., 4¾″ H. ...$750.00

A-OH April 1980   *Garth's Auctions, Inc.*

ROW I, L To R

PAPERWEIGHT, Blown Glass Fruit On Clear Base, Yellow To Peach Shading, Sm. Broken Blister & Stem Rough, 3½″ D. $400.00

JIGGER, Clear Blown W/Jumbled Candy Base, Rim Flake, 2¼″ H. $75.00

PAPERWEIGHT, Blown Fruit On Clear Base, Yellow To Pink Shading, 3½″ D. $400.00

ROW II, L To R

PAPERWEIGHT, Pink & Gr. Rose On Wh. Ground, 2⅝″ D. $375.00

PAPERWEIGHT, Cranberry Cut To Wh. To Clear W/Sulphide Of John Kennedy On Cobalt Ground, "Baccarat", 3⅛″ D. $105.00

PAPERWEIGHT, Wh. Cut To Clear W/Sulphide Of John Kennedy On Cobalt Ground, "Baccarat", 3⅛″ D. $105.00

PAPERWEIGHT, Red & Gr. Poinsettia On Wh. Latticinio Ground, 3″ D. .. $400.00

ROW III, L To R

PAPERWEIGHT, Violet In Gr., Yellow & Purple, Sm. Surface Bruise, 3″ D. $375.00

PAPERWEIGHT, 6 Animal Canes Surrounded By Gr. Canes On Field Of Red Canes, Minor Surface Wear, 2⅝″ D. $325.00

PAPERWEIGHT, Blue & Gr. Flower, 2¾″ D. $375.00

A-MA Aug 1980   *Robert C. Eldred Co., Inc.*
BACCARAT PAPERWEIGHTS

ROW I, L To R

ABRAHAM LINCOLN, Aubergine & Wh. Double Overlay, Clear Cushion, Sulphide Portrait, "G.P. 1953" On Cameo, Etched On Beveled Edge "Baccarat 1954", 3⅛″ D. $300.00

THEODORE ROOSEVELT, Opaque Wh. Overlay, Sulphide Portrait, Flashed Gr. Cushion, Etched Baccarat Mark On Underside, Limited Edition, 3⅛″ D. $275.00

ROW II

DWIGHT D. EISENHOWER, Sulphide Portrait, Clear Cushion, Etched On Beveled Edge "Baccarat 1953", 2¾″ D. ... $125.00

A-WA D.C. May 1980 *Adam A. Weschler & Son*
L To R

LILY, Clear W/Tiered Bouquet, 2¾″ D. $50.00*

LILY, Clear W/Multicolored Flowers, 3″ D. $50.00*

CANDY CANE & LACY, Clear W/Red-Wh.-Blue, 2¾″ D. $65.00*

A-MA Aug 1980   *Robert C. Eldred Co., Inc.*
PAPERWEIGHTS

ROW I, L To R

PAUL YSART, Dragonfly W/Blue Body, Goldstone Wings, Red Eyes, Jasper Ground, Sgn., 2⅞″ D. $400.00

SAINT LOUIS, Overlay Wh. Cut To Clear Faceted Windows, Sgn. & Dated 1970, 3″ D. $250.00

ROW II, L To R

BACCARAT, Butterfly Over Wh. Clematis, Star Cut Base, 2¾″ D. $2500.00

KAZIUN, Double Overlay W/Blue Cut To Wh. Cut To Clear Windows Displaying Yellow Rose, Sgn., 2⅜″ D. $3000.00

ROW III, L To R

BACCARAT, Rose & Wh. Double Overlay W/Sulphide Portraits, "G. Pouillett" On Cameo, Cross Cut Base, Etched On Beveled Edge "Baccarat 1953", 3″ D. $225.00

BACCARAT, Spaced Millefiori, Lrg. Floret, Silhouette Canes, Sgn. & Dated "B 1847", 3¼″ D. $1200.00

A-WA D.C. May 1980 *Adam A. Weschler & Son*

BACCARAT PAPERWEIGHTS

ROW I, L To R

LILY, Clear W/Multi. Flowers & Pebble Base, 3¼″ D. $35.00*

BOUQUET, Clear W/Mauve To Wh. Petals, 2″ D. $50.00*

LILY, Clear W/Wh. To Gr. Petals, Inscribed M49 On Base, 3″ D. $50.00*

ROW II, L To R

FLOWERS, 2, Pansy & Floating Bouquet, Clear Glass Set, 2¼″ D., 1¾″ D. $75.00*

FACETED SULPHIDE, Clear W/Seven Windows, ¾ Portrait Of Martin Luther, Sgn. Luther 1485-1546-G.P. 1955, Stenciled B. 1957, 2½″ D. $40.00*

SULPHIDE, Clear Domed W/Double Portrait Of Queen Elizabeth & Prince Phillip, Sgn. G. Poillerat, Stenciled Baccarat 1953 .... $60.00*

ROW III, L To R

FACETED SULPHIDE, Clear Glass W/ J. Kennedy, Cobalt Blue Base, Sgn. A. David 63, Stenciled Baccarat, 2¾″ D. ... $100.00*

FACETED SULPHIDE, Clear W/7 Windows-Marquis De LaFayette, Cobalt Blue Ground, Sgn. B.G.P. 1955, 2¾″ D. .. $60.00*

FACETED SULPHIDE, Ruby Double Overlay, 6 Windows-Gen. Eisenhower, Diamond Cut Base, Dated B1954, 3¼″ D. .. $100.00*

ROW IV, L To R

FACETED SULPHIDE, Clear W/7 Windows-Abraham Lincoln, Amethyst Ground, Sgn. G.P. 1953, Stenciled Baccarat 1954, 2¾″ D. $50.00*

FACETED SULPHIDE, Clear W/7 Windows-Thomas Jefferson, Clear Diamond Cut Base, Sgn. G.P. 1953, Stenciled B1954, 2¾″ D. $60.00*

FACETED SULPHIDE, Clear W/ 7 Windows-Gen. Eisenhower, Clear Diamond Cut Base, Stenciled B1954, 2¾″ D. $90.00*

*Price does not include 10% buyer fee.

A-OH Mar 1980   *Garth's Auctions, Inc.*
ROW I, L To R
LACY SALT, Canary W/Rim Flakes, 3" H.
.... $150.00
FOOTED TUMBLER, Fiery Opalescent,
Colonial Patt., Flake At Open Bubble On
Foot, 3¾" H. $155.00
TOILET WATER BOTTLE, Sapphire
Blue, Blown 3-Mold, Rim Chipped & Broken
Blister Near Base, 5½" H. $47.50
BLOWN CREAMER, Deep Cobalt Blue,
W/Applied Handle & Foot, 12 Ribs, Check
At Base Of Handle & Tiny Rim Flake, 4" H.
.... $55.00
PRESSED TUMBLER, Cobalt Blue, 9
Panels, Flake On Base, 3¼" H. $10.00
ROW II, L To R
PRESSED CASTER SET, Blue, Daisy &
Button W/3 Jars, Pewter Caps, 7" H. ....
.... $55.00
BLOWN INK, 3-Mold, Olive Amber, 2¾"
D. $80.00
PITTSBURGH SUGAR BOWL, Cobalt
Blue, Flint Paneled, No Lid, Sm. Rim Flakes,
5¾" H. $45.00
INK, Oliver Amber, 2¼" H. $45.00
PRESSED FLINT GOBLET, Cobalt
Blue, Flute Patt., 6" H. $55.00
ROW III, L To R
PITTSBURGH COLOGNE BOTTLE,
Deep Amethyst, 8 Panels & Applied Lip,
6¼" H. $155.00
BLOWN SADDLE FLASK, Amber
W/Applied Handle, 9" H. $20.00
PINT FLASK, Olive Amber, Double Eagle
W/"Pittsburgh PA" On 1 Side, 7¼" H.
.... $75.00

A-NY May 1980   *Calkins Auction Gallery*
L To R
BOTTLES, 2, 19th C., Sm. Sq. Olive Gr.
Bottle W/Pontil Mark & Drk. Amber Bottle
"Warner's Safe Kidney & Liver Cure, Ro-
chester, NY, 5" H., 9¾" H. $20.00
BOTTLES, 2 Drk. Gr. Embossed "Clarke
& White, NY", Lrg. Chip From Top Of
Neck, & Free Blown Drk. Amber Chestnut
Shaped Bottle W/Applied Handle, 9½" H.,
7" H. $20.00
HISTORICAL FLASK, 1 Qt., Cobalt Blue,
By Dyottville Glass Works, Philada., Pontil
Mark, 8" H. $50.00
FLASK & BOTTLE, 19th C., 8¾" H., 8¼" H.
.... $10.00
BOTTLES, 2, 19th C., Olive Gr. Gin Bottle
& Drk. Amber Bottle In Shape Of Fish, 10½"
H., 6¼" H. $20.00

A-NY May 1980   *Calkins Auction Gallery*
L To R
MEDICINE BOTTLES, 2, Late 19th C.,
1st In Row "The Great Dr. Kilmer's Swamp
Root Kidney, Liver & Bladder Remedy",
Last In Row "Healey & Bigelow Indian
Sagwa", 8¼" H., 8¾" H. $20.00
SQ. BOTTLES, Pr., 2nd & Next To Last
Items, 8½" H. $15.00
BOTTLES, 2, 19th C., 3rd & 3rd To Last
Items, 10" H. $20.00
CATHEDRAL PICKLE BOTTLES, Pr.,
Middle Items, 19th C., Aqua, Blown In Mold,
Applied Top, 13¼" H. $85.00

◄ A-MA April 1980   *Robert W. Skinner Inc.*
L To R
HISTORICAL FLASK, G. Washington-
Eagle, Pt., Pale Gr., Some Inside Stain, PA,
Ca. 1820-1840................. $1400.00*
SUNBURST PICTORIAL FLASK, Pt.,
Clear Gr., Sm. Mouth Chip, Keene Marl-
boro Street Works, NH, Ca. 1814-1830
.... $400.00*

A-NY May 1980   *Calkins Auction Gallery*
L To R
BOTTLES, 2, 19th C., 1st Bottle Is 12 Sided
W/Whittle Marks In Pale Gr., 2nd Is Flat On
2 Sides W/Molded Corners, Pontil Mark,
Blown In Mold, Whittle Marks, Pale Gr., 5"
H., 6½" H. $10.00
BOTTLES, 2, 19th C., 1st Bottle Is Aqua
Colored Embossed "Fellows Syrup Of Hypo-
phosphites", 2nd Bottle Is Aqua W/Whittle
Marks, Embossed "Gibson's Fruit Tablets,
Established 1840", 7¾" H., 12½" H. .. $15.00
CHESTNUT TYPE BOTTLE, 19th C.,
Aqua, Blown In Mold, Pontil Mark, Over-
all Quilted Patt., 5½" H. $35.00
BOTTLES, 2, 19th C., 1st Bottle Is Beer
Bottle Embossed "T.W. Miller, Malone, NY",
2nd Bottle Is 8 Sided, Embossed "Rumford
Chemical Works", "Patented Mar. 10 1868",
Minor Rim Chip, 7" H., 5¾" H. $10.00

A-MA April 1980   *Robert W. Skinner, Inc.*
L To R
HISTORICAL CALABASH FLASK,
"Jeny Lind"-Factory, Qt., Sapphire Blue,
Attrib. To Ravenna Glassworks, OH, Ca.
1850-1860 .... $900.00*
HISTORICAL FLASK, "Gen. Washington"-
"J.R." Eagle, Pt., Clear W/Amethyst Tint,
John Robinson, PA, Ca. 1820-1840 .. $2100.00*

A-MA April 1980   *Robert W. Skinner, Inc.*
L To R
**"WHEAT PRICE" - SHORT HAIR - "FAIR-
VIEW WORKS"** Portrait Flask, VA Ca.
1830-40 .... $5500.00*
HISTORICAL FLASK, Prospector-Eagle,
Pt., Aqua, Ca. 1860-1875 .... $60.00*

A-MA April 1980 *Robert W. Skinner Inc.*
HISTORICAL CALABASH FLASK, "Jenny Lind" "Facroty & S. Huffsey/Glass Works", Qt., Blue Gr., Ca. 1850-1860
.... $650.00*

A-MA April 1980 *Robert W. Skinner Inc.*
RIBBED CHESTNUT FLASK, ½ Pt., Golden Yellow, Midwestern, Ca. 1815-1830
.... $450.00*

A-MA April 1980 *Robert W. Skinner Inc.*
RIBBED CHESTNUT FLASK, ½ Pt., Aqua, Body Crack, Midwestern, Ca. 1815-1830 .... $35.00*

A-MA April 1980 *Robert W. Skinner Inc.*
HISTORICAL FLASK, Jenny Lind Lyre, Pt., Aqua, Mouth Roughness, M'Carty & Torreyson Works, WV, Ca. 1845-1855
.... $800.00*

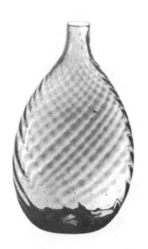

A-MA April 1980 *Robert W. Skinner Inc.*
SWIRLED FLASK, Swirled To Left, Pt., Citron, Midwestern, Early 19th C ...$475.00*

A-MA April 1980 *Robert W. Skinner Inc.*
PITKIN TYPE FLASK, Ribbed & Swirled To Rt., ½Pt., Lt. Olive Amber, N. Eng., Ca. 1783-1830 .... $150.00*

A-MA April 1980 *Robert W. Skinner Inc.*
HISTORICAL FLASK, Jenny Lind, Qt., Aqua, Attrib. To M'Carty & Torreyson, WV, Ca. 1845-1855.................. $850.00*

A-MA April 1980 *Robert W. Skinner Inc.*
PITKIN TYPE FLASK, Ribbed & Swirled To Rt., ½ Pt., Lt. Olive Amber, N. Eng., Ca. 1783-1830...................... $125.00*

A-MA April 1980 *Robert W. Skinner Inc.*
PITKIN TYPE FLASK, Ribbed & Swirled To Rt., Pt., Olive Gr., Mouth Chip, Midwestern, Ca. 1815-1830 .... $90.00*

*Price does not include 10% buyer fee.

A-MA April 1980   *Robert W. Skinner Inc.*
HISTORICAL FLASK, Railroad-Eagle, Pt., Deep Olive Amber, Coventry Glass Works, CT, Ca.1830-1848 ...... $120.00*

A-MA April 1980   *Robert W. Skinner Inc.*
HISTORICAL FLASK, Taylor & "Rough & Ready" - "Major Ringgold" & Bust, Pt., Lavender, Attrib. To Baltimore Glass Works, MD, Ca. 1830-1850 .... $1000.00*

A-MA April 1980   *Robert W. Skinner Inc.*
PICTORIAL FLASK, "Jared Spencer" - Manchester, CT., Pt., Lt. Olive Amber, Shoulder Bruise, Ca. 1815-1825 .. $5000.00*

A-MA April 1980   *Robert W. Skinner Inc.*
HISTORICAL FLASK, "Success To The Railroad", Pt., Blue Gr., Lancaster Glass Works, NY, Ca. 1830-1840 ..... $1500.00*

A-MA April 1980   *Robert W. Skinner Inc.*
HISTORICAL FLASK, "Success To The Railroad", Pt., Clear Gr., Lancaster Glass Works, NY, Ca. 1830-1840 ...... $650.00*

A-MA April 1980   *Robert W. Skinner Inc.*
JARED SPENCER TYPE PICTORIAL FLASK, No Inscription, Pt., Olive Amber, Mouth Repair, Pitkin Glass Works, CT, Ca. 1815-1825 .... $6000.00*

A-MA April 1980   *Robert W. Skinner Inc.*
HISTORICAL FLASK, "Rough & Ready" & Taylor Bust-Eagle, Pt., Lt. Yellow Gr., Pittsburgh District, PA, Ca. 1820-1840 .... $4750.00*

A-MA April 1980   *Robert W. Skinner Inc.*
HISTORICAL FLASK, "Success To The Railroad", Pt., Yellow, Lancaster Glass Works, NY, Ca. 1830-1850 ..... $1300.00*

A-MA April 1980   *Robert W. Skinner Inc.*
PICTORIAL FLASK, Gentlemen Arguing-Grotesque Head, ½ Pt., Sapphire Blue, Ca. 1830-1850 .... $800.00*

*Price does not include 10% buyer fee.

A-MA April 1980 *Robert W. Skinner Inc.*
PICTORIAL FLASK, Summer Tree-Spring Tree, Qt., Deep Sapphire Blue, ½ Of Neck Missing, Am., Ca. 1840-1850 ..... $450.00*

A-MA April 1980 *Robert W. Skinner Inc.*
SCROLL PICTORIAL FLASK, Qt. Sapphire Blue, Sm. Base & Rib Chips, Ca. 1840-1860 .... $750.00*

A-MA April 1980 *Robert W. Skinner Inc.*
HISTORICAL FLASK, Eagle-Cornucopia, Pt., Olive Amber, Body Cracks, Keene Marboro Street Works, NH, Ca. 1830-1850 .... $35.00*

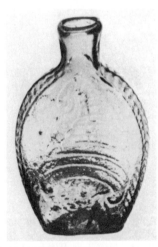

A-MA April 1980 *Robert W. Skinner Inc.*
MEDALLION PICTORIAL FLASK, Cornucopia-Star, ½ Pt., Pale Blue, Gr., Midwestern, Ca. 1820-1840 ..... $2500.00*

A-MA April 1980 *Robert W. Skinner Inc.*
SCROLL PICTORIAL FLASK, Pt., Olive Yellow, Ca. 1845-1860 .... $550.00*

A-MA April 1980 *Robert W. Skinner Inc.*
HISTORICAL FLASK, Eagle-Cornucopia, ½ Pt., Aqua, PA, Ca. 1820-1840 ... $400.00*

A-MA April 1980 *Robert W. Skinner Inc.*
PICTORIAL FLASK, Cornucopia-Urn, Pt., Olive Amber, Base Bruises, Coventry Glass Works, CT, Ca. 1830-1848........ $40.00*

A-MA April 1980 *Robert W. Skinner Inc.*
PICTORIAL FLASK, Cornucopia-Urn, Pt., Bright Gr., Medial Rib Flake, Ca. 1830-1848 .... $160.00*

A-MA April 1980 *Robert W. Skinner Inc.*
HISTORICAL FLASK, Eagle-Corncucopia, ½ Pt., Pale Blue Gr., Ca. 1820-1840 .... $600.00*

*Price does not include 10% buyer fee.

A-MA April 1980   *Robert W. Skinner Inc.*
HISTORICAL FLASK, Eagle-Medallion, Pt., Clear, PA, Ca. 1820-1840 . . . . $6500.00*

A-MA April 1980   *Robert W. Skinner Inc.*
HISTORICAL FLASK, Columbia-Eagle, Pt., Lt. Grey Blue, Kensington Glass Works, PA, Ca. 1815-1825 . . . . $4500.00*

A-MA April 1980   *Robert W. Skinner Inc.*
HISTORICAL FLASK, Masonic-Eagle, Pt., Lt. Gr., Keene Marlboro Street Works, NH, Ca. 1814-1830. . . . . $225.00*

A-MA April 1980   *Robert W. Skinner Inc.*
HISTORICAL FLASK, Eagle-Lyre, Pt., Aqua, Kentucky Glass Works, Louisville, KY, Ca. 1840-1850. . . . . $750.00*

A-MA April 1980   *Robert W. Skinner Inc.*
HISTORICAL FLASK, Columbia-Eagle, ½ Pt., Pale Yellow Gr., Kensington Glass Works, PA, Ca. 1815-1830 . . . . . . $2000.00*

A-MA April 1980   *Robert W. Skinner Inc.*
HISTORICAL FLASK, Masonic-Eagle, Pt., Shaded Yellow Olive To Clear, Keene Marlboro Street Works, NH. $2250.00*

A-MA April 1980   *Robert W. Skinner Inc.*
HISTORICAL FLASK, Double Eagle, ½ Pt., Olive Amber, Body Bubble Burst, Stoddard Glass House, NH, Ca. 1840-1860 . . . . $55.00*

A-MA April 1980   *Robert W. Skinner Inc.*
HISTORICAL FLASK, Masonic-Eagle, Pt., Purple, Base Flake, Keene Marlboro Street Works, NH, Ca. 1815-1830 . . . . . $7500.00*

A-MA April 1980   *Robert W. Skinner Inc.*
HISTORICAL FLASK, Masonic-Eagle, Pt., Yellow Gr., Keene Marlboro Street Works, NH, Ca. 1814-1830 . . . . $950.00*

*Price does not include 10% buyer fee.

A-MA April 1980   *Robert W. Skinner Inc.*
HISTORICAL FLASK, Double Eagle, Pt.,
Amber, Lrg. Base Bubble Burst, Stoddard
Glass House, NH, Ca. 1842-1860 . . . .
. . . . $65.00*

A-MA April 1980   *Robert W. Skinner Inc.*
HISTORICAL FLASK, "Genl LaFayette"
Eagle, Pt., Blue, Gr., Ca. 1820-1830
. . . . $1600.00*

A-MA April 1980   *Robert W. Skinner Inc.*
HISTORICAL FLASK, "Washington" -
Taylor & "Bridgeton, NJ", Pt., Peacock Gr.,
Bridgeton Glass Works, NJ, Ca. 1830-1850
. . . . $650.00*

A-MA April 1980   *Robert W. Skinner Inc.*
HISTORICAL FLASK, "Rough & Ready"
& Taylor Bust-Masterson Eagle, Qt., Aqua,
Mouth Bruise, Midwestern, Ca. 1820-1840
. . . . $1100.00*

A-MA April 1980   *Robert W. Skinner Inc.*
HISTORICAL FLASK, Washington-
Taylor, Qt., Amethyst, Tiny Base Flake &
Some Inside Stain, Dyottville Glassworks,
PA, Ca. 1840-1860 . . . . $800.00*

A-MA April 1980   *Robert W. Skinner Inc.*
HISTORICAL FLASK, Eagle-Flag, Pt.,
Deep Golden Amber, Attrib. To Coffin &
Hay, NJ, Ca. 1820-1840 . . . . $1700.00*

A-MA April 1980   *Robert W. Skinner Inc.*
HISTORICAL FLASK, "LaFayette"-Ma-
sonic, Pt., Olive Amber, Mt. Vernon Glassworks, NY, Ca. 1820-1830 . . . . . . $2100.00*

A-MA April 1980   *Robert W. Skinner Inc.*
HISTORICAL FLASK, "Washington" -
Taylor "Bridgeton, NJ", Pt., Deep Golden
Amber, Ca. 1830-1850 . . . . $1100.00*

A-MA April 1980   *Robert W. Skinner Inc.*
HISTORICAL FLASK, Washington-Taylor, Qt., Sapphire Blue, Dyottville Glassworks, PA, Ca. 1840-1860 . . . . . . $1300.00*

*Price does not include 10% buyer fee.

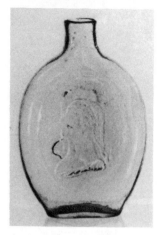

A-MA April 1980   *Robert W. Skinner Inc.*
HISTORICAL FLASK, Washington-Taylor, ½ Pt., Dyottville Glass Works, PA, Ca. 1840-1860 . . . . $60.00*

A-MA April 1980   *Robert W. Skinner Inc.*
HISTORICAL FLASK, "General Washington"-Eagle, Pt., Deep Aqua, Ca. 1820-1840 . . . . $500.00*

A-MA April 1980   *Robert W. Skinner Inc.*
HISTORICAL FLASK, Washington-Sailing Ship, Albany Glass Works, NY, Pt., Lt. Sapphire Blue, Tiny Inside Mouth Bruise, Ca. 1830-1850 . . . . $2500.00*

A-MA April 1980   *Robert W. Skinner Inc.*
HISTORICAL FLASK, Gen. Jackson-Floral Motif, Pt., Yellow Olive, PA, Ca. 1820-1840 . . . .,. . $7500.00*

A-MA April 1980   *Robert W. Skinner Inc.*
HISTORICAL FLASK, "General Washington"- Eagle, Pt., Deep Aqua, Ca. 1820-1840 . . . . $500.00*

A-MA April 1980   *Robert W. Skinner Inc.*
HISTORICAL FLASK, Washington-Baltimore Monument, Qt., Lt. Amethyst, Baltimore Glass Works, MD, Ca. 1820-1840 . . . . $2600.00*

A-MA April 1980   *Robert W. Skinner Inc.*
HISTORICAL FLASK, "G. Washington" -Eagle, Pt., Deep Aqua, Base Chip & Some Inside Stain, Ca. 1820-1840 . . . . . . $325.00*

*Price does not include 10% buyer fee.

A-MA April 1980   *Robert W. Skinner Inc.*
HISTORICAL FLASK, "Washington" - "Baltimore Glass Works" Monument, Pt., Cornflower Blue, 2 Sm. Body Bruises, MD, Ca. 1830-1850 . . . . $900.00 *

A-MA April 1980   *Robert W. Skinner Inc.*
HISTORICAL FLASK, "Washington" - Jackson, Pt., Yellow Amber, Keene Marlboro Street Works, NH, Ca. 1820-1940 . . . . $120.00*

A-OH Mar 1980   *Garth's Auctions, Inc.*
ROW I, L To R
PEWTER COFFEE POT, Mkd. "A. Porter", Finial Incomp. & Spout Battered, 10½" H.
.... $205.00
PEWTER PLATE, Engraved "J.C.M.", Faint Touch, 9" D. $65.00
PEWTER PITCHER W/Hinged Lid, Unmarked Am., 6" H. $100.00
PEWTER COFFEE POT, Tip Of Spout Damaged & Hinge Rep., Unmarked Am., 11" H. $80.00
ROW II, L To R
TIN DOUBLE CRUISE LAMP, 9½" H.
.... $27.50
PEWTER PORRIGER W/Crown Handle, Battered & Tiny Hole, 6½" L. $135.00
PEWTER PORRIGER W/Crown Handle, 5½" L. $185.00
PEWTER FOOTED BOWL, Unmarked, 6" D., 4¾" H. $115.00
WRT. IRON BETTY LAMP HOLDER, To Be Driven Into Wall, Tooled & Cut Out Ornaments, 2" D. $165.00
TIN LAMP, Saucer W/Rust Damage & Old Rep., 6" H. $62.50
ROW III, L To R
PEWTER MEASURE W/Brass Rim, ½ Pint, London Maker, 4" H. $45.00
PEWTER MEASURE W/Brass Rim, ½ Gill, 2½ H. $42.50
PEWTER MEASURE W/Brass Rim, Quart, Imperial Measure, 6" H. $70.00
PEWTER MEASURE W/Brass Rim, ½ Pint, 3½" H. $45.00
BRASS PITCHER & PEWTER STRAINER, 4" H., 3¼" D. $35.00

A-OH April 1980   *Garth's Auctions, Inc.*
PEWTER
ROW I, L To R
SM. CANDLESTICKS, Pr., Unmarked Am., 5¼" H. $550.00
TEA POT, Battered & Lid Hinge Rep., Unmarked Am., 6" H. $85.00
FUNNEL, Slightly Battered, 4⅜" H. ...$55.00
ROW II, L To R
PLATE, Touch Mark For David Melville, Newport, 8" D. $325.00
WATER JUG, Unmarked Am., 10" H.
.... $525.00
PLATE, Touch Marks Of Thomas Danforth II, 8" D. $175.00
ROW III, L To R
PLATE, Touch Marks Of Thomas Badger, "Boston", Pitted, 8½" D. $135.00
PORRIGER W/Cast Crown Handle, Mkd. "I.G.", 4¼" L. $375.00
CHARGER, "Love" Touch, Deep Surface Scratch, 11" D. $200.00
PLATE, Eagle Mark For Nathaniel Austin, MA, 8⅞" D. $460.00

A-MA July 1980   *Robert W. Skinner Inc.*
STERLING FLATWARE, Newcastle Patt., Gorham Mfg. Co. 13 Pc. Setting, 164 Pcs. RI, 20th C., 172 Troy Oz. $2200.00*

A-WA D.C. Feb 1980 *Adam A. Weschler & Son*
L To R
ROCOCO 800-SILVER CANDELABRA, Pr., German, L. Eckert, Late 19th C., 7-Light, Reich Silvermark, 24" H. ... $4100.00*
ROCOCO 800-SILVER COVERED TUREEN, German, Friedlander, Late 19th C., Reich Silvermark, Verso Dated Berlin 15. Oct. 1897, 18½" L., 11½" H. $4100.00*
ROCOCO 800-SILVER FOOTED PLATEAU, Mirrored, German, Friedlander, Late 19th C., 17" L. $1100.00*

A-OH April 1980   *Garth's Auctions, Inc.*
COIN SILVER TEASPOON, Mkd. "C.D.", 6" L. $12.00
COIN SILVER TEASPOONS, 3, (1 Illus.), Mkd. "E. & D. Kinsey", 6⅛" L. $37.50
COIN SILVER 37 Pcs., (4 Illus.), Twisted Handles, Mkd. "Duhme" $740.00
COIN SILVER TEASPOONS, 2, (1 Illus.), Mkd. "James Watts", 5⅞" L. $26.00
COIN SILVER DEMITASSE SPOON, 5½" L. $11.00
COIN SILVER TABLESPOON, Mkd. "I.D.", 10" L. $60.00
COIN SILVER TABLESPOON, Mkd. "E. & D. Kinsey", 8⅛" L. $35.00
SILVER SAUCE LADLE, Hallmarked, 7¼" L. $65.00
FLATWARE, 12 Pc. Set, (2 Illus.), Wood Handles, Mkd. "Am. Cutlery Co.", 9½" L. $55.00
COIN SILVER SPOONS, 3, (1 Illus.), Mkd. "D.B. Warren", 1 Tablespoon W/Repair
.... $24.00
FLATWARE, 12 Pc. Set, (2 Illus.), Wood Handles, Mkd. "U.S. Cutlery Co. Bellville, NJ.", 9½" L. $55.00
SILVER LADLE W/Strainer Bowl, Bowl Resoldered, 7½" L. $55.00
COIN SILVER SERVING SPOON, Mkd. "Duhme 1867", 8¼" L. $35.00
SILVER SERVING SPOONS, 6, (1 Illus.), Mkd. "J. Doll", 1 Handle Broken & Resoldered, 9" L. $120.00

A-MA Aug 1980   *Robert C. Eldred Co., Inc.*
COIN SILVER TABLESPOONS By Edward Winslow, MA, Ca. 1669-1753, 3 Oz. Troy
.... $950.00
COIN SILVER TEA STRAINER, Mkd. "IB" In Oval, Am., 2 Oz. Troy $320.00*

*Price does not include 10% buyer fee.

A-VA Jan 1980 *Laws Auction & Antiques*
STERLING SILVER FLAT TABLE SERVICE, Reed & Barton Intaglio Patt., Cased, 187 Pcs. $1250.00

A-WA D.C. Feb 1980 *Adam A. Weschler & Son*
STERLING COFFEE-TEA SERVICE, 6 Pcs., Am., Jocobi & Jenkins, Late 19th C., 170 Oz. $7000.00*

A-WA D.C. May 1980 *Adam A. Weschler & Son*
GEORGE III SILVER CRUET SET, 6-Bottles, Paul Storr, London, Ca. 1814, Rosette Stoppers Orig., 11½" L., 35 Oz. .. $4600.00*

A-WA D.C. Dec 1980 *Adam A. Weschler & Son*
REPOUSSE STERLING
L To R
GOBLETS, Set Of 8, Stieff, Chalice-Form W/Rosebud Medallions On Concave Stems W/Trumpet Bases, 48 oz., 6½" H. $1100.00*
FOOTED PUNCH BOWL, J. E. Caldwell & Co., Phila., 7-Qt., Vine Decor., Late 19th C., 50 oz., 11" D., 8¾" H. $1500.00*

A-MA July 1980 *Robert W. Skinner Inc.*
REPOUSSE TEA SET, Sterling Silver, 5-Pcs., RI, Ca. 1891 .... $4200.00*

A-MA Sept 1980 *Richard A. Bourne Co., Inc.*
PEWTER
ROW I, L To R
OCTAGONAL TOBACCO JAR, Eng., Surface Pitted, Brass Finial Loose, 4½" H. $35.00
TOBACCO JAR, Eng., Inner Press & Human Head Finial, Minor Imperfections, Pitted Surface, 5½" H. $70.00
COVERED JELLY MOLD, 5½" H. $100.00
HALF PINT MEASURES, 2, 1 By James Yates, Both 19th C. $100.00
ROW II, L To R
TEAPOT By Rufas Dunham, ME, 1837-1861, Sgn., 7¼" H. $225.00
TEAPOT By Smith & Co., Sgn., Badly Bent, 6¼" H. $50.00
PINT MEASURE, Eng., By G. Farmiloe & Son, 19th C. $135.00
ROW III, L To R
QUART MEASURE, Eng., 19th C., Some Pitting $100.00
COMMUNION CHALICE, Am., Unmarked, 19th C., Sl. Dents & Bent At Base, 8⅜" H. $140.00
QUART MEASURE, Scottish, By H. Reid, 19th C., Minor Dents & Sm. Repairs Needed $75.00

Left
A-WA D.C. Feb 1980 *Adam A. Weschler & Son*
GEORGE III SILVER SERVICE PLATES, Set Of 12, Paul Storr, London, Ca. 1807, 10" D. $29500.00*
Right
A-MA Oct 1980 *Robert W. Skinner Inc.*
PEWTER TEAPOT, Wooden Wafer Finial, Mkd. "TD & SB", Wafer Broken, Base Ring Damaged, CT, Ca. 1825, 4½" D., 7¼" O.H. $975.00*

A-MA Aug 1980 *Robert C. Eldred Co., Inc.*
STERLING SILVER TEA & COFFEE SERVICE By Gorham, Fluted Bands, Plume Scroll Handles, 170 Oz. Troy $2300.00

A-Ma Aug 1980 *Robert C. Eldred Co., Inc.*
L To R
STERLING SILVER REPOUSSE PLATTER W/Monogram, By S. Kirk & Son, Early 20th C., 22 Oz. Troy $350.00
SILVER HANDLED BASKET, Pierced & Engraved Masonic Decor., Dutch, 18th C., 22 Oz. Troy $1500.00
STERLING SILVER TRAY By Reed & Barton, 22 Oz. Troy $310.00

*Price does not include 10% buyer fee.

A-WA D.C. Feb 1980 *Adam A. Weschler & Son*
REPOUSSE STERLING FLAT TABLE SERVICE, Rose Patt. By Stieff, Am., 98 Pcs., 100 Oz. $3800.00*

A-MA May 1980 *Paul J. Dias, Inc.*
COPPER CANDY KETTLES, Set Of 6, Dovetailed W/Iron Handles, Polished
.... $750.00

A-MA July 1980 *Robert W. Skinner Inc.*
BURL WOOD BOWL, Hand Carved, Chip At Rim, Am., 18th C., 14" D., 5" H.
.... $725.00*

A-NY May 1980 *The Auction Gallery*
BELLOWS, Carved & Painted, Leather, Wood & Tin, 19 C., "19th S. 4th St. Phila. Pat.", 24" L. $70.00

*Price does not include 10% buyer fee.

A-OH April 1980 *Garth's Auctions, Inc.*
WOODEN BUTTER PRINT, 1 Pc. W/ Turned Handle, Flower, Weathered & Age Cracks, 4¼" D. $45.00
WOODEN BUTTER PRINT, 1 Pc. W/ Turned Handle, Pineapple, 5" D.
.... $125.00
IRON SKEWER HOLDER, 4" H. . $35.00
WOODEN BUTTER PRINT, 1 Pc. W/ Turned Handle, Flowers, Air Hole, 4⅛" D.
.... $65.00
TIN COOKIE CUTTER, Rooster, 4¾" H.
.... $67.50
TIN COOKIE CUTTER, Crow, 6" L.
.... $50.00
WOODEN BUTTER PRINT, 1 Pc. W/ Wooden Handle, Eagle, Air Hole, 4¾" D.
.... $135.00
TIN COOKIE CUTTER, Sm. Bird, 4" L.
.... $20.00
TIN COOKIE CUTTER, Deer W/Antlers, 4¾" H. $105.00
TIN COOKIE CUTTER, Sm. Bird, 4" L.
.... $25.00
WOODEN BUTTER PRINT, 1 Pc. W/ Wooden Handle, Rooster, Minor Age Cracks, 4½" D. $285.00
WOODEN BUTTER PRINT, 1 Pc. W/ Wooden Handle, Cow, 4⅜" D. ... $130.00
WOODEN BUTTER PRINT, Rectangular, Thistle & Rose On 1 Side & Geometric Bar Design On Other, Stamped "W.T.", 4¼" x 7½" $75.00
WOODEN BUTTER PRINT, 1 Pc. W/ Turned Handle, Eagle, 4⅜" D. ... $105.00

Left
A-MA Sept 1980 *Richard A. Bourne Co., Inc.*
HANGING CANDLE BOX, Oak Sliding Cover, Eng., 18th C., 17½" H. $150.00

Right
A-WA D.C. Feb 1980 *Adam A. Weschler & Son*
SILVER LAZY SUSAN, Eng., 20th C., Cobalt Lined Crystal Condiment Urns, Hot Water Base, Soup Tureen, 4 Oval Covered Entree Dishes, 25" D. $950.00*

A-OH April 1980 *Garth's Auctions, Inc.*
WOODEN BUTTER PRINT, 1 Pc. W/Turned Handle, Pineapple & Tulip, Edge Chip & Age Crack, 4⅛" D. $35.00
WOODEN BUTTER PRINT, 1 Pc. W/Turned Handle, Eagle, 3⅝" D. .. $45.00
WROUGHT IRON CURLING IRON, Button End Handles, 11⅜" L. $15.00
TIN PRIVY LAMP, Oval Font, Brass & Tin Whale Oil Burner, 9" L. $30.00
TIN COOKIE CUTTER, Abraham Lincoln On Horseback, 8½" L. $405.00
SM. CANDLE SNUFFERS, Scissor Shaped, 4" L. $70.00
TURNED WOODEN COOKIE ROLLER, 12" L. $37.50
PEWTER CANDLE MOLD, Single Tube, Threaded Tip Marked "M", 9¾" L. .. $20.00
WOODEN FEED SACK STAMP, "D", 5" L. $22.50
WOODEN BUTTER PRINT, 1 Pc. W/Turned Handle, Pineapple, 4⅝" D.
.... $80.00
WOODEN BUTTER PRINT, 1 Pc. W/Turned Handle, Sheaf, 3⅜" D. .. $35.00
RELIEF CARVING, Eagle & 1802, Sgn., 5" x 7¾" $95.00
CAST IRON TARGET, Bird, 4" L. ...$20.00
WOODEN BUTTER PRINT, 1 Pc. W/Turned Handle, Star, 3⅞" D. $30.00
WOODEN BUTTER PRINT, 1 Pc. W/Turned Handle, Flower, Edges Weathered, 4¾" D. $35.00

A-MA May 1980 *Paul J. Dias, Inc.*
FLOOR MODEL COFFEE GRINDER, Enterprise Mfg. Co., Cast Iron, Ca. 1878, Orig. Red, Blue & Gold Paint & Stenciling, Orig. Tin Painted Drawer, Sm. Break On 1 Leg W/Brace Repair, 5'7" H. $2300.00

A-OH April 1980   *Garth's Auctions, Inc.*
WRT. IRON DIPPER W/Scrolled Hanger, Handle Bent, 20" L. $30.00
WRT. IRON FORK W/Scrolled Hanger, 7¾" L. $35.00
WOODEN BUTTER PRINT, Acorn, 1 Pc. W/Turned Handle, Age Crack, 3½" D. $30.00
WOODEN BUTTTER PRINT, Dished Out W/Carved Lamb, 1 Pc. W/Turned Handle, Scrubbed Finish, 4¾" D. .. $130.00
WOODEN BUTTER PRINT, Acorn, Turned & Inserted Handle, 3¾" D. ..$100.00
WRT. POKER, Brass Handle, Polished, 14¾" L. $10.00
WRT. IRON POKER, Twisted Shank & Eye Hanger, 17" L. $7.50
WRT. IRON SPATULA W/Scrolled Hanger, Sm. Split In Blade, 22¾" L. ... $20.00
WOODEN BUTTER PRINT, Flower & Leaves, Age Cracks, 1 Pc. W/Turned Handle, 3¾" D. $30.00
CAST IRON PAN, Decor. Handle, 5" D. $25.00
WOODEN BUTTER PRINT, Pineapple, 1 Pc. W/Turned Handle, 3½" D. .. $60.00
WOODEN BUTTER PRINT, Hexagonal, Stave Const. Case, Drk, Varnish Finish, 4" D. $40.00
WOODEN BUTTER PRINT, Flower, Drk. Finish, 1 Pc. W/Turned Handle, 2⅞" D. $25.00
WRT. IRON SUGAR NIPPERS, 9¾" L. $80.00

A-OH Feb 1981   *Garth's Auctions, Inc.*
CAST IRON TRIVETS
ROW I, L To R
TRIVETS, 2 (1 Illus.), "Howell H", 6" L. $10.00
TRIVET, "O.M. Co.", 4¾" Sq. .. $17.50
TRIVETS, 2 (1 Illus.), Oblong Waffle, 3¼" x 4½" $10.00

*Price does not include 10% buyer fee.

A-OH Mar 1980   *Garth's Auctions, Inc.*
ROW I, L To R
WOODEN BUTTER WORKING PADDLE, Crack In Blade, 10" L. $60.00
WROUGHT STEEL FOOD CHOPPER W/ Wooden Handle, Corner Of Blade Chipped, 6½" W. $25.00
BUTTER PRINT, Compass Star Designs, 7¼" D. $165.00
ROW II, L To R
IRON TOOL, Stamped "H. Huber, Phila., PA", Curly Maple Handle, 9½" L. ... $55.00
WROUGHT IRON SUGAR NIPPERS, 8" L. $47.50
CAST IRON SPIDER, 6¾" L. $20.00
WROUGHT STEEL FOOD CHOPPER W/Wooden Handle, 6¼" W. $17.50
WROUGHT IRON SUGAR NIPPERS, Stamped "Burton", 8¼" L. $95.00
WROUGHT IRON SPATULA W/Twisted Handle, 9½" L. $45.00
ROW III, L To R
WOODEN BUTTER PRINT, Tulip & "B.M.", Handle Missing, 4¼" D. ... $130.00
WOODEN BUTTER PRINT, Paisley Design, Handle Missing, 4½" D. ... $75.00
WOODEN BUTTER PRINT, Tulip & Stars, Turned 1 Pc. Handle, 4¾" D. $195.00
WOODEN BUTTER PRINT, Tulip & Sm. Stars, Turned 1 Pc. Handle Chipped, 4¾" D. $90.00
WOODEN BUTTER PRINT, Seals W/Initials, Sm. Handle Relief Carved, 4½" D. $55.00

TRIVET, "Ober" Waffle, 4½" Sq. ... $7.50
TRIVET, Lacy Urn, 6" L. $10.00

ROW II, L To R
TRIVET, Lacy, 8" L. $22.50
TRIVET, Round Petal, 5" D. $45.00
TRIVET, "Good Luck To All Who Use This Stand.", 8" L. $15.00
TRIVET, 6 Petal, 5⅜" D. $47.50
TRIVET, "A. In S.", 6¾" L. $8.00

ROW III, L To R
TRIVET, Round Lattice, 5⅜" D. ... $20.00
TRIVETS, 2 (1 Illus.), Lantz #2 ... $35.00
TRIVETS, 2 (1 Illus.), Ober Sq. ... $35.00

ROW IV, L To R
TRIVETS, 2 (1 Illus.), "Sensible", 6" L. $42.50
TRIVET, "Ferro Steel" Urn, 6" L. .. $12.50
TRIVET, Spider Web Variant, 6" L. $22.50
► **TRIVET**, "J. T. & Co.", 7⅜" L. ... $40.00

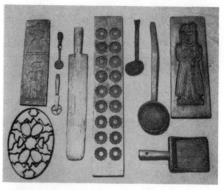

A-OH Sept 1980   *Garth's Auctions, Inc.*
CARVED WOODEN COOKIE BOARD, Insect Damage $90.00
PASTRY CUTTER, Wooden Handle, Iron Jaws That Hold Brass Wheel, 6½" L. $25.00
PASTRY CUTTER, Wooden Handle, Pewter Wheel, 7" L. $50.00
WOODEN FEATHER BED THUMPER, 22¼" L. $55.00
MAPLE SUGAR BOARD, Maple W/18 Carved Flowers, 5" x 27" $90.00
WOODEN SPOON, Chip Carved Handle, 10½" L. $30.00
DIPPER, 1 pc. Of Wood, 19½" L. .. $40.00
CARVED WOODEN COOKIE BOARD, Figure Outlined In Tin, 6½" x 17½" .. $215.00
TIN COOKIE CUTTER, Several Joints Need Resoldered, 7½" x 11"....... $65.00
WOODEN SCOOP, 11¼" L. $50.00

A-NY May 1980   *The Auction Gallery*
TABLE TOP DOUGH BOX, Covered, Early 19th C., Splayed & Dovetailed Sides, Orig. Red Paint, 30" L., 18" W., 12" H. $250.00

A-MA Sept 1980   *Robert W. Skinner Inc.*
CARVED KNIFE BOX, Pine, Dovetailed Const., Blue-Gray Paint Over Old Red, Some Wear & Minor Paint Loss, Late 18th C., N. Eng., 6½" H. $275.00*

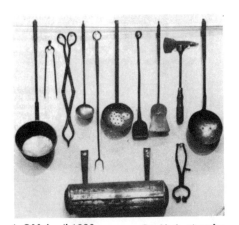

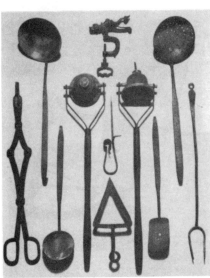

A-MA Aug 1980   *Robert C. Eldred Co., Inc.*
CHIPPENDALE BRASS ANDIRONS,
Pr., Am., 18″ H. $300.00

A-OH Mar 1980   *Garth's Auctions, Inc.*
ROW I, L To R
BRASS TRIVET, Heart Center & Turned
Feet, 9⅜″ L. $45.00
BRASS TRIVET, Striped Center, 11″ L.
. . . . $30.00
TIN CANISTER W/Double Compartments,
3⅝″ D. $40.00
BRASS TRIVET, Quarterfoil Center, 9½″L.
. . . . $75.00
BRASS TRIVET, Heart Center & Shoe
Form Feet, 9″ L. $70.00
ROW II, L To R
CAST BRASS TRIVET, Eagle, Not Pol-
ished, 10¼″ L. $65.00
FOOD CHOPPER W/Polished Brass Han-
dle, 7¾″ L. $32.50
CAST BRASS TRIVET, Not Polished,
9¼″ L. $22.50
HOOF CLEANER, Civil War Era, Nickel
Plated & Mkd. "C.W.Mc", 5½″ L. . . $12.50
CAST IRON TRIVET, 2 Interlocking
Hearts, 7½″ L. $25.00
ROW II, L To R
WROUGHT IRON TRIVET, Stamped
"G.G.", 10″ L. $25.00
CAST IRON TRIVET, Rectangular W/
Handle, 8″ L. $22.50
CAST IRON TRIVET, Urn W/Fern, 8¼″L.
. . . . $17.50
CAST IRON TRIVET, Lacy Urn W/Smooth
Rail, 6″ L. $15.00
WROUGHT IRON TRIVET, Scrolled Feet
& Turned Handle, 11¾″ L. $57.50

A-OH April 1980   *Garth's Auctions, Inc.*
BRASS DIPPER, Wrought Iron Handle,
19½″ L. $200.00
WROUGHT IRON PIPE TONGS, 8⅛″ L.
. . . . $165.00
WROUGHT IRON PIPE TONGS, Accord-
ian, Comb. Of Iron & Copper Fastening
Rivets, 16″ L. $105.00
BRASS TASTER, Wrought Iron Handle,
13½″ L. $170.00
WROUGHT IRON FORK, 19½″ L.
. . . . $175.00
BRASS STRAINER, Wrought Iron Handle,
15½″ L. $165.00
WROUGHT IRON SCRAPER, 15″ L.
. . . . $30.00
BRASS SPATULA, Wrought Iron Handle,
15½″ L. $165.00
IRON TOMAHAWK, Turned Wooden Han-
dle, 12″ L. $35.00
BRASS DIPPER, Wrought Iron Handle,
19½″ L. $75.00
TIN HANGING CANDLE BOX, 15″ L.
. . . . $245.00
WROUGHT IRON SUGAR NIPPERS,
8½″ L. $65.00

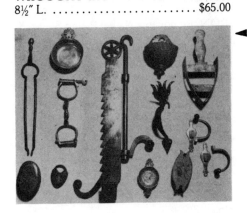

A-OH July 1980   *Garth's Auctions, Inc.*
WROUGHT IRON UTENSILS, Set of 4
W/Brass Bowls & Blade, Handles Have
Tooled Vines & Mkd. "1854 M.C." Set
Includes Wrought Iron Ladles 18″ & 15″,
Spatula 15″ L. & Skimmer 18½″ L.
. . . . $2100.00
CAST IRON SEWING DRAGON, 7″ H.
. . . . $255.00
PEWTER CAMPAIGN TORCHES, Pr.,
Bell Shaped, Wrought Iron Arms & Turned
Wooden Handles, 1 Handle Split, 23½″ L.
. . . . $170.00
WROUGHT IRON SCISSORS TONGS,
20″ L. $75.00
**WROUGHT IRON STICKING TOMMY
CANDLEHOLDER,** 9″ L. $65.00
WROUGHT IRON FORK, 19¾″ L.
. . . . $35.00
WROUGHT IRON TRIVET, Triangular,
Pitted, 9″ L. $55.00

◄ A-OH Nov 1980   *Garth's Auctions, Inc.*
**WROUGHT IRON & BRASS PIPE
TONGS,** 16½″ L. $65.00
PEWTER PORRINGER, Cast Old Eng.
Handle Resoldered To Bowl, 4½″ D.
. . . . $45.00
WROUGHT IRON TRAMMEL, Sawtooth,
Adj., 24″ L. $190.00
REDWARE WALL POCKET, Wheel
Thrown & Tooled, Chipped, 6½″ H. . . . $60.00
BRASS TRIVET, 10½″ L. $50.00
STEEL HANDCUFFS, Pr., "Hiatt Best
Warranted Wrt.", W/Key, 9½″ L. . . $70.00
WROUGHT IRON THUMB LATCH,
Tulip Top, Thumb Pc. Complete, Pivot Pin
Missing, 10″ L. $160.00
BRASS JAMB HOOKS, Pr. . . . $130.00
OVAL TIN BOX, Hinged Lid W/Punched
Diamond Shape, 3″ x 4½″ $27.50
IRON PADLOCK, Brass Keyhole, Stamped
"I.S.", Some Rust, 2⅞″ L. $10.00
PEWTER PORRINGER, Double Handled,
2¾″ D. $30.00
WOODEN OVAL BOX, Spring Clip Lid,
Worn Red & Gr. Heart & Flower Designs,
5¼″ L. $20.00

◄ A-MA Aug 1980   *Robert C. Eldred Co., Inc.*
BRASS ANDIRONS, Pr., Ca. 1790, 18½″ H.
. . . . $700.00

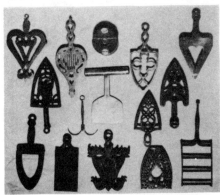

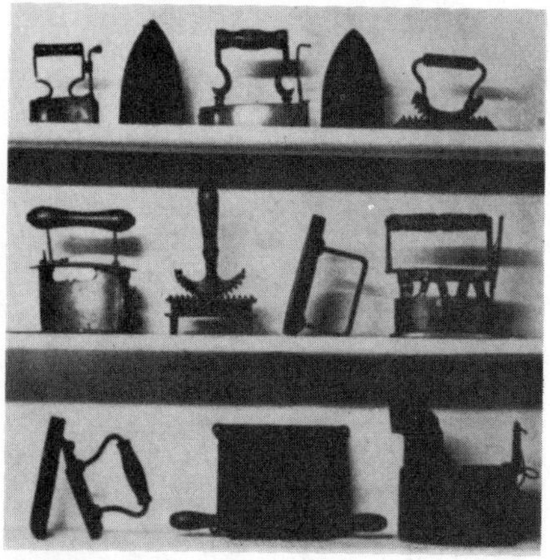

A-OH Oct 1980 *Garth's Auctions, Inc.*

ROW I, L To R

SM. IRON, Turned Wooden Handle & Insert, 5″ H. $37.50

CAST IRON FLAT IRON, Medallion & "Gerdame No 5.", 6½″ L. $20.00

BRASS IRON, Turned Wooden Handle & Decor. Detail, Engraved "A. Christin", Insert Missing, 6¼″ L. $47.50

WOODEN MODEL, Patt. Maker For Flat Iron, 6¼″ L. $6.00

CAST IRON FLUTER, 2-Pc., Mkd. "Pat'd Aug. 21, 1866", 6″ L. $25.00

ROW II, L To R

BRASS CHARCOAL IRON, Wooden Handle, 8″ L. $10.00

IRON & BRASS FLUTER, 3-Pc., Turned Wooden Handle, Damaged, 8½″ H. .. $20.00

CAST IRON FLAT IRON, Mkd. "D.C.", 7″ L. $15.00

BRASS & COPPER CHARCOAL IRON, Wooden Handle, Repaired, 8″ L. .. $20.00

ROW III, L To R

CAST IRON FLAT IRON, 7″ L. .. $27.50

CAST IRON TOOL, 2-Pc., Mkd. "Pat'ed Jan. 8, 1873 By H.E.Fuller, Princeton MO", 6″ x 8″ $37.50

CAST IRON CHARCOAL IRON W/ Chimney, Wire Bail & Wooden Handles, Face Of Bearded Man On Vent Cover, 8¼″ H. $15.00

A-OH April 1980 *Garth's Auctions, Inc.*

BURL BUTTER PADDLE, 8″ L. ... $230.00

WOODEN BUTTER PRINT, Pheasant Eating Berries, Threaded Handle Missing, 3⅝″ D. $70.00

WOODEN BUTTER PADDLE, Carved Prints On Each Side, Cherry & Leafy Plant, 11¾″ L. $460.00

WOODEN BUTTER PRINT, Star Flower, Minor Edge Cracks, 3⅜″ D. $52.50

WOODEN BUTTER PADDLE W/Serrated Blade, 9½″ L. $12.50

BUTTER PRINT, Heart Shaped, 2½″ H. $85.00

BUTTER PRINT, Fan Shaped, 2¾″ H. $75.00

WOODEN BUTTER PRINT, Leaf Design, 4⅜″ D. $60.00

PAPER CUT-OUT, Daniel & 2 Lions In Den, Framed, 5⅜″ x 5½″......... $85.00

BUTTER PRINT, Rectangular, 2 Sheaves, 2¾″ x 4⅞″ $55.00

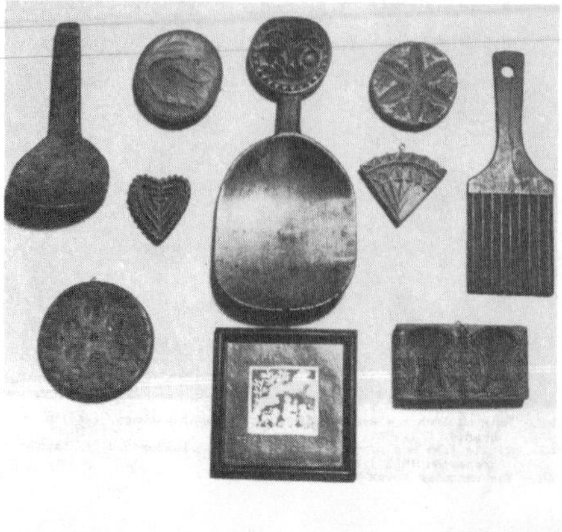

A-OH Oct 1980 *Garth's Auctions, Inc.*

MINIATURES

ROW I, L To R

IRON, Wrought Handles, 2¾″ L. ... $7.50

FLAT IRON, 3¼″ L. $7.50

TAILOR'S IRON, Mkd. "Chagrin Falls, O. Ober", 4⅝″ L. $20.00

FLAT IRON, Decor. Handle, 3¼″ L. $15.00

FLAT IRON, 3¼″ L. $7.50

ROW II, L To R

SAD IRON, Nickel Plated W/Wooden Handle, Embossed Head Of Classical Lady & Trivet, 3⅞″ L. $17.50

SAD IRON, Removable Iron & Wood Handle, "Patented May 9, '98", 4″ L. $22.50

SAD IRON, Trivet, Enterprise Mfg. Co., Phila., 3″ L. $20.00

SAD IRON, "Geneva Fluter, Pat'd 1866", 3½″ L. $35.00

SAD IRON, Trivet, Worn Nickel Plating, 3⅝″ L. $22.50

ROW III, L To R

SAD IRON, Worn Nickel Plating, 4¼″ L. $15.00

IRON, Removable Nickel Plated Sleeve & Handle, 5″ L. $7.50

IRON, Removable Wooden Handle & Trivet Mkd. "Willards", 5″ L. $22.50

IRON, Removable Wooden Handle, "Sensible No 6", 4″ L. $30.00

ROW IV, L To R

TAILOR'S GOOSE, Twisted Wrought Handle, 4¼″ L. $27.50

SAD IRON, Trivet, 3″ L. $22.50

SAD IRON, Removable Handle & 2 Bases, 3¾″ L. $25.00

SAD IRON, Trivet, Enterprise Mfg. Co., Phila., Pat'd Jan 1, '77", Handle W/Cooling Holes, 3⅞″ L. $25.00

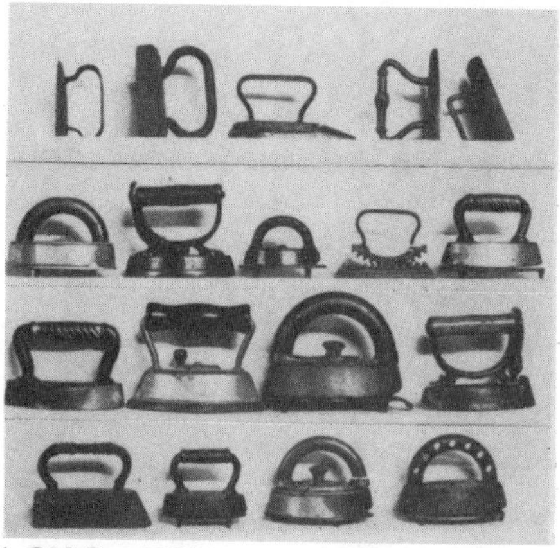

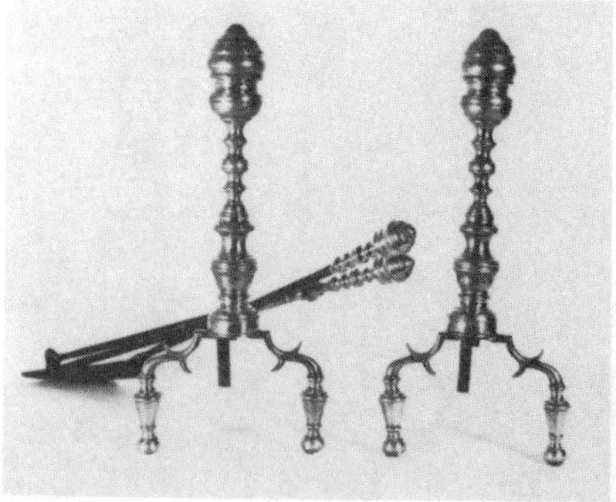

A-MA Aug 1980 *Robert C. Eldred Co., Inc.*

BRASS ANDIRONS, Pr., Sgn. "H. Smylie 3 Patent", Matching Shovel & Tongs, 20½″ H. $600.00

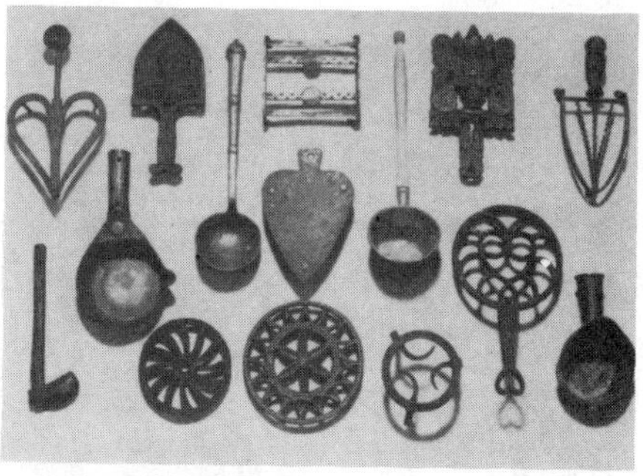

A-OH Oct 1980 *Garth's Auctions, Inc.*

ROW I, L To R

WROUGHT IRON TRIVET, Heart W/ Scrolled Handle, 10¼″ L. $155.00

CAST IRON TRIVET, Geo. Washington, 9¼″ L. $45.00

PEWTER LADLE, Mkd. "C.H.B.", 14″ L. $25.00

WROUGHT IRON TRIVET, Filed Designs, 1 Cross Member Missing, 5¼″ x 5½″ $25.00

DIPPER, Pewter Bowl W/Turned Wood Handle, Somewhat Battered, 14½″ L. $35.00

CAST IRON TRIVET, Vintage Design, 9″ L. $30.00

WROUGHT IRON TRIVET, Penny Feet & Crimped Iron, Scorched Wooden Handle, 9¼″ L. $30.00

ROW II, L To R

WROUGHT IRON LADLE, Made To Accept Wooden Handle, 9¾″ L. ... $45.00

WROUGHT IRON TRIVET, Spade Shaped W/3 Legs, 7½″ L. $135.00

CAST IRON TRIVET, Circular W/Heart Designs, 10¾″ L. $65.00

ROW III, L To R

FILE MAKER'S HAMMER, 9″ L. .. $27.50

CAST IRON TRIVET, Circle W/Spiral Designs, 5¼″ D. $27.50

CAST IRON TRIVET, Circle W/Compass Star Flower, 6¾″ D. $55.00

WROUGHT IRON TRIVET, Circle W/ Curved Legs, 4¼″ D., 3″ H. $100.00

CAST BRONZE CHINESE IRON, 7″ L. $17.50

A-MA Aug 1980   *Robert C. Eldred Co., Inc.*
L To R
ANDIRONS, Pr., Am., Brass Finials, 15″ D., 22½″ H. $375.00
BRASS ANDIRONS W/Log Guards, Pr., Am., 23″ D., 16″ H. $175.00
FEDERAL BRASS ANDIRONS, Pr., 1 Re-Posted, Ca. 1800, 22½″ H. $425.00

A-OH April 1980   *Garth's Auctions, Inc.*
ROW I, L To R
SM. COPPER SAUCE PAN, Iron Handle, Dovetailed Seams, Polished & Sl. Battered, 4¼″ D., 6″ O.H. $50.00
IRON HOG SCRAPER, Wooden Handle, 5″ L. $12.50
PEWTER CANDY MOLD, "A. Wilke, Brooklyn, NY", 6″ H. $70.00
TIN TELESCOPING HORN, Embossed "Pat. May 12, 1903", Extends To 13¾″ L.
. . . . $22.50
TIN FLY CATCHER, Embossed "Patent Applied For, Feb. 1865, W.P.R.", 7⅝″ H.
. . . . $30.00
ROW II, L To R
TIN GRATER W/Hand Crank & Remov. Base, Porcelain Knob Chipped, Old Soldered Rep., 6¾″ O.H. $15.00
TIN TEA CADDY, 5¾″ H. $20.00
TIN COTTAGE CHEESE SIEVE, Matching Pan Not Illus., 5¾″ D., 5″ H. . . $110.00
TIN MILK CAN, 5½″ H. $17.50
TIN MILK CAN, 8¼″ H. $17.50
ROW III, L To R
GAS FLAT IRON W/Rotating Handle, "Pat. Sept. 29, '85", 8¼″ L. $12.50
TIN MELON RIB MOLD, 5½″ L.
. . . . $17.50
CAST IRON GOFFERING IRON, 6¾″ H.
. . . . $50.00
CAST CHARCOAL IRON, Tin Heat Deflector Under Wooden Handle & Chimney, Fastening Pin Replaced W/Nail $25.00

A-OH April 1980   *Garth's Auctions, Inc.*
WOODEN TASTER, Bowl Edge Worn, 8¼″ L. $20.00
WOODEN SPATULA, 11¼″ L. . . . $5.00
KENTUCKY PISTOL, By Halback Of Baltimore, MD, Converted To Percussion, Ca. 1780, 6¾″ Barrel, 12″ O.L. . . . $975.00
WOODEN LADLE, 7¾″ L. $45.00
BURL BUTTER PADDLE W/Bird Head Handle, 10¼″ L. $675.00
WOODEN LADLE, 6″ L. $110.00
CARVED WALKING STICK, Parrot, Wooden, Orig. Gr. Paint, Glass Eyes, Damaged, 13″ L. $55.00
POWDER HORN W/Iron & Brass Dispenser Tip, "J. Leavitt", Ca. 1780, Wooden End W/Threaded Insert Cap, 14″ L.
. . . . $475.00
PRINT BLOCK, Tree Form, Surface Deteriorated & Cracked, 3″ H. $2.50
PRINT BLOCK, Leaf Shape, Turned Handle, 2½″ L. $55.00
IRON SUGAR TONGS & CUTTER, 5¾″ L. $60.00
IRON CANDLE SNUFFER, Scissor W/Pick At End, 4¾″ L. $80.00
CUT-OUT. Almond Shaped W/Tulips, Red Cloth Back & Corner Block Frame, Glass Has Corner Crack, 4½″ x 5″ . . . $110.00
CAST BRASS SCISSOR WICK TRIMMERS & TRAY, 9¾″ L. $50.00

Left
A-MA Oct 1980   *Robert W. Skinner Inc.*
IRON GRISSETTE, Riveted Handle, Am., Late 17th-Early 18th C., 14½″ L., 11½″ W.
. . . . $475.00*

Right
A-NY May 1980   *The Auction Gallery*
WROUGHT IRON CHAIN TRAMMEL, 18th C., N. Eng., Adj., 40″ L. $45.00

A-OH Mar 1980   *Garth's Auctions, Inc.*
SEWER TILE BOOK FLASK, "Constatution Of The Know Nothing", Chip On Base, 5¼″ L. $90.00
WROUGHT IRON LOCK W/KEY, Snake Head Keeper Initialed "P.S.A.", 5¾″ x 6″
. . . . $65.00
SEWER TILE EAGLE, Incised "E.J.E.", Ca. 1950, 5″ H. $50.00
WROUGHT IRON SUGAR NIPPERS, 8¼″ L. $50.00
FOOD MOLD, Tin & Cooper W/Embossed Ear Of Corn, Handle Added, 5″ x 6½″ . . $65.00
WROUGHT IRON SUGAR NIPPERS, 6″ L. $45.00
REDWARE HOT PLATE, Clear Glaze W/ Br. Splotches, Rim Flakes, Impressed "John Bell, Waynesboro", 8⅛″ D. $555.00
LEATHER CUTTER W/Steel Blade, Brass Ferrule Stamped "C.C.", Rosewood Handle, 7″ L. $25.00
FOOD MOLD, Tin & Copper W/Embossed Ear Of Corn, 5¼″ x 7″ $70.00
FOOD CHOPPER W/Turned Wooden Handle, 6″ W. $10.00
FOOD CHOPPER W/Turned & Cut Out Wooden Handle, Crescent Blade, 8¼″ W.
. . . . $15.00
FOOD CHOPPER W/Turned Wooden Handle, 6½″ W. $12.50

A-OH April 1980   *Garth's Auctions, Inc.*
L To R
WROUGHT IRON DIPPER, Scrolled Hanger, 18″ L. $25.00
WROUGHT IRON DIPPER, Scrolled Hanger, 14¾″ L. $40.00
WROUGHT IRON UTENSILS, 5 Pc. Set, Polished, Scrolled Hanger . . . $275.00
WROUGHT IRON STRAINER, Scrolled Hanger, 18″ L. $30.00

A-OH Oct 1980   *Garth's Auctions, Inc.*
ROW I, L To R
SHENANDOAH POTTERY FRAME,
Buff Clay W/Br. Running Glaze, Attrib. To
John Bell, 8¼" x 9¼" $75.00
CAST IRON FIRE MARK, Eagle, Repro.,
8¾" x 11¼" $7.50
SHENANDOAH POTTERY FRAME,
Buff Clay W/Br. Running Glaze, Attrib. To
John Bell, 8½" x 9¼" $75.00
ROW II, L To R
WOODEN DIPPER, Turned Bowl W/Brass
Bands, Inserted Handle, 12¼" L. ... $6.50
NOISE MAKER, Wood & Brass, 7¼" L.
.... $7.50
CAST BRONZE MONKEY, 2¾" L.
.... $35.00
**WROUGHT IRON BUTTERFLY
HINGES,** 2, 4" x 5" $30.00
WOODEN NUT CRACKER, Head Of
"Old Salt", 8" L. $22.50
WOODEN NUT CRACKER, Threaded
Thumb Screw, 5" L. $5.00
WOODEN SPOONS, 2, 1 W/Scratch
Carving, Other W/Heart Shaped Handle,
7½" L. $27.50
SHENANDOAH POTTERY TRIVET,
Buff Clay W/Br. Sponging On Embossed
Surface, Impressed "John Bell, Waynes-
boro", 9" D. $25.00
WALNUT SLICER, 10" L. $25.00

A-OH April 1980   *Garth's Auctions, Inc.*
L To R
TIN HANGING MATCH BOX W/
Hinged Lid & Striking Surface, Worn Blk.
Paint W/Gold Stencil, 4½" L. $35.00
TOLE DEED BOX, Orig. Br. Japanning,
Handle Replaced, Wear & Scratches, 8½"
L. $205.00
TOLE SHAKER, Orig. Drk Br. Japanning,
2¾" H. $165.00
TIN MINI. HOUSE, Orig. Br., Wh., & Red
Paint, 3½" H. $125.00
TOLE DEED BOX, Beveled Edge Lid &
Orig. Gold Japanning, Sm. Ring For
Hanging But Orig. Lid Handle Missing, 4" x
5¼" x 5¾" $25.00

A-OH Mar 1980   *Garth's Auctions, Inc.*
ROW I, L To R
TIN COOKIE CUTTER, Rabbit, 5½" L.
.... $45.00
WOODEN BUTTER PRINT, Pinwheel W/
Stars, 1 Pc., 3⅞" D. $195.00
TIN COOKIE CUTTER, Animal, 5⅞" L.
.... $25.00
ROW II, L To R
TIN COOKIE CUTTER, Woman, 5⅜" H.
.... $17.50
**WROUGHT IRON SCISSORS WICK
TRIMMER,** 6¾" L. $32.50
STEEL SCISSORS WICK TRIMMER, 7"
L. $45.00
BRASS SHOT FLASK, Spring & Nozzle
Gone, 7¼" H. $20.00
LUTZ PATENT FIRE LIGHTER W/Orig.
Instruction Sheet, 8¾" L. $20.00
STEEL SCISSORS WICK TRIMMER, 1
Leg Missing, 6½" L. $15.00
TIN COOKIE CUTTER, Deer, 5" L.
.... $50.00
ROW III, L To R
WOODEN BUTTER PRINT, Flower,
Some Wear, 4" D. $100.00
WOODEN BUTTER PRINT, Pineapple,
Slightly Weathered, 4" D. $60.00
WOODEN BUTTER PRINT, Tulip,
Leaves, & Stars, 1 Pc. W/Turned Handle,
4¼" D. $165.00
WOODEN BUTTER PRINT, Chicken,
Treaded Handle Missing, 4" D. ... $235.00
WOODEN BUTTER PRINT, Concentric
Circles W/3 Leaf Center, Weathered & Age
Cracks, 1 Pc. W/Turned Handle, 4" D.
.... $75.00

A-OH April 1980   *Garth's Auctions, Inc.*
L To R
TOLE CANISTER, Orig. Br. Japanning,
Decor, Very Worn, 8¼" H. $40.00
TOLE TALL POT, Orig. Drk. Br.
Japanning, Wear & Spout Battered, 11¼"
H. $800.00
TOLE TRAY, Orig. Br. Japanning W/
Heart Shaped Floral Design, Little Wear,
6½" x 10½" $175.00

A-OH Mar 1980   *Garth's Auctions, Inc.*
HOMESPUN, Red & Wh. W/Center Seam,
48" x 68" $95.00
HANGING SHELVES, Mahogany, 15"
W., 7½" D., 25" H. $135.00
ROW I, L To R
WOODEN BUTTER PRINT, Tulip &
Circle Design, 1 Pc. W/Turned Handle, 3¼"
D. $95.00
WOODEN BUTTER PRINT, Eagle &
Stars, Turned Handle, 3" x 5" $450.00
WOODEN BUTTER PRINT, Star Design,
Surface Worn, 3¾" D. $40.00
ROW II, L To R
WOODEN BUTTER PRINT, Rose, 1 Pc.
W/Turned Handle, 2⅝" D. $40.00
SM. WOODEN BUTTER PRINT, Fluted
Circle, 1 Pc. W/Wooden Handle, 1⅞" D.
.... $60.00
WOODEN BUTTER PRINT, Star Design,
Inserted Whittled Handle, Back Carved
"Mrs. W.", 4¾" D. $205.00
TURNED WOODEN BUTTER PRINT,
Sun, 3¼" L. $40.00
WOODEN BUTTER PRINT, Star Flower,
1 Pc. W/Wooden Handle, 2½" D. .. $85.00
CLEAR BLOWN LAMP FONT W/Tin
Drop Burner & Turned Wooden Base, 8" H.
.... $130.00
HANGING SCONCE W/Turned Walnut
Shelf & Poplar Back, 9" H. $165.00
ROW III, L To R
WOODEN BUTTER PRINT, Fat Sheaf
Of Grain, 1 Pc. W/Turned Handle, 3¾" D.
.... $245.00
BUTTER PRINT, Heart & Tulup Design,
Sm. Brass Knob On Back, 3" x 5¾"...$500.00
WOODEN BUTTER PRINT, Tulip W/In-
serted Turned Handle, 4⅜" D. ... $135.00

A-NY May 1980   *The Auction Gallery*
L To R
WROUGHT IRON PIGTAIL ANDIRONS,
12" D., 18" H. $100.00
**WROUGHT IRON KNIFE BLADE AND-
IRONS,** 18th C., Brass Finials, Repaired,
14" D., 16½" H. $150.00

A-MA Mar 1980   Robert W. Skinner Inc.
L To R
TIFFANY TABLE LAMP Leaded Glass Shade & Dore Bronze Standard, Shade Stamped "Tiffany Studios, NY", Early 20th C., 21½" O.H. $3250.00*
TIFFANY FAVRILLE DESK LAMP, Glass & Bronze, Base Stamped "Tiffany Studios", Bears Trademark, Chips Under Shade Fitting, NY, Late 19th C., 12" O.H. $1900.00*

A-MA Mar 1980   Robert W. Skinner, Inc.
STEUBEN CUT BACK LAMPS, Pr., Fittings Are Cast Brass, Finials Hung W/2 Faceted Amethyst Glass Bells, Orig. Silk Shades Complete, NY, 20th C., 28" O.H. $2800.00*

A-MA Aug 1980   Robert C. Eldred Co., Inc.
L To R
TIFFANY BRONZE LILY LAMP, 7-Light, Irid. Gold Glass Shades Sgn. LCT. Favrille, Base Plate Missing, Rewired, 20½" H. $4000.00
TIFFANY ART NOUVEAU TABLE LAMP, Gr. Leaded Shade, Sgn., Metal Base, Shade: 14" D., 16" O.H. .. $2000.00

Price does not include 10% buyer fee.

Left
A-WA D.C. Dec 1980 *Adam A. Weschler & Son*
BRONZE TIFFANY TABLE LAMP, Octagonal Shade, Scalloped Rim 1/8 Lrg. Spider Web Medallions W/Crackled Clear Glass, Opalescent & Colored Glass Beneath, Round Terrain Base Enclosing Baluster Mosaic Glass Base In Tesseraie & Setiliae, Electrified Conv. Fuel Canister, Imp. Tiffany Glass & Decorating Co., Tiffany Studios, NY, Gr.-Br. Patina, 20" D., 29" H. $210000.00*

Right
A-WA D.C. Feb 1980 *Adam A. Weschler & Son*
TIFFANY TABLE LAMP, Glass & Bronze, Shade Labelled Tiffany Studios, Base Impressed, Shade, 16" D., Base 21" H. $3100.00*

Left
A-MA Mar 1980   Robert W. Skinner, Inc.
TABLE LAMP, Leaded Glass Shade, Bronze Standard, "Handel" Molded Into Base, Shade Restored, Am., Early 20th C., 23" O.H. $1200.00*
Right
A-MA July 1980   Robert W. Skinner Inc.
TIFFANY TABLE LAMP, Leaded Brickwork Shade, Bronze Standard, Base & Shade Sgn. "Tiffany Studios-NY", Early 20th C., 24" H. $6500.00*

A-MA Mar 1980   Richard A. Bourne Co., Inc.
MIRRORED TIN WALL SCONCES W/ Single Candleholders & Circular Reflectors, Orig. Blue & Gold Striped Paint Well Preserved, Diam. 9½" $1250.00

Left
A-MA Oct 1980   Robert W. Skinner Inc.
BRASS CHANDELIER, 19th C., 12½" H. $800.00*

Right
A-WA D.C. Oct 1980 *Adam A. Weschler & Son*
GLASS BASKET CHANDELIER, 6-Light, European, Early 20th C., 24" D., 36" H. $400.00*

Left
A-MA July 1980   Robert W. Skinner Inc.
TIFFANY LILY TABLE LAMP, Glass & Bronze, 10-Light, 5 Shades & Base Sgn., NY, Early 20th C., 20½" H. $7500.00*
Right
A-MA Aug 1980   Robert C. Eldred Co., Inc.
TIFFANY BRONZE LILY LAMP, 3-Light, Gold Irid. Shades Mkd. LCT, Base Mkd. Tiffany Studios, NY, 13" H. $3000.00

Left
A-WA D.C. Oct 1980 *Adam A. Weschler & Son*
HANDEL LAMP, Landscape Decor., Br. Patinated Bronze Standard Shade Sgn., Ca. 1925, Shade 18" D., 24" O.H. .. $1300.00
Right
A-MA Mar 1980   Robert W. Skinner Inc.
TABLE LAMP, Reverse Painted Shade, Wavy Edge Sq. Base, Chips Under Shade Cap, Am. 20th C., 21" O.H. $450.00*

A-WA D.C. May 1980 *Adam A. Weschler & Son*
L To R
DAUM NANCY DESK LAMP, Bronze Dore & Gold Painted Bronze, Ca. 1910, Cameo Glass Shade, 18½" H. ... $550.00*
FRENCH ART GLASS TABLE LAMP, Wrought Metal Base W/Applied Floral Decor., Inscribed Daum Nancy, 15" H. $700.00*

Left
A-MA Mar 1980   *Robert W. Skinner Inc.*
CHANDELIER, Dome-Shaped Irregular Leaded Glass Rim Shade, Green On Cream Ground, Am., 20th C., 28½" D. $1400.00*
Right
A-MA Aug 1980   *Robert C. Eldred Co., Inc.*
PAIRPOINT TABLE LAMP, 3-Dolphin Base, Reverse Painted Shade, Sgn. C. Durand, Mkd. Pairpoint On Base & Shade, 15½" D., 20" H. $1300.00

Left
A-MA Mar 1980   *Robert W. Skinner Inc.*
TABLE LAMP, Reverse Painted Shade, Brass Standard, Base Stamped Pairpoint Mfg. Co. Trademark, MA, 20th C., 18½" O.H. $1750.00*
Right
A-MA July 1980   *Robert W. Skinner Inc.*
BRADLEY & HUBBARD BANQUET LAMP, Cranberry Glass & Silver Plated, "Soldat Spartiste", Lighting Adaptation, Am., Late 19th C., 18" L. $325.00*

Left
A-MA Aug 1980   *Robert C. Eldred Co., Inc.*
TIFFANY BRONZE FLOOR LAMP, Gold Irid. Shade In Peacock Design, Sgn. LCT Favrille, Base Mkd. Tiffany Studios, NY, Shade, 12" D. $1800.00

Right
A-MA Oct 1980   *Robert W. Skinner Inc.*
ASTRAL LAMP, Brass & Overlay Glass, Clear Blown Shade W/Etched Designs, Brass Font & Stepped Base, Prism Ring Missing, Electrified, Shade Has Chips, Ca. 1850, 29" O.H. $400.00*

A-MA Mar 1980   *Robert W. Skinner Inc.* ▶
TABLE LAMP, Reverse Painted Shade, Bronzed Metal Standard, Rim Chips, Am., 20th C., 25½" O.H. $1100.00*

*Price does not include 10% buyer fee.

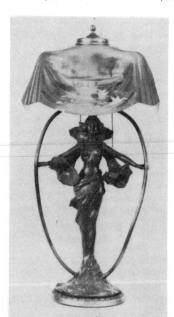

A-MA July 1980   *Robert W. Skinner Inc.*
CARVED ALABASTER FLOOR LAMP, "Three Graces", European, 20th C., 78½" H. $1800.00*

A–MA April 1980   *Richard A. Bourne Co., Inc.*
LEADED GLASS HANGING SHADE, Pink & Wh. Flowers, Few Glass Panels W/Cracks, 23" D. $325.00

A-OH July 1980 *Stratford Auction Center*
L To R
WELLER LAMP, Not Converted, Orig. Lamp From Factory, LaSa. Unsigned, 19½" H.
.... $300.00
WELLER LAMP, Dickensware, Br. Shiny Glaze W/Yellow Roses, Brass Oil Font, Imp. Sgn., 12" H. $400.00

A-MA Mar 1980 *Robert W. Skinner Inc.*
L To R
TABLE LAMP, Reverse Painted Shade, Ring On Shade Stamped "Jefferson", Bronze Standard, Orig. Felt Pad On Base Bearing Handel Fabric Label, Am., 20th C., 23½" O.H. $1400.00*
HANDEL BOUDOIR LAMP, Reverse Painted, Sgn. "F.L. Handel", CT, Early 20th C., 12½" O.H. $1500.00*

A-MA July 1980 *Robert W. Skinner Inc.*
KEROSENE LAMPS, Pr., Glass & Lithophane, European, Late 19th C., 20" H.
.... $1050.00*

*Price does not include 10% buyer fee.

A-MA July 1980
L To R
PAIRPOINT BOUDOIR LAMP, Painted Glass & Metal, Base & Shade Sgn., MA, Early 20th C., Shade, 8" D., 15½" H.
.... $1100.00*
DAUM NANCY TABLE LAMP, Mottled Glass & Wrt. Iron, Wired For Illumination, Inscribed, Early 20th C., 12" D. .. $1800.00*

A-MA July 1980 *Robert W. Skinner Inc.*
STUDENT'S LAMP, Nickel Plated, Kerosene Fed, Am., Late 19th C., 25" H.
.... $750.00*

A-MA April 1980 *Robert W. Skinner Inc.*
HANGING HALL CANDLE LAMP, Clear Glass Geometric Cut Globe W/Smoke Bell, Brass Frame Holder, Early 19th C., 17" H.
.... $400.00*

Left
A-WA D.C. Oct 1980 *Adam A. Weschler & Son*
MEISSEN CANDELABRUM, 7-Light, Late 19th-Early 20th C., 23" H. ... $600.00*

Right
A- MA July 1980 *Robert W. Skinner Inc.*
VIC. PORCELAIN LAMP, Brass Base, Polychrome Painted Decor., Gold Overglazing, Brass Mounts, Sgn. "Wagner", Austrian, Late 19th C., 14" H. $400.00*

Left
A-MA Jan 1981 *Robert W. Skinner Inc.*
TIFFANY FAVRILLE TABLE LAMP, Gr. Daffodil Cone Shaped Shade, Bronze Standard, Sgn. On Base & Shade, Ca. 1900, 23" O.H. $10000.00*

Right
A-MA Nov 1980 *Robert W. Skinner Inc.*
TIFFANY TABLE LAMP, Early 20th C., NY, Shade In Acorn Patt. W/Gr. Brick Work, Bronze Baluster Base, Sgn. Both Base & Shade, 22" O.H. $3100.00*

A-MA Nov 1980 *Robert W. Skinner Inc.*
HANGING GLASS SHADE, Am., Late 19th C., Caramel, Gr. & Purple Slag Glass W/Tulip Motif, Shade: 26¼" D. ... $750.00*

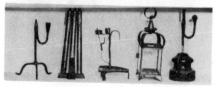

Left

A-MA Nov 1980   *Robert W. Skinner Inc.*
HANDEL TABLE LAMP, Early 20th C.,
Reverse Painted Glass Shade, Bronze Base,
Shade Artist Sgn. Bedigie, 23¼" O.H.
.... $8100.00*

Right

A-MA Jan 1981   *Robert W. Skinner Inc.*
HANDEL LAMP, CT, Tree Decor., Sgn.
"Handel", Cast Bronze Base, Ca. 1915, 22"
H. $2500.00*

Left

A-MA Jan 1981   *Robert W. Skinner Inc.*
AURENE FLOOR LAMP, Corning, NY,
Br. Shade Over Calcite Glass W/Zig-Zag
Motif, Brass Harp, Ca. 1910, Shade: 10" D.,
58" O.H. $1100.00*

Right

A-OH Oct 1980   *Early Auction Co.*
ROYAL FLEMISH LAMP BASE, 2-Tiers,
Decor. W/Shields & Lions, 28¾" H.
.... $700.00*

Left

A-MA Oct 1980   *Robert W. Skinner Inc.*
STANDING CANDLE HOLDER, Iron
Candle Socket, Scroll Shape Splint Holder,
Am., Mid 18th C., 27" H. $225.00*

Right

A-MA Feb 1980   *Robert W. Skinner Inc.*
CANDLESTAND, Iron & Brass, Acorn
Finial On Rounded Stem, Double Adj. Can-
dle Sockets, Cont., 18th Or 19th C., 63" H.
.... $700.00*

*Price does not include 10% buyer fee.

A-OH April 1980   *Garth's Auctions, Inc.*
ROW I, L To R

**IRON HOG SCRAPER CANDLE-
STICKS,** Pr., W/Pushups & Lip Handle,
5½" H. $230.00

**IRON HOG SCRAPER CANDLE-
STICKS** W/Pushup & Lip Handle, "Patented 1853", 4¼" H. $95.00

TIN CAMPAIGN TORCH, 5½" H.
.... $20.00

PEWTER WHALE OIL LAMP, Marked
"Calder" & "Providence", Orig. 1 Spout
Burner, Stem Soldered To Base, 4½" H.
.... $290.00

REDWARE PA CANDLE LAMP W/
Handle, Clear Glaze, 6" H. $250.00

ROW II, L To R

CAST IRON BETTY LAMP, Attached
Saucer Base, Wrought Hanger & Wire Pick,
5⅜" D. $135.00

**WROUGHT IRON DOUBLE CRUISE
LAMP** W/Ram's Horn Finial, On Hanging
Pan, 5¾" H. $200.00

**SHEET & WROUGHT IRON BETTY
LAMP** W/Swivel Cover, 4¼" H. .. $140.00

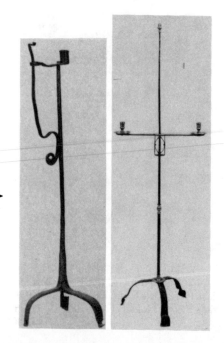

A-OH Feb 1981   *Garth's Auctions, Inc.*
LIGHTING DEVICES

ROW I, L To R

WROUGHT IRON BETTY LAMP, Chain
W/Pick But No Hanger, 4½" H. $65.00

BRASS MINER'S LAMP, 2¾" H. .. $50.00

TIN BURGLAR'S LAMP, Clear Bulls-eye
Lens & Brass Crown Top, Orig. Burner &
Font, 6¼" H. $65.00

TIN MINER'S LAMP, Spout W/Copper
Extension, 3½" H. $20.00

**WROUGHT IRON DOUBLE CRUISE
LAMP,** 5" H. $40.00

ROW II, L To R

TIN BURGLAR'S LAMP, Clear Bulls-eye
Lens & Double Scalloped Top, Damaged,
6½" H. $12.50

TIN DRK. ROOM LAMP, "Kodak", Worn
Orig. Red Paint, Brass Burner & Red Glass,
8½" H. $10.00

TIN & BRASS LAMP, Conical Chimney
W/Mica Window, Repaired, 7½" H.
.... $10.00

TIN BURGLAR'S LAMP, Clear Bulls-eye
Lens, Orig. Worn Br. Japanning, 6⅝" H.
.... $45.00

ROW III, L To R

**WROUGHT IRON RUSH LIGHT
HOLDER,** Twisted Arm & Stem W/Candle
Socket Counter Weight, 9" H. $215.00

TIN CANDLE MOLD, 3-Tube, 10½" H.
.... $50.00

WROUGHT IRON CANDLE HOLDER,
Twisted Stem & 2 Sockets, Repaired, 7½" H.
.... $165.00

TIN CANDLE LANTERN, 2 Of 4 Glasses
Cracked, 11" H. $10.00

**WROUGHT IRON RUSH LIGHT
HOLDER,** Faceted Knob Counter Weight,
Turned Wooden Base W/Lrg. Crack, 10¾"
H. $165.00

A-OH Oct 1980   *Garth's Auctions, Inc.*
GOING TO BED LAMPS
ROW I, L To R
TREEN, 2⅝″ H. $30.00
PERSIAN BRASS, Engraved W/Animals
& Hunters, 2⅞″ H. $12.50
CAST IRON, Knight In Armour, 3⅝″ H.
.... $30.00
MARBLE, Crown, Chips, 3 5/7″ H. ...$10.00
EXOTIC WOOD, Carved Flutes, Ivory
Finial, 5¾″ H. $20.00
BRASS, Worn Gilding, 2⅞″ H. ... $17.50
TREEN, Transfer Of Shells, 2″ H. .. $20.00
ROW II, L To R
TREEN, Transfer Of Dunkell, Ivory Finial,
2¾″ H. $30.00
TREEN, Threaded Cap, 2¼″ H. .. $17.00
SM. BRASS, 1⅞″ H. $30.00
CARDBOARD, Floral Decoupage, 2″ H.
.... $20.00
OVAL PORCELAIN, Tan Glaze, 2⅝″ H.
.... $17.50
BRASS, Embossed Foliage, 2¼″ H. .. $15.00
LIGNUM VITAE, Threaded Cap, 2⅜″ H.
.... $37.50
TURNED ANTLER, Wooden Lid, Antler
Base Broken, 3″ D. $15.00

A-MA Sept 1980   *Richard A. Bourne Co., Inc.*
PEWTER
ROW I, L To R
CAMPHENE LAMP By Capen & Moli-
neaux, Sgn. Ca. 1844-1854, Pitted, 2¾″ H.
.... $125.00
CAMPHENE LAMP By Capen & Moli-
neaux, Sgn., Damage To Saucer Rim, Burner
Not Orig., 3¼″ H. $80.00
CAMPHENE LAMP, Am. Unmarked,
Double Burner, Rough Cond., 2¾″ H.
.... $90.00
CAMPHENE LAMP W/Tin Parts, Rust
On Surface, 3½″ H. $45.00
ROW II, L To R
WHALE OIL LAMPS, Pr. Am., Unmarked,
Both Dented & Bent, 6¾″ H. $175.00
PINT MUGS, 2 Prs., (1 Item Illus.), Eng., 1
Pr. W/Monograms, 1 Pr. Mkd. "Pint"
.... $125.00

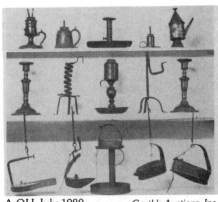

A-OH July 1980   *Garth's Auctions, Inc.*
ROW I, L To R
PEWTER LAMP, 6¼″ H. $160.00
PEWTER PETTICOAT LAMP, Cast Ear
Handle & Single Spout Burner, Snuffer
Missing, Dent & Sm. Pc. Missing, 4½″ H.
.... $70.00
BRASS CHAMBER STICK, 5″ H. $155.00
SM. PEWTER CHAMBER LAMP, Simple
Spout Burner, Cast Mrk. On Bottom
.... $125.00
TIN SINGLE SPOUT LAMP, Incomplete
& Needs Repair, 6″ H. $15.00
ROW II, L To R
PEWTER CANDLESTICKS, Pr. W/
Inserts, Sl. Battered, 8″ H. $230.00
WRT. IRON CANDLESTICKS W/Spiral
Adj. Stem, Rust Damage, 9¼″ H. .. $145.00
PEWTER LAMP W/Saucer Base, "Houghton
& Wallance, Pat. Nov. 15, 1843", 8¼″ H.
.... $390.00
WRT. IRON RUSH LIGHT HOLDER,
9½″ H. $220.00
ROW III, L To R
HANGING GREASE LAMP, Wrt. & Cast
Iron, 5″ O.H. $170.00
WRT. IRON CRUISE LAMP, Swivel Lid,
Adj. Angle & Pick, 7½″ O.H. $235.00
TIN BETTY LAMP & STAND W/Pick &
Hanger, 10″ H. $285.00
TIN BETTY LAMP W/Pick, Solder Repair,
4½″ O.H. $90.00
COPPER BETTY LAMP W/Pick, 4½″ O.H.
.... $155.00

A-OH April 1980   *Garth's Auctions, Inc.*
L To R
**WROUGHT IRON RUSH LIGHT
HOLDER**, Candle Socket Counterweight,
Wooden Block Base, 10¼″ H. $150.00
TURNED WOODEN CANDLESTICK
W/Pushup, Attrib. To Peter Derr, Brass
Insert, Age Crack, 6¾″ H. $350.00
TIN LAMP, Orig. Worn Drk. Blue Paint W/
Stenciled Gold Label, "Drummond's Patent,
T. Sewell, Manufacturer, Feb. 20, 1846",
7½″ H. $415.00
BENNINGTON CANDLESTICK W/
Flint Enamel Glaze, 9½″ H. $375.00
WROUGHT IRON RUSH LIGHT, Worn
Mod. Blk. Paint, Old Rep., 10½″ H. ...$175.00

A-OH Nov 1980   *Garth's Auctions, Inc.*
CHRISTMAS TREE LIGHTS
ROW I, L To R
BLOWN GLASS ORNAMENTS, Santas
W/Sm. Tree In Arms, 1 W/Red Coat, 1
W/Wh. Coat, 4¾″ H. $105.00
TIN LIGHT, 8 Stained Glass Panels, 3¼″ H.
.... $55.00
TIN LIGHT, 4 Stained Glass Panels, Insert
Missing, 2 Panels Broken, 4¾″ L. ... $5.00
ROW II, L To R
HOBNAIL LIGHTS, Lot Of 2 (1 Illus.),
Chicago Lamp Candle Co., Gr. & Blue, 4¼″
H. $22.50
FOLDING TIN LIGHT, Mica Windows &
Gold Japanning, 4½″ H. $50.00
TIN LIGHTS, Lot Of 2 (1 Illus.), 8 Panels,
Worn Color, 1 W/Wire Handle, 2¾″ H.
.... $50.00
BLOWN LIGHT, Amber W/Expanded
Diamond Netting & Folded Rim, 2½″ H.
.... $40.00
DIAMOND QUILTED LIGHTS, Set Of 4
(1 Illus.), 2 Clear, 2 Amber, 1 Sgn. Made In
France, Rim Flakes, 3½″ H. $7.50
ROW III, L To R
LIGHT, Acanthus Leaf Patt., Hearn Wright
& Co., London, 3½″ H. $35.00
BLOWN GLASS ORNAMENT, Drum,
2½″ L. $60.00
TIN LIGHT, 4 Stained Glass Panels, Wire
Hanger, 3¼″ H. $37.50
DIAMOND QUILTED LIGHT, Harrods
Stores Limited, Rim Flakes, 3½″ H. ... $10.00
DIAMOND QUILTED LIGHTS, Lot Of 3
(1 Illus.), Blue, Gr. & Aqua, Rim Flakes, 3½″
H. $7.50

A-MA Oct 1980   *Robert W. Skinner Inc.*
TIN TINDER BOXES, 2, Applied Handles, Candle Sockets, Am., 18th C., 4½″ D.
.... $325.00*

*Price does not include 10% buyer fee.

A-OH Mar 1980   *Garth's Auctions, Inc.*
ROW I, L To R
SM. HAND LANTERN W/Embossed Case & 3 Orig. Glasses W/Copper Wheel Engraved Doe On Front, 6" H. $50.00
TIN HAND LANTERN, Old Worn Gr. Paint W/Gold Striping, 6" H. $140.00
TIN LANTERN W/Ring Feet, Sm. Whale Oil Font In Candle Socket, 5½" H.
.... $80.00
SHEET BRASS WHALE OIL LAMP W/Lemon Shaped Font, Soldered Rep., 6¾" H. $75.00
TIN BURGLAR'S LANTERN W/Clear Bullseye Lens, 7" H. $30.00
ROW II, L To R
WROUGHT IRON RUSH HOLDER, Twisted W/Coiled Counterweight, Wooden Base, 9" H. $255.00
CAST & WROUGHT IRON MINER'S LAMP, Betty Type W/Lid Latch & Brass Semicircle W/Stamped Crossed Hammers, Old Gold Paint, 3¾" O. H. $270.00
TIN FOOT WARMER, Wrought Iron Handle W/Wooden Extension At One Time $55.00
WROUGHT IRON RUSH LIGHT HOLDER W/Candle Socket Counterbalance & Old Turned Wooden Base, 9" H. $195.00

ROW III, L To R
TIN CANDLESTICK W/Lip Handle & Brass Rim, Coiled Wire Pushup, 6" H.
.... $60.00
WROUGHT IRON ALPINE CANDLEHOLDER, 7½" H. $95.00
TIN KINNEAR'S PATENT LAMP, Worn Br. Japanning, 7½" H. $155.00
SHEET IRON CANDLESTICK W/Lip Handle, 3 Position Pushup, Old Breaks In Stem, 5¾" H. $55.00
WROUGHT IRON SPIRAL CANDLESTICK, Turned Wooden Base, Lip Hanger & Pushup, 8½" H. $190.00

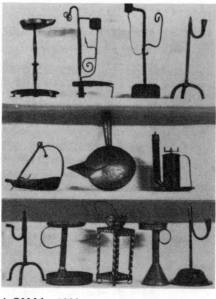

A-OH Mar 1980   *Garth's Auctions, Inc.*
ROW I, L To R
WROUGHT IRON GREASE LAMP, Old Blk. & Gold Paint, Base Sgn. "J. Herr, 1825", 10¼" H. $1025.00
WROUGHT IRON CANDLE HOLDER, Scrolled Spring Feet & Handle, 12¼" H. $275.00
WROUGHT IRON CANDLE HOLDER, Wooden Base, 12½" H. $155.00
WROUGHT IRON RUSH LIGHT HOLDER, 11" H. $155.00
ROW II, L To R
WROUGHT IRON GREASE LAMP, Spout Bit Battered, 5¾" H. $85.00
CANDLE WAX POURING LADLE, Copper, Made For Wooden Handle, Old Spout Rep., 10" L. $100.00
TIN LAMP, Damage & Rep., 7¾" H. $150.00
ROW III, L To R
WROUGHT IRON RUSH LIGHT HOLDER, 9½" H. $225.00
TIN BETTY LAMP STAND, Crimped Pan & Weighted Base, Saucer Base Bit Crooked, 8" H. $135.00
TIN CANDLE LANTERN, Painted Gr., Wh., Blue, & Red, 8¾" H. $45.00
TIN BETTY LAMP STAND, Weighted Base, 7¾" H. $115.00
WROUGHT IRON RUSH LIGHT HOLDER, Candle Socket Counterweight, Wooden Base Not Orig. But Old, 10¼" H.
.... $145.00

A-MA Oct 1980   *Robert W. Skinner Inc.* ▶
L To R
TIN BETTY LAMP W/Stand, Wick Pick & Hanger, Am., 18th C., 12" H. .. $350.00*
TIN PARADE LANTERN, 4 Glass Panels, 1 Mkd. "Abraham The Faithful, Hannibal The Brave", Int. W/Camphene Burner, Cam., Ca. 1860, 10" H. $400.00*

◀ A-MA Oct 1980   *Robert W. Skinner Inc.*
TIN LARD LAMPS, 2, 1 W/Orig. Gr. Paint Stenciled "Sam'l Davis Patented May 6th 1856", Other W/Orig. Br. Paint, PA, 7½" H.
.... $350.00*

A-MA Aug 1980   *Richard A. Bourne Co., Inc.*
ROW I, L To R
COPPER SHIP'S LANTERNS, Pr., Brass Mounting, Made By Russell & Stoll Co., NY, Minus Burners, Sm. Restorations, 18" O.H. $200.00
GALVANIZED SHIP'S ANCHOR LIGHT, Copper Mounted Top, Clear Magnifying Lens, Orig. Oil Fixture, Weathered, 15" O.H. $40.00
SM. BOAT LANTERN, Single Lamp, Brass Top, Orig. Oil Burner, 12" O.H. ... $80.00
ROW II, L To R
LRG. BRASS SHIP'S LANTERN, Needs Polishing, Electrified, 14" H. $110.00
COPPER SHIP'S LANTERN, Early Electric Bulb, Glass Cracked, Needs Polishing, 14" O.H. $50.00
LRG. ONION LANTERN, Copper Or Brass Mountings W/Wire Guards & Ruby Glass Globe, Electrified, Shows Wear & Use, 20" O.H. $90.00
LRG. SHIP'S COPPER LANTERNS, Pr. Electrified, Weathered To Gr. Color, 28" O.H. $275.00

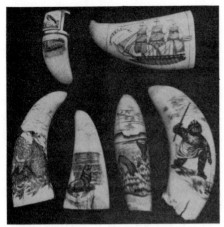

A-MA Aug 1980 *Richard A. Bourne Co., Inc.*
SCRIMSHAW
ROW I, L To R
SM. SPERM WHALE'S TOOTH, Mounted On Silver For Hanging, Engraved In Color, Sgn. "JB", 2⅝" L. $175.00
SM. SPERM WHALE'S TOOTH, Engraved W/Use Of Color, 4" L. ... $150.00
ROW II, L To R
WHALE'S TOOTH, Engraved W/Use Of Color, Sgn. "Jane Hough", 4½" L. .. $425.00
SM. SPERM WHALE'S TOOTH, Engraved W/Water & Sky In Blue, Sgn. "JB", 3⅝" L. $300.00
SM. WHALE'S TOOTH, Engraved W/Blue Whale Against Aurora Borealis, Sgn. "CM", 4⅜" L. $225.00
WHALE'S TOOTH, 5½" L. $425.00

Left
A-MA Aug 1980 *Richard A. Bourne Co., Inc.*
BULL WHALE'S TOOTH, Colored Scrimshaw, Sl. Age Cracks, 7" L. $6000.00
Right
A-MA Sept 1980 *Robert W. Skinner Inc.*
WHALE'S TOOTH, Cracks & Heel Chip, Am., Ca. 1840, 7" L. $700.00*

A-MA Aug 1980 *Richard A. Bourne Co., Inc.*
ROW I, L To R
WATCH CASE, Prisoner-Of-War Bone, Temple-Form, Dated 1813 In Bonnet, Battery-Operated Clock Work, Minor Loss Of Bone, Finial Broken, Repl. Clock Dial, 6½" W., 4" D., 10" O.H. $600.00
JEWELRY BOX, Prisoner-Of-War Bone, Early 19th C., Velvet-Lined Int., Tiny Chip In Bone, 9" L., 6¼" D., 5¼" H. ... $500.00

A-MA Aug 1980 *Richard A. Bourne Co., Inc.*
SCRIMSHAW
ROW I, L To R
WHALE'S TOOTH, Some Use Of Color On 1 Side, "Newport VA 1862", 5¼" L. $250.00
WHALE'S TOOTH, Some Use Of Color, 6" L. $500.00
WHALE'S TOOTH, Sgn. "GM", 6" L. $450.00
ROW II
WHALE'S TOOTH, Engraved On 1 Side, Sgn. By Artist W. Dean, Chip & Minor Age Cracks, 6½" L. $350.00

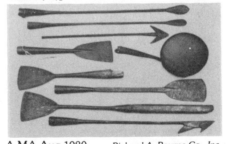

A-MA Aug 1980 *Richard A. Bourne Co., Inc.*
Top To Bottom
WHALING LANCE, Unmounted, Branded A. Peters & Cast Steel, 36½" L. .. $125.00
LANCE, Unmounted, Rusted Surface $70.00
ARCTIC OR DOUBLE-FLUE HARPOON, Initialed "FS", Cone Cut Off, Sl. Bent, 26¾" L. $95.00
BONE SPADE, Unmounted, Branced Cast Steel, Worn & Rusted, 19¾" L. ... $50.00
SM. SKIMMER, Hand Wrought Iron, 19" L. $90.00
BONE SPADE, Worn, 21" L. $35.00
BONE SPADE, Hand Wrought Shank, Initials "NG", Rusted, 30¼" L. ... $130.00
HEAD SPADE, Worn-Down, Rusted, Traces Of Orange Paint, 38" L. ... $50.00
TEMPLE TOGGLE HARPOON, Maker's Brand "JBD", Orig. Twine Wrapped Around Cone, 32" L. $225.00

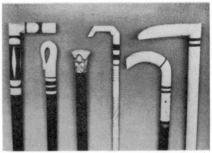

A-MA Aug 1980 *Richard A. Bourne Co., Inc.*
SCRIMSHAW
L To R
CANE, Whale Ivory Handle W/Ebony Inlays, Ebony Shaft, Age Crack, Tip Of Cane Missing, 34" L. $200.00
CANE, Carved Whale Ivory Serpent's Head Handle, Baleen Inlaid Rings, Wooden Shaft W/Brass Tip, 37½" L. $275.00
CANE, Leather Rings W/Clear Amber-Colored Tip, Carved Ivory Knob, 36½" L. $75.00
LADY'S CANE, Carved Whalebone Shaft, Baleen Inlays Between Shaft & Handle, 1 Ring Missing, 29½" L. $200.00
CANE, Island Wood Shaft W/Inlaid Whale Ivory Handle, Age Cracks, Pins Missing, 32" L. $100.00
CANE, Tapered Whalebone Shaft, Whale Or Walrus Ivory Handle, 35" L. .. $225.00

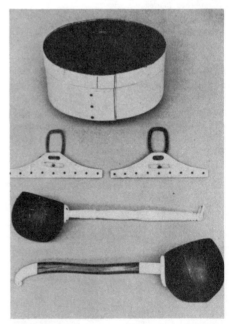

A-MA Aug 1980 *Richard A. Bourne Co., Inc.*
SCRIMSHAW
Top To Bottom
DITTY BOX, Panbone W/Pine Top & Bottom, Paint Shows Wear, 7⅞" W., 10¼" L., 4¾" H. $900.00
HAMMOCK FRAMES, Pr., Panbone, Rawhide-Bound Rope Hanger, 8⅜" L. $1100.00
DIPPER, Cocoanut Shell Bone W/Lrg. Whalebone Handle, Bone Hanging Ring, 12¼" L. $500.00
DIPPER, Cocoanut Shell Bowl, Wooden Handle W/Whale Ivory Attachment, Scrolled Whale Ivory Tip, 12" L. $450.00

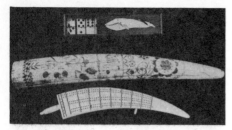

A-MA Aug 1980   *Richard A. Bourne Co., Inc.*
Top To Bottom
SCRIMSHAW DOMINOES, Lt. Mahogany Box W/Sliding Cover W/Applied Ivory Whale, 2 Sm. Chips............ $350.00
LRG. WALRUS TUSK, Engraved On Both Sides W/Much Use Of Color, Repaired, 22" L.
.... $300.00
SCRIMSHAW CRIBBAGE BOARD, Eskimo Engravings, Walrus Tusk Mounted On 4 Ivory Feet, Repaired, 22" L. $300.00

A-MA Aug 1980   *Richard A. Bourne Co., Inc.*
ROW I, L To R
WALRUS IVORY WHALE FIGURES, 2, Carved, 3", 4½" L. $120.00
JAGGING WHEEL, Form Of Sperm Whale, 5⅛" L. $180.00
ROW II, L To R
SCRIMSHAW WAX SEALER, Female Leg W/Incised Carving In Red & Blk., 2½" L.
.... $150.00
SCRIMSHAW JAGGING WHEEL, From Nantucket, Whale Ivory W/Br. Patina, 5⅜" L.
.... $225.00
SCRIMSHAW JAGGING WHEEL, From Nantucket, Whale Ivory, Br. Patina, 5¼" L.
.... $225.00
SM. SCRIMSHAW BOX, Sliding Cover Made Of Ivory, 2¾" L. $160.00

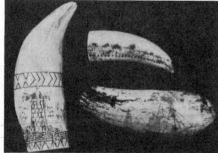

A-MA Aug 1980   *Richard A. Bourne Co., Inc.*
SCRIMSHAW
LRG. BULL WHALE'S TOOTH, Wigglework Scrimshaw Carving Of Ship & Lighthouse, 6⅞" L. $650.00
SM. WHALE'S TOOTH, Engraved On Both Sides W/Panoramic Sea & Landscapes, Sl. Worn, 4½" L. $225.00
BULL WHALE'S TOOTH, Sgn. "EDR" & "1843", 7¼" L. $350.00

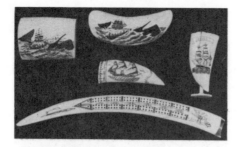

A-MA Aug 1980   *Richard A. Bourne Co., Inc.*
SCRIMSHAW
ROW I, L To R
SECTION OF IVORY, ½ Pound, Engraved Scene "The Capture", 4½" L. $260.00
WHALE'S TOOTH, Engraving Of "The Capture", 6¾" L. $300.00
SCRIMSHAW VASE, Inverted Sperm Whale's Tooth Mounted On Turned Whale Ivory Foot, Age Split, 5" H. $200.00
WHALE'S TOOTH, Engraved W/Portrait Of "The Black Ball Packet Neptune Oct 1861", 5¾" L. $300.00
CRIBBAGE BOARD, Eskimo Engraving, Pegs Missing, Door Arrangement At Butt End Missing, 16¾" L. $175.00

A-MA Aug 1980   *Richard A. Bourne Co., Inc.*
Top To Bottom
BULL WHALE'S TOOTH, Engraved On 1 Side W/Some Use Of Color, Early 19th C., 3½" W., 5¾" L. $1300.00
WHALE'S TOOTH, Pinpoint Scrimshaw Work On Both Sides, Some Use Of Color On 1 Side, 6" L. $500.00

A-MA Aug 1980   *Richard A. Bourne Co., Inc.*
SCRIMSHAW
LRG. BULL WHALE'S TOOTH, Engraved On Both Sides, "Hunting The Great White Bear"/"The Artic W/Boats Fast To A Whale", Titles Sl. Worn, 6¾" L. .. $375.00
WHALE'S TOOTH, "Oh Give Not Way To Sorrow", 7¼" L. $300.00
SPERM WHALE'S TOOTH, "Nantucket Sleighride", Sl. Age Crack, 5⅞" L. .. $200.00

A-MA Aug 1980   *Richard A. Bourne Co., Inc.*
SCRIMSHAW
TOP To BOTTOM
WHALE'S TOOTH, Engraving Of Eagle Done In Br. Tones, Sgn. "R. Spring", Dated "74", 5" L. $120.00
WHALE'S TOOTH, Engraving Of "The Capture", 5" L. $125.00
SM. WALRUS TUSK, Am. Engravings W/ Date 1874, Sm. Chip, 8¼" L. $150.00
SM. ELEPHANT TUSK, Engraved Overall W/Whaling Scene, 8⅞" L. $175.00

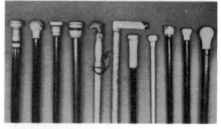

A-MA Aug 1980   *Richard A. Bourne Co., Inc.*
SCRIMSHAW
L To R
CANE, Island Wood Shaft W/Whalebone-Turned Head, Baleen Rings, Icicle-Like Inlays, Ivory Tip, Sl. Age Cracks, 33½" L.
.... $350.00
CANE, Blk.-Painted Hardwood Shaft W/ Carved Whale Ivory Turk's Head, 34" L.
.... $250.00
CANE, Island Wood Shaft, Turned Whale Ivory Head, 35½" L. $100.00
CANE, Wooden Shaft W/Whale Ivory Head Engraved "GCD", Bone Tip, 36" L. ..$150.00
CANE, Carved Whalebone Shaft W/Gold-Colored Metal Eagle's Head, 34½" L.
.... $125.00
CANE, Bone Shaft W/Simple Walrus Ivory Handle, Silver Tip W/Initials "WPR", Repaired, Tip Dented, 36" L. $175.00
CANE, Wooden Shaft W/Twist-Carved Bone Handle W/Whale Ivory Knob, 34¼" L.
.... $125.00
LADY'S CANE, Whalebone Shaft W/ Simple Turned Whale Ivory Head, Baleen Or Ebony Set In Top, 32¾" L. ... $200.00
CANE, Island Wood Shaft, Whale Ivory Knob Carved W/14 Facets, 35¼" L. .. $100.00
CANE, Island Wood Shaft W/Simple Turned Ivory Knob, 33" L. $50.00
CAPTAIN'S CANE, Whale Ivory Knob & Baleen Or Horn Tip, Sl. Age Cracks, 35¾" L.
.... $150.00

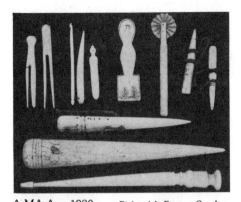

A-MA Aug 1980   *Richard A. Bourne Co., Inc.*
SCHRIMSHAW
ROW I, L To R
WHALEBONE CLOTHES PINS, 2, 4¼"
& 5" $125.00
UTILITARIAN OBJECTS, Lot Of 3,
Whalebone Sailor's Needle, Crochet Hook
& Needle Case................. $100.00
WHALEBONE SEAM RUBBER, En-
graved W/Flowers, Plants, Urn & Dog's
Head, 5" L. $150.00
JAGGING WHEEL, Ivory W/Plain Whale-
bone Handle, 6⅛" L. $200.00
SAILOR'S SAILMAKING NEEDLES, Lot
Of 2, Leather Thumb Pcs., 3⅞" L. ...$120.00
ROW II, TOP To BOTTOM
WHALEBONE FID, Leather Thong, En-
graved "WF", 8" L. $125.00
LRG. WHALEBONE FID, 12" L.
.... $225.00
PC. OF TURNED WHALEBONE, Unfin-
ished, 11¾" L. $160.00

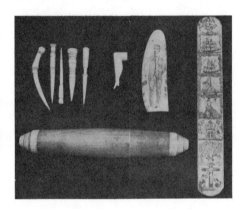

A-MA Aug 1980   *Richard A. Bourne Co., Inc.*
ROW I, L To R
SCRIMSHAW BODKINS, Lot Of 5, 4 Of
Whale Ivory, 1 Of Whalebone $150.00
HANDLE, For Lady's Cane, Whale Ivory,
Never Completed Though Fully Carved,
2¾" L. $50.00
SECTION OF BULL WHALE'S TOOTH,
Flat, Engraved On Curved Side, 6¼" L.
.... $50.00
CORSET BUSK, Whalebone, Engraved
On Both Sides, ⅛" Thick, 13⅜" L. .. $325.00
ROW II
SCRIMSHAW ROLLING PIN, Turned
Whale Ivory Tips, Mahogany Roller, Wood
W/Age Split, 13" L. $300.00

A-MA Aug 1980   *Richard A. Bourne Co., Inc.*
SCRIMSHAW
Top To Bottom
BULL WHALE'S TOOTH, Engraved W/
Use Of Color On 1 Side, Blk. Ink Engraving
On Other, 3⅝" W., 7⅛" L. $1800.00
LRG. BULL WHALE'S TOOTH, En-
graved On 1 Side, Tooth Malformed On
Back Side, 3½" W., 7¾" L. $1000.00

A-MA Aug 1980   *Richard A. Bourne Co., Inc.*
SCRIMSHAW
Top To Bottom
WHALE'S TOOTH, Engraved On 1 Side,
5¾" L. $425.00
WHALE'S TOOTH, Engraved On Both
Sides, Sgn. "R. Spring 74", 6¾" L. ...$375.00

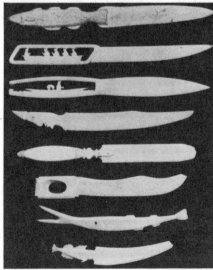

A-MA Aug 1980   *Richard A. Bourne Co., Inc.*
ESKIMO SCRIMSHAW ITEMS, Collec-
tion Of 8, 7 Letter Openers & Fork Made Of
Walrus Ivory, Whale Ivory & Bone, Some
Chips $150.00

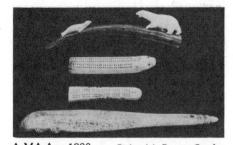

A-MA Aug 1980   *Richard A. Bourne Co., Inc.*
Top To Bottom
ESKIMO SCULPTURE, Carved Whale
Ivory Polar Bear Attacking Seal, Mounted
On Walrus Ivory, 11¾" L. $375.00
SCRIMSHAW CRIBBAGE BOARD, Es-
kimo Carving, Ivory, Complete W/Pegs,
Cover Missing, 7⅛" L. $225.00
SCRIMSHAW CRIBBAGE BOARD, Es-
kimo Carved Bone, Decor. W/2 Totems In
Color, 6" L. $25.00
CLUB, Carved Bone, 16½" L. ... $225.00

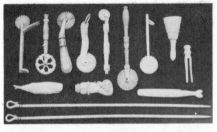

A-MA Aug 1980   *Richard A. Bourne Co., Inc.*
ROW I, L To R
JAGGING WHEEL, Whale Ivory W/3-
Tined Fork, Heart & Club Carved Handle,
Repaired, 6½" L. $200.00
JAGGING WHEEL, Turned Whalebone
Handle W/Whale Ivory Wheel, Nantucket
Type, 6" L. $275.00
JAGGING WHEEL, Whale Ivory W/2
Bands Of Baleen Inlay, Good Patina, 6⅛" L.
.... $300.00
JAGGING WHEEL, Whale Ivory W/Ring
Handle & Lrg. Wheel, 5⅞" L. $275.00
JAGGING WHEEL, Whalebone W/Sm.
Whale Ivory Wheel, Mother-Of-Pearl Inlays,
Sm. Chip, Pcs. Missing, 6½" L. ... $225.00
JAGGING WHEEL, Nantucket-Type,
Turned Whalebone Handle W/Lrg. Whale
Ivory Wheel, 8⅜" L. $400.00
JAGGING WHEEL, Walrus Ivory W/Pin-
ned Movable Handle & Open-Cut Hearts-
Diamonds, 6" L. $150.00
PICK-WICK, Bell-Shaped, Turned Whale's
Tooth W/Hand Wrought Pick, 4¼" H.
.... $400.00
CLOTHES PIN, Turned Whalebone, 3¾" L.
.... $70.00
ROW II, L To R
CARVED SPERM WHALE, Whale Ivory,
Repaired, 4⅞" L. $130.00
CANE HEAD, Carved Ivory, Engraved "G.
Harrison/Hotel", 3½" L. $320.00
LETTER OPENER, Whale Ivory, 2 Parts,
6⅜" L. $80.00
ROW III
SCRIMSHAW KNITTING NEEDLES,
Pr., Bone W/Carved Whale Ivory Serpent
Handles, Double Inlay Rings Of Baleen,
19 13/16" L. $600.00

A-MA Aug 1980   *Richard A. Bourne Co., Inc.*
L To R
SHIP CAPTAIN'S LIQUOR CHEST,
Orig. Engraved Label "Drk. Otard Brandy",
Minor Damages, 5 Lrg. Case Bottles, 4 Sm.
Case Bottles, 2 Stemmed Wines, Whiskey
Tumbler, 16½" L., 11⅜" W., 11" H. . . . $325.00
BELAYING PINS, Pr., From Charles W.
Morgan, Mounted On Custom-Made Board
W/Brass Plate, 24" O.H. $200.00
LOAN LIBRARY, Issued By Am. Sea-
man's Friend Society, Pine Case, Complete,
12⅞" W., 7¼" D., 26" H. $1100.00

A-MA Sept 1980   *Richard A. Bourne Co., Inc.*
L To R
SM. TABLE GLOBE, Am., "Perce's Mag-
netic Globe-NY, Charles Scribner", Ca.
1864, Moving Axis, Worn & Darkened, 5" D.,
12" H. $225.00
CELESTIAL TABLE COVER, "Cruch-
ley's Globe", London, Early 19th C., 8¾" D.,
14" O.H. $450.00
TERRESTRIAL GLOBE, "Phillip's Globe",
Late 19th C., 8½" D., 16½" H. $75.00

A-MA Aug 1980   *Robert C. Eldred Co., Inc.*
DOUBLE-CASED CHRONOMETER By
T.S. Negus & Co., NY, Brass-Mounted
Walnut Case W/Oak Carrying Case, Minus
Second Hand $1200.00

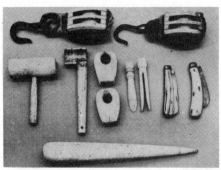

A-MA Aug 1980   *Richard A. Bourne Co., Inc.*
ROW I, L To R
SCRIMSHAW BLOCK, Whalebone W/
Iron Hook, 8½" L. $650.00
SCRIMSHAW BLOCK, Whalebone W/
Iron Hook $650.00
ROW II, L To R
ROPE SERVER, Whalebone, 5⅝" L.
. . . . $250.00
ROPE SERVER, 1-Pc. Whalebone, 7½" L.
. . . . $300.00
DEADEYES, Pr., Whale Ivory, 2¾" W., 3" L.
. . . . $350.00
CLOTHES PINS, Whalebone, Non-Match-
ing Pr., 1 W/Side Broken Off, 4¾" L.
. . . . $50.00
SAILOR'S JACK KNIFE, 2 Blades, Bone
Darkened & Split, Blade Worn, 4¾" L.
. . . . $50.00
SAILOR'S JACK KNIFE, Single Blade,
Darkened Areas, Blade Worn, 5" L.
. . . . $60.00
ROW III
LRG. FID, Panbone, 13½" L. $200.00

A-MA Aug 1980   *Richard A. Bourne Co., Inc.*
L To R
ARTIFICIAL HORIZON, Sailor-Made, Ma-
hogany, 17½" L. $250.00
BRASS TELESCOPE, 2-Draw, By Harris
& Co., London, Day Or Night Glass, Leather
Casing Worn, Lens Cap Missing . . $175.00
TELESCOPE, 2-Draw, Hagger & Bro.,
MD, Day Or Night, Painted Sailor-Made
Ropework, Mahogany Beneath . . . $275.00
TELESCOPE, Single-Draw, By G. Chris-
tian, Liverpool, Leather Bound, Missing
Lens Cap $200.00
TIN SPEAKING TRUMPET, Orig. Gr.
Paint, Rusted $70.00

A-MA Aug 1980   *Robert C. Eldred Co., Inc.*
L To R
TELESCOPE, Brass & Mahogany, Some
Dents, 24" L. $140.00
TELESCOPE, 26X German, "Voigtlander
& John A-G, Braunschweig" $110.00
TELESCOPE, Eng., Brass & Walnut, Mkd.
"C. West, London-Day Or Night", 23" L.
. . . . $160.00
SHIP'S TELESCOPE, Brass, 19th C., Tube
Mkd. "Day Or Night", 39" L. $180.00
TELESCOPE, Eng., Brass, "Cutts, Lon-
don", Leather Cover, 36" L. $150.00

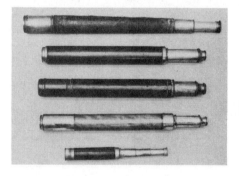

A-MA Aug 1980   *Richard A. Bourne Co., Inc.*
Top To Bottom
TELESCOPE, Single-Draw, "U.S. Navy/
Power 30/Bardou & Son/Paris/150", Leather
Bound, Minus Lens Caps, Aged . . $225.00
TELESCOPE, Single-Draw, By Willson &
Dixey, London, Day Or Night Glass
W/Mahogany Case, Minus Lens Cap
. . . . $225.00
TELESCOPE, Single-Draw, By W. Gerard,
Liverpool, Day Or Night Glass, Leather
Wrapped, Lens Cap Missing $170.00
TELESCOPE, Single-Draw, By Messer,
London, Day Or Night Glass, Mahogany
Case $400.00
TELESCOPE, 3-Draw, Leather Bound,
Complete W/Lens Cap. $130.00

A-MA Aug 1980   *Richard A. Bourne Co., Inc.*
ROW I, L To R
SHIP'S BELL CLOCK, Seth Thomas, 8-Day, 7-Jeweled Movement, Brass Dial, 7⅛" D. $200.00
SHIP'S BELL CLOCK, Brass-Cased, Seth Thomas, 6⅞" D. $275.00
SHIP'S BELL CLOCK, Seth Thomas, Brass-Cased, Strike Works, Threading Damaged, 7¼" D. $200.00
ROW II, L To R
ANEROID BAROMETER, Eng., Brass-Cased, 6½" D. $60.00
HOLOSTERIC BAROMETER By S. Thaxter & Son, MA, Brass Case Dented, 4¾" D. $80.00
ANEROID BAROMETER, Brass-Cased, By The Tailor Instrument Co., Case Dented, 5¼" D. $40.00

A-MA Aug 1980   *Richard A. Bourne Co., Inc.*
ROW I
TELESCOPE, Single-Draw, 18th Or Early 19th C., Mahogany Casing, Sailor Ropework On End, Brass Draw & Lens Pcs., Lens Cover Missing, 51½" L. $900.00
ROW II, L To R
BRASS PARALLEL RULES, Pr., 24" L. $200.00
BRASS SHIP'S CAPTAIN'S SPEAKING TRUMPET, Dented, Orig. Red Paint On Int., 18" L. $220.00
ROW III, L To R
U.S. NAVY SEXTANT, Cased, Model Mark II, Few Parts Missing $175.00
DRY CARD COMPASS, For Sm. Boat, In Box W/Sliding Cover $150.00

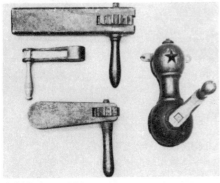

A-MA Aug 1980   *Richard A. Bourne Co., Inc.*
RATTLES, Collection Of 4, Used On Board Ship $475.00

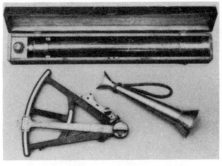

A-MA Aug 1980   *Richard A. Bourne Co., Inc.*
CASED TELESCOPE By A. Carins, Liverpool, Single-Draw Tapered Scope W/Leather Wrapping, Complete W/Cap & Additional Lens $600.00
BRASS SHIP'S SPEAKING TRUMPET, Oriental Engraving.............. $350.00
QUADRANT, Ebony W/Brass Mountings & Ivory Inlays, Parts Missing $475.00

A-MA Aug 1980   *Richard A. Bourne Co., Inc.*
SHIP'S INSTRUMENTS
ROW I, L To R
QUADRANT, Brass Mounted, Cased Ebony, Engraved Ivory Insets, Sm. Ivory Finial, Orig. Case Is Oak, Bears "John Ormand/Ulverston/1852" $1300.00
QUADRANT, Brass Mounted, Cased Ebony, By Spencer & Co., London, Inlaid Ivory Insets, Mahogany Case..... $800.00
ROW II, L To R
SEXTANT, Mahogany Case, Brass Mounted Ebony, Ivory Inlays........... $900.00
SEXTANT, Cased Brass, By Janet Taylor, London, Ca. 1833-1859 .... $900.00

A-MA Aug 1980   *Richard A. Bourne Co., Inc.*
L To R
SEWING OR JEWELRY BOX, Prisoner-Of-War Bone, Silk Pin Cushion Top, Orig. Lining, 7⅝" L., 9¼" D., 5" H. $250.00
SEWING OR JEWELRY BOX, Prisoner-Of-War Bone, Several Repl. Pcs. Of Bone, Top Loose, Minus Hinges, 8¾" L., 5¾" D., 4½" H. $200.00

A-MA Aug 1980   *Richard A. Bourne Co., Inc.*
ROLLING PIN, Heavy Teak-Like Wood W/Turned Whalebone Handles, 1 Handle Repaired, 18" L. $450.00

A-MA Aug 1980   *Richard A. Bourne Co., Inc.*
CALIPERS, Pr., Used To Measure Whale Oil Casks, Normal Wear $275.00
TOGGLE HARPOON, Bent By Whale, Bears "Cole" $100.00
LRG. COPPER DIPPER, For Removing Case Oil, Dented.............. $110.00
IRON SHIP BOLLARD, Bearing Name "W. & B. Douglas, Midd. Conn.", 8½" H. $40.00

A-MA Aug 1980   *Richard A. Bourne Co., Inc.*
WHALING MEMORABILIA, Of John R. Cumin, 2 Journal Log Books, Scrimshaw Seam Rubber, 2 Unfinished Cane Handles, Lrg. Undied Pc. Of Native Tapa Cloth, Ca. 1842-1846 .... $2800.00

A-MA Aug 1980   *Richard A. Bourne Co., Inc.*
JOURNAL, 2-Volumes By John Bubier, Of A Number Of Voyages In U.S. Warships, 1920's, Orig. Covers $2800.00

A-MA Aug 1980   *Richard A. Bourne Co., Inc.*
Top To Bottom
SAILOR'S VALENTINE, Octagonal
Double Case, 9⅛" W. $900.00
SAILOR'S VALENTINE, Picture Frame
Made Of Shells In Shadow Box W/Steel
Engraving, 8¾" x 10⅜" $300.00

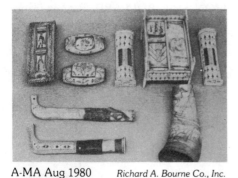

A-MA Aug 1980   *Richard A. Bourne Co., Inc.*
ROW I, L To R
GAME BOX, Prisoner-Of-War, Sliding
Cover, Set Of Bone Dominoes, Slight Dam-
age, 6¾" L. $225.00
SNUFF BOXES, Pr., Prisoner-Of-War, 4" L.
.... $300.00
GAME BOX, Prisoner-Of-War, Poly-
chromed Work, Sliding Covers Under
Domed Covers, 5½" L. $450.00
ROW II, L To R
ESKIMO KNIVES, 2, Carved & Engraved
Bone Sheaths & Bone Handles, Minor Dam-
ages, 8½" O.L. $135.00
SCRIMSHAW POWDER HORN, Minus
Its Attachments, 6½" L. $100.00

A-MA Aug 1980   *Richard A. Bourne Co., Inc.*
WHALE'S TOOTH, Sgn. "P. Ingle 71",
6¼" L. $300.00

A-MA Aug 1980   *Richard A. Bourne Co., Inc.*
Top To Bottom
SCRIMSHAW OVAL POCKETBOOK,
Form Of Ditty Box, Engraved Whaling
Scene On Side, Carved Whale On Rosewood
Lid, Lined W/Suede, 6" W., 8½" L., 10" O.H.
.... $1150.00
DITTY BOX,   Plain Panbone W/Plum
Pudding Mahogany Top & Base, Bottom
Lined W/Red Velvet, 8" D., 4" H. ... $1250.00

A-MA Aug 1980   *Richard A. Bourne Co., Inc.*
SCRIMSHAW WHALE'S TOOTH, Whal-
ing Scene On 1 Side, Some Use Of Color,
Br. Patina, Sl. Age Cracks, 7" L. ...$5250.00

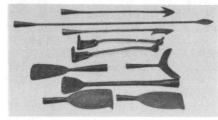

A-MA Aug 1980   *Richard A. Bourne Co., Inc.*
WHALING GEAR
Top To Bottom
ARCTIC DOUBLE-FLUE HARPOON,
Incised "HH", End Sl. $300.00
LANCE, Long Shaft, 58" L. $200.00
TOGGLE HARPOON, Restored, Some
Rust, 32" L. $100.00
CASK LITTER, Rusted $350.00
CUTTING SPADE, Unmounted, Branded
"Snow & Purrington", 20¼" L. ... $100.00
FLENCING KNIFE, Unmounted, Y-
Shaped, 14" L. $225.00
CUTTING SPADE, Hand Wrought, Un-
mounted, Blade Worn, 30" L. $70.00
FLENCING SPADE, Unmounted, 17" L.
.... $75.00
FLENCING SPADE, Unmounted, 17" L.
.... $50.00

A-MA Aug 1980   *Richard A. Bourne Co., Inc.*
Top To Bottom
DARTING HARPOON, Branded A. Peters
& Initials "BB", Traces Of Orig. Paint, 37" L.
.... $150.00
EXPERIMENTAL HARPOON, Fold-Out
Flukes, 1 Fluke Broken Off, Rusted, 30" L.
.... $40.00
TOGGLE HARPOON, Branded A. Peters,
31½" L. $175.00
TOGGLE HARPOON, Branded A. Peters,
32¾" L. $120.00
TOGGLE HARPOON, Various Impressed
Letterins, 31" L. $170.00
TOGGLE HARPOON, Branded A. Peters,
Shaft Bent, 31" L. $175.00

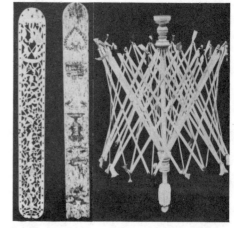

A-MA Aug 1980   *Richard A. Bourne Co., Inc.*
L To R
SCRIMSHAW CORSET BUSK, Whale-
bone, 13⅝" L. $450.00
SCRIMSHAW CORSET BUSK, Busk
Once Had Backing & Brass Rivets Held 2
Pcs. Together, Elaborately Carved, 13¼" L.
.... $800.00
SCRIMSHAW DOUBLE SWIFT, 21½"
O.H. $1600.00

A-MA Feb 1980   *Robert W. Skinner Inc.*
AM. FLAG, Hand Sewn W/34 Stars, Hand
Written Date "1861", Minor Repairs, 102" x
69" $160.00*

A-MA Aug 1980   *Richard A. Bourne Co., Inc.*
SCRIMSHAW SEWING BOX, Int. Con-
tains Tray Made Of Various Woods, Whale
Ivory Knobs & Some Wooden Knobs, Ext.
W/Inlaid Whale Ivory, Baleen, Ebony &
Mother-Of-Pearl, 10⅜" D., 14¾" L., 6½" H.
.... $750.00

A-WA D.C. Oct 1980 *Adam A. Weschler & Son*
CANTON FAMILLE ROSE
TEA SET, 3-Pc., Ca. 1900 . . . . $275.00*
COVERED CUPS & SAUCERS, Set Of 10, (1 Illus.), Ca. 1900 . . . . $300.00*

A-WA D.C. Oct 1980 *Adam A. Weschler & Son*
CANTON FAMILLE ROSE
L To R
TABLE ARTICLES, Set Of Candlesticks (Illus.), Vase (Not Illus.), Ca. 1900 . . $550.00*
BOTTLE W/Cover, Ca. 1880, 15½" H.
. . . . $500.00*

A-WA D.C. Oct 1980 *Adam A. Weschler & Son*
CANTON FAMILLE ROSE
Top To Bottom
COVERED VEGETABLE DISH, Ca. 1800, Marquis-Form, 12" L. $450.00*
FOOTED PLATEAU, Ca. 1880, Marquis-Form, 14¾" L. $450.00*

*Price does not include 10% buyer fee.

A-WA D.C. Oct 1980 *Adam A. Weschler & Son*
CANTON FAMILLE ROSE VASES, Pr., Ca. 1860, 14½" H. 900.00*

A-WA D.C. Oct 1980 *Adam A. Weschler & Son*
CANTON FAMILLE ROSE TABLE ARTICLES, Set Of 4, Late 19th-Early 20th C. $350.00*

A-WA D.C. May 1980 *Adam A. Weschler & Son*
CANTON FAMILLE ROSE
SERVING PCS., Tazza & Leaf-Form Dish
. . . . $225.00*
SALAD PLATES, 17, (1 Illus.), 7¾" D.
. . . . $300.00*
DEEP PLATES, 14 (1 Illus.), 9¾" D.
. . . . $575.00*
DINNER PLATES, 12, (1 Illus.), 9½" D.
. . . . $825.00*
TEA SET, 3-Pc., Teapot W/Wrapped Handle, Hog Snout Creamer & Covered Sugar
. . . . $250.00*
CUPS & SAUCERS, 19, (1 Illus.) . . . $300.00*
CUPS & SAUCERS, 16, (1 Illus.), 2 Sizes
. . . . $200.00*
COVERED SOUPS & SAUCERS, 10, (1 Illus.), Early 20th C. $250.00*

A-WA D.C. May 1980 *Adam A. Weschler & Son*
CANTON FAMILLE ROSE
GLOBULAR COVERED GINGER JARS, Pr., Kang Hsi Marks, 19th C., Underglaze Blue Chop Marks, 6½" H. $475.00*
COVERED BOXES, 2, Rectangular W/Int. Divider, Square $500.00*

A-WA D.C. May 1980 *Adam A. Weschler & Son*
CANTON FAMILLE ROSE
Top
DEEP BOWL, 11" D. $500.00*
Bottom, L To R
PUNCH BOWL, 13½" D. $700.00*
PUNCH BOWL, 15" D. $900.00*

A-WA D.C. Oct 1980 *Adam A. Weschler & Son*
FLOOR SCREEN, 4-Fold, Chinese, 19th C., 64" W., 72" H. $1300.00*

A-WA D.C. May 1980   *Adam A. Weschler & Son*
CANTON FAMILLE ROSE
L To R
BOTTLE VASE, Long Neck, 12½" H.
.... $450.00*
CEREMONIAL URN & COVER, Pilgrim,
Flask-Form, 15¾" H. $800.00*
BALUSTER PITCHER, 12½" H. ..$375.00*

A-WA D.C. May 1980   *Adam A. Weschler & Son*
CANTON FAMILLE ROSE
L To R
BALUSTER VASES, Pr., 10" H. ..$400.00*
BALUSTER VASES, 2, 1 W/Cover, Taller:
11" H. $250.00*

A-WA D.C. May 1980 *Adam A. Weschler & Son*
ROW I
NANKING BLUE & WH. PLATES, 13, (2
Illus.), Rice Patt., 19-20th C., Each W/River
Landscape W/Pagoda .... $200.00 *
ROW II, L To R
NANKING BLUE & WH. PLATES, 24, (1
Illus.), 19-20th C., Each W/River Landscape
Medallion W/Pagodas .... $275.00 *
**CHINESE EXPORT BLUE FITZHUGH
PLATES**, 11, (1 Illus.), Late 19th C., Medal-
lion W/4 Animals Centered By 4 Fan Medal-
lions W/Floral Blossoms, 9½" D. .. $250.00 *

*Price does not include 10% buyer fee.

A-WA D.C. Feb 1980 *Adam A. Weschler & Son*
FAMILLE ROSE JARS, Pr., Chinese,
19th C., Carved Wooden Bases, Removable
Wooden Tops W/Blue Peking Glass Finials,
44" O.H. $210.00*

A-OH July 1980   *Garth's Auctions, Inc.*
ROSE MEDALLION
ROW I, L To R
SUGAR BOWL, Strap Handle, Lid Miss-
ing, 4¼" H. $65.00
CREAMER, 3½" H. $35.00
COVERED JAR, 4¼" H. $155.00
COVERED BOX, Lid Glued But Not Good
Fit, 3¼" H. $20.00
SUGAR BOWL, Lid Missing, Mkd. "China",
4" H. $20.00
ROW II, L To R
PLATE, Octagonal, 7⅛" D. $15.00
CUPS & SAUCERS, 4, (1 Illus.), Minor
Flakes $45.00
TEA POT, Cane Wrapped Wire Handles,
Lid W/Minor Rim Flakes, 6½" H. .. $95.00
CUPS & SAUCERS, 5, (Illus.), Mkd. "Made
In China"......................... $37.50
FLOWER POT & SAUCER, Glued Rim
Chip, 5¼" H. $155.00
ROW III, L To R
COVERED VEGETABLE, Rectangular,
Lemon Peel Glaze, 9" x 7¾" $335.00
SPOON, Edge Flakes, 6" L. $8.00
PLATE, Mkd. "Made In China", 8½" D.
.... $15.00
HANDLELESS CUP & SAUCER .. $6.00
DISH, Leaf-Shaped, Minor Flakes On Rim &
Underside, 7¾" L. $120.00

Left
A-MA Oct 1980   *Robert W. Skinner Inc.*
**ROSE MEDALLION PORCELAIN UM-
BRELLA STAND**, Mid 19th C., 25" H.
.... $1450.00*

Right
A-WA D.C. May 1980 *Adam A. Weschler & Son*
**CANTON FAMILLE ROSE URN &
COVER**, Baluster Form, 26" H. .. $900.00*

Left
A-MA Oct 1980   *Robert W. Skinner Inc.*
**ROSE MEDALLION WATER PIT-
CHER**, Mkd. On Base "Made In China",
Base Chip, Early 20th C., 9" H. .. $525.00*
Right
A-MA Oct 1980   *Robert W. Skinner Inc.*
**ROSE MEDALLION PORCELAIN
JARDINIERE**, Mid 19th C., 12" D.
.... $675.00*

A-MA Aug 1980   *Robert C. Eldred Co., Inc.*
ROSE MEDALLION
L To R
BOWL, Early 19th C., Figural Garden
Scenes, Minor Flake To Rim, 13½" D., 5¼" H.
.... $525.00
LRG. COVERED GINGER JAR, 19th C.,
Decor. W/Panels Of Flower, Birds, & Fig-
ures, Double Underglaze Blue Circular Mrk.
On Foot, Minor Line In Cover.... $500.00

A-MA April 1980   *Richard A. Bourne Co., Inc.*
CANTON ROSE MANDARIN
ROW I, L To R
LRG. CIRCULAR PLATTER, 19th C.,
14¾" D. $250.00
OVAL PLATTER, 19th C., Minute Rim
Nicks, 14⅝" L. $175.00
ROW II
PUNCH BOWL, Late 19th C., Or Early
20th C., Teakwood Base, 13" D. . . $450.00

A-MA Feb 1980   *Robert W. Skinner Inc.*
**ORIENTAL EXPORT PORCELAIN
TEMPLE JARS,** Polychrome Decor., China,
Ca. 1900, 18" H. $650.00*

A-MA Oct 1980   *Robert W. Skinner Inc.*
**ORIENTAL EXPORT PORCELAIN
TEMPLE VASES,** Pr., Overall Polychrome
Decor., 1 Vase Repaired, Other W/Damage
To Handle, China, Ca. 1900, 34" H.
. . . . $3350.00*

Left
A-MA Aug 1980   *Robert W. Skinner Inc.*
ROSE MEDALLION TRAY, Gold Trim
& Background, Bottom Unglazed, China,
Early 19th C., 7¼" W., 1¾" D., 14" L.
. . . . $600.00*

Right
A-WA D.C. Oct 1980 *Adam A. Weschler & Son*
**CANTON FAMILLE ROSE PUNCH
BOWL,** Ca. 1880, 13½" D. $700.00*

A-WA D.C. May 1980   *Adam A. Weschler & Son*
CANTON FAMILLE ROSE
L To R
CHAMBER POT & COVER, 19th C.,
10¾" H. $650.00*
COVERED TUREEN & UNDERTRAY,
Tray: 12" L., Tureen: 9" H. $850.00*
**COVERED OVAL TUREEN & UNDER-
TRAY,** Tray: 8¼" L. $600.00*

A-WA D.C. Dec 1980 *Adam A. Weschler & Son*
CHINESE CINNABAR
ROW I
ROUND COVERED BOXES, Pr., Re-
movable Tops, Garden Landscape & Dragon
W/Carp In Clouds, Footed Bases, Carved
Wood Stands, Late 19th-Early 20th C., 6" D.
. . . . $250.00*
ROW II, L To R
SQ. BOX, Removable Top, Figures In
Garden Landscape, Greek Key Incised
Decor., Notched Corners, Late 19th C.,
7¼" Sq. $175.00*
BOX & TRAY, Removable Top W/River
Landscape & Figures Within Greek Key
Borders, Early 20th C., Tray: 8" L.
. . . . $50.00*
ROW III, L To R
QUATREFOIL-FORM COVERED BOX,
Removable Top, Figures Beneath Hawthorn
Tree, Footed Base, Late 19th C., 6½" L.
. . . . $375.00*
SQ. BOX, Removable Top W/Figures In
Balcony, Late 19th-Early 20th C., 4¾" Sq.
. . . . $80.00*

A-MA April 1980   *Richard A. Bourne Co., Inc.*
ORIENTAL ART OBJECTS
ROW I, L To R
CLOISONNE VASE, Worked On Silver,
4⅝" H. $275.00
PEKING ENAMEL TEAPOT, Decor. Of
Flowers & Birds, Minor Chips, Imperfec-
tions To Enamel Inlay, 7" H. $400.00
PEKING ENAMEL RICE BOWL W/
Cover, Decor, Of Dragons, Repair In Rim
Of Bowl, 4¾" D. $75.00
ROW II
CLOISONNE VASES, Pr., Mkd. China,
9" H. $175.00

A-MA Aug 1980   *Robert C. Eldred Co., Inc.*
ROSE MEDALLION
L To R
COVERED VEGETABLE DISH, Early
19th C., 9¼" x 8", 5½" H. $250.00
COVERED TUREEN, Early 19th C., 11½"
L., 8½" H. $450.00
COVERED VEGETABLE DISH, Early
19th C. $225.00
DEEP DISH, Early 19th C., 11" L.
. . . . $175

*Price does not include 10% buyer fee.

A-MA April 1980   *Richard A. Bourne Co., Inc.*
L To R
KUTANI OR SATSUMA BOWL, Japanese, 19th C., Partially Glazed W/Raised Figures In Landscape, Repaired, 9⅜″ D.
.... $125.00
IMARI BOWL, Japanese, 19th C., 12″ D.
.... $625.00

A-MA Aug 1980   *Robert C. Eldred Co., Inc.*
L To R
CHINESE EXPORT PORCELAIN BOWL, Blue & Wh. Decor. Of Flowers, Mid 19th C., 12¾″ D. $600.00
CHINESE EXPORT PORECLAIN PLATTER, Landscape Decor., Ca. 1800, 14½″ L.
.... $150.00
CHINESE EXPORT PORCELAIN TEA-POT, Blue & Wh. W/Silver Mounts, Hinged Cover, Single Side Handle, 18th C., 8½″ H.
.... $500.00
BLUE & WH. CANTON PLATTER, 14½″ x 11½″ $275.00

A-WA D.C. Dec 1980 *Adam A. Weschler & Son*
CHINESE SNUFF BOTTLES
ROW I, L To R
LAPIS LAZULI, Late 19th C. $160.00*
PEKING ROSE OVERLAY, Clear Glass W/Bats & Foliage, Agate Stopper, Late 19th C. $140.00*
PEKING ROSE GLASS, Clear Quartz Stopper, Late 19th C. $60.00*
PEKING INT. PAINTED GLASS, River Landscape, Sgn. In Calligraphy, Gr. Jade Stopper, Late 19th C. $90.00*
ROW II, L To R
CINNABAR, Gourd Shaped, Applied Stones Of Fruit & Flowers W/Greek Key Border, Late 19th C. $180.00*
CINNABAR, High Relief Lilies & Butterflies, Chop Marks On Bottom, Late 19th C.
.... $70.00*
FAMILLE JAUNE PORCELAIN, Gr. Hardstone Stopper, Calligraphy On Bottom, Early 20th C. $45.00*
PEKING INT. PAINTED GLASS, Rose Quartz Stopper, Late 19th C. $50.00*
ROW III, L To R
PEKING SMOKED GLASS, Low Relief Of Old Sages, Gr. Swirl Glass Stopper, Early 20th C. $25.00*
CINNABAR, High Relief Hawthorn Tree & Flowering Branch W/Exotic Birds, Chop Marks On Bottom, Late 19th-Early 20th C.
.... $60.00*
CORAL, High Relief Lily Blossom, Cat's Eye Stopper, Late 19th-Early 20th C.
.... $150.00*
CLOISONNE, Trellising Vine, Leaf & Flowers On Blue Ground, Coral Stopper, Late 19th C. $175.00*
ROW IV, L To R
CLUB-FORM, Cobalt Glazed, Agate Stopper, Early 20th C. $45.00*
HORN, Painted River Landscape, Verso W/Calligraphy, Horn Stopper, Early 20th C.
.... $60.00*
PEKING ROSE OVERLAY & OPAQUE GLASS, Late 19th C. $160.00*
CLOISONNE, Floral Medallions On Powder Blue Ground, Clear Glass Stopper, Late 19th C. $110.00*

*Price does not include 10% buyer fee.

A-WA D.C. Dec 1980 *Adam A. Weschler & Son*
CHINESE CLOISONNE
L To R
VASE, Emerald Gr. Ground, Chop Mark On Base, 18th-19th C., 10¼″ H. $250.00*
MEI PING VASE, Blue Ground, 19th C., 11½″ H. $300.00*
GOURD SHAPED VASE, Powder Blue Ground, 19th C., 11″ H. $550.00*

A-VA Jan 1980   *Laws Auction & Antiques*
MANDERIAN ARM CHAIRS, Pr., Carved Kinoki Wood $1600.00

A-WA D.C. Dec 1980 *Adam A. Weschler & Son, Inc.*
CANTON GARDEN SEAT, Early 19th C., 18½″ H. $1600.00*

A-WA D.C. Feb 1980 *Adam A. Weschler & Son*
FAMILLE VERTE GARDEN SEATS, Pr., Barrel-Form, Late Ch'ing Dynasty, Carved & Pierced Wooden Stands, 12″ H. . . $650.00*

A-WA D.C. Dec 1980 *Adam A. Weschler & Son*
CHINESE CLOISONNE
L To R
BALUSTER-FORM VASES, Pr., Blue Ground, Late 19th C., 5″ H. $175.00*
BARREL-FORM COVERED JARS, Pr., Removable Top, Pierced Brass Finial, 19th C., 5½″ H. $325.00*
BALUSTER-FORM VASES, Powder Blue Ground, Brass Handles, Early 20th C., 5½″ H. $175.00*

A-MA July 1980   *Robert W. Skinner Inc.*
THEOREM ON VELVET, Polychrome
Watercolor, Am., Early 19th C., 15½″ x 19″
.... $600.00*

Left
A-MA May 1980   *Paul J. Dias, Inc.*
LITHO. ON PAPER, Bicycle Advertising
Poster, No Company Name, Framed, 17½″
x 21½″ $87.50

Right
A-WA D.C. May 1980 *Adam A. Weschler & Son*
GRECO-RUSSION ICON, The Deesis,
18th-19th C. $600.00*

A-WA D.C. Oct 1980   *Adam A. Weschler & Son*
CURRIER IVES LITHOGRAPHS, The
Celebrated Trotting Mare Lucy & The CA
Wonder Occident, Colored W/Eglomise
Matted Frames, 11″ x 15″ $550.00*

A-MA Sept 1980   *Richard A. Bourne Co., Inc.*
ROW I
SILHOUETTES, Set Of 3, Patchen
Family, 1 Mkd. "Peales Museum", Modern
Frames, 4½″ x 3½″ $150.00
ROW II
SILHOUETTES, Set Of 3, Marshall Family,
Impressed "Museum", Some Foxing, Mod-
ern Frames, 4½″ x 3½″ $225.00
ROW III, L To R
SILHOUETTES IN THE OVAL, Pr., 18th
C., Paper Toned, Orig. Blk. Lacquer Frames,
2¾″ x 2⅛″ $150.00
SILHOUETTE, Blk. On Wh. W/Painted In
Details, Modern Frame $75.00

A-MA July 1980   *Robert W. Skinner Inc.*
WATERCOLOR MEMORIAL, On Paper,
Some Foxing, Am., Ca. 1811, 12″ x 73″
.... $2050.00*

*Price does not include 10% buyer fee.

A-MA Aug 1980   *Robert C. Eldred Co., Inc.*
L To R
SILHOUETTE, By August Edouart, Ca.
1826-1849, Birdseye Maple Frame 13½″ x 8¼″
.... $240.00
SILHOUETTE, Inscribed "M. Locke Fecit",
1839, Beveled Frame, 13½″ x 11″ .. $200.00

A-MA Feb 1980   *Robert W. Skinner, Inc.*
OIL ON BOARD, "Pima Papoose", Artist:
George Clough, Unsigned, Gilt Frame, 3½″
W., 5½″ H. $1350.00*

Left

A-MA April 1980   *Robert W. Skinner Inc.*
NEEDLEWORK LANDSCAPE, Glass
Reverse Painting, Blk. Paint Loss, Minor
Damage To Frame, Am., Early 19th C., 4¾"
D. $550.00*

Right

A-MA Feb 1980   *Robert W. Skinner Inc.*
NEEDLEWORK OF "VANITAS", Ca.
1820, 11½" x 9½" $350.00*

A-MA April 1980   *Robert W. Skinner Inc.*
WATERCOLOR MEMORIAL, Reverse
Painted Border On Glass, Sgn, "Abigal
Smith Thaxter", Orig. Gold Leaf Frame,
Some Paint Loss & Chips On Frame, Ca.
1825, 18" x 22" $650.00*

A-MA Sept 1980   *Richard A. Bourne Co., Inc.*
Top To Bottom
FOLIO N. CURRIER LITHOGRAPH,
"Falls Of Niagra", Margins Cut Some, Paper
Toned & Foxed, Old Mahogany Veneer
Frame $75.00
**SMALL FOLIO CURRIER & IVES LITHO-
GRAPH,** "NY Ferry Boat", Faded & Foxed,
Toned, Full Margins, Sm. Waterstain
.... $175.00

Left

A-VA April 1980   *Laws Auction & Antiques*
FOLK ART PAINTING, Oil On Canvas, 2
Children W/Kitten, Period Molded Walnut
Gilt-Lined Frame, Cleaned & Relined, Ca.
1825, 30" x 24" $555.00

Right

A-MA Oct 1980   *Robert W. Skinner Inc.*
**WATERCOLOR THEOREM ON VEL-
VET,** Fruits In Double Handled Basket On
Fringed Mat, Some Discoloration To
Velvet, Am., Ca. 1835, 13" x 15" .. $1300.00*

A-NY May 1980   *The Auction Gallery*
WATERCOLOR ON PAPER, Mourning
Picture, N. Eng., Early 19th C., Orig. Gilt
Frame, Reverse Painted Glass, Sm. Paint
Deterioration, 14½" x 16½". $200.00

A-MA Sept 1980   *Richard A. Bourne Co., Inc.*
NEEDLEWORK ON SILK, Framed,
Eng., Late 18th C., Paint On Glass Flaking,
Old Birdseye Maple Frame, 16⅜" x 14⅝"
.... $400.00

A-MA May 1980   *Paul J. Dias, Inc.*
LITHOGRAPHS ON CARDBOARD, Set
Of 4, Singer Sewing Machine, Orig. Frames,
1 W/Lt. Water Staining, 1 W/Sm. Tear,
14½" x 19½" $50.00

A-MA Mar 1980   *Robert W. Skinner Inc.*
SARAH BERNHARDT POSTER, Pub-
lished By Champenois 1896, Lithograph In
Colors W/Silver, Mounted To Cloth, Minor
Damages, 27⅜" x 82" $3200.00*

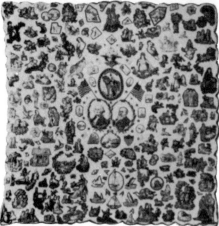

CALICO PIECED QUILT, Cloverleaf In Red, Gr., Gold, Yellow, Pink & Salmon W/Ribbon, Bowknot & Swag Border, 19th C., 99″ x 84″ $550.00*****

CALICO PIECED QUILT, Diagonal Rows Of Gr. Panels W/Red Strawberry Patt., Wh. Sawtooth Framing, 19th C., 96″ x 77″ $275.00*****

Top To Bottom
EMBROIDERED CREWEL COVERLET, Silk, 19th C., Fr. Knots, Long & Short, Chain & Lace Stitches, 91″ x 82½″ . . $5400.00
QUILT, Am., Colorful Appliqued Decoration Depicting Extremely Diverse Scenes W/ Central Needlework Medallion Of Washington Leaning Against His Horse, Dated 1789/ 1889, 84″ Sq. $2800.00

CALICO PIECED QUILT, Tulip On Wh. Ground, 19th C., 100″ x 88″ $350.00*****

CALICO PIECED QUILT, Snowflake Field In Printed Rust On Wh. Ground, Drapery & Festoon Border, Scalloped Edge, 19th-20th C., 80″ x 98″ $400.00*****

HAND LOOMED COVERLET, NY, Red, Wh. & Blue W/Wh. Fringe, Center Seam, 72″ x 80″ $145.00

JACUARD COVERLET, Floral Design In Red, Br. & Tan, By Jos. Klar, Reading 1844, Minor Fringe Loss, PA, 7½′ x 6′ . . $300.00 *****

HAND WOVEN CANDLEWICK BED— SPREAD, Indigo Blue & Wh., Early 19th C., 80″ x 64″ $155.00

A-OH April 1980   *Garth's Auctions, Inc.*
APPLIQUE QUILT TOP, Gr. Calico W/
Red, Goldenrod, Blue-Green, & Yellow-
Green, 90″ x 92″ $295.00

A-NY May 1980   *Calkins Auction Gallery*
APPLIQUE QUILT, "Star Of Bethlehem",
VT, 19th C., Lavender On Wh. Ground, 82″
x 80″ $475.00

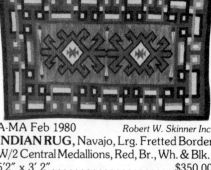

A-MA Feb 1980   *Robert W. Skinner Inc.*
INDIAN RUG, Navajo, Lrg. Fretted Border
W/2 Central Medallions, Red, Br., Wh. & Blk.,
5′2″ x 3′ 2″ $350.00*

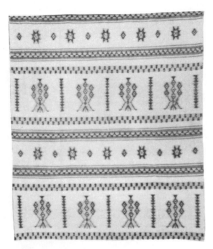

A-NY May 1980   *Calkins Auction Gallery*
HOMESPUN BEDSPREAD, Gr. & Br.,
19th C., Candlewick On Natural, 70″ X 100″
.... $260.00

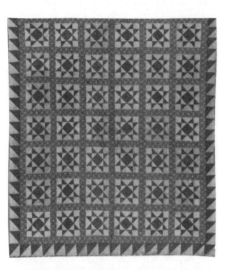

A-WA D.C. Dec 1980 *Adam A. Weschler & Son*
CALICO PIECED QUILT, Star On Gold
Ground W/Blue Framing, 2-Pieced Saw-
tooth Border, 19th C., 109″ x 92″
.... $400.00*

A-NY May 1980   *Calkins Auction Gallery*
**HAND LOOMED OVERSHOT COV-
ERLET,** NY, 19th C., Center Seam, 66″ x 84″
.... $120.00

A-NY May 1980   *Calkins Auction Gallery*
HAND LOOMED COVERLET, Early 19th
C., Red & Wh. Patt. W/Wh. Fringe, 76″ x 88″
.... $175.00

A-OH April 1980   *Garth's Auctions, Inc.*
PIECED QUILT, Red, Goldenrod & Blue-
Green, Wh. Homespun Back, 79″ x 87″
.... $450.00

A-NY May 1980   *Calkins Auction Gallery*
SHOW TOWEL, Am., 19th C., Red &
Wh. Linen, 20″ x 40″ $150.00

*Price does not include 10% buyer fee.

A-NY May 1980   *Calkins Auction Gallery*
QUILT, "Star Of Bethlehem", Sgn. & Dated "By E.J. McDonald, 1858", Sm. Deterioration, 88½" x 90½" $500.00

A-WA D.C. May 1980 *Adam A. Weschler & Son*
ANTIQUE SHIRVAN RUG, Shaded Red Ground, 3 Medallions On Blue To Gold Ground, Palmette Guard Border On Ivory Ground, 5.9′ x 4.1′ $1300.00*

A-MA Jan 1981   *Robert W. Skinner Inc.*
QUILTED COVERLET, Am., Mid 19th C., Quilted W/Wh. Cotton Background, Patch Design W/Tan Circle & Sm. Patt. Gr. Corner Spears, Some Fading, 72" x 90" ... $325.00*

*Price does not include 10% buyer fee.

A-WA D.C. May 1980 *Adam A. Weschler & Son*
KILIM RUG, Sand-Beige Ground W/4 Medallions, Crab Guard Border, 8.3′ x 5.1′ $2000.00*

A-WA D.C. May 1980   *Adam A. Weschler & Son*
SEMI-ANTIQUE CABISTAN PRAYER RUG, Beige Ground, 4′ x 3.3′ $500.00*

A-WA D.C. Oct 1980   *Adam A. Weschler & Son*
BANQUET CLOTH W/12 Matching Napkins, Italian Lace, Ecru Linen & Drawnwork, 145" x 70" $425.00*

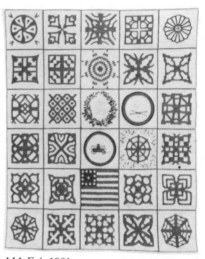

A-MA Feb 1981   *Robert W. Skinner Inc.*
APPLIQUE COMMEMORATIVE COVERLET, W/Legend Reading "Ladies Donation To The Fireman's Fair, Yale Engine Co. No. 1, South Reading July 1853*, Size: 93" Sq. $2700.00*

A-MA April 1980   *Robert W. Skinner, Inc.*
HEARTH RUG, Appliqued & Embroidered, Moth Damage, 62" x 28" .. $6750.00*

A-WA D.C. May 1980   *Adam A. Weschler & Son*
SEMI-ANTIQUE CABISTAN RUG, Br. Ground W/Red Border, 6.9′ x 3.4′.. $725.00*

A-MA Dec 1980   *Robert W. Skinner Inc.*
SCHOENHUT HUMPTY DUMPTY CIRCUS, Orig. Paint & Fabrics, Am., Early 20th C. $1750.00*

A-MA Dec 1980   *Robert W. Skinner Inc.*
TEDDY BEAR, Honey Plush, Button Eyes, Embroidered Nose, Excelsior Stuffing, German, Early 20th C., 15″ H. $600.00*
SCHOENHUT TOY PIANO W/Stool, Painted On Blk. Keys, Imitation Wood Graining, Trademark On Front, PA, Early 20th C., 17½″ H. $200.00*
TEDDY BEAR, Drk. Br. Plush W/Blk. Stripes, Glass Eyes, Cotton Stuffing, Minor Damages, Am., Early 20th C., 16¾″ L. $60.00*

A-MA Dec 1980   *Robert W. Skinner Inc.*
CAST IRON TOY STOVE, Repousse Scroll Design, 4 Cooking Pots, Am., Late 19th C., 13½″ H. $110.00*

*Price does not include 10% buyer fee.

A-CT Nov 1980   *Lloyd W. Ralston*
KITCHEN, Embossed, Stained Tin, 9¼″ W. $90.00

A-CT Nov 1980   *Lloyd W. Ralston*
LIONEL PEOPLE, Papier Mache W/House & Tree $25.00

A-MA Dec 1980   *Robert W. Skinner Inc.*
MUSICAL AUTOMATION TOY, Mkd. "Gbk", Comp. Limbs-Bisque Head Doll, Celluloid Baby, Germany, Ca. 1900, 12″ W., 8″ D., 10½″ H. $1500.00*

A-MA Dec 1980   *Robert W. Skinner, Inc.*
REINDEER CANDY CONTAINERS, Pr., Papier Mache, Brushed Cotton Fur, Glass Eyes, Sm. Damages, German, Late 19th C., 9½″ L., 11″ H. $160.00*
SANTA CLAUS, Papier Mache & Cloth, Woven Back Pack, Wood Stand, Feet Damaged, German, Late 19th C., 10½″ H. $130.00*

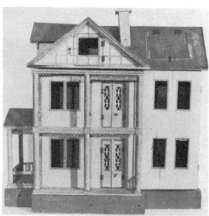

A-MA D.C. Dec 1980   *Robert W. Skinner Inc.*
DOLL HOUSE, Colonial-Style, Electrified, Orig. Wall & Floor Coverings, Some Damage, Am., Early 19th C., 32″ W., 31¾″ H. $550.00*

A-MA Mar 1980   *Richard A. Bourne Co., Inc.*
MINIATURES
FRENCH PORCELAIN TEASET, 6 Plates, 6 Saucers, 6 Cups, Sugar, Creamer, & Teapot, Gold Decor. Has Minor Wear .. $100.00
CHINA TEASET, 6 Plates, 6 Saucers, 5 Teacups, Sugar Bowl, Creamer & Teapot, Minor Wear To Decor., Finial Broken Off Teapot Cover, Age Crack In 1 Plate & 1 Saucer $70.00

A-MA Mar 1980   *Richard A. Bourne Co., Inc.*
DOLLHOUSE FURNITURE & MINIATURES
ROW I, L To R
CHAISE LOUNGE, Orig. Paper On Back, Upholstered In Red Velvet, 1 Leg Replaced $160.00
ROYAL GRAND PIANO, Petite Princess Fantasy Furniture, Orig. Box & Catalogue $40.00
ROW II, L To R
SALON WING CHAIRS, 2, Petite Princess Fantasy Furniture, 1 Red & 1 Gold, Orig. Boxes & Catalogues $30.00
GRANDFATHER CLOCK W/Folding Screen, Petite Princess Fantasy Furniture, Orig. Box & Catalogue $25.00
REGENCY HEARTHPLACE, Petite Princess Fantasy Furniture, Orig. Box & Catalogue $45.00

A-MA Mar 1980   Richard A. Bourne Co., Inc.
DOLLHOUSE FURNITURE, Near-Matching Set, Marble-Top Table & Lady's Desk, Upholstery On Chairs & Sofa Shows Wear $725.00

A-MA July 1980   Robert W. Skinner Inc.
CHILD'S HOBBY HORSE, Pine, Rocking Platform W/Captain's Chair, Orig. Blk. Paint, Am., Early 19th C., 11½" W., 36" L., 16" H. $300.00*

A-NY May 1980   Calkins Auction Gallery
CHILD'S HOBBY HORSE, Rocking Chair In Orig. Blue Paint & Yellow Striping W/Floral Decor., Orig. Cond., 39" L., 13" W., 18" H. $270.00

A-MA July 1980   Robert W. Skinner Inc.
CARVED WOODEN HOBBY HORSE, Grey Decor., Padded Leather Saddle, Horsehair Tail Am., Early 19th C., 44" H. $400.00*

*Price does not include 10% buyer fee.

A-MA Mar 1980   Richard A. Bourne Co., Inc.
MECHANICAL TOYS
ROW I, L To R
THREE-WHEELED CYCLE W/Bisque-Headed Girl Rider, Cycle Made Of Iron Complete W/Key, Most Of Orig. Paint Worn Away, Mechanism Working, 10" H. $850.00
THREE-WHEELED CYCLE W/Blk. Rider, Cycle Made Of Iron & Comes W/Key, Retains Some Of Orig. Paint, Mechanism Working, 8" H. $475.00
ROW II, L To R
THREE-WHEELED CYCLE W/Comp.-Headed Girl Rider, Mechanism Dated 1870, Retains Most Orig. Paint, Mechanism Working, 8" H. $825.00
WALKING DOLL, Pushes A Three-Wheeled Carriage, Doll Has Comp. Head, Molded Hair & Comp. Body, Clothing Orig. W/Leather Boots, Key Missing, Mechanism Works, 10½" H. $550.00

A-MA Mar 1980   Richard A. Bourne Co., Inc.
L To R
DOLL'S CARRIAGE, Orange & Gold Stencil-Decor. Body, Natural Wood-Finished Handle & Wheels W/Blk. Striping On Spokes, Orig. Leather Canopy, 25" H. $160.00
DOLL'S CARRIAGE, Iron Frame, Br. & Blk. Wooden Body, Leather Upholstered Int., Refinished In Spots, Upholstery Sl. Torn & Frayed, Canopy Top Missing, 27½" O.H. $60.00

A-MA Mar 1980   Richard A. Bourne Co., Inc.
L To R
WOODEN STAGE COACH, 2 Wh. Horses & Wooden Undercarriage, Ref. Crazed, 16" H. $175.00
CHILD'S ROCKING HORSE, Orig. Br. & Wh. Horsehide Covering, Wh. Mane & Tail, Leather Reins & Wooden Rockers, 31" H. $200.00

A-OH May 1980   Garth's Auctions, Inc.
CAP PISTOLS
CAST IRON, "Pluck, Made In U.S.A.", 3½" L. $27.50
PLATED STEEL, "Big Bill, Made In U.S.A.", 5½" L. $15.00
CAST METAL, "Dick", 4¼" L. $5.00
TIN, "Sure Shot Safety", 5½" L. ... $4.00
CAST WHITE METAL & PLASTIC, "Atomic Disintegrator", 7½" L. $20.00
PLATED STEEL & PLASTIC, "Gene Autry 44", 11" L. $17.50
CAST IRON, "Tiger", Worn Blk. Paint, 6¾" L. $15.00

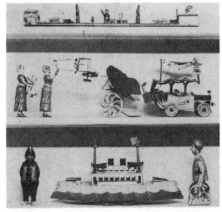

A-OH May 1980   Garth's Auctions, Inc.
TIN TOYS
ROW I
MAIN STREET, Windup, Track W/Busses Trucks, Etc. $90.00
ROW II, L To R
WOMAN & BABY, Windup, Made In Germany, Flaked Paint, 7" H. $285.00
WOMAN & BABY, Windup, Made In Germany, Baby Missing, 7" H. $60.00
BIPLANE, Windup, 1 Vane Of Propeller Missing, Does Not Run, 8" L. $300.00
BUTTERFLY, Push Toy W/Cast Iron Wheels, Worn Paper Covering On Wheels, 9¼" W. $15.00
HI-WAY HENRY, Windup, Made In Germany, Working Cond., 10" L. ... $2200.00
ROW III, L To R
STANDING CLOWN, Windup, Old Paint Varnished, Gears Somewhat Stripped, 8" H. $55.00
BATTLESHIP, Pull Toy W/Old Paint, 18½" L. $155.00
G.I. JOE & HIS K-9 PUPS, Windup, Unique Art, Working Cond., 8¾" H. $35.00

A-MA Mar 1980   *Richard A. Bourne Co., Inc.*
TOYS
ROW I, L To R
**LIONEL MICKEY MOUSE HAND
CAR,** Minor Wear.............. $500.00
**LIONEL STANDARD GUAGE LOCO-
MOTIVE,** Ca. 1927-36, Cars Complete
W/Orig. Boxes & Transformer, Some Paint
Wear $700.00
ROW II
LIONEL STEAM ENGINE W/Coal Car
& Livestock Car, Minor Parts Missing
.... $425.00

A-MA Mar 1980   *Richard A. Bourne Co., Inc.*
CAST IRON TOYS
ROW I, L To R
REPRO. CARRIAGE, Drawn By Blk.
Horse, Complete W/Driver, Gr. Carriage,
10″ L. $10.00
PULL BELL TOY, Iron Horse Jockey,
Remaining Parts Tin, Rust Surface To Some
Tin Parts, 7″ L. $100.00
CARRIAGE W/Driver & Drawn By 1 Horse,
Carriage Painted Maroon W/Gold Trim &
Red Wheels, Driver & Horse Have No Paint,
Paint Somewhat Flaked, 7¾″ L. ... $60.00
ROW II, L To R
CARRIAGE W/Driver & Passenger, Car-
riage Is Blue W/Yellow Wheels & Drk. Blue
Canopy, Minor Paint Loss, 11½″ L. .. $70.00
HOSE CARRIER, Ca. 1910, Drawn By 1
Wh. Horse & 1 Blk. Horse, Carrier Is Red
W/Br. Wheels, Complete, Paint Worn, 20″ L.
.... $225.00
ROW III, L To R
IRON & TIN FARM WAGON, Ca. 1910,
Blue Wagon W/Yellow Undercarriage &
Red Tin Side Gates, Drawn By 2 Blk. Horses,
Complete W/Orig. Driver, Some Paint Wear,
17″ L. $175.00
FIRE PATROL WAGON, Red Wagon W/
Yellow Wheels, Drawn By 2 Blk. Horses &
Complete W/Driver, Almost All Paint Worn
Away, 2 Drivers Missing, 14″ L. 80.00

A-OH May 1980   *Garth's Auctions, Inc.*
TIN TOYS
ROW I, L To R
COWBOY RIDER, Wind-Up, By Marx,
Unused Cond. In Orig. Box, 8″ H. .. $50.00
KENTUCKY DERBY RACE, Wind-Up,
Gears Stripped, 13½″ Sq. $35.00
COO-COO CAR, Wind-Up, Embossed
Marx Emblem, Gas Tank Missing, Working
Cond., 8″ L. $65.00
ROW II, L To R
HI-WAY HENRY, Wind-Up, "Made In
Germany", Working Cond., 10″ L. .. $2075.00
SUBMARINE, Wind-Up, Orig. Box, "Mar-
usan Toys, Japan", 1 Fin Broken Off, 13″ L.
.... $25.00
GIRL, Pull Toy W/Wood, Old Paint, 8″ L.
.... $35.00
ROW III, L To R
G.I. JOE & K-9 PUPS, Wind-Up, Working
Cond., By "Unique Art", 9″ H. $35.00
CRUISE SHIP, Wind-Up, Some Rust, Pro-
peller & Key Missing, 19½″ L. $35.00
GOOFY & DONALD DUCK, Wind-Up,
"Walt Disney's Donald Duck Duet", Donald
Missing Arm, 10″ H. $65.00

A-MA Mar 1980   *Richard A. Bourne Co., Inc.*
SCHOENHUT TOYS
L To R
UPRIGHT PIANO, Finish Worn, 20 Of 22
Keys Work, Keys Repainted, 23½″ W., 11½″ D.,
21″ H. $60.00
BABY GRAND PIANO W/STOOL, Nor-
mal Scratching & Flaking, Keys Repainted, All
Keys In Working Order, 24″ W., 21½″ D., 18″ H.
.... $290.00
UPRIGHT PIANO, Orig. Finish W/Some
Wear & Flaking, None Of Keys Functional, 19″
W., 9¾″ D., 17½″ H. $55.00

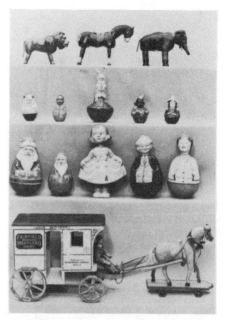

A-MA Mar 1980   *Richard A. Bourne Co., Inc.*
SCHOENHUT ANIMAL FIGURES & TOYS
ROW I, L To R
LION, Minor Wear To Paint $100.00
HORSE, Some Paint Wear To Body, Chip
Out Of Left Shoulder, Straps To Leather
Saddle Missing, Replaced Ear $60.00
ELEPHANT, Paint Wear........ $60.00
ROW II, L To R
CLOWN ROLLY DOLLY, Held Together
By Tape, Orig. Paint, Minor Wear, 4½″ H.
.... $40.00
CHINAMAN ROLLY DOLLY, Body Split,
Minor Paint Flaking, 4½″ H. $50.00
RABBIT ROLLY DOLLY, "Schoenhut
Rolly Dolly" Label & Encircling Label "Pat-
ented/December 15, 1908", Minor Wear To
Paint, Minor Flaking, 8¾″ H. $225.00
BLK. CLOWN ROLLY DOLLY, Minor
Bruises & Flaking, 4½″ H. $70.00
ADMIRAL ROLLY DOLLY, Appears To
Be Retouched In Areas, Flaked, 4½″ H.
.... $70.00
ROW III, L To R
LRG. SANTA CLAUS ROLLY DOLLY,
Portions Of Metal Label Remain, Upper &
Lower Sections Rejoined, Flaking, 9″ H.
.... $260.00
SANTA CLAUS ROLLY DOLLY, Orig.
Label "Schoenhut/Toys/Made In/USA",
Paint Flaking & Retouched, 6½″ H. .. $75.00
**LRG. COMPOSITION GOOGLY-EYED
DOLL,** Minor Paint Flaking, 11″ H. .. $40.00
FOXY GRANDPA ROLLY DOLLY, Labeled
On Bottom, Minor Crazing & Some Retouch-
ing To Body, 8½″ H. $175.00
SCHNICKLEFRITZ ROLLY DOLLY, Minor
Paint Flaking, 8½″ H. $275.00
ROW IV
SCHOENHUT TOY, Fairfield Western Mary-
land Dairy Milk Wagon, Drawn By Br. Horse
On Wooden Platform W/Iron Wheels, Orig.
Milk Man Figure, Minor Repair & Minimal Loss
Of Paint, 29″ L., 10½″ H. $550.00

A-OH May 1980   *Garth's Auctions, Inc.*
CAST IRON TOYS
ROW I, L To R
CART W/BELL, Pull Toy, Heart Wheels, Ringing Bell, Open Work Shields & Stars, "1776-1876, Independence", Old Red, Gold & Silver Paint, 9½" L. $375.00
KENTON SURREY, 2 Horses, Driver & Lady Passenger, Orig. Paint & Cloth Top, Unmarked, 13" L. $105.00
PULL TOY, Heart Wheels W/2 Figures & Bell, "Ding Dong Bell, Pussy's Not In The Well", Worn Old Paint, 9¼" L. ... $480.00
ROW II, L To R
MONKEY ON LOG, Pull Toy, Heart Wheels, Worn Old Paint, 6" L. ... $250.00
LANDAU, 2 Horses, Driver & Footman, Old Worn Repaint, Section Of Harness Chain Repl., 15½" L. $405.00
NODDING WOMAN, Pull Toy, Donkey On Wheels, Worn Old Paint, 6" L. ...$165.00
ROW III, L To R
KENTON FARM WAGON, 2 Horses & Driver, Worn Old Paint, Unmarked, 15" L. $135.00
KENTON HANSOM CAB, 1 Horse, Driver & Woman Passenger, Orig. Paint, Unmarked, 15¾" L. $175.00

Left
A-NY May 1980   *Calkins Auction Gallery*
FOLK ART TOY, "The Jolly Jiggers", 17" L., 15" H. $325.00

Right
A-MA Dec 1980   *Robert W. Skinner Inc.*
IVES CLOCKWORK TOY, Lady Made Of Metal & Wood, Papier Mache Head & Feet, Wooden Base, Paper Label "Patented Mar. 31st, 1874", Am., 8½" H. $1550.00*

A-MA Mar 1980   *Richard A. Bourne Co., Inc.*
ROW I,
LITHOGRAPHED WOODEN TRAIN SET, Engine & 4 Cars, Each Train Car Carries Alphabet Blocks, Reverse Side Are 2 Puzzles, Paint Worn, Some Crazing & Flaking, Stack Of Engine Missing, 28" L. $230.00
ROW II, L To R
DECORATED TIN DOLLHOUSE STOVE W/5 Cooking Accessories & 1 Pan To Go Inside Stove, Minor Wear To Paint & Sl. Rusting, 9" L., 4" O.H. $90.00
ELECTRIC RACE CAR, "Patent Applied For/Electricar/KoKoMo", Complete W/ Track & Transformer, Sl. Paint Wear, Track Dirty & Car Will Not Function On Track, 11" L. $50.00
ROW III, L To R
PULL TOY, Wooden Horse On Platform W/Cast Iron Wheels, Restorations & Minor Repainting, 10" H. $130.00
MECHANICAL TOY, Fur Kitten W/Key Wind Mechanism & Wheels On Feet, Orig. Key, 20" L. $180.00

A-CT Nov 1980   *Lloyd W. Ralston*
L To R
TRICK BEAR & SKIPPING DOG, German Tin Painted Windup, Working, 6¼" H. $275.00
KNIGHT ON HORSEBACK, Penny Toy, German Tin Windup $80.00
MOTHER PUSHING GIRL IN SLEIGH, Penny Toy, German Tin Windup, Wheels Missing, 1 Side Rough $210.00

A-CT Nov 1980   *Lloyd W. Ralston*
L To R
RUCK RUCK, Tellus, German Tin Windup, Working, Varnished, 6" L. $90.00
NAUGHTY BOY, Lehmann, German Tin Windup, Painted, Working $275.00

A-OH May 1980   *Garth's Auctions, Inc.*
TOYS
ROW I, L To R
TIN DUMP TRUCK, Wooden Wheels & Old Red, Blk. & Yellow Paint, 5¾" L.
.... $15.00
CAST IRON ROAD GRADER, Rubber Wheels & Gr. Paint, 7½" L. $50.00
CAST IRON TRUCK, Worn Yellow Paint, Metal Wheels Mkd. "Hamilton Corhart", 4¼" L. $22.50
ROW II, L To R
CAST IRON PICK UP TRUCK, Old Worn Gr. & Blk. Repaint, 7¼" H. .. $37.50
CAST IRON TRACTOR & WAGON, Tractor Mkd. "Allis Chalmers", Wagon Mkd. "Arcade", Wh. Rubber Wheels & Gr. & Red Paint, 9½" L. $25.00
ROW III, L To R
CAST IRON DUMPER WAGON & TRACTOR, Wheels On Tractor Repl., 12¾" L. $35.00
CAR W/RUMBLE SEAT, Old Red & Blk. Paint W/Yellow Wheels, 5" L. $22.50

A-CT Nov 1980   *Lloyd W. Ralston*
L To R
JOE PENNER, Marx, Tin Windup, Working, 8¼" H. $160.00
PORKY PIG, Marx, Tin Windup, Working, 7¾" H. $85.00
B.O. PLENTY, Marx, Tin Windup, Orig. Box, Not Comp., 8½" H. $65.00

A-CT Nov 1980   *Lloyd W. Ralston*
L To R
ST. BERNARD DOG, Lehmann, Tin Windup, Rust Face, Working, 6½" L.
.... $170.00
DANCING DARKY, Lehmann, Jointed Tin, 8" H. $325.00

A-CT Nov 1980   *Lloyd W. Ralston*
L To R
ROLLO-CHAIR, Strauss-Stock, Tin Wind-up, Not Working, 7¾" L. $260.00
JAZZBO JIM, Unique Art, Tin Windup, Needs Adjusting, Faded, Rust, Poor Cond.
.... $110.00

A-CT Nov 1980   *Lloyd W. Ralston*
L To R
BUCKING BRONCO, Lehmann, German Tin Windup, Painted, Working, 7½" L.
.... $275.00
BUSY LIZZIE, German Tin Windup, Working, Faded, 7" H. $250.00

A-MA July 1980   *Robert W. Skinner, Inc.*
LAMB PULL TOY, Wood & Wool, Metal Wheels, Am., Early 19th C., 17" L., 13" H.
.... $500.00*

A-CT Nov 1980   *Lloyd W. Ralston*
CRANDALL'S DISTRICT SCHOOL, Orig. Box, Painted Wood $265.00

A-CT Nov 1980   *Lloyd W. Ralston*
SCHOENHUT FIGURES
LOT, Sm. Elephant, Hippo, Donkey, Horse, Bareback Rider Girl $220.00
LOT, Lrg. Goat, Cow, Lion, Clown, 4 Ladders, 2 Barrels $400.00
LOT, 3 Sm. Clowns, Sm. Lion, Horse, Donkey, Elephant, Ringmaster ... $375.00

A-CT Nov 1980   *Lloyd W. Ralston*
PRETTY VILLAGE, McLaughlin, Box Rough, Ca. 1890, 14¾" x 20½" $375.00

A-CT Nov 1980   *Lloyd W. Ralston*
L To R
UNCLE SAM RIDING BICYCLE, Tin, Am. Flyer, Faded, 8" L. $300.00
ARCHIE, Ronson Toy, Tin Head, Not Working $40.00

A-CT Nov 1980   *Lloyd W. Ralston*
FIRE HOOK & LADDER WAGON, Bliss, Paper Litho. On Wood, 31" L. .. $2350.00

A-CT Nov 1980   *Lloyd W. Ralston*
STABLE, German, Wooden, Horse Missing Leg, 22½" x 23" $155.00

A-CT Nov 1980   *Lloyd W. Ralston*
NOAH'S ARK, Bliss, 10 Carved Wooden Animals, Minor Repair, 13¼" L. .. $270.00

A-CT Nov 1980   *Lloyd W. Ralston*
HORSE DRAWN BELL TOY, Nursery Rhymes On Drums, Paper Litho. On Wood, Mechanical Chimes, Hubley, Cast Iron Horse, 12" x 11" $190.00

A-CT Nov 1980   *Lloyd W. Ralston*
RACING SULKY, Geo. Brown, Am. Painted Tin, 8¾" L. $475.00

A-CT Nov 1980   *Lloyd W. Ralston*
LIMOUSINE, German Tin Windup Missing, Shellaced, 14" L. $550.00

A-CT Nov 1980   *Lloyd W. Ralston*
AUTOMOBILE, German Tin Windup, Working, 7¼" L. $500.00

A-CT Nov 1980   *Lloyd W. Ralston*
MOTORCYCLE & SIDECAR, Tipp, Tin Windup, Working, 10" L. $450.00

A-CT Nov 1980   *Lloyd W. Ralston*
UL UL, German Painted Tin Windup, Working, 7" L. $195.00

A-CT Nov 1980   *Lloyd W. Ralston*
SUMMER TROLLEY, Converse "City Hall Park #175", Painted Pressed Steel, 16" L. $360.00

A-CT Nov 1980   *Lloyd W. Ralston*
GLASS CANDY CONTAINERS, Barney Google & Sparkplug, Painted .. $230.00

A-CT Nov 1980   *Lloyd W. Ralston*
GLASS CANDY CONTAINERS, Charlie Chaplin & Camera On Tripod, Painted
.... $90.00

A-CT Nov 1980   *Lloyd W. Ralston*
ARMY FLAT CARS W/CAISSON, Marklin, German Painted Tin, 1 Ga. ... $425.00

A-CT Nov 1980   *Lloyd W. Ralston*
TROLLEY & TRAILER, Carette, Ca. 1905, Orig. Electrical System $1950.00

A-CT Nov 1980   *Lloyd W. Ralston*
TRAIN STATION, Central Bahnhof, Marklin, German Painted Tin, Painted Glass Windows, Candle Operation, 12" x 16¾"
.... $2700.00

A-CT Nov 1980   *Lloyd W. Ralston*
GLASS CANDY CONTAINERS, 2 Santas In Chimneys, 2nd W/Few Flakes .. $90.00

A-CT Nov 1980   *Lloyd W. Ralston*
PEACOCK EBO PAO-PAO, German Tin Windup, Working, Retouched, Squeaker Not Working, 9½" L. $120.00

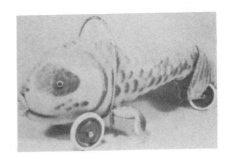

A-CT Nov 1980   *Lloyd W. Ralston*
FISH ON WHEELS, Steiff #100, Stuffed Plush, 33" L. $175.00

A-CT Nov 1980   *Lloyd W. Ralston*
ZEPPELIN ROUNDABOUT, M&K, German Painted Tin Windup, Working, 13" H.
.... $2450.00

A-CT Nov 1980   *Lloyd W. Ralston*
BIRDS ON SWING, German Painted Tin Windup, Working, 14½" H. $875.00

A-CT Nov 1980   *Lloyd W. Ralston*
L To R
HUNTER, German Painted Tin, Mechanical, 9" H. $450.00
BLK. COUPLE, German Painted Tin Windups, Not Working, 8¼" H., 7" H. $400.00

A-CT Nov 1980   *Lloyd W. Ralston*
L To R
BLK. YELLOW KID, Ringing Dinner Bell On Frying Pan, Pot Metal Head, Cloth Dressed Wooden Body & Base, Painted Tin Pan, 8¾" H. $450.00
POPEYE OVERHEAD PUNCHER, Chein Tin Windup, 9¾" H. $1300.00

A-CT Nov 1980   *Lloyd W. Ralston*
CIRCUS TRAIN, Cole Bros. & Wardie Jay, Painted Wood & Pot Metal Accessories
.... $650.00

A-CT Nov 1980   *Lloyd W. Ralston*
POPEYE THE SAILOR ROWBOAT, Hoge N.Y.C., Painted Tin Windup, Orig. Oars, Working, 14¾" L. $2000.00

A-CT Nov 1980   *Lloyd W. Ralston*
MAGGIE & JIGGS, German Tin Windup, Working, 8½" H. $1500.00

A-CT Nov 1980   *Lloyd W. Ralston*
MICKEY & MINNIE MOUSE ACROBATS, Japan Celluloid Windups, Not Working, 17" H. $350.00

A-CT Nov 1980   *Lloyd W. Ralston*
LIVE STEAM ENGINE, "GBN" Bing German Painted Tin & Nickel Plating, Orig. Directions, Makes Electricity, 12⅝" L. $200.00

A-CT Nov 1980   *Lloyd W. Ralston*
LIVE STEAM ENGINE, Bing, Painted Tin, Nickel Plated, Wood Base, Burner Missing, 6¼" Sq. $25.00

A-CT Nov 1980   *Lloyd W. Ralston*
LIVE STEAM POWER PLANT, Jensen, Nickel Plated & Painted, 10" x 11" $55.00

A-CT Nov 1980   *Lloyd W. Ralston*
TURBINE ENGINE, Empire, Nickel Plated & Painted Cast Iron, Electric, Orig. Box, Incomp. $25.00

A-CT Nov 1980   *Lloyd W. Ralston*
WEEDEN LIVE STEAM ATTACHMENTS, Painted Tin $70.00

A-CT Nov 1980   *Lloyd W. Ralston*
L To R
BOY RIDING ST. BERNARD, Rocker, Painted Tin, Poor Cond. 5" L. $35.00
CLOWN ON PIG, German Tin Windup, Wheels Not Connected, 4" L. $75.00

A-CT Nov 1980   *Lloyd W. Ralston*
L To R
CHILD IN HIGH CHAIR, Penny Toy, German Tin $150.00
BABY CARRIAGE, Penny Toy, German Tin $150.00

A-CT Nov 1980   *Lloyd W. Ralston*
SAND MILL CONSTRUCTION TOY, Am., Painted Tin, Mechanical, 11" L. $55.00

A-CT Nov 1980   *Lloyd W. Ralston*
DRUM MAJOR, Wolverine, Tin Windup, Orig. Box, Working, 13½" L. $160.00

A-CT Nov 1980   *Lloyd W. Ralston*
SCHOENHUT FIGURES, Lot Of 3, Restored Ringmaster, Retouched Tiger & Stool $200.00

A-CT Nov 1980   *Lloyd W. Ralston*
ELVES SEASAW, Mechanical Pull Toy, Painted Cast Iron, 7½" x 7½" $300.00

A-CT Nov 1980   *Lloyd W. Ralston*
L To R
CLOWN IN BARREL, Penny Toy, Stock, German Tin, 3" L. $400.00
AIRPLANES ON POLE, Penny Toy, Spring Action $150.00
MERRY GO ROUND, Penny Toy, Mechanical, Not Working $80.00

A-CT Nov 1980   *Lloyd W. Ralston*
L To R
CARROUSEL, 4 Girls On Swings, Painted Tin Windup, Working, 10" H. $400.00
MATADOR & BULL, Tin Windup, Working, 7" L. $160.00

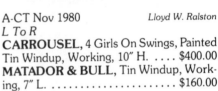

A-CT Nov 1980   *Lloyd W. Ralston*
MILK WAGON, #16, Am. Tin & Wood, 13" L. $175.00

A-CT Nov 1980   *Lloyd W. Ralston*
FIRE HOUSE W/PUMPER & PATROL, Orobr, German Tin Windup, Working $275.00

A-CT Nov 1980   *Lloyd W. Ralston*
LIMOUSINE, Carette, German Painted Tin, Wh. Rubber Wheels, Incomp., 16" L. $3250.00

A-CT Nov 1980   *Lloyd W. Ralston*
GARAGE W/2 CARS, Tipp & Co., German Tin, Battery Operated, Orig. Box $900.00

A-CT Nov 1980   *Lloyd W. Ralston*
DUMP TRUCK, Buddy L., Painted Pressed Steel, 2' L. $500.00

A-CT Nov 1980   *Lloyd W. Ralston*
TOURING CAR, Carette, Painted Tin Windup, Working, 8½" L. $3200.00

A-CT Nov 1980   *Lloyd W. Ralston*
GORDON BENNET RACER, Tin Windup, Damaged Wheel, Nor Working, 7¼" L. $1000.00

A-CT Nov 1980   *Lloyd W. Ralston*
FIRE PATROL, Buddy L., Painted Pressed Steel, Poor Cond., 25" L. $140.00

A-CT Nov 1980   *Lloyd W. Ralston*
TOURING CAR, Converse, Painted Pressed Steel, Incomp., 16" L. ... $370.00

A-CT Nov 1980   *Lloyd W. Ralston*
YELLOW TAXI, German Tin Windup, Repaired, Working, 10½" L. $525.00

A-CT Nov 1980   *Lloyd W. Ralston*
POLICE PATROL VAN, Dent, Painted Cast Iron, Orig. Driver, 8¾" L. ... $725.00

A-CT Nov 1980   *Lloyd W. Ralston*
SEDAN, Gunthermann, Tin Windup, Working, 9½" L. $125.00

A-CT Nov 1980   *Lloyd W. Ralston*
SPECIAL DELIVERY VAN, Rothschild & Co., Turner Tin Friction, Not Working, 13¼" L. $425.00

A-CT Nov 1980   *Lloyd W. Ralston*
POLICE PATROL, Painted Cast Iron & Tin, Recast Men, 15½" L. $1100.00

A-CT Nov 1980   *Lloyd W. Ralston*
L To R
TAXI, German Tin Windup, Working, 7¼" L. $900.00
OHO, Lehmann, Tin Windup, Pc. Of Winder Missing, Working, 4" L. $320.00

A-CT Nov 1980   *Lloyd W. Ralston*
MODEL T PICKUP, Buddy L., Painted Pressed Steel, 12" L. $430.00

A-CT Nov 1980   *Lloyd W. Ralston*
SPECIAL DELIVERY VAN, Gately, Fitzgerald & Co., German Tin Windup, Repl. Doors $600.00

A-CT Nov 1980   *Lloyd W. Ralston*
L To R
JACKIE THE HORNPIPE DANCER,
Strauss, Tin Windup, Not Working, Faded,
9" H. $130.00
ALABAMA COON JIGGER, Strauss
"Tombo", Tin Windup, Repl. Arms, Working, 19½" H. $100.00
CHARLIE MCCARTHY CRAZY CAR,
Marx, Tin Windup, Working, 7½" L.
.... $125.00

A-OH May 1980   *Garth's Auctions, Inc.*
CAST IRON TOYS
ROW I, L To R
TRUCK, "Hubley", Worn Red Paint &
Cracked Rubber Wheels, 3½" L. .. $15.00
FORDSON TRACTOR, Worn Red Paint,
3⅝" L. $50.00
STEAM SCOOP, Worn Red Paint, 4½" L.
.... $35.00
SOLDIER ON HORSEBACK, Worn Paint,
3½" H. $17.50
LADDER WAGON, Worn Red Paint, Wh.
Rubber Wheels, 3½" L. $12.50
ROW II, L To R
RACER, Worn Blue Paint, "Hubley", 4¼" L.
.... $27.50
SIDE WHEELER, Worn Old Paint, ½ Chimney Repl., 7¾" L. $90.00
AIRPLANE, Worn Silver Paint, 4¾" L.
.... $35.00
ROW III, L To R
FORDSON TRACTOR, Wh. Rubber
Wheels, "Arcade", Worn Red Paint & Gr.
Dump Wagon By Arcade (Not Illus.), 3" x
5¼" L. $45.00
CALVARY, 35 Pc. Set, Orig. Box "Am.
Calvary", 5½" x 6¼" $60.00
FORDSON TRACTOR, Worn Red Paint,
"Arcade" & Farm Wagon (Not Illus.), 3¾" x
4" L. $40.00

A-NY May 1980   *Calkins Auction Gallery*
L To R
TIN WINDUP TOY, Jazzbo Jim, By
Unique Art Mfg. Co., Ca. 1921, Working
Cond., 5" W., 10½" H. $140.00
TIN WINDUP TOY, The Shoopee Car,
By Louis Marx & Co., Ca. 1930, Working
Cond., 8½" L., 6½" H. $110.00
TIN WINDUP TOY, Joe Penner, By Louis
Marx & Co., Ca. 1930, 3½" W., 8½" H.
.... $130.00
FOLK ART WOODEN MUSICAL TOY,
Jolly Jigger, Orig. Paint, 8" W., 10¼" H.
.... $190.00

A-CT Nov 1980   *Lloyd W. Ralston*
ROW I, L To R
SIGHTSEEING SHIP, Revolving Airplanes,
German Tin Windup, Rusty, Wheels Need
New Axle, 9¼" L. $250.00
TOONERVILLE TROLLEY, German Tin
Windup, Working, 1 Drk. Side ... $310.00
ROW II, L To R
POOL PLAYER, Penny Toy, German Tin
Mechanical $105.00
WHISTLE AIRPLANE, Penny Toy, Fr.
Tin, Stained, Working........... $85.00
ALLIGATOR & BEETLE, Penny Toys,
German Tin $75.00

A-CT Nov 1980   *Lloyd W. Ralston*
Top To Bottom
TRUCK, Turner Toy, Friction Dump, Painted Pressed Steel, 15½" L. $135.00
DELIVERY VAN, Friction, Painted
Pressed Steel, Orig. Tin Driver, 11" L.
.... $195.00

A-CT Nov 1980   *Lloyd W. Ralston*
TOYLAND DAIRY & TRAILER, Painted
& Stenciled Pressed Steel, Girard, Orig.
Box, 17" L. $110.00

A-CT Nov 1980   *Lloyd W. Ralston*
SONNY MOVING VAN, Orig. Labels,
Painted Pressed Steel, Back Gate Missing,
26" L. $200.00

A-CT Nov 1980   *Lloyd W. Ralston*
Top To Bottom
LOCOMOTIVE & TENDER, Friction,
Painted & Stenciled Pressed Steel, 17½"
L. $80.00
LOCOMOTIVE & TENDER, Mason &
Parker, Tin & Paper, Painted Wood, Cast
Iron, Incomp., 28" L. $145.00

A-CT Nov 1980   *Lloyd W. Ralston*
LOCOMOTIVE & TENDER, Ives #187,
Electrified, Cars W/Repl. Wheels, Broken
Conductor, 25" L. $170.00

A-CT Nov 1980   *Lloyd W. Ralston*
BIG 6 LOCOMOTIVE, Stevens, Painted Cast Iron Engine, Nickel Plated Painted Cast Iron Passenger Car........ $170.00

A-CT Nov 1980   *Lloyd W. Ralston*
Top To Bottom
1 HORSE CAB, Kenton, Painted Cast Iron, 10" L. $160.00
WALKING HORSE CART, Ives, Painted Cast Iron & Pressed Steel, Poor Cond., 10¼" L. $155.00

A-CT Nov 1980   *Lloyd W. Ralston*
HORSE DRAWN RACK DRAY, Kenton, Painted Cast Iron, Recast Wilkins Driver, Pc. Of Rack Missing, 15" L. $100.00

A-CT Nov 1980   *Lloyd W. Ralston*
MULE DRIVEN ICE WAGON, Painted Cast Iron, Pressed Steel, 11" L. ... $95.00

A-CT Nov 1980   *Lloyd W. Ralston*
HAY CART, Pratt & Letchwood, Painted Cast Iron & Wood, Driver Missing, 10½" L. $225.00

A-CT Nov 1980   *Lloyd W. Ralston*
MOTORCYCLES, Lot Of 4, Painted & Nickel Plated Cast Iron.......... $160.00

A-CT Nov 1980   *Lloyd W. Ralston*
L To R
YELLOW CAB, Arcade, Painted & Stamped Cast Iron, Wh. Tires Retouched, 8" L. $340.00
MODEL T 2-DOOR SEDAN, Painted Cast Iron, Repl. Driver, Wh. Rubber Tires, 6½" L. $240.00

A-CT Nov 1980   *Lloyd W. Ralston*
L To R
FIRE PUMPER, Hubley, Painted & Nickel Plated Cast Iron, Wh. Rubber Tires On Wood Hubs, 8½" L. $160.00
ICE TRUCK, Kenton, Painted Cast Iron, Orig. Tongs & Glass Ice, 7½" L. .. $260.00

A-CT Nov 1980   *Lloyd W. Ralston*
L To R
ARTIC ICE CREAM TRUCK, Kilgore, Cast Iron, Repainted, 8" L. $120.00
CHEVROLET PICKUP TRUCK, Arcade, Painted Cast Iron, 8½" L. $410.00

A-CT Nov 1980   *Lloyd W. Ralston*
CENTURY OF PROGRESS SIGHT-SEEING BUS, Greyhound Lines Chicago '33 Arcade, Painted Cast Iron, Rubber Wheels, 14¼" L. $175.00

A-CT Nov 1980   *Lloyd W. Ralston*
LIVE STEAM LAUNCH, Wheeden, Painted Tin, Poor Paint, 20" L. $350.00

A-CT Nov 1980   *Lloyd W. Ralston*
CRAFT SPEEDBOAT ON CRADLE, Lionel, Painted Tin Windup, Working, Incomp., 18" L. $300.00

A-CT Nov 1980   *Lloyd W. Ralston*
Top To Bottom
AIRPLANE, Girard, Painted Tin Windup, Working, 10" W., 12½" L. $150.00
AIRPLANE IN HANGER, Painted Pressed Steel, Rubber Tires, 16" L. $185.00
TRIMOTOR AIRPLANE, Kingsbury, Pressed Tin, Repainted, Working, 15½" L. $195.00

A-CT Nov 1980   *Lloyd W. Ralston*
SPEEDBOAT, Painted Wood, 2 Electric Motors, Orig. Box, 24" L. $250.00

A-CT Nov 1980   *Lloyd W. Ralston*
MERCHANT MARINE SHIP, Ives, Painted Tin Windup, Working, Restorations, Incomp., 11" L. $160.00

A-CT Nov 1980   *Lloyd W. Ralston*
SPEEDBOAT, Hess #7, Tin Friction, 12" L. $130.00

A-CT Nov 1980   *Lloyd W. Ralston*
TRAIN SET, Am. Flyer Locomotive, Tender, 4 Freight Cars, Painted Cast Iron & Tin $195.00

A-CT Nov 1980   *Lloyd W. Ralston*
L To R
AUTO TRUCK, Pierce Arrow, Take Apart, Rubber Tires, Wood Hubs, 6½″ L. ... $70.00
SILVER ARROW, Arcade, Painted Cast Iron, Nickel Plated Grill, Wh. Rubber Tires, 7″ L. $100.00

A-CT Nov 1980   *Lloyd W. Ralston*
L To R
SEDAN, Hubley, Painted Cast Iron, 5¼″ L. $65.00
LIMOUSINE, Hubley, Painted Cast Iron, 7″ L. $65.00
LINCOLN TOURING CAR, Williams, Painted Cast Iron, 7″ L. $120.00

A-CT Nov 1980   *Lloyd W. Ralston*
OIL TRUCKS, Champion Gas & Motor Oil, Painted Cast Iron, Rubber Tires, Wood Hubs, 4¾″ L., 8″ L. $145.00

A-CT Nov 1980   *Lloyd W. Ralston*
L To R
CHAMPION MACK RACK TRUCK, Painted Cast Iron, Rubber Tires, Wood Hubs, 7½″ L. $250.00
MODEL T COUPE, Arcade, Painted Cast Iron, 6½″ L. $250.00

A-CT Nov 1980   *Lloyd W. Ralston*
NUCAR TRANSPORT, Hubley, Painted Cast Iron, Rubber Tires, Wood Hubs, 16½″ L. $650.00

A-CT Nov 1980   *Lloyd W. Ralston*
L To R
SEDAN, Hubley, Painted & Nickel Plated Cast Iron, Rubber Tires On Wood Hubs, 6¾″ L. $150.00
MODEL A COUPE W/Rumble Seat, Arcade, Painted & Nickel Plated Cast Iron, Orig. Label, 5″ L. $200.00
SEDAN, 4-Door, Arcade, Painted & Nickel Plated Cast Iron, 5″ L. $100.00

A-CT Nov 1980   *Lloyd W. Ralston*
L To R
SPEEDSTER, Kenton, Painted Cast Iron, 7¾″ L. $90.00
FORDSON TRACTOR & PLOW, Arcade, Painted & Nickel Plated Cast Iron
.... $145.00

A-CT Nov 1980   *Lloyd W. Ralston*
L To R
MACK TRUCKS, Lot Of 2, Painted Cast Iron, 1 W/Nickel Plated Wheels .. $100.00
CREW CAB TRUCK, Williams, Painted & Nickel Plated Cast Iron, 7″ L. $285.00

A-CT Nov 1980   *Lloyd W. Ralston*
AUTOMOBILE, Carl Bubb, German Tin Windup, Working, 6″ L. $1000.00

A-CT Nov 1980   *Lloyd W. Ralston*
LOCOMOTIVE, Ives, Painted Cast Iron, Clockwork Not Working, Headlight Missing, 9½″ L. $420.00

A-CT Nov 1980   *Lloyd W. Ralston*
LOCOMOTIVE & TENDER, Wilkins #33, Painted Cast Iron, Repl. Wheels .. $160.00

A-CT Nov 1980   *Lloyd W. Ralston*
TRAIN SET, Ives #11 Electric Painted Cast Iron Locomotive, Homemade Tender, Incomp. Baggage, 2 Coaches, O Ga., Yale & Harvard..................... $240.00

A-CT Nov 1980   *Lloyd W. Ralston*
TRAIN SET, Ives, #3238 Electric Painted Cast Iron Locomotive, Baggage, Combination & Passenger Car, Coach, O Ga.
.... $350.00

A-CT Nov 1980   *Lloyd W. Ralston*
TRAIN SET, Am. Flyer, Cast Iron Locomotive, Tin Tender, 2 Coaches, O Ga.
.... $100.00

A-CT Nov 1980   *Lloyd W. Ralston*
TRAIN SET, Marklin, O Ga., Live Steam
Locomotive, 7 Cars, Painted Tin . . $1500.00

A-CT Nov 1980   *Lloyd W. Ralston*
TRAIN SET, Ives, Painted Tin, Most Pcs.
Flaking, Orig. Box $275.00

A-CT Nov 1980   *Lloyd W. Ralston*
TRAIN SET, Ives #3241, Red, Painted &
Stamped Tin, Cast Iron Base, Orig. Box,
Crossing Gate $250.00

A-CT Nov 1980   *Lloyd W. Ralston*
TRAIN SET, Bing Locomotive, Painted
Cast Iron, Windup, Working, 4 Cars, Track
Key, Orig. Box $375.00

A-CT Nov 1980   *Lloyd W. Ralston*
TRAIN SET, Ives #3236, Electric Locomotive, 2 Cars, Std. Ga., Set Restored . . $225.00

A-CT Nov 1980   *Lloyd W. Ralston*
TRAIN SET, Ives #3236, Std. Ga., Painted
& Stamped Tin, Cast Iron Base, Orig. Box,
Flaking Roofs $290.00

A-CT Nov 1980   *Lloyd W. Ralston*
LOCOMOTIVE, Ives #10, Electric, Std.
Ga., Peacock, Restored $120.00

A-CT Nov 1980   *Lloyd W. Ralston*
WILKINS' LARGEST TRAIN SET, Painted Cast Iron, Am. Style, Locomotive, Tender, Coupler Missing, Baggage-Passenger &
Passenger Car, Repaired $750.00

A-CT Nov 1980   *Lloyd W. Ralston*
MILLWRIGHT & SAWYER, Live Steam
Attachments, German Painted Tin . . . $65.00

A-CT Nov 1980   *Lloyd W. Ralston*
SLEEPING COACH, Marklin, Painted Tin,
1 Ga., Incomp., 16″ L. $500.00

A-CT Nov 1980   Lloyd W. Ralston
CLAM SHELL DREDGER, Buddy L.,
Painted Pressed Steel, Working, 33" L.
.... $450.00

A-CT Nov 1980   Lloyd W. Ralston
TANK TRUCK, Buddy L., Painted Pressed
Steel, Rubber Tires, 25½" L. $850.00

A-CT Nov 1980   Lloyd W. Ralston
ROADSTER, Dayton, Friction, Painted
Pressed Steel, 2 Rubber Tires Missing, 13½"
L. $340.00

A-CT Nov 1980   Lloyd W. Ralston
GMC TANDEM DUMP TRUCK, Re-
painted Pressed Steel, Firestone Rubber
Tires, 29" L. $125.00

A-CT Nov 1980   Lloyd W. Ralston
HILLCLIMBER TOYS, Lot Of 2, Moving
Van & Fire Truck, Both Painted Pressed
Steel & Incomp., 11¾" L., 14½" L. $140.00

A-CT Nov 1980   Lloyd W. Ralston
MOTORIZED FIRE PUMPER, Kingsbury,
Painted Cast Iron & Pressed Steel, Work-
ing, 11" L. $220.00

A-CT Nov 1980   Lloyd W. Ralston
LOCOMOTIVE & TENDER, Carette,
Live Steam, German Painted Tin, Brass
Broiler, 13½" L. $310.00

A-CT Nov 1980   Lloyd W. Ralston
TRAIN SET, Carette, Locomotive, Tender,
2 Coaches, Live Steam, German Painted
Tin, 3 Ga. $2300.00

A-CT Nov 1980   Lloyd W. Ralston
CROSSING PLATFORM, Marklin, Candle Lit, German Painted Tin $120.00

A-CT Nov 1980   Lloyd W. Ralston
TRAIN SET, Ives Locomotive, Cast Iron &
Painted Tin, Am. Flyer & Ives Cars, Includes
Ives Water Tower & Sm. Station (Not Illus.)
.... $245.00

A-CT Nov 1980   Lloyd W. Ralston
DART TRAIN SET, Weeden, Am. Live
Steam Tin Locomotive, Dated 1887, Tender
& Coach $425.00

A-CT Nov 1980   Lloyd W. Ralston
BRIDGE W/POSTAL COACH, German
Painted Tin $110.00

A-CT Nov 1980   Lloyd W. Ralston
PACIFIC EXPRESS LINE, J.A.J., German Painted Tin, O Ga., Needs Restoration,
29" L. $410.00

A-CT Nov 1980   Lloyd W. Ralston
PAINTED TIN TOYS, Marklin Snow Plow
& Flat Car, Both 1 Ga., 8" L., 10" L.
.... $375.00

A-CT Nov 1980   *Lloyd W. Ralston*
L To R
AUTOMOBILE, German Tin Friction,
5¾" L. $140.00
LEAPING LENA, Strauss, Tin Windup,
Working, 8½" L. $140.00

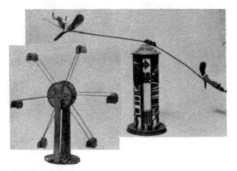

A-CT Nov 1980   *Lloyd W. Ralston*
L To R
HY-LO, Buffalo Toys, Tin, 15½" H.
. . . . $65.00
SKY HAWK, Marx, Tin Windup, Working,
19" D., 8" H. $95.00

A-CT Nov 1980   *Lloyd W. Ralston*
MERRY GO ROUND, German Painted
Tin, Paint Poor, 10¾" W. $400.00

A-CT Nov 1980   *Lloyd W. Ralston*
L To R
AERIAL SPINNER, Am. Toyland, Tin &
Stained Wood, 18½" H. $270.00
FERRIS WHEEL, German Tin Windup, 4
Figures Missing, Not Working, 10½" H.
. . . . $130.00

A-CT Nov 1980   *Lloyd W. Ralston*
L To R
FERRIS WHEEL,8 Gondolas, Live Steam
Attachment, German Painted Tin, 10¾" H.
. . . . $155.00
CLOWN, Papier Mache, Cloth Dressed,
Wood Rockers, Mechanism Working, 8" H.
. . . . $275.00

A-CT Nov 1980   *Lloyd W. Ralston*
L To R
WILD ANIMAL PICTURE CUBES,
McLaughlin Puzzle, 8½" x 11" $110.00
LOCOMOTIVE PICTURE PUZZLE,
McLaughlin Box, Ca. 1887, 9¼" x 12½"
. . . . $125.00

A-CT Nov 1980   *Lloyd W. Ralston*
CRISS CROSS SPELLING STRIPES,
McLaughlin, Orig. Box, 3 Strip Puzzles, All
Framed $60.00

A-CT Nov 1980   *Lloyd W. Ralston*
CUT-UP TRAVEL, Parker Bros., Orig.
Box, 5 Strip Puzzles, All Framed . . $180.00

A-CT Nov 1980   *Lloyd W. Ralston*
BROWNIE BLOCK PUZZLE, Palmer Cox
McLaughlin, New Glass Case, Cubes: 12½"
Sq. $140.00

A-CT Nov 1980   *Lloyd W. Ralston*
L To R
MODEL T, 4-Door Sedan, Bing, Tin Wind-
up, Headlight Missing, Working, 6½" L.
. . . . $250.00
MOTORCOACH, Lehmann, Tin Windup,
Working $290.00

A-CT Nov 1980   *Lloyd W. Ralston*
HESSMOBILE TOURING CAR, Tin
Windup, Not Orig. Figure, Not Working, 9" L.
. . . . $105.00

A-CT Nov 1980   *Lloyd W. Ralston*
ROW I, L To R
J.L. HUDSON CO. DELIVERY VAN,
Painted Cast Iron, Rubber Tires, 8" L.
. . . . $200.00
JAEGER CEMENT MIXER, Kenton, Re-
stored Paint, 9¼" L. $310.00
ROW II, L To R
AIRFLOW, Hubley, Painted & Nickel Plated
Cast Iron, Electrified, Wh. Rubber Tires On
Wood Hubs, 8" L. $600.00
MODEL T ROADSTER, Bing, German
Painted Tin Windup, Working, 6¼" L.
. . . . $310.00

A-CT Nov 1980   *Lloyd W. Ralston*
L To R
MAGIC LANTERN, Ernst Plank, Orig. Box
.... $140.00
MAGIC LANTERN, Satyr Figure, Brass
Plated Tin, Wood Case, 10¾″ x 8½″
.... $160.00

A-CT Nov 1980   *Lloyd W. Ralston*
TOOTSIE TOYS, Lot Of 33, Cars, Trucks
& Trains $400.00

A-CT Nov 1980   *Lloyd W. Ralston*
Top To Bottom
BELL TELEPHONE TRUCK, Hubley,
Painted & Nickel Plated Cast Iron, Repl.
Tools, Orig. Rubber Tires On Wood Hubs,
14″ L. $500.00
FIRE PUMPER, Kenton, Painted & Nickel
Plated Cast Iron, Hubley Drivers, 14½″ L.
.... $220.00

A-CT Nov 1980   *Lloyd W. Ralston*
FAGEOL BUS, Arcade, Painted Cast Iron,
12¼″ L. $140.00

A-CT Nov 1980   *Lloyd W. Ralston*
TOOTSIE & BARCLAY TOYS, Lot Of
13, Vehicles & 1 Chair, Some Orig., Some
Restored $110.00

A-CT Nov 1980   *Lloyd W. Ralston*
SOLDIERS & DIE CASTS, Lrg. Lot
.... $185.00

A-CT Nov 1980   *Lloyd W. Ralston*
DINKY TOYS, Lrg. Lot $130.00

A-CT Nov 1980   *Lloyd W. Ralston*
TOOTSIE & BARCLAY TOYS, Lrg. Lot
.... $150.00

A-CT Nov 1980   *Lloyd W. Ralston*
SOLDIERS, Milton Bradley, Paper Litho
.... $45.00

A-CT Nov 1980   *Lloyd W. Ralston*
SOLDIERS, Lrg. Lot $200.00

A-CT Nov 1980   *Lloyd W. Ralston*
L To R
HERCULES JAZZ BANK, Chein Tin,
Orig. Box, 11½″ x 12″ $165.00
CANDY CONTAINERS, 2, Glass Santa,
Papier Mache Egg $85.00

A-CT Nov 1980   *Lloyd W. Ralston*
L To R
UNCLE SAM FLIPPING HIS HAT, Paper
Litho., Cloth Dressed, Ca. 1916, 9½″ H.
.... $110.00
JOCKEY ON HORSE, Mechanical, Paper
Litho. & Painted Tin, 10½″ L. $205.00

A-CT Nov 1980   *Lloyd W. Ralston*
L To R
GENERAL GRANT FIGURE, For Ives
Smoker, Redressed $600.00
JFK, In Rocking Chair, Music Box, Nor
Working, Wood & Plastic, Japan, Ca. 1963
.... $45.00

A-CT Nov 1980   *Lloyd W. Ralston*
SCHOENHUT FIGURES, Ostrich, Restored Acrobat, Lrg. Horse, Repl. Platform
.... $425.00

A-CT Nov 1980   *Lloyd W. Ralston*
SCHOENHUT FIGURES, Lrg. Giraffe, Elephant W/Repl. Tail & Drum ... $150.00

A-CT Nov 1980   *Lloyd W. Ralston*
SCHOENHUT FIGURES, Rhino W/Repl. Tail & Glass Eyes, Mule W/Repl. Ears, & Stool $210.00

A-CT Nov 1980   *Lloyd W. Ralston*
SCHOENHUT FIGURES, Lion, Monkey W/New Hat-Foot, & Hippo W/Glass Eyes
.... $310.00

A-CT Nov 1980   *Lloyd W. Ralston*
SCHOENHUT FIGURES, Camel & Horse W/Repl. Tail $225.00

A-CT Nov 1980   *Lloyd W. Ralston*
L To R
AMOS & ANDY FRESH AIR CAB, Tin Windup, Not Working, 8" L. $350.00
TEDDY BEAR, BOY & CART, German Tin Windup, Working, 5½" L. $210.00

A-CT Nov 1980   *Lloyd W. Ralston*
L To R
DANCING COUPLE, German Painted Tin Windup, Working, 6¾" H. ... $300.00
TOURING CAR, Hessmobile, Tin Friction, Mechanism Jammed, 11" L. $450.00

A-CT Nov 1980   *Lloyd W. Ralston*
L To R
POOL PLAYER, German Tin Windup, Working, 6½" L. $195.00
CAT ON SCOOTER, Chein Tin Windup, Not Working, 7¼" L. $85.00
CHARLESTON TRIO, Marx, Tin Windup Not Working $120.00

A-CT Nov 1980   *Lloyd W. Ralston*
L To R
KING RACER ROADSTER, Marx, Tin Windup, Working, Orig. Box, 9" L. $260.00
TURKEY, German Painted Tin, Lever Action, 6" H. $245.00

A-CT Nov 1980   *Lloyd W. Ralston*
BOY RIDING ALLIGATOR, Tin Windup, Working, 15" L. $100.00

A-CT Nov 1980   *Lloyd W. Ralston*
L To R
PADDY & PIG, Lehmann, Tin Windup, Working, Cloth Dressed.............. $500.00
ONKLE, Lehmann, Tin Windup, Not Working, Incomp. $90.00

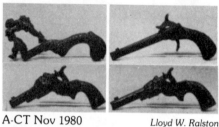

A-CT Nov 1980   *Lloyd W. Ralston*
ROW I, L To R
SHOOT THE HAT, Animated Cap Pistol, Ives, Japanned Cast Iron $350.00
VOLUNTEER, Cap Pistol, Japanned Cast Iron, 5¼" L. $50.00
ROW II, L To R
LOOK OUT CAP PISTOL, Bulldog Face, Stevens, Japanned Cast Iron $190.00
LION CAP PISTOL, Stevens, Japanned Cast Iron $100.00

A-CT Nov 1980   *Lloyd W. Ralston*
L To R
SURPRISE BOX, Cap Shooter, Japanned & Gold Painted Cast Iron, Minor Chip, 4¾" L.
.... $2400.00
PRETZEL VENDOR-CHIMNEY SWEEP, Lehmann, Tin Windup, Working, Incomp.
.... $130.00

A-CT Nov 1980   *Lloyd W. Ralston*
L To R
NAUGHTY BOY, Lehmann, Tin Windup, Working, 5" L. $400.00
BOY SLEDDING, Hess, German Tin Friction, 6¼" L. $310.00
ONKELS, Lot Of 2, Lehmann, German Painted Tin Windup, Working $625.00

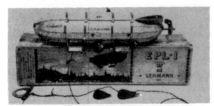

A-CT Nov 1980 *Lloyd W. Ralston*
EPL-1 ZEPPELIN, Lehmann, Tin Windup, Working, Incomp., Orig. Box $430.00

A-CT Nov 1980 *Lloyd W. Ralston*
ROW I, L To R
PAAK-PAAK, Lehmann, Tin Windup, Working $240.00
MOTORCYCLE & SIDECAR, G & K, German Tin Windup, Working, 7" L.
.... $425.00
ROW II, L To R
AUTO, G & K, German Tin Windup, Working, 4½" L. $210.00
AUTO, Vis A Vis, Tin Friction, 4" L.
.... $200.00

A-CT Nov 1980 *Lloyd W. Ralston*
L To R
LADY IN 3 WHEEL AUTO, Stock, Tin Windup, Working, Missing Tiller, 4¾" L.
.... $235.00
BLK. MAN PUSHING CART, German Tin Windup, Working, 6½" L. $200.00

A-CT Nov 1980 *Lloyd W. Ralston*
L To R
DARKY BANJO PLAYER, German Painted Tin Windup, 6¾" H. $525.00
MOTHER DUCK & DUCKLINGS, German Painted Tin Windup $140.00
DOG CHASING MONKEY, Stock, Tin Windup, Working, 6½" L. $325.00

A-CT Nov 1980 *Lloyd W. Ralston*
L To R
CARROUSEL, German Painted Tin Windup, Working, Velvet Cloth Canopy, Orig. Price Tag, Poor Cond., 17" H. ... $575.00
FERRIS WHEEL, German Painted Tin, Litho. Figures, Reverse Wind Mechanism Working, 15" H. $625.00

A-CT Nov 1980 *Lloyd W. Ralston*
L To R
RUNNING PIG, German Painted Tin Windup, Working, 6" L. $260.00
WALKING LADY, German Painted Tin Windup, Working, 6" H. $210.00
CAT, German Painted Tin Windup, Working, 6½" H. $190.00

A-CT Nov 1980 *Lloyd W. Ralston*
SIGNAL TOWERS, Lot Of 3, German Painted Tin $100.00

A-CT Nov 1980 *Lloyd W. Ralston*
ROUND HOUSE, 5-Stall, O Ga., German Painted Tin, 25" W. $190.00

A-CT Nov 1980 *Lloyd W. Ralston*
STATION, Lionel $110.00

A-CT Nov 1980 *Lloyd W. Ralston*
NEWSPAPER STAND, For Railroad Station, German Painted Tin & Glass, 5¼" H.
.... $95.00

A-CT Nov 1980 *Lloyd W. Ralston*
BEAN BAG TARGET, Paper Litho. On Wood, 14¼" H. $300.00

A-CT Nov 1980 *Lloyd W. Ralston*
DOLL HOUSE, Bliss, Paper Litho. On Wood, Missing Chimney & Curtain, 9½" x 7½" x 4¾" $310.00

A-CT Nov 1980   *Lloyd W. Ralston*
L To R
MOTORCYCLE W/SIDECAR, Arnold, Tin Windup, Working, 8½″ L. $275.00
PENNY FIRE TOY, German Nickeled Tin Windup, Working, 4½″ L. $200.00

A-CT Nov 1980   *Lloyd W. Ralston*
L To R
CHINA HEAD DOLLS, Lot Of 2, 16½″ H., 12″ H. $100.00
DOLL, Tin Momentum Action, Working, Cloth Dressed, Felt Hat, Orig. Box, 4½″ H. . . . $90.00

A-CT Nov 1980   *Lloyd W. Ralston*
PLAYSKOOL PULLMAN, Am. Flyer, 9½″ x 11½″ $150.00

A-CT Nov 1980   *Lloyd W. Ralston*
MILTON BERLE CAR, Marx, Tin & Plastic, Windup, Working, Orig. Box, 6½″ L.
. . . . $95.00

A-CT Nov 1980   *Lloyd W. Ralston*
TIN WINDUP TOYS, Lot Of 2, Gunthermann Bus & Gama Funny Harry, Both Working Cond., 8¾″ L., 5¼″ L. . . $185.00

A-CT Nov 1980   *Lloyd W. Ralston*
L To R
GIRL ON POTTY, German Tin, Mechanical, Working, 5″ H. $125.00
DARKY IN ROCKING CHAIR, German Painted Tin, Cloth Clothes, 6½″ H.
. . . . $325.00

A-CT Nov 1980   *Lloyd W. Ralston*
SCHOENHUT FIGURES, Lot Of 2, Lion Tamer & Chinaman, Both Restored . . $250.00
SCHOENHUT FIGURES, Lot Of 3, Gorilla W/Restored Face & 2 Barrels $400.00

A-CT Nov 1980   *Lloyd W. Ralston*
SCHOENHUT FIGURES, Lot Of 2, Barney Google W/New Coat & Spark Plug
. . . . $500.00
SCHOENHUT FIGURES, Lot Of 2, Maggie & Jiggs W/New Pants $1275.00

A-CT Nov 1980   *Lloyd W. Ralston*
LITTLE GIRLS PAPER DOLL, 1 Doll, 6 Dresses, 3 Hats, 1 Flower, No Stand Orig. Box $700.00

A-CT Nov 1980   *Lloyd W. Ralston*
SCHOENHUT FIGURES, Lot Of 4, Bulldog, Restored Hobo, Restored Poodle & Barrel $150.00

A-CT Nov 1980   *Lloyd W. Ralston*
SCHOENHUT FIGURES, Lot Of 3, Buffalo, Farmer & Goat, All Restored
. . . . $310.00

A-CT Nov 1980   *Lloyd W. Ralston*
SCHOENHUT FIGURES, Lot Of 3, Kangaroo W/New Ears, Acrobat & Zebra W/New Tail $450.00

A-CT Nov 1980   *Lloyd W. Ralston*
JENNY LIND PAPER DOLL, 1 Doll, 10 Dresses, 5 Hats, 1 Stand, Orig. Box, Ca. 1850 . . . . $775.00

A-CT Nov 1980   *Lloyd W. Ralston*
MACK DUMP TRUCK, Arcade, Painted Cast Iron, 3 Labels, 12″ L. $650.00

A-CT Nov 1980 *Lloyd W. Ralston*
PLOW, Wilkins, Painted Cast Iron, Horse's Leg Missing, 10½" L. $1200.00

A-CT Nov 1980 *Lloyd W. Ralston*
L To R
SKIDOODLE, Nifty, German Tin Windup, Working, 10½" L. $550.00
YELLOW CAB CO., Arcade, Painted & Stenciled Cast Iron, 5" L. $550.00

A-CT Nov 1980 *Lloyd W. Ralston*
DOUBLE DECKER BUS, Kenton, Painted Cast Iron, Rubber Tires On Wood Hubs, 3 Orig. Figures, 10" L. $650.00

A-CT Nov 1980 *Lloyd W. Ralston*
L To R
DRAY, Welker & Crosby-Pratt & Letchworth, Painted Cast Iron, Poor Cond., 14½" L. $155.00
COW ON PLATFORM, Painted Cast Iron, Poor Cond., 6¼" L. $130.00

◄ A-CT Nov 1980 *Lloyd W. Ralston*
HUBER ROAD ROLLER, Hubley, Painted Cast Iron, Incomp., 14" L. $250.00

A-CT Nov 1980 *Lloyd W. Ralston*
L To R
ANDY GUMP CAR, Painted Cast Iron, Restored, 7" L. $550.00
POPEYE SPINACH MOTORCYCLE, Painted Cast Iron, Restored Figure, Repaired Motorcycle, 5¼" L. $210.00

A-CT Nov 1980 *Lloyd W. Ralston*
L To R
MICKEY & MINNIE MOUSE HANDCAR, Lionel, Tin & Painted Composition, Clockwork Not Working $500.00
POPEYE EXPRESS, Marx, Tin Windup, Working, 20" W. $600.00

A-CT Nov 1980 *Lloyd W. Ralston*
L To R
POPEYE & OLIVE OYL, Marx, Tin Windup, Working $525.00
MOON MULLINS & KAYO HANDCAR, Marx, Tin Windup, Working, 6½" L. $360.00

A-CT Nov 1980 *Lloyd W. Ralston*
L To R
FELIX THE CAT, Schoenhut, Painted Wood, Decals, Tail Incomp., 4" H. $45.00
CHARLIE MCCARTHY CRAZY CAR, Marx, Tin Windup, Working, 8" L. $160.00
POPEYE IN BARREL, Chein Tin Windup, Working, 7" H. $200.00

A-CT Nov 1980 *Lloyd W. Ralston*
BUCK ROGERS ROCKET SHIP, Tin Windup, Working, 12" L. $310.00

A-CT Nov 1980 *Lloyd W. Ralston*
ROADSTER, Girard, Painted Pressed Steel, Rubber Tires, Electrified But Missing, 14½" L. $55.00

A-CT Nov 1980 *Lloyd W. Ralston*
EXPRESS LINE, Buddy L., Painted Pressed Steel, Body Loose, 25" L. $610.00

A-CT Nov 1980 *Lloyd W. Ralston*
GRAHAM PAIGE SEDAN, Painted Pressed Steel, Electric, 20" L. $500.00

A-CT Nov 1980 *Lloyd W. Ralston*
HOOK & LADDER, Big Boy, Painted Pressed Steel, Varnished Wood Extension Ladders, 38" L. $725.00

A-CT Nov 1980   *Lloyd W. Ralston*
RAILROAD STATION, Marklin, Painted
Tin, Electric, 19″ L. $65.00

A-CT Nov 1980   *Lloyd W. Ralston*
SPIRIT OF COLUMBIA AIRPLANE,
Am. Flyer, Ca. 1930, Pressed Tin Friction,
18″ W., 20″ L. $525.00

A-CT Nov 1980   *Lloyd W. Ralston*
SPIRIT OF AMERICA, Am. Flyer, Ca.
1928, Pull Toy, Pressed Tin, Not Working,
18″ W., 18½″ L. $165.00

A-CT Nov 1980   *Lloyd W. Ralston*
AIRPLANE, Jepp, Fr. Tin Windup, Working, 11⅛″ W., 7⅝″ L. $260.00

A-CT Nov 1980   *Lloyd W. Ralston*
L To R
ACROBATS BELL TOY, Gong Bell #54,
Painted Cast Iron, 6″ x 6″ $1600.00
W.C. FIELDS LOOKALIKE, German Paint-
ed Tin Windup, Working, 8″ H. . . $245.00

A-CT Nov 1980   *Lloyd W. Ralston*
L To R
CARROUSEL, German Painted Tin Wind-
up, Working, Missing Top Flag, 13″ H.
. . . . $700.00

A-CT Nov 1980   *Lloyd W. Ralston*
HI-WAY HENRY, German Tin Windup,
Working, 10½″ L. $2000.00

A-CT Nov 1980   *Lloyd W. Ralston*
ICE WAGON, Dent, Painted Cast Iron, 16″
L. $165.00

A-CT Nov 1980   *Lloyd W. Ralston*
CHIEF WAGON, Kenton, Painted Cast
Iron, 12¼″ L. $700.00

A-CT Nov 1980   *Lloyd W. Ralston*
DRAY, Wilkins, Painted Cast Iron & Pressed
Steel, 17½″ L. $580.00

A-CT Nov 1980   *Lloyd W. Ralston*
CIRCUS CHARIOT, Hubley, Painted Cast
Iron, Repro. Figure, Restorations, 9½″ L.
. . . . $250.00

A-CT Nov 1980   *Lloyd W. Ralston*
FIRE PUMPER, Kingsbury, Painted Cast
Iron, 17½″ L. $240.00

A-CT Nov 1980   *Lloyd W. Ralston*
BIX 6 CIRCUS WAGON, Arcade, Painted
& Stenciled Wood & Cast Iron, Plumes
Missing, 14½″ L. $270.00

A-CT Nov 1980   *Lloyd W. Ralston*
HOOK & LADDER, Dent, Painted Cast
Iron & Wood, 27″ L. $275.00

A-CT Nov 1980   *Lloyd W. Ralston*
TRAIN SET, Locomotive, Tender, 2 Coaches,
Painted Cast Iron, 26½″ L. $75.00

A-CT Nov 1980   *Lloyd W. Ralston*
BIG PARADE, Marx, Tin Windup, Orig.
Box, Working, 2′ L. $225.00

A-CT Nov 1980   *Lloyd W. Ralston*
MERRY MAKERS, Marx, Tin Windup, Orig. Box, Working $750.00

A-CT Nov 1980   *Lloyd W. Ralston*
TOPSY TURVY TOM, H.E. Nurenburg, Tin Windup, Orig. Box, Working, 10¼" L.
. . . . $650.00

A-CT Nov 1980   *Lloyd W. Ralston*
L To R
AMOS & ANDY, Marx, Tin Windup, Moving Eyes, Orig. Arms, Working, 12" H.
. . . . $1100.00
HEY-HEY THE CHICKEN SNATCHER, Marx, Tin Windup, Working, 9" H. . . . $575.00

A-CT Nov 1980   *Lloyd W. Ralston*
RACING SCULL, U.S. Hdw., Painted Cast Iron, Mechanical, 14" L. . . . $1300.00

A-CT Nov 1980   *Lloyd W. Ralston*
L To R
CHARLIE CHAPLIN, German Tin Windup, Iron Feet, Orig. Arms, Working, 8½" H.
. . . . $550.00
RABBIT W/CARROT, German Painted Tin Windup, Working, Cloth Carrot, 7½" L.
. . . . $310.00
BEACH PATROL SURFER, Hubley, Painted Cast Iron, Paper Janzen Label, Orig. String, 8" L. $825.00

A-CT Nov 1980   *Lloyd W. Ralston*
PEDAL CAR RACER, #93 Pioneer, Painted Tin, Wood Frame, Rubber Tires, Chain Drive, 44" L. $525.00

A-CT Nov 1980   *Lloyd W. Ralston*
PACKARD PEDAL CAR, Am. National, Battery In Trunk, Seats & Canvas Restored, Can Be Pedaled By 2 Children . . . $4200.00

A-CT Nov 1980   *Lloyd W. Ralston*
PEDAL CAR, Sideway, Nash, Rubber Tires, Orig. Wood, Missing Windshield, 34" L.
. . . . $400.00

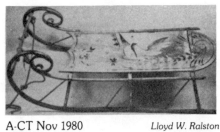

A-CT Nov 1980   *Lloyd W. Ralston*
SLED, 41" L. $400.00

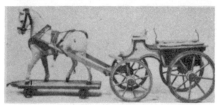

A-CT Nov 1980   *Lloyd W. Ralston*
HORSE & CARRIAGE, Stuffed Skin Horse, Decor. Wooden Carriage, Upholstered, 28" L. $330.00

A-CT Nov 1980   *Lloyd W. Ralston*
VOLUNTEER, Fallows, Am. Painted & Stained Tin, Stenciled, Some Touch Up, Repl. Parts, Working $1200.00

A-CT Nov 1980   *Lloyd W. Ralston*
FIRE PUMPER, Fallows, Am. Painted & Stenciled Tin, 18" L. $5700.00

A-CT Nov 1980   *Lloyd W. Ralston*
HORSE DRAWN FISH WAGON, Fulton Market #240, Am. Painted & Stenciled Tin, 11¼" L. $1250.00

A-CT Nov 1980   *Lloyd W. Ralston*
DOCTOR'S BUGGY, Geo. Brown, Am. Painted Tin, Cast Iron Wheels, 14" L.
. . . . $975.00

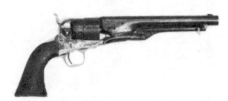

A-MA Feb 1980   *Robert W. Skinner Inc.*
PERCUSSION PISTOL, Colt Model 1860 Army Percussion Revolver, Cal. 44, Walnut Grips, Ca, 1860-1865 . . . . $450.00*

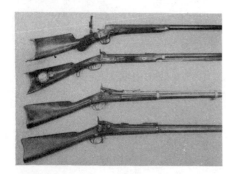

A-MA May 1980   *Richard A. Bourne Co., Inc.*
Top To Bottom
SHORT RANGE TARGET RIFLE, Remington-Hepburn #3, Factory "B" Quality, .38-40 Caliber, Eng. Walnut Stock W/Nickel-Plated Trim, Minor Blemish, 98% Orig. Blue Finish, 28″ Barrel $1200.00
RIFLE, ½-Stock, Percussion, Mkd. "Robertson Phila", Bearing Birmingham Proof Marks, .50 Caliber, German Silver Engraved Trim, 98% Orig. Twist Br. Finish, 35¼″ Barrel
. . . . $2500.00
SPRINGFIELD RIFLE, Model 1866, Dated 1864, 3-Bands, 90% Orig. Finish, Walnut Stock, Faded Inspection Mark . . . $550.00
SPRINGFIELD RIFLE, Model 1873, Modifications Of 1878, Inspector's Mark . . . $500.00

A-MA Sept 1980   *Robert W. Skinner Inc.*
PERCUSSION RIFLE, .45 Cal., Walnut ½ Stock, Lock Mkd. "J.H. Johnston, Pittsburgh, PA", Barrel Mkd. "J.H. Johnston, Great Western Gun Works", Am., Ca. 1865, 33″ L. $400.00*

A-MA Feb 1980   *Robert W. Skinner Inc.*
PERCUSSION TARGET RIFLE, Tiger Maple Half Stock, Barrel Stamped "G.A. Stufegen", Silver Plate Inset In Cheek Rest Inscribed "T.J. Craner", Am., Ca. 1860, Barrel: 33″ L. $550.00*

*Price does not include 10% buyer fee.

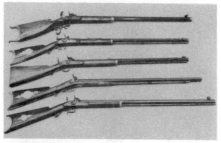

A-MA May 1980   *Richard A. Bourne Co., Inc.*
Top To Bottom
SCHUETZEN RIFLE. NY, Percussion, .45 Caliber, Stamped "Zettler/NY", Nickel-Plated Brass Fore-End Tip, Trigger Guard & Butt Plate, Figured European Walnut Stock, Double-Set Triggers, Minor Flaws, 31⅛″ Barrel $2700.00
HUNTING & TARGET RIFLE, ½-Stock, Percussion, NY, .40 Caliber, Stamped "W. Dixon/Adams, NY/Cast Steel", Walnut Stock, Brass Trigger Guard, German Silver Patch Box, 95% Orig. Br. Finish, Minor Damages, 32″ Barrel $650.00
RIFLE, ½-Stock, Percussion, NY, .45 Caliber, Stamped "C. Werner/Rochester", "Remington", Walnut Stock, Polished In Oil W/ Plain Brass Mounts, Single-Set Trigger, Bayonet Lug Dovetailed Into Side Of Barrel, 75% Orig. Br. Finish, Minor Damages, 30″ Barrel $900.00
COMBINATION GUN, Remington, Factory-Made, Percussion, Double-Barrel Side-By-Side, .38 Caliber, Figured Walnut Stock, Worn Stain, 31″ Barrel $850.00
HUNTING & TARGET RIFLE, ½-Stock, NY, Percussion, Stamped "G.H. Ferriss/ Utica/NY", .38 Caliber, Reddish Walnut Stock, 98% Orig. Glossy Br. Finish, Some Handling Marks, 32¼″ Barrel $1600.00

A-MA Sept 1980   *Robert W. Skinner Inc.*
MILITARY POWDER FLASK, Double Embossed Sides, "N.P. Ames" & "1838" Stamped On Collar, Am., Early 19th C., 9¼″ H. $175.00*

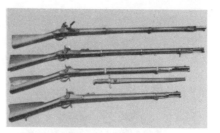

A-MA May 1980   *Richard A. Bourne Co., Inc.*
Top To Bottom
U.S. FLINTLOCK MUSKET, Model 1816, Lock Plate Stamped, Barrel Polished, Untouched Br. Patina, Repl. Hammer Screw & Lock Plate Screw, Walnut Stock . . $500.00
RIFLE MUSKET, Muzzle-Loading, Enfield-Type, 3-Band, Stamped On Lock Plate "1862/ L.A. Co.", Brass Trigger Guard & Butt Plate, Iron Bands, Nipple Protector & Chain, 90% Orig. Blue Finish $800.00
U.S. RIFLE-MUSKET, Special Model 1863, So Called Remington Zouave Rifle, 98% Orig. Blue Finish, Toned Brass Furniture, Oil-Finished Walnut Stock, Repl. Front Sight
. . . . $950.00
SABER BAYONET, Brass-Hilted, Recurved, For Preceding Rifle, Leather Sheath, Discolored $185.00
U.S. SPRINGFIELD RIFLE-MUSKET, Model 1863, Type II, Mkd. "Springfield 1864"
. . . . $275.00

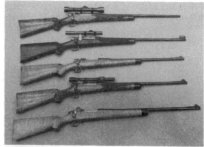

A-MA May 1980   *Richard A. Bourne Co., Inc.*
Top To Bottom
CUSTOM SPORTING RIFLE, Springfield Action, .220 Donaldson Ace Caliber, Silver Nameplate, Walnut Chest W/Loading Dies, Headspace Gauge, Cutter & Die, 24″ Barrel
. . . . $750.00
CUSTOM SPORTING RIFLE, Springfield, By Robert G. Owen, NY, Action Extensively Refined, Figured Fr. Walnut Stock, Sl. Wear To The Blue, .30-06 Caliber . . . $1900.00
CUSTOM SPORTING RIFLE, Springfield, Made & Mkd. By M.S. Risley, .30-06 Caliber, Action Refined W/Low Bolt Handle, 24″ Barrel $350.00
CUSTOM SPORTING RIFLE, Springfield, Made & Mkd. By M.S. Risley, .257 Roberts Caliber, Action Refined, Stock In Curly Maple W/Tortoise-Shell Finish, Telescope Adjusting Screw Cap Missing, 22″ Barrel
. . . . $500.00
CUSTOM SPORTING RIFLE, Made & Mkd. By M.S. Risley, Remington 720 Action, 300 H & H Magnum Caliber, Engraved, Curly Maple Stock, 24″ Barrel $500.00

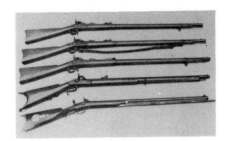

A-MA May 1980   *Richard A. Bourne Co., Inc.*
Top To Bottom
U.S. RIFLE, Model 1879, .45-70 Caliber, Inspector's Stamp, 95% Orig. Blue Finish, Minor Handling Marks $300.00
U.S. RIFLE, Model 1879, .45-70 Caliber, Inspector's Stamp, 98% Blue Orig. Finish, Sl. Storage Marks $400.00
U.S. RIFLE, Model 1888, .45-70 Caliber, Inspector's Stamp, Suggestions Of Orig. Blue Finish, Repl. Breech Block, Fitted W/ Sliding Ramrod Bayonet, Walnut Stock W/ Lt. Storage Marks $200.00
SWISS FEDERAL SEMI-MILITARY RIFLE, Muzzle-Loading, Percussion, .39 Caliber, Lock Engraved "Th. Niederer A. Heiden", Double-Set Triggers, Full Walnut Stock W/Swiss Butt Plate, Drk. Br. Patina, Partial Line Crack $750.00
NY SPORTING & TARGET RIFLE, ½-Stock, Percussion, .415 Caliber, Engraved German Silver Patch Box & Mountings, Blued Iron Parts, 34" Barrel $450.00

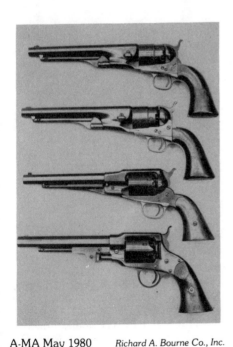

A-MA May 1980   *Richard A. Bourne Co., Inc.*
Top To Bottom
COLT 1860 ARMY, 8" Barrel, 3-Screw Model, Refinished $700.00
COLT 1860 ARMY, 8" Barrel, 3-Screw Model, Reblued, Lt. Pitting, Walnut Grips $450.00
REMINGTON NEW MODEL NAVY, .36 Caliber, Reblued & Polished, Varnished Walnut Grips $400.00
ROGERS & SPENCER REVOLVER, Reblued, Orig. Grips W/Inspector's Marks $450.00

*Price does not include 10% buyer fee.

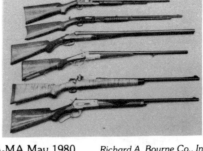

A-MA May 1980   *Richard A. Bourne Co., Inc.*
Top To Bottom
REMINGTON REPEATING RIFLE, Model 12, Slide-Action, .22 LR Caliber, Factory-Engraved Receiver, Custom Pistol-Grip Stock W/Cheekpiece Of Fr. Walnut W/ Matching Slide Handle, 22" Barrel .. $450.00
REMINGTON REPEATING RIFLE, Model 25, Slide-Action, .25-20 Caliber, Sl. Storage Or Rack Marks, 24" Barrel ..$325.00
REMINGTON SHOTGUN, Double-Barrel, Hammerless, 12 Gauge W/Side Locks, Stamped "E. Remington Sons, Llion, NY", Pistol Grip Stock, Forearm Of Veined European Walnut W/Inlaid Gold, 95% Orig. Twist Br. Finish $600.00
SHOTGUN-STYLE HUNTING RIFLE, J.P. Sauer Und Sohn, Suhl, Single-Barrel, 8.15 x 46R Caliber, Fluid Steel, Fully Proof Mkd., Frame, Lock, & Furniture Finished In Wh. Plating, Sl. Wear $250.00
CUSTOM SPRINGFIELD SPORTING RIFLE, Model 1903, .400 Whelen Caliber, Curly Maple Stock, Barrel Mkd. Griffin & Howe, 24" Barrel $400.00
WINCHESTER LT. WT. RIFLE Model 1886, .45-70 Caliber, ½ Magazine, Solid Frame, Pistol Grip Stock & Forearm Of Figured Wood W/Rubber Shotgun Butt Plate, 98% Orig. Blue, 24" Barrel .. $1600.00

A-MA Sept 1980   *Robert W. Skinner, Inc.*
KENTUCKY RIFLE, Unmarked, Flintlock, Conv. To Percussion, Plate Mkd. "J. Ridout & Co.", Tiger Maple Stock W/Silver Inlay, Stock Chipped, Ramrod Missing, Stock & Barrel Cut, Am., 29¼" L. $950.00*

A-MA Feb 1980   *Robert W. Skinner Inc.*
WOODEN GUNSMITH'S SIGN, Carved & Polychrome Decor. Rifle W/Inscription On Butt "The Winchester Store", Repaired, Am., Late 19th C., 67" L. $700.00*

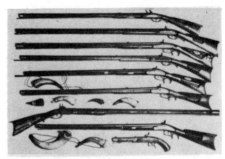

A-OH Sept 1980   *Garth's Auctions, Inc.*
Top To Bottom
KENTUCKY RIFLE, Full Stock, Curly Maple, Barrel Mkd. "G. Bear", 56" L. $1300.00
KENTUCKY RIFLE, Full Stock, Curly Maple, Lock Engraved "W.W.", 62" L. $525.00
KENTUCKY RIFLE, Full Stock, Curly Maple, Perc. Lock, Engraved Silver Inlays, 60" L. $875.00
KENTUCKY RIFLE, Full Stock, Curly Maple, Perc. Lock Mkd. "Jas. Golcher", 57" L. $375.00
KENTUCKY RIFLE, ½ Stock, Curly Maple, Perc. Lock, Silver Inlays W/"G.W.B. 1880", 55" L. $400.00
KENTUCKY RIFLE, Full Stock, Curly Maple, Perc. Lock Mkd. "Jas. Golcher", 57" L. $400.00
POWDER HORN, Simple Carved End, 9" L. $17.50
KENTUCKY RIFLE, Full Stock, Curly Maple, Perc. Lock W/Brass Plate, Mkd. "Peter Neff & Sons, Cincinnati", Old Brass Repair, 56" L. $300.00
SM. POWDER HORN, Engraved "A. Young 1834", Wooden End W/Brass Tacks, 4¾" L. $40.00
HORN SHOT FLASK, Brass Spring Cap, Simple Diamond Engraving, 7" L. .. $20.00
SM. POWDER HORN, Turned Wooden Ends, 5" L. $30.00
POWDER HORN, Engraved Bird, End Has Sm. Splits, 7" L. $30.00
KENTUCKY RIFLE, Full Stock, Curly Maple, Perc. Lock, Silver Inlays, Repaired Stock, 60" L. $700.00
KENTUCKY RIFLE, ½ Stock, Walnut, Perc. Lock, Barrel Mkd. "H. Sheet", 51½" L. $350.00
POWDER HORN, Engraved, 12½" L. $105.00
POWDER HORN, Simple Carved End, 8" L. $17.50
PERC. PISTOL, 16¼" L. $100.00

A-MA Feb 1980   *Robert W. Skinner, Inc.*
CAVALRY CARBINE, Model 1865, Spencer Cal. 56-60, 20" Barrel, Mkd. "Spencer Repeating Rifle Co. Boston, MA, Pat'd Mar.6, 1860", Am., Ca. 1865-1870 .. $425.00*

A-OH April 1980   *Garth's Auctions, Inc.*
COPPER WEATHERVANE, Old Worn Gilt, Head Somewhat Battered, Resoldered, 28½" H $625.00
CANDLE MOLD, Tin, 12-Tube, Some Rust, 13¼" H......................... $365.00
BURL BOWL, 2 Carved Handles, 16" D., 6¾" H......................... $1025.00
PUNCHED TIN PAUL REVERE LANTERN, Rusted And Candle Socket Missing, 14½" O.H. $75.00
TAVERN TABLE, Maple & Birch, Dovetailed Drawer W/Curly Front, Ref., Top Reattached, 28" x 34", 29½" H $550.00
STONEWARE CROCK, 5-Gal., Impressed Label "Burger & Co., Rochester, NY", Cracks, Applied Handles & Albany Slip Int., 12¼" H......................... $115.00

A-NY May 1980   *Calkins Auction Gallery*
TRENCHER, Hand Hewn, Painted, Maple, 19th C., 25½" L., 12" W., 5" H. ... $170.00
BENNINGTON CUSPIDOR, Diamond Patt., Ca. 1849, Mottled Br. Glaze, Tiny Chip, 8" D., 5" H. $65.00
DOVETAILED BOX, Grain Painted, Early 19th C., Pine W/Hinged Door, 14" L., 8" W., 5½" H. $75.00
HEPPLEWHITE SWING LEG TABLE, Cherry, N. Eng., Ca. 1800, Orig. Cond., 42" L., 15¼" W., 29" H. $425.00
LRG. OVOID STONEWARE CROCK, Double Incised Lines, 12" D., 13" H. $25.00
OVOID STONEWARE CROCK, 2-Gal., By J. Hart, Cobalt Blue Decor., 10" D., 10" H. $45.00
SPLINT BASKET W/Swing Handle, Orig. Red Paint, 19th C., Wooden Bottom W/Reinforcing Straps Up The Side, 14" D., 10½" H. $90.00
REDWARE CROCK, 19th C., Mottled Orange & Br. Glaze, Sm. Crack & Flaking, 10" H. $25.00
SLED, 19th C., Painted & Decor., Stamped On Brass Plate "G.R. Wyman 1887", 60" L., 11½" W. $225.00

A-OH June 1980   *Garth's Auctions, Inc.*
CARVED PINE SHIELD, Stars & Stripes, Relief Carved W/Worn Red, Wh. & Blue Paint, 20th C., 19" H. $180.00
LIVERY STABLE TRADE SIGN, Fully Molded Horses Head, Zinc, Worn Gilding, Minor Splits & Damage, 23" H. .. $680.00
INDIAN LITHOGRAPH, Handcolored, By "J.O. Lewis, 1825, Litho By Lehman & Duval", Playing Fox Wearing Peace Medal, Tear In Rt. Side, Framed, 19" x 23½" $105.00
COBBLERS BENCH, 1 Pine Board W/ Whittled Legs & Divided Working Surface, 19½" x 48½" x 17" H. $370.00
WRITING ARM CHAIR, Dovetailed Drawer, Ref. $280.00
WOVEN SPLINT BASKET, Varnished, 13¾" D., 8½" O.H. $32.50
CARVED DECOY, Balsa Body & Wooden Head, Blk. Duck W/Glass Eyes & Worn Paint, 19" L. $25.00
LRG. POTTERY JAR, Mottled Br. Color, Incised, NC, 19½" H. $27.50
CARVED DECOY, Balsa Body & Wooden Head, Mallard Drake W/Glass Eyes & Worn Paint, 19¼" L. $20.00
PENNY RUG, Wool Felt, 1 Medallion Missing, 43" x 58"................... $25.00

A-MA Aug 1980   *Robert C. Eldred Co., Inc.*
ENG. PEWTER CHARGER By Bush & Perkins Of Bristol & Bitton, Ca. 1790 .. $170.00
WHIELDON PLATE, Gr. & Yellow Mottled Glaze, Ca. 1750-1780, 9½" D. $220.00
SHERATON MIRROR, Reverse Painted Upper Panel, 32¼" x 20½" $300.00
HEPPLEWHITE DROP LEAF TABLE, Am., Curly Maple, 36" L., 28" H. .. $400.00
BOW-BACK WINDSOR ARMCHAIR, Am., 13-Spindle $350.00

A-OH April 1980   *Garth's Auctions, Inc.*
LITHOGRAPH, Blk. & Wh., Mahogany Shadow Box Frame W/Gilted Liner, Carved Insurance Co. Label, 26½" x 32½" .. $75.00
PEWTER SOUP PLATE, Mark "London" W/Crowned Rose Touch Marks, Minor Pitting, 10½" D. $95.00
HANGING BOX, Poplar, Rosehead Nails, Carved Date "1770", 5¾" W., 7" D., 12¾" H. $140.00
PEWTER BASIN, English Touch W/"T.C.," Polished, 9"D., 2½"H. $175.00
QUEEN ANNE TAVERN TABLE, Maple Base, Overlapping Drawer W/Single Dovetailed Corners, Pine Breadboard Top, 30¼" x 38½", 26" H. $4100.00
WOVEN SPLINT BASKET, Natural, Br. & Tan, 10½" x 19", 10" O.H. $60.00

A-OH Feb 1981   *Garth's Auctions, Inc.*
DECOR. ROCKER, Orig. Red & Blk. Graining W/Yellow Striping & Stenciling $135.00
TIN LANTERN, Clear Globe, Orig. Font. Sl. Battered W/Worn Br. Japanning, 12 3/5" O.H. $45.00
ROCKINGHAM BOWL, 6½" D. .. $15.00
BEDSIDE STAND, Cherry, Dovetailed Drawers, Old Finish, 17¾" x 20", 28¾" H. $300.00
BENTWOOD BRIDE'S BOX, Lid W/Chip Carved Design, Dated "1796", Worn Blk. Paint, 10¾" x 17¾" $300.00

A-OH Feb 1981   *Garth's Auctions, Inc.*
CAMPAIGN TORCH, Tin On Wooden Pole, Rust Damage, Sm. Hole In Font, 50" H. $10.00
HARPOON, Wrought Iron On Wooden Pole, 59" L. $15.00
CAMPAIGN TORCH, Tin On Short Wooden Pole, Rust Damage, Repaired, 27" L. $20.00
ROUND CUTTING BOARD, Poplar, 18" D. $35.00
VIC. JIG-SAW BRACKETS, Pr., Wooden, Partially Stripped, 18" x 35" $35.00
CAST IRON FOOT SCRAPER, Dachshund, 21½" L. $65.00
WOVEN SPLINT BASKET, Bow Decor., Some Damage, 20" H. $10.00
BENCH, Pine W/Pencil Post Legs, Ref., 15" x 42½", 16½" H. $45.00
CHRISTMAS TREE HOLDER, Cast Iron, "A Merry Xmas" & "Smart, Brockville, Pat. 1931", Worn Gr. Paint, 7½" H. $25.00
CAST IRON BAKING MOLD, Lamb, Crusty Blk. Paint, 14½" L. $30.00

A-OH Feb 1981   *Garth's Auctions, Inc.*
EMBROIDERY ON SILK, Child In Garden, Watercolor Head, Colors Faded, Backing Tattered, Framed, 14" x 16½" $55.00
LITHOGRAPH, Handcolored, Child & Dog, "Fidelity", Paper Damaged, Shadow Box Frame W/Gilded Trim, 27½" x 33½" $45.00
PEWTER TEAPOT, Octagonal W/Cast Handle, Unmarked, Repaired, 8½" H. $55.00
PEWTER TALL POT, Mkd. "Dixon & Son", Wooden Handle & Finial, 11¼" H. $80.00
PEWTER TEAPOT, Mkd. "Dixon & Son", Wooden Handle & Finial, 10" H. ... $65.00
SIDE CHAIRS, Pr., Hitchcock-Type, Old Blk. Repaint, Orig. Stenciling, Cane Seats $110.00
DRESSING TABLE, Pine, Eng., Dovetailed Drawer, Orig. Lt. Gr. Paint W/Wh. Striping, 35½" W., 19½" D., 29" H. $110.00
KETTLE SHELF, Wrought Steel, Polished, 10¼" x 14", 12¾" H. $95.00

A-OH Feb 1981   *Garth's Auctions, Inc.*
EMBLEM, Odd Fellows, Embroidered, Red, Wh., Yellow, Beige Ground, 21¾" x 23¾" $12.50
WINDSOR ARM CHAIR, Bamboo W/Writing Arm, Dovetailed Drawer, Restorations, Ref., 17½" Seat H. $600.00
CHALK BASKET OF FRUIT, Top W/Faded Yellow Paint, Base Unpainted, 11" H. $40.00
VIC. CANDLESTAND, Walnut W/Turned Cherry Top, 17¾" D., 19¾" H... $55.00
KNIFE BOX, 2-Part, Poplar, Worn Gray Paint, 8" x 12½", 6" H. $85.00

A-OH Feb 1981   *Garth's Auctions, Inc.*
HANGING TOWEL RACK, Poplar, 4 Dowels, 20th C., 24¼" W., 10" D., 26½" H. $65.00
WROUGHT IRON EMBER TONGS, 28¾" L. $25.00
JACQUARD COVERLET, 2-Pc. Single Weave, Blue, Red & Wh. W/Bird Border, Sgn. "Sommerset OH 1848. L. Hesse Weaver", Edge Wear, No Fringe, 75" Sq. $155.00
WROUGHT IRON PEEL, 39½" L. $30.00
HARNESS MAKER'S VISE, Leather Covered Seat, Stamped "1857", Sm. Repair, Ref., 43" H. $85.00
STOOLS, Set Of 6 (1 Illus.), Woven Cane Seats, Traces Of Red Paint, Ref., 17" H. $510.00
CAST IRON DOOR STOP, Boston Bull W/Repaint, 8¾" H. $30.00

A-NY May 1980   *Calkins Auction Gallery*
DOUBLE SILHOUETTE, NY, Early 19th
C., Backed W/Blk. Cloth & Sewn To Paper,
Inscribed "Norman Beckwith & His Wife
Fanny About 1800", 10¾" x 7⅝" .. $255.00
CANDLE STAND, 18th C., Peg Footed,
N. Eng., Painted, 17" D., 29¾" H. .. $150.00
BED WARMER, Brass & Wood, Am.,
Early 19th C., 10½" D., 42" L. $185.00

A-NY May 1980   *Calkins Auction Gallery*
MINI. PRICKET CANDLESTICK, Early
19th C., 13½" H. $80.00
SHAKER SEWING BOX, 3-Tiered, NY,
Ca. 1870, Pincushion On Top, Orig. Finish,
9" L. $80.00
**CHIPPENDALE ACCOUNTANT'S
DESK,** 19th C., Old Red Finish, 32" W., 24"
D., 38" H. $325.00
SHAKER SPLINT BASKET W/Swing
Handle, High Push-Up Bottom, 14½" D., 9"
H. $130.00
CANADA GOOSE DECOY, By Wildflow-
er, Ca. 1930, Orig. Paint, 20" L., 11" H.
.... $130.00

A-OH June 1980   *Garth's Auctions, Inc.*
TIN CANDLE SCONCES, Set Of 3, (2
Illus.), Ribbed Edge Back W/Crimped Top
& Drip Pan, 14" H. $585.00
CURRIER & IVES LITHOGRAPH, Hand-
colored Folio, "View Of Harpers Ferry,
VA", Old Frame, 20¾" x 25½" $105.00
GAUDY IRONSTONE PLATE, Minor
Wear, 7½" D. $15.00
GAUDY STICK SPATTER BOWL, Blue,
Red & Gr., Mkd. "Adams, England", 6¼" D.
.... $45.00
GAUDY IRONSTONE PITCHER, Oc-
tagonal, Minor Edge Wear, 8" H. .. $105.00
GAUDY STICK SPATTER BOWL, Blue,
Red & Gr., Mkd. "Adams, England", 7" D.
.... $60.00
SPONGE SPATTER BOWL, Red & Blue
Border W/Gaudy Red & Gr. Rose Design,
8⅞" D. $100.00
SHERATON TABLE, Maple, Dovetailed
Drawer W/Orig. Embossed Brass Pull, Some
Curl & Worn Old Refinishing, Orig. Top
Has Replaced Strip Added, Brass Caster
Feet Missing, 20" x 42" W/14¼" Leaves,
27½" H. $300.00
STICK SPATTER BOWL, Red, Blue & 2
Shades Of Gr., Mkd. "Tunstall, England",
9¾" D. $70.00
**HISTORICAL BLUE STAFFORDSHIRE
PLATTER,** Drk. Blue, "Sussex Place,
Regents Park, London", Back W/Lrg. Sur-
face Chips, 17¼" L. $85.00

A-OH Oct 1980   *Garth's Auctions, Inc.*
CANDLE DRYING RACK, 8 Remov.
Disks, Revolving Wheel, 1 Disk W/Repaired
Split, No Finish, 48" D., 42½" H. .. $335.00
WROUGHT IRON CHOPPER, 25¼"
H. $40.00
KRAUT CUTTER, Walnut W/Chip Carv-
ing At Ends, 20¼" x 28½" $75.00
**WROUGHT IRON GOOSE NECK
ANDIRONS,** Pr., 23" H. $110.00
WOVEN SPLINT BASKET, Bushel W/
Wooden Side Handles, Minor Damage, 21½"
D., 12" L. $110.00
SHAKER QUILTING TABLE, Mt. Leba-
non, NY, 34" x 59½" x 31¼" H. .. $850.00

A-OH Sept 1980   *Garth's Auctions, Inc.*
**OIL ON WOODEN PANEL POR-
TRAITS,** Pr., Cleaned, Restorations,
Modern Frames, 26¾" x 33" $420.00
PEWTER PLATES, Set Of 4, "London",
Touchmarks, Knife Scratches, 8⅞" D.
.... $380.00
PEWTER CHARGER, Surface Dents, De-
terioration, Rim Break, Partially Cleaned,
16½" D. $85.00
PEWTER CHALICE, Pr., Unmarked, 6⅜"
H. $270.00
PEWTER TANKARDS, Pr., Glass Bot-
tomed, Inscribed "Lincoln College, 1859",
8¾" H. $120.00
PEWTER TEAPOT, "Armitages & Stand-
ish", MA, Repair, Make Do Tin Lid, 9¾" H.
.... $55.00
WORK TABLE, Walnut, Dovetailed Draw-
ers, Orig. Remov. Top Secured W/Pins,
Top Finish Cleaned Off, Old Finish On Base,
36" x 54¼", 29½" H. $550.00
SPUN BRASS KETTLE, Wrought Iron
Rim, Bale Handle, Damaged, 21" D. . $75.00
CAST IRON DOOR STOP, Horse, Old
Worn Paint, 10" H. $70.00
CAST IRON DOOR STOP, Scottie, Old
Worn Paint, 8" H. $50.00

A-OH Mar 1980   *Garth's Auctions, Inc.*
NEEDLEWORK HOMESPUN PANELS,
Pr., Sgn. "Elizabeth Fowls Feb. 15 (& April
25) 1800", Framed, 15" x 17" $1240.00
PINE BOX, Orig. Old Watermelon Colors,
10½" x 7" x 5½" $65.00
PINE MULE CHEST, Old But Not Orig.
Graining, Feet Replaced, Engraved Brasses,
36" W., 18" D., 41" H. $600.00
CARVED WOODEN DECOY, Canada
Goose Attrib. To Jim Pierce, Havre De
Grace, Orig. Worn Paint, Cracks In Neck &
Block, 24" L. $185.00

A-OH June 1980   *Garth's Auctions, Inc.*
CURRIER & IVES LITHOGRAPH, Hand-
colored, "The Old Oaken Bucket", Damage,
20¾" x 24½" $45.00
TILT-TOP TEA TABLE, Bird Cage & 3
Board Top Old Replacements, 2 Pads On
Feet Repl., Ref., 37" D., 28½" H. .. $350.00
WINDSOR BOW-BACK CHAIR, Carved
Scroll On Arms Rather Worn Flat, 1 Arm
W/Repairs, Old Worn Red & Blk. Paint, Seat:
18" H. $625.00
CARVED WOODEN DECOY, Canvas-
back Drake, Detroit River, Glass Eyes &
Worn Flaking Repaint, 17¼" L. $35.00

A-OH June 1980   *Garth's Auctions, Inc.*
CARVED WOODEN EAGLE, Old Gild-
ing, 68" W. $710.00
PEWTER CANDLESTICKS, Pr., Am.,
Unmarked, 9¾" H. $290.00
CARVED WOODEN DECOY, Pintail Sgn.
"Arness", CA, Glass Eyes, 11¾" L.
.... $60.00
WOODEN FACTORY DECOY, Mam-
outh Mason Canvasback Hen, VA, Split In
Underside Of Block, Working Repaint, Glass
Eyes, 19¼" L. $105.00
CARVED WOODEN DECOY, Bluebill W/
Glass Eyes & Repaint, 13½" L. $25.00
HARVEST TABLE, Poplar, Top Is Replace-
ment, Some Alterations, Ref., 20" x 69",
10¼" Leaves, 30" H. $575.00
STONEWARE JAR, Applied Vintage,
Running Gr. Glaze, Incised "Lanier Mead-
ers", 10¾" H. $125.00
**WOVEN SPLINT BUTTOCKS BASK-
ET,** Some Damage & Wear, 17" x 16", 7¾"
O.H. $125.00
STONEWARE PLANTER JAR, Incised
"Lanier Meaders", 15½" H. $40.00

A-OH July 1980   *Garth's Auctions, Inc.*
PORTRAIT OF YOUNG WOMAN, Oil
On Cottom Ticking, Ca. 1836, Backed On
Transparent Material, Repl. Stretcher,
Cleaned, Minor Restorations, 26½" x 31½"
.... $600.00
PRE-COLUMBIAN REPRO., Ceramic
Jaguar, 13" L., 7½" H. $7.50
PIMA BASKET, Stepped Geom. Design,
7¼" D., 7" H. $70.00
DOVETAILED BOX, Pine, Orig. Wrought
Iron Hasp & Lock, Orig. Red Paint W/Drk.
Border Stripe, 17¾" L. $175.00
PAPAGO BASKET, Yucca W/Animal
Figures, 9" D., 4½" H. $70.00
HEPPLEWHITE PEMBROKE TABLE,
Birch, Hinges Reset, Old Worn Red, Top
Board W/Some Curl, 16½" x 42", 11" Leaves,
28½" H. $195.00
WROUGHT IRON ANDIRONS, Pr., 13"
H. $25.00
APACHE BURDEN BASKET, Leather
Bottom & Fringe, Stripe Design, 12" D., 10"
H. $160.00

◄ A-OH May 1980   *Garth's Auctions, Inc.*
BAROMETER, English, Mahogany On Pine
W/Line Inlay, Inscribed "Barnascone, Shef-
field", Center Clock An Addition & Broken
Arch Pediment Repl., Mercury Tube
Cracked, 38½" H. $150.00
COLORED MEZZOTINT, Napoleon,
Crest W/"N", Sgn, In Pencil, Old Frame
Has Damage, 14" x 18" $25.00
HANDCOLORED MAP, Engraved,
"Melitae Vulgo Malte", Framed, 18½" x 22½"
.... $45.00
OVERLAY LAMP, Rose Cut To Opaque
Wh. To Clear, Brass Connector & Collar,
13" H. $320.00
EMPIRE SIDE CHAIR, Mahogany, Sabre
Leg W/Flame Veneer, Slip Seat, Stamped "E.
Clark", Repairs $95.00
SHERATON STAND, Mahogany On Pine,
Dovetailed Drawers, Worn Old Finish, 17" x
19¾", 28¾" H. $310.00

A-OH Oct 1980   *Garth's Auctions, Inc.*
CHAIR TABLE, Maple & Pine, Mortised
Const., Pins Repl., Old Red Repaint, 42½" x
43½" 27½" H. $1000.00
COMPASS STAR, On Pine Board, Gr.,
Blk. & Wh., 9¾" x 13" $15.00
TIN CAMPAIGN HORN, Old Red, Wh.
& Blue Paint Worn, 29" L. $40.00
TIN RAILROAD OIL CAN, Embossed
"NKP RR", 30" H. $10.00
TIN FOOT WARMER, Punched In Wooden Frame W/Turned Posts, 8¾" Sq., 6¼" H.
.... $75.00
CAST IRON RABBIT, Paint Removed,
12" H. $85.00

A-OH Oct 1980   *Garth's Auctions, Inc.*
OVAL TIN CANDLE SCONCE, Crimped
Pan, 11¾" H. $175.00
TIN WEATHERVANE, Layers Of Old
Paint & Gilt, Modern Wooden Base, 24" H.
.... $95.00
TIN CANDLE SCONCE, Crimped Top
& Edge Pan, Rusted, 13½" H. $30.00
OBLONG WOODEN BOWL, 1 Pc. Of
Wood, Age Cracks, Scrubbed Int., Ext. W/
Worn Old Red, 17" x 25½" $14.00
TAVERN TABLE, Maple W/Old Red On
Base, 2 Board Top W/Cut Corners, 35" x
37¾", 24¼" H. $350.00
WOVEN SPLINT BASKET, Minor Rim
Damage, 13" D., 8" O.H. $45.00

A-OH Sept 1980   *Garth's Auctions, Inc.*
SPLINT WOOD ½-BUSHEL, Wire Bale
Handle, Some Damage, 14¾" L. ... $10.00
WROUGHT IRON ROTARY BROILER,
Penny Feet, 23" L. $90.00
BENTWOOD STORAGE BOX, Old Blk.
Paint, Edge Damage, 20" D., 14" H. .. $57.00
WOVEN SPLINT BASKET, Filled W/Rag
Carpet Balls, 11" x 18" $15.00
YARN WINDER, Oak W/Mortised Base,
Chamfered Stand, 32" D., 36" H. .. $40.00
CAST IRON HITCHING POST, Dog's
Head, Painted Blk., 46½" H. $245.00
HEPPLEWHITE TABLE, 2 Board Pine
Bread Board Top, Old Faded Salmon Paint
On Base, Top Worn, Splits, Repair, 28" x 48",
27½" H. $150.00
POTTERY CROCK, Br. Glaze, Open
Side Handles, Sm. Rim Flakes, 11½" H.
.... $17.50

A-OH Mar 1980   *Garth's Auctions, Inc.*
EMPIRE POLE SCREEN, Mahogany W/
Veneered Base On Ball Feet & Turned
Post, Floral Needlepoint, Veneer Damage,
54½" H. $55.00
COLORED LITHOGRAPHS, Pr., George
& Martha Washington, Old Frames, 9¼" x
11½" $50.00
HITCHCOCK SIDE CHAIR, Old Br.
Paint, New Rush Seat $40.00
HITCHCOCK SIDE CHAIR, New Rush
Seat $40.00

A-OH July 1980   *Garth's Auctions, Inc.*
SAMPLER ON HOMESPUN, "Evaline
McDonal, Mar. 8, 1842, Framed, 15⅝" x
19⅝" $350.00
**FAN BACK WINDSOR ARMCHAIR
ROCKER,** Orig. Worn Red & Blk. Graining $700.00
ROCKINGHAM DOG, Muzzle Restored,
10¾" H. $250.00
TILT TOP CANDLESTAND W/Birdcage, Orig. Drk. Reddish Br. Finish, 18¾"
D., 28¼" H. $1000.00
PUNCHED TIN FOOT WARMER
W/Wooden Frame, 10" Sq., 6" L. .. $350.00

A-MA April 1980   *Richard A. Bourne Co., Inc.*
DIMINUTIVE DAGUERREOTYPES,
Collection Of 10, Gutta-Percha Case W/
Raised Decor., Minor Damage To Cover, 2
Pcs. Of Beading Missing $120.00

A-OH April 1980   *Garth's Auctions, Inc.*
TIN CANDLE SCONCES, Pr., Punched Crown Shaped Top, Minor Rust, 14" H.
. . . . $600.00
OIL ON POPLAR PANEL, Cleaned, Old Gilded Frame, Attrib. To Ethan Allen Greenwood, 21" x 24½" $2450.00
BURL BOWL W/Carved Handles, Old Crack, 14¾" x 18½", 6" H. $525.00
PEWTER PLATE, 2 Eagle Touchmarks For Sylvester Griswold, Baltimore, 8¾" D.
. . . . $600.00
PEWTER PLATE, Mate To Above, Same Touch Marks, 8¾" D. $550.00
QUEEN ANNE TAVERN TABLE, Cherry Base, Curly Maple 2 Board Top, Ref., Minor Rep., 33½" x 38½", 27¼" H. $1300.00
OVOID STONEWARE JAR, 4-Gal., Impressed "4, J. Weaver", Applied Handles & Brushed Floral Decor. In Cobalt, Crack & Old Chips, 14" H. $155.00

A-MA Aug 1980   *Robert C. Eldred Co., Inc.*
L To R
YARN WINDER, Am., Early 19th C., Walnut. $90.00
CANDLESTAND, Am., 18th C., Ref., Top: 13" Sq., 27" H. $500.00
Q.A./CHIPPENDALE SIDE CHAIR, Walnut, Am. $550.00

A-OH Jan 1980   *Garth's Auctions, Inc.*
SPOON RACK, Orig. Worn Stylized Floral Decor., 15½" H. $100.00
WOODEN FISH, Old Yellow Paint, 21" L.
. . . . $80.00
MIRROR, Orig. Red Painted Frame, Mirror Cracked, 8½" H. $210.00
GREEN GLASS DEMIJOHN, Landscape Painting, Minor Wear, 17½" H. . . . $285.00
BENTWOOD BOX, Old Red Stain, 8¼" D., 3½" H. $50.00
BENTWOOD BOX, Orig. Red Paint W/ Design Of Yellow, Wh., Blue, & Orange, 8" D., 4½" H. $185.00
POPLAR DOUGH BOX, Turned Splayed Legs, Orig. Drk. Br. Paint Has Wear, 1 Board Top W/Chip Carving On Ends, 19" x 42½", 31" H. $375.00
CHILD'S CHAIR, Decor., Worn Rush Seat
. . . . $95.00
DOLL SIZE ROPE BED, 10½" x 15½", 9¼" H. $75.00

A-NY May 1980   *Calkins Auction Gallery*
OIL ON CANVAS, Am. 19th C., 24¾" x 20¼"
. . . . $140.00
CHIPPENDALE CANDLESTICKS, Pr., English, 18th C., Brass, Weighted Bottoms, 7¾" H. $55.00
TOLEWARE DEED BOX, 19th C., Painted Gr. W/Orange & Yellow Stenciled Decor., 9½" L., 6" W., 7" H. $95.00
HEPPLEWHITE STAND, Splayed Leg, Cherry, 1 Drawer, Late 18th C., 27½" H.
. . . . $350.00
BRACED BOW BACK WINDSOR, 18th C., Painted Gr., Split Seat Repaired, 36½" O.H. $275.00
WATER BUCKET, 19th C., Wooden W/ Metal Bands, Orig. Red Paint, Wire Swing Handle, 12" D., 12" H. $25.00
STONEWARE ADVERTISING JUG, 1-Gal., 19th C., "L. Lehman, Cash Grocer, 464 Broad St., Newark, NJ", 5¾" D., 9½" H.
. . . . $90.00
HOOKED RUG, Am., Multi-Colored, 19th C., 42" x 30" $110.00

A-NY May 1980   *Calkins Auction Gallery*
WROUGHT ROTATING BROILER, 18th C., 33" L. $100.00
WROUGHT IRON BROILER, Late 18th Or Early 19th C., 19½" L. $65.00
WROUGHT IRON BROILER, Late 18th Or Early 19th C., 14½" L. $60.00
TABLE SWIFT, Carved & Turned, 19th C., Maple & Wire W/Wooden Screw Arrangement To Fasten To Table Top, 34" L.
. . . . $70.00
WROUGHT IRON RAM'S HORN PEEL, 18th C., 28" L. $105.00
HAND HEWN BURL BOWL, Am., 18th Or 19th C., Good Patina, Repair, 16" D., 4" H.
. . . . $325.00
MORTAR & PESTLE, Turned & Painted, Early 19th C., Orig. Red Paint $70.00
STEP DOWN WINDSORS, Set Of 4, Early 19th C., Ref., 34½" O.H. . . $1040.00
HEPPLEWHITE TAP TABLE, Early 19th C., 1 Board Scrubbed Top, Old Blue Paint Over Orig. Red, 28½" H. $300.00
WROUGHT IRON FIREPLACE TOASTER W/Penny Feet, 18th C., 13½" W., 16" H.
. . . . $225.00
SPLINT BASKET W/Double Handle, 19th C., Pushed Up Bottom, 15½" D., 10½" H.
. . . . $90.00

A-OH Oct 1980   *Garth's Auctions, Inc.*
UTENSIL RACK, Pine, 7 Wrought Iron Hooks, 32" L. $90.00
WROUGHT IRON UTENSILS, 2, Skimmer W/Damaged Bowl & Fork, 16" L., 18¾" L. $12.50
WROUGHT IRON DIPPER, 16" L. $12.50
WROUGHT IRON PEEL, 22¾" L. $15.00
WROUGHT IRON TASTER, Hammered Copper Bowl, 15" L. $50.00
WROUGHT IRON DIPPER, Simple Tooling On Handle, 17¼" L. $25.00
WROUGHT IRON FORK, Simple Tooling On Handle, 15½" L. $15.00
HATCHEL W/Iron Spikes & Cover, Punched Tin Rim, Ca. 1812, 17¼" L. $40.00
WORK TABLE, Birch Base & Pine Breadboard Top, Repaired, 25¾" H. ... $600.00
STONEWARE JAR, 10" H. $17.50

A-OH Mar 1980   *Garth's Auctions, Inc.*
WATERCOLOR MEMORIAL, Framed, 18½" x 22" $430.00
LADDER-BACK ARM CHAIR, Alligatored Br.-Red Paint & Old Woven Splint Seat, Rep. $450.00
TOLE DOCUMENT BOX, Orig. Drk. Br. Japanning W/Swags In Blue, Red, & Wh., 8" L. $350.00
CARDBOARD TRAY, Wallpaper Covered, Minor Tears, 9" D. $30.00
TILT-TOP TEA TABLE, Old Worn Red Paint, Rep. To 1 Leg, 25½" D., 24¾" H. $525.00
CARVED WOODEN DECOY, Pintail Drake By Lee Burgess, VA, Ca. 1910, Working Repaint, 17" L. $115.00
CAST IRON HORSE WINDMILL WEIGHT, 16½" H. $240.00

A-OH Mar 1980   *Garth's Auctions, Inc.*
CURRIER & IVES LITHOGRAPH, Hand-colored, "G. Washington", Stains, Gilt Frame, 13½" x 17¾" $30.00
BLK. & WH. ENGRAVING, Theodore Roosevelt, Sgn. "Sidney L. Smith" Engraver, Modern Frame, 25½" x 32½" $55.00
N. CURRIER LITHOGRAPH, Hand-colored, "George Washington", Beveled Frame, 14½" x 17½" $25.00
ARROWBACK MAMMY'S BENCH, Baby Guard Missing, Ref., Sm. Rep., 51" L. $235.00
CORK BODIED DECOY W/Carved Wooden Head, Tail & Bottom, Mallard Drake, Old Paint & Glass Eyes, 15½" L. $30.00
CARVED WOODEN DECOY, Masons Redhead Drake W/Worn Paint & Glass Eyes, 13½" L. $105.00
CORK BODIED DECOY W/Carved Wooden Head, Tail & Bottom, 15½" $35.00
CARVED WOODEN DECOY, Canvasback Drake, Glass Eyes & Working Repaint, 14½" L. $60.00
CORK BODIED DECOY W/Wooden Bottom, Head & Tail, Am. Brandt, WI, Working Repaint & Glass Eyes, 13" L. .. $50.00
CORK BODIED DECOY W/Wooden Bottom, Tail & Carved Head, Canvasback Drake, WI, Old Paint & Glass Eyes, 17" L. $40.00

A-WA D.C. May 1980 *Adam A. Weschler & Son*
RUSSIAN ICON, Virgin Percherskaya, 19th C., Repousse Gilt Metal Rizza W/Applied Haloes $500.00*

◄ A-OH April 1980   *Garth's Auctions, Inc.*
OIL ON POPLAR PANEL, Sgn. "Edward Allen Pt. AD 1829", Crack In Upper Rt., Mahogany Veneer Frame, 29" x 35" .. $1510.00
PEWTER CANDLESTICKS, Pr., Am., 9¾" H. $360.00
SHAKER SEWING STAND, Birch W/Mahogany Veneer Drawer Fronts, Ivory Eyelets For Thread, 6¼" x 8¾", 8¾" H. $165.00
DECORATED DRESSING TABLE, Pine, Dovetailed Drawers, Edge Wear, Orig. Brass Pulls, 36" W., 17¾" D., 37¾" H. .. $600.00
MINI. SHERATON CHEST, Curly Maple, Dovetailed Drawers W/Walnut Cockbeading & Inlaid Escut., Orig. Removable Mirror, 10¼" W., 6½" D., 13½" O.H. $925.00

A-OH Jan 1980   *Garth's Auctions, Inc.*
MIRRORED TIN SCONCES, Pr., Glass Mosaic Incomplete On Each, Worn Blk. Paint, 9½" D. $550.00
HAND COLORED COPPER ENGRAVINGS, Pr., "Sauvagesse Iroquise & Sauvage Iroquise", Paris, 1796, Framed, 13½" x 16½" $170.00
REDWARE BOWL, Wavy Line Yellow Slip Decor., Some Glaze Wear, 9½" D., 3" H. $185.00
REDWARE BOWL, Br. Combed Slip W/Gr. Dashes, Center W/Old Glaze Wear, 11¾" D., 2¼" H. $500.00
REDWARE MILK BOWL W/POURING SPOUT, Rim W/Br. Sponging, Minor Glaze Wear & Rim Chip, 10½" D., 4½" H. ..$115.00
HEPPLEWHITE OVAL TEA TABLE, Maple, 2 Board Top, Old Worn Drk. Br. Paint, Top Cleaned Off, 27¾" x 37½", 26" H. $1600.00
WINDSOR SIDE CHAIRS, Set Of 4 (2 Illus.), Orig. Red & Blk. Graining W/Yellow Striping & Gold Stenciled Crest, Show Wear $580.00
TIN LIDDED CONTAINER W/Orig. Smoked Wh. Paint, Wear, 12½" D., 14" H. $165.00
WROUGHT IRON TRIVET, 5¾" D., 11½" L. $85.00
WROUGHT IRON SKILLET, Old Rep. At Handle & Surface Pitted, 12½" L. .. $350.00

A-OH Mar 1980   *Garth's Auctions, Inc.*
TIN WALL SCONCE W/Deep Pocket For Burner, Old Blk. Paint, 13½" H. ...$125.00
REVERSE PAINTED GLASS CHECKERBOARD, Minor Flaking To Colors, Oak Frame, 20½" Sq. $210.00
TIN CANDLE SCONCE W/Reflector Top, 12" H. $85.00
CARVED WOODEN FISH By Miles Davis, 20th C., 25" L. $105.00
LADDER BACK SIDE CHAIR, Front Stretcher Has Wear, Repaint, Feet Built Up, No Seat $65.00
SM. BRASS WIRE FIRE SCREEN, 21" x 27" $65.00
TIN CANDLE MOLD, 10-Tube, Rust, 10½" H. $245.00
PAPIER MACHE DECOYS, Mallard Drake & Pintail Drake, Worn Orig. Paints & Some Damage To Drake, 14" & 16¾" L. $22.50
TIN CANDLE LANTERN W/Vent Top, Glass Missing, Wire Cross Bars Old Addition, Some Damage, Painted Blk., 12" O.H. $45.00

A-OH April 1980   *Garth's Auctions, Inc.*
SM. CHIPPENDALE SCROLL MIRROR, Mahogany, 1 Ear Old Replacement, 11" x 18" $205.00
PIPE BOX, Pine, Dovetailed Case & Drawer, Orig. Worn Red Paint, 5¼" x 20¾" $375.00
WINDSOR SIDE CHAIR, Ref. W/Traces Of Old Blk. Paint, 16" H. $325.00
DOME TOP BOX, Orig. Blk. Lacquer, Gilded Tooled Brass Hdw. & Chinoiserie Decor., Some Flaking, 8¾" W., 5" D., 5¾" H. $105.00
CANDLESTAND, Painted, Sm. Splits & Sm. Burned Hole, 17¼" D., 26¼" H. $500.00
CAST IRON ENGLISH GRISSET, For Soaking Rush In Grease, Sm. Pc. Broken From Rim, 12½" L. $175.00

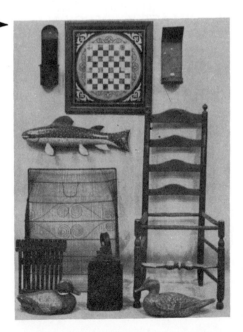

A-OH July 1980   *Garth's Auctions, Inc.*
HEPPLEWHITE BOX, Ebony Colored Veneer On Pine W/2 Inlaid Oval Shells, Orig. Brass Bail Side Handles, Mahogany Tray Insert, Some Damage To Veneer & Inlay, 7½" x 7¾" x 10¾" $295.00
FAN-BACK WINDSOR SIDE CHAIR, Old Blk. Paint Shows Gr. Beneath, Branded "W. Cox", Legs Chipped, 16½" H. $900.00
CHERRY STAND, Dovetailed Drawer, Damaged & Worn Finish, 15" x 18¼", 29¼" H. $150.00
CAST IRON FIGURAL CLOCK, Worn Paint, Does Not Run, 16" H. $825.00
SM. SPUN BRASS PAIL, Am. "Hayden's" Patent Label, Iron Bail Handle, 8½" D. $70.00

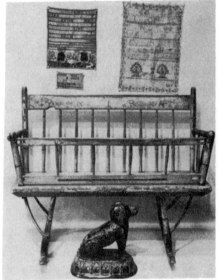

A-OH July 1980   *Garth's Auctions, Inc.*
SAMPLER ON HOMESPUN, Bright Orig. Colors, Ca. 1788, Unframed, 10½" x 12" $1775.00
SAMPLER ON HOMESPUN, Faded Colors, Hole In Fabric, Ca. 1829, Unframed, 12½" x 17¾" $170.00
MINI. SAMPLER ON HOMESPUN, Unframed, 3¼" x 5¾" $235.00
SM. WINDSOR MAMMY'S BENCH, Bamboo Turnings W/Bentwood Leg Braces, Remov. Baby Guard, Worn Orig. Yellow Paint, Repaired, 37" W. $3200.00
ROCKINGHAM SEATED DOG, Br. Shiny Glaze, 12" H. $300.00

A-OH Mar 1980   *Garth's Auctions, Inc.*
WOODEN LADLE, Repaired Crack In Bowl, 13½" L. $27.50
HANGING RACK, Slots For Spoons, Towel Bar & Holder For Mortar & Pestle, Ref., 26½" W., 5" D., 21" H. $55.00
WROUGHT IRON TRIVET, Triangular Turned Handle W/Brass Ferrule, 12¼" L. $75.00
JACQUARD COVERLET, 2-Pc., Single Weave, Ca. 1854, OH, Overall Wear, 70" x 84" $205.00
YARN WINDER, Chip Carved Block W/ Wooden Counter & Gears, 26½" D., 33" H. $75.00
CHILD'S HIGH CHAIR, Arrow Back, 1 Arm Replacement, Gr. Paint $120.00
BOBBINS, 3, Maple In Pine Frame, Flange Of 1 Chipped, 12¾" H. $50.00
CARVED WOODEN DECOY, Bluebill By H. H. Ackerman, Glass Eyes & Working Repaint, 13" L. $40.00

A-OH June 1980   *Garth's Auctions, Inc.*
OIL ON CANVAS, "Jonathan Smith, Esquire, Bath NH", Cleaned & Some Restorations, Modern Frame, 34" x 39" . . . $525.00
TIN CANDLE SCONCES, Pr., Diamond Shaped Back & Drip Pan W/Crimped Edges, 11½" H. $260.00
CARVED WOODEN DECOY, Redhead Hen, Glass Eyes, Orig. Paint, 15½" L. $55.00
DOME TOP BOX, Poplar W/Worn Orig. Wallpaper Covering, Int. Lined W/CT Newspaper Dated 1805, Orig. Handmade Hinges & Wire Handle, 12" L. $45.00
CARVED WOODEN DECOY, Mate To Previous Decoy, 16½" L. $90.00
WORK TABLE, Walnut W/Removable 2 Board Top, Dovetailed Drawers, Mortised & Pinned Frame, 36" x 54", 29¼" H. $400.00
VICTOR FACTORY DECOY, Mallard Drake, Glass Eyes Missing, Old Paint, 15 1/5" L. $35.00
WOODEN TUB, Stave Const., Orig. Worn Gray Paint, 18" D., 19" H. $70.00
VICTOR FACTORY DECOY, Mate To Previous Decoy, 1 Glass Eye Broken, 15½" L. $25.00

◄ A-OH July 1980   *Garth's Auctions, Inc.*
REVERSE PAINTING ON GLASS, The Last Supper, Some Flaking, Orig. Frame, 11⅝" x 14¾" $175.00
CALENDAR CLOCK, "Terry's Patent, Mfg. By Ansonia Brass & Copper Co.", CT, Painting Worn & Minor Veneer Damage, Metal Face Crazed, Key & Pendulum, 25¼" H. $625.00
BOW BACK WINDSOR SIDE CHAIR, Worn Blk. Paint, 1 Leg Split, Seat: 17" H. $550.00
CLAMBROTH CANDLESTICKS, Pr., Minor Roughness & Flakes, 6¾" H. . . $170.00
EMPIRE TABLE, Mahogany, Dovetailed Drawers, Worn Finish, Veneer Repair Necessary, 21¾" W., 15½" D., 29" H. $850.00

A-NY May 1980   *Calkins Auction Gallery*
SHAKER OVAL BOX, Maple & Pine, 19th C., Copper Rivets, 9" x 6¼" . . $55.00
APOTHECARY CHEST, 13-Drawer, 19th C., Orig. Built Into Corner, 1 Side & Top Have No Paint, Remaining Case Painted Red & Blue, Drawers Dovetailed, Moldings Restored, 18½" W., 10½" D., 56½" H. $800.00
SHAKER ARMCHAIR W/Tilters, Orig. Tape Seat, Old Varnish Finish, 1 Rung Repl., 43¼" O.H. $1400.00
REDWARE BUTTER CHURN W/Handle & Wooden Dasher, Br. Glaze W/Blk. Band, 19th C., 3-Gal., Rim Chip, 14" H. . . $60.00
WROUGHT IRON FOOTED GRIDDLE, Late 18th Or Early 19th C., 18" L., 10" W. $30.00
CAST IRON KETTLE, 3 Legged W/ Wrought Bail Handle, Early 19th C., 11¾" D., 7¾" H. $50.00

A-MA July 1980   *Robert W. Skinner Inc.*
VIC. BRASS FIRE SCREEN & AND-IRONS, Am., Ca. 1900 .... $500.00*

A-WA D.C. May 1980 *Adam A. Weschler & Son*
HINGED COMPACTS, 3, (2 Illus.), 14 Karat Yellow Gold, R. Blackington & Co., MA, Mirrored Int. Lid, Monogrammed, 3.5 Oz. $800.00*

A-NY May 1980 *Calkins Auction Gallery*
OIL ON CANVAS, 19th C., Am., 24½" x 34"
.... $400.00
OIL ON CANVAS, 19th C., Am., 24½" x 34"
.... $800.00
CORNER HEPPLEWHITE WASH STAND, Bow Front, Ca. 1800, Mahogany, Dovetailed Arched Gallery, 31½" H.
.... $235.00
DOME TOP BOX, Dovetailed, Early 19th C., 24" L., 13" W., 12" H. $200.00
CAPTAINS CHAIR, Painted, Ca. 1840, Worn Paint On Arms, 31" O.H. $185.00
HOOKED RUG, Am., 19th C., Shades Of Gray, Br., Tan & Blk., 50" L., 30" W.
.... $225.00

—————————————————————

A-OH Mar 1980 *Garth's Auctions, Inc.*
HEARTH BROOM W/Turned Wooden Handle & Woven Fibre Head, 39" L.
.... $150.00
SCOOP W/Heavy Copper Bowl, Wrought Iron & Wooden Handle, Crack In Wood, 16½" L. $40.00
TIN HANGING LANTERN W/Hinged Door, Whale Oil Burner, 1 Old Glass Cracked, Old Blk. Paint, 9½" W., 4¾" D., 12¾" H. $175.00
COPPER SKIMMER W/Wrought Iron & Wooden Handle, 24½" L. $60.00
KITCHEN MASHER, Curly Maple, Ref., 11½" H. $37.50
CANDLE MOLD, Single Tube, 11¾" H.
.... $75.00
KITCHEN MASHER, Curly & Birdseye Maple, Ref., 11" H. $22.50
CANDLE DRYING RACK, Pine, Ref., Minor Insert Damage, 24" W., 27" H.
.... $95.00
CANDLE MOLD, Tin, 48-Tube, 15" W., 6¾" D., 10½" H. $255.00
WROUGHT IRON TOASTER, Old Pitting & 1 Twisted Flame Finial Missing, 16½" L. $315.00

A-OH Mar 1980 *Garth's Auctions, Inc.*
WROUGHT IRON BROILER W/Remov. Drip Pan, 10" x 19" $55.00
RYE STRAW BASKET W/Rim Handle, Minor Wear, 13" D. $30.00
FAN BACK WINDSOR SIDE CHAIR, Worn Blk. Paint, Spindle Rep., 1 Leg Built Up, 18" H. $135.00
WROUGHT IRON LIGHTING STAND, Chip Carved Base, Pitted, 39½" H. ..$185.00
WROUGHT IRON TRAMMEL, Adj. Rod Replacement, From 20" L. $55.00
SHEET IRON LIGHTING STAND, Crown Base W/4 Spout Burner, 14¼" H.
.... $145.00
STONEWARE CROCK, 2-Gal., Stenciled Cobalt Label "Hamilton & Jones, Greensboro, PA", 10" H. $150.00
WROUGHT IRON TOASTER W/Twisted Handle, Wooden Grip Scratched, 13¼" W., 23" L. $50.00

A-OH Mar 1980 *Garth's Auctions, Inc.*
WATERCOLOR, Paper Has Minor Staining & 2 Margin Tears, Grained Frame, 18½" x 23" $375.00
COMB BACK WINDSOR ARM CHAIR, Worn & Alligatored Blue Repaint, 17½" Seat H. $2200.00
CARVED WOODEN SHOREBIRD, Snipe Stick Up W/Split Tail, MA, Copper Tack Eyes, 9¼" H. $215.00
INDIAN POTTERY JAR, Worn Surface & 2 Rim Chips, 5¾" H. $155.00
QUEEN ANNE TAVERN TABLE, Maple W/2 Board Oval Top, Old Worn Red Paint On Base & Top Ref., 22½" x 32¾", 27" H.
.... $2400.00
CARVED WOODEN DECOY, Blk. Duck, MI, Glass Eyes & Shallow Relief Carving W/ Orig. Paint, 15½" L. $65.00
BLOWN MILK BOWL, Pale Gr., 14½" D., 5⅝" H. $285.00

A-NY May 1980 *Calkins Auction Gallery*
STEP BACK SPICE CABINET, 10 Drawer, N. Eng., 19th C., Brass Pulls, Painted Blue, Dovetailed Drawers, 18½" W., 16½" H. $425.00
BRANT DECOY, Carved & Painted, 16" L., 8" H. $80.00
DECORATED SUGAR BUCKET, Iron Handle On Cover, Bail Handle, Metal Bands, PA, Late 19th C., 9" D., 7½" H. $50.00
CHIPPENDALE BLANKET CHEST, Grain Painted Pine, N. Eng., Early 19th C., 40½" L., 16½" W., 20" H. $300.00
OVOID STONEWARE PITCHER, Union Pottery Co., NJ, 19th C., Cobalt Blue Decor., Chips & Cracks Near Top, 10¼" H.
.... $70.00
OVOID JUG, Early 19th C., Cobalt Blue Decor. W/Incised Lines, 16" H. $55.00

A-OH July 1980   *Garth's Auctions, Inc.*

WATERCOLOR PORTRAIT, 2 Holes In Margin, Orig. Corner Block Frame, Old Glass Cracked, 9¾″ x 13¾″ $4500.00

SHELF CLOCK, Eli Terry, Mahogany On Pine W/Orig. Reverse Glass Painting, Minor Damages, Orig. Wooden Face & Works, Paper Label, CT, Orig. Finials & Weights & Pendulum, 31¼″ H. $1100.00

BANNISTER BACK SIDE CHAIR, Blk. Paint, Rush Seat Frame Has Worn Cloth Covering $225.00

HEPPLEWHITE TABLE, Walnut W/2-Board Top, Finish Removed, 22¼″ x 26¾″ $1450.00

BRASS ANDIRONS, 18″ H. ... $625.00

A-OH Feb 1980   *Garth's Auctions, Inc.*

CHIPPENDALE SCROLL MIRROR W/ Old Glass, Mahogany, All 4 Ears Replaced & Other Repairs, 12″ x 20″ $130.00

AUDUBON BIRD PRINTS, 4 (1 Illus.), Octavo Edition, Handcolored Lithographs By "J.T. Bowen, Phila.", Well Matted & Unframed, 11″ x 14″ $140.00

WINDSOR HIGHCHAIR, Bamboo W/ Rabbit Ear Spindle Back, Old Worn Blk. Paint W/Yellow Striping & Stenciled Crest Shows Red Beneath, Top Of 1 Back Post Split $120.00

HEPPLEWHITE TEA CADDY, Inlaid Mahogany On Pine W/Ivory Escut., Ball Feet Are Replacements, 5″ x 5½″ x 9″ .. $105.00

HEPPLEWHITE STAND, Cherry, Dovetailed Drawer & 1 Board Top, Ref. & Rep. To Top Of 1 Leg, 14½″ x 15¼″, 22½″ H. $155.00

A-OH Sept 1980   *Garth's Auctions, Inc.*

CURRIER & IVES LITHOGRAPH, Handcolored, "The Old Oaken Bucket", Margins Trimmed, Framed, 12½″ x 16½″ .. $125.00

TIN MOLD, Fish, Mkd. "Germany", 12½″ W. $17.50

MINI. CHEST OF DRAWERS, Dovetailed Drawers, Cherry, Pine & Poplar, Repl. Crest, 11½″ W., 6″ D., 12¾″ H. $135.00

ARROW-BACK, COMB-BACK ROCKER, Repairs, Ref. $255.00

STAND, Pine W/Orig. Red Graining, Alterations, 17″ x 22″, 28½″ H. $85.00

SPLINT BASKET, Wood Side Handles, Faded Blue Design, 14″ D. $45.00

GROTESQUE STONEWARE JUG, Incised "Lanier Meaders", 9″ H. ... $105.00

CANDLE MOLD, 12-Tube, Tin, 11¼″ H. $40.00

A-OH April 1980   *Garth's Auctions, Inc.*

STEP DOWN WINDSOR SIDE CHAIR, Orig. Drk. Red Paint W/Yellow Striping & Shell Design On Crest, 17¾″ H. .. $325.00

TOLE COFFEE POT, Orig. Drk. Br. Japanning W/Yellow, Orange, Gr., Blk. & Wh. Decor., Scratched, 8½″ H. $575.00

WALNUT STAND, Top Old Replacement, 14½″ D., 24″ H. $100.00

PEA PICKING BASKET, All Wood, Worn Old Red Paint, 5½″ x 10¼″ $115.00

CARVED EAGLE, Pine, Fish In Talons, Worn Br. Stain, Initialed "C.S.", 16¼″ W. $265.00

RYE STRAW BASKET, 11½″ D. .. $35.00

A-OH Jan 1980   *Garth's Auctions, Inc.*

◄ **SAMPLER ON HOMESPUN,** "Mary Kirkbride, Aged 12, 1825", Framed, 15¼″ x 23½″ $325.00

CHIPPENDALE SCROLL MIRROR, Mahogany On Pine, Minor Rep. To Crest & Sm. Section Of Gilt Liner Missing, 15½″ x 23″ $590.00

BOW-BACK WINDSOR SIDE CHAIR, Orig. Blk. Paint W/Yellow Striping, Seat: 18″ H. $325.00

HANDLELESS CUPS & SAUCERS, Pr., Soft Paste, Pink & Purple Lustre, Minor Wear, 1 Cup W/Chip On Rim $95.00

SALOPIAN DOME TOP TEAPOT, Polychrome Enameled Blk. Transfer Decor., Old Spout Chips & Rim Hairline, 10¾″ H. $300.00

HEPPLEWHITE STAND, Cherry, 1 Dovetailed Drawer, Orig. Brass Bail, 19½″ x 20″, 25¾″ $400.00

STONEWARE JAR, Gr. Running Glaze, 11½″ H. $95.00

CAST IRON SHOE LAST, Old Blk. W/ Yellow Striping, 8¼″ H. $25.00

A-OH July 1980   *Garth's Auctions, Inc.*
LYRE FROM BANJO CLOCK, Mahogany W/Figured Veneer Facade, Reverse Painting, Orig. Works, Pendulum & Weights, Hands, Finial & Drop Missing, Repair Needed, 33½″ H. $2900.00
WAG-ON-THE-WALL CLOCK, Wood Case W/Brass Gears, Painted Metal Face W/Polychrome Decor., Paint Worn, 18″ H.
.... $650.00
WRITING ARM CHAIR, Orig. Red & Blk. Graining W/Yellow Striping & Free Hand Decor., Worn Finish & Repaired ....
.... $2800.00

A-OH Mar 1980   *Garth's Auctions, Inc.*
QUEEN ANNE SIDE CHAIR, Old Reddish Br. Finish W/Worn Rush Seat, Rep. To Crest & Surface Damage To Front Legs & Feet $425.00
PASTEL DRAWING, Framed, 13½″ x 16¼″
.... $425.00
GAUDY DUTCH CUPS & SAUCERS, 3, 1 Set W/Minor Damage $705.00
HEPPLEWHITE STAND, Dovetailed Drawer, Sgn. "Mrs. E. Smith Rollsburgh", Replaced Brass Pull & Old Finish, 17¾″ x 18″, 28½″ H. $295.00
TIN MELON FOOD MOLD, Ribbed, Mkd. "Kreamer", 6½″ x 9″ $15.00
CARVED WOODEN DECOY, Canvasback Drake From Eastern Shore, VA, Ca. 1910, Weathered W/Age Cracks & Old Working Repaint, 13½″ L. $47.50

A-OH Mar 1980   *Garth's Auctions, Inc.*
OIL ON CANVAS, Decor. Frame, Sm. Patch, 18½″ x 25¼″ $550.00
WATERCOLOR, Basket Of Fruit, Old Gilded Frame, 10″ x 11″ $480.00
SEWER TILE SQUIRREL, 6¾″ H.
.... $250.00
STORAGE BOX, 2 Finger Const., Copper Tacks, Orig. Red Varnish, 5½″ x 8″ ...$135.00
STORAGE BOX, 3 Finger Const., Copper Tacks, No Finish, 7¾″ x 10¾″ $105.00
PLANK SEAT SIDE CHAIR, Old Br. Paint W/Wh. & Gold Striping & Stenciled Crest 50.00
HEPPLEWHITE STAND, Dovetailed Drawer, Ref., 18¾″ x 19″, 26¾″ H. .. $400.00
WOVEN SPLINT BASKET, Worn Wh. Paint, 11¾″ x 12½″, 8″ O.H. $75.00
WOVEN SPLINT BASKET, Blk. & Red, 11″ D., 6½″ H. $20.00

A-OH Oct 1980   *Garth's Auctions, Inc.*
SINGLE WEAVE COVERLET, 2-Pc., Red, Wh. & Blue, 82″ x 96″ $215.00
CRADLE, Dovetailed Pine W/Hood, Old Red Paint, Repl. Rockers, 44″ L., 26″ H.
.... $170.00
WOVEN SPLINT BASKET, Filled W/ Handsewn Carpet Balls, 11″ x 17″ ... $55.00

A-OH July 1980   *Garth's Auctions, Inc.*
JACQUARD COVERLET, 1-Pc., Double Weave, Blue & Wh. W/Gen. Washington In Corners, Edge Wear, 70″ x 84″ ... $900.00
PENCILPOST BED, Walnut W/Orig. Rope Side Rails, Old Drk. Finish, 52½″ x 76½″ $3700.00
CAST IRON JOCKEY HITCHING POST, Rusted, Bill Of Cap Restored, Ring Missing, 48″ H. $500.00
CHILD'S LADDER-BACK ARMCHAIR ROCKER, Broken Out Splint Seat, Worn Orig. Blk. Paint $375.00
DOLL SIZE PENCILPOST BED, Headboard & 1 Rail Replacements, 12½″ x 23¼″, 21½″ H. $70.00

A-OH July 1980   *Garth's Auctions, Inc.*
DOUBLE WEAVE JACQUARD COVERLET, 2-Pc., Blue & Wh. Edge Wear, 80″ x 86″
.... $700.00
CRADLE, Curly Maple Brackets At Head, 40½″ L. $475.00
WH. CLAY PITCHER, Albany Slip Glaze, Rim Flakes, 12½″ H. $25.00
WROUGHT IRON LIGHTING DEVICE, Adj. Betty Lamp On Rod W/Circular Base, Complete W/Chain & Pick, 21½″ H.
.... $700.00
STONEWARE GROTESQUE JUG, Blk./ Br. Glaze, Sm. Spout & Lrg. Filler Hole In Back, Open Handle Missing, Flake On Lip Of Hole, Attrib. To White Cottage, OH, 10″ H. $2850.00

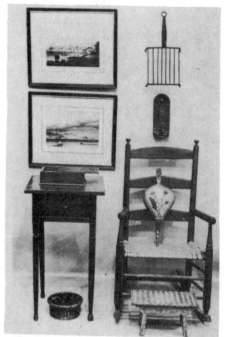

HANDCOLORED LITHOGRAPHS, "Valparaiso" & "Rio-Janeiro", Framed, 17½" 21" $110.00
WROUGHT IRON BROILER, Scrolled Feet, 16½" L. $55.00
TIN CANDLE SCONCE, 9½" H. . $25.00
LADDER-BACK ARM CHAIR ROCKER, New Woven Splint Seat, Rockers Worn Flat
.... $45.00
SPICE BOX, Dovetailed Cherry, Sliding Lid, Old Varnish Finish, Lid W/Minor Lip Damage, 6¼" x 9½" x 2¾" H. $65.00
SM. STAND, Maple, Slender Turned Legs, Dovetailed Drawer, 1 Board Top, 16" Sq., 27¾" H. $150.00
DECOR. TURTLE BACK BELLOWS, Brass Nozzle, Orig. Wh. Paint W/Salmon Striping, Gr.-Red Floral Decor., Old Leather Removed, 18" H. $155.00
ROCKINGHAM SPITTOON, Base Flakes, 7¾" D. $10.00
FOOT STOOL, Worn Wh.-Gr. Paint In Plaid Design, 7¼" x 13½", 7" H. ... $25.00

WINDSOR SIDECHAIRS, Maple & Ash, Bow-Back, 7 Spindles, Ref., Ca. 1790
.... $375.00
Q. A. TAVERN TABLE, Pinned Const., Maple, Am., Ca. 1730-40, 21" W., 30" L., 23" H. $650.00
FOLK ART EAGLE, Am., Carved Gilt, Wood Plinth, Ca., 1850, 14¼" L., 14¼" H.
.... $275.00
MORTAR & PESTLE, Lignum Vitae, Mortar W/2-Tone Coloring $100.00

SAMPLER ON HOMESPUN, "Sibel Wyman, Londonderry Born, Sept. 21, 1810, Aged 9 Years In 1819", Framed, 8" x 18¼"
.... $195.00
NEEDLEWORK SAMPLER, Homespun Filled In W/Cross Stitch Or Satin Stitch, "Wrought By Lydia S. Rice, AE 10 Years 1820, Charlotte Baker Ins.", Some Old Restitching, Shadowbox Frame, 24½" Sq.
.... $550.00
LADDER-BACK SIDE CHAIR, Old Woven Splint Seat, Worn Old Brownish Red Repaint $125.00
CARVED WOODEN DECOY, Decor. Blue Wing Teal Drake, MD, Orig. Paint, 12¾" L. $80.00
SM. WOODEN KNIFE BOX, Alligatored Blk. Paint W/Bird & Tulip Design, 7" x 12", 4½" H. $65.00
TEA TABLE, 1 Board Top Old Replacement, Worn & Alligatored Blue Green Paint, 20" x 30", 23" H. $625.00
WOVEN SPLINT BASKET, Old Gr. Paint, 13½" D., 7" O.H. $100.00
CARVED WOODEN DECOY, Hollow Goldeneye Drake, Lake Ontario, Ca. 1910, Turned Head, Tack Eyes, Old Working Repaint, 14¼" L. $100.00
WOVEN SPLINT ½ BUTTOCKS BASKET, Gr. & Natural, 5" x 9", 4" O.H.
.... $95.00

BANISTER BACK ARM CHAIR, Repairs & Insect Damage, Split In Back Stretcher, Old Worn Finish & Rush Seat $600.00
WAG-ON-THE-WALL CLOCK, Painted Wooden Face, Brass Gear Movement, Flaked Paint, Case Inscribed, 13½" x 19"
.... $600.00
CHILD'S LADDER-BACK ARM CHAIR, Woven Splint Seat, Orig. Worn Olive Paint
.... $400.00
WRT. IRON KNIFE BLADE ANDIRONS, Pr., Rusted, 15½" H. $420.00
HATCHEL, Wrt. Iron & Wood, Punched & Chip Carved Detail, 14¾" L. $65.00

_____

OIL ON CANVAS, Portrait Of A Man W/ Wh. Lace Collar, Rebacked On Plywood W/ Several Patches, Yellowed Varnish, Wide Gilded Frame, 20" x 24" $185.00
FEDERAL MIRROR, Mahogany W/Fluted Frame, Orig. Reverse Painting Quite Worn, 12" x 18½" $72.50
WINDSOR BOW-BACK CHAIR, Partially Stripped Of Old Paint, Seat: 16½" H.
.... $675.00
CARVED WOODEN DECOY, Old Squaw Drake, Sgn. "Frank Dobbins, Jonesport, ME", Orig. Paint, 12" L. $85.00
CARVED WOODEN DECOY, Redhead Drake From St. Lawrence River, Glass Eyes, Orig. Paint W/Shot Wounds & Wear, Ca. 1910, 13½" L. $75.00
HEPPLEWHITE TABLE, Walnut, Simple Line Inlay On Edge, Orig. Top W/New Glue Blocks & Center Brace Replacement, Ref., 20" x 30½" $875.00
STONEWARE JUG, 2-Gal., Impressed "R.W. Russel", Brushed Cobalt Blue Flowers & Applied Handles, Flake On Lip, 11¼" H.
.... $135.00
CARVED WOODEN DECOY, Redbreasted Merganser Drake, Northern MI, Glass Eyes, Old Worn Working Repaint, Age Cracks In Block, 15¾" L. $145.00

A-OH Feb 1980   *Garth's Auctions, Inc.*
OIL ON CANVAS, Sgn. "D.A.", Modern Gold Finished Metal Frame, 12¼" x 18¼"
.... $45.00
CARVED WOODEN DECOY, Canvasback W/Oversize Head, Old Worn Working Repaint, Neck Split & Mismatched Glass Eyes, 15" L. $45.00
BRASS VIC. CANDLESTICKS, Pr., Pushups Missing, 9¾" H. $110.00
TABLE TOP DESK BOX, Pine, Old Worn Blk. Paint, 24" W., 18½" D., 7¼" H.
.... $85.00
CARVED WOODEN DECOY W/Inset Head, Old Worn Blk. & Wh. Working Repaint, 15½" L. $40.00
WORK TABLE, Pine, Dovetailed Drawer, 2 Board Top, Old Rep. & Much Use, Ref., 28" x 38", 29¼" H. $125.00
DOUGH BOX, Poplar, Dovetailed, Old Red Paint, 15" x 27", 13" H. $95.00
CARVED WOODEN DECOY, Oversize Eider Hen By Warren Wass, ME, Ca. 1910 Orig. Worn Paint W/Age Cracks & Chip On Tail, Inset Head, 20" L. $50.00

A-NY May 1980   *Calkins Auction Gallery*
SILVER DOLLAR CRIB QUILT, VT, 19th C., Multi-Colored Calico Pcs. Tied To Cotton Backing, 40" x 60" $70.00
REDWARE JUG, N. Eng., 19th C., Incised Lines, Drk. Gr. Dripped Glaze, 7½" H.
.... $35.00
REDWARE PRESERVE JAR, Covered, N. Eng., 19th C., Orange Glaze W/Br. Drip Decor., Few Chips, 5¾" D., 8½" H. .. $60.00
REDWARE JUG, Handled, N. Eng., 19th C., Br. Glaze, 7" D., 10½" H. $35.00
REDWARE OVOID CROCK, N. Eng., 19th C., Incised Lines, Grey Ground W/Drk. Br., 2 Minor Chips, 9" D., 10" H. .. $75.00
REDWARE JUG, Handled, N. Eng., 19th C., Speckled Br. On Tan Glaze, 4" D., 9" H.
.... $20.00
REDWARE OVOID JAR, N. Eng., 19th C., Br. Glaze, Minor Flaking, 6" D., 7½" H.
.... $20.00
REDWARE JUG, Handled, 19th C., Dribbled Glaze On Br. & Gr. Glaze, Sm. Chip On Neck, 4¾" D., 8" H. $35.00
SHAKER BLANKET CHEST, Pine, Early 19th C., Dovetailed Drawer W/Sm. Brass Pulls, Some Damage To Lip Of Drawer, 48½" W., 17½" D., 34½" H. $300.00

A-OH April 1980   *Garth's Auctions, Inc.*
"CURRIER & IVES" LITHOGRAPH, "Summer In The Country", Margins Trimmed, Sm. Holes In Lt. Margin, Old Beveled Mahogany Veneer Frame, 13" x 17"
.... $65.00
SHERATON SHAVING MIRROR, Mahogany On Pine, Dovetailed Drawers, Hdw. Incomplete, Veneer Rep., 15¼" W., 9½" D., 24" H. $100.00
PEWTER LIGHTHOUSE COFFEE POT, Unmarked Am., 11" H. $150.00
WINDSOR SIDE CHAIR, Ref., Holes In Seat, 16¾" H. $450.00
CHERRY STAND W/Curly Maple Veneer Facade, Dovetailed Embossed Brass Pulls, Ref., 18¾" x 22", 28¼" H. $375.00
SM. STONEWARE CROCK, Impressed Label "White Utica", 7" H. $315.00
PINE BOX, Dovetailed, Till & Int. Drawer, Ref., 14" L. $85.00

A-OH Jan 1980   *Garth's Auctions, Inc.*
SM. QUEEN ANNE MIRROR, Mahogany On Pine, Splits In Frame & Old Worn Finish, 8¼" x 14½" $275.00
LEEDS CHARGER, Blue Feather Edge W/ Pot Of Flowers In 5 Colors, 14½" D. .. $500.00
FANBACK WINDSOR SIDE CHAIR, Bamboo, Old Blk. Paint W/Gold Striping, Break In Crest Rail, Seat: 16¾" H. .. $125.00
◄ **LEEDS GAUDY TEA POT,** Blue Floral, Flakes On Spout & Rim Of Lid, 6¾" H.
.... $85.00
LEEDS GAUDY PITCHER, Floral Decor., 4 Colors, Spout Chipped & Hairline, Shallow Flakes On Base, 6⅜" H. $90.00
LEEDS GAUDY HANDLELESS CUP & SAUCER, Floral Decor., 4 Colors, Saucer Has Rim Flakes $75.00
LEEDS GAUDY SUGAR BOWL, Blue Floral Decor., Edge Chips & Hairlines, 5¾" H.
.... $95.00
HEPPLEWHITE DROP LEAF SWING LEG TABLE, Birch, Ref., Stains In Top, 13¾" x 30¾", W/8" Leaves, 27¼" H. .. $555.00
BOX, Pine W/Hinged Lid, Ref., 11" W., 9¾" D., 13¼" H. $175.00

A-MA May 1980   *Paul J. Dias, Inc.*
L To R
CASH REGISTER, Am. Cash Register Co., Saginaw, MI, Bronze, Rings Up To $9.99, Oak Base $375.00
CASH REGISTER, National Series 1064-G, Bronze, 1-Drawer, Oak Base, Rings Up To $99.99 .... $300.00
CASH REGISTER, Barbershop, MI, Nickel Plated, Registers To $1.75, Amt. Purchased Sign On Top $450.00

A-OH Aug 1980   *Garth's Auctions, Inc.*
NAVAJO RUG, Crystal Pound Blanket, Red On Natural Ground, Edge Wear, Bottom End W/Ext. Damage, 41″ x 73″ . . $35.00
ROPE BED, Orig. Red & Blk. Graining, Orig. Rails, 51¼″ x 75″, 60½″ H. . . $500.00
ZINC DOG, On Iron Base, 2 Breaks In Zinc, 16″ x 27½″, 19″ H. $1900.00
CARVED WOODEN DECOY, Redhead Hen By Frank Schmidt, MI, Glass Eyes, Orig. Paint, 15½″ L. $85.00
CARVED WOODEN DECOY, Redhead Hen By Frank Schmidt, MI, Glass Eyes, Orig. Paint, 15½″ L. $85.00
CARVED WOODEN DECOY, Bluebill Drake, Attrib. To Tom Schroders, MI, Glass Eyes, Old Paint W/Shots, 17¼″ L. . . $65.00

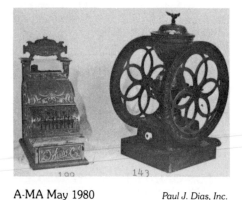

A-MA May 1980   *Paul J. Dias, Inc.*
L To R
CASH REGISTER, Nickel Plated Cast Iron Audit Barbershop, Rings Up To 50¢, Amt. Purchased Sign, Marble Cracked $275.00
COUNTER TOP COFFEE GRINDER, Enterprise Mfg. Co., Cast Iron W/Wooden Base & Drawer, Orig. Paint & Stenciling $500.00

A-OH July 1980   *Garth's Auctions, Inc.*
DOUBLE WEAVE JACQUARD COVERLET, 2-Pc., Blue, Red, & Wh. Sgn. "William Stroud, Cadiz, OH 1836", Edge Wear & Damage To Fringe, 74″ x 84″ $425.00
COPPER HORSE WEATHERVANE, Bullet Holes, No Standard, 24″ L. . . $550.00
COPPER BED WARMER, Floral Engraved Lid & Turned Wooden Handle, 53″ L. $325.00
SM. LADDER-BACK ROCKER, Old Red Paint W/Gilt Striping & Woven Splint Seat $475.00
STONEWARE JAR, 3-Gal., Brushed Floral Decor. In Cobalt Blue, 13½″ H. $425.00
WROUGHT IRON TOASTER, Minor Damage & Leg Replaced, 17″ L. . . . $150.00
TIN RAILROAD LANTERN, Removable Font & Oil Burner, Cobalt Blue Globe, 9¾″ L. $185.00
BRASS DIPPER, Dovetailed W/Wrt. Iron Handle, Sm. Rim Split & Repair, 22½″ L. $115.00

––––––––––––––––––––––––

A-OH Jan 1980   *Garth's Auctions, Inc.*
PA SAWTOOTH QUILT, Red & Yellow, Reversible W/Red & Gr. Calico On Back, 78″ x 86″ $350.00
NESTING KITCHEN SPATTER BOWLS, Set Of 6, Blue & Tan Sponging On Wh., 11½″ x 5½″ D. $390.00
BRASS BED WARMER W/Turned Wooden Handle, Worn Gr. Graining, 40½″ L. $220.00
EMPIRE CHEST OF DRAWERS, Cherry, 6 Dovetailed Drawers, Orig. Br. Graining W/ Stylized Design On Facade, 43″ W., 20¼″ D., 48″ H. $350.00
FULL STOCK LONG RIFLE, Old Replaced Flint Lock W/Percussion Striker Fastened In Jaws, Mkd. "Haws", Brass Fittings, Part Of Stock Split, 44″ Barrel, 60″ O.L. $375.00
WOVEN SPLINT WEAVERS BASKET, Some Damage & Old Breaks, 14½″ W., 6″ D., 14″ H. $85.00

A-OH July 1980   *Garth's Auctions, Inc.*
CHIPPENDALE SCROLL MIRROR, Mahogany, Orig. Glass Discolored, Missing Ornament Off Crest, 19½″ x 39¾″ . . $375.00
WALKING STICK, Blown Pale Aqua W/Multi-Colored Swirls, 60¾″ L. . . $175.00
COURTING MIRROR W/Reverse Painting, Figured Veneer On Pine Needs Repair & Painting Cracked, 10″ x 15⅜″ . . $375.00
WINDSOR ARMCHAIR, Bamboo, Arm Broken, Seat: 18½″ H. $875.00
LAMP, Opaque Wh. Base & Pale Blue Ribbed Font W/Wh. Swirls, Brass Connector & Collar, 8½″ H. $275.00
OVERLAY LAMP, Opaque Wh. Foot W/Brass Stem & Amethyst Cut To Clear Font, Brass Collar, Sm. Flake, 11¼″ H. $200.00
LAMP, Cranberry Font, 8¼″ H. . . $125.00
EMPIRE TILT TOP STAND, Cherry, Dish Turned Top, Repairs & Worn Finish, 22¾″ D., 29″ H. $400.00
LAMP, Stepped Marble & Brass Base, Clear Blown Font W/Wh. Swirls, 11¾″ H. $150.00

◀

A-OH Sept 1980 *Garth's Auctions, Inc.*
HOOKED RAG RUG, Polychrome Floral Design W/Blk. Border, 40" x 80" . . . $95.00
MESCALERO APACHE TRAY, Yucca Fibre W/Pinwheel Design, 11½" D. . . $25.00
CARVED WOODEN SHOREBIRD, Glass Eyes, Wire Bill W/Distressed Paint, Stamped "R.A.M. '70", 12" H. $30.00
CANDLESTAND, Chestnut, Orig. Top, Ref., 13" x 20¼", 29½" H. $135.00
WOODEN INDIAN, Carved & Polychromed, Sgn. "Made In 1923, A.A. Solman", Repair On Feathers, 26" H. $400.00

A-OH Mar 1980 *Garth's Auctions, Inc.*
INDIAN RUGS Canada, Ca. 1910-20, 3' 4" x 5' 4" $175.00
WOODEN EAGLE W/Flag, Orig. Worn Paint, Eagle Missing Part Of 1 Wing, 21" H. $775.00
LADDER BACK SIDE CHAIR, Alligatored Br. Repaint & New Rush Seat $125.00
SM. REDWARE TURKSHEAD MOLD W/Clear Glaze, 7" D. $23.00
REDWARE BOWL W/Cream Slip & Br. Running Splotches & Clear Glaze, Minor Flaking In Bottom, 8" D. $25.00
REDWARE TURKSHEAD MOLD, Br. W/ Puddles Of Wh. Slip, 7" D. $25.00
QUEEN ANNE TEA TABLE, Maple & Pine, Old Blue-Grey Paint Worn On 1 Board Top, 21" x 29¼", 26½" H. $1750.00
POTTERY CANDY MOLD, Golden Amber Glaze, Hairline, 8¾" x 14½" $315.00

A-OH June 1980 *Garth's Auctions, Inc.*
MIRROR, Curly Maple Frame, Age-Not Period, Ref., 13" x 29½" $425.00
LITHOGRAPH, Handcolored Folio, By "J.T. Bowen, Phila. 1845", "Annulated Marmot Squirrel", Modern Walnut Frame, 26¾" x 31¾" $230.00
CARVED WOODEN DECOY, Canvasback Drake Bobtail W/Snakey Neck, Glass Eyes, Splits, Worn Repaint, 14" L. . . $50.00
WOVEN SPLINT BUTTOCKS BASKET, Minor Breaks, 11" x 12", 5½" O.H. $75.00
CARVED WOODEN DECOY, Goldeneye Drake, Turned Head, Glass Eyes, Old Paint, Split, 13½" L. $135.00
DOUGH BOX, Poplar, Dovetailed Tray, 1 Board Top, Ref., 22" x 43¼", 28" H. . . $370.00
CORNER CHAIR, Cherry, Made As Commode, Solid Seat Repl., Ref. $200.00
CARVED WOODEN DECOY, Canvasback Drake Bobtail W/Lowhead, Round Body, Glass Eyes, Weathered Repaint, 14" L. $30.00
CARVED WOODEN DECOY, Mallard Drake W/Glass Eyes, Worn Paint, Gordon Hamilton, MI, 14" L. $35.00
CARVED WOODEN DECOY, Canada Goose Preener W/Carved Feathers, Glass Eyes, Orig. Paint, MI, 22" L. $215.00

A-OH Mar 1980 *Garth's Auctions, Inc.*
TIN SCONCE, 9 Pointed Star Design & Circular Crimped Top, 13½" H. $220.00
TIN SCONCE, Circular Crimped Top, 13" H. $115.00
HOLLOW CUT SILHOUETTE, Inscribed "Rebecca Jones, Drawn By Sarah Hustler At Undercliff From Her Shadow. 1787", Birdseye Frame, 14" x 19½" $105.00
TIN BETTY LAMP W/Matching Stand, Wire Pick & Hanger, Some Rust Damage, 11¼" H. $230.00
WROUGHT IRON RUSH LIGHT HOLDER W/Twisted Arm & Candle Socket Counter Weight, Old Whittled Base W/Age Cracks, 12½" H. $110.00
WROUGHT IRON KETTLE LAMP, Worn Old Gold Paint, Arms Bent Slightly, 13" H. $300.00
DECORATED CHAIRS, Set of 6 (1 Illus.), Plank Seat, Old But Not Orig. Graining $630.00
BEDSIDE STAND, Dovetailed Drawer, Cherry, 1 Board Top, Old Finish, 19¼" x 20", 29½" H. $260.00
STONEWARE JUG, 2 Gal., Stenciled Snowflake Design In Cobalt Blue, Mkd. "F.H. Cowden, Harrisburg", Sm. Rim Chips, 10¼" H. $65.00
TIN CANDLE LANTERN, Horn Has Deteriorated, Old Flaking Blk. Paint, 11¾" O. H. $95.00

A-OH Mar 1980 *Garth's Auctions, Inc.*
WATERCOLOR, Stain Along Rt. Side, Old Gilded Frame, 14¼" x 19¼" . . . $85.00
WATERCOLOR, Old Gilded Frame, 14¼" x 19" $95.00
CANNON BALL ROPE BED, Orig. Drk. Red Over Yellow Sponged Graining, Orig. Side Rails, 51¾" x 96", 57½" H. . . $2300.00
WOODEN NOAH'S ARK W/Orig. Painted & Decoupage Decor., 23 Animals, 4 People, Some Wear On Ark & Few Animals Have Minor Damage, 31½" L. $850.00

A-OH Mar 1980   *Garth's Auctions, Inc.*
HOOKED WOOL RUG, 27½" x 39"
.... $315.00
REDWARE CHARGER, Yellow Slip, Initials "J.P.D.", Rim Chips, 13¼" D. .. $900.00
POTTERY DOG, Mottled Br. & Amber Glaze, Rim Chips On Base, Paper Label Attrib. To Berner Pottery, PA, 10¾" H.
.... $95.00
REDWARE CHARGER, 3 Line Yellow Slip Decor., Coggled Edge & Old Rim Chips, 13¼" D. $570.00
HEPPLEWHITE WORK TABLE, Maple Base, 1 Dovetailed Drawer & Old Worn Red Paint, 3-Board Pine Breadboard Top Scrubbed, 26" x 41", 27" H. $600.00
CARVED WOODEN DECOY, Canada Goose W/Old Worn Paint, Glass Eyes, & Splits In Block, 23" L. $455.00

A-OH Feb 1980   *Garth's Auctions, Inc.*
APPLIQUE QUILT W/Dutchy Tulip Design In Red & Green on Wh., Some Stains, 74" x 80"
.... $155.00
WATERCOLOR & PENCIL, Modern Frame, 8" x 10" $185.00
CARVED WOODEN SHOREBIRD W/Turned Head, Sgn. "Stevens", 13½" H.
.... $80.00
WOODEN BOX, Made From Cigar Boxes, Hinged Removed, 8" Sq., 4½" H. .. $17.50
DECORATED SIDE CHAIR, Spindle Back, Rabbit Ear, Plank Seat, Orig. Red & Blk. Graining W/Yellow Striping & Leaf Stenciled Crest $75.00
HEPPLEWHITE CANDLESTAND, Cherry & Maple, Sm. Repairs & Ref. W/Traces Of Old Red, 14¼" D., 28¼" H.
.... $250.00

A-OH Sept 1980   *Garth's Auctions, Inc.*
SHAKER PIE LIFTER, 14½" L. $40.00
WOODEN SMOOTHING BOARD, Decor. Cut-Outs, Carved initials "JK", Glued Repair, 21" L. $110.00
SHAKER PIE LIFTER, 15" L. ... $40.00
LADDER-BACK SIDE CHAIR, Old Drk. Red Paint W/Gilt Striping, Woven Splint Seat $25.00
ROUND BENTWOOD MEASURE, Turned Handle, Minor Rim Damage, Shaker, 6" D. $70.00
TURNED WOODEN DARNER, 8¾" L.
.... $10.00
SISTER'S DESK, Pine, Attrib. To NY Shakers, Old Red Paint, Leather Hinges Repl., 24½" W., 19½" D., 20½" H. $150.00
CARVED WOODEN DECOY, Am. Goldeneye Hen, By Fitch, MI, Glass Eyes, Old Paint, 13½" L. $45.00
WOODEN NIDDY-NODDY, 18" L.
.... $50.00
STONEWARE JUG, 2-Gal., Cobalt Stenciled, PA, Rim Repair, 10" H. $40.00

A-OH Jan 1980   *Garth's Auctions, Inc.*
LAMP W/Clambroth Base & Clear Star & Punty Font, Brass Collar & Stem, Electrified, Minor Check In Base, 19½" H.
.... $105.00
SHAVING MIRROR, Walnut Frame, 17¼" H. $85.00
FRAKTUR DESIGN, Hand Drawn, Paper Stained, Old Grained Frame, Dated "1823" In Urn, 13¼" x 15½" $520.00
ARROW-BACK ARM CHAIR, Bamboo Turnings & Plank Seat, Old Worn Blk. Paint Shows Yellow Beneath $150.00
FEDERAL STAND, Curly Maple, 2 Dovetailed Cockbeaded Drawers & Drop Leaf Top, Old Br. Finish, 18" x 19¾" W/10¾" Leaves, 28½" H. $1250.00
REDWARE JAR, Speckled Lt. Amber Glaze W/Splashes Of Yellow Slip & Gr. Glaze, Applied Handles, Glaze Wear, Lid Fits But Decor. Varies From Base, 12½" H. ...$295.00
SHAKER FOOTSTOOL, Orig. Blk. Paint W/Gold Label, 11¾" x 11½", 6½" H. .. $205.00

A-OH Sept 1980   *Garth's Auctions, Inc.*
DOUBLE WEAVE COVERLET, 2-Pc., Red, Blue & Wh., Wear, 70" x 82½" .. $25.00
CANNON BALL BED, Cherry, Orig. Rails Lengthened, Repairs, 52½" x 80¾", 50" H.
.... $475.00
DECOR. HITCHCOCK SIDE CHAIRS, Pr., Youth Size, Old Red Paint W/Blk. Striping, Yellow Floral Decor., Paint Worn, Repairs $50.00
TIN LANTERN, Glass Sides, Top Handle, Ring In Base To Hold Font, 15" H.
.... $35.00

A-OH Mar 1980   *Garth's Auctions, Inc.*
HOOKED RAG RUG, 29" x 45" . . $350.00
CHILD'S LADDER BACK ARM CHAIR ROCKER, Ref., New Woven Splint Seat
. . . . $85.00
SINGLE ROPE BED, Narrow Size, Ref., 28" W., 75" L., 28" H. $310.00
ROLLING PIN, Curly Cherry, 18½" L.
. . . . $42.50
WOODEN CANDLE LANTERN W/Glass In Door & 3 Sides, 8½" O.H. $265.00
TIN PAUL REVERE CANDLE LANTERN, Worn Gold Paint, Hinge Needs Rep., 13" O.H. $95.00
SM. COPPER TEAPOT, Dovetailed Stems, Short Spout W/Flap, 6¼" $95.00
FOOT STOOL, Worn Green & Yellow Design, 8" x 14", 7¾" H. $25.00
BRASS PAUL REVERE LANTERN, 13" H. $215.00

A-OH July 1980   *Garth's Auctions, Inc.*
DOUBLE WEAVE JACQUARD COVERLET, 1 Pc., Blue & Wh. Coin Center Medallion, 76" x 100" $4000.00
PENCILPOST ROPE BED, Walnut W/Cherry Head & Foot Boards, Orig. Rails, 50¼" x 75", 84½" H. $600.00
FIREPLACE FENDER, Wire Grill & Brass Feet, Rail & Finials, 56" W., 17" D., 16½" H. $250.00
CAST IRON CAMP STOVE, Remov. Decor. Wire Grill, Pitted, 11½" D., 10" H. $85.00
CAST IRON MORTAR & PESTLE, Pitted, 5" H. $25.00

A-OH Feb 1980   *Garth's Auctions, Inc.*
OPAQUE WATERCOLOR, Sgn. "Spoonamore '68", Framed 23" x 26½" $27.50
ROPE BED, Maple, Replaced Metal Side Rails, Ref., 52" W. $200.00
TRAMP ART BOX, Old Blue & Gold Paint, 14" x 20", 12½" H. $85.00
SM. BLANKET CHEST, Pine, Till At Each End, Removable Divider Board A Replacement, Old Worn Br. Paint, 36" W., 14" D., 14¼" H. $150.00
CARVED WOODEN DECOY, Hollow Bufflehead W/Old Worn Working Repaint Glass Eyes & Bill Damage, 12" L. . . $85.00
CARVED WOODEN DECOY, Mate To Above, 12¾" L. $85.00

A-MA Sept 1980   *Robert W. Skinner Inc.*
PARLOUR STEREO VIEWER, Rosewood, Label Reads "Alex Beckers, NY, Patent April 7, 1857", Some Varnish Flaking, Frosted Glass Missing From Back, 25 Glass Stereo Views Of Foreign Subjects, 18¾" H.
. . . . $300.00*

A-OH Feb 1980   *Garth's Auctions, Inc.*
COPPER ARCHITECTURAL ORNAMENT, Gr. Patina & Wooden Floor Stand, 57" H. $360.00
WALL CUPBOARD, Pine, 1-Pc., Picture Frame Molding, Ref., Int. Painted Blue, 33¾" W., 19¾" D., 73" H. $225.00
STONEWARE JUG, 4-Gal., Cobalt Slip Decor., Impressed Label "E.E. Hall & Co. 171 Blackstone St. Boston, MA", 17" H.
. . . . $225.00

A-OH May 1980   *Garth's Auctions, Inc.*
SILHOUETTES, Pr. Of George & Martha Washington, Oval Shadow Box Frames W/Gilded Lines, 11½" x 13½" $110.00
CAST IRON FIRE GRATE, English W/Brass Trim, 32" W., 17½" D., 33½" H.
. . . . $455.00

A-OH Sept 1980   *Garth's Auctions, Inc.*
WOODLAND ROACH, Orange Dyed & Wh. Deer Hair & Porcupine Hair Attached To Woven Yarn Core, 14″ L. $60.00
NAVAJO SADDLE BLANKET, Natural Wool W/Analine Red Central Cross, Ca. 1920, 31″ x 36″ $45.00
OSAGE TYPE ROACH, Horsehair Dyed W/Gr.-Red, Wood Feathers Socket, Ca. 1910, 13″ D. $30.00
CARVED WOODEN DECOY, Canvasback Drake, Attrib. To Joe Begin, MI, Balsa Body, Working Repaint, Glass Eyes, 14½″ L. $45.00
CAST IRON DOOR STOP, Cat, Painted Blk., 13½″ L. $210.00
CARVED WOODEN DECOY, Hollow Bluebill Drake W/Tacked Canvas Bottom, Torn, Worn Old Paint, Glass Eyes, 14½″ L. $55.00
CHEST OF DRAWERS, Pine, 6 Nailed Drawers, Sponged Blk. & Red Paint, 45½″ W., 12½″ D., 22″ H. $155.00
DECOY, Cork Body, Carved Wooden Head, Mallard Drake, Attrib. To Enwright, Toledo, Tack Eyes, Old Worn Paint, 16¼″ L. $40.00
CARVED WOODEN DECOY, Canada Goose W/Hollowed Out Bottom, Tack Eyes, Old Worn Paint, 24½″ L. $100.00
CARVED WOODEN DECOY, Mallard Hen W/Old Working Repaint, Tack Eyes, Lake Erie Marshes, 15¼″ L. $35.00

A-OH Jan 1980   *Garth's Auctions, Inc.* ▶
CARVED WOODEN DECOY, Merganzer Drake, Eyes Gone & Old Worn Paint, Checking 13″ L. $55.00
CARVED WOODEN DECOY, Blk. Duck W/Old Worn Paint, Split in Head, MI, 19¾″ L. $75.00
CARVED WOODEN DECOY, Mate to lst Decoy, Orig. Tack Eyes, 13″ L. . . $95.00
GRAINED MANTLE, Orig. Yellow & Br. Graining, Opening: 30″ x 31½″; 56″ W., 6″ D., 52″ O.H. $350.00
STUFFED CANVAS DECOY, Canada Goose W/Old Blk. & Grey Paint, 26″ L.
. . . . $135.00

A-OH Mar 1980   *Garth's Auctions, Inc.*
HOOKED RAG RUG, 27″ x 44″ . . $175.00
HANGING CANDLE BOX, Walnut, Dovetailed, Leather Hinge Replaced By Piano Hinge, 13½″ W., 8½″ D., 16″ H. . . $260.00
WROUGHT IRON RUSH LIGHT & CANDLE HOLDER, Twisted Stem, 12¼″ H.
. . . . $85.00
CAST IRON EAGLE SNOW BIRDS, Pr., 6½″ W. $50.00
WROUGHT IRON RUSH LIGHT HOLDER W/Lead Filled Turned Wooden Base, 12½″ H. $145.00
WROUGHT IRON RUSH LIGHT HOLDER W/Tooled Stem & Candle Socket Counter Balance, Wooden Base Old Replacement, 15¾″ H. $140.00
BLANKET CHEST, Pine & Poplar, Dovetailed Case & Drawers, Till & Trap Lock W/Key, Orig. Drk. Red "Vinegar" Graining Over Yellow Ground, Rep. To Lid Hinge On Till, 48½″ W., 21¾″ W., 21¾″ D., 29¾″ H.
. . . . $750.00
CARVED WOODEN DECOY, Pintail Drake, Worn Working Repaint, Bottom Mkd. "Barto IL, 1880-1959", Glass Eyes & Split In Neck, 17″ L. $100.00
CARVED WOODEN DECOY, Canada Goose W/Root Head, Weathered Paint, Age Cracks, Tail Chipped, 21½″ L. $105.00
CARVED WOODEN DECOY, Goldeneye, Old Working Repaint & Crack In Bottom, 13½″ L. $60.00

A-OH Oct 1980   *Garth's Auctions, Inc.*
MANGLE BOARD, Highly Chip Carved, Sgn. "Anno 1711", Scandanavian, 31⅜″ L.
. . . . $370.00
SMOOTHING BOARD & ROLLER, 2-Pc., PA, Red Paint W/Wh. & Gr. Floral Decor., "1867" On Board, Roller Not Illus., Minor Insect Damage, 28¼″ L. . . . $230.00
APPLIQUE QUILT, Gr. & Red Calico Floral Decor. W/Yellow Centers, Feather Quilting, 92″ x 94″ $580.00
WATERCOLOR PORTRAIT, Young Man, Mkd. "Meprs Kury 1848", Framed, 9¼″ x 12¼″ $165.00
TABLE TOP DESK, Pine, Dovetailed, Old Red Paint, Orig. Brass Side Handles, 19¾″ W., 20¼″ D., 8″ H. $205.00
BLANKET CHEST, Walnut, Dovetailed, Alterations, 43½″ W., 19¼″ D., 8″ H.
. . . . $245.00
CAST IRON DOOR STOP, Ram, 9″ L.
. . . . $45.00

A-NY May 1980   *Calkins Auction Gallery*
PANTRY BOX, Orig. Gray Paint, 19th C., 12″ D., 6½″ H. $55.00
COVERED SUGAR BUCKET W/Swing Handle, Orig. Gray Paint, Lapped Wooden Bands, 19th C., 10″ D., 9″ H. $35.00
SHAKER BENTWOOD ROCKER, Newly Taped Red & Blk. Seat & Back, Painted Blk., 37″ O.H. $175.00
SHAKER BLANKET CHEST, Paneled, CT, Orig. Red Paint, Orig. Cond., 32″ L., 16½″ W., 20″ H. $275.00
SHAKER ARMED ROCKER, Newly Taped Red & Blk. Seat & Back, Orig. Drk. Finish, 1 Rocker Repaired, 42″ O.H. . . $250.00

A-OH Mar 1980 *Garth's Auctions, Inc.*
RUG, Made From Patches Of Cloth, Some
Wear & Minor Rep. Necessary, 31" x 44"
.... $45.00
FLOWER POTS, Pr., White Clay, Attached Saucers & Drk. Amber Glaze, 1
Has Hairline, 5½" H. $25.00
WOOD CARVING, 20th C., 10" x 16½",
15" H. $65.00
CHEST OF DRAWERS, Pine, Orig. Worn
Painted Decor., Cast Iron Tassel Pulls W/
Worn Bronzing, 19th C., 37¼" W., 18¾" D.,
33¼" H. $110.00
BRASS LUCERNE LAMP, 20th C., 28½" H.
.... $35.00

A-OH Mar 1980 *Garth's Auctions, Inc.*
BLK. & WH. ENGRAVING, "Washington Irving & His Literary Friends At
Sunnyside", NY, Ca.1864, Old Gilded
Frame, 29¾" x 39½" $27.50
HITCHCOCK CHAIRS, Set Of 6, Blk. &
Br. Graining W/Gilt Striping, Repairs, Rush
Seats $450.00
FIREPLACE FENDER, Wire Decor.
Work & Brass Trim, 35" W., 16" H. .. $225.00

A-OH July 1980 *Garth's Auctions, Inc.*
JACQUARD COVERLET, 2-Pc., Double
Weave, 2 Shades Of Blue & Red, Some
Wear & Center Seam Resewn, 72" x 84"
.... $350.00
**HEPPLEWHITE CORNER WASH-
STAND,** Mahogany, Sm. Corner Shelf Replaced, Dovetailed Drawer & Gallery, Worn
Finish & Veneer Damage, Restorations, 23"
W., 41½" H. $225.00
**STEP DOWN WINDSOR ARMCHAIR
ROCKER,** Late 19th C., Pieced Oak Seat,
Iron Rod & Braces $200.00
YELLOWWARE POTTERY PITCHER,
Embossed Decor., Minor Wear & Chip, 8¼"
H. $35.00
PITCHER, Embossed Decor. W/Greenish
Gray Glaze, Impressed "S & JB", Hairline,
10¼" H. $35.00
ROCKINGHAM PITCHER W/Hound
Handle, Embossed Decor., Minor Glaze
Flakes, 10⅛" H. $85.00
ROCKINGHAM BED PAN, 16½" L.
.... $25.00

A-OH June 1980 *Garths's Auctions, Inc.* ▶
OIL ON CANVAS, Portrait, Subdued
Colors, Initialed "D.W.", Old Gilded Gesso
Frame, 24" x 27½" $225.00
STAFFORDSHIRE COTTAGE, Polychrome Enameling W/Blue "Cole Slaw" Trim
& Gilding, 6¼" H. $125.00
IRONSTONE TUREEN & PLATTER,
Indian Tree Patt., Mkd. "Mintons", Chips On
Rim Of Tray, 6¼" H. $25.00
STAFFORDSHIRE TOBY, Orange & Yellow Coat W/Gr. — Blk. & Gilt, Lid Repaired,
5" H. $25.00
SHERATON CHEST OF DRAWERS,
Cherry W/Curly Maple Veneer Facade, Dovetailed Drawers, Repl. Oval Brasses, 39¾" W.,
20¼" D., 40 ¾" H. $725.00
CARVED WOODEN DECOY, Coot By
Edgar Pilson, Ca. 1810-1848, Weathered &
Neck Repairs W/Old Working Repaint, 13¼"
L. $80.00
CARVED WOODEN DECOY, Redbreasted Merganser Drake, MI, Branded Monogram & Orig. Paint, 15½" L. $65.00

A-OH Oct 1980 *Garth's Auctions, Inc.*
INDIAN RUG, Blk., Red & Wh., 32½" x 50"
.... $120.00
ROCKINGHAM BOWL, 6⅝" D., 3¼" H.
.... $10.00
ROCKINGHAM BOWL, Old Flake &
Hairline, 6½" D., 3⅝" H. $15.00
ROCKINGHAM TEAPOT, Rebecca At
The Well, Flakes & Hairline, 9¾" H. . $45.00
ROCKINGHAM BOWL, 8¼" D., 3⅞" H.
.... $25.00
ROCKINGHAM BOWL, 6½" D., 3¼" H.
.... $30.00
SHERATON PEMBROKE TABLE, Dovetailed Drawer, Orig. Red Paint, 19" x 39",
29¼" H. $250.00
ROCKINGHAM FOOT WARMER, Repaired Spout, 8¾" H. $65.00
ROCKINGHAM CUSPIDOR, Embossed
Shell Rim, 7½" D. $35.00
FLINT ENAMEL FOOT WARMER, Embossed Foliage At Spout, 9¼" H. .. $115.00

A-OH Oct 1980   *Garth's Auctions, Inc.*
HOOKED RAG RUG, Polychrome Floral Design On Blue-Blk. Ground, 36" x 59"
.... $100.00
WOODEN SHOREBIRD, On Drift Wood Base, 15½" H. $12.50
CARVED WOODEN DECOY, Canvasback Drake By Nick Purdo, MI, Glass Eyes, Old Worn Paint, 14¾" L. $50.00
WOODEN SHOREBIRD, Sgn. "H.V. Shourds", Drift Wood Base, 10½" H.
.... $50.00
SM. BOX, Pine, Dovetailed, Wrought Iron Corner Braces & Lock, Some Damage, 17" W., 10½" D., 8¾" H. $50.00
SHAKER WORK TABLE, Poplar & Butternut, Dovetailed Drawer, Lt. Varnish Finish, NH, 30" x 48½", 28½" H. $550.00
REDWARE JAR, Gr. Glaze Shades To Orange To Clear, Chipped, 10¾" H.
.... $5.00
TIN FIRESIDE OVEN, Remov. Shelf, 14" W., 8½" D., 14½" H. $85.00
REDWARE PITCHER, Speckled Br. Glaze, Rim Flakes, 9¾" H. $65.00

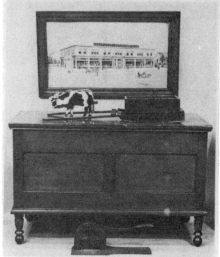

A-OH Feb 1980   *Garth's Auctions, Inc.*
ARCHITECTS WATERCOLOR, Orig. Oak Frame, 20½" x 34¾" $80.00
WOODEN OXEN, Pr., Old Blk., Wh. & Tan Paint, 11½" L. $47.50
TOY WOODEN SLED, Old Drk. Red Paint, 15" O.L. $32.50
BLANKET CHEST, Poplar, Old Red Stain, Repr. To Back Rail & Lid For Till Missing, 43¾" W., 18¼" D., 26½" L. $130.00
CAST IRON TOBACCO CUTTER, "Red Tin Tag, Chew Climax Plug, Lorrillard's Climax Plug, 17½" L. $35.00

A-OH Feb 1980   *Garth's Auctions, Inc.*
SM. HOOKED RAG RUG, Some Edge Wear, 17½" x 35" $20.00
CRADLE, Poplar, Dovetailed, Worn Br. Finish, 44" L. $140.00
BLANKET CHEST, Walnut, Dovetailed, Till Missing Lid, Hinges Reset, Back Missing, 50" W., 22½" D., 25½" H. $215.00

◄ A-OH Mar 1980   *Garth's Auctions, Inc.*
CHARCOAL DRAWING, Framed, 20½" x 26½" $185.00
CANNON BALL BED, Old Red Paint, All Rails Missing, 51" W., 40" H. $140.00
DOLL SIZE CANNON BALL BED, Old Worn Blue Paint, 20¼" x 29¾", 23½" H.
.... $290.00
DOLL SIZE TABLE, Pine W/Worn Finish, 1 Leg Rep., 8" x 12", 7¼" H. $45.00

A-OH Jan 1980   *Garth's Auctions, Inc.*
APPLIQUE PANEL, Applique Is Hand Work, Border Machine Stitched, 32" x 34"
.... $50.00
EMPIRE TALL POST BED, Walnut, Ref., Orig. Side Rails, 56¼" x 80", 8" H. $1250.00
PICKET FENCE BASKET, Wooden Bottom, Turned Wooden Handles, Worn Old Yellow Paint, 11¼" x 18½", 8" H.
.... $72.50
PICKET FENCE BASKET, Wooden Bottom, Bentwood Handles, 18½" D., 13" H.
.... $165.00

A-OH Feb 1980   *Garth's Auctions, Inc.*
TIN ADVERTISING PICTURE, "Southern Railway System. High Bridge, Kentucky River", Spotted W/Rust, 25¾" x 37¾" ...$45.00
COUNTRY STORE DISPLAY CASE, Walnut, Dovetailed W/Lift Lid W/Lrg. Glass Window, 22¾" x 34½", 6¾" H. ..$85.00
WORK TABLE, Pine, 2 Board Top, Base W/Old Br. Stain, Top Ref., 32" x 50", 28¾" H. $225.00
TRICYCLE, Steel Frame W/Wire Spoke Wheels, Old Leather Seat & Turned Wooden Handles, Repair To Handle Bars, 31" H. $205.00

A-OH Feb 1981   *Early Auction Co.*
APPLIQUE QUILT, Swags & Pinwheel In Red, Ecru, & Golden Rod, Pencil Patt. Still Intact On Backing, Few Sm. Stains, 84″ Sq. $385.00
TIN DISHPAN W/Lid, 18¼″ D. ... $25.00
BENTWOOD BOX, Oval W/Wood Spring Fastener On Lid, "I.P.I.S.", 6¼″ x 14″ $45.00
TIN COLLANDER, Sheet Tin Cover, 17″ D. $10.00
HUTCH TABLE, Pine, Restorations & Ref., 35″ x 69″, 30″ H. $475.00
STOOL, 3-Leg, Worn Gr. Paint ... $45.00
FOOT STOOL, Pine W/Birds-eye Maple Top, 9″ x 15½″, 12″ H. $60.00

A-OH Feb 1981   *Garth's Auctions, Inc.*
JACQUARD COVERLET, 2-Pc. Double Weave, Blue & Wh. W/Peacocks & Turkeys, Some Moth Damage, 74″ x 92″ $275.00
ROPE BED, Poplar, Worn Br. Finish, Orig. Side Rails, 52¼″ W., 56″ H. $200.00
STONEWARE JUG, Imp. Label "J. Fisher Lyons, N.Y.", Cobalt Slip Label "P. F. Rauber De Bac Rochester N.Y.", Minor Hairline, 14″ H. $40.00
SPUN BRASS KETTLE W/Wrought Iron Handle, Stamped "The Am. Brass Kettle Co.", 17¾″ D., 11″ H. $65.00
TIN LANTERN W/Reflector, "Dietz", Damaged & Incomp., 15½″ H. $15.00

A-OH Feb 1981   *Garth's Auctions, Inc.*
JACQUARD COVERLET, 2-Pc. Double Weave, Blue, Wh. & Red, Corners W/Date "1850", 76″ x 82″ $450.00
WROUGHT. SAWTOOTH TRAMMEL, Adj. From 44″ L. $50.00
TINSEL PICTURE, Red & Blue Floral W/Wh. Reverse Painted Ground, Gold Frame, 17½″ x 21½″ $35.00
WROUGHT. IRON SAWTOOTH TRAMMEL, Adj. From 46″ L. $55.00
WOODEN BOWL, Hollowed From 1 Pc. Of Wood, Varnished, 16″ x 35½″, 6″ H. $67.50
CRADLE, Pine, Poplar & Cherry, Ref., 39½″ W., 15″ D., 26½″ H. $160.00
WOVEN SPLINT BASKET W/Lid, Faded Red Band, 14″ D., 10½″ H. $50.00
STONEWARE JUG, 3-Gal., "3" & Wavy Line In Cobalt, 15″ H. $25.00

A-OH Feb 1981   *Garth's Auctions, Inc.*
JACQUARD COVERLET, 2-Pc. Single Weave, Drk. Blue, Teal Blue, Red & Wh. W/Eagle & Vintage Borders, Sgn. "Jacob Stephen Springvil, Seneca, Co., OH 1853", Top End Worn, 72″ x 81″ $200.00
WROUGHT & CAST IRON BRACKET LIGHT, From Tavern In St. Louis, Ca. 1894, 28″ x 52½″ $215.00
WOODEN HOBBY HORSE, Worn Orig. Red & Wh. Paint, Orig. Saddle & Harness, 43″ L. $370.00
BRASS SHIP'S LIGHTS, Set Of 3, Red, Clear & Blue Lens, "Perkins Marine Lamp, Brooklyn, N.Y.", 8″ H. $135.00

A-OH Feb 1981   *Garth's Auctions, Inc.*
WEATHERVANE, Iron Standard & Directionals W/Copper Wind Cups & Cut-out Conestoga Wagon & Team Arrow, 70½″ H. $130.00
POSTER, Blk. & Wh. Advertising, "Sears, Roebuck & Co", Framed, 15″ x 23¼″ $32.50
WROUGHT IRON PEEL, Ram's Horn Finial, 43″ L. $85.00
LADDER—BACK ARM CHAIR, Rush Seat, 19½″ Seat H. $300.00
YARN WINDER, Walnut W/Chip Carving On Base, Clicker Bar Missing, 27″ D., 41″ H. $65.00
BENTWOOD BOX, Round W/Lid & Bail Handle, 9″ D., 5½″ H. $65.00
BENTWOOD BOX, Oval W/Lid & Finger Const., Minor Damage, 9¾″ x 12½″, 5″ H. $75.00
CHILD'S ARM CHAIR, Woven Splint Seat, Old Damage & Repair, Ref. $50.00

A-OH Feb 1981   *Garth's Auctions, Inc.*

KEGS, Set Of 4 (1 Illus.), Stave Const., No Openings Into Hollow Int., 10¾" H.
.... $80.00

DOME TOP BOX, Dovetailed, Tulip Wood W/Orig. Blk. Paint W/Mustard & Red Striping, Wrought Iron Lock, Hasp & Escut. Missing, 26" L. $120.00

TIN CANDLE MOLD, 12-Tube, 11" H.
.... $75.00

CUPBOARD BASE, Poplar & Birch, Orig. Cast Iron Hdw., Worn Ref., 47" W., 20¼" D., 37½" H. $100.00

TIN BUTTON MOLD, Embossed, 10" x 15" $100.00

CLAY JAR, Buff W/Wh. Glaze, Blk. Spots & Mismatched Stoneware Lid, Some Flaking, 8½" H. $25.00

BENTWOOD BOX, Tin Corners & Orig. Varnish Finish, Stenciled Label "Spices", 9½" D., 3½" H. $45.00

STONEWARE CROCK, Imp. Label "W. H. Farrar & Co., Geddes, N.Y." W/Splashes Of Cobalt Blue, Cracked, 8" D., 7" H.
.... $65.00

A-OH Feb 1981   *Garth's Auctions, Inc.*

JACQUARD COVERLET, 2-Pc. Double Weave, Blue & Wh. Floral Design W/"1848" In Corners, Minor Edge Wear, 74" x 86"
.... $150.00

TIN LANTERN, Base Embossed "Empire", Kerosene Burner Altered For Candle, Clear Globe, Minor Rust, 12" H. $30.00

TIN CANDLE LANTERN, Rust & Repairs, 12½" O.H. $50.00

TIN LANTERN, "Dietz Victor", Kerosene Burner W/Clear Globe, Rust, 13" H.
.... $17.50

WRITING BOX, Pine, Dovetailed W/Iron Lock, Hasp Missing, Int. Lids Removed, Ref., 7" x 10" x 20" $30.00

JELLY CUPBOARD, Pine W/Single Board Doors & Well In Top, 42" W., 15¼" D., 43¼" H. $420.00

CHILD'S LADDER-BACK ARM CHAIR ROCKER, Worn Red Paint W/Gold Striping & Decals On Slats, Worn Woven Cane Seat
.... $205.00

A-OH Feb 1981   *Garth's Auctions, Inc.*

◄ **QUILT**, Basket Design In Pink, Gold & Purple Calico W/Wh., Some Wear, 67½" x 82"
.... $170.00

ROPE BED, Poplar W/Turned Posts & Acorn Finials, 55½" W. $160.00

POTTERY JUG, Running Gr. Ash Glaze, Handle Stamped "W.D.", Ca. 1890, 11¼" H.
.... $105.00

WOVEN SPLINT BASKET W/Side Handles, Minor Rim Damage, 1 Handle Damaged, 22" D. $70.00

POTTERY JUG, Blk. Glaze W/Blue Highlights, 11½" H. $22.50

HOOKED RAG RUG, Bowl Of Flowers W/Foliage Border, Backed W/New Burlap, Some Wear & Repair, 26" x 53" ... $170.00

A-MA Jan 1981   *Robert W. Skinner Inc.* ►

TIN TEA STORAGE BINS, Pr., PA, Slanted Lift Lids W/Bow Fronts, Oriental Scenes In Gold, Paper Labels "Henry Troemner" Maker, Minor Paint Loss, Ca. 1870, 22½" H.
.... $750.00*

A-OH Feb 1981   *Garth's Auctions, Inc.*

MEMORIAL, Embroidery In Shades Of Br., Olive & Gr. W/Watercolor Sky, Face & Hands Of Woman Also Watercolored, Tomb Inscribed "Sacred To The Memory Of An Affectionate Father", Eglomise Surround Is Blk. & Gold W/"Rachel Oakford 1818", Minor Tears, Orig. Gilded Gesso Frame, 23¾" x 30¼" $375.00

TIN SCONCES, Pr., Urn Shaped Reflectors W/Cobalt Glass Inserts Surrounded By Pcs. Of Mirror, Cast Pewter Finials, Electric Candles & Tin Sockets Are Old Additions
.... $275.00

BRASS VIC. CANDLESTICKS, Pr., Pushups, 9⅝" H. $165.00

LAMP, Clear Pressed Thumb Print & Waffle Font, Gr. Base W/Worn Gilding, Repaired, 10¼" H. $100.00

TELESCOPING CANDLESTICK, Silver On Copper, Sl. Crooked W/Worn Silver, 7¾" H. $40.00

GLASS BALL ON BASE, Gr. Mercury Ball, 11" H. $95.00

BLANKET CHEST, Pine, Dovetailed, Orig. Worn Br. Sponging Over Salmon Ground W/Blk. Trim, Paint Alligatored W/Wear, 40½" W., 21" D., 25" H. $300.00

REDWARE DISH, Oval W/Scalloped Rim, Yellow Ship W/Sgraffito Stylized Flowers, Incised "L. & B. Breininger, Robesonia, 1972", 8¾" x 11½" $45.00

HOOKED RAG RUG, Edge Wear, 29" x 52" $30.00

A-OH Nov 1980 *Garth's Auctions, Inc.*
WROUGHT IRON GATE, 34″ x 81″
. . . . $110.00
WROUGHT IRON SKILLET, Long Handle, 13″ D., 26½″ L. $125.00
WROUGHT IRON PEEL, Faceted Knob Handle, 24½″ L. $40.00
IRON SKIMMER, Worn Tinning, Stamped Label, 16¾″ L. $15.00
WROUGHT IRON & BRASS SPATULA, Home Made Reproduction, 17¾″ L. . . $25.00
PEEL, Reticulated Copper Blade, Wrought Iron Handle, Traces Of Tinning On Copper, 24″ L. $75.00
WROUGHT IRON FORK, Long Handles, 27½″ L. $25.00
WROUGHT IRON & BRASS DIPPER, Mkd. "J. Sloan", 20th C., 17½″ L. . . $45.00
CARVED WOODEN DECOY, Mallard Drake, Sgn. "O'Brien, Oshkosh, WI", Worn Orig. Paint & Glass Eyes, Ca. 1925, 17″ L.
. . . . $115.00
STAND W/ROUND BASE, Chamfered Columns, Octagonal Top, Worn Layers Of Red, Blue & Gr., 17½″ D, 29½″ H. . . $30.00
BURL STOMPER, Hickory Handle, 29½″ H. $55.00
CAST & WROUGHT IRON ANDIRONS, Pr., Ball Top, Hand Made, Early 20th C., 23¼″ H. $40.00
CARVED WOODEN DECOY, Bluebill Hen, Sgn. "David Cowan", NY, Repainted Ca. 1920, 13¾″ L. $35.00

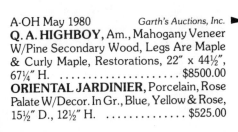

A-OH May 1980 *Garth's Auctions, Inc.* ▶
Q. A. HIGHBOY, Am., Mahogany Veneer W/Pine Secondary Wood, Legs Are Maple & Curly Maple, Restorations, 22″ x 44½″, 67¼″ H. $8500.00
ORIENTAL JARDINIER, Porcelain, Rose Palate W/Decor. In Gr., Blue, Yellow & Rose, 15½″ D., 12½″ H. $525.00

A-NY May 1980 *Calkins Auction Gallery*
LRG. SPLINT BASKET W/Double Fixed Handle, 19th C., Wooden Bottom, 20″ D., 14″ H. $130.00
COVERED SUGAR BUCKET W/Swing Handle, Lapped Wooden Bands, Orig. Red Paint, 12½″ D., 12½″ H. $45.00
FOOTED DRYING RACK, Pine, 19th C., Orig. Red Paint, 39½″ L., 7½″ W., 41½″ H. $100.00
CAST IRON SHAKER STOVE, 2 Parts, Hinge Repaired, 27″ L., 11½″ W., 19″ H. $125.00
OVOID STONEWARE JUG, 19th C., By L. Seymour, Chips On Neck, Cracked Handle, 15″ H. $35.00
HATCHEL, 18th C., Maple, Tin & Wrought Iron, 5″ W., 24″ L. $20.00
FOOT STOOL, Pine, Early 19th C., Painted Red & Blk. Graining Over All W/Yellow Stenciling, 11″ L., 7″ W., 6″ H. $50.00

A-OH April 1980 *Garth's Auctions, Inc.*
WATER BENCH, Pine, Ref., Wear & Deterioriation, 34″ W., 11″ D., 51½″ H.
. . . . $525.00
WROUGHT IRON HANGING LIGHTING DEVICE, Rush Light W/Candle Socket & Drip Pan Counterweight, Orig. Pushup, Pitted Surface, Sawtooth Trammel Hanger Adj. From 36″ L. $625.00
POTTERY SHAVING MUG, Drk. Br. Glaze, Flake On Rim, 3⅜″ H. $30.00
SEWER TILE HEN, Flakes On Beak & Wings, 6″ H. $75.00
SALT CROCK, White Clay, Eagle On Front & Br. Speckled Glaze, 4½″ D.
. . . . $65.00
HANDCOLORED LITHOGRAPH, "Currier & Ives", "Am. Fruit Piece", Margins Trimmed & Modern Birdseye Frame, 13¾″ x 17″ $85.00
REDWARE COTTAGE CHEESE SIEVE, Applied Handle, Gr. Clear Glaze W/Running Br., NH, Edge Wear & Flakes, 5″ H.
. . . . $185.00
REDWARE BEAN POT, Applied Handle, Mottled Gr. Clear Glaze W/Br. Splotches, Chips, Mismatched Lid, 6½″ H. . . . $95.00
SM. BIN, Pine, Ref., 17¾″ W., 12¾″ D., 24″ H.
. . . . $105.00
SHEET COPPER BUCKET W/Iron Handle, 9¼″ H. $50.00

A-NY May 1980 *Calkins Auction Gallery*
MARBLE GRAVE MARKER, Early 19th C., 15¾″ W., 11″ H. $165.00

A-OH Mar 1980   *Garth's Auctions, Inc.*
BROOM HOLDING RACK, 16½″ D.
.... $85.00
BENTWOOD SPICE BOX, Oval W/
Divided Int., Poplar, Lid Has Inlaid Walnut
Pinwheel, & Initials "H.H.W.", 6″ x 10¾″,
2¾″ H. $110.00
TIN TEA KETTLE, Copper Bottom, 8″ H.
.... $45.00
TOY ICE CREAM FREEZER, Complete,
Mkd. "Wonder", 7½″ H. $75.00
BLANKET CHEST, Poplar W/Sq. Walnut
Posts Terminate In Pencil Post Feet W/Scal-
loped Apron & Mortised Panels, Lid Old
Replacement, 33″ W., 17″ D., 23″ H.
.... $140.00
STAVED CASK, Old Red Paint & Bent
Hickory Handle, 12″ D., 5¾″ H. ... $70.00
TIN TEA POT, Pewter Finial, 5½″ H.
.... $40.00
CORK BODIED DECOY, Wooden Bot-
tom, Tail & Head, Redhead Drake W/Work-
ing Repaint & Glass Eyes, 14½″ L. .. $30.00
TIN BOX, Oval W/Hinged Lid, 3¼″ x 4½″,
3″ H. $15.00
FOOT WARMER, Mortised W/Sausage
Turned Posts, Punched Tin Box W/Hinged
Door, 9¼″ x 11″, 6¾″ H. $65.00

A-OH Sept 1980   *Garth's Auctions, Inc.*
SHEET IRON SHOVEL, Turned Wooden
Handle, 16″ H. $10.00
HOOKED RAG RUG, 23″ x 30½″ .. $90.00
TIN SHAVING MIRROR, Embossed W/
Shelf, 9½″ x 12¼″ $39.00
SM. RYE STRAW BASKETS, 2, 6″, 7″ D.
.... $5.00
RYE STRAW BASKET, 12½″ D. .. $10.00
RYE STRAW BASKET, 13″ D. .. $17.50
BLANKET CHEST, Paneled, Poplar, Till,
Old Yellow Steel Comb Graining, Repl.
Hinges, Sm. Damages, 45¾″ W., 21½″ D.,
25¼″ H. $210.00
STONEWARE JUG, 2-Gal., Impressed
Label "Ottman Bros Port Edwards, NY",
14″ H. $70.00

A-OH Feb 1980   *Garth's Auctions, Inc.*
MORAVIAN TYPE CHAIRS, Pr., Ref.
.... $70.00
COPPER KETTLE W/Pouring Spout,
Dovetailed, Wrought Iron Handle, Middle
Eastern, 10½″ D. $67.50
PEWTER CHARGER, Rim W/Stamped
initials, Partial Torch Mark On Back, Sm.
Repr. Split, 13″ D. $55.00
PEWTER CHARGER, Rim W/4 Sets Of
Stamped Initials, 13¾″ D. $40.00
PANELED BLANKET CHEST W/Till,
Wrought Iron Strap Hinges & Bear Trap
Lock & Key, Old Rose Mulled Decor., Dated
1835, 50″ W., 25½″ D., 24″ H. $500.00

A-OH June 1980   *Garth's Auctions, Inc.*
INDIAN PRINTS, Handcolored, Published
By E.C. Biddle, Phila. 1835, Litho By Leman
& Duval, Modern Frames, 17¼″ x 22¾″
.... $230.00
CARVED WOODEN DECOY, Canvas-
back Drake Hi-Head Bobtail, Clinton River,
MI, Ca. 1910, Glass Eyes & Old Worn Re-
paint, 15½″ L. $75.00
CARVED WOODEN DECOY, Bluebill
Drake W/Hump Back & Long Tail, NY,
Glass Eyes & Old Worn Paint, 12½″ L.
.... $65.00
CARVED WOODEN DECOY, Mallard
Drake, WI, Glass Eyes & Old Repaint, Bill
Damage, 14¾″ L. $110.00
BLANKET CHEST, Poplar, Dovetailed,
Repainted Blue W/Red Trim & Yellow Strip-
ing, Strap Hinge Old Replacements, Feet &
Base Molding Repl., Lock Missing, Brass
Hdw. Repl., 51″W., 23″D., 30″H. ... $35.00
CARVED WOODEN DECOY, Bluebill
Drake Bobtail, Hollowed Out Block, Turned
Head An Old Replacement, 15¼″ L. ...$35.00
GROTESQUE STONEWARE JUG,
Greenish Matt Glaze, Incised "Lanier Mead-
ers", 9″ H. $205.00
CARVED WOODEN DECOY, Canvas-
back Drake, Attrib. To Dane Hibbert, MI,
Glass Eyes & Old Weathered Paint, 15¼″ L.
.... $75.00

A-NY May 1980   *Calkins Auction Gallery*
L To R
HITCHING POST, Cast Iron, "Black
Boy", Am., Late 19th C., Blk. Painted Base,
37½″ H. $225.00
CAST IRON JENNY LIND MIRROR,
Am., 19th C., 13″ W., 20″ H. $90.00

A-MA Mar 1980   *Robert W. Skinner Inc.*
SIGN, Gilt & Cast Iron, "Golden Boar Inn",
Imbossed "J.J. Ducel M'de Forges Paris",
France, Late 19th C., 24″ W., 13″ D., 23″ H.
.... $425.00*

*Price does not include 10% buyer fee.

A-OH June 1980   *Garth's Auctions, Inc.*
ENGRAVINGS, 4, (2 Illus.), English, Hand-colored In 1802 & 1803 To Illus. Peter Simon Pallas' Travels, 13½" x 16¼" $50.00
FEDERAL MIRROR, 2-Part, Orig. Reverse Painting, Frame Redecor. Blk., Yellow & Gilt, 13¼" x 31½" $135.00
WINDSOR SIDE CHAIR, Old Worn Finish, Seat: 16¾" H. $215.00
CANDLESTAND, Turned Wood W/Tin Sockets & Polychrome Paint, Henry Ford Museum Reproduction $55.00
WINDSOR SIDE CHAIR, Old Worn Finish, Seat 17¼" H. $215.00
CARVED WOODEN DECOY, Goldeneye Hen From St. Lawrence River, Feather Stamping Old Worn Repaint, Glass Eyes Not Matching, Ca. 1930, 14¾" L. .. $50.00
CARVED WOODEN DECOY, Goldeneye Drake, Tack Eyes, Bill Damage, 13½" L. $30.00

A-OH Mar 1980   *Garth's Auctions, Inc.*
THEOREM ON VELVET, 20th C., Modern Painted Frame, 17¼" x 22½" ... $30.00
VIC. CHILDREN'S PRINTS, Pr., Beveled Maple Birdseye Veneer Frames, "The Playmates", 8½" x 9" $60.00
CARVED WOODEN SHOREBIRD, Driftwood Base, 8¾" H. $50.00
SIDE CHAIRS, Set Of 4 (1 Illus.), Curly & Birdseye Maple, Old Finish $260.00
BEDSIDE STAND, Curly Maple, Dovetailed Drawer, Ref., Repairs, 19¾" x 20¼", 28½" H. $200.00
TIN FOOT WARMER, Pierced Rim & Embossed Crest, Int. Pan For Coals, 7½" x 10½", 5¾" H. $110.00
OVAL TIN FOOD MOLD W/Melon Ribs, 6¼" x 8¼", 4¼" H. $20.00

A-OH April 1980   *Garth's Auctions, Inc.*
TIN CHANDELIER, Made By PA Tinsmith From Tin Covered Walls Of 1845 Tin Shop, 13" O.H. $575.00
WOODEN LIGHTING SHELF, Adjustable, 23¾" H. $175.00
MIRROR, Mahogany On Pine, Old Beveled Mirror, 11½" x 21½" $325.00
WINDSOR SIDE CHAIR, Ref., Rep. Splits In Seat, 18" H. $450.00
INDIAN CARVED WOODEN BOWL, N.W. Coast, Animal Form, Maple W/Worn Finish & Rim Damage, Int. W/Water Damage & Hole, 21" L. $400.00
SM. TAVERN TABLE, Maple Legs, Beaded Pine Apron & 1 Dovetailed Drawer, Pine Bread Board Top, Old Red Paint, 21" x 30½", 25" H. $405.00
INDIAN BASKET, Papago, Br. Design, Ca. 1930, 11" D., 6 " H. $210.00
OVOID REDWARE JAR, Spotted Gr. Glaze, Sm. Rim Flakes & Mismatched Lid, 7½" H. $255.00

◄ A-OH Feb 1980   *Garth's Auctions, Inc.*
SINGLE WEAVE JACQUARD COVERLET, 1 Pc., Sgn. Border "Made By Wm. Ney, Myerstown Lebanon Co. PA", Colors Faded & Overall Wear, 80" Sq. .. $160.00
FISH DECOY, Wooden Body & Metal Fins, 9½" L. $30.00
MAKE DO CAKE STAND, Clear Pressed Base & Tin Top, 11¾" D., 8½" H. .. $80.00
PEWTER INKWELL, Ironstone Insert, 7" D. $125.00
LRG. WOODEN FISH DECOY, Tin Fins Incomplete & Tail Chips, Old Worn Paint, 13¾" L. $60.00
PIE SAFE, Poplar, 6 Punched Tin Panels In Doors, Feet Rep., Old But Not Orig. Gr. Paint, 41½" W., 15½" D., 46¾" H. .. $460.00
CARVED WOODEN DECOY, Worn Blk. W/Working Repaint & Tack Eyes, 11¼" L. $35.00
CARVED WOODEN DECOY, Brandt W/Chipped Bill & Old Worn Blk. Repaint, 17½" L. $40.00

A-OH Feb 1980   *Garth's Auctions, Inc.*
JACQUARD COVERLETS, Pr., Blue & Wh., 2 Pc. Single Weave, Ca. 1837, Both W/Wear, 72" x 90" $350.00
SM. SETTEE, Plank Seat, Shaped Arms, & Spindle Back, Ref., 72" L. $340.00
CARRY ALL, Pine, Ref., 27" L. .. $75.00

A-OH Feb 1980   *Garth's Auctions, Inc.*
IRON WEATHERVANE W/Zinc Running Horse, 33″ L. $105.00
TIN HORN, Orig. Worn Wh. Paint W/Blue & Red Japanning, 19½″ L. $5.00
TIN HORNS, 2, Orig. Worn Blue & Gold Japanning, Wooden Mouth Pc. On Lrg. One, 10¾″ L., 13½″ L. $5.00
TIN HORN, Unpainted, 12¾″ L. $5.00
WOODEN DECOY, Blk. & Wh. Working Repaint, 14″ L. $25.00
HOLLOW WOODEN DECOY, Blk. Duck W/Worn Working Repaint, Glass Eyes Chipped, 13¾″ L. $80.00
BLANKET CHEST, Pine, Orig. Reddish Br. Graining, Lock & Key & Till, 43¾″ W., 20¾″ D., 26″ H. $300.00
CARVED WOODEN DECOY, Old Blk. & Wh. Working Repaint W/Yellow Painted Eyes, 14½″ L. $30.00
STONEWARE CROCK, 4 Gal., Cracked, 11½″ H., ... $60.00
WOODEN DECOY, Old Worn Blk. & Wh. Paint, 14¾″ L. $20.00

A-OH Sept 1980   *Garth's Auctions, Inc.*
BOX, Dovetailed Pine W/Slant Lift Lid, Worn Red-Gr. Repaint, 8½″ x 14¾″, 7½″ H. $25.00
BLANKET CHEST, Poplar, Old Red Paint, Repair, 39¼″ W., 16¼″ D., 22″ H. ... $150.00
WROUGHT IRON TOOLS, 2, Spoon & Fork, Rusted, 17¾″ L. $60.00
SPUN BRASS DIPPER, Wrought Iron Handle, 20¼″ L. $37.50
CARVED DIPPER, Made From 1 Pc. Of Wood, Chip Carved, 9″ L. $45.00
OVAL RYE STRAW BASKET, Flared Foot W/Damage, 6″ x 10″, 3″ H. ... $7.50
HORN, Decor. Of Carved Mermaid, 7″ L. $20.00
METAL SCHOOL BELL, Turned Wooden Handle, Damage To Handle, 10¾″ H. $32.50
BLANKET CHEST, Poplar, Dovetailed Drawers, Till & Orig. Lock, Orig. Worn Red Paint, Minor Repairs, 47″ W., 19¼″ D., 25″ H. $190.00
ROUND WOVEN SPLINT BASKET, Faded Red Design, Some Damage, 16″ D., 11″ H. $12.50

A-OH Sept 1980   *Garth's Auctions, Inc.*
DOLL SIZE CANNON BALL ROPE BED, Orig. Drk. Red Finish W/Stenciled Gilded Flowers, Ball Finials Removed, 7½″ x 11″ $85.00
ROUND SHAKER STORAGE BOX, Finger Const., Lt. Colored Finish, 5″ D. $60.00
BOX, Dovetailed Poplar, Orig. Red & Drk. Br. Striped Graining, Wrought Iron Hasp, Lock W/Brass Escutcheon, 6¼″ x 8″ x 15″ $100.00
LADDER-BACK CHAIR, Doll Size, Orig. Faded Red & Blk. Graining, Woven Splint Seat, 13″ H. $85.00
CAST IRON HITCHING POST, Ring Missing From 1 Side, 63½″ H. $65.00
BLANKET CHEST, Dovetailed Pine, Bracket Feet, Worn Orig. Red & Blk. Graining W/Yellow Striping, Foliage Medallion, 41¼″ W., 16″ D., 21¼″ H. $150.00
BLANKET CHEST, Dovetailed Pine, Till, Orig. Br. Graining, Repair, 44½″ W., 20½″ D, 24¼″ H. $90.00
SEWER TILE VASE, Form Of Tree Trunk, Incised "H.T. Funk", 12″ H. $55.00
REDWARE PITCHER, Sgraffito Decor., "Samuel Rumbelow, Aug. 28th 1881", Repair, 11½″ H. $165.00

A-MA Mar 1980   *Richard A. Bourne Co., Inc.*
SCULPTURES
L To R
PORTRAIT BUST, Benjamin Franklin, Fr. 19th C., Drk. Pat., 11½″ H. $300.00
BRONZE, Benjamin Franklin, 19th C., Wh. Marble Pedestal W/Polished Drk. Marble Base, Gr. Pat., Leans To Left, 12″ O.H. $300.00
BRONZE, Benjamin Franklin, 19th C., Boulle-Style Pedestal, Gr.-Br. Pat., Repaired, 12¼″ O.H. $350.00

◄ A-OH Mar 1980   *Garth's Auctions, Inc.*
DECORATED CHEST OF DRAWERS, Pine, Dovetailed Drawers, Orig. Yellow Paint, Assort. Embossed Brass Pulls, Some Wear To Top Surface, 45½″ W., 22″ D., 43″ O.H. $900.00
PITTSBURGH FLINT TUMBLER, Clear W/8 Panels, 6¼″ H. $12.50
PRESSED HAND LAMP, Clear W/Applied Handle & Brass Collar, 4″ H. $22.50
PRESSED HAND LAMP, Cobalt W/Applied Handle & Brass Collar, 3″ H. .. $42.50
PITTSBURGH BLOWN FOOTED GOBLET, Clear W/Applied Handles & Baluster Stem, 6½″ H. $45.00
PITTSBURGH BLOWN FOOTED ALE, Clear W/Applied Foot & Baluster Stem, 7″ H. $25.00
FOOT STOOL, Mahogany, Old Rep. & Cane Top Needs Restored, 9¼″ x 12¼″, 6″ H. $80.00

A-OH Feb 1980   *Garth's Auctions, Inc.*
OIL ON CANVAS, Framed, 20¾" x 28"
.... $155.00
BRASS VIC. CANDLESTICKS, Pr., W/
Pushups, Marked "The King Of Diamonds",
12⅜" H. $310.00
STAFFORDSHIRE PLAQUE, Orange
Lustre Frame & Blk. Transfer W/Polychrome
Enameling "The Pensioner's Yarn", 8¼" x 9¼"
.... $30.00
DROP LEAF TABLE, Cherry, 22" x 39",
28½" H. $300.00
CANADA GOOSE DECOY, Canvas
Stretched On Wood & Wire Frame W/Wood-
en Head, 25" L. $25.00

A-OH Sept 1980   *Garth's Auctions, Inc.*
GAUDY STICK SPATTERWARE, Gr.
& Blk. Border Design W/Red Strips & Poly-
chrome Floral Centers, 44 Pc. Set, Most W/
Minor Damages $160.00
EMPIRE CHEST OF DRAWERS, Curly
Maple & Cherry, Dovetailed Drawers, Repl.
Wooden Pulls, Ref., 49" W., 24" D., 50" H.
.... $375.00
CAST IRON DOOR STOP, Airdale W/Old
Worn Paint, 8¼" H. $55.00
CAST IRON ALUMINUM DOOR STOP,
Irish Setter W/Flaked Paint, 16" L. .. $20.00

A-OH Mar 1980   *Garth's Auctions, Inc.*
OIL ON CANVAS, Cleaning & Tightening
Necessary, Orig. Beveled Frame & Stretcher,
30" x 34½" $30.00
WOODEN SHOREBIRD, Sickel Billed
Curlew, Factory Decoy, 13¼" H. .. $25.00
EMPIRE INSPIRED BOX, Mahogany, Rep.
& Chipped, 11½" H. $25.00
WOODEN SHOREBIRD, Factory De-
coy 13" H. $20.00
MULE CHEST, Pine, Dovetailed Drawers,
Lift Lid W/Staple Hinges & Till, Brass Bails
Repl., 43¼" W., 16½" D., 37¾" H. .. $450.00
CARVED WOODEN DECOY, Mallard
Hen W/Laminated Body, Glass Eyes, By
Dewey Wright Sr., IL, Ca. 1910, 15" L.
.... $80.00
TURNED BURL MORTAR, Ref., 7" H.
.... $120.00
CARVED WOODEN DECOY, Masons
Broadbill, Glass Eye Missing, Weathered
Paint & Wood, 13" L. $65.00

A-OH Feb 1980   *Garth's Auctions, Inc.*
BRASS VIC. CANDLESTICKS, Pr.,
W/Pushups, 8¾" H. $100.00
WOODEN DOLL HOUSE, Orig. Red &
Wh. Paint W/Clear & Blue Glass Glazed
Windows, Back Opens & Rooms Wired For
Electricity, 12¼" x 19½", 14" H. .. $135.00
HEPPLEWHITE CHEST OF DRAWERS,
Cherry, Dovetailed Cockbeaded Drawers,
Brass Pulls Replacements, 41½" W., 18½" D.,
43¾" H. $700.00
SM. LEMON TOP BRASS ANDIRONS,
Pr. 1 Missing Finial, Blk. From Use & 1 Set
Of Legs Split, 18th C., 13" H. $105.00

A-OH Mar 1980   *Garth's Auctions, Inc.*
CUT OUT WOODEN WEATHERVANE,
Old Blk. Alligatored Paint, 20th C., 25¼" L.
.... $235.00
CARVED WOODEN DECOY, ½ Size Sea
Gull, MI, Orig. Paint & Glass Eyes, 12" L.
.... $115.00
PINE BOX, Orig. Yellow Ochre Paint & Blk.
Brushed Polka-Dots, Replaced Leather Hinges,
6¼" x 7" x 10¼" $140.00
CARVED WOODEN DECOY, Mallard Hen
W/Turned Head, NY, Tack Eyes & Old Worn
Paint, Carved Initials "J.H.O.", 13¼" L. .. $225.00
CARVED WOODEN DECOY, Decor.
Pidgeon Hen Branded "Pete", VA, 1979,
13½" L. $55.00
BLANKET CHEST, Pine, 6 Board, Orig.
Red Paint W/Blk. Striping, 39" W., 17¼" D.,
19¼" H. $400.00
BUCKET, Stave Const., Wire Bail &
Wooden Handle, Orig. Yellow Paint W/Br.
"Stamped" Graining & Vintage, 12" D., 9"
H. $85.00
CARVED WOODEN DECOY, Bluebill
Hen By H.H. Ackerman, MI, Ca. 1950,
Glass Eyes, Old Working Repaint & Shot
Scars, 15½" L. $45.00
CARVED WOODEN DECOY, Bluebill
Hen By Jim Pierce, Havre De Grace, MD,
Stamped "J.P.", Split In Neck & Orig. Paint,
14¼" L. $75.00

A-NY May 1980 *Calkins Auction Gallery*
OIL ON ART BOARD, Am., 19th C., Orig. Gilt Frame, 16″ x 22″ $150.00
PENCIL & WATERCOLOR ON PAPER, Am., 19th C., "Dunmore" Freight Engine W/ Rutland Railroad On Coal Tender, Newly Framed, 13½″ x 11″ $120.00
WOODEN TUB, Painted Red W/Cutout Handles & Lapped Wooden Bands, 18″ D. 12½″ H. $85.00
TOLEWARE TRAY, 19th C., Painted Blk. W/Gold Stenciled Decor. & Floral Border, 20″ x 14¾″ $35.00
OVOID REDWARE CROCK, N. Eng., Early 19th C., Partly Unglazed, Incised Lines Around Shoulder, Some Flaking, 9½″ D., 12″ H. $45.00
BLANKET CHEST, Early 19th C., Grain Painted, Lift Top W/Till, Sgn. B. Coff Or Copp, Repair, 18½″ W., 23¾″ H. .. $225.00
FOOT STOOL, N. Eng., Late 18th Or Early 19th C., Woven Splint Top, Orig. Cond., 14″ L., 11½″ W., 9″ H. $50.00
TIN CANDLE LANTERN, N. Eng., 19th C., Iron Ring Hand Holder, 4¼″ Sq., 17″ H. $70.00
TIN CANDLE LANTERN, 19th C., Footed, Ring Handle, 5″ Sq., 13½″ H. $45.00
HATCHEL W/Cover, 18th C., Tiger Maple Thumb Molded & Notched, Pine Cover Put Together W/Wooden Pins, 24″ L., 6½″ W. 6″ H. $25.00
OVOID STONEWARE CROCK, Made By Orcutt & Wait, MA, Early 19th C., Blue Slip, Cracked, 13″ H. $35.00
EARTHENWARE JAR, 18th C., Br. Glaze At Top, Tan Glaze At Bottom, Few Chips, 15″ H. $55.00

A-OH June 1980 *Garth's Auctions, Inc.* ▶
Q.A. HIGHBOY, Overlapping Dovetailed Drawers, Married & Converted From Flat Top, Repl. Hdw., Ref., 38″ W., 20¼″ D., 81″ H. $3200.00

WRT. IRON ANDIRONS, Pr., Twisted Stems Topped W/Double Sunflowers, 17½″ H. $475.00

A-OH July 1980 *Garth's Auctions, Inc.*
OVERLAY LAMP, Clambroth Base W/ Wh. To Opaque Yellow Gr., Brass Connector & Collar, 2 Sm. Bruises On Base, 14¼″ H. $260.00
OVERLAY LAMP, Stepped Marble & Brass Base W/Bronze & Gold Gilded Stem, Cobalt To Clear Font & Brass Collar, 16¼″ H. $325.00
OVERLAY LAMP, Opaque Wh. Base & Cranberry Font, Brass Connector & Collar, Minor Chips On Base, 13½″ H. .. $375.00
HUNT BOARD, Cherry W/Figured Walnut Veneer Facade, Ref., & Repl. Clear Lacy Knobs, Veneer Damage, PA, 42½″ W., 20″ D., 39″ H. $1250.00
BRASS BALL TOP ANDIRONS, Pr., Matching Brass Log Stops, 12¾″ H. .. $220.00

A-NY May 1980 *Calkins Auction Gallery*
FEDERAL LOOKING GLASS, Gilded Pine, Early 19th C., Reverse Painted Top Panel, Glass Cracked, 15″ W., 29½″ H. $150.00
RIDING ACADEMY SIGN, Carved & Painted, NY, 19th C., 2″ Pc. Of Wood, Blk., Gold, Red & Gr., 30″ L., 14″ W. .. $1100.00
REDWARE JUG, Handled, N. Eng., Early 19th C., Tannish Gr. Glaze, Chip On Bottom, 8″ H. $50.00
OVOID REDWARE JUG, Handled, N. Eng., Early 19th C., Lt. Gr. & Tan Glaze, 7″ H. $40.00
BENNINGTON MIXING BOWL, Sgn., Ca. 1840, Br. Mottled Glaze, Hairline Crack, 13″ D., 3½″ H. $325.00
REDWARE CROCK, Wide Mouth W/Ears, N. Eng., 19th C., Br. & Orange Glaze, Spider In Bottom, 10″ D., 6″ H. ... $25.00
Q. A. SIDE CHAIR, Spanish Foot, N. Eng., 18th C., Rush Seat, Old Drk. Finish, 41½″ O.H. $150.00
HOLLOW PINTAIL HEN DECOY, Carved & Painted, Long Island, Paint Somewhat Worn, 15½″ L. $80.00
EMPIRE CHEST OF DRAWERS, Grain Painted, NY, Ca. 1830, Orig. Sandwich Opalescent Pulls On Top Drawer & Free Blown Glass Pulls On Others, 45″ W., 19¼″ D., 50½″ H. $950.00
REDWARE MILK PAN, N. Eng., 19th C., Unglazed Outside, Yellow Glaze Inside, 14″ D., 3½″ H. $40.00
HOOKED RUG, Am., 19th C., 3 Color Line Border, 28″ x 38″ $65.00
STONEWARE CROCK, 4 Gal. W/Ears, 19th C., Cobalt Blue Decor., 10¼″ D., 13½″ H. $180.00
WOODEN DUCK DECOY, Carved & Painted, Attrib. To Frank Combs, NY, Early 20th C., Some Repaint, 16″ L. .. $100.00
WOODEN DUCK DECOY, Attrib. To Chauncy Wheeler, NY, Early 20th C., Carved & Painted, Some Repaint, 14½″ L. .. $65.00
DOME TOP CHEST, Grain Painted, 19th C., Overall Wavy Blk. Decor. Over Red, Orig. Lock, 19¾″ L., 9½″ W., 9½″ H. .. $400.00
WOODEN WATER BUCKET, N. Eng., Interlocking Wooden Bands & Wooden Swing Handle, Orig. Paint, 13″ D., 11¾″ H. $90.00

A-OH Feb 1980   *Garth's Auctions, Inc.*
OIL ON CANVAS, Orig. Stretcher & New
Frame, 13″ x 29″ $170.00
WOODEN KEG, Turned From 1 Pc. Of
Wood W/Ends Inserted, 8″ H. $7.50
FISH DECOY, Carved Wooden Body
W/Curved Tail & Metal Fins, Old Paint, 5¾″
L. $20.00
WRITING BOX, Walnut, Dovetailed, Ref.,
15″ W., 12″ D., 6¼″H. $105.00
STONEWARE PITCHER, Br. Albany
Slip Decor., 8½″ H. $70.00
EMPIRE JELLY CUPBOARD, Pine,
Paneled Doors & Dovetailed Drawers, Old
Graining Shows Red Beneath, Cast Iron
Latches Incomplete, 43¼″ W., 18¼″D., 44½″
H. $195.00
WOVEN SPLINT BASKET, Some Wear,
10″ x 16″, 8″ O.H. $50.00

A-OH Feb 1980   *Garth's Auctions, Inc.*
PAINTED SIGN, Blk. & Wh., 38¾″ x 13½″
.... $80.00
COPPER WEATHERVANE, Running
Horse, Cast Zinc Head, Bullet Holes & Gr.
Patina W/Traces Of Gold Leaf, Modern
Standard Base, 26½″ L. $265.00
SPINDLE BACK SIDE CHAIR, Ref. &
New Paper Rush Seat $25.00
HANGING PIE SAFE, Poplar Frame, Top
& Bottom Boards W/Tin Punched Side
Panels, 30″ W., 20″ D., 31″ H. $185.00
COPPER FRYING PAN W/Long Wood-
en Handle, 42½″ L. $85.00
CARVED WOODEN DECOY, Eider
Drake From Nova Scotia, Old Worn Work-
ing Repaint, Orig. Keel, 14¾″ L. $25.00

A-OH Mar 1980   *Garth's Auctions, Inc.*
OIL ON ARTIST BOARD, Sgn. "J. Nash",
Old Gilded Frame, 22″ x 28″ $155.00
REDWARE MUG, Br. Running Glaze, Im-
pressed "John Bell, Minor Rim Chip & Hair-
line, 5¾″ H. $435.00
REDWARE FLOWER POT W/Attached
Saucer Base, Running Br. Glaze & Im-
pressed "John Bell", 5¾″ H. $300.00
REDWARE SOAP DISH, Br. Running
Glaze, Impressed "John Bell, Waynesboro",
5¼″ D. $360.00
REDWARE JUG, Br. Running Glaze, Rim
Impressed "John W. Bell, PA", 7¼″ H.
.... $205.00
WOODEN YARN WINDER, Chip Carved
Base & Turned Reel, Click Does Not Work,
29½″ D. $85.00
BLANKET CHEST, Pine, Till Lock Miss-
ing & Rep. To Hinge, Old Red Repaint, 35″
W., 15¾″ D., 18″ H. $105.00
BLANKET CHEST, 6-Board, Poplar W/
Till & Int. Drawer, Orig. Worn Blue Paint,
Replaced Front Foot, 43¾″ W., 18″ D., 22″ H.
.... $85.00
CARVED WOODEN DECOY, Mallard
Hen, Upper Chesapeake Bay, MD, Orig.
Paint, 16¼″ L. $55.00
CARVED WOODEN DECOY, Bufflehead
Hen, Capt. Harry Jobes, MD, Orig. Paint,
14¾″ L. $60.00

A-OH Mar 1980   *Garth's Auctions, Inc.*
OIL ON CANVAS, Cleaned & Profes-
sionally Rebacked, Framed, 19th C., 25¼″
x 29″ $1900.00
COVERED CARDBOARD BOX,Wall-
paper W/Zig-Zag Rim & Domed Lid, Some
Wear & Damage, 6½″ x 9″, 5½″ O.H.
.... $35.00
CHEST OF DRAWERS, Pine, Queen
Anne W/Wide Dovetailing In Case, Dove-
tailed Overlapping Drawers, Worn Old
Reddish Br. Paint & Replaced Brasses, 37¾″
W., 19″ D., 53″ H. $975.00
CARVED WOODEN DECOY, Redhead
Drake By Robert Michels, MI, Ca. 1940,
Glass Eyes & Old Paint W/Few Shot Scars,
16″ L. $50.00

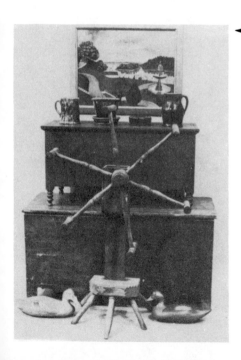

A-NY May 1980   *Calkins Auction Gallery*
WOODEN FOLK ART WHIMSY, Carved
& Painted, NY, Late 19th C., Orig. Paint,
19½″ L., 2½″ W., 12¼″ H. $300.00

A-OH Jan 1980　　　*Garth's Auctions, Inc.*
DECORATED TURTLE BACK BEL-LOWS, Orig. Yellow Paint W/Gr. Border & Stenciled, Brass Nozzle & Deteriorated Leather, 17½″ L. $150.00
SAMPLER ON HOMESPUN, Stains & Some Tears In Upper Border, Gold Leaf Frame, 19¾″ x 23½″ $300.00
SHAKER PIE LIFTER, Wire W/Wooden Handle, 18½″ L. $55.00
REDWARE W/Shiny Glaze, 5½″ H. . .$22.00
CAST IRON FLOWER POT, Urn Shaped, Worn Wh. Paint, 6¼″ H. $20.00
CLAY JAR, Wh. W/Albany Slip, 5¼″ H.
. . . . $10.00
DESK, Cherry, Dovetailed Drawers, Slant Top, Ref., 41½″ W., 18½″ D., 39¼″ O.H.
. . . . $725.00
REDWARE APPLEBUTTER JAR, Clear Speckled Glaze W/Sm. Edge Flakes, 7¼″ H.
. . . . $22.50
TIN STORAGE BOX, 12″ D., 3½″ H.
. . . . $85.00
REDWARE APPLEBUTTER JAR, Lrg. Size, Int. Glaze & Ext. Patina, 8¾″ H.
. . . . $85.00

A-NY May 1980　　　*Calkins Auction Gallery*
CHILD'S ROCKING HORSE, Am., 19th C., 2 Flat Carved Horses, 1 Blk. & 1 Wh., Mounted On Red Rockers, Upholstered Orig., 52″ L., 14″ W., 20″ H. $225.00

A-OH Jan 1980　　　*Garth's Auctions, Inc.*
TOLE URNS, Pr., Fr. W/Polychrome Floral Decor. On Yellow Gr., Cast Grape Finials, 8¼″ H. $350.00
DELFT CHARGER, Polychrome Floral Center W/Swag Decor. Rim, Old Minor Edge Flakes & Rim Hairline, Late 19th C., 13″ D. $160.00
CHIPPENDALE CHEST OF DRAW-ERS, Mahogany, Dovetailed Drawers, Replaced Brasses, Old Mellow Finish, 34¼″ H. $2600.00

A-OH July 1980　　　*Garth's Auctions, Inc.*
OVERLAY LAMP, Stepped Marble & Brass Base, Opaque Wh. Cut To Opaque Gr. W/ Brass Collar & Connector, Plugged Hole, 16¾″ H. $1625.00
TRIPLE OVERLAY LAMP, Marble Foot, Gilded Brass Stem, Blue Cut To Clear Font, Brass Collar, Worn Stenciled Vintage Design, Sm. Split, 14″ H. $350.00
TRIPLE OVERLAY LAMP, Opaque Blue Base & Blue Cut To Wh. Cut To Clear Font, Cracks, 12¾″ H. $360.00
OVERLAY LAMP, Stepped Marble & Brass Base, Opaque Wh. Cut To Cranberry Font W/Worn Gilding, 11¾″ H. . . $350.00
DUNCAN PHYFE DROP LEAF TABLE, Mahogany, Dovetailed Cockbeaded Drawer, Drawer Pull Repl. & Worn Finish, 22½″ x 39″, 12″ Leaves, 27½″ H. $400.00

A-OH Feb 1980　　　*Garth's Auctions, Inc.*
WOODEN STICK UP DECOY, Canada Goose W/Old Worn Paint & Adj. Head, 20″ L.
. . . . $110.00
SHEET METAL STICK UP DECOY, Canada Goose W/Old Worn Paint & Adj. Head, Rod Gone, 20½″ L. $65.00
SHEET METAL STICK UP DECOY, Canada Goose W/Old Worn Paint, Wrought Iron Rod, 19″ H. $65.00
KNIFE BOX, Walnut, Dovetailed, Old Worn Finish, 14¼″ x 10½″ $145.00
SM. CHEST OF DRAWERS, Cherry, Dovetailed Drawers, Ref., New Corner Blocks, 38″ W., 18½″ D., 34¾″ H. . . $375.00
WOVEN SPLINT BASKET, Old Rim Repair, 13″ x 17½″, 8½″ O.H. $30.00

Left
A-MA Aug 1980　　　*Robert W. Skinner Inc.*
CARVED FIGURE, Pine Standing Indian, Gilt Highlighting On Unfinished Pine, Am., 20th C., 66″ H. $700.00*

Right
A-NY May 1980　　　*Calkins Auction Gallery*
CAST IRON HITCHING POST, Painted, "Black Sambo", 19th C., Orig. Cond., 45″ H.
. . . . $250.00

A-OH Mar 1980   *Garth's Auctions, Inc.*
THEOREM ON VELVET, 20th C., Framed, 20″ x 24″ $200.00
DECORATED BOX, Pine & Poplar, Orig. Paint, Wooden Hinges & Hand Made Hasp, Dated "1836", 16½″ W., 10¼″ D., 12¼″ H. $875.00
CARVED WOODEN CARDINAL W/ Hinged Tin Wings, Worn Orig. Red & Blk. Paint, 11¼″ H. $165.00
CARVED WOODEN SHOREBIRD, Blk. Bellied Plover, VA, 10½″ H. $45.00
BLANKET CHEST, Poplar, Old Hat Wing Escut. & Worn Red Paint, 32″ W., 17½″ D., 19½″ H. $275.00
CARVED WOODEN DECOY, Blue Bill Hen, MI, Glass Eyes, Turned Head & Carved Wing Detail, Orig. Paint, 11½″ L. $80.00
WOODEN STORAGE BOX, 4 Finger Const. W/Copper Tacks, Worn & Alligatored Gr. Paint, 10″ x 13¾″, 5″ H. .. $215.00

A-MA Aug 1980   *Robert C. Eldred Co., Inc.*
SHAKER COVERED BOX W/Handle, Curly Maple & Pine, 9½″ x 6½″, 3½″ H. $170.00
SHAKER COVERED BOX, Drk. Br. Stain, 10″ D., 2¼″ H. $130.00
SHAKER COVERED BOX, Med. Br. Stain, 9¾″ x 7¼″ x 3″ $130.00
LRG. SHAKER COVERED BOX, Waxed Natural Finish, 12″ x 15″, 6½″ H. .. $175.00

A-OH Mar 1980   *Garth's Auctions, Inc.*
WROUGHT IRON WEATHERVANE, 60″ L. $75.00
WROUGHT IRON BALANCE SCALES, Wire Hook Added, 17½″ L. $65.00
WROUGHT IRON STRAP HINGES, Pr., From Blanket Chest, 40½″ L. $45.00
KRAUT CUTTER, Ash W/Heart Cut Out & Heart Shaped Thumb Screws, 19½″ L. $55.00
WROUGHT IRON GRISETTE LIGHTING DEVICE, Old Rep., 14¼″ H. .. $30.00
WROUGHT IRON BROILER, Made To Hang Over Fire Place Rod, Brass Knob On Rod, 12¼″ L. $90.00
BRASS SPOUT LAMP W/Weighted Base, Polished & Soldered Rep., 19½″ H. $45.00
BLANKET CHEST, Poplar, Dovetailed, Orig. Red & Blk. Graining, Lock Missing, 40¾″ W., 19½″ D., 22½″ H. $260.00
TIN CANDLE LANTERN, Replaced Glass, 13″ O. H. $465.00
TIN CANDLE LANTERN W/Vent Top, Sliding Glass Panel Replacement, Rust, 11½″ H. $145.00

A-OH Mar 1980   *Garth's Auctions, Inc.*
POLITICAL BANNER, Tear Over Eagle, 2′ 11″ x 11′ 5″ $40.00
BLK. & WH. LITHOGRAPH, "Patriae Pater", Shadow Box Frame W/Gilded Liner, 22″ x 26¼″ $25.00
BLK. & WH. ENGRAVING, "Theodore Roosevelt", Sgn. "Sidney L Smith", Old Oak Frame, 26¾″ x 33½″ $70.00
BLK. & WH. ENGRAVING, Painting Of Thomas Jefferson By Gilbert Stuart, Sgn. "Albert Rosenthal" Engraver, Old Frame, 23¼″ x 27½″ $30.00
MAMMY'S BENCH, Arm Repair, Ref., & Baby Guard Missing, 85″ L. $275.00
WOODEN DOLL BUGGY, Metal Rim Wood Spoke Wheels, Orig. Painted Leatherized Cloth Top W/Fringe, 34″ L. .. $305.00
WOODEN HORSE PULL TOY, Saddle & Bridle Worn, 15¼″ L. $165.00

A-NY May 1980   *Calkins Auction Gallery*
OIL ON CANVAS, Portrait Of Lady Holding Dog, Ca. 1840, Hardboard Mounting, Orig. Gilt Frame, 32″ x 38″ $175.00
TIN CANDLE LANTERN, N. Eng., 19th C., Blk. Paint, 1 Wire Guard Missing, 4½″ Sq., 14″ H. $45.00
CANDLE BOX, Pine W/Sliding Cover, N. Eng., Early 19th C., Painted Drk. Gr., Nailed Const., Wrought Nails, 12½″ L., 7½″ W., 6″ H. $50.00
STONEWARE BUTTER CROCK, 19th C., Cobalt Blue Decor., 7″ D., 4″ H. $140.00
BIRD CAGE WINDSOR ARM CHAIR, Sgn. C. Sheppard, Ca. 1820, Worn Varnish Finish, Repair To 1 Leg, 30½″ O.H. .. $300.00
HEPPLEWHITE BLANKET CHEST, Grain Painted, 2 Drawer, Early 19th C., Orig. Brasses, 39″ W., 18″ D., 36½″ H. $375.00
SHERATON WASH STAND, Painted & Decor., 19th C., Dovetailed, 16″ W., 13½″ D., 35″ H. $100.00
WINDSOR FOOT STOOL, Painted Gr., N. Eng., Early 19th C., 13″ L., 6″ W., 5½″ H. $30.00
MILK PAN, Yellowware, 19th C., 13″ D., 3½″ H. $35.00
REDWARE SPITTOON, N. Eng., 19th C., Mottled Br. & Yellow Glaze, 8″ D., 4¾″ H. $45.00
OVOID STONEWARE JUG, NY, 19th C., Cobalt Blue Decor., 13″ H. $50.00
REDWARE BEAN POT W/Handle, N. Eng., 19th C., Partly Unglazed, 7½″ D., 6″ H. $15.00

A-OH Mar 1980   *Garth's Auctions, Inc.*
OIL ON WOODEN PANEL, Minor Dents & Restor. Needed, Old Gilt Frame 24½″ x 32½″ $175.00
REDWARE PIE PLATE, 3 Line Yellow Slip Design, Coggled Edge & Minor Edge Chips, 9¾″ D. $125.00
TIN CANDLE MOLD, 24-Tube, Side Handles Flattened, 11″ H. $75.00
WROUGHT IRON RUSH LIGHT HOLDER W/Candle Socket Counterweight, Wooden Base Replacement, 10½ H. $135.00
REDWARE PIE PLATE, Worn 3 Line Yellow Slip Design, Coggled Edge, 9 3/8″ D. $105.00
MULE CHEST, Pine, Nailed Drawer, Lift Lid, Orig. Red Graining, 39″ W., 14½″ D., 32″ O.H. $250.00
CAST IRON SCREW PRESS, Orig. Blk. Paint W/Gilded Designs, 9″ x 11¾″ .. $45.00

A-NY May 1980   *Calkins Auction Gallery*
FOLK ART CUT OUT FIGURE, Uncle Sam, Early 20th C., Red, Wh. & Blk., 33″ W., 75″ H. $75.00
CURRIER & IVES PRINT, "Genesta", Ca. 1885, Matted, Some Water Stain, 17″ x 19¾″ $100.00
FOLK ART ADVERTISING SIGN, Echo Cigars, Late 19th C., Oil On Canvas, Minor Repair To Canvas, 27½″ W., 37″ H. .. $185.00

A-OH Mar 1980   *Garth's Auctions, Inc.*
DOME TOP BOX, Dovetailed, Poplar, Orig. Lock & Hasp, 14″ x 24″, 12¾″ H. $450.00
CHEST OF DRAWERS, Maple, Dovetailed Case & Drawers, Old Worn Red Paint & Replaced Brasses & Escut., Orig. Cornice Split & Damaged At One End, 40″ W., 19″ D., 44″ H. $300.00
WROUGHT IRON STRAP HINGES, Set Of 4 (2 Illus.), Old Worn Gr. Paint, 29½″ To 32″ L. $80.00

———————————————

A-OH Mar 1980   *Garth's Auctions, Inc.*
DRAWING, Pen, Ink, & Watercolor, "The Saturn", Sm. Tear In Left Margin, Framed, 27¼″ x 42″ $300.00
CARVED WOODEN DECOY, Bluebill Hen, MI, Ca. 1920, Glass Eyes & Worn Paint, Age Crack In Block, 10¼″ H. .. $40.00
CARVED WOODEN DECOY, Redhead Drake, WI, Ca. 1940, Glass Eyes, Balsa Body, Worn Repaint, 12½″ L. $35.00
WATER BENCH, Pine, Worn Grey Paint Shows Blue Beneath, 43½″ W., 12½″ D., 39″ H. $475.00
CARVED WOODEN DECOY, Bufflehead Drake, MI, Ca. 1930, Glass Eyes, Worn Working Repaint W/Age Cracks In Block & Split In Bill, 13″ L. $50.00
SM. REDWARE SPITTOON, Br. Sponged Glaze, Short Hairline & Minor Edge Flakes, 5¼″ D. $140.00
CARVED WOODEN DECOY, Hollow Bluebill Drake, Lake Ontario, Ca. 1910, Old Paint, Shot Scars, 13½″ L. $60.00
STONEWARE JUG, Simple Brushed Cobalt Design, Label "A. Clark, Jr. Athens, NY", 14″ H. $95.00
OVOID STONEWARE JUG, Simple Brushed Cobalt Design, Impressed Label "L. Norton & Son", 10¾″ H. $250.00
STONEWARE JUG, 2 Gal., Floral Design In Cobalt Slip, Impressed Label "J. Norton & Co. Bennington, VT", 13½″ H. .. $305.00

A-OH Sept 1980   *Garth's Auctions, Inc.*
TOLE TRAY, Orig. Blk. Paint W/Polychrome Scene, Minor Touch-Up Repair, 29″ L. $105.00
CARVED SHOREBIRD, Branded "B", 12½″ H. $60.00
CARVED WOODEN SHOREBIRD, Hollow Redhead Drake, Attrib. To Benjamin Elsholtz, MI, Old Worn Paint, Neck Repair, 14″ L. $60.00
CARVED WOODEN SHOREBIRD, Mate To Above, Glued Break In Neck, 14″ L. $50.00
CARVED WOODEN SHOREBIRD, Base Branded "Richard Morgan", 10¾″ H. $75.00
HEPPLEWHITE CHEST OF DRAWERS, Dovetailed-Cockbeaded Drawers, Cherry, Repl. Brass Knobs, Feet Ended Out, Ref., 42½″ W., 20½″ D., 42¼″ H. $625.00
CARVED WOODEN DECOY, Blk. Duck From Kettle Point, IN, Worn Old Repaint, 16″ L. $70.00

A-OH Feb 1980 *Garth's Auctions, Inc.*
OIL ON CANVAS, Sgn. "F. Lincoln 1963",
Framed, 13¼" x 15½" $9.00
OIL ON CANVAS, Mate To Above, 13¼"
x 15½" $5.00
SM. BRASS CANDLESTICKS, Pr., W/
Pushups, 6" H. $77.50
INKWELL, Clear Pressed Swirled Well In
Brass Stand, 8¼" Sq., 7¼" H. $150.00
HEPPLEWHITE SLANT TOP DESK,
Cherry, Dovetailed & Cockbeaded Drawers,
Ref. W/Repairs To Lid, Replaced Brasses &
Feet, 38½" W., 21" D., 44" O.H. .. $1320.00

A-OH Sept 1980 *Garth's Auctions, Inc.*
METAL SCHOOL BELL, Turned Curly
Maple Handle, 10⅜" H. $35.00
REDWARE SGRIFFITO BOWL, Stamped
"GVP 1970", Gr.-Br. Glaze Design, 15¾"
D., 4½" H. $35.00
REDWARE JUG, Slip Design Gr. W/Cream
Spots, Cracked, Not Am., 9" H. .. $10.00
SLANT TOP DESK, On Frame, Curly
Maple, Dovetailed Drawers, Birdseye Lid,
Repl. Brasses, Finish On Lid Worn, 37¼" W.,
18¾" D., 44½" H. $2650.00
CAST IRON DOOR STOP, Boxer W/Old
Worn Paint, 9½" H. $25.00
CAST IRON DOOR STOP, Rabbit W/Old
Worn Paint, 10¼" H. $110.00
CAST IRON DOOR STOP, Boxer W/Old
Worn Paint, 8½" H. $25.00

◄ A-OH Mar 1980 *Garth's Auctions, Inc.*
OIL ON CANVAS, Rebacked & Rep. To
Background, Shadow Box Frame, 19th C.,
21¾" x 26½" $375.00
CLAMBROTH CANDLESTICKS, Pr.,
Chips, 8¾" H. $120.00
BLOWN PITTSBURGH COMPOTE,
Clear W/Applied Foot, Baluster Stem & Lid
W/Applied Finial, Broken Blister & Sm.
Flakes, 10" H. $55.00
DOME TOP BOX, Orig. Decor., Poplar,
Orig. Leather Hinges, 5½" x 9¼", 5¼" H.
.... $270.00
SANDWICH VASE, Canary, 10" H. ....
.... $175.00
SLANT FRONT DESK, Maple W/Dove-
tailed Feet, Case, & Drawers, Old Worn Br.
Steel Comb Graining, Oval Embossed Eagle
Brasses Old Replacements, 38" W., 19¼"
D., 43¼" O.H. $3500.00
CARVED WOODEN DECOY, Bluebill
Drake, MI, Ca. 1930, Glass Eyes & Old
Worn Working Repaint, 14" L. $50.00
CARVED WOODEN DECOY, Mallard
Hen, Canada, Ca. 1930, Old Working
Repaint & Bill Repair, 15½" L. $40.00

A-OH June 1980 *Garth's Auctions, Inc.*
CORNER CUPBOARD, Cherry, 1-Pc., Repl.
Cornice, 51" W., 83½" H. $900.00
CARVED WOODEN DECOY, Canada
Goose, Old Blk. & Wh. Repaint, Barnegat Bay,
N.J., 23¾" L. $105.00

A-OH Oct 1980 *Garth's Auctions, Inc.*
WALL CUPBOARD, 2-Pc., Walnut, Dove-
tailed Case, Drawers & Pie Shelf, Cove
Molded Cornice, Minor Repairs, 60½" W.,
20" D., 88" H. $1700.00
ROCKINGHAM SEATED DOG, Sm.
Chips & Flakes, 10¾" H. $135.00
ROCKINGHAM BOWL, Base Chips &
Hairline, 13" D., 5¾" H. $35.00
ROCKINGHAM PITCHER, 9" H.
.... $45.00
WOVEN SPLINT BASKET, Covered, 2
Wooden Handles, Faded Red Design, Minor
Damages, 13¾" x 20", 10" H. $50.00

A-OH June 1980   *Garth's Auctions, Inc.*
ELI TERRY CLOCK, Mahogany Case, Orig. Label, CT, Works Repl. W/Spring Driven Movement, Orig. Painted Wood Face, Reversed Painting In Door Has Res. & Finials Repl., Repair To Crest, 31¼″ H.
.... $350.00
PEWTER PLATE, Continental Touch, 8⅜″ D.
.... $75.00
PEWTER PLATE, "Made In London, Townsend", Touch Marks, 8¼″ D. $55.00
HEPPLEWHITE DROP LEAF TABLE, Cherry, Boards In Top & Leaves Old Replacements, Leaves Braced, Old Worn Ref., 20½″ x 47½″, 19″ Leaves, 29½″ H. .. $255.00
PEWTER SOUP PLATE, Continental Touch Marks, 11″ D. $85.00
PEWTER CHARGER, 20th C., 13″ D.
.... $25.00
PEWTER TALL COFFEE POT, Wooden Handle, "James Dixon & Sons", 13½″ H.
.... $145.00
PEWTER PLATE, Knife Scratches & Repair, Engraved Rim W/Initials & Date 1871, 9⅛″ D. $65.00

A-OH Jan 1980   *Garth's Auctions, Inc.*
WATERCOLOR MEMORIAL, "Abigail Duke, Died October 24th, 1789", Damage At Inscription, Framed, 12¼″ x 13″ .. $250.00
REDWARE OVID JUG, Minor Glaze Flaking At Lip, 6″ H. $125.00
HANGING BOX, Orig. Yellow W/Gr. Paint, Made From Cigar Boxes, 10½″ x 10½″ x 4¾″ $175.00
CARVED TOBACCO BOX, Walnut, 8″ H. $85.00
SCHOOL MASTERS DESK, Pine, Dovetailed Removable Slant Top Desk W/ Fitted Int., Dovetailed Drawers, Bottom 2 Drawers Added, Old Worn Red Paint, 31¾″ W., 22″ D., 38½″ H. $450.00
STEP DOWN WINDSOR SIDE CHAIR, Orig. Worn Red Paint, Splits In Seat, 17½″ Seat H. $175.00
STONEWARE CROCK, 6 Gal., Cobalt Blue Slip Decor., Hairline, 13½″ H. .. $65.00
STONEWARE BUTTER CROCK W/ LID, Cobalt Blue Brushed Design, Sgn, "John Bell, Waynesboro", Hairline In Base, 9″ D. $575.00

A-NY May 1980   *Calkins Auction Gallery*
SANDPAPER PICTURE, Wh., Gray, Gr. & Blk., Ca. 1835, Gold Frame, 11½″ x 13½″
.... $265.00
OIL ON CANVAS, Portrait Of Young Boy In Military Uniform, Ca. 1830, Gilt Frame, Mounted On Hardboard, Damage To Frame, 15″ x 17″ $200.00
SANDPAPER PICTURE, Wh., Gray, Gr. & Blk. Tortoise Shell & Gilt Frame, 13″ x 14¾″ $275.00
TOLEWARE BUN TRAY, Blk. Ground W/ Gold Decor., 9¼″ W., 13½″ L. ... $55.00
TOLEWARE CADDY, Painted Blk. W/Red & Yellow Decor., 4⅛″ D., 8″ H. ... $50.00
SHERATON CHEST OF DRAWERS, Painted Yellow & Burnt Umber Swirl Decor., Ca. 1820, Orig. Brasses, 41″ W., 18½″ D., 42″ H. $785.00
RECTANGULAR BOX, Pine W/Orig. Red Paint, Nailed Const., 24″ L., 10″ W., 9″ H.
.... $265.00
HOOKED RUG, Am., Multicolored Geometric Design, 28″ W., 43″ L. $95.00
SPLINT BASKET W/Fixed Handle, 14″ D., 9″ H. $50.00

A-OH Aug 1980   *Garth's Auctions, Inc.*
OIL ON ARTISTS BOARD, Vic. Woman, Sgn. "W.M. Weisse", Gilt Frame, 27½″ x 31¼″
.... $145.00
BLK. & WH. ETCHING, Fitted, Numbered, Sgn. In Pencil "Debussy 74/250, Sidney Chafetz", 14½″ x 18¾″ $25.00
SHERATON CORNER WASHSTAND, Mahogany, Eng., 1 Dovetailed Drawer W/ Fake Drawers, 25½″ W., 18″ D., 43″ H.
.... $300.00
STAFFORDSHIRE FIGURE, Little Red Riding Hood & Wolf, Polychrome Enamel, 10″ H. $55.00
BED STEPS, Mahogany W/Turned Legs, Lift Top, Slide Out Commode Drawer, Top Step W/Hinged Lid, Tooled Leather On Steps, 19″ W., 27″ D., 26″ H. ... $150.00
STAFFORDSHIRE FIGURE, Lion W/ Animal, Repaired, Polychrome Enameling, 11″ H. $40.00

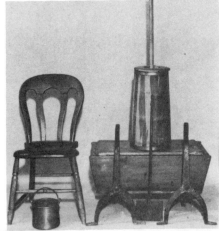

A-OH Feb 1981   *Garth's Auctions, Inc.*
CHURN, Stave Const., Brass Bands & Orig. Dasher, 19″ H. $35.00
SIDE CHAIRS, Pr. (1 Illus.), Balloon Back, Ref. $100.00
CAST IRON WAFFLE IRON W/Wrought Iron Handles, 28¼″ L. $25.00
DOUGH BOX, Poplar, Ref., 14″ x 28½″
.... $75.00
WROUGHT IRON ANDIRONS, Pr., 22″ H. $32.50
COPPER PAN W/Wire Bale Handle, 5″ H.
.... $85.00

A-NY May 1980   *Calkins Auction Gallery*
OILS ON CANVAS, Pr. Am., Ca. 1835, Orig. Mustard Yellow Frames, Annonymous, Repair To Portrait Of Lady, 35¼″ x 41¾″
.... $2300.00
DECORATED CHAIRS, Set Of 6, (2 Illus.), NY, 19th C., Cane Seats Are New, Mahogany Graining, 35″ O.H. $600.00
DECORATED FOOT WARMER, Wood, Tin, Glass, Brass & Iron, NY, Ca. 1865, Mfg. By B.F. Sanborn, 8¼″ L., 5½″ W., 9½″ H.
.... $160.00
DECORATED DRESSING TABLE, Late 18th Or Early 19th C., Orig. Cond., Sm. Amount Of Wear On Top, 36¼″ W., 20½″ D., 28″ H. $525.00
STONEWARE COOLER, 4-Gal., Barrel Shaped, 19th C., Molded & Multi-Colored Decor., Cracked, 10½″ D., 12½″ H. ..$110.00
BOAT CANDLE LANTERN, Brass & Glass, Early 19th C., Opens From The Bottom, Candle Holder Missing, 6″ D., 13¼″ H.
.... $70.00
DOME TOP BOX, Grain Painted, Early 19th C., Dovetailed, Orig. Lock, Repair To Crack In Top, 25″ L., 12¼″ W., 12¾″ H.
.... $350.00
WOODEN MORTAR & PESTLE, Turned & Painted, Am., 19th C., Retains Most Orig. Red Paint, 6½″ D., 7¾″ H. $100.00
OVOID CROCK, Cobalt Blue Slip Decor., Incised Lines, Tiny Chips, 13″ H. .. $45.00

A-OH Oct 1980   *Garth's Auctions, Inc.*
TIN MOLD, Rabbit, ½ Only, 15½″ H.
.... $30.00
OVAL BENTWOOD STORAGE BOX, Worn Old Blue Paint, 5″ x 6½″.... $100.00
OVAL BENTWOOD STORAGE BOX, Copper Tacks, Watervliet Shaker, 7¼″ x 10⅝″ $145.00
CARVED WOODEN MORNING DOVE, Tack Eyes, Old Repairs, Modern Base, 7¾″ L. $35.00
OVAL BENTWOOD STORAGE BOX, Watervliet Shaker, 5¼″ x 7″ $95.00
ROUND BENTWOOD STORAGE BOX, Mt. Lebanon, NY, Shaker, Rim Split, Traces Of Gr. Paint, 7½″ D. $65.00
SHAKER HERB CHEST, Walnut W/Poplar Ends, Dovetailed Drawers, Restorations, Ref., 39″ W., 25¾″ D., 46″ H. $800.00
OVAL BENTWOOD STORAGE BOX, Multiple Finger Const., Copper Tacks, Watervliet, 8½″ x 11½″, 4¾″ H. .. $165.00
WOODEN SUGAR BUCKET, Stave Const., Old Grey Paint, Canterbury, NH, 9½″ H. $75.00

A-OH April 1980   *Garth's Auctions, Inc.*
PEWTER PLATE, 2 Eagle Touch Marks, "S.D.", 8″ D. $85.00
TIN CANDLESTICKS, Pr., W/Sand Weighted Bases & Pushups W/Turned Brass Knobs, 9¾″ H. $150.00
PEWTER CHARGER, Mkd. W/4 Cartouche Of Thomas Danforth Family W/ "T.D.", 13¼″ D. $300.00
PEWTER TEA POT, Mkd. "L.J. Curtiss", Handle Reattached, 8″ H. $195.00
PEWTER PLATE, Eagle Touch & "T. Danforth", 7¾″ D. $420.00
HEPPLEWHITE CHEST OF DRAWERS, Pine, Dovetailed Drawers W/Wooden Knobs, Old Red Paint, Pc. Of Front Foot Missing, 40¾″ W., 18½″ D., 37″ H. ... $550.00
OVOID STONEWARE JUG, Incised Swag Design W/Cobalt Blue, "Commeraws Stoneware", Base Chips & Handle Restored, 12″ H. $255.00
STONEWARE JUG, Floral Design In Cobalt Blue Slip, Impressed "J. & E. Norton, Bennington VT", 10¾″ H. $265.00

A-NY May 1980   *Calkins Auction Gallery*
WEATHERVANE, Tin & Wood, NY, Late 19th C., Weathered W/Traces Of Old Blk. & Wh. Paint, Arms Of Hunter Missing, 29½″ L., 12″ H. $50.00

*Price does not include 10% buyer fee.

Left
A-MA Feb 1980   *Robert W. Skinner Inc.*
COPPER WEATHERVANE, Horse & Rider, Am., Ca. 1900, 31″ L. $1500.00*

Right
A-MA Oct 1980   *Robert W. Skinner Inc.*
COPPER WEATHERVANE, Hackney Horse, Lead Head, Am., Early 20th C., 7½″ W., 33″ D., 27″ H. $1250.00*

Left
A-MA Oct 1980   *Robert W. Skinner Inc.*
COPPER WEATHERVANE FIGURE, Cow, Gilt Finish, Am., Early 20th C., 28″ L., 10″ H. $450.00*

Right
A-NY May 1980   *Calkins Auction Gallery*
COW WEATHERVANE, Copper & Zinc, Molded & Gilded, 19th C., Few Bullet Holes & Minor Damage, 33″ L., 21″ H. .. $650.00

A-OH Jan 1980   *Garth's Auctions, Inc.*
REDWARE JAR, Br. Speckled Glaze, Rim Flake, 5″ H. $17.50
TIN CANDLE MOLD, 12 Tubes, Base Of Handle Loose, 10½″ H. $40.00
PRINTED FRAKTUR, "Taufschein" Certificate, Printed In "Ephrata" By "G. Baumann", PA, Ca. 1810, Modern Gr. Frame, 15¾″ x 18¾″ $165.00
PUNCHED TIN PAUL REVERE LANTERN, 14″ O.H. $105.00
REDWARE JAR W/Br. Speckled Int. Glaze, Impressed "H", 4½″ H. $60.00
FIREPLACE MANTLE, Pine, OH, Old Worn Blk. Paint, Opening: 29″ x 35″, 51″ W., 7″ D., 53″ H. $35.00
TIN CANDLE LANTERN, 3 Glass Panes Protected By Wire & Sliding Tin Door, 1 Wire Replaced, 12½″ H. $90.00
DOUBLE LEMON TOP BRASS ANDIRONS, Pr., 18th C., 19¼″ H. $550.00

Left
A-MA May 1980   *Paul J. Dias, Inc.*
LIGHTNING ROD WEATHERVANE, W.C. Schinn Mfg. Co., Glass Ball & Zinc Car, 1 Side Shows Damage, 47″ x 27½″ $175.00

Right
A-NY May 1980   *Calkins Auction Gallery*
FOLK ART SHEET IRON WEATHERVANE, Painted, N. Eng., 19th C., Part Of 1 Foot Missing, 28″ H. $300.00

A-OH July 1980   *Garth's Auctions, Inc.*
HISTORICAL BLUE STAFFORDSHIRE PLATE, Med. Blue Transfer "South Carolina", Wear & Flakes, 7½″ D. $250.00
TABLE TOP DESK, Cherry, Dovetailed, Base Molding Missing, Old Varnish Finish, 34″ W., 17″ D., 13″ H. $350.00
HISTORICAL BLUE STAFFORDSHIRE PLATE, Drk. Blue Transfer "Commodore MacDonnough's Victory", Impressed "E. Wood & Sons", Edge & Glaze Wear, 9¼″ D. $250.00
HISTORICAL BLUE STAFFORDSHIRE PLATE, Med. Drk. Blue Transfer "Library Philadelphia", I. & W. Ridgway, 8¼″ D. $175.00
HISTORICAL BLUE STAFFORDSHIRE PLATE, Drk. Blue Transfer "The Valentine", Impressed "Clews", Minor Knife Scratches & Flakes, 9″ D. $75.00
CHIPPENDALE CHEST OF DRAWERS, Mahogany, Serpentine, Dovetailed Drawers, Repair Needed, 43¾″ W., 21⅜″ D., 40″ W. $4600.00

A-NY May 1980   *Calkins Auction Gallery*
FISH WEATHERVANE, Carved, 19th C., Red Paint Over Orig. Salmon Color, 20″ L. $150.00

A-NY May 1980   *Calkins Auction Gallery*
FOLK ART TINSEL PICTURE, 19th C., NY, Orig. Walnut Frame W/Gold Liner, 21″ x 25″ $400.00
WATERCOLOR ON PAPER, Am., Stenciled & Free Hand, 19th C., Matted & Framed, 27½″ x 32½″ $2100.00
LOOKING GLASS, Pine, N. Eng., Ca. 1820-1830, Stenciled Sections Ebonized, Remainder Is Mahogany, 17½″ W., 36¾″ H. $200.00
BELLOWS, Painted & Decor., Pine, Leather & Brass, NY, Ca. 1820, Shows Wear, 17½″ L. $65.00
SHAKER BASKET W/Swing Handle, NY, 19th C., 7¾″ D., 5″ H. $190.00
OVOID REDWARE JAR W/Double Handle, N. Eng., 19th C., Incised Lines, Orange Glaze W/Umber Splotches, Few Chips, 9″ D., 9″ H. $95.00
REDWARE DEEP DISH, Glazed W/Slip Decor., 19th C., 13½″ L., 10¾″ W., 2½″ H. $80.00
SHERATON CHEST OF DRAWERS, Vinegar & Putty Grain Painted, 19th C., Brasses Repl., Paint Restoration To Top, 42¼″ W., 18¾″ D., 44¼″ H. $1100.00
CHILD'S ROCKER, Painted & Decor., PA, 19th C., 23″ O.H. $435.00
FOLK ART WOODEN GREBE DECOY, Carved & Painted, Long Island, 19th C., Weathered, 11″ L. $75.00
WINDSOR FOOT STOOL, Cross Stretchered, N. Eng., Early 19th C., Needlepoint Top & Old Finish On Base, 12½″ L., 8″ W., 8″ H. $45.00
DOME TOP BOX, Grain Painted, 19th C., 18¾″ L., 9¼″ W., 8½″ H. $275.00
TOLEWARE FIREPLACE COAL BOX & TOOL HOLDER, Am., 19th C., Decor., Minor Paint Damage On Portrait, 13½″ W., 18″ D., 24½″ H. $200.00

◄ A-MA Aug 1980   *Robert C. Eldred Co., Inc.*
PEDDLER'S CART, Iron-Banded Wooden Wheels, PA, 50″ L. $1300.00

A-OH Sept 1980   *Garth's Auctions, Inc.*
WOVEN PLAQUES, Set Of 3, Single Star Designs Are Papago, Double Star Is Pima, 8″ To 10½″ D. $110.00
GALLUP THROW, 2 Yei Figures In Br./-Red/-Orange On Wh. Ground, 17″ x 34″ $65.00
REDWARE PIE PLATE, 3 Line Yellow Slip Design, Worn & Old Chips, 10″ D. . . $50.00
REDWARE CHARGER, Yellow Slip Puddles, Hairline, 12½″ D. $155.00
REDWARE PIE PLATE, 3 Line Yellow Slip Design, Worn & Old Chips, 10″ D. . . $25.00
APPLIQUE WOOL PENNY RUG, Blk. Braided Edge, Some Wear, 28″ x 46″ . . . $75.00
CHEST, Poplar, Applied Cut-Outs Form Apron, Overlapping Dovetailed Drawers, 2 Fake Drawers W/Lift Top, Tooled Brass Hdw. Old Repl., Worn Blue Paint W/Color Beneath, 40″ W., 18½″ D., 43½″ H. . . . $700.00
CARVED WOODEN DECOY, Canvasback, W/Worn Old Paint, 14¾″ L. . . $20.00
CARVED WOODEN DECOY, Bluebill Drake, Evans Factory 1921-32, Orig. Worn Paint, Glass Eyes, Neck Joint Glued, 15¼″ L. $85.00

A-OH April 1980   *Garth's Auctions, Inc.*
HISTORICAL BLUE STAFFORDSHIRE PLATE, Drk. Blue, "Winter View Of Pittsfield, MA", Impressed "Clews", 10½″ D. $250.00
HISTORICAL BLUE STAFFORDSHIRE PLATTER, Med. Blue, Doctor Syntax "A Noble Hunting Party", Impressed "Clews", Sm. Rim Flake, 17⅛′ L. $625.00
HISTORICAL BLUE STAFFORDSHIRE PLATE, Med. Drk. Blue, "Fair Mount Near Philadelphia", 10¼″ D. $175.00
HISTORICAL BLUE STAFFORDSHIRE PLATE, Drk. Blue, "Winter View Of Pittsfield, MA", Impressed "Clews", Sm. Rim Flake, 6¾″ D. $225.00
CHIPPENDALE CHEST OF DRAWERS, Pine, Dovetailed Drawers, Worn Old Red Repaint, Orig. Embossed Eagle Brasses, Restorations, Sm. Section Missing Of 1 Back Foot, 38½″ W. x 18¾″ D., 38¾″ H. . $675.00
TIN PAUL REVERE LANTERN W/ Punched Design, Rust & Ring Handle Replaced, 14″ H. $65.00
FOOT STOOL, Maple, Whittled Legs, Ref., 8¼″ x 12¼″ $20.00

A-OH Sept 1980   *Garth's Auctions, Inc.*
PEWTER CHARGER, Faint Touchmarks, Surface Corrosion, 15⅝″ D. $115.00
PEWTER BASIN, Side Handles, Repaired Splits, Unmarked, 13½″ D. $100.00
PEWTER TEAPOT, "Sellew & Co, Cincinnati", Repaired, Polished, 7½″ H. . . $95.00
PEWTER MUGS, Pr., 4¼″ H. . . . $55.00
PEWTER BELLIED TANKARD MEASURE, Repairs, 6⅜″ H. $70.00
CUPBOARD TOP, Walnut, Dovetailed Cockbeaded Drawers In Base, OH, Ref., 37½″ W., 12″ D., 39″ H. $300.00
LADDER-BACK ARM CHAIR, Worn Drk. Red Paint, Worn Splint Seat, Damages $35.00
STONEWARE CHURN, 5 Gal., Cobalt Blue "5" & Leaf, 16¾″ H. $75.00
CAST IRON ANDIRONS, Pr., Key Handle Finials, 12½″ H. $35.00

A-OH July 1980   *Garth's Auctions, Inc.*
MANTLE, Carved Pine, Worn Orig. Polychrome Paint On Carvings, Br. Patina Background, Restored Shelf, 9″ x 64¾″, 60″ H. $8000.00
IRON FIRE SET, 3-Pc., Brass Handles, Rusted, 32″ L. $200.00
DOUBLE LEMON DROP ANDIRONS, Pr., Brass, 1 W/Seam Separation, 19¼″ H. $350.00
SERPENTINE FIREPLACE FENDER, Iron W/Wire Grill & Brass Top Rail, Rust On Rail, 45″ W., 16″ D., 13″ H. . . $450.00
WROUGHT IRON TRIVET, 14″ L. $305.00

A-OH Jan 1980   *Garth's Auctions, Inc.*
WARDROBE, Walnut, 1-Pc., OH, Hooks Removed & Supports Added For Removable Book Shelves, Ref., 44″ W., 15½″ D., 72″ H. $325.00
CAST IRON WAFFLE IRON, Heart Shaped Patt., 22½″ L. $105.00
MINI. BLANKET CHEST, Poplar, 6 Board, Worn Old Red Paint, 12″ W., 7¼″ D., 10½″ H. $150.00
FOOTSTOOL, Pine W/Orig. Br. Steel Comb Graining, 8¼″ x 17½″, 9″ H. $85.00

A-OH July 1980   *Garth's Auctions, Inc.*

OVERLAY LAMP, Opalescent Base & Gr. Cut To Clear Font, Brass Connector & Collar, Flake, 13¼" H. $250.00
ASTRAL LAMP, Stepped Marble & Brass Base, Triple Overlay Stem, Cut Prisms & Embossed Cast Brass Detail, Frosted Cut To Clear Shade, No Burner, 23" H. . .$925.00
OVERLAY LAMP, Opaque Wh. Base W/ Worn Gilding & Gr. Cut To Clear Font, Brass Connector & Collar, 9⅝" H. ...$175.00
ASTRAL LAMP, Blk. Stone Foot, Embossed Brass Base, & Ruby Red Cut To Clear & Frosted Stem, Brass Font, Cut To Clear Shade, Burner & Chimney, 28¼" H. $1100.00
OVERLAY LAMP, Amethyst Base & Cobalt Blue Cut To Clear Font, Brass Stem & Collar, 9½" H. $200.00
ASTRAL LAMP, Stepped Marble & Brass Base, Red Cut To Clear Stem & Brass Font W/Cut Prisms, Oil Burner & Chimney W/Frosted Cut To Clear Shade, 25" H. $650.00
OVERLAY LAMP, Opaque Blue Base W/ Gilding & Cobalt Blue Cut To Clear Font, Brass Stem & Collar, 12½" H. ... $400.00
HEPPLEWHITE SERPENTINE SIDE— BOARD, Mahogany, Dovetailed Drawers, Drk. Old Finish & Veneer Repair Necessary, Pine & Poplar Sec. Woods, Orig. Brasses, VA, 72" W., 27" D., 41" H. $4500.00
BRASS LEMON DROP ANDIRONS, Pr., 19" H. $550.00
MINI HEPPLEWHITE CHEST, Walnut W/Line Inlay, Dovetailed Drawers & Orig. Embossed Brasses, Worn Dry Finish, Repairs Necessary, Ca. 1871, 14" W., 8½" D., 16½" H. $2600.00

A-OH Sept 1980   *Garth's Auctions, Inc.* ▶
WALL CUPBOARD, 2-Pc., Walnut, Old Worn Gray Paint, 43" W., 19½" D., 82¾" H. $475.00
WROUGHT IRON SPOON, 15¾" L. $27.50
CAST IRON WINDMILL WEIGHT, Horse, 16¼" H. $185.00
WROUGHT IRON SPATULA, 17¼" L. $50.00
FOOT STOOL, Pine W/Legs Mortised Through Top, Old Drk. Red Finish, 7¼" x 14", 6½" H. $15.00

A-OH Mar 1980   *Garth's Auctions, Inc.*
CAST WH. METAL EAGLE, Old Worn Gilding, Oval Wooden Base, 19" D. . . $20.00
SM. CUPBOARD, Poplar, Door W/Twin Chestnut Panels, Ref., 33½" W., 11" D., 40" H. $130.00
CHILD'S LADDER-BACK ARM CHAIR ROCKER, Ref. & New Woven Splint Seat $115.00
ROLLING PIN, Curly Maple, Ref., 20½" L. $55.00
TURNED WOODEN KITCHEN MASHERS, 2, 10½" L. x 11" L. $12.50
TURNED WOODEN KITCHEN MASHER, Ref., 17" L. $17.50

A-OH June 1980   *Garth's Auctions, Inc.*
CHALK FIGURE GROUP, Boy & Girl Wearing Tams, Very Worn, Drk. Old Paint, 8¼" H. $60.00
TABLE TOP WRITING DESK, Mahogany & Other Veneer On Pine, Shaped Dovetailed Drawer, Repair & Some Repl., Ref., 18" W., 11¾" D. $325.00
BRASS CANDLE SCONCES, Pr., Scrolled Arms W/Removable Brackets, Extends From Wall, 12½" $460.00
HEPPLEWHITE BOW FRONT CHEST OF DRAWERS, Eng., Figured Mahogany On Pine, Dovetailed Drawers, Oval Brasses Replacements, Repairs, 41½" W., 19¾" D., 41" H. $300.00
CARVED WOODEN DECOY, Canvasback Drake Lowhead, MI, Ca. 1930, Worn Old Working Repaint, 14¼" L. $35.00
CORK BODIED DECOY, Wooden Inset Tail & Head, Bluebill W/Glass Eyes, 14" L. $20.00

Left
A-MA Aug 1980   *Robert C. Eldred Co., Inc.*
BRONZE FIGURE, "The Bronco Buster", Mkd. Copyright By Frederick Remington, 21⅝" H. $2100.00

Right
A-MA Mar 1980   *Richard A. Bourne Co., Inc.*
BRONZE, 19th C., Benjamin Franklin, Drk. Pat., Minor Damages, Wooden Base Beneath Slate, 16" O.L., 13" O.H. $1800.00

A-NY May 1980   *Calkins Auction Gallery*
OIL ON CANVAS, Mounted On Hardboard, Am., Ca. 1840, 28" x 34" .. $250.00
SPLINT BASKET W/Double Handle, N. Eng., 19th C., 12½" D., 5½" H. $55.00
STONEWARE INK BOTTLES, Pr., London, 19th C., Br. Glaze, 1 W/Pouring Spout, 7¼" H. $8.00
CANDLE BOX, Pine, Painted, Dovetailed W/Sliding Cover, Wrought Nails, 14¼" L., 5¼" W., 4" H. $70.00
Q. A. SIDE CHAIR, 18th C., Old Drk. Finish, 38½" O.H. $150.00
Q. A. CHEST OF DRAWERS, N. Eng., 18th C., Maple, Tiger Maple & Pine, Dovetailed Top, Brasses Repl., 2 Backboards Repl., Lip Repair, 34¾" W., 18" D., 40" H. $775.00
CHIPPENDALE SIDE CHAIR, Painted, MA, Late 18th C., 35" O.H. $105.00
BENNINGTON TYPE CUSPIDOR, N. Eng., 19th C., Mottled Br. Glaze, Beading Around Top, 10" D., 6½" H. $25.00
OVOID STONEWARE JUG By L. Seymour, Cobalt Blue Decor., 11½" H. .. $45.00
STONEWARE JUG, 3 Gal., By Hamilton & Jones, PA, Cobalt Blue Decor. On Gray Ground, 16½" H. $155.00

A-OH April 1980   *Garth's Auctions, Inc.*
WALL CUPBOARD, 2 Pc., Poplar, Dovetailed Drawers, Ref., 56" W., 22¼" D., 86¼" H. $1050.00
KENTUCKY RIFLE ½ STOCK, Curly Maple, Engraved Lock Replaced Percussion Hammer, 49½" O.L. $300.00
BRASS VIC. CANDLESTICKS, Pr., W/Pushups, 10¾" H. $170.00
PEWTER BASIN, Partial Touch Mark For Gershom Jones, Providence, 7¾" D. $350.00
PEWTER BASIN, Partial Touch Mark For "Samuel Hamlin", 7¾" D. $175.00
PEWTER BASIN, Partial Touch Mark For Samuel Kilbourn, Baltimore, 7⅞" D. $600.00

────────────

◄ A-OH Sept 1980   *Garth's Auctions, Inc.*
OPAQUE WATERCOLOR DRAWING, Prussian On Horseback, "Johann Christmann, 1853", Framed, 18¼" x 24½" ...$115.00
TOLE DEED BOX, Orig. Orange-Yellow Decor. On Drk. Br. Japanned Ground, Touch Up, Varnish, Orig. Brass Bale, 8" L. $115.00
TRAMP ART BOX, Hinged Lid, Orig. Varnish W/Gold-Silver Paint, Minor Damage, 14¼" x 8", 7" H. $80.00
TOLE DEED BOX, Orig. Blk. Ground W/Stenciled Flowers, Yellow Stiping, Int. W/Modern Blue Paint, 8¾" L. $50.00
CHEST OF DRAWERS, Curly Maple, Dovetailed Drawers, Cherry Paneled Ends, Repl. Curly Maple Top, Orig. Clear Blown Glass Knobs, Ref., 43¾" W., 22" D., 37" H. $425.00
CAST IRON DOOR STOP, Bull Dog, Old Repaint, 6" H. $75.00
PUNCHED TIN FOOT WARMER, Wooden Frame W/Turned Posts, Repairs, 7½" x 8½", 6" H. $30.00
CAST IRON DOOR STOP, Boxer, Old Worn Paint, 8¾" H. $25.00

A-OH Mar 1980   *Garth's Auctions, Inc.*
OPEN PEWTER CUPBOARD, 1-Pc., Pine, Board & Batten Door, Old Worn Red Paint, Backboards Incomplete, 47" W., 21" D., 73½" H. $300.00
CARVED WOODEN DECOY, Am. Merganser Drake, MI, Stamped "RWC", Orig. Paint, 14½" L. $80.00
CARVED WOODEN DECOY, Mallard Drake Bobtail By William Williams, MI, Ca. 1930, Orig. Worn Paint & Tack Eyes, 17½" L. $55.00
CARVED WOODEN DECOY, Wood Duck Drake, MI, Glass Eyes & Worn Orig. Paint, 12¼" L. $150.00
CARVED WOODEN DECOY, Canvasback Drake, Havre De Grace, MD, Orig. Worn Paint, 16" L. $100.00
CARVED WOODEN DECOY, Bluebill Drake Low Head, MI, Ca. 1930, Glass Eyes & Old Repaint, 10¼" H. $50.00
CARVED WOODEN DECOY, Canvasback Drake, MI, Ca. 1930, Glass Eyes, Old Repaint & Split In Neck, 14½" L. .. $55.00
REDWARE PITCHER, Cream Colored Slip W/Running Gr. & Clear Glaze, Impressed "S. Bell & Son, Strasburg", 10" H. $515.00
SPLINT BASKET, Old Drk. Stain, 12½" x 19", 9" H. $85.00
STONEWARE JAR, Impressed "T. M' Granger", 9" H. $45.00

A-MA Oct 1980   *Robert W. Skinner Inc.*
PISTOL TINDER LIGHTER, Notch Carved Handle, Am., Early 18th C., 9" L. $500.00*

A-OH Sept 1980   *Garth's Auctions, Inc.*
VIC. SECRETARY, Walnut, W/Dovetailed
Drawers, Crown Mold Cornice, 40″ W., 27¼″
D., 84¾″ H. $1025.00
WOVEN SPLINT BASKET, Wooden Side
Handles, Wear & Damage, 12¼″ D.
.... $12.50
LRG. WOVEN SPLINT BASKET, Hand
Holds, Wear & Damage, 12″ D., 14″ H.
.... $20.00
WOVEN SPLINT BASKET W/LID, 2
Handles, Yellow Varnish, 10″ D., 8″ H.
.... $55.00
RYE STRAW BASKET, Some Damage,
9½″ D. $35.00

A-OH June 1980   *Garth's Auctions, Inc.*
WALL CUPBOARD, Pine, 2-Pc., Dove-
tailed Drawers, Repl. Brasses, Ref., 54½″ W.,
18½″ D., 85½″ H. $1000.00
CARVED WOODEN DECOY, Red
Breasted Merganser Hen, Turned Head,
Orig. Paint, Chesapeake Bay, VA, 16″ L.
.... $175.00
YARN HOLDER, Turned Treen, Sm. Hole
Cut In Rim For Yarn, 8¼″ H. $205.00
CARVED WOODEN DECOY, Mate To
First Decoy, 17″ L. $195.00
CARVED WOODEN DECOY, Canada
Goose, Lower Ontario, Inset 2-Pc. Head &
Neck, Weathered W/Old Blk. & Wh. Re-
paint, 18″ L. $125.00

A-OH Sept 1980   *Garth's Auctions, Inc.*
WALL CUPBOARD, 2-Pc., Walnut &
Poplar, Dovetailed Drawers, Ref., 48″ W.,
17¾″ D., 84″ H. $675.00
CARVED WOODEN DECOY, Masons
Mallard Drake, Challenge Grade, Glass
Eyes, Orig. Worn Paint, Putty At Neck
Incomp., 16″ L. $80.00
STONEWARE PITCHER, Albany Slip W/
Sgraffito Label "Mrs. Mary Harman, Colum-
bus, OH", Sm. Rim Flakes, 9¾″ H. .. $85.00
CARVED WOODEN DECOY, Worn
Orig. Paint, Glass Eyes, Head Splits, Repairs,
16½″ L. $35.00
VICTORY FACTORY DECOYS, 2, Mal-
lard Drakes W/Old Paint, Glass Eyes, Neck
Repairs, 16½″ L. $40.00

A-OH April 1980   *Garth's Auctions, Inc.*
WALL CUPBOARD, 2 Pc., Curly Maple
& Poplar, 48″ W., 20″ D., 90″ H. .. $3200.00
PEWTER PLATE, 2 Eagle Touch Marks
For Blakeslee Barns, Philadelphia, Wear, &
Knife Scratches, 7⅞″ D. $205.00
PEWTER PLATE, 2 Eagle Touch Marks
For Thomas Boardman, 7¾″ D. .. $295.00
PEWTER PLATE, 2 Eagle Touch Marks
For Samuel Pierce, Greenfield, MA, Some
Wear, Knife Scratches, 8″ D. $380.00
PEWTER PLATE, 2 Eagle Touch Marks
For Thomas Boardman, 7¾″ D. .. $285.00

A-OH Mar 1980   *Garth's Auctions, Inc.*
WOVEN SPLINT BASKET, Colors Faded,
15″ D., 5½″ H. $70.00
WOODEN SPLINT BASKET, 21½″ D.,
11″ O.H. $55.00
WOVEN SPLINT BASKET W/Hinged
Lid, 11½″ x 18″, 8¼″ O.H. $50.00
CORNER CUPBOARD, Poplar & Pine,
2-Pc., Dovetailed Drawers, Ref., Porcelain
Pulls Repl., 54½″ W., 85½″ H. $550.00
WROUGHT IRON ANDIRONS, Pr.,
Twisted Stem & Ram's Horn Finials, 16″ H.
.... $65.00

A-OH April 1980   *Garth's Auctions, Inc.*
PEWTER PLATE, Samuel Danforth, Hartford, Some Repair $235.00
PEWTER CANDLESTICKS, Pr., W/Push-ups, 1 W/Split At Base & Missing Pushup, 9½" H. $250.00
PEWTER PLATE, Touchmarks Of Thomas Danforth I, 8⅞" D. $305.00
PEWTER TALL COFFEE POT, Leather Finial On Lid, Tip Of Spout Damaged, Eagle Touch Of Ashbil Griswold, CT, 11" H. $225.00
PEWTER SOUP PLATE, 3 Eagle Touchmarks, 9⅝" D. $360.00
PEWTER PLATE, 2 Partial Touchmarks Of Rampant Lion, Pitting & Knife Scratches, 8" D. $240.00
HEPPLEWHITE CHEST OF DRAWERS, Pine & Poplar, Dovetailed Cockbeaded Drawers, Orig. Oval Gilded Brasses, 40½" W., 20¼" D., 43" H. $3300.00
WHITE CLAY PITCHER, Hound Handled, Drk. Cobalt Blue, Glaze, 12½" H. $220.00

A-OH April 1980   *Garth's Auctions, Inc.*
OPEN PEWTER CUPBOARD, 1 Pc., Pine W/Wrought Iron "H" Hinges, Restored, 48" W., 16½" D., 80" H. $650.00
BELLIED PEWTER MEASURES, Set Of 6, Cast Ear Handles, "Quart" To ¼ Gill, English, 6¼" To 2" H. $600.00
PEWTER PLATE, Touch Marks For "Townsend & Compton, London", 8⅝" D. . . $95.00
PEWTER TANKARD MEASURE, "½ Pint", English, Battered & Rim Split, 3½" H. $45.00
PEWTER TANKARD MEASURE, "Pint", English, 4¾" H. $65.00
PEWTER BEAKER, "Quart", "I. Thompson, C & M 1884", English, 6" H. . . $75.00
PEWTER PLATE, Touch Marks Of David Melville, Newport, RI, 8¼" D. $245.00
PEWTER PLATE, Faint Touch, "S.E.", 8¼" D. $90.00
PEWTER PLATE, Continental Touch, 9" D. $55.00

A-OH Feb 1980   *Garth's Auctions, Inc.*
POTTERY COOLER, Doulton Type, Applied Decor., Wooden Spigot, Sm. Flakes Around Rim, 12¼" H. $65.00
JOINTED WOODEN TOY W/Long Stick Support, Old Paint, 11¾" H. $60.00
ROCKINGHAM OVAL SOAP DISH, 4" x 5½" $55.00
ROCKINGHAM BOWL, 6½" D., 3¼" H. $55.00
JOINTED WOODEN TOY W/Long Stick Support, Old Paint, 13¼" H. $60.00
PIE SAFE, Poplar, Punched Tin Panels, Ref. & Several Panels W/Rust Damage, 39" W., 17" D., 48" H. $300.00
WROUGHT IRON ANDIRONS, Pr., W/ Ring Tops, 11¼" H. $55.00
ROCKINGHAM BOWL, 9¾" D., 4¼" H. $35.00

A-OH Mar 1980   *Garth's Auctions, Inc.*
CORNER CUPBOARD, Walnut, 1-Pc., Paneled Doors Set Into Beaded Frame, 46½" W., 79¾" H. $1100.00
CANVAS BACK DECOY, Cloth Cork Body & Carved Wooden Head & Tail, Old Paint & Glass Eyes, 14" L. $35.00

A-OH Sept 1980   *Garth's Auctions, Inc.*
CORNER CUPBOARD, 2-Pc., Curly Maple, Ref., All Latches Removed, Feet Restored, 69" W., 80½" H. $2300.00
CARVED WOODEN DECOY, Bluebill Drake, Attrib. To Benjamin Elsholtz, MI, Old Worn Paint, Bill Split, 13¾" L. . . $35.00
SGRIFFITO CHARGER REPRODUCTION, Redware W/Yellow Slip & Br.-Gr. Glaze, Sm. Bit Of Glaze Flaking On Center Of Peacock, 13" D. $25.00
CARVED WOODEN DECOY, Bluebill Hen By Gerald Fitch, MI, Old Gold Paint, Glass Eyes, 13½" L. $55.00
WOVEN REED BASKET, Wooden Bottom, Gr. Rope Design, 11½" x 24" . . $35.00

A-OH Jan 1980   *Garth's Auctions, Inc.*

WOVEN SPLINT BASKET, Faded Gr. &
Red Design, 11" x 16½", 8" O.H. .. $35.00

STONEWARE JUG, Albany Slip Glaze W/
Incised Label, 6¼" H. $40.00

OPEN WEAVE SPLINT BASKET W/
Wooden Bottom, Old Red Paint, 14¼" D.,
11½" H. $45.00

STONEWARE JUG, Blue Stenciled Label
"Hamilton & Jones, Greensboro, PA", 9¾" H.
.... $35.00

WOVEN SPLINT BASKET, Gr. & Yellow
Design, Minor Rim Damage, 11½" x 15", 9"
O.H. $50.00

POPLAR CUPBOARD, 1 Pc., Worn Old
Alligatored Red Paint, 54" W., 24" D., 80" O.H.
.... $1600.00

REDWARE MUG, Clear Glaze W/Bands
Of Br. Sponging, 6½" H. $395.00

REDWARE COVERED PITCHER, Incised Band W/Br. Sponging & Clear Glaze,
Some Glaze Wear & Sm. Chips, 7" H.
.... $165.00

REDWARE PITCHER, Br. Sponging &
Clear Glaze, Lid Missing, Chip At Spout,
6¼" H. $60.00

REDWARE OVOID JAR, 2 Incised Rings
At Shoulder & Flared Lip, Mottled Gr. & Br.
Glaze, Hairline In Base & Int. Calcium
Deposits, 10¼" H. $55.00

SEWER TILE COLLIE, Broken From
Base & Reattached, Base Incised "Kyte",
11¼" H. $135.00

REDWARE PITCHER, Incised Bands
Around Shoulder & Lip, Chip On Lip, Gr. &
Br. Running Glaze, 7¾" H. $225.00

WOODEN BUCKET W/Wooden Lid,
Stave Const., Metal Bands On Both, Wire
Handle Off Center, Old Drk. Blue Paint, 12"
D., 9½" H. $115.00

A-OH June 1980   *Garth's Auctions, Inc.*

WALL CUPBOARD, Cherry, 1 Pc., Dove-
tailed Drawers, Handmade Reproduction,
Age But Not Period, 48½" W., 20¾" D., 80½"
H. $750.00

MASON'S WOODEN DECOY, Bluebill
Hen, Glass Eyes Do Not Match, Working
Repaint, 13½" L. $37.50

WOODEN DECOY, Cut-Out W/Whittled
Base, Old Worn Paint, 16" L. $30.00

CARVED WOODEN DECOY, Bluebill
Drake, Repl. Tack Eyes & Old Working
Repaint, Ca. 1910, 13¼" L. $25.00

A-OH Feb 1980   *Garth's Auctions, Inc.*
ROW I, L To R
CARVED WOODEN WHIMSY, Made
From 1 Pc. Of Wood, 13½" H. ... $105.00
STONEWARE PITCHER, Sm. Size, 7" H.
.... $77.50
CAST IRON TOBACCO CUTTER,
Blade Worn, 13½" L. $145.00
WOOD CARVING, Worn Br. Finish,
12¼" H. $60.00
ROW II, L To R
CARVED DUCK DECOY, Old Paint, 9½"
L. $50.00
FOLK ART CARVING, Unfinished Pine
W/Pencil Inscript. On Base, Animal's Tail
Broken, 7¼" Sq., 5¾" H. $52.50
CARVED DUCK DECOY, Mate To 1st
Decoy $80.00
ROW III, L To R
LAMINATED WOOD TURNING, Chalice
W/2 Free Rings, 4½" H. $17.50
INLAID WALL BRACKETS, Pr., 6½" H.
.... $30.00
STONEWARE PIG BOTTLE, Hairline &
Chipped Ears, 8" L. $170.00
SM. WINDSOR FOOT STOOL, Bamboo
Turned Legs & Worn Old Red Paint W/Yel-
low Stiping, 5¼" x 11¾", 5½" H. ... $45.00
FEED SACK STAMP, Carved Walnut,
"R.T. Keys", 6½" L. $27.50
TURNED WOOD WHIMSEY, 7⅝" H.
.... $13.00

◄ A-OH Sept 1980   *Garth's Auctions, Inc.*
WALL CUPBOARD, 1-Pc., Walnut, Soft
Wood Cornice Painted Blk., Old Finish,
48½" W., 22¼" D., 85¼" H. $495.00
**PEWTER BELLIED TANKARD
MEASURES,** Set Of 7, ¼ Gill To Qt., Most
W/Repair Or Damage, 2" To 6¼" .. $225.00
STONEWARE CROCK, 3 Gal., Impressed
Label "Fort Edward Stoneware Co., NY",
Floral Design In Cobalt, Cracked, 10½" H.
.... $70.00
STONEWARE CROCK, 2 Gal., Impressed
Label "L.S. Benedict & Son, CT", Bird On
Branch In Cobalt, Cracked, 9½" H. .. $85.00

A-OH June 1980   *Garth's Auctions, Inc.*
CARVED WOODEN DECOY, Blk. Duck, Glass Eyes & Working Repaint, 17″ L. . . . $40.00
CARVED WOODEN DECOY, Swimming Scoter W/Inset Head, Overpaint Removed To Show Orig. Blk. & Wh., 14½″ L. . . . $25.00
PIE SAFE, Poplar, 1-Pc., Dovetailed Drawer, Punched Panels In Top Doors & Sides W/ Star & Circle Designs, Repaired & Ref., 36½″ W., 16¼″ D., 72″ H. $400.00
CARVED WOODEN DECOY, Goldeneye Drake, Toledo, OH, Glass Eyes, Carved Wing Detail & Orig. Paint, 12¾″ H. . . $70.00
CARVED WOODEN DECOY, Mate To The Above $115.00

A-OH Oct 1980   *Garth's Auctions, Inc.*
KITCHEN CUPBOARD, 2-Pc., Poplar, Old Red Repaint, Repairs, 40½″ W., 19½″ D., 80″ H. $175.00
SEWING BOX, Pine W/1 Drawer, 6 Thread Holders, Cut-Out Carrying Handle, Old Drk. Varnish Finish, 8¾″ x 7″, 7½″ H. $25.00
GROTESQUE STONEWARE JUG, Incised "Lanier Meaders", Teeth Damaged, 9½″ H. $75.00
GROTESQUE STONEWARE CHURN, Impressed "B.B. Craig, Vale NC", Ash Gr. Glaze W/Blue Streaks, 14¼″ H. . . . $80.00
GROTESQUE STONEWARE PITCHER, Gr. Ash Glaze W/Blue Highlights, Impressed "B.B. Craig, Vale NC", Inscribed "Nov. 1878", 9¼″ H. $75.00

A-OH April 1980   *Garth's Auctions, Inc.*
WALL CUPBOARD, 1 Pc., Pine, Ref. W/Traces Of Old Red, 37½″ W., 19″ D., 82″ H. $575.00
CUT-OUT WOODEN CROW, Some Rep., 35″ H. $145.00
STONEWARE CROCK W/Cover, Brushed Cobalt Rim Design, Impressed Label "Solomon Bell, Strasburg VA", Applied Handles, Chips & Firing Crack, 9½″ D., 9″ H. $220.00
OVOID STONEWARE COOLER, Incised Leaf Design Filled W/Cobalt Blue, Impressed Label "N. Clark & Co. Lyons", Applied Handle, Minor Flakes, Lid Missing, 14″ H. . . $475.00
WINDSOR FOOT STOOL, Old Gr. Paint, 10″ x 13¾″, 11″ H. $145.00

A-OH Mar 1980   *Garth's Auctions, Inc.*
OIL ON CANVAS, Mt. Vernon, Needs Cleaning, Flaking & Tear, Gilded Fr., 35¾″ x 27¾″ $510.00
HATCHEL ON BOARD W/Heart Cut Outs, Worn Finish, Ca. 1853, 27″ L. . . $145.00
SM. SPINNING WHEEL, "E. Washburn", Bobbin & Support Replacements, Wheel 19½″ D. $205.00
CAST IRON FIRE BACK, Crack In Base, 21½″ x 27″ $190.00
CARVED WOODEN DECOY, Mallard Drake, Hollow & Tack Eyes, By Robert Michesl, MI, Ca. 1940, 14″ L. $40.00
CAST BELL METAL PAN, Engraved "Mrs. Nading, Sept. 2, 1844", Wrought Iron Bail, 11″ D. $75.00
CARVED WOODEN DECOY, Mallard Drake By Ackerman, Glass Eyes, 15¾″ L. $35.00

A-MA July 1980   *Robert W. Skinner Inc.*
DOUBLE-SEATED SURRY, Upholstered Seats W/Blk. & Red Orig. Painted Decor., Wood Covered Top, Labeled "Sargent & Hann", MA, Late 19th C. $1300.00*

*Price does not include 10% buyer fee.

A-OH Sept 1980   *Garth's Auctions, Inc.*

CARVED WOODEN DECOY, Redhead Drake, By Ben Schmidt, MI, Glass Eyes, Old Worn Paint, 14¼″ L. $165.00

WALL CUPBOARD, Cherry, 2-Pc., Dovetailed Drawers, Hdw. Repl., Ref., 52″ W., 19″ D., 83¼″ H. $1800.00

CARVED WOODEN DECOY, Blk. Duck By Frank Cummings, MI, Glass Eyes, Orig. Paint, 19¼″ L. $80.00

CARVED WOODEN DECOY, Mallard Drake By Frank Cummings, MI, Glass Eyes, Orig. Paint, 18½″ L. $60.00

CARVED WOODEN DECOY, Canada Goose, MI, Hollow, Old Patches On Neck, Old Working Repaint, 23″ L. $105.00

A-OH Mar 1980   *Garth's Auctions, Inc.*

WALL CUPBOARD, 2-Pc., Poplar, Dovetailed Drawers, Orig. Red Paint Shows Wear, Assorted Hdw., 48″ W., 18¼″ D., 86½″ H. $1300.00

ROCKINGHAM PITCHER W/Embossed Tulips, Some Glaze Flaking, 8¼″ H. $22.00

ROCKINGHAM BOWL, Sm. Rim Flake, 9″ D. $45.00

ROCKINGHAM TANKARD PITCHER, Minor Flake On Base & 1 On Spout, 9″ H. $55.00

CARVED WOODEN DECOY, Bluebill, VA, Ca. 1920, Old Working Repaint Over Weathered Surface, 14½″ L. $40.00

A-OH Jan 1980   *Garth's Auctions, Inc.*

COPPER EAGLE WEATHERVANE, Traces Of Old Gilding, Weathered Wood Base, 24″ At Wings $650.00

SM. BELL METAL POT W/Wrought Iron Handle, 5½″ D. $105.00

BELL METAL POT W/Wrought Iron Handle, 8″ D. $105.00

CHEST OF DRAWERS, Cherry W/Old Brownish Red Steel Comb Graining On Frame & Sponged Graining On Drawers, Dovetailed, Wooden Knobs Replacements, 40½″ W., 21½″ D., 75¼″ H. $700.00

◄ A-MA Mar 1980   *Richard A. Bourne Co., Inc.*

CARRIAGE, Blk. Body W/Orig. Gold & Gr. Stenciling, Wooden Wheels, Orig. Leather Top & Leather Upholstered Seat, Minor Wear To Decor., 40″ O.H. $650.00

CARRIAGE, Wh., Yellow, Gr. & Blk. Decor. Orig. Carriage Lamps & Decor. Wheels, Top Releathered, Seat Reupholstered, Carpet Redone, 42″ O.H. $550.00

A-OH Mar 1980   *Garth's Auctions, Inc.* ►

OPEN PEWTER CUPBOARD, Pine, 2-Pc., Red Paint & Rep., 42½″ W., 19″ D., 76″ H. $675.00

PEWTER TANKARD MEASURES, Set Of 6, 1¾″ To 5¾″ H. $180.00

ANIMATED WHIRLY-GIG, Tiger & Billy Goat, Worn Paint, ;18½″ L. $205.00

DOUGH BOX, Poplar W/Cut Out Hand Holds, Ref., 15″ x 25″, 15½″ H. $95.00

CARVED WOODEN DECOY, Hollow Pintail Drake, Sgn. "Edward Schueller, Thomson, IL", Glass Eyes & Orig. Paint, 18¾″ L. $110.00

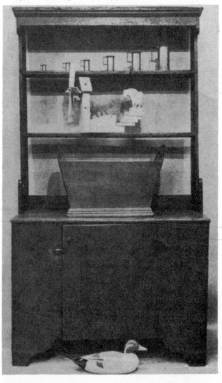

A-OH Feb 1981   *Garth's Auctions, Inc.*
WALL CUPBOARD, 2-Pc., Poplar, Married W/Repl. Bracket Feet, Dovetailed Drawers, Old Red Repaint, 56½" W., 19½" D., 81½" H. $475.00
CRAIG POTTERY, 2 Pcs., Jug & Pitcher, Gray W/Wh. Swirls, Impressed & Dated 1978, 5¼" x 6½" H. $15.00
CAST IRON SCALES, Tin Plated Brass Pan, "Perfection Scales, Size 2, Am. Mfg. Co., Philadelphia.", Worn Orig. Red Paint, 15" L. $47.50
GROTESQUE POTTERY JUG, Gray Glaze, Imp. "B. B. Craig, Vale, N.C.", 7½" H. $25.00
GROTESQUE POTTERY JUG, Grayish Gr. Glaze, Imp. "B. B. Craig, Vale, N.C.", 6" H. $20.00

A-OH Feb 1981   *Garth's Auctions, Inc.*
WOVEN SPLINT BASKET, Rim Damage, 13" x 18", 8" O.H. $25.00
WALL CUPBOARD, 2-Pc., Walnut, Dovetailed Drawers, 2 Panes Cracked, 46" W., 18½" D., 84" H. $850.00
GROTESQUE POTTERY JUG, Gray, W/Wh. Swirls, Imp. "B.B. Craig Vale, N.C.", 6½" H. $35.00
CRAIG POTTERY, 2 Pcs. (1 Illus.), Covered Jar & Jug, Gray W/Wh. Swirls, Imp. "B.B. Craig Vale N.C.", Dated 1978, 5¼" & 5⅞" H. $35.00

A-OH Feb 1981   *Garth's Auctions, Inc.*
WOVEN SPLINT BASKET, Minor Rim Damage, 14½" x 24", 9" O.H. $55.00
WALL CUPBOARD, 2-Pc., Poplar, Dovetailed Drawers Need Pulls, Ref., 46½" W., 18½" D., 78½" H. $385.00
REDWARE PIE PLATE, Sgraffito Distelfinks & Tulip, Incised "L. & B. Breininger, Robesonia PA, July 23, 1974, Cool, Very Dry", 9½" D. $40.00
REDWARE PIE PLATE, Sagraffito Tulips & Flowers, Incised "L. & B. Breininger, Robesonia PA, 1974", 10¼" D. $35.00
TIN DUTCH OVEN, Tooled Design On Door, Rust Damage, Spit Missing, 23" L. $55.00

◄ A-OH Feb 1981   *Garth's Auctions, Inc.*
CORNER CUPBOARD, 1-Pc., Pine, "H" Hinges, Extensive Alterations, Ref., 47" W., 77" H. $400.00
TIN CHURN, 13½" H. $75.00
TIN TEAPOT, Ceramic Double Boiler Insert, 8" O.H. $25.00

A-OH Feb 1981   *Garth's Auctions, Inc.* ►
CORNER CUPBOARD, 2-Pc., Walnut, Brass "H" Hinges, 28" W., 70" H. $300.00
PETIT POINT ON PAPER, 2 Girls By A Brook, "E. K. Fece 1862", Minor Border Damage, Unframed, 13¼" x 16" $30.00
MASONIC APRON, Printed & Embroidered, Blue Binding W/Metallic Thread & Sequins, Some Wear, 13" x 14" $30.00
IMARI PORCELAIN BOWL, Polychromed W/Minor Surface Flakes In Interior, 8¼" D., 3½" H. $40.00
VIC. CANDLESTAND, Drk. Varnish Stain Finish, Cracks In Top, 13¼" D., 30¼" H. $45.00

A-OH Oct 1980   *Garth's Auctions, Inc.*
ROW I, L To R
CAST IRON DOOR STOPS, Pr., Parrots W/Old Polychrome Paint, 6″ H. . . . $75.00
CAST IRON DOOR STOP, Basket Of Flowers W/Old Polychrome Paint, 8¼″ H. $25.00
CAST IRON DOOR STOP, Basket Of Flowers W/Old Polychrome Paint, 5¾″ H. $25.00
TREEN THREAD CADDY W/Pine Cushion Top, Clear Varnish W/Blk. Striping, 8″ H. $77.50
CAST IRON DOOR STOP, Lady W/ Bouquet, Rusted Paint, 6½″ H. $22.50
ROW II, L To R
CAST IRON DOOR STOP, Boxer, Old Worn Paint, 8½″ H. $42.50
HANGING SALT BOX, Poplar, Red Repaint Shows "Salt" Beneath, Late Sq. Dovetails, 6¾″ x 7″, 6½″ H. $45.00
CAST IRON DOOR STOP, Girl W/Basket Of Flowers, Old Polychrome Repaint, 8¾″ H. $70.00
SM. WOODEN BUCKET, Stave Const., No Finish, 6″ D., 6″ H. $100.00
ROW III, L To R
ROUND BENTWOOD BOX, 6¼″ D. $12.50
CAST IRON NUT CRACKER, Dog, Worn Old Paint, 11″ L. $20.00
BUTTER MOLD, Rec. Cased, Line Design, 3″ x 5½″ $15.00
ROUND BENTWOOD BOX, Copper Tacks, Old Yellow Varnish, 7⅝″ D. . . $50.00
ROUND BENTWOOD BOX, Copper Tacks, Paper Label "High Bush Blueberries, NH", 6½″ D. $80.00
TAPE LOOM, Shaker, NY, 4″ x 12″ $80.00

A-OH Oct 1980   *Garth's Auctions, Inc.*
L To R
WROUGHT IRON STRAP HINGES, Pr., 21¼″ L. $50.00
WROUGHT IRON FORK, Wooden Handle, 17¼″ L. $45.00
IRON SCISSORS WICK TRIMMERS, 4½″ L. $10.00
IRON SCISSORS WICK TRIMMERS, Mkd. "Challenge Cutlery Co.", 5¾″ L. $20.00
IRON SCISSORS WICK TRIMMERS, 6⅝″ L. $15.00
SHENANDOAH POTTERY BOTTLE, Bluff Clay W/Tooling, Drk. Br. Glaze, 5 Ears, 8¼″ D. $20.00
CAST IRON LION ORNAMENT, Holes In Eyes & Forehead, 8½″ D. $50.00
OVAL SOAPSTONE PICTURE FRAME, 4½″ x 6″ $25.00
WOODEN SPINNING BOBBINS, 2, 6¼″, 7¾″ L. $15.00
WOODEN SPINNING BOBBIN, 9″ L. $10.00
BRASS & WROUGHT IRON TASTER, Break In Iron, 12¾″ L. $75.00
WROUGHT IRON SPIKES, 5, (1 Illus.), Tulip Form Tops, 4½″ L. $25.00

A-OH Mar 1980   *Garth's Auctions, Inc.*
POSTER, "Our Country & Our Flag", Printed In Red Wh. & Blue, 35 Stars In Flag, Ca. 1864, 2⅝″ x 7¾″ $35.00
STICK PIN, Brass Embossed Eagle & Shield W/"I", 6¼″ L. $5.00
PRINTED RIBBON, "Miami Valley Convention", Ca. 1840, Glued To Cardboard, 2½″ x 8¼″ $45.00
BRASS METAL, Star Shaped, "Grand Army Of The Republic, 1861-1866-Veteran", 1¾″ D. $25.00
COLLAR BUTTON, "Tippecanoe & Morton Too", ¾″ D. $42.50
BRASS CLIP ON BUTTON, "Protection", McKinley Campaign, ⅞″ D. . . $9.00
CAMPAIGN BUTTON, Image Of McKinley, ⅞″ D. $9.00
COLLAR BUTTON, "Harrison & Morton", Worn Paint ¾″ D. $5.00
BRASS EAGLE INSI NIA, 1⅝″ D. . . $15.00
POSTER, "The Union, Constitution", 34 Stars In Flag, Ca. 1860, 2¾″ x 7½″ . . $12.50

*Price does not include 10% buyer fee.

A-OH Aug 1980   *Garth's Auctions, Inc.*
JADE BEADS, Double Strand In Gr. & Several Colors, Carved Jade Clasp . . .$215.00
ORIENTAL SILVER CHAIN, Simply Tooled Ring, Mkd. $25.00
INDIAN SILVER BROACH, 13 Pcs. Of Turquoise, 1⅞″ x 3″ $55.00
PURPLE JADE EARRINGS, Pr., Enameled Wh. Metal Fittings $15.00
ID BRACELET, Yellow Gold, "RMCKM", Mkd. 14K, 5.85 Troy Oz. $2500.00
ENAMELED SILVER BELT, Middle Eastern, 28″ L. $165.00
WEDGWOOD BUTTON & COLLAR BUTTON, Lavender W/Blk. Basalt Arms, Mkd. "Wedgwood England" $80.00
YELLOW GOLD BOX, Lid Cross Set W/ 19 Sm. Diamonds, Mkd. "22", 1¾″ D. $250.00
RHINESTONE BROACH, Pine Back Incomp., 2⅛″ L. $10.00
YELLOW GOLD KEY CHAIN, Capitol Bldg. Eng., Mkd. 14K, 2.05 Troy Oz $450.00
BRACELET, Gr. Jade & Yellow Gold, Mkd. "14" $70.00

Left
A-WA D.C. May 1980   *Adam A. Weschler & Son*
GEORGE III CASE WATCH & FOB, 18 Karat Yellow Gold, L. Lawrence, London, Ca. 1816, Chain Drive W/Lever Move $1100.00*

Right
A-NY May 1980   *Calkins Auction Gallery*
LRG. WOODEN TUB, NY, 19th C., Laced Wooden Bands, Never Painted, Orig. Cond., 22″ D., 21½″ H. $115.00

A-OH Feb 1981   *Garth's Auctions, Inc.*
ROW I, L To R
TIN KEROSENE LAMP, Horizontal Cylindrical Font, Brass Burner, Chimney Not Illus., Worn Olive Paint, 13" H. $20.00
OCTAGONAL SUNDIAL, Engraved: "Time Passeth 1722", 11" D. $245.00
TIN KEROSENE LAMP, Brass Burner, Crimped Edge Reflector Stamped "Climax", 9½" O.H. $25.00

ROW II, L To R
TIN SKATER'S LAMP, Split In Threaded Top, 6¾" H. $25.00
KEROSENE COACH LAMP, Clear & Red Lens, "Dietz Eureka", 7¼" H. .. $27.50
TIN LAMP FILLER, 5" H. $25.00
WROUGHT IRON GREASE LAMP, 9" H. $95.00
BRASS TAPER LAMP, Chain But Pick Missing, Embossed, 4" H. $25.00
CANDY CONTAINER, Lantern Shaped, 6½" H. $50.00

ROW III, L To R
PEWTER LAMP, Weighted Base, Worn Gilding, No Burner, 7½" H. $50.00
WROUGHT IRON DOUBLE CRUSIE LAMP, 5½" O.H. $65.00
BRASS CANDLESTICK, Sq. Base, 5⅝" H. $145.00
PEWTER LAMP, Base Mkd. "Smith & Co.", Damaged, 6¾" H. $115.00
PEWTER LAMP, Foot W/Tin Addition, Brass Collar W/Old Repair, 8¾" H. $60.00

A-OH July 1980   *Garth's Auctions, Inc.* ▶
PEWTER CHARGER, Corroded & Pitted, 15" D. $90.00
HANGING SPICE RACK, Walnut, 10¼" x 19" $180.00
PEWTER CHARGER, Partial London Touch, Sm. Split & Rim Damaged, 15" D. $75.00
SECRETARY TOP, Pine, 4 Panel Door W/Dentilated Cornice, Mustard Color Paint Shows Red Beneath, 13½" x 39¾", 41½" H. $300.00
DOLL CRADLE, Poplar, Dovetailed, Orig. Br. Varnish, Repair, 25¾" L. .. $160.00

A-OH Oct 1980   *Garth's Auctions, Inc.*
BLK. PAPER CUT-OUT, 2 Deer W/Floral Border, Applied Gilded Paper Ornaments, Walnut Cross Corner Frame, 11" x 13" $135.00
OIL ON CANVAS, Portrait Of Young Man, Orig. Cond. W/1 Patched Tear, New Stretcher, Framed, 25½" x 30½" .. $600.00
ARROW-BACK BOSTON ROCKER, Worn Drk. Paint W/Yellow Striping .. $85.00
CLEAR BLOWN CAKE STAND, Applied Foot & Stem, 8½" D., 6½" H. $65.00
BLOWN APOTHECARY JAR, 2 Applied Rings, Lid W/Applied Finial, 9¾" H. .. $55.00
SHERATON STAND, Dovetailed Drawer, Orig. Top Has Shrinkage & Warpage-Refastened, Orig. Worn Red Paint, Repl. Brass Bale, 17½" x 18", 27" H. $250.00
TIN BEVERAGE URN, Cast Pewter Paw Feet & Handles, Burner Missing, Removable Base, Ivory On Spout Incomp., 14¾" H. $15.00

A-OH Feb 1981   *Garth's Auctions, Inc.*
ROW I, L To R
TURNED WOODEN THREAD CADDY, 6 Holders, Crack In Base, 6¾" H. .. $15.00
SLEIGH BELLS ON LEATHER STRAP, 15½" L. $50.00
BUCKET, Stave Const. W/Metal Bands & Wire Bale W/Wood Handle, Decoupage "The Moss Covered Bucket", 4¾" D., 3¾" H. $17.50

ROW II, L To R
PINE BASKET, Orig. Decor. W/Inscription Around Rim, 6" Sq., 4½" H. $130.00
CAST IRON SEWING MACHINE, Worn Orig. Painted Decor., 13½" L. $135.00
TIN BUCKET, Embossed W/Wire Bale & Wooden Handle, Orig. Red Japanning, 5¼" H. $20.00

ROW III, L To R
BOX, Fruitwood Veneer W/Hinged Bowed Lid & Gr. Velvet Int., Engraved Brass Shield On Lid W/"G", 5" H. $30.00
ICE CREAM FREEZER, Child Size, "Wh. Mountain Junior", Cylinder Missing .. $42.50
PEWTER FOOD MOLD, Mkd. "A Ramage", Threaded Lid, 6½" H. $45.00
LIGNUM VITAE COVERED JAR, Sm. Age Cracks, 8" H. $15.00
SHENANDOAH WALL POCKET, Redware W/Cream Slip, Gr. & Br. Glaze W/Applied Flower, Chipped & Hairlines, Top Handle Missing, 5¾" H. $75.00

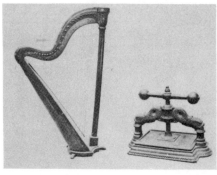

A-MA Sept 1980   *Richard A. Bourne Co., Inc.*
L To R
SM. HARP OR LYRE, Ca. 1874, Metal & Wood, 31" H. $1100.00
IRON BOOK PRESS, Dolphin-Form Arms, 20" L., 17" H $260.00

A-MA Feb 1980   *Robert W. Skinner Inc.*
L To R
SNARE DRUM, Brass Shell W/Single Vent
Hole, Wood Rims W/Trace Of Red Paint,
Top Head Has Several Splits, 15¾" D., 10½"
H. $250.00*

MILITARY SNARE DRUM, Polychromed
Am. Spread Eagle Decor, Brass Plate Reads
In Script "F.J. Lunt, Newburyport", Both
Heads Split, Snare Detached, Mid 19th C.,
11" O.H. $675.00*

A-MA Aug 1980   *Robert C. Eldred Co., Inc.*
FIRE BUCKETS, Pr., NH, Gr. W/Gold
Letters, 1 Handle Needs Repair, 13" H.
.... $350.00

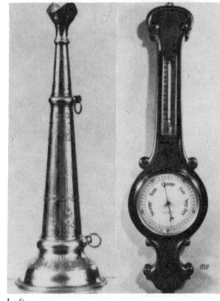

Left

A-MA Aug 1980   *Robert W. Skinner Inc.*
FIREMAN'S SPEAKING TRUMPET, Silver Plated Decor. W/Stylized Floral & Geometric Designs, Inscribed "Citizens Engine
Co. No. 2", Am., Ca. 1880, 19¾" L. . .$500.00*

Right

A-VA April 1980   *Laws Auction & Antiques*
BAROMETER, Mahogany, Ca. 1820, 36" H.
.... $220.00

A-MA Mar 1980   *Richard A. Bourne Co., Inc.*

ROW I, L To R
FIRE BUCKET, "No 1 Prince Gardner
1832", Surface Worn, Handle Broken Free
On 1 Side, 13" H. $375.00

FIRE BUCKET, Name Partially Rubbed
Off, Ca. 1833, Handle Broken Free On 1
Side, 12" H. $350.00

ROW II, L To R
LEATHER FIRE BUCKET, "A. Porter",
"1821", Orig. Handle, 12" H. $375.00

FIRE BUCKET, "J. Barrows. No. 1, 1827",
Orig. Handle Broken Free On 1 Side, 12½" H.
.... $200.00

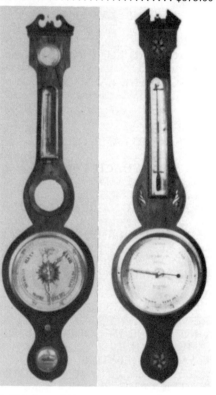

A-MA Aug 1980   *Robert C. Eldred Co., Inc.*
L To R

BANJO BAROMETER, Eng., Walnut, 19th
C., Ivory Finial, 39" L. $300.00

BANJO BAROMETER, Walnut Inlay, By A.
Riva, Glasgow, Broken Arch Pediment, 39" H.
.... $550.00

A-MA Aug 1980   *Robert C. Eldred Co., Inc.*
L To R
FIRE ALARM BOX, Walnut Case W/Glass
Door, 14" W., 15½" H. $425.00
BRASS BUGLE, Inscribed, Used On Bos-
ton's Ladder No. 4, 11½" L. $300.00

A-MA Oct 1980   *Robert W. Skinner Inc.*
MILITARY SHAKO, Bell Crowned Leather
Helmet W/Duckbill Visor, Brass Scale Chin
Strap, Gilt Cord, Label Inside (Illus.), Am.,
Ca. 1820-1830, 15" O.H. $750.00*

A-MA Feb 1980   *Robert W. Skinner, Inc.*
STERN BOARD CARVING, Eagle
Above 2 Gathered Am. Flags, Sgn., MA,
Ca. 1900, 59" L., 22" H. $1900.00*

*Price does not include 10% buyer fee.

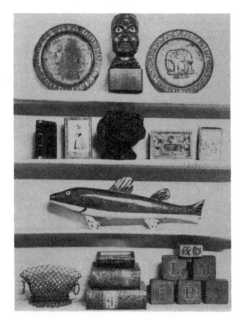

A-OH Mar 1980   Garth's Auctions, Inc.
ROW I, L To R
TIN "ABC" PLATES, 2 (1 Illus.), Not A Pr., 6½" D. $30.00
CARVED WOODEN HEAD W/Painted Eyes, 20th C., 7" H. $35.00
TIN "ABC" PLATE, "Jumbo", Rust, 6¼" D. $30.00
ROW II, L To R
SM. BOOK SHAPED BOX, Velvet & Paper Trim, Mirror On Inside Lid, 2¼" x 3¼" $15.00
SM. BOOK SHAPED BOX, Rev. Painted Front & Back, 2½" x 3⅝" $17.50
POTTERY HEAD, Hand Formed, Blk. Shiny Glaze, 20th C., 4¼" H. $15.00
SM. CARDBOARD BOX W/Rev. Painting On Lid & Int. Mirror, Hinge Torn, 2¾" x 3¾" $15.00
SM. BOOK SHAPED BOX, Rev. Decor., Hinge Torn, 2¼" x 3" $13.00
ROW III
CARVED WOODEN FISH By Miles Davis, 14" L. $95.00
ROW IV, L To R
SM. ROOT BASKET, Clear And Amber Beads Strung On Wire, 2¾" H. $5.00
BOOK SHAPED BOX W/Glass Front & Back, Blk. & Gold Binding, 2½" x 3¾" $37.50
BOOK SHAPED BOX W/Glass Front & Back, Rev. Painted Glass, 1 Cracked, 3" x 4½" $7.50
BOOK SHAPED BOX, Printed & Marbelized Bindings, Rev. Painted Glass Worn, 3¾" x 5" $55.00
EMBOSSED WOODEN BLOCKS, Set Of 9, 2" Sq. $35.00

*Price does not include 10% buyer fee.

Left
A-WA D.C. Oct 1980   Adam A. Weschler & Son
GEORGE III CISTERN BAROMETER, Inlaid Mahogany, Francis Roncorone, London, Ca. 1810, Broken Arch Pediment, Brass Urn Above Hinged Glazed Door, Feather Crossbanded Satinwood Line Edge Waist, 38" H. $1200.00*
GEORGE III CISTERN BAROMETER, Mahogany, T. Ribright/Poultry, London, Ca. 1810, Broken Arch Pediment Above Hinged Glazed Door, Brass Workings, 38" H. $750.00*

Right
A-MA Aug 1980   Richard A. Bourne Co., Inc.
STICK BAROMETER By George Inch, London, Brass-Mounted Rosewood Case, Complete W/Thermometer, Engraved Ivory Dials $1550.00

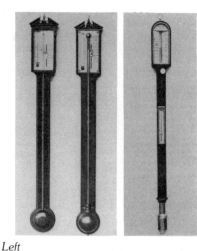

A-OH Oct 1980   Garth's Auctions, Inc.
BENNINGTON CUSPIDOR, Impressed "1849" Mrk., Rockingham Glaze, 9½" D. $65.00
YELLOWWARE CUSPIDOR, Rockingham Glaze, 9" D. $20.00
WOVEN SPLINT BUTTOCKS BASKET, 13" x 17½", 7½" O.H. $70.00
WOVEN SPLINT BUTTOCKS BASKET, 13½" x 16", 6" O.H. $65.00

◄ A-MA Sept 1980   Robert W. Skinner Inc.
L To R
WALL BOX, Pine, Painted & Grained, Int. Worn, Minor Paint Loss, Early 19th C., 12½" W., 4½" D., 11½" L. $2400.00*
DECOR. COVERED WOODEN BOX, Dovetailed Const., Sliding Cover W/Divided Int., N. Eng., Ca. 1824, 3½" H. $1900.00*

A-OH Oct 1980   Garth's Auctions, Inc.
BENTWOOD MEASURES, 2, Old Gr. Paint, 5", 5½" D. $30.00
BENTWOOD MEASURE, Old Red Paint, 7½" D. $30.00
STONEWARE JAR, Applied Wh. Clay Vintage, Ash. Gr. Glaze, Incised "Lanier Meaders", 11" H. $40.00
REDWARE BOWL, Gr. Glaze W/Old Chips, 16¾" D., 3½" H. $40.00
TIN CANDLE MOLD, 12-Tube W/Handle, 10" H. $55.00
REDWARE BOWL, Glaze Chips, 14½" D., 3" H. $30.00
WH. CLAY PRESERVING JAR, Albany Slip W/Stenciled Label "Donagho Co. Parkersburg", 10" H. $22.50
BOOKCASE, 5-Section, Dovetailed, Pine, Orig. Worn Br. Graining, Harvard Shaker, 48" W., 14" D., 63" H. $1150.00
SHENANDOAH REDWARE PLATE, Br. Radiating Design W/Clear Glaze, Some Flaking, 8¼" D. $110.00
ROCKINGHAM CUSPIDOR, Yellowware, 8" D. $12.50
WH. CLAY PLATE, Clear Int. Glaze, 7⅞" D. $80.00
ROCKINGHAM SHAVING MUG, Mkd. "Bennett, Canton Ave, Baltimore MD", 4¼" H. $65.00
REDWARE PIE PLATE, Clear Int. Glaze, Edge Flakes, Impressed "John W. Bell, Waynesboro, VA", 9⅛" D. $135.00
SHENANDOAH REDWARE JAR, Gr. Glaze W/Orange & Br. Decor., Rim Flakes, 7¾" H. $175.00
REDWARE BOWL, Thrown As Jug, Cut In ½ Before Glazing & Firing, Applied Handle, Clear Glaze, 15" D., 3¾" H. $90.00
SHENANDOAH REDWARE JAR, Mottled Br., Blk., & Yellow W/Tooling, Impressed "Winchester, VA", 7⅝" D. .. $85.00
POTTERY JAR, Tan Glaze, Impessed "Cowen & Wilcox", 6½" H. $20.00
SHENANDOAH POTTERY LAMP, Wh. Clay W/Worn, Flaking Wh. Paint, 1 Ear Broken Off, 9" H. $115.00
REDWARE JAR, Drk. Br. Int. Glaze, Impressed "John Bell, Waynesboro", 7⅝" H. $65.00

A-OH Aug 1980   *Garth's Auctions, Inc.*
ROW I, L To R
BRONZE ORIENTAL VASE, Dragon Handles, Early 19th C., Minor Damage On Rim Of Foot, 6″ H. $32.50
ORIENTAL NODDING FIGURE, Bisque Head & Hands W/Glazed Robe, Minor Flakes, 5½″ H. $65.00
CAST WH. METAL BODHISATTVA, Lotus Throne, Blk. Lacquer, Worn Gilding W/ Worn Red Stripe, 7¼″ H. $25.00
ROW II, L To R
IMARI CUP, Polychrome Floral & Butterfly Design, Mid 19th C., 2⅝″ H. ... $13.00
SM. IMARI CUP, Matches Above, 1¾″ H. $10.00
KUTANI MAGIC HAMMER, Symbol Of Good Fortune, Pine, Plum, Bamboo Design, Meiji, 5¼″ L. $55.00
SM. ORIENTAL PORCELAIN JAR, Red, Blk. & Gilded Landscape Design, 2⅞″ H. $7.50
LACQUER BOX, Blk. & Gilt, Peacock On Lid, Minor Chip, 3⅝″ D., 2¾″ H. .. $15.00
ROW III, L To R
SATSUMA DISHES, Set Of 5, (1 Illus.), Chrysanthemum & Butterfly Design, Meiji, 5″ D. $30.00
ORIENTAL PORCELAIN DISH, Boat Shaped, Polychrome Floral Cloisonne W/ Blue & Wh. Key Rim, Floral Int., 7½″ L. $365.00
IMARI DISH, Polychrome Design W/Landscape Center & Medallion Rim, 4½″ D. $16.00

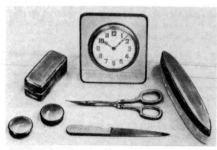

A-WA D.C. Oct 1980   *Adam A. Weschler & Son*
8-DAY TRAVELING CLOCK, Sterling & Powder Blue Enameled, Early 20th C., Am. $200.00*
LADY'S TRAVELING DRESSER SET, 6 Pcs., Vermeil Sterling & Lavender Enamel, Early 20th C., Fitted In Cagreen Leather Carrying Case $200.00*

*Price does not include 10% buyer fee.

A-OH Sept 1980   *Garth's Auctions, Inc.*
ROW I, L To R
ROCKINGHAM FLASK, Potato Shaped, Chips, 5¾″ H. $50.00
PEWTER SHAKERS, Pr., 5″ H. .. $15.00
PEWTER PORRIGER, Old Eng. Handle, 4½″ D. $250.00
ROCKINGHAM TOBY BANK, Chipped, 5¼″ H. $55.00
ROW II, L To R
PEWTER BELLIED MEASURE, 1/16 Pt., Soldered Split, 2″ H. $35.00
PEWTER FOOTED SALT, Unmarked, 2⅜″ H. $55.00
PEWTER BELLIED MEASURE, ½ Pt., Repairs, 3¾″ H. $40.00
PEWTER FOOTED SALT, Unmarked, 2⅛″ H. $105.00
PEWTER FOOTED SALT, Unmarked, 1⅞″ H. $55.00
ROW III, L To R
MINI. BRASS CANDLESTICKS, Pr., 4″ H. $50.00
PEWTER ICE CREAM MOLD, Makes Card W/Club, 3″ x 4″ $22.50
SM. BRASS DOOR KNOCKER, Figure In Lotus Position, 4″ H. $10.00
MINI. BRASS CANDLESTICKS, Pr., 4¼″ H. $60.00

A-MA Sept 1980   *Richard A. Bourne Co., Inc.*
BATTERSEA ENAMELS
SNUFF BOX, Form Of Reclining Spaniel In Natural Colors, Ca. 1770, Old Repairs $375.00
OVAL BOX, Romantic Scene On Cover, Cracks.......................... $80.00
ROUND BOXES, Lot Of 3, Each W/Different Verse, Ca. 1770, 1 Chipped & 1 W/ Cracks.......................... $300.00

A-OH Nov 1980   *Garth's Auctions, Inc.*
CHRISTMAS TREE ORNAMENTS
TEARDROPS, 2, Paper Label "Germany", 11¼″ L., 10″ L. $10.00
CHILD, 2½″ H. $30.00
CHILD'S HEAD, Satin Face W/Worn Red & Gold, 3½″ H. $47.50
PARROT, Fibre Tail & Tin Clip, 6″ L. $12.50
FISH, Gold & Red, 3″ L. $35.00
BIRD, Silver, Red & Gr., Tin Clip Missing, 6¾″ L. $30.00
CHILD'S HEAD, Glued In Glass Eyes, Silver W/Worn Color, 3″ H. $30.00
TREE TOP, Blue W/Applied Silver Glitter, 10½″ H. $5.00
VASES, 2, Gold W/Painted Flowers, 3½″ H. $10.00
BIRD, Fibre Tail & Wings, 4½″ L. .. $32.50
CLOWN, Red Suit, 4⅛″ H. $42.50
WAX CHERUB, Arms & Legs Have Repair, 3⅝″ D. $65.00
ROUND, Drk. Gr. W/Floral Enameling, 2″ H. $5.00
TEARDROP, Red W/Tinsel Wrapping, Cut Out Paper Angel, 8¾″ L. $30.00
LRG. SANTA, Magenta Coat, 5¼″ H. $40.00
BLIMP, Gr. W/Tinsel Wrapping & Paper Santa, 5¾″ H. $60.00
HEAD W/CONICAL CAP, Minor Damage, Hanger Gone, 2½″ H. $5.00
HOUSE, Red Roof, Gr. Evergreens, Minor Damage, Hanger Gone, 2½″ H. ... $22.50
CHILD'S FACE, Glass Eyes, Flesh Colored W/Red Hood, 3″ H. $57.50
ROUND, Red W/Embossed Parrot, 2½″ H. $27.50
CANDLE HOLDERS, Set Of 16, Counter Balanced, Tin & Wire, Gilded, 5″ L. .. $90.00
TINSEL & PAPER, Red W/Gold Flowers, 6½″ L. $15.00

A-WA D.C. May 1980 *Adam A. Weschler & Son*
DRESSER SET, 6 Pcs., 14 Karat Yellow Gold Mounted, William B. Kerr & Co., Am., Monogrammed, 12 Oz. $2600.00*

A-OH Nov 1980   *Garth's Auctions, Inc.*
ROW I, L To R
WROUGHT IRON & BRASS TASTER,
11¾" L. $75.00
WROUGHT IRON & BRASS TASTER,
9" L. $125.00
TINY STEEL FORKS, Set Of 3 (1 Illus.),
Gr. Stained Bone Handles, 8" L. .. $24.00
WROUGHT IRON SPLINT LIGHT
HOLDER, 8¾" L. $35.00
JEW'S HARP, Eagle Brand, Made In Eng.,
4½" L. $12.50
WROUGHT IRON & BRASS LADLE,
Lrg. Shallow Bowl, 10" L. $150.00
WROUGHT IRON & BRASS DIPPER,
13" L. $95.00
ROW II, L To R
BRASS FISHING REEL, Ivory Handle, 3"
L. $55.00
WROUGHT STEEL CHOPPER, Turned
Wooden Handle, 6¼" W. $15.00
BRASS & STEEL BLEEDER, 3½" L.
.... $85.00

A-OH Mar 1980   *Garth's Auctions, Inc.*
SILVER DEMI TASSE SPOON, Marked
& Monogramed, 5⅝" L. $17.50
STEEL KNIFE & FORK W/Antler Han-
dles, 9¾" L. $27.00
VELVET PILLOW, Purple W/Beaded
Decor., 6½" x 8". $20.00
MEERSHAUM PIPE, Carved Lion's Head
& Amber Mouth Pc., Fitted Case, 6½" L.
.... $52.50
FIGURAL PEWTER SPOON, Continen-
tal Angel Mark, 5" L. $8.00
HOLLOW CUT SILHOUETTE, Wh. &
Blk. Ink, Embossed "Day's Patent", Orig.
Embossed Brass On Wood Frame, 4½" H.
.... $200.00
SM. BELLOWS W/Hand Painted Scene,
Some Wear, Releathered, 11½" L.
.... $45.00
PAPIER MACHE SNUFF BOX, Decou-
page Scene Hand Painted, 2⅝" D.
.... $23.00
DELFT TILE, Purple & Wh., Minor Glaze
Wear, 4½" Sq. $7.00
COIN SILVER SPOONS, 4, "W.M. Root
& Brother", 5¾" L. $44.00
COIN SILVER SPOON, Marked "A.P.",
Sm. Dent In Bowl, 7" L. $10.00
SILVER SPOON W/Shell Bowl, Marked
"M. Gibney Patent 1846", 6½" L. $30.00
COIN SILVER SPOONS, 4, Monogramed
"P.C.C.", 6" L. $40.00

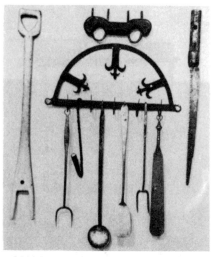

A-OH Mar 1980   *Garth's Auctions, Inc.*
WOODEN CLOTHES WASHING
FORK, 27" L. $42.50
MINI. WOODEN YOKE, Old Blk. Paint,
9" L. $17.50
PRUNING SAW, Burl Handle W/Horn
Ferrule, 22½" L. $35.00
WROUGHT IRON UTENSIL RACK,
18½" x 9½" $85.00
WROUGHT IRON FORK, 15½" L.
.... $60.00
WROUGHT IRON CANDLE HOLDER,
10½" L. $140.00
WROUGHT IRON DIPPER W/Tooled
Handle, 19" L. $55.00
WROUGHT IRON SPATULA, Hanger A
Bit Askew, 17" L. $35.00
WROUGHT IRON FORK, 14¼" L.
.... $17.50
IRON WIDE BLADE SPATULA, 15" L.
.... $80.00

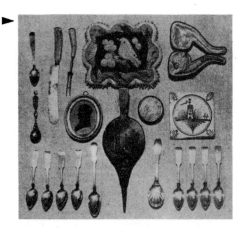

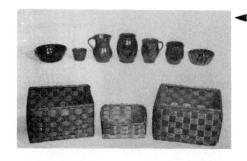

A-OH Mar 1980   *Garth's Auctions, Inc.*
SPOON RACK, Pine, Mortised Const.
W/Scalloped Edges, Old Worn Blue Paint,
PA, 20½" W., 21½" H. $235.00
WROUGHT IRON SPATULA, 16½" L.
.... $30.00
CUT OUT WOODEN DOUGH WORK-
ING KNIFE, Sm. Split, 17½" L. .. $37.50
WOODEN LIGHTING STAND, Whittled
Legs Set Into Block W/Applied Gallery, 42"
H. $235.00
TIN CANDLE LANTERN, Pierced Star
Top & Ring Handle, Old Worn Gold Paint,
12" O.H. $80.00
SIFTER, Bentwood Rim, 17½" D. .. $22.50
TIN CANDLE MOLD, 3-Tube, 10½" H.
.... $50.00
TIN CANDLE MOLD, 4-Tube, 10" H.
.... $50.00
WROUGHT IRON ANDIRONS, Pr., 14½"
H. $105.00
WOVEN SPLINT BASKET, 15½" D.
.... $45.00

A-NY May 1980   *Calkins Auction Gallery*
ROW I, L To R
BENNINGTON BOWL, Tulip Decor. In
Bottom, Rim Flake, 3¼" H. $45.00
REDWARE CUSTARD CUP, Handleless,
Flared W/Red & Blk. Drip Decor., Minor
Rim Flake, 4" D., 2¾" H. $40.00
REDWARE MILK PITCHER, Gr. W/Mot-
tled Decor., Incised Lines Around Center,
5½" D., 7" H. $55.00
REDWARE OVOID JAR, Orange W/Br.
Splotches, Incised Lines Near Rim, 6" D.,
7½" H. $95.00
REDWARE HANDLED JAR, Orange W/Br.
Mottled Decor., Incised Lines Near Rim,
Minor Rim Chips, 5" D., 6" H. ... $120.00
REDWARE JAR, Olive W/Orange Spots,
PA, 5" D., 5½" H. $85.00
REDWARE CAKE MOLD, PA, Red
Ground W/Blk. Seaweed Decor., 8" D., 3" H.
.... $55.00
ROW II, L To R
POTATO STAMPED INDIAN BASKET,
Algonquin, 16½" L., 10½" W., 10" H.
.... $120.00
POTATO STAMPED INDIAN BASKET,
Algonquin, 12" Sq., 4" H. $70.00
POTATO STAMPED INDIAN BASKET,
Algonquin, Damaged, 17" L., 13" W., 10" H.
.... $140.00

A-MA April 1980   *Richard A. Bourne Co., Inc.*
POLITICAL MEMORABILIA, 7 Cards Commemorating The Presidency & Assasination Of William McKinley, Partially Illus.
.... $550.00

A-OH Feb 1981   *Garth's Auctions, Inc.*
TIN
ROW I, L To R
PENNY BANK, Punched Sides, Worn Wh. & Gr. Paint, 3¼" H. $15.00
CHOCOLATE MOLD, 2-Part Chicken, "Germany", 3" H. $22.50
CHOCOLATE MOLD, 2-Part Rabbit, "Burn Brothers N.Y.C.", 5¼" H. ... $22.50
COTTAGE CHEESE SIEVES, Pr., Heart Shaped, 3¾" H. $80.00

ROW II, L To R
CANNISTERS, Set Of 4, Br. Japanning, Smallest Stenciled "Coffee", 1 Stenciled "Tea", Some Worn, Ca. 1851, 6" To 9" $35.00
CANNISTER, Embossed Pinwheels W/ Worn Gold Japanning, 6½" H. $15.00

ROW III, L To R
SQ. BOXES, Lot Of 2, Br. Japanning, Lrg. 1 W/"Ginger" Label, 2⅞" Sq., 3½" Sq.
.... $15.00
HINGED CHOCOLATE MOLD, Rooster, Repaired, Brass Hinges $50.00
MINI. PAILS, Wire Bales, Worn Blue Japanning, 2⅜" & 3" D. $40.00

A-OH Mar 1980   *Garth's Auctions, Inc.*
PRINTED CAMPAIGN RIBBON, "Henry Clay, 1844", 3½" x 9½" $65.00
POSTER, "James K. Polk", Minor Edge Rep. Unframed, 9¼" x 24" $70.00
TIN CANTEEN, "We Drank From The Same Canteen, Chicago 1900", 5¾" L.
.... $25.00
PENCILED NOTE, On White House Stationery, McKinley, Framed, 6¾" x 8¼"
.... $150.00
STEVENGRAPH, "Centennial In Philadelphia 1876", George Washington, Framed, 5" x 13½" $100.00
BRASS LAMP, For Sterilizing Medical Instruments, Civil War, Burner W/Twin Wicks & Cover, 5" L. $50.00
PRINTED ELECTION TICKET, Lincoln & Johnson, Nov. 8, 1864, OH, Framed, Fold Lines, 7¾" x 12" $80.00

A-MA April 1980   *Richard A. Bourne Co., Inc.*
POLITICAL MEMORABILIA, Campaign Items Mounted On 9 Cards Including Buttons, Tickets, Badges, Etc. $1900.00

A-MA Feb 1980   *Robert W. Skinner Inc.*
ROW I
INDIAN BASKETRY BOWL, Pomo, Stepped Triangle Designs & Quail Feathers & Shell Bead Decor., 6½" D., 2½" H.
.... $525.00*

ROW II, L To R
INDIAN BASKET, Tlingit, 3 Central Bands Of False Embroidered Decor., Red, Blk., Gr. & Yellow, 7" D., 5½" H. $150.00*
INDIAN BASKET, Tlingit, 3 Bands Of Alternating Triangle Designs W/Openwork Sections Between, Red, Blk. & Wh. On Natural, 4½" D., 4½" H. $360.00*
INDIAN BASKET, Tlingit, 2 Bands Of Stepped Geometric False Embroidered Designs, Br., Orange & Wh. On Natural, 7" D., 6" H. $175.00*

A-MA Aug 1980   *Richard A. Bourne Co., Inc.*
NANTUCKET BASKETS
ROW I, L To R
TINY BASKET, 1-Egg Size, 2¾" D.
.... $300.00
POCKETBOOK, Sgn. Jose Formoso Reyes, W/Drawstring, Top 6½" Sq. $200.00
LIDDED BASKET, 8¾" D. $850.00
ROW II, L To R
CIRCULAR BASKET, Incised "W" In Handle, 9¼" D. $400.00
CIRCULAR BASKET, 11" D. .. $550.00
ROW III, L To R
SHALLOW BASKET, Sm. Loop Side Handles, 15" D. $350.00
CIRCULAR BASKET, Hoop-Shaped Side Handles, 15" D. $500.00

A-MA Mar 1980   *Richard A. Bourne Co., Inc.*
ROW I, L To R
FIRE BUCKET, "Mechanic Fire Society", "Isaac Dow", "No. 3 1811", Orig. Handle Broken Free On 1 Side & In Half, 11¾" H. $850.00
FIRE BUCKET, "P.F.D. No 1", 12½" H. $150.00
ROW II, L To R
LEATHER FIRE BUCKET, Partially Repainted, 13½" H. $75.00
FIRE BUCKETT, "D.B. Chapin", 13¾" H. $125.00

A-NY May 1980   *Calkins Auction Gallery*
SPLINT BASKET W/Double Swing Handle, Old Blk. Paint, 10" W., 8½" D., 16" L. . .$80.00
SPLINT BASKET W/Shaker Swing Handle, Copper Rivets, Sl. Damage, 14½" D., 11" H. $120.00
SPLINT BASKET W/Double Fixed Handle, Pushed Up Bottom, 15½" D., 9" H. . . $80.00
CHEESE BASKET W/Handle, Rails Supporting Bottom, Good Patina, 17½" D., 7" H. $210.00
CHEESE CURD BASKET, Shaker, 11" D., 4½" H. $90.00
SPLINT CHEESE BASKET, Single Wrap, Good Patina, Minor Damage, 21" D., 8" H. $110.00
SPLINT DRYING BASKET, Fixed Handle, Double Wrapped Oak, 14½" L., 9" W., 6" H. $100.00
MINI. MELON BASKET W/Fixed Handle, Minor Break In Rim, 8" L., 4" H. . . $90.00

A-NY May 1980   *Calkins Auction Gallery*
SPLINT BASKET, Late 19th C., 23" L., 15" W., 8" H. $80.00

A-MA Aug 1980   *Richard A. Bourne Co., Inc.*
L To R
NANTUCKET EVENING BAG, Made By Stanley M. Ropp, Ca. 1972, Whale Ivory Starfish & Rosewood Top, 4" D., 8" H. $700.00
OVAL NANTUCKET BASKET, Made By Stanley M. Ropp, Ca. 1969, Sgn., 8½" W., 11½" L., 6" H. $400.00

A-MA April 1980   *Richard A. Bourne Co., Inc.*
L To R
NANTUCKET LIGHTSHIP BASKET, Made As Lady's Pocketbook W/Carved Whale On Lid, Minor Repair Necessary To Hinge Loops, 7" W., 8" L., 7" H. . . $300.00
NANTUCKET LIGHTSHIP BASKET By Stanley M. Roop, Sgn., Ca. 1965, Rosewood Top W/Carved Whale Ivory, 6" W., 8" L., 7" H. $450.00

A-MA Aug 1980   *Robert C. Eldred Co., Inc.*
POWDERHORN, Engraved "Gideon Webb's Horn Dat'd At Crown Pt. Sept. 8, 1762", Sm. Hole, 12" L. $4600.00

A-MA Mar 1980   *Richard A. Bourne Co., Inc.*
ROW I, L To R
FIRE BUCKET, 18th C., "R. Brown" & "1794", Orig. Frail Handle, 11" H. . . $350.00
LEATHER FIRE BUCKET, "No. 1 C-Hardy 1806", Replaced Handle, 11" H. $325.00
ROW II
LEATHER FIRE BUCKETS, Pr., Orig. Paint, "Ira Barrow", "1836", Both Handles Off, 1 Missing, 1 Holed In Bottom, 12¾" H. $325.00

A-OH Jan 1980   *Garth's Auctions, Inc.*
PA GERMAN BIBLE, Published By Samuel Saur 1791, Illuminated Fraktur Book Plate Date 1795, Blk., 4" x 7" $325.00
LEATHER BOUND BOOK, "Clavis Universalis" Printed In German By Joseph Bauman, Ca. 1818, 3¾" x 6" $30.00
HAND LETTERED BOOKLET, Of Mathematical Exercises, "Jacob F. Stoltzfuls Book, March 2, 1858;;, 8½" x 13" . . $200.00
SM. LEATHER BOUND GERMAN BOOK, Published By Michael Billmeyer In Germantown, 1812, Illuminated Fraktur Book Plate, 3½" x 5¼" $75.00
LEATHER BOUND SONG BOOK, Handwritten, "Henry Thomas's Book Written This 20th Day Of February 1839". . . $52.50
KENTUCKY PISTOL, Flint Lock W/Walnut Stock, Ca. 1790. 14¾" H. . . $1300.00
FRENCH PISTOL, Flint Lock W/Silver Mountings & Silver Wire Inlay, 16" L. $275.00

A-MA Sept 1980   *Richard A. Bourne Co., Inc.*
BISCUIT TINS
ROW I, L To R
HUNTLY & PALMER, Form Of 8 Multi-colored Books, Some Wear To Finish, Cover Tab Missing, 6¼″ H. $125.00
ENGLISH, Form Of 8 Books W/Red Bindings, Unsigned, 6¼″ H. $125.00
HUNTLY & PALMER, Form Of China Cabinet, Rusting On Bottom, 7″ H. . .$100.00
ROW II, L To R
HUNTLY & PALMER, Form Of Marble Pedestal, Hinge Pin Broken, 7″ H. . . $100.00
MCVITIE & PRICE, Scottish, Form Of Louis XV Commode, 6″ H. $110.00
HUNTLY & PALMER, Form Of Box Camera, 4″ H. $220.00
HUNTLY & PALMER, Form Of Cannon, Finish Worn, 4″ H. $100.00

A-OH June 1980   *Garth's Auctions, Inc.*
BRASS SCISSORS WICK TRIMMERS W/Tray, 9¼″ L. $70.00
WROUGHT IRON KEROSENE WICK TRIMMER W/Attached Brush That Removes Char From Wick, 5⅜″ L. . . . $20.00
HOLLOW CUT SILHOUETTES, Mini., Pr., Pen & Ink Detail & Matching Embossed Gilded Frames, 2″ x 2½″ $200.00
WROUGHT IRON DOUGH SCRAPER W/Brass Handle, Blade Stamped "B.L.S. 1860", 4″ L. $65.00
SALESMAN'S SAMPLE, Wagon Jack, Wood & Brass, 7¼″ H. $60.00
TIN LAMP, 3 Burner W/Shallow Rectangular Font, Old Blk. Paint, 3″ x 6½″ $65.00
WROUGHT IRON CANDLE CUTTER, Shape Of Bird, 7″ L. $315.00
COPTIC POTTERY LAMP W/Embossed Designs, 5th-7th C. A.D., Syria Or Palestine, 4″ L. $17.50
BRASS CEREMONIAL LAMP, 5 Compartments Each W/Lion On Hinged Lid, Pcs. Missing, 4½″ D. $60.00
SUGAR MOLD, Maple, Leaf Shaped, 3½″ L. $10.00
BRONZE ROMAN LAMP, 4¾″ L. . .$15.00

A-OH Jan 1980   *Garth's Auctions, Inc.*
TIN NUTMEG GRATER, 6¾″ H. . . $55.00
BRASS PASTRY CUTTER, 4¼″ L. . .$65.00
TIN COOKIE CUTTER, Heart Shaped, 1½″ L. $30.00
TIN COOKIE CUTTER, Stylized Horse, 7″ L. $80.00
TIN COOKIE CUTTER, Seated Cat, 4″ H. $82.50
NUTMEG GRATER, Turned Wood W/Brass Fittings & Spring Feed, Cup Marked "Patent Apr. 2, 1861", 7¾″ L. $165.00
TIN & WOOD PASTRY CUTTER W/Turned Handle, 6″ L. $60.00
BRASS PASTRY CUTTER, 6″ L. . .$105.00
CAST IRON COOKIE BOARD, Octagonal, 10¼″ x 10½″ $475.00
PASTRY CUTTER, Scrimshaw Carved Whale Bone, 7″ H. $150.00
WROUGHT IRON TASTER, 6⅝″ L. $65.00
WROUGHT IRON FORK W/Designed Handle, 7¼″ L. $125.00
FOOD CHOPPER W/Curly Maple Handle, Marked "N. Cody", 8½″ L. . . $195.00
TIN COOKIE CUTTER, Stylized Horse, 6″ L. $90.00
FOOD CHOPPER W/Wrought Blade & Wooden Handle, 5¼″ L. $20.00

A-OH Sept 1980   *Garth's Auctions, Inc.*
CAST IRON PARLOR STOVE, Orig. Urn Finial, NY, Ca. 1852, 40″ H. . . $280.00
HEXAGONAL HALL LIGHT, Tin Frame W/Embossed Decor., Frosted Cut To Clear Panels, Clear Blown Smoke Bell, Candle Socket, 17″ H. $105.00
TURTLE BACK BELLOWS, Decorated, Orig. Gr. Paint W/Pumpkin & Yellow Striping & Gold Stenciled Basket of Fruit, Brass Nozzle, 17″ L. $175.00
SM. COPPER TEA KETTLE, Dovetailed Seams, Battered, Wooden Knob Repl. 6½″ O.H. $105.00
KETTLE SHELF TRIVET, Cast & Wrt. Iron, Cast Scroll Work Top Damaged, 10½″ x 13″, 10″ H. $80.00
OVERSIZE DECOY, Cork Body, Carved Wooden Head, Canvasback Drake By Whitney Labeau, MI, Orig. Paint & Glass Eyes, 17¾″ D. $30.00

A-MA Sept 1980   *Robert W. Skinner Inc.*
BRASS SPOOL RACK, Sm. Emery Finial W/3 Tiers Of 5 Spool Holders On Each, Eng., Mid 19th C., 5″ D., 12½″ H. . . $230.00*

A-NY May 1980   *Calkins Auction Gallery*
BURL BOWL, Am., Painted Salmon & Gr., 7″ D. $85.00
CANDLELIGHTING REFRACTOR, 18th C., Dovetailed Const., Orig. Red Paint & Glazing, 5″ H. $70.00
SCRIMSHAW POWDER HORN By Thomas Stucklas, NY, Ca. 1812, Good Patina, 12½″ L. $300.00
SAW TOOTH TRAMMEL, 18th C., Wrought Iron $125.00

*Price does not include 10% buyer fee.

A-MA Feb 1980   *Robert W. Skinner Inc.*
INDIAN BASKETRY BOWL, Mission, Double Handles W/Banded Stylized Decor., Break In 1 Handle, 17½″ D., 9¾″ H. . . . $150.00*

A-MA Feb 1980   *Robert W. Skinner Inc.*
L To R
INDIAN BASKET, Tlingit, 3 Bands Of False Embroidered Decor. W/Openwork Sections Between, Blue, Orange & Wh. On Natural, 8″ W., 3″ D., 8″ H. . . . $150.00*
INDIAN COVERED BASKET, Tlingit, 7 Bands Of False Embroidered Decor., Red, Gr. & Wh. On Natural, 6½″ D., 5½″ H. $400.00*
INDIAN BASKET, Tlingit, Solid Decor. W/5 Bands Of False Embroidered Designs, Yellow, Red, Gr. & Blk. On Natural, Sl. Tear, 5″ D., 7″ H. $175.00*

A-MA Feb 1980   *Robert W. Skinner Inc.*
L To R
INDIAN BEADED PIPE BAG, Sioux, Rawhide W/Yellow Pigment, Solid Quilled Bottom & Fringe Suspensions, Some Damage To Quills, 25″ x 8″ $350.00*
INDIAN PIPE BAG, Kiowa, Beaded Decor. On Base W/Scalloped Mouth & Fringe Bottom, 21″ L. $250.00*
INDIAN PIPE BAG, Sioux, Beaded Decor. W/Quill Work & Fringe On Bottom, 23½″ L. $675.00*

A-MA Feb 1980   *Robert W. Skinner, Inc.*
L To R
INDIAN COVERED BASKET, Hupa, Lt. Ground, Blk., Br. & Natural, 7½″ D., 5½″ H. $300.00*
INDIAN BASKETRY OLA, Apache, Loss Of Stitches Throughout, 24″ W., 20″ H. $850.00*

A-MA Feb 1980   *Robert W. Skinner Inc.*
INDIAN SALLY BAG, Wasco, 7½″ W., 8″ L. $900.00*

A-MA Feb 1980   *Robert W. Skinner, Inc.*
L To R
INDIAN BASKETRY BOWL, Pomo, Bell-Shaped W/Stylized Designs & Shell Beads Hung Around Top Half, 11″ D., 4½″ H. $475.00*
INDIAN BASKETRY BOWL, Pomo, Stylized Triangle Motif On Sides, Blk. On Natural, 4″ D., 2″ H. $500.00*

A-MA Feb 1980   *Robert W. Skinner, Inc.*
L To R
INDIAN BASKETRY OLA, Apache, Natural W/Drk, Stepped & Stylized Designs, 12″ H. $550.00*
INDIAN SHOULDERED BASKET, Yokut W/Stepped Geometric Designs, 8″ D., 7″ H. $350.00*

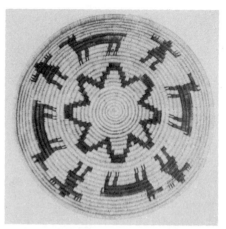

A-MA Feb 1980   *Robert W. Skinner Inc.*
INDIAN BASKETRY TRAY, Apache, Few Stitches Lost On Rim, 12″ D. $300.00*

A-MA Feb 1980   *Robert W. Skinner Inc.*
INDIAN BASKET, Pomo, Canoe-Shaped W/Stylized Stepped Designs & Quill Feather Decor., 6″ L., 4″ D., 2″ H. $700.00*
MOCCASINS, Northern Plains, Blue Silk Ribbon Edging & Cotton Lining . . . $275.00*
INDIAN RAWHIDE DOLL, Northern Plains, Fringed Clothing W/Simple Beaded & Red Wool Decor., 11½″ L. $80.00*

A-MA Feb 1980   *Robert W. Skinner Inc.*
INDIAN BASKETRY BOWL, Apache, 6″ D., 6″ H. $275.00*

A-MA Feb 1980   *Robert W. Skinner, Inc.*
L To R
INDIAN BASKETRY BOWL, Hupa, Break On 1 Side, Rim Roughness, 15″ D., 11½″ H. $250.00*
INDIAN COVERED BASKET, Eskimo W/Carved Ivory Finial, 10″ D., 6″ H. $275.00*

A-OH Mar 1981   *Garth's Auctions, Inc.*
OIL ON ACADEMY BOARD, Winter Landscape, Preparer's Label "Syracuse NY", Old Gilded Frame, 24½" x 30½" ... $135.00
PENCIL Drawing Of Gentleman On Paper, Old Gilded Frame, 13½" x 15½" $85.00
CARVED WOODEN SHOREBIRD SLEEPER, Tack Eyes, Shot Wounds, 7¼" H. $55.00
WORK BOX, Star & Floral Inlay, Few Turnings Missing, 6½" x 10", 12½" H. ... $85.00
CARVED WOODEN SHOREBIRD, 8¼" H. $60.00
ARROWBACK SIDE CHAIRS, Set Of 4, Plank Seats, Old Blk. Repaint, 2 W/Seat Damage $150.00
HEPPLEWHITE STAND, Pine & Poplar, 1 Dovetailed Drawer, 1 Board Top, Old Worn Finish, Splits In Top, 22½" x 26", 27" H. $135.00
CARVED WOODEN DECOY, Red-Breasted Merganser Hen, Carved Wing Detailing, Branded "Clare", Glass Eyes, 17½" L. $90.00
WOVEN SPLINT BUTTOCKS BASKET, Some Wear, 14½" D., 9" H. .. $105.00
CARVED WOODEN DECOY, Canvas Back Drake By John Roth, WI, Ca. 1930, Glass Eyes, Old Repaint, 18½" L. .. $105.00

A-OH Mar 1981   *Garth's Auctions, Inc.*
SINGLE WEAVE JACQUARD COVERLET, 2-Pc., Wh., Blue, Red, Pink & Gold, Corners Sgn., Colors Faded, Some Edge Wear, Ca. 1849, 72" x 87" $115.00
ROPE BED, Poplar, Partially Stripped Of Old Drk. Red Paint, Posts W/Age Splits, Orig. Side Rails, 43½" W., 43½" H. $100.00
TRADE SIGN, Pocket Watch, Cast Iron Frame, Zinc Face, Old Blk. Paint, 30" D. $280.00
STONEWARE CROCK, 2-Gal., Brushed Cobalt Decor., Imp. Label "T. Harrington, Lyons", Glaze Flaking, 9" H. $65.00
CAST IRON SNOW BIRDS, Set Of 2, 6½" D. $80.00
CARVED WOODEN DECOY, Redhead Drake, Dodge Factory, Working Repaint, Glass Eyes, Damaged, Ca. 1884-94, 14" L. $65.00
STONEWARE JAR, 2-Gal., Brushed Cobalt Floral Decor., Imp. "Lyons", Glaze Flaking, 11¾" H. $75.00

A-OH Mar 1981   *Garth's Auctions, Inc.*
OVERSHOT COVERLET, 2-Pc., Blue & Ochre Wool & Natural Colored Linen, Sm. Wear, Minor Stains, 64" x 84" $130.00
WOVEN SPLINT BUTTOCKS BASKET, Old Gr. Paint, 19" x 21½", 10" H. .. $295.00
SM. OVOID STONEWARE JUG, Splash Of Blue At Shoulder, Hairline, 10½" H. $45.00
WH. CLAY JUG, Reddish Br. Albany Slip, Orig. Tin Lids On Spout & Top, Wire Bale Handle, Sm. Flakes, 9" H. $50.00
DROP LEAF TABLE, Hickory Pencil Post Legs, Chesnut Top, Base Cleaned To Old Gr. W/Matching Gr. Stained Top, Sl. Warp In Top, 17½" x 48½", 28½" H. $100.00
SHENANDOAH REDWARE CUSPIDOR, Cream Slip W/Running Br. & Gr., Base Chips, 6¾" D. $180.00
MINI. BLANKET CHEST, Dovetailed Const., Restorations, 22" W., 12½" D., 14" H. $250.00
CARVED WOODEN DECOY, Hollow Bluebill Hen, Ca. 1930, 14½" L. $115.00
WOODEN DODGE FACTORY DECOY, Redhead Hen, Glass Eyes, Worn Repaint, Ca. 1880, 14¼" L. $155.00
CARVED WOODEN DECOY, Canvas Back Hen, MI, Glass Eyes, Worn Repaint, Branded "L.F.B.", Ca. 1935, 15" L. $75.00

◄ A-OH Mar 1981   *Garth's Auctions, Inc.*
CARVED WOODEN EAGLE, Hand Carved W/Old Painted & Varnished Surface, Some Damage, 27½" W. $225.00
CARVED WOODEN DECOY, Bluebill, Glass Eyes, Old Repaint, 13¼" L. .. $30.00
CARVED WOODEN DECOY, Worn Paint, 14" L. $30.00
BLANKET CHEST, Poplar, Dovetailed Const., Orig. Br. Flame Graining, 38" W., 20" D., 21¾" H. $400.00
CARVED WOODEN DECOY, Mallard Drake, Glass Eyes, Old Paint, 14" L. $20.00
CARVED WOODEN DECOY, Blk. Duck, Glass Eyes, Old Worn Paint, 15¾" L. $30.00

A-MA Jan 1981   *Robert W. Skinner Inc.*
PIPE BOX, N. Eng., Early 19th C., Pine, Sq. Nail Const., Dovetailed Drawer, Brass Knob, Red Paint Loss, 10⅞" H. $550.00*

A-OH Mar 1981   *Garth's Auctions, Inc.*
PASTEL ON PAPER, 20th C. Folk Art, Grained Frame, 20½" x 28¼" H. ... $65.00
TERRA COTTA BUST, Ears Damaged, 10" H. $20.00
PLANT STAND, Curly Maple, Worn Varnish Finish, Top Warped, 11¼" Sq., 33½" H. $65.00
LADDER-BACK WAGON SEAT, Woven Splint Seat, Worn Drk. Red Paint, 33½" W. $390.00
CARVED WOODEN DECOY, Canada Goose, Glass Eyes, Old Paint, 21½" L. $105.00
CARVED WOODEN SIZING DECOY, Sturgion From Blk. Lake MI, Ca. 1920, Metal Fins, Tack Eyes, Age Splits W/Old Repaint, 36" H. $435.00

A-OH Mar 1981   *Garth's Auctions, Inc.*
PA WOVEN RAG CARPET, 4 Strips, Beige W/Colorful Stripes........ $260.00
HANDCOLORED ENGRAVINGS, Set Of 4 (1 Illus.), "Amphibien", Each Framed In Linen Matt, 13½" x 15" $120.00
SLAT-BACK SIDE CHAIR, Old Blk. Paint W/Gold Striping Shows Red Beneath, Old Cloth Seat $80.00
CARVED WOODEN CROW DECOY, Simple Stylized Rendition, 17" H. .. $95.00
ROCKINGHAM JARDINIERE, Indian Head In Relief, 8" D., 6¾" H. $95.00
TABLE, Poplar, 2 Board Top, Old Worn Blk. Paint, Sm. Break & Groove Where Boards Meet, 26¼" D., 26½" H. $60.00
CARVED WOODEN DECOY, Glass Eyes, Old Blk. Paint, Simple Detail, Wire Legs & Base, 17½" L. $200.00
WOVEN SPLINT BASKET, Wooden Base, Stationary Rim W/Swivel Handle, Old Br. Varnish, 11½" D. $135.00
GROTESQUE POTTERY JUG, Incised "Lanier Meaders", 8" H. $155.00

A-OH Mar 1981   *Garth's Auctions, Inc.*
CHARCOAL DRAWING W/Pastel Coloring, 27¼" x 32¾" $85.00
CARVED WOODEN DECOY, Bluebill Drake By Baumgardner, Houghton Lake MI, Glass Eyes, Worn Repaint, Ca. 1930, 12" H. $60.00
CARVED WOODEN DECOY, Bluebill Hen, Picton, Ontario, Tack Eyes, Orig. Paint, 13" L. $95.00
CARVED WOODEN DECOY, Bluebill Hen, Low Head Position, Tack Eyes, Simple Feather Carving, Orig. Paint, Upper NY State, Ca. 1930, 13½" L. $80.00
EMPIRE CHEST OF DRAWERS, Cherry W/Mahogany Veneer Facade, Dovetailed Drawers W/Birdseye Veneer, Ref., 45" W., 20¼" D., 45" H. $140.00
CARVED WOODEN DECOY, Coot By Paul Doering, Princeton, WI, Glass Eyes & Orig. Paint, Branded "P.R.D.", 10¾" L. $85.00
MINI. CHEST OF DRAWERS, Orig. Blk. & Br. Flame Graining, 15¾" W., 8" D., 15¾" H. $145.00
CARVED WOODEN DECOY, Bluebill Drake Sleeper, PA, Ca. 1940, Glass Eyes, Old Paint, 11¾" L. $55.00
CARVED WOODEN DECOY, Goldeneye Drake, NY, Glass Eyes, Old Paint, Simple Wing Carving, Ca. 1930, 14" L. $75.00

◄ A-OH Jan 1981   *Garth's Auctions, Inc.*
NAVAHO RUG, Red & Natural Brown Shades, 44" x 74", Ca. 1910 ...... $425.00
WINDSOR SIDE CHAIRS, Set Of Six Matching Bow-Backs W/7 Spindles, Old Worn Paint. Repair To One Bow & One A Replacement, CT Origin $7,200.00

A-OH Mar 1981   *Garth's Auctions, Inc.*
WRT. IRON PEEL, 41½" L. $50.00
SINGLE SIZE BED, Poplar, Age Splits, Worn Finish W/Traces Of Red, 36¾" W., 36" H. $45.00
WRT. IRON PEEL, Faceted Knob Finial, 36" L. $30.00
CAST IRON PARLOR STOVE, "Johnson Cox & Fuller Troy NY Home Parlor #4, Patented 1852", 26½" H. $195.00
CAST IRON BOOT SCRAPER, 9½" x 13½" $55.00

A-OH Mar 1981   *Garth's Auctions, Inc.*
SINGLE WEAVE JACQUARD COVER-LET, 2-Pc., Wh., Red, blue & Gr. W/4 Rose Medallions, Eagle Border, Corner Blocks Sgn. "Samuel Hippart, Mount Joy, L. C., PA, 1833", Worn, 80" x 94" $175.00
FEDERAL ARCHITECTURAL MIRROR, 2-Part, Ref. W/Traced Of Old Red, Base Molding Incomp., 14¼" x 26¾"
. . . . $40.00
CARVED WOODEN SHOREBIRD, Glass Eyes, Sgn. "Moore", Sm. Repair, 14¼" O.H. $85.00
SM. LADDER-BACK SIDE CHAIR, 3-Slat Back, Ref., New Woven Splint Seat, Legs Worn, Sm. Repairs $20.00
CARVED WOODEN DECOY, Gr. Wing Teal Drake, CA, Mkd. "Arness" Glass Eyes, 12" L. $65.00
SM. CHERRY STAND, 2 Dovetailed Drawers, 2 Board Top Reattached, Wooden Knobs Recent Addition, 16¾" x 17¼", 24" H.
. . . . $310.00
CARVED WOODEN DECOY, Bluebill Drake, WI, Glass Eyes, Worn Orig. Paint, Ca. 1920, 12½" L. $70.00
CARVED WOODEN DECOY, Goldeneye Drake, Tack Eyes, Repaint, Ca. 1945, 13½" L. $35.00
MAUL, Burl W/Hickory Handle, 16¾" L.
. . . . $35.00

A-OH Mar 1981   *Garth's Auctions, Inc.*
L To R
MINI. TOLE BUCKET W/Lid, Orig. Gr. Paint W/Gold Stenciling "My Boy", Worn & Faded, 2¼" D. $50.00
TIN PAIL, Lid & Wire Bale, 3¾" D.
. . . . $20.00
TOLE MUG, Worn Gold Japanning & Stenciled Label "My Girl", 2¾" D. . . $42.50

A-OH Mar 1981   *Garth's Auctions, Inc.*
INK ON LINED PAPER, Pr., Drawings By J. O. Miller, Sm. Amount Of Paper Damage On Both, Framed Together In Gilded Frame, 18" x 22¼" $105.00
PENCIL DRAWING, Young Girl Watering Plants, Gilded Frame, 13" x 15" . . . $160.00
LADDER-BACK ARM CHAIR, Woven Splint Seat, Ref. $140.00
KNIFE BOX, Dovetailed, Figured Birch, Old Varnish Finish, 6¼" x 12¼" . . . $175.00
SM. MAT, Pieced From Multi. Velvet Patches, 11" x 18" $30.00
HEPPLEWHITE STAND, Pine & Poplar, 1 Nailed Drawer, 1 Board Top, Very Worn, Old Red Finish, 20" x 20¼", 28" H.
. . . . $180.00
CARVED WOODEN DECOY, Goldeneye Hen, Upper NY State, Ca. 1930, 15½" L.
. . . . $25.00
WOVEN SPLINT BASKET, 15" x 16½", 9½" O. H. $60.00
CAST IRON DOOR STOP, Scottie, Old Blk. Paint, 8½" H. $45.00
CARVED WOODEN DECOY, Canvas Back Drake, Attrib. To Frank Strey, WI, Ca. 1930, Splits In Block, Glass Eyes, Orig. Paint, 17½" L. $95.00

A-OH Mar 1981   *Garth's Auctions, Inc.*
L To R
MINI. TOLE BUCKET, Orig. Gold Japanning W/Red Striping & Blk. Stenciled Label "A. Present", Some Wear, 3" H. . . . $25.00
SM. WOODEN ACCORDIAN, Tin Keys, Paper Bellows, Orig. Red & Blk. Graining W/Blue & Gold Comma Border, 6¼" L.
. . . . $25.00
TIN ADVERTISING PAIL, Embossed Label "N. K. Fairbank & Co., Chicago, NY", 3" H. $30.00

A-OH Mar 1981   *Garth's Auctions, Inc.*
TOILE, Blk. Hunting Scenes Block Printed On Linen, Framed, 15½" x 21¾" . . . $45.00
SM. HEXAGONAL MIRROR, Carved Walnut Frame, 11" D. $75.00
LADDER-BACK ARM CHAIR, Woven Splint Seat, Blk. Repaint $105.00
IRON HOG SCRAPER CANDLE-STICKS, Pr., Pushups Stamped "Patent Secured", 5⅛" H. 170.00
CARVED WOODEN DECOY, Goldeneye Drake W/Glass Eyes, MI, 12" L.
. . . . $75.00
STAND, Walnut & Chestnut, 2 Board Top W/Some Warp, 20" x 24", 27¼" H.
. . . . $150.00
CARVED WOODEN DECOY, Mallard Drake, Glass Eyes, Orig. Paint, 16" L.
. . . . $240.00
OVOID STONEWARE JAR, 3-Gal., Mottled & Spotted Glaze, 13" H. . . . $45.00
CAST IRON DOOR STOP, Scottie, Old Worn Paint, 8" H. $55.00

A-OH Mar 1981   *Garth's Auctions, Inc.*
L To R
TOLE ADVERTISING MUGS, Set Of 2, Orig. Paint W/Stenciled Labels, 3¼" H.
. . . . $80.00
MINI. BRASS CANDLESTICK, 3⅜" H.
. . . . $35.00
TOLE CREAMER, Orig. Br. Japanning W/Gold Stenciled Floral Spray, Has Wear, 5¼" H. $22.50
SM. BOX, Paper Covered Cardboard, Red Satin Pincushion Top Rimmed W/Vic. Shell Work, Labeled "Maude Cooks Old Box", 2¾" D. $7.50

A-OH Mar 1981   *Garth's Auctions, Inc.*
BAG FILLER, Pine, Adj. Hopper Holds
Grain Sacks, Worn Amish Blue Paint, 52" H.
.... $95.00
WROUGHT IRON TRAMMEL, Adj. From
35½" L. $35.00
PRINTED FRAKTUR, "Geburts Und Tauf-
schein", Records 1828 PA Birth, 18¼" x 22¾"
.... $65.00
WROUGHT IRON TRAMMEL, Adj. From
37" L. $40.00
LRG. COPPER KETTLE, Dovetailed
Seams, Wrought Iron Base & Attachment
Ears, Stamped "Sidney Shepard, Buffalo,
NY", 28" D., 16" H. $375.00
WROUGHT IRON TOASTER, Feet De-
teriorated, Twisted Handle, 18" L. .. $145.00
CAST IRON SHIP LIGHT, Double Spout
W/Orig. Lid, Mkd. "Jarechi", Edge Chip
.... $90.00

A-OH Mar 1981   *Garth's Auctions, Inc.*
CARVED WOODEN DECOY, Canada
Goose Swimmer, Glass Eyes, Old Paint, 27"
L. $110.00
CORNER CUPBOARD, 2-Pc., Curly
Maple, Dovetailed Drawers, Old Wavy Glass
& Worn Finish, 55½" W., 82½" H.
.... $1740.00
CARVED WOODEN DECOY, Pidgeon
Drake, Upper NY State, Ca. 1940, Working
Repaint, 13¼" L. $52.50
STONEWARE CUSPIDOR, Cobalt
Brushed Foliage Designs, 7¾" D. .. $145.00
CARVED WOODEN DECOY, Lowhead
Mallard Hen, MN, Ca. 1920, Glass Eyes,
Orig. Paint W/Some Restoration, 14¼" L.
.... $55.00

A-OH Mar 1981   *Garth's Auctions, Inc.*
CAST IRON LAWN CHAIR, Urn & Vin-
tage Back, Worn & Rusted Wh. Paint
.... $150.00
WROUGHT IRON COOKING PAN,
15½" D. $65.00
**WROUGHT IRON TRIVET W/FORK
REST,** Stamped Tooling, Scrolled Feet, 32"
L. $75.00

◀ A-OH Mar 1981   *Garth's Auctions, Inc.*
TOILE PANEL, Red On Wh., Scene Of
"Jeanne Hachette", Framed, 15½" x 30"
.... $25.00
BRASS VIC. CANDLESTICKS, Pr. W/
Pushups, 12" H. $135.00
CLEAR COMPOTE, Blown & Cut, Straw-
berry Diamond & Fan Patt., Minor Chips &
Flakes, 10¼" H. $65.00
SHERATON CHEST OF DRAWERS,
Am., Bow Front, Mahogany Veneer On Pine,
Repl. Brasses, Some Veneer Repair, 41" W.,
19½" D., 45½" H. $350.00
CAST IRON ANDIRONS, Pr., Eagle Fin-
ials, Need Restoration, 11½" H. $25.00
CAST IRON DOOR STOP, Bull Dog, Old
Repaint, 6¼" H. $40.00

A-OH Mar 1981   *Garth's Auctions, Inc.*
WOODEN BUTTER PRINT, Hexagonal
Design, Worn, 1 Pc. W/Turned Handle, 4¼"
D. $30.00
BRASS CHAMBER STICK, Decor. Han-
dle, 4" D. $40.00
WROUGHT IRON TRIVET, 9" L.
.... $30.00
WOODEN BUTTER PRINT, Crisp Floral
Design, 1 Pc. W/Turned Handle, 3⅞" D.
.... $45.00

ROW II, L To R
WROUGHT IRON SHEARS, Flattened
Screw Driver Handle, 6¾" L. $12.50
PEWTER PORRIGER, Cast Handle W/
Break, Bowl Battered & Sm. Hole, 5½" D.
.... $145.00
WROUGHT IRON MOUSE TRAP, 8¼"
L. $35.00

ROW III, L To R
SCISSOR WICK TRIMMERS, 2 Pr. (1
Illus.) $20.00
PEWTER LADLE, Mkd. "A.D. Britannia",
Sm. Breaks, 15" L. $35.00
IRON WEAPON BLADE, Attrib. To Ro-
man Occupation Of British Isles, Excavated
In Ireland, 10" W. $55.00
WHALEBONE BUSK, (At Far Right) Scrim-
shaw Work Includes Lady Liberty, Eagle,
Etc., 13" L. $250.00

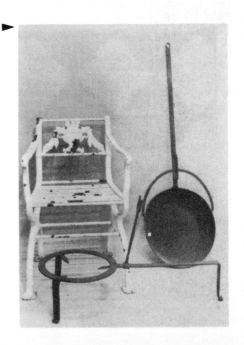

A-OH Sept 1980   *Garth's Auctions, Inc.*
HANGING SHELVES, Made For Corner, Old Red Paint, 23¾" W., 7¼" D., 40" H.
.... $125.00
ROW I, L To R
PIN CUSHION, Form Of Ladies Leg, Some Wear, 12" H. $20.00
TIN FOOD MOLDS, 2, Mellon Ribs, Both Mkd. "Kreamer" $20.00
ROW II, L To R
WROUGHT IRON DOUBLE CRUSIE LAMPS, 7" O.H. $20.00
VIC. PIN CUSHIONS, 2, Blue & Ecru, Pink & Blk., 4½" D. $27.50
ROUND WOODEN BUTTER PRINT CASED, Strawberry Design, 4¼" D.
.... $40.00
ROW III, L To R
TIN COTTAGE CHEESE SIEVE, Heart Shaped W/Round Holes, 4¼" H. .. $40.00
TIN COTTAGE CHEESE SIEVE, Round W/Dot-Dash Punching, 6" D. $40.00
TIN STRAINER, Cup Shaped W/2 Size Holes, 4½" D., 3¾" H. $27.50

A-NY May 1980   *Calkins Auction Gallery*
OIL ON CANVAS, Am., Ca. 1892, 21" x 17"
.... $105.00
LRG. COPPER POT W/Iron Handle, Am., 19th C., Dovetailed Bottom, Sgn. S & A Co., Has Cover, 12¼" D., 25¾" L. $105.00
SPLINT BASKET W/Fixed Handle, 19th C., 12½" D., 9" H. $40.00
LADLE, Carved Maple, 19th C., 15" L.
.... $65.00
COPPER DIPPER W/Long Handle, Am., 18½" L. $50.00
SHALLOW COPPER PAN W/Wrt. Iron Handle, Early 19th C., Sm. Split In Bottom, 17" L. $45.00
EARTHENWARE JAR, Br. & Tan, Minor Rim Chips, 5½" D., 7½" H. $150.00
TIN CANDLE LANTERN, Painted Blue W/4 Wire Bands Around Glass, Candle Holder Missing, 10½" H. $85.00
BURL MALLET, Am., 18th Or Early 19th C., 11½" L. $13.00
TIN MOLDS, Pr., 19th C., 5¾" x 4¼"
.... $40.00
CARVED WOODEN CHEESE PRINT, PA, 18th Or Early 19th C., 2 Wooden Bars On Back W/Dowels, 11⅝" D. $215.00
COVERED PANTRY BOX, Wooden W/ Traces Of Orig. Paint, 19th C., 10" D., 4½" H.
.... $45.00
SAWBUCK TABLE, N. Eng., 18th Or Early 19th C., Orig. Red Finish On Base, Wrt. Head Nails, 28" H. $300.00
TIN CANDLE LANTERN, N. Eng., 18th Or Early 19th C., Painted Blk. W/Wire Bands Around Glass, Lrg. Loop Handle, 17" H.
.... $50.00
TIN CANDLE LANTERN, N. Eng., 18th Or Early 19th C., Wire Bars In Front Of Glass, Loop Handle, 13" H. $55.00
HAND HEWN TRENCHER, Maple, NY, Early 19th C., Orig. Green Paint, 31" L., 19½" W., 6" H. $160.00
WOODEN CANTEEN, 18th C., Locked Wooden Bands, Ref., 6" D., 9¾" L. .. $85.00
LRG. REDWARE JAR, N. Eng., Early 19th C., Drk. Br. Glaze, Sl. Roughness On Rim, 7" D., 12" H. $45.00

A-OH Sept 1980   *Garth's Auctions, Inc.*
WALL CUPBOARD, 1-Pc., Pine, Single Board & Batten Door In Base, Upper Shelves Painted Coral, Ref., Base Restored, 38½" W., 20¾" D., 72¼" H. $450.00
DECORATIVE WOODEN DECOYS, Pr., Mallards Sgn. "Ben Bull", Drake Has Neck Repair, 10¼" D. $50.00
CARVED WOODEN DECOY, Mallard Hen, Glass Eyes, Orig. Paint, 11¼" L.
.... $60.00
CARVED WOODEN DECOY, Bufflehead Drake, Glass Eyes, Orig. Paint, 11¼" L.
.... $40.00
DECOY, Foam Body, Carved Wooden Head, Mallard Drake, Worn Orig. Paint, Glass Eyes, 16½" L. $55.00
VICTORY FACTORY COOT, Old Worn Repaint, 1 Glass Eye Missing, Lead Wt. & Line, 12½" L. $45.00
WOODEN FACTORY DECOY, Bluebill Drake, Glass Eyes, Old Paint, 15" L.
.... $45.00
CARVED WOODEN DECOY, Blk. Duck W/ Worn Orig. Paint, 1 Glass Eye, 14" L. $45.00
CARVED WOODEN DECOY, Cork Body, Redhead Drake By Whitney Labeau, MI, Glass Eyes, 18½" L. $25.00
CARVED WOODEN DECOY, Canada Goose, Balsa Body, Pine Head & Tail, Old Paint, Damaged, 23" L. $105.00

A-MA Mar 1980   *Robert W. Skinner Inc.*
FIREPLACE COAL STOVE, Enameled Forest Green, Wh. & Br., England, Late 19th C., 24" W., 28" H. $550.00*

*Price does not include 10% buyer fee.

A-OH Mar 1981   *Garth's Auctions, Inc.*

CARVED WOODEN RAINBOW TROUT, Polychrome Enameling, By Miles Carpenter, 20th C., 25½" L. $175.00

WOODEN CHIMNEY CUPBOARD, Worn Br. Patina, Not Free Standing, 17½" W., 10¾" D., 73" H. $350.00

WOODEN BIRD CAGE, Old Red & Wh. Paint, 16½" x 12½", 18¼" H. $85.00

GABLE END VENT, Decorative Cutouts, Pine, Ref., 21" D. $50.00

CARVED WOODEN DECOY, Hollow Duck W/Red Head & Glass Eyes, 12½" L. $85.00

CARVED WOODEN DECOY, Bluebill Drake Preener, MI, Branded "Clare", Unused Cond., Glass Eyes, 12¾"L. $95.00

CHILD'S SLED, Iron Rails, Wood W/ Orig. Worn Gr. Paint, Yellow Striping & Floral Decor., 11" x 35½" $135.00

CARVED WOODEN DECOY, Wood Duck W/Glass Eyes, Branded "Cabela's", 13½" L. $105.00

TIN COFFEE POT, Copper Bottom, Some Resoldering, 13½" H. $45.00

CHILD'S WAGON, Wooden Spoke Wheels, Removable Side Rails, Orig. Red Paint W/"Climax" On Rails, Old Repairs, 41" L. $275.00

CARVED WOODEN DECOY, Alert Head Bluebill Hen, Alexandria Bay, Ca. 1920, Glass Eyes, Old Repaint, 11¾" L. $155.00

CARVED WOODEN DECOY, Canada Goose, Long Necked Sentinal, MI, 21" L., 23" H. $255.00

STONEWEAR JUG, 3-Gal., Imp. Eagle & Swan Highlighted In Blue, 16" H. $105.00

CARVED WOODEN DECOY, Canvasback Drake W/Turned Head, Glass Eyes, Worn Orig. Paint, WI, 15½" L. $105.00

A-OH Mar 1981   *Garth's Auctions, Inc.*

HOOKED RAG RUG, Semicircular, Clipper Ship, Colors Faded, Minor Edge Wear, 37" x 51" $105.00

OVOID STONEWARE JAR, Cobalt Brushed Band Of Foliage, 9¼" H. .. $155.00

WOVEN SPLINT BUTTOCKS BASKET, Br. Varnish, Some Wear & Breaks, 15" x 17", 9" O. H. $75.00

STONEWARE CROCK, 2-Gal., Rose In Cobalt Slip, 9½" H. $85.00

BLANKET CHEST, Poplar, Dovetailed Const., Wrt. Iron Strap Hinges, Orig. Bear Trap Lock, Br. Varnish Finish, 52" W., 22" D., 24½" H. $160.00

OVOID STONEWARE JUG, 3-Gal., Brushed Cobalt Decor., 15" H. $95.00

WOVEN SPLINT BUTTOCKS BASKET, Br. & Natural Wood Patt., 11½" x 13½", 5½" O. H. $125.00

STONEWARE JUG, 3-Gal., Brushed Cobalt Blue Decor., 16" H. $95.00

A-OH Mar 1981   *Garth's Auctions, Inc.*

PANELED DOORS, Pr., Orig. Flame Graining In Faded Br. W/Red Panels, Poplar, 36¾" x 76½" $280.00

WOODEN SIGN, Wrought Iron Hdw. & Scrollwork, Turned Acorn Drops, Weathered Blk. Paint W/Yellow Letters, Some Repair, 45" W., 41" H. $425.00

STONEWARE CHURN, 6-Gal. Brushed Cobalt Blue Decor., Hairline Cracks, 19" O. H. $225.00

COPPER WEATHERVANE, Layers Of Old Worn Paint, 24½" H. $95.00

STONEWARE JUG, 3-Gal., Imp. Label "Ottman Bros & Co, Fort Edwards", Pecking Chicken In Cobalt, Shallow Flake On Lip, 16½" H. $270.00

CARVED WOODEN DECOY, Bluebill W/Old Paint & Shot Scars, 14¼" L. $40.00

CARVED WOODEN DECOY, Bluebill W/Glass Eyes & Old Paint, 14¼" L. $65.00

CARVED WOODEN DECOY, Redhead W/Old Paint & Glass Eyes, Split In Neck, 13½" L. $40.00

A-OH Mar 1981   *Garth's Auctions, Inc.*

CAST PLASTER BUST, Lincoln, Orig. Frame, Casting Mkd. "J. Powell, Patented 1865", 15⅝" D. $50.00

STONEWARE TANKARD, Pewter Top, Blue Slip Decor., Minor Chips, 13¼" H. $165.00

METTLACH PITCHER, Br. Glazed Embossed Bark Finish, Mkd. & Stamped "1028", 14½" H. $300.00

STONEWARE JAR, Applied Classical Decor., Tan Pebbly Glaze, Minor Flakes, 8" H. $55.00

DRY SINK, Pine, Orig. Blk. Brushed Graining On Reddish Ground, 29½" W., 16¾" D., 30" H. $310.00

HIGH CHAIR, Orig. Drk. Graining W/Yellow Striping & Stylized Birds On Crest, Break In Crest, 31½" H. $155.00

CARVED WOODEN DECOY, Bufflehead Drake By Mallory, Kingston, Ontario, Glass Eyes, Orig. Paint, 11" L. $85.00

CARVED WOODEN DECOY, Elongated Blk. Duck From Picton, Ontario, Tack Eyes, Worn Old Repaint, Ca. 1930, 18" L. $70.00

CARVED WOODEN DECOY, Redhead Drake, MI, Ca. 1920, Worn Paint, 13¾" L. $55.00

INDEX